Dictionary
of
20th Century History

David M. Brownstone
Irene M. Franck

Prentice Hall

New York London Toronto Sydney Tokyo Singapore

First Edition

Prentice Hall

Simon & Schuster, Inc.
15 Columbus Circle
New York, NY 10023

DISTRIBUTED BY PRENTICE HALL TRADE SALES

Manufactured in the United States of America

1 2 3 4 5 6 7 8 9 10

Library of Congress Cataloging-in-Publication Data

Brownstone, David M.
   Dictionary of 20th-century history / David Brownstone, Irene M. Franck.
      p. cm.
   ISBN 0-13-209883-0
   1. History, Modern—20th century—Dictionaries. I. Franck, Irene M.
II. Title. III. Title: Dictionary of twentieth-century history.
D419.B76   1990
909.82′03—dc20

Preface

So much has happened—this century has seen the first flight out to the stars, atomic weapons that threaten all life on earth, an enormous cycle of wars and revolutions, the discovery of the secret of life, and even Gorbachev's attempt to dismantle much of what was only a little while ago Lenin's new world system. Some, like us, chronicle what has gone before; all of us wonder what will surprise us next in these most interesting times.

In writing this work, our main aim has been to identify and briefly discuss the central events, people, movements, ideas, and discoveries of the twentieth century. Our main focus has been on political, military, economic, religious, scientific, and medical matters, though we have included a small number of relevant cultural entries. The highlights of the cultural life of the century will be taken up in our forthcoming companion volume, the *Dictionary of 20th Century Culture*.

Please note that where small capitals have been used within entries, they indicate the presence of another entry with further directly related information. In the World War II overview entry, for example, you will find references out to the PEARL HARBOR attack, MIDWAY, EL ALAMEIN, STALINGRAD, and the other major events of that war.

Please also note that we have included brief entries on countries that are new in the century, and those that have experienced massive systemic changes, but have otherwise treated major events in discrete entries, rather than as part of long country-by-country histories, feeling that this approach best meets the specific inquiries of most readers.

Our thanks go to our editors and publishers, Kate Kelly, Ken Wright, and Charles Levine, ably assisted by Susan Lauzau, and to editors Jill Schoenhaut and Michael Lisk, who so capably shepherded the book through the production process. As always, we also thank the staff of the Chappaqua Library, and their colleagues throughout the northeastern library network, who so equably and successfully fulfill our sometimes rather esoteric research needs.

David M. Brownstone
Irene M. Franck
Chappaqua, New York

A

AA, popular shorthand for ALCOHOLICS ANONYMOUS, a mutual-support group founded in the United States in 1935.

AAA, the initials of the AGRICULTURAL ADJUSTMENT ADMINSTRATION, by which this NEW DEAL Federal agency of the 1930s was best known.

Aachen, Battle of (October 20, 1944), the first large German city to be taken by Allied forces in World War II; it fell to American troops on October 20 as they pierced the SIEGFRIED LINE.

Abadan Theater fire (August 19, 1978), a fire in an Iranian movie theater set by Shiite fundamentalist arsonists, killing 350–400 people; the gasoline-induced fire spread so quickly that most of those inside died from smoke and in the accompanying panic.

Abbott, Grace (1878–1939), U.S. social worker, writer, teacher, and social reformer, who was especially concerned with questions of legal and social justice for the flood of immigrants who arrived in the United States early in the 20th century. She was director of the Chicago-based Immigrants' Protective League (1908–1917) and active with Jane ADDAMS in Chicago's HULL HOUSE during the same period; she worked with the U.S. Children's Bureau during and after World War I and as its director 1921–24.

ABC (**A**tanasoff-**B**erry **C**omputer), world's first fully electronic COMPUTER, conceived 1937–38 and built 1939–42 by U.S. physicist John Vincent ATANASOFF, assisted by Clifford E. Berry. Unknown for 25 years, the ABC came to public attention during a 1967 lawsuit over royalties paid to the creators of ENIAC, long regarded as the first American

computer. In 1973 a U.S. federal judge voided the ENIAC patent, concluding that Atanasoff's work had contributed significantly to its development, in effect affirming that the ABC was the world's first computer. In the ABC, Atanasoff pioneered in using electron tubes as on–off switches, employing a binary system for mathematical calculations. He also set the pattern of separating the computer's memory from the area in which computations are carried out, and many of his other choices are still reflected in modern computers.

Abd el-Krim (1892–1963), Moroccan national leader in the RIF WAR (1921–26), in which his forces defeated the Spanish army at the BATTLE OF ANUAL in 1922, establishing the Rif Republic, but were themselves defeated in 1926 by far stronger combined French and Spanish armies. He was imprisoned by the French on Réunion Island in the Indian Ocean and in 1947 was sent to France, but en route he escaped to asylum in Cairo. He has been regarded by many 20th-century North African and other third world revolutionaries as an early hero of their own battle against colonialism.

abdication crisis (November 16–December 10, 1936), the period between the announcement by Britain's King EDWARD VIII that he wished to marry American divorcee Wallis SIMPSON and his abdication. Winston CHURCHILL supported his right to marry Simpson and remain king, but Prime Minister Stanley BALDWIN and the great majority of British and Dominion church and state figures did not. Edward chose Wallis, and abdicated. They were later made duke and duchess of Windsor by his brother, who became GEORGE VI.

Abdul-Hamid II (1842–1918), Turkish ruler (1876–1909), who took the throne professing liberal and constitutional sympathies but soon suppressed all opposition, developed a powerful secret police, and attempted to crush dissident political and ethnic national movements throughout the Turkish empire. His forces were responsible for the Armenian massacres of the late 1870s in Constantinople and for the massacres of the mid-1890s, in which hundreds of thousands of Armenians died, prefiguring the greater massacres of the ARMENIAN HOLOCAUST. He was forced by the YOUNG TURKS to grant a measure of constitutional government to Turkey in 1908 and was removed in 1909.

Abdullah Ibn Husein (1882–1951), son of HUSSEIN IBN ALI. After the successful ARAB REVOLT during World War I, he became Emir of Transjordan, then part of British-dominated Palestine. In 1946, he became the first king of independent TRANSJORDAN, participating in the FIRST ARAB–ISRAELI WAR of 1948 and later annexing the WEST BANK of the Jordan River. He was assassinated on July 20, 1951.

Abdullah, Mohammed ("Lion of Kashmir;" 1905–1982), Kashmiri aristocrat, who founded the Kashmir Muslim Conference, became a leader of the Indian CONGRESS PARTY during the struggle for independence, and became leader of Kashmir in independent India (1948–53). He was ousted and imprisoned by the Indian government in 1953, after advocating Kashmiri independence, but became chief minister of Kashmir again after gaining his freedom in 1973.

Abdul Rahman, Tunku (1903–　　), Malaysian lawyer, who became president of the United Malays National Organization (UMNO) in 1951. He took his party into the succeeding Alliance party, a Malay-Chinese coalition that became the ruling party of the new nation of Malaya in 1957, and became first prime minister of his country (1957–

63). He was the key negotiator of the union of Malaya, Singapore, Sabah, and North Borneo into the Federation of Malaysia in 1963, becoming first prime minister of the Federation of MALAYSIA (1963–70); but he agreed to the independence of Singapore in 1965 and resigned after Chinese-Malay rioting in 1969.

Abdul Razak, Tun (1922–1976), Malaysian lawyer, who became a leader of the United Malays National Organization (UMNO) in the mid-1950s, deputy prime minister, and then second prime minister of Malaysia (1970–76), succeeding TUNKU ABDUL RAHMAN.

Abel, Rudolph Ivanovich (1902–1971), a Soviet intelligence colonel who operated an espionage organization in the United States 1948–57, was captured and sentenced to a 30-year term and then exchanged for U-2 INCIDENT pilot Francis Gary POWERS in 1962.

Abernathy, Ralph David (1926–　　), U.S. Baptist minister and associate of Martin Luther KING, Jr., who became a leader of the CIVIL RIGHTS MOVEMENT in the mid-1950s. With King he led the MONTGOMERY BUS BOYCOTT, was a founder and the first secretary-treasurer of the SOUTHERN CHRISTIAN LEADERSHIP CONFERENCE (SCLC), and was second president of the SCLC (1968–77) after King's assassination. As president of the SCLC, he led a series of demonstrations and campaigns for Black economic and civil rights, including the Poor People's Campaign of 1968, which established a squatters' settlement—Resurrection City—in Washington, D.C.

ABM, popular shorthand for ANTIBALLISTIC MISSILE.

A-bomb, popular shorthand for the ATOMIC BOMB, first developed in the United States in the MANHATTAN PROJECT in 1945.

Abraham Lincoln Battalion, the American battalion in the INTERNATIONAL BRIGADES during the SPANISH CIVIL WAR, numbering about 2,800 volunteers, of whom an estimated 900 were killed and many others injured. The battalion first went into action on February 17, 1937, at the Battle of Jarama, near Madrid; of 450 men, 120 were killed and 175 wounded. Most of its surviving members were withdrawn with the rest of the International Brigades in November 1938.

Abrams, Creighton Williams, Jr. (1914–1974), U.S. officer, who saw service in World War II, held several substantial army field and staff positions during the 1960s, became deputy to General William WESTMORELAND in VIETNAM in 1967, was U. S. commander in Vietnam 1968–72, and was army chief of staff 1972–74.

Abscam (Abdul scam), a 1978–79 Washington, D.C., FEDERAL BUREAU OF INVESTIGATION "sting" operation, in which FBI agents, posing as wealthy Arab businessmen, offered bribes to scores of public officials. Ultimately, seven federal legislators were indicted; all were tried and convicted, although one conviction was later reversed on appeal. Senator Harrison A. Williams, Jr., and Congressmen John W. Jenrette, Jr., Raymond F. Lederer, Michael O. Myers, John M. Murphy, and Frank Thompson, Jr., were convicted as a result of Abscam.

Abyssinian War, an alternate name for the ETHIOPIAN–ITALIAN WAR of the mid-1930s.

accelerator, in physics, a device for speeding up charged atomic PARTICLES to high velocities and energy levels and often forcing collisions among them to produce other kinds of subatomic particles; a type of machine basic to modern nuclear research and particle physics, popularly called an "atom smasher." The earliest accelerators were linear, starting with the machine built 1929–31 by U.S. physicist R. J. van de Graaff, and employed various methods of forcing acceleration. Working at the University of California at Berkeley, Ernest O. LAWRENCE pioneered in building circular accelerators, starting with his CYCLOTRON 1930–32. From 1946 more sophisticated accelerators were built, including the proton linear accelerator designed by Luis W. ALVAREZ. Many early accelerators were used for de-

cades, notably in producing radioactive ISOTOPES for medical treatment and research. But ever larger and more sophisticated machines were built for nuclear research, such as the CERN accelerator in Geneva, built in the early 1970s, and the Super Superconducting Collider (SSC), popularly dubbed the Desertron, being constructed in the late 1980s and planned to be tens of miles across.

Acheson, Dean Gooderham (1893–1971), U.S. lawyer, who began his career as a clerk to Supreme Court Justice Louis B. BRANDEIS in 1920, thereafter practicing law, with a brief period of government service at the Treasury Department in 1933, until becoming an assistant secretary of state in 1941. In 1945, he moved up to the post of undersecretary of state under George C. MARSHALL, in that period developing such major early COLD WAR initiatives as the MARSHALL PLAN and the TRUMAN DOCTRINE. He became secretary of state in the TRUMAN administration and supported the formation of the NORTH ATLANTIC TREATY ORGANIZATION (NATO) in 1949, U.S. participation in the KOREAN WAR, and CHIANG KAI-SHEK'S government after it fled to Taiwan. He was attacked by Senator Joseph MCCARTHY for his defense of Alger HISS and other state department personnel who had been charged with being Communists or Communist sympathizers, and he was also blamed by McCarthy and others for not strongly enough supporting Chiang in the CHINESE CIVIL WAR.

Achille Lauro **hijacking** (October 1985), the October 7 seizure of the Italian cruise ship *Achille Lauro*, carrying over 400 passengers and crew, by four Palestinian terrorists, off the coast of Egypt. The hijackers demanded release of Palestinian prisoners held by Israel, threatening to kill the ship's passengers; they did kill disabled American passenger Leon Klinghoffer on October 8, afterward throwing his body and wheelchair overboard. Syria refused permission to land; Egypt, however, promised safe-conduct to the terrorists after being assured by the ship's captain that no one had been hurt. On October 10, U.S. naval aircraft forced the Egyptian airliner carrying the hijackers to land in Sicily, an action sharply protested by Egypt; Italy took them into custody, along with two PALESTINE LIBERATION ORGANIZATION (PLO) leaders on the airplane, but did not arrest the PLO officials.

acid rain, atmospheric water in which industrial pollutants released into the air, notably sulfur dioxide and nitrogen oxides, form sulfuric and nitric acids, which then fall to earth in raindrops. The long-term effects of acid rain are devastating, such as creating lifeless lakes in America's Northeast and killing trees in Germany's Black Forest. Despite warnings of the effects of such pollution, governments responded slowly to the threats, opposed by industry most of the way. Air pollutants knowing no borders, acid rain was a subject of hot dispute between countries, as between the United States and Canada in the 1980s.

ACLU, the initials of the AMERICAN CIVIL LIBERTIES UNION.

acquired immune deficiency syndrome, full name of the deadly viral disease known as AIDS.

Action Française, French rightist, anti-Jewish, monarchist, largely Catholic group formed by Charles MAURRAS in 1899, which from 1908 published its own newspaper and engaged in street violence as well. It was seriously damaged by the condemnation of Pope PIUS XI in 1926, kept some of its strength in the 1930s, collaborated with Vichy and the Nazis during World War II, and was smashed after the war.

ADA, the initials of AMERICANS FOR DEMOCRATIC ACTION, the liberal group founded in 1947.

Adair v. *United States* (1908), a landmark U.S. Supreme Court decision upholding the "yellow dog" contract, an agreement forced on workers by their employers, that made union membership grounds for discharge.

Adams, Sherman, U.S. presidential aide, former governor of New Hampshire, who in 1958 was accused of taking gifts, notably a vicuña coat, from his friend Bernard Goldfine in return for attempting unethically to influence government agency proceedings against Goldfine. Adams was strongly defended by president Dwight D. EISENHOWER and exonerated by a congressional committee, but ultimately resigned as the public campaign against him continued to grow.

Addams, Jane (1860–1935), pioneer U.S. social worker, women's rights worker, peace activist, and writer, who established Chicago's HULL HOUSE in 1889 and there in the next four decades developed many of the approaches and structures central to the settlement house movement of the early 20th century. She was president of the WOMEN'S INTERNATIONAL LEAGUE FOR PEACE AND FREEDOM, co-recipient of the Nobel Peace Prize in 1931, and is probably best known for her book *Twenty Years at Hull House*.

Aden, a former British colony; on November 30, 1967, Aden became part of the new nation of SOUTH YEMEN, which became the YEMEN PEOPLE'S REPUBLIC (PEOPLE'S DEMOCRATIC REPUBLIC OF YEMEN) IN 1970.

Adenauer, Konrad (1876–1967), German lawyer, who became mayor of Cologne (1917–33) and was a leading member of the Catholic Center Party before the Nazi takeover in 1933. He was removed from office by the Nazis and held no office of any kind during the Nazi period. Going back into public life after the war, he became a leader of the Christian Democratic Union, had major responsibility for the drafting of a new Basic Law for West Germany in 1948, and became first chancellor of the FEDERAL REPUBLIC OF GERMANY, 1949–63. During the period in which he was chancellor, West Germany became fully independent, joined the NORTH ATLANTIC TREATY ORGANIZATION (NATO), and redeveloped major economic strength.

Adkins v. *Children's Hospital* (1923), a landmark U.S. Supreme Court decision invalidating a federal minimum wage law for women workers in the District of Columbia.

Adler, Alfred (1870–1937), Austrian psychiatrist, who developed the idea of the inferiority complex and the corollary that many people's drive for superiority is in compensation for feelings of inferiority. Adler was an early disciple of Sigmund FREUD, but broke with him in 1912 over the primacy of sex, believing power relations to be more important.

adrenaline (epinephrine), vital HORMONE excreted by the adrenal gland, which lies above the kidney, discovered in 1901 independently by Japanese-American chemist Jokichi Takamine and Thomas Bell; later found to mobilize the body's systems to react to environmental conditions, such as danger.

Afars and Issas, Territory of the, name 1966–77 of the former colony FRENCH SOMALILAND, now DJIBOUTI.

Affluent Society, The, a book by John Kenneth GALBRAITH (1958), which sharply criticized wasteful U.S. consumption patterns, urging redirection of wealth for social service and for national and international society-building purposes. The book title then moved into the language, often being used critically, as intended, but sometimes being used to admiringly describe the excesses originally criticized.

Afghan–British War (May 1919), a short-lived holy war (*jihad*), mounted by Afghan king AMANULLAH KHAN, who had succeeded his assassinated father in February. His troops attacked across the Indian border and were soon repulsed and then pursued by superior British–Indian forces with air power, forcing an end to hostilities in less than a month, although guerrilla war then continued along that far-from-peaceful border.

Afghan Civil War (1978–   ) and **Afghan–Soviet War** (1979–1989), a civil war that drew massive Soviet intervention. In April 1978 a coup organized by the radical wing of the People's Democratic Party toppled the government of Sardar Mohammed DAUD KHAN, who was killed during the coup. The new government instituted radi-

cal changes and was opposed by many other groups, who began to form themselves into MUJAHEDDIN resistance groups. Civil war broke out, with the Mujaheddin rebels soon winning most of the country and threatening to topple the government. The Soviets were dissatisfied with government handling of the rebellion and ultimately intervened; divisional-strength airborne and land invasions of Afghanistan on December 25, 1979, took Kabul. Afghan premier Hafizullah Amin died during the invasion; Babrak KARMAL was installed by the Soviets as premier. Then followed a 9-year Afghan-Soviet war; Soviet troops numbering an estimated 130,000, with massive air and armor support, proved unable to defeat the Mujaheddin, who were headquartered in Pakistan and there supplied with U.S. weapons. An estimated 2–3 million Afghan refugees fled to Pakistan. In 1986 newly installed Soviet premier Mikhail GORBACHEV began to negotiate Soviet withdrawal; on April 14, 1988, a withdrawal agreement was signed at Geneva, and Soviet disengagement began, concluding in February 1989. However, no end to the continuing civil war was negotiated.

Afghanistan (Republic of Afghanistan), until 1919 a de facto British protectorate, becoming a monarchy under AMANULLAH KHAN until the republican coup of 1973. The republic was overthrown by the coup of April 1978; Afghanistan then became a one-party Communist state led by Babrak KARMAL and from 1986 by Mohammad NAJIBULLAH. The coup was followed by the AFGHAN CIVIL WAR (1978–   ), and the 9-year Soviet occupation of the country. After the Soviet troop withdrawal, which was completed in February 1989, the civil war continued.

AFL, initials of the AMERICAN FEDERATION OF LABOR, by which the organization was best known.

African National Congress (ANC), the leading organization of the Black and other nonwhite peoples of South Africa from 1912, seeking the creation of a multiracial, fully integrated, democratic state; the party of Albert LUTHULI, Nelson MANDELA, Winnie MANDELA, and Oliver TAMBO. Until the SHARPEVILLE MASSACRE of 1960, the dominant philosophy in the ANC was that of Gandhian nonviolence, even during the years of increasing government-directed repression and violence following the institution of APARTHEID in 1948. After Sharpeville, ANC policy began to change, and after the outlawing of the ANC in 1961, followed by the life imprisonment of Nelson Mandela and other ANC leaders, it changed decisively toward the development of a guerrilla war against the South African government, including acts of sabotage and terrorism directed against noncombatants. In early 1990, the ANC was once again legalized by the South African government.

Agadir Incident (1911), an alternative name for the MOROCCO CRISIS OF 1911.

Agent Orange, U.S. Army code name for a highly toxic herbicide, containing DIOXIN, that was used to defoliate large forest areas during the VIETNAM WAR. In the late 1970s many Vietnam veterans involved in the spraying discovered that they themselves had been severely poisoned and that their children had been affected; ultimately, mass lawsuits forced the Agent Orange manufacturers to set up a compensation fund, though they continued to deny liability.

Agnew, Spiro Theodore (1918–   ), U.S. lawyer, Republican governor of Maryland (1967–69), and Richard M. NIXON'S vice-president (1969–73) who strongly opposed anti–VIETNAM WAR protesters, liberalism, and immorality. Under investigation for possible corruption while in office in Maryland, he denied wrongdoing and pleaded "no contest" to a single charge of income tax evasion, later being heavily fined and placed on probation. He resigned his vice-presidency on October 10, 1973.

Agricultural Adjustment Administration (AAA), U.S. federal agency established in 1933 by the Agricultural Adjustment Act, a NEW DEAL measure aimed at controlling farm production by using a combination of subsidies, quotas, and taxes, that was de-

clared unconstitutional by the Supreme Court in UNITED STATES V. BUTLER in 1936. Congress then accomplished much the same goals by authorizing a system of parity and soil conservation payments, storage of surplus products, and production quotas, these functions being taken over by the Department of Agriculture in 1946.

Aguinaldo, Emilio (1869–1964), president of the first Phillipine Republic, and its leader during the PHILIPPINE WAR OF INDEPENDENCE and PHILIPPINE-AMERICAN WAR.

Ahidjo, Ahmadou (1924–   ), Cameroon political leader, who entered his country's assembly in 1947, when it was still a French trust territory. He became premier of French Cameroons in 1958 and was first president of the Republic of Cameroon from 1960 until his retirement in 1982. As president, he instituted a federal form of government that allowed the unification of several diverse peoples to proceed with minimum abrasion, developing a more unified single government form in 1972.

AIDS (acquired immune deficiency syndrome), viral disease that attacks the body's immune system, leaving it defenseless against infections, such as candidiasis or *Pneumocystis carinii* pneumonia, or rare cancers, such as Kaposi's sarcoma; a deadly illness with an incubation period of possibly 5–10 years and a mortality rate of perhaps 100%. Thought to have originated in Africa, AIDS was recognized as a new disease in the United States in 1981, though records showed that the earliest cases there were probably seen in 1977. The virus causing it was identified in 1984 by Robert Gallo of the National Cancer Institute and independently by Luc Montagnier of the Pasteur Institute in Paris. That same year saw the first test for AIDS. At first, it seemed—in the United States, at least—to be associated with homosexual males, hemophiliacs, Haitians, and needle-using drug addicts; though homosexual males and addicts continued to be at high risk unless they took steps to protect themselves, it was soon found that others were also at risk, including heterosexuals. In fact, in Africa the disease—perhaps of a more powerful strain—spread very quickly in heterosexual populations. Before the disease was recognized and tests developed to screen for it, the AIDS virus entered the blood supply, and many BLOOD BANKS unknowingly spread the disease. In the mid-1980s there was widespread concern that the disease would be spread by casual contact, leading to ostracism of some people who had, or were thought to have, AIDS. Medical experts assured the public that the HIV (human immuno-deficiency virus, also called HTLV, or human T-lymphotropic virus) that causes AIDS could be transmitted only through intermixing of blood or blood products. As experience largely bore out their contention and people became better educated about AIDS, hysteria eased somewhat. Widespread discrimination remained, however. Many people feared testing for the disease lest results be made public; yet without testing, infected individuals could unknowingly spread the disease to others. The conflicting needs of the individual's right to privacy and the public's right to be protected against infection came into conflict in many places along a wide front. Oddly, when a home test was developed in the late 1980s, the U.S. government blocked its sale, arguing that testing must be linked with counseling. The U.S. FOOD AND DRUG ADMINISTRATION also was criticized for retaining its slow, careful process for approving medications (a policy eased somewhat in 1989), the disease being so deadly that it spurred many AIDS patients to spend thousands of dollars on desperate remedies, many from quacks and charlatans. In the late 1980s various drugs were used to slow the effects of the disease, but none to cure it. AIDS also sharply tested the medical community, at risk through their care of patients; some health care workers refused to treat AIDS patients, especially to operate or do autopsies. The disease added a tremendous burden to an already overstrained hospital and social welfare system. By the end of the 1980s, though the number infected continued to rise around the world and the social questions remained acute, physicians

had found that, by early detection and preventive anti-infection treatment, they could extend the length and quality of life for many AIDS patients, perhaps by years.

Air America, a U.S. CENTRAL INTELLIGENCE AGENCY (CIA) covert air force operating in southeast Asia from 1959 through the VIETNAM WAR.

air-cushion vehicle (ACV), craft designed to travel over land or water on a self-generated air cushion, the best known being the HOVERCRAFT designed by British engineer Christopher Cockerell in 1955, seeing regular service from 1968. ACVs were much developed from then on, but practical problems persisted, so applications were largely limited to industry.

Air India explosion (June 23, 1985), explosion of an Air India 747 in midair over the Irish Sea, off Ireland, killing 329 people. Although the cause of the explosion remained unknown, there was thought to have been a bomb aboard.

airplane, engine-powered, heavier-than-air machine for piloted flight, first developed by American inventor-brothers Wilbur and Orville WRIGHT and flown successfully on December 17, 1903, at Kill Devil Hills, near Kitty Hawk, North Carolina. Lightweight wooden biplanes, with two sets of wings connected by struts, were used in small numbers—but drew great public attention—in World War I; in 1915 the Fokker craft became the first to have its machine guns synchronized with the propeller. Biplanes also were flown by early record-breaking aviators such as Charles LINDBERGH and by mail pilots, who made the first coast-to-coast airmail flight in 1920. The first seaplane was developed in 1911 by American aviator-inventor Glenn Hammond CURTISS. In the 1920s monoplanes (with single wings) began to replace biplanes; all-metal airplanes were standard by the 1930s and during World War II. Daily scheduled airplane flights were begun in Europe in 1919; by the 1930s European and American planes could carry 30–40 passengers; and by 1939 Pan American had begun regular trans-Atlantic and trans-Pacific service, flying the famous "Clippers" built by Igor SIKORSKY. During World War II most aircraft were propeller-driven, though some JETS—airplanes driven by JET PROPULSION—came into use late in the war. After World War II, the British Vickers Viscount turboprop, a propeller-driven airplane with a turbine engine, went into commercial service in 1953 and was the standard craft until supplanted for general use by jets. In the 1980s scientists were experimenting with fuelless airplanes, designed to fly on a MICROWAVE beam sent up from the ground.

Aisne Offensive (May 27–June 6, 1918), the third of five major German offensives in 1918, all of them aimed at winning World War I with the help of the Eastern Front troops freed by Soviet withdrawal from the war. German forces attacked French armies on the Aisne, advancing 20 miles to the Marne, where they were stopped by French and American forces. The Americans fought their first substantial battles of the war at this time, at CHATEAU-THIERRY and BELLEAU WOOD, and began to make a significant difference in the course of the war.

Aitken, William Maxwell, the given name of the British press baron, Lord BEAVER-BROOK.

Alamogordo, site of the TRINITY test, where the first experimental ATOMIC BOMB was exploded, at a U.S. air base in New Mexico on July 16, 1945.

Albania (People's Socialist Republic of Albania), until 1912 part of the Ottoman empire, then lapsing into near-anarchy until establishment of a republic in 1925. The republic lasted 3 years; its leader became King Zog I in 1928, ruling over a de facto Italian protectorate, which was occupied by Italy in 1939 and then by Axis troops during World War II. Albania became a one-party Communist state on January 11, 1946, led by Enver HOXHA; it was part of the Soviet bloc until 1961, leaned toward China until 1977, and thereafter pursued an independent course.

Albania, annexation of (April 7, 1939), the taking of Albania by fascist Italy, 13 years after the Italian-Albanian treaties of 1926 and 1927, which had made Albania essentially an Italian protectorate.

Albizu Campos, Pedro (1891–1965), Puerto Rican lawyer and leader of the Nationalist Party, who advocated violent revolution to establish Puerto Rican independence. He spent 20 years in prison for his views: 1936–43, on a charge of conspiracy to mount an insurrection; 1950–53, after Puerto Rican nationalists attempted to assassinate U.S. president Harry S. TRUMAN; and 1954–64, after Puerto Rican nationalists wounded five Congressmen in the House of Representatives.

Alcoholics Anonymous (AA), a worldwide organization of recovering alcoholics, all of whom preserve public anonymity and hold themselves available to help others who wish to recover from alcoholism. Founded in the United States in 1935 by Bill Wilson and Bob Smith, AA now has over 1.5 million members.

Aldermaston marches, a series of antinuclear demonstrations organized by the British CAMPAIGN FOR NUCLEAR DISARMAMENT in the late 1950s and early 1960s, in which demonstrators marched from London to Aldermaston, the site of the British Atomic Weapons Research Establishment, to protest the development of nuclear arms.

Alemán Valdées, Miguel (1902–83), Mexican lawyer, governor, and cabinet officer, who was president of Mexico 1946–52. His presidency was marked by industrial development but also by growing economic problems, despite large-scale foreign investment and loans.

Alexander I (1888–1934) self-created dictator of Yugoslavia, in 1929, after efforts to bring Serbs, Croats, Slovenes, Montenegrins, and others together in a united country. He was assassinated by Croatian nationalists in Marseilles, France, on October 9, 1934.

Alexander, Harold (1891–1969), British officer and World War II general, who saw action in World War I and was commander of the British forces during the final evacuation of DUNKIRK in 1940 and the last man off the beach. Two years later, in 1942, he commanded British forces in Burma, falling back before the invading Japanese. That summer he became British Middle Eastern commander and thereafter the chief organizer of Allied victory in North Africa. He commanded joint British-American forces invading Italy and later all Allied forces in the region, in 1944 becoming a field marshal.

Alfonsin Foulkes, Raúl (1927–　　　），Argentinian lawyer and political leader, who became president in 1983, succeeding the military government that had lost the Falklands War and conducted the DIRTY WAR. He immediately moved to restore democracy, prosecute those who committed and authorized the murders of the dirty war, and revive Argentina's seriously damaged economy.

Algeciras Conference (1906–1907), meeting that ended the MOROCCO CRISIS OF 1905.

Algeria (Democratic and Popular Republic of Algeria), until 1962 a French colony, becoming an independent nation on July 3, 1962, after the 1954–62 ALGERIAN WAR OF INDEPENDENCE, and then a one-party Islamic Socialist state, led successively by Ahmed Ben BELLA, Houari BOUMEDIENNE, and Ben-Jedid CHADLI.

Algerian War of Independence (1954–62), a successful Algerian rebellion against French rule, initiated by the FLN (National Liberation Front) after almost a decade of growing Arab nationalism following World War II. By 1956 heavy guerrilla fighting had spread throughout the country's rural areas, then moving into Algiers. During the late 1950s an estimated 60,000–100,000 Algerian guerrillas, operating within a wholly friendly Arab population and receiving arms and support from bases in Tunisia, confronted 400,000–500,000 French army troops. In May 1958 a revolt of French officers in Algiers, led by General Jacques MASSU, nearly triggered a civil war in France, brought down the Fourth Republic, and brought Charles DE GAULLE's Fifth Republic to power. In September 1958 the Algerian rebels set up a provisional government in Tunis. De Gaulle continued the war but sought peace. During 1958 he offered self-determination to Algeria, put down the officers' revolt, released some captured FLN leaders, and resisted SECRET ARMY ORGANIZATION (OAS) terrorism from the right. The French army put down a right-wing French colonists' revolt in Algiers in 1960 and a French army mutiny led by General Raoul SALAN in 1961. In March 1962 negotiations at Evian-les-Bains in France brought about an Algerian ceasefire. Ahmed BEN BELLA became premier of the new Algerian government; independence came on July 3, 1962.

All power to the Soviets, a BOLSHEVIK slogan put forward by Vladimir Illich LENIN on his return from exile in April 1917.

All the President's Men (1974), book by Washington *Post* reporters Robert WOODWARD and Carl BERNSTEIN about the uncovering of the WATERGATE scandal, which eventually forced the resignation of U.S. president Richard M. NIXON.

Allenby, Edmund Henry Hynman (1861–1936), British general, who first fought in France during World War I and in 1917 became commander of the British Expeditionary Force in Egypt, from there taking Palestine and Syria.

Allende Gossens, Salvador (1908–73), Chilean physician, Marxian socialist, and political leader, a founder of the Chilean Socialist Party in 1933, in congress 1937–70. Allende unsuccessfully ran for the presidency as head of a leftist coalition three times (1952, 1958, 1964) before winning a plurality in 1970. As president he moved to put his socialist program into effect, nationalizing much of the economy and instituting land reforms, while encountering powerful domestic opposition from the right and center. As the first elected Marxist head of state in Latin America, he also encountered powerful U.S. opposition, the U.S. CENTRAL INTELLIGENCE AGENCY (CIA) joining his domestic enemies in seeking to unseat his government, which was toppled by the military coup of September 11, 1973. Allende died during the coup; he was widely reported to have been murdered, as were large numbers of his supporters during and after the coup, although the new military government claimed that he had committed suicide.

allergy, hypersensitivity to foreign substances. The most extreme form of allergy is anaphylaxis, extreme sensitivity to the injection of a foreign substance, such as penicillin or a bee sting; a subsequent injection can provoke a severe reaction and if the patient is untreated can lead to shock and possibly death. French researcher Charles R. Richet first identified anaphylaxis in 1902, for which he received the 1913 Nobel Prize for Physiology or Medicine. Other allergies are less serious but far more common. The term "allergy" was introduced in 1906 to refer to people who became ill after receiving medications and to hay fever sufferers, for whom pollen desensitization treatments were begun in 1910, the same year that asthma was first seen as an allergy. Gradual recognition of the role of histamines in the allergic reaction led in 1937 to the development of antihistamines by French pharmacologist Daniele Bovet, for which he won the 1957 Nobel Prize for Physiology or Medicine.

Alliance for Progress, an inter-American initiative proposed by president John F. KENNEDY in March 1961, and formally stated by the ORGANIZATION OF AMERICAN STATES in August 1961. Its aim was to join massive U.S. aid to internally generated Latin American funds, creating programs to help stimulate economic and educational self-development in Latin America. In practice, the initiative proved to be more slogan than substance.

Allies, during WORLD WAR I, the major acting participants on the Allied side were France, the British Empire, Russia, the United States, Serbia, Italy, Belgium, Greece, Rumania, and Montenegro. During WORLD WAR II, the major Allies were ultimately the United States, the Soviet Union, the British Commonwealth, France, China, Poland, and Yugoslavia. There were 19 other Allied signatories to the original Declaration of the United Nations.

Alliluyeva, Svetlana, (1926–   ) the daughter of Joseph STALIN, who defected from the Soviet Union in 1967, returned in 1984, and emigrated again in 1986.

alpha particles, one of the three products of natural RADIOACTIVITY, found to be the nuclei of helium atoms, without the usual ELECTRONS; discovered and named by Ernest RUTHERFORD in the early 1900s.

alpha rhythms, type of brain wave associated with relaxation, first discovered by Hans Berger using his ELECTROENCEPHALOGRAPH (EEG).

Alsace-Lorraine, a disputed French-German border region in eastern France, that was taken by Germany in 1871 after its victory in the Franco-Prussian War, taken back by France in 1918 after its victory in World War I; retaken by Germany in 1940, and won back by France in 1945.

Alsop, Joseph Wright, Jr. (1910–89), U.S. journalist, who played an influential role in developing support for government policy during the early years of the COLD WAR and for American intervention in the VIETNAM WAR.

Alvarez, Luis Walter (1911–88), U.S. physicist, who developed a much-enhanced BUBBLE CHAMBER and with it detected many previously unknown subatomic PARTICLES, resulting in new theories by physicists such as Murray GELL-MANN. Early in World War II, Alvarez worked on RADAR, developing a microwave beam that permitted all-weather landing; in 1944 he joined the team building the ATOMIC BOMB at Los Alamos and flew in the *ENOLA GAY'S* companion plane when the bomb was dropped on HIROSHIMA. After the war his work with the bubble chamber, and with linear ACCELERATORS won him the 1968 Nobel Prize for Physics.

In 1980, with his geologist son Walter, he developed the controversial theory that dinosaurs became extinct some 65 million years ago at the end of the Cretaceous and beginning of the Tertiary periods because the Earth was hit by a huge meteorite, an idea sparking fears for a NUCLEAR WINTER in case of future atomic war.

Alzheimer's disease, debilitating illness that causes progressive loss of intellectual functioning; long thought a routine part of the aging process for much of the population, it was first recognized as a disease in 1906 by German neurologist-pathologist Alois Alzheimer. Despite much research, however, diagnosis remained difficult late in the century, and effective treatment was likewise elusive.

Amal (al-Amal; Movement of the Deprived), Shiite Moslem Lebanese political organization and militia, supported in some periods by Syria and influenced by Iran, that during the 1980s became an increasingly strong military and political factor in the LEBANESE WARS.

Amanullah Khan (1892–1960), king of Afghanistan (1919–29), who succeeded to the throne after the assassination of his father, Habibullah Khan, in February 1919 and in May began the short-lived AFGHAN-BRITISH WAR. He ruled until 1928, when a revolt drove him into exile.

America First Committee, an organization opposed to American entry into World War II, which terminated its activities after December 7, 1941. Although it was largely dominated by pro-Nazi organizations, it attracted many conservatives as well, including aviator Charles A. LINDBERGH, its most prominent member and spokesperson.

American Civil Liberties Union (ACLU), an organization founded in 1920 by Jane ADDAMS, Helen KELLER, Roger BALDWIN (its director 1920–50), and many other likeminded Americans for the purpose of preserving and developing the constitutionally guaranteed rights of all Americans, whatever their beliefs. With the sole exception of a weakening of this resolve during the witchhunts of the MCCARTHY period, that purpose has been followed, from such cases as those of SCOPES and SACCO AND VANZETTI in the 1920s to a defense of the right of American Nazis to march in Skokie, Illinois, in 1978. The organization came under attack by then-presidential candidate George BUSH during the 1988 presidential campaign, who accused his opponent, Michael DUKAKIS, of being a "card-carrying member" of the ACLU, a charge widely criticized for its associations with the "card-carrying Communist" charges of Senator Joseph MCCARTHY during the witchhunts of the 1950s.

American Expeditionary Force (AEF), the U.S. army in France during World War I.

American Federation of Labor (AFL), a U.S. labor organization organized in 1886, consisting of a group of craft unions seeking to improve the wages and working conditions of its members and opposing direct union participation in politics, though acting as a special interest group in political matters. Led successively by Samuel GOMPERS, William GREEN, and George MEANY, the AFL generally resisted the organization of the unskilled and of industrial unions, splitting in 1935–36 over the organization of industrial unions. Some AFL unions then formed the Committee for Industrial Organizations, which became the CONGRESS OF INDUSTRIAL ORGANIZATIONS (CIO). The great organizing success of the CIO in the next decade created a rival labor federation as large as the AFL itself. But both organizations faltered somewhat in the post–World War II period, with racketeering a great problem for the AFL; the CIO split over COLD WAR political issues, the passage of the TAFT-HARTLEY ACT, and a turn toward conservatism in the United States. George Meany led the AFL into a merged AFL-CIO in 1955.

American Federation of Labor–Congress of Industrial Organizations (AFL-CIO), from 1955 the single organization that joined the AFL and CIO, which had developed as separate organizations since the mid-1930s split in the AFL over the industrial union question and the organization of the CIO. Walter REUTHER led the CIO and George MEANY led the AFL into the joined federation; Meany was its first president, succeeded by Lane KIRKLAND in 1979. The federation expelled the Teamsters Union for corruption in 1957, and Reuther led the United Automobile Workers (UAW) back out of the federation in 1968, the union later reaffiliating. The AFL-CIO generally supported Democratic candidates from the 1950s through the 1980s, but evidenced little power to organize the unorganized or to strongly influence the course of political events after the 1960s.

American Friends Service Committee (AFSC), an American Quaker-based pacifist, nonviolent, and peace-fostering organization that educates and campaigns against all forms of war and for nuclear and all other forms of disarmament.

American Indian Movement (AIM), a radical activist organization, that in the 1970s mounted a series of demonstrations, in an attempt to capture national support for a series of economic and civil rights demands on behalf of American Indians; the best known of these was the 1973 occupation of the Wounded Knee massacre site in South Dakota.

Americans for Democratic Action (ADA), U.S. anti-Communist liberal organization founded in 1947, as leading American liberals attempted to distance themselves from Communism during the early years of the COLD WAR, and the postwar anti-Communist hysteria that developed into the MCCARTHY period. Members of the ADA exerted some influence in liberal Democratic politics through the early 1960s, but thereafter the organization had little influence.

Amiens Offensive (August 8–September 4, 1918), World War I push in which Allied forces attacked weakened German forces at Amiens and then along much of the Western Front, forcing German withdrawal to the HINDENBURG LINE. These attacks and the clearing of the ST.-MIHIEL salient cleared the way for the final Allied offensives of the war.

Amin, Idi (Idi Amin Dada Oumee; 1925–), Ugandan officer, who became armed forces chief in 1966 and in 1971 headed the military coup that toppled President Milton OBOTE. Amin then became president and dictator of Uganda, in the process instituting an 8-year reign of terror, replete with atrocities that attracted worldwide condemnation. He was deposed during the UGANDA–TANZANIA WAR of 1979 by Tanzanian troops invading Uganda in support of Ugandan insurgents; he then fled to Libya and later lived in Saudi Arabia.

Amnesty International, a worldwide London-based human rights organization, founded in 1961, that works to free prisoners of conscience in all countries, ameliorate their conditions of imprisonment, abolish the use of torture, and help the families of those imprisoned; a recipient of the 1977 Nobel Peace Prize.

amniocentesis, withdrawal of fluid from the amniotic sac surrounding the fetus in a pregnant woman, to analyze shed fetal cells for genetic problems; a procedure pioneered in 1952 by British physician Douglas Bevis. If a serious disease or defect is found, such as DOWN'S SYNDROME, the parents may choose to have the fetus aborted or the defect corrected through FETAL SURGERY. Amniocentesis is most often used when mothers are over 35 or family medical history may suggest serious genetic problems, and its use sparked the growth of genetic counseling.

Amoco Cadiz, a supertanker that broke up on rocks in a storm off Portsall, Brittany, on March 17, 1978, spilling 1.6 million barrels of oil into the sea, the worst oil spill to date. The spill created a massive environmental disaster on the coast of western Europe, seriously affecting 200 miles of coastline, as well as coastal waters.

Amritsar massacre (April 13, 1919), killing of at least 379 people and wounding of 1,200 more when British troops in India's Punjab, commanded by General Reginald

Dyer, fired on a crowd of an estimated 10,000 unarmed demonstrators trapped in an open plaza called the Jallianwalla Bagh, which had only one exit. The massacre, accompanied by martial law and followed by a wave of repressive activities, was a central event in the development of the Indian independence movement, immensely aiding the growth of anti-British feeling and nationalist organization.

Amundsen, Roald Engelbregt (1872–1928), Norwegian explorer, who led the first party to reach the SOUTH POLE, arriving on December 14, 1911, one month before Robert SCOTT's ill-fated party. In 1903–06 Amundsen had been the first to sail the fabled NORTHWEST PASSAGE; in 1918–20 he was the second person, the first in the 20th century, to traverse the NORTHEAST PASSAGE without wintering over. In 1926, he, Lincoln ELLSWORTH, and Umberto NOBILE were the first to fly in a DIRIGIBLE over the North Pole, though their claim was disputed by some. Amundsen died 2 years later searching for Nobile, whose dirigible had crashed near Spitsbergen.

An Loc, Siege of (April–July 1972), a divisional-strength VIETNAM WAR engagement, in which North Vietnamese forces attacking in the spring EASTER OFFENSIVE ultimately were repelled by the South Vietnamese with U.S. air support.

analog computer, type of COMPUTER that deals in continuous variables, such as temperature or voltage, unlike DIGITAL COMPUTERS, which work with discrete variables, such as numbers or on-off signals. The first analog computers, prototypes for later electronic versions, were the "network analyzer" and "differential analyzer" developed by Vannevar BUSH 1925–30. Most modern computers are of the digital type, analog computers being best suited to network analysis in special areas such as electrical power networks, telephone systems, hydraulic systems, and psychoneurological networks.

anaphylaxis, extreme type of ALLERGY that can lead to shock and possibly death, first identified in 1902 by French researcher Charles R. Richet.

anarchism, the replacement of the state and all other centralized political forms by free, uncoerced cooperation between individuals, who can then develop a completely egalitarian society. From the late 19th century, in a protracted attempt to destroy state power, some individuals and small groups of anarchists in many countries made assassination attempts on leaders in many countries, as in the 1901 assassination of U.S. president William McKINLEY. Anarchism was then strongly linked with TERRORISM, though the use of assassination and other kinds of terrorism was by no means limited to anarchists, then or later in the century. During the 20th century, anarchism became associated with SYNDICALISM, as anarcho-syndicalism, in that form joining trade unionism with anarchist philosophy in advocating the development of unions that would radicalize masses of workers, paralyze society by means of a general strike, and take power directly without developing other political forms. This was the basic approach of the INDUSTRIAL WORKERS OF THE WORLD and had considerable labor movement strength in Spain, France, and Latin America until the 1930s. In the 1960s a strong stream of anarchist thinking was present in the student movements of the time, although in many instances it was not recognized as such by those attempting to attack state power.

anarcho-syndicalism, 20th-century movement marrying ANARCHISM with SYNDICALISM, advocating the development of unions that would radicalize masses of workers, paralyze society by means of a general strike, and take power directly without developing other political forms.

Anastasia, the youngest child of Czar NICHOLAS II and Alexandra Fyodorovna, a possible survivor of her family's murder in 1918; several have claimed her identity since but without conclusive evidence. The story of Anastasia has generated many books, and two American films, including the classic 1956 Anatole Litvak film, *Anastasia*, with Ingrid Bergman in the title role.

Anderson, John Bayard (1922–   ), U.S. lawyer, in Congress as a Republican from 1960, who ran for the presidency as an independent in 1980 after failing to win the Republican presidential nomination. He secured 7% of the popular vote and no electoral votes.

Anderson, Marian (1902–   ), U.S. singer, one of the most celebrated artists of her time, who because of her race was in 1939 denied the use of Constitution Hall in Washington, D.C., by the Daughters of the American Revolution (DAR). Eleanor ROOSEVELT then intervened, sponsoring a concert on Easter Sunday 1939 at the Lincoln Memorial; an estimated 75,000–100,000 came to hear Anderson sing, and to affirm their own democratic beliefs.

Anderson, Terry, one of the American LEBANON HOSTAGES, an Associated Press Middle East correspondent who was kidnapped on March 15, 1985.

Andrea Doria **sinking** (June 26, 1956), the sinking of the Italian liner *Andrea Doria* in fog off Nantucket Island, after the prow of the Swedish liner *Stockholm* struck it amidships; rescue ships found most of the survivors, but 51 died.

Andrews, Roy Chapman (1884–1960), U.S. explorer and naturalist, long associated with New York City's American Museum of Natural History, who made many expeditions searching for plants and animals, live and extinct. After early specialization in whales, working off Alaska and East Asia, he conducted land explorations in east and central Asia, discovering major new fossil fields, including the first complete dinosaur eggs ever found, and writing popular books about his travels.

Andropov, Yuri Vladimirovich (1914–84), Soviet Communist Party official, who saw service in World War II, was Soviet ambassador to Hungary 1954–57, and was head of the KGB 1967–82. In November 1982, he became his party's general secretary and leader of the Soviet Union, adding the title

of president in June 1983. Although he was ill during most of his brief tenure, he strongly supported the new generation of Soviet leaders then emerging, led by Mikhail GORBACHEV, and many of the anticorruption and other reforms then being discussed, preparing the way for the massive changes of the Gorbachev era.

anemia, insufficiency of red blood cells, a condition first treated with a diet high in liver in 1926 by George Minot and William Murphy, following George Whipple's 1920 experiments with dogs, work for which all three received the 1934 Nobel Prize for Physiology or Medicine. Later it was found that liver was high in VITAMIN B_{12}. By 1947 Mary Shorb had developed a liver extract used for treating anemia.

Angel Island, an island in San Francisco Bay that was used as a U.S. immigration station 1910–40. Until the mid-1920s the island was the site of a major U.S. immigration service attempt to impede Chinese immigration, with immigrants often detained for periods of up to 2 years in conditions much like those of a poorly maintained prison.

Anglo-Japanese Alliance (1902), mutual assistance pacts regarding Chinese and Korean interests, which encouraged Japan to enter the RUSSO-JAPANESE WAR of 1904–05, to annex Korea in 1911, and to enter World War I on the ALLIED side; the pacts were abrogated in 1923.

Anglo-Russian Entente, the St. Petersburg agreement of August 31, 1907, delineating but not entirely settling Russian and British spheres of influence in Central Asia; it was part of the settling of the European powers into two rival systems that characterized the period before World War I.

Angola (People's Republic of Angola), until 1975 a Portuguese colony, winning independence on November 10, 1975, after the long ANGOLAN WAR OF INDEPENDENCE (1961–74), followed by the even longer (1975–   ) ANGOLAN CIVIL WAR. In 1975 the country became the one-party, Marxist-oriented People's Republic of Angola.

Angolan Civil War (1975–), conflict that began on November 11, 1975, the day after the Portuguese pulled out of Angola, ending the long ANGOLAN WAR OF INDEPENDENCE. The three insurgent groups that had fought for independence split the next day; when the Soviet-backed POPULAR MOVEMENT FOR THE LIBERATION OF ANGOLA (MLPA), led by Augustinho NETO, proclaimed the People's Republic of Angola, the NATIONAL FRONT FOR THE LIBERATION OF ANGOLA (FNLA), led by Holden ROBERTO, and the NATIONAL UNION FOR THE TOTAL INDEPENDENCE OF ANGOLA (UNITA), led by Jonas SAVIMBI, joined in armed opposition to the new government. Operating in the north, the FNLA was by 1979 completely defeated by the MPLA, which was joined by an estimated 40,000 Cuban troops and also by Soviet advisors and heavily supplied by the Soviet Union. UNITA, operating in the south, received backing from Portuguese exiles and the South African government, including the support of an estimated 5,000 South African troops early in the conflict. When the South African troops were withdrawn, at the end of 1975, UNITA successfully went over to the same sort of hit-and-run guerrilla war that all three organizations had conducted against the Portuguese, with continuing South African war material support. In some periods, UNITA was also supported by South African trooops moving across the Namibian border in search of Namibian guerrillas based in Angola. After 13 years of civil war, in August 1988 the United States mediated an agreement between Angola, Cuba, and South Africa, providing for the staged withdrawal of Cuban troops from Angola and the cessation of South African aid to UNITA. In November the same parties agreed on a timetable for Cuban withdrawal and on independence for Namibia. UNITA, which was not a participant in the peace talks, vowed to fight on. A UNITA-MPLA truce was signed on June 22, 1989, but held for only 2 months. The Namibian Independence agreement did hold, and free elections, which gave SWAPO a majority, were held in November, 1989.

Angolan War of Independence (1961–74), a long guerrilla war against the Portuguese, conducted by three major organizations. From 1961, the Soviet-backed POPULAR MOVEMENT FOR THE LIBERATION OF ANGOLA (MPLA), led by Augustinho NETO, fought in central Angola, mainly out of bases in Zambia. The NATIONAL FRONT FOR THE LIBERATION OF ANGOLA (FNLA), led by Holden ROBERTO, fought in northern Angola, mainly out of bases in Zaire. In 1966 these were joined by the NATIONAL UNION FOR THE TOTAL INDEPENDENCE OF ANGOLA (UNITA), led by Jonas SAVIMBI, which operated in southern and eastern Angola. Although the insurgent forces could not take Luanda, the capital, by the early 1970s they controlled much of the countryside, tying down an estimated half of the Portuguese army in a long, fruitless colonial war. In 1974 an army coup in Lisbon toppled the Portuguese government; the new government then negotiated independence with the temporarily united insurgents, the Portuguese finishing their withdrawal on November 10, 1975. On November 11 the MPLA announced formation of the People's Republic of Angola, the FNLA and UNITA went into armed opposition, and the ANGOLAN CIVIL WAR began.

Anhwei Incident (1941), an alternate name for the NEW FOURTH ARMY INCIDENT, in which Chinese Nationalist troops attacked their communist allies during the SINO-JAPANESE WAR, presaging the renewed civil war that would come after the defeat of Japan.

Animal Farm (1945), a George ORWELL novel, bitterly satirizing Soviet society during the STALIN era, charging that the RUSSIAN REVOLUTION had been betrayed by its leadership.

Anual, Battle of (1921), RIF WAR battle, in which Moroccan republican forces ambushed and destroyed a much larger, 20,000-strong Spanish force, killing an estimated 12,000 and capturing most of those left alive.

Anschluss (March 12, 1938), the German annexation of Austria, after several years of German attempts to take over the country by use of indigenous Nazi organizations; the annexation was part of the run-up to World War II, for total lack of resistance, within or outside Austria, encouraged Hitler's adventurism. Austria was itself a dictatorship at the time; in 1934 Chancellor Engelbert DOLLFUSS had dissolved all other political parties and put down a subsequent Social Democratic uprising before being assassinated in a failed German-directed Austrian Nazi coup. His successor, Kurt von SCHUSCHNIGG, had continued the dictatorship and tried for a time to resist Nazi takeover but could not do so when his Italian support evaporated.

Antarctic Treaty (December 1959), a multinational treaty effective June 1961, providing that Antarctica would be a nuclear test–free zone, adopting the principle of multinational Antarctic scientific research, and agreeing to defer resolution of territorial claims in the area until the December 1989 treaty expiration.

Antarctica, world's southernmost continent, site of the SOUTH POLE and hence the target of numerous 20th-century expeditions, as well as many research efforts in the INTERNATIONAL GEOPHYSICAL YEAR (1957–58), after which the region was proclaimed an unmilitarized zone kept open for international research.

Anti-Comintern Pact (November 25, 1936), a German-Japanese treaty, in which both countries agreed to support each other against the countries of the COMMUNIST INTERNATIONAL, led by the Soviet Union. The agreement was part of the run-up to World War II, but did not result in Japanese invasion of the Soviet Union after the German 1941 invasion.

antiballistic missile (ABM), type of interceptor missile that destroys incoming BALLISTIC MISSILES in flight however the incoming missiles originate; in use from the 1970s.

antibiotic, organic substance that kills bacteria without killing the body infected by them, the first found and most notable of them being penicillin, discovered by Alexander FLEMING in 1928. René DUBOS was the first person to deliberately search in the soil for naturally occurring antibiotics, finding two—gramicidin and tyrocidin—in 1939, a search widened by others with the success of penicillin, refined and available for medical use by 1940. In 1943 Selman A. Waksman and others discovered streptomycin and in 1949 neomycin; in 1944 Benjamin Duggar and others discovered Aureomycin, the first of the tetracycline antibiotics, made available for medical use by 1948. Other discoveries followed, some from soil and fungi, some synthesized by researchers. And the search continues, for with widespread use of antibiotics new strains of antibiotic-resistant bacteria have developed, especially since many livestock raised for food are routinely fed antibiotics.

antielectron, alternate name for the POSITRON, the first known particle of ANTIMATTER.

Antigua and Barbuda, until 1958, a British colony, Antigua and the neighboring Caribbean island of Barbuda then became a territory and on November 1, 1981, an independent member of the COMMONWEALTH. Except for the period 1971–75, the country has since 1961 been led by Prime Minister Vere Cornwall Bird.

antimatter, atomic PARTICLES of equal size but opposite electrical charge to other atomic particles; on meeting, particles and antiparticles annihilate each other, their mass being converted to energy. British physicist Paul DIRAC first predicted the existence of antimatter in 1928, confirmed in 1932 when U.S. physicist Carl Anderson discovered the positron (or antielectron), the positively charged counterpart of the negatively charged ELECTRON. In 1934 Louis DE BROGLIE introduced the term *antiparticle*. In 1955 Italian-American physicist Emilio

Segré and Owen Chamberlain discovered the antiproton, and a year later a California team found the antineutron. Before long some scientists were talking about the possible existence of whole galaxies of antimatter in the universe.

Antonescu, Ion (1882–1946), a Rumanian fascist who took power in 1940, bringing Rumania into World War II on the side of the AXIS. In August 1944, with Soviet armies about to take Rumania, he was overthrown and in 1946 was executed by the Rumanian government.

Anvil-Dragoon, Operation, the Allied code name for the August–September 1944 French Mediterranean coast landings and subsequent pursuit of German forces in the SOUTHERN FRANCE CAMPAIGN.

Anzio landings, World War II invasion of Italy by Allied seaborne forces on January 22, 1944, landing at Anzio, south of Rome and north of the GUSTAV LINE, the strongly held German defensive line running across Italy. The troops landed were to move inland, cut German communications lines, and link up with Allied forces advancing from the south, across the Gustav Line. The landing was made, but Allied troops were then pinned for 4 months on their small beachhead, much like the Allied troops at GALLIPOLI in World War I, while the advance failed to materialize. Ultimately, in May, the Gustav Line was breached; Allied troops broke out of the Anzio beachheads and joined those coming north from the smashed Gustav Line.

A-1, first French SATELLITE, launched November 26, 1965, making France the third nation in the world to achieve space capability, after the Soviet Union and the United States.

Apalachin Conference, meeting attended by most of the leaders of organized crime in the United States, at the Apalachin, New York, home of Joseph Barbara, Sr. A raid on the meeting by New York state police on November 14, 1957, led to 58 arrests, with great attendant publicity but no significant convictions.

apartheid, the South African system of racial segregation, aimed at institutionalizing racism and preserving the dominance of the country's minority white population. The term was a plank in the 1948 electoral platform of the NATIONAL PARTY; the election brought the MALAN government to power, which then proceeded to create the system promised by the slogan. The apartheid laws adopted from the late 1940s through the early 1960s included a great many punitive provisions aimed at Blacks, other nonwhites, and all opponents of the regime, including internal deportations and exiles, educational segregation, prohibition of interracial marriages and sexual activities, abolition of the right of Blacks to strike, and the creation of Black "homelands." These were accompanied by the Suppression of Communism Act of 1950, which was the basic vehicle for the creation of the police state that South Africa then became. Apartheid also became an excuse for the widespread abuse of dissidents of all races, with an increasingly powerful secret police wielding more and more power as South African society was pulled apart by apartheid, four decades of civil disorders, and a growing guerrilla war. Apartheid also made South Africa a pariah among the nations of the world, being condemned by the UNITED NATIONS repeatedly from 1952 on and by the other nations of the COMMONWEALTH in 1961, after the SHARPEVILLE MASSACRE of 1960. Apartheid has brought worldwide boycotts of South African goods and sports, the withdrawal of many foreign business firms, and widespread internal disturbances, including the massive SOWETO RIOTS of 1976. During the 1980s, facing enraged world opinion and an intransigent internal freedom movement, the BOTHA government took a series of steps aimed at easing some of the most objectionable features of apartheid, but had little success in altering world opinion or braking internal opposition. In the autumn of 1989, the new South African government, led by F.W. de Klerk took a series of steps aimed at relieving tensions, including the release of Walter Sisulu and other long-imprisoned leaders of the AFRICAN NATIONAL CONGRESS and the legalization of the ANC.

Apollo, series of U.S. spacecraft that in 1969 first put humans on the Moon, following President John F. KENNEDY's May 1961 promise to do so within the decade. The Apollo program built on the manned MERCURY and GEMINI space flights and also earlier U.S. unmanned spacecraft programs, including Ranger, which transmitted TELEVISION pictures of the Moon before making a "hard" or crash landing on it; Surveyor, which developed the techniques for making a "soft" landing on the Moon; and Lunar Orbiter, which explored possible landing sites. Tragedy struck in January 1967, when Virgil I. (Gus) GRISSOM, Edward H. White II, and Roger B. Chaffee died in a fire on the ground during a flight rehearsal. But NASA recovered. On July 20, 1969, Neil ARMSTRONG stepped from the lunar module onto the Moon's surface, followed by Edwin Aldrin, Jr.; Michael Collins remained in lunar orbit aboard the *Apollo 11*'s command module. Other Apollo landings followed, bringing back lunar samples and carrying out various experiments, the final mission being *Apollo 17*, launched on December 7, 1972. *Apollo 18* and the U.S.S.R.'s *SOYUZ 19*, both launched on July 15, 1975, docked together in space, on the first joint U.S.–U.S.S.R. mission.

appeasement, Neville CHAMBERLAIN's policy, joined in by the French government, of allowing Germany to have its way in Europe, which from the mid-1930s allowed the NAZIS to occupy the RHINELAND and part of Austria, and take Czechoslovakia. Appeasement paved the way for World War II, rather than bringing the "PEACE FOR OUR TIME" that Chamberlain thought his policy had bought when he gave away Czechoslovakia at MUNICH in 1938. The policy ended after the German takeover of the rest of Czechoslovakia, in March 1939, by then too late to avert the coming war.

Aqualung, underwater breathing apparatus developed in 1943 by Jacques COUSTEAU

and Émil Gagnan, popularly called SCUBA gear.

Aquino, Corazon (Corazon Cojuangco; 1933–   ), president of the Philippines, who took over the leadership of the Liberal Party after her husband, opposition leader Benigno Aquino, was assassinated in August 1983, on his return from exile. In 1986 she ran for the presidency against Ferdinand MARCOS in an election that generated the events of the PHILIPPINE REVOLUTION. She emerged from the revolution president of the Republic of the Philippines, turning her country toward democracy and constitutional government, while at the same time attempting to bring an end to continuing Communist insurgency, repeated coup attempts, and threats from the right, all within the context of a national economy in considerable difficulty.

Arab League (League of Arab States), organization formed in Cairo in March 1945 by Egypt, Saudi Arabia, Iraq, Jordan (then Transjordan), Syria, Lebanon, and Yemen, later joined by several other Arab and partly Arab states and by the PALESTINE LIBERATION ORGANIZATION (PLO). Although largely concerned with the long Arab–Israeli conflict and with economic, political, and propaganda pressure against Israel, the League also functioned as a forum for competing groups of Arab states and supported the Iraqi side during the IRAN-IRAQ WAR. In 1979, Egypt, until then the leading member of the League, was suspended for making a separate peace treaty with Israel.

Arab Legion, the Jordanian army, organized after World War I and trained and commanded by British officers 1921–56, during much of that period being the most effective fighting force in the Arab world. It was commanded by John Bagot GLUBB (Glubb Pasha) 1939–56. In 1948, during the FIRST ARAB-ISRAELI WAR (ISRAELI WAR OF INDEPENDENCE), the Arab Legion defeated the Israeli army at Jerusalem and held much of what is now the WEST BANK for Jordan.

Arab Revolt (June 5, 1916), an insurrection in the Arabian Hejaz region; Arabs led by HUSSEIN IBN ALI, Sharif of Mecca, declared their independence from Turkish rule, attacked Medina, and took Mecca, beginning the war for Arab independence as associates of the Allies in World War I.

Arabian Civil War (1919–25), the long civil war fought in western Arabia (the Hejaz), between the forces of IBN SAUD and those of the Hashemite king of Arabia, HUSSEIN IBN ALI. Hussein abdicated in October 1924, the war then being carried on by his son Ali; Ibn Saud captured Mecca in October 1924, and Medina and Jidda in December 1925, ending the war.

Arafat, Yasir (1929–   ), Palestinian engineer, who became a Palestinian Arab student organizer in the 1950s, was a founder of FATAH in 1959 and became its leader during the 1960s, and from 1969 has been head of the PALESTINE LIBERATION ORGANIZATION (PLO) and chief spokesperson for the Palestinian Arab nationalist movement. Although deeply engaged in conducting a guerrilla and terrorist war against Israel since the 1950s, he is also widely regarded as a moderate in the Arab world, who since 1974 has focused on attempting to negotiate establishment of a Palestinian state on the WEST BANK of the Jordan River. He has publicly disavowed all responsibility for terrorism and in 1988 offered to help find and eliminate terrorists, but is consistently accused of complicity in terrorism by the Israelis and from time to time by some Western governments. His leadership of the PLO has survived all attacks, including expulsions of the PLO from Jordan in 1971 and from Lebanon in 1983, as well as attacks and secessionist movements by elements opposing what they perceived as his moderate policies. He addressed the UNITED NATIONS in 1974 and again in 1988, when the UN moved its General Assembly meeting to Geneva to hear him after the United States refused to admit him.

Aramburu, Pedro (1903–70), Argentinian officer, an anti-Peronist who was provisional president 1955–58, in that period conducting a purge of Juan PERON's supporters and in 1958 conducting free elections. He was assassinated in June 1970 by Peronist guerrillas.

Arbenz Guzmán, Jacobo (1913–71), Guatemalan officer, defense minister 1949–1950, and president 1950–54. His tenure ended with the success of U.S.-backed forces in the GUATEMALAN CIVIL WAR; he then fled into exile.

Arbuckle case, the indictment and trial of film star Roscoe "Fatty" Arbuckle for the alleged rape and murder of actress Virginia Rappe during a 1921 Labor Day weekend party, highly publicized afterward as a Hollywood orgy. Arbuckle was tried twice before hung juries, and was acquitted at his third trial but was then blacklisted by the film industry.

Arcadia Conference (December 1941–January 1942), a wartime ROOSEVELT-CHURCHILL conference held in Washington, that identified the war in the west as the key American-British priority, with the Pacific war to be largely defensive until the near-desperate situation in Europe and the Atlantic improved; the meeting also set up the Combined Chiefs of Staff.

Ardennes, Battle of (August 20–25, 1914), one of the World War I Battles of the FRONTIERS, in which the second major French offensive of World War I was stopped with huge losses.

Ardennes, Battle of (May 12–15, 1940), the decisive battle of early World War II in the west. The German army invaded northern France on May 10, moving through the difficult country of the Ardennes and reaching the Meuse River on May 12. The French were surprised, having expected the main German thrust to come from the north, through Belgium; their negligible forces in the Ardennes were quickly defeated. On May 13, before the French could adequately respond, German armor had broken through near Sedan and crossed the Meuse; by May 15, defending French armies had been smashed, the Allied armies had been split, and the Germans were headed for the

Channel ports, which they reached a week later, forcing the surrender of the Belgian army on May 28, followed by the British evacuation at DUNKIRK.

Ardennes, Battle of the (December 1944–January 1945), an alternative name for the BATTLE OF THE BULGE.

Arendt, Hannah (1906–75), German-American political philosopher and writer, who fled Nazi Germany in 1933. Her major works, including *The Origins of Totalitarianism* (1951), *On Revolution* (1963), and *On Violence* (1970), dealt with freedom, the loss of societal cohesion, and the rise of totalitarianism.

Arias Sánchez, Oscar (1941–   ), Costa Rican economist, who held several economic planning and National Liberation Party posts before becoming president of Costa Rica in 1986. He quickly emerged as a leading force in the search for Central American peace, convening a Latin American summit immediately following his inauguration. His "Arias Plan" of February 1987, for which he was awarded the 1987 Nobel Peace Prize, was a major step toward resolution of the NICARAGUAN CIVIL WAR.

Arktika, U.S.S.R. ship that was the first surface vessel to reach the NORTH POLE, in 1977.

Armenian earthquake (December 7, 1988), a massive earthquake that struck Soviet Armenia, leveling many cities and towns, including the city of Leninakan. An estimated 55,000 people were killed and 500,000 left homeless. Soviet premier Mikhail GORBACHEV cut short a visit to New York on learning of the earthquake. For the first time in decades the Soviet Union welcomed help from abroad in the aftermath of the disaster, and much foreign medical and disaster relief help came.

Armenian Holocaust, the massacres of an estimated 1–1.5 million Armenians by the Turkish government during World War I, most of them dying from famine and disease while in Turkish concentration camps in the Syrian desert. This enormous set of massacres had been preceded by many

other massacres of Armenians by Turks, notably the Constantinople massacres of the late 1870s, the massacres of the mid-1890s, in which hundreds of thousands died, and the 1909 massacres. Most of the surviving Armenians dispersed, large numbers going to what became Soviet Armenia and Azerbaijan, and smaller numbers to the Levant.

Armstrong, Neil Alden (1930–   ), U.S. aviator and astronaut, who became the first human to land on the Moon. After service during the Korean War, Armstrong became a test pilot, then an astronaut. In 1966 he was launched in *Gemini 8*, performing the first U. S. docking in space, and on July 20, 1969, in command of *Apollo 11*, he stepped onto the Moon, saying as he alighted: "That's one small step for a man, one giant leap for mankind."

Army–McCarthy hearings (April–May 1954), 36 days of televised hearings, beginning on April, 22, 1954, in which Senator Joseph R. MCCARTHY accused the U.S. Army of covering up subversive activities at Fort Monmouth, New Jersey, and was himself accused, with his counsel, Roy COHN, of improperly seeking preferential treatment for G. David Schine. These hearings were a turning point for McCarthy; Army counsel Joseph WELCH definitively exposed McCarthy's recklessness and inhumanity, a Senate censure following in December that effectively ended McCarthy's witchhunting career. The national distaste for McCarthy and his methods that followed the hearings also considerably contributed to the subsidence of the anti-Communist hysteria of the period.

Arnhem, Battle of (September 1944), establishment of a bridgehead across the Rhine on September 17, 1944, by British and Polish troops, who were held there by opposing German forces, losing 7,000 of 9,000 men involved in the action before retreating; part of the failed OPERATION MARKET GARDEN.

Arnold, Henry Harley "Hap" (1886–1950), pioneer U.S. aviator, who saw service in World War I, advocated air force development during the interwar period, becoming U.S. Army Air Corps commander in 1938. He was Army Air Corps chief throughout World War II, finishing the war as a five-star general.

Aron, Raymond Claude (1905–83), French journalist, historian, and sociologist, who edited the FREE FRENCH London-based publication *La France Libre* during World War II, and wrote from a left-centrist position on politics for *Le Figaro* 1947–77, while also teaching and writing several substantial works in politics and sociology.

Arras, Battle of (April 9–15, 1917), World War I attack on German forces at Arras, in France, by British troops, among them troops of the Canadian Corps, in support of the much larger NIVELLE OFFENSIVE that was to begin April 16. The Canadians suffered 11,000 casualties while taking VIMY RIDGE on the first day of the battle; combined British and German casualties numbered at least 150,000. The attack failed; the German line was not broken.

arsenal of democracy, phrase coined by U. S. president Franklin Delano ROOSEVELT on December 29, 1940, in a broadcast to the nation; from "We must be the great arsenal of democracy."

artificial heart, mechanical blood-pumping device designed to aid or replace—temporarily or permanently—an ailing human heart. In the mid-1930s, Alexis CARREL and Charles LINDBERGH pioneered in developing a pumping machine, popularly called the Lindbergh machine, to supply blood to a patient's organs, keeping them alive outside the body. This prototype of an external artificial heart was further developed by others, notably by John H. Gibbon, Jr., who developed a heart-lung machine and in 1953 used it keep his patient, Cecelia Bavolek, alive during heart surgery; and by Denton COOLEY, who developed a widely used heart-lung bypass machine in 1955. In 1967 U.S. surgeon Michael DE BAKEY made the first actual implant of an artificial heart, to aid the heart of his patient, who lived for 4 days. In 1969 Dr. Cooley made the first

temporary implant of an artificial heart to replace a patient's own heart, for 5 days while a donor was sought. The patient, Haskell Karp, died the day after the second operation. Numerous artificial heart designs were tried over the decades. In 1982 a team of surgeons led by William DeVries made the first permanent implant of a mechanical heart designed by Robert K. Jarvik and W. J. Kolff; the patient was Barney Clark, who lived with the polyurethane Jarvik-7 device for 112 days. The survival rate was so poor, however, that by the late 1980s replacement was being phased out in favor of aiding the heart, notably with artificial pump-assist devices or with muscle transplanted from elsewhere in the body.

artificial intelligence (AI), so-far theoretical machine recreation of the workings of the human brain; a possibility seen by a few pre-20th-century visionaries, but actively explored only since the mid-20th century with the rise of COMPUTERS. Exploring the question in the 1930s, Alan TURING developed a theoretical test to distinguish between a human brain and a machine. In the 1930s and 1940s various scientists, notably Norbert WIENER, codified ideas about FEEDBACK—in essence, the ability of a machine to "learn" from experience and modify its workings to meet changing conditions. Early computer experts, who coined the term "artificial intelligence" in the early 1950s, met at Dartmouth College in 1956 to begin a concerted drive toward achieving it. Though their work spawned no electronic brains to approach human ones in their manner of operation, especially in their ability to deal with imprecise or incomplete data, the increasing power and sophistication of supercomputers at least made such a possibility more realistic. Among the practical offshoots of their work has been the development of ROBOTS and sophisticated diagnostic programs, those used by physicians. The anticipated "fifth generation" of computers is to be built around ideas of artificial intelligence.

ASEAN, the initials of the ASSOCIATION OF SOUTHEAST ASIAN NATIONS.

Asian flu, worldwide influenza pandemic of 1957–58; it affected more people than the INFLUENZA PANDEMIC of 1918–19 but was less lethal, probably because ANTIBIOTICS had been developed to treat secondary infections.

Ask not what your country can do for you; ask what you can do for your country, statement by U.S. president John Fitzgerald KENNEDY, in his Inaugural Address, January 20, 1961.

Asquith, Herbert Henry (1852–1928), British barrister, Liberal MP, and cabinet member, who was prime minister 1908–16. Asquith was a moderate social reformer who found it difficult to deal with such major social movements of his time as the rise of trade unionism and the campaign for WOMAN SUFFRAGE, and whose long intraparty feud with David LLOYD GEORGE seriously damaged the Liberal party. He lost his position to Lloyd George in 1916.

Assad, Hafez al (1928–   ), Syrian air force officer, who was the leader of the BA'ATH PARTY coup of 1963, then becoming air force commander, and minister of defense after the coup of 1966. He took power in his own 1970 coup and formally assumed the office of president in 1971, becoming sole ruler except for a period of ill health in 1983–84. His government has maintained a close alliance with the Soviet Union, opposed Israel and suffered several defeats at their hands, defeated a MOSLEM BROTHERHOOD revolt at Hama in 1982, intervened in force in Lebanon and partially occupied that country during the LEBANESE WARS, and supported Iran during the IRAN-IRAQ WAR of the 1980s.

Association of Southeast Asian Nations (ASEAN), a regional association of six non-Communist southeast Asian nations, established in 1967, which until the mid-1970s was primarily concerned with regional political matters but since then has increasingly been involved in developing common economic cooperation and attempting to correct growing trade imbalances.

Astor, Nancy Langhorne (1879–1964), American-born Conservative, who became the first woman to sit in the British parliament (1919–45). During her career she was both a reformer and, with her husband, Waldorf Astor, a leader of the right-wing CLIVEDEN SET, a group that in the 1930s saw COMMUNISM as a greater menace than FASCISM, and sought to appease HITLER.

Aswan High Dam, a large Egyptian dam near the first cataract of the Nile, built in the 1960s with the help of Soviet loans after withdrawal of promised British and U.S. funding had led Egyptian president Gamal Abdel NASSER to nationalize the Suez Canal, precipitating the SUEZ CRISIS and the SINAI-SUEZ WAR (SECOND ARAB-ISRAELI WAR).

Atanasoff, John Vincent (1903–   ), theoretical physicist who, with Clifford E. Berry, built the world's first fully electronic COMPUTER, the ABC (**A**tanasoff-**B**erry **C**omputer), 1939–42, after more than 2 years of planning. In the confusion of wartime Atanasoff obtained no patents for his computer, and by 1946 the ENIAC, funded heavily by the government for military purposes, had been built. Atanasoff had spent several days in 1941 showing his machine to John Mauchly, one of ENIAC's creators. But he and most other people did not realize the extent of his contribution to modern computers until 1973, when, in a lawsuit regarding royalties paid to ENIAC's creators, a U.S. federal judge voided the ENIAC patent because it was based on Atanasoff's work in so many respects.

Atanasoff-Berry Computer, full name of the world's first fully electronic computer, built 1939–42 by John Vincent ATANASOFF and Clifford E. Berry; better known as the ABC.

Atatürk, Mustapha Kemal (1881–1938), Turkish commander at GALLIPOLI during World War I, leader of the Turkish revolution that deposed the Ottomans in the early 1920s, commander of Turkish forces during the GREEK-TURKISH WAR of 1920–22, and founder and first president of the Turkish Republic. After Turkish victory in the Greek-Turkish War he forced replacement of the very severe Treaty of SÈVRES of 1920 with the much more favorable Treaty of LAUSANNE of 1923. As virtual dictator of Turkey, he stifled all internal dissent, while at the same time moving Turkey away from traditional Islam and toward Western society. Originally Mustapha Kemal, in 1933 he renamed himself Atatürk, or Father of the Turks.

Athens-Beirut airport hijacking (June 14–30, 1985), hijacking of a Trans World Airlines (TWA) Boeing 727, en route from Athens to Rome with 153 passengers, by ISLAMIC HOLY WAR terrorists. The plane flew to Beirut, where the terrorists demanded release of over 700 Shiite Moslem Israeli prisoners, then to Algiers, and back to Beirut. At the first two stops some passengers were released; at the third, the terrorists murdered U.S. Navy diver Robert Stethem. The plane then flew back to Algiers, where the release of a terrorist arrested at Athens was negotiated in return for the release of more passengers. The plane then flew back to Beirut, where 2 weeks of negotiations, in which AMAL leader Nabih BERRI took a leading part, ultimately led to the freeing of the hostages and release of over 300 Arab prisoners by the Israelis. All of the hijackers escaped into Beirut.

Atlanta mass murders, killings of 28 young Black people, most of them children, in Atlanta during the period 1979–81. Prompted by enormous national concern, complete with a special grant of $1.5 million authorized by President Ronald REAGAN and a visit to Atlanta by Vice-President George BUSH, a massive hunt for the supposed single murderer ensued. Wayne B. Williams of Atlanta was indicted for two of the murders on July 17, 1981; he was convicted of both on February 27, 1982, and subsequently sentenced to life imprisonment. Whether he committed all of the murders is as yet unknown; however, the murders stopped after his arrest and imprisonment.

Atlantic, Battle of the, in both World Wars, the battle of the British and American navies against German SUBMARINE WARFARE.

In both wars the German submarine fleet was ultimately defeated but not without enormous Allied shipping losses.

Atlantic Charter (1941), the statement of war aims issued by ROOSEVELT and CHURCHILL after their wartime conference off Newfoundland August 9–12, 1941, which affirmed joint American-British desires for world peace, freedom, and self-determination. The Atlantic Charter was a powerful ideological motivator during the war; much of it was included in the UNITED NATIONS Charter.

Atlantic City Conference, meeting of most of the leaders of organized crime in the United States, including Al CAPONE, Charles "Lucky" LUCIANO, Frank Costello, Meyer Lansky, Louis "Lepke" Buchalter, and many others. Held at the President Hotel in Atlantic City in May 1929, the conference resulted in an agreement to set up the first national crime syndicate.

Atlantic Wall, the series of German fortifications along the shoreline of Western Europe, aimed at barring invasion from the sea, which little impeded the NORMANDY invasion on D-DAY, June 6, 1944.

Atlantis, fourth of the U.S. SPACE SHUTTLES, launched initially in 1985; on its third flight, in 1989, it was used to launch the first space probe from a shuttle, the *Magellan,* headed toward VENUS.

atomic bomb (A-bomb), explosive device employing NUCLEAR FISSION, used to destroy HIROSHIMA and NAGASAKI, Japan, on August 6 and August 9, 1945, quickly bringing World War II to a close and beginning the period of fear for the survival of life on Earth that is the Nuclear Age. Concern as to possible German development of the bomb led Albert EINSTEIN and others to urge President Franklin D. ROOSEVELT to authorize accelerated American development of the bomb. The result was the MANHATTAN PROJECT, 1942–45, which produced the first atomic bomb, exploded in a test code-named TRINITY at ALAMOGORDO, New Mexico, on July 16, 1945. Though the atomic bomb ended the war without a costly invasion of Japan, many people—including many who worked on the bomb—soon began to fear its power and urge its strict control. Despite the fears, nuclear technology spread: the Soviet Union had its own atomic bomb by 1949, Britain by 1952, France by 1960, and China by 1964. By 1949, the atomic bomb was being used as a triggering device for the far more powerful HYDROGEN BOMB (H-bomb).

atomic clock, device that uses atomic or molecular oscillations to keep time, far more accurately than conventional timekeeping devices; the first was built by the U.S. Bureau of National Standards in 1948, using ammonia molecules. The Bureau later developed an even more accurate clock, using cesium 133, and popularly called the cesium clock; its oscillations were adopted as the new international standard "atomic second" in 1964. By 1979 U.S. scientists had developed a hydrogen MASER clock that they calculated could, if kept in a constant environment, run 50 million years without losing a second.

Atomic Energy Commission (AEC), U.S. agency to regulate development of nuclear weapons—the ATOMIC BOMB and the HYDROGEN BOMB—and nuclear energy, whether from NUCLEAR FISSION or NUCLEAR FUSION; established by the 1946 Atomic Energy Act to replace the MANHATTAN PROJECT. In a major controversy the AEC in 1953 removed J. Robert OPPENHEIMER, former head of the Manhattan Project, from chairmanship of its General Advisory Committee. From 1954 the AEC allowed private companies to work in atomic production and research under government supervision. The AEC was disbanded in 1974 and replaced with two agencies: the Energy Research and Development Administration (ERDA) and the Nuclear Regulatory Commission (NRC).

atomic pile, early alternate name for a NUCLEAR REACTOR, more specifically the conglomerate of material massed for the NUCLEAR FISSION reaction.

atomic structure, basic model of the atom as a positively charged central NUCLEUS, including one or more uncharged NEUTRONS and one or more positively charged PROTONS, surrounded by rings or a "cloud" of negatively charged spinning ELECTRONS. In 1904 Joseph THOMSON, discoverer of the electron, first suggested that electrons sat in orbits around a positively charged sphere; and Japanese physicist Hantaro Nagaoka posed the idea of the central nucleus, which was then rejected as impossible. But in 1911 Ernest RUTHERFORD, with Hans GEIGER and Ernest Marsden, developed the first practical nucleus-centered model (in 1914 Rutherford also discovered the PROTON). Two years later Niels BOHR modified the atomic model, drawing on Max PLANCK'S QUANTUM THEORY to suggest that electrons circle the nucleus in fixed concentric orbits or "shells," emitting energy in discrete units as they jumped from orbit to orbit. Also in 1913, British physicist Henry Gwyn Jeffreys Moseley, using X-RAY analysis, first equated the atomic number assigned to each element on chemistry's periodic charts with the electric charge on an atom's nucleus. In 1925 Wolfgang PAULI posited that each electron occupied a unique state in an atom, an idea called the EXCLUSION PRINCIPLE; in the same year Dutch-American physicists Samuel Goudsmit and George Eugene Uhlenbeck contributed the idea that electrons must have an intrinsic spin; and in 1932 James Chadwick discovered the NEUTRON. These completed the general picture of the atom at this level, but by the 1950s physicists had found that some of these atomic elements were themselves further subdivisible into even smaller PARTICLES.

Attica Prison riot, hostage-taking and seizure of part of the Attica, New York, state prison on September 9, 1971, by approximately 1,000 inmates. After 4 days of negotiations, and spurred by charges of atrocities being committed by the inmates upon their hostages, 1,500 police stormed and took the prison, killing 29 inmates and 9 hostages, who were caught in police crossfire. Later investigation indicated that the atrocity reports had little or no factual basis.

Attlee, Clement Richard (1883–1967), British barrister, who in 1905 took up the cause of the poor, went to live in the slums of London's East End, and became Labour MP for Limehouse. He was leader of the British Labour Party 1935–55, a member of Winston CHURCHILL'S wartime coalition cabinet, and postwar prime minister 1945–51. In the 1930s he supported anti-Fascist causes such as the Loyalist side in the SPANISH CIVIL WAR, and opposed APPEASEMENT. As prime minister he carried out Labour's nationalization of much of Britain's basic industry and establishment of the NATIONAL HEALTH SERVICE while also presiding over the dissolution of much of the British Empire.

Auchinleck, Claude (1884–1981), British officer, who served in India, saw action in World War I, and again served in India during the interwar period. A field marshal during World War II, he scored early North African successes as British Middle Eastern commander in 1941, but was relieved of command after a series of German victories, returning to command British forces in India.

Aung San (1914–47), Burmese nationalist leader, who fought with the Japanese during World War II, then organized and led the Burmese National Army revolt against the Japanese in March 1945, going over into an anti-Japanese guerrilla war on the side of the ALLIES. In 1947, after British withdrawal plans from Burma were announced, he became prime minister of the Burmese government then in formation, but was assassinated, with five members of his cabinet, on July 19, 1947, and was succeeded as prime minister by U NU.

Auschwitz-Birkenau (Oswiecim), a German CONCENTRATION CAMP complex in central Poland, near Cracow, opened in 1940, at which during the period 1942–44 at least 2 million people were murdered by the Nazis, most of them from Poland and the Soviet Union and mostly Jews. The estimates of the numbers of those murdered may be on the low side.

Australia (Commonwealth of Australia), in 1901, the British colonies of New South Wales, Queensland, South Australia, Tasmania, Victoria, and Western Australia, which then became states within the new Commonwealth of Australia, a member of the COMMONWEALTH.

Austria (Republic of Austria), until November 1918 part of the Austro-Hungarian empire, afterward a republic. In 1934, after socialist–fascist clashes, Austria became a fascist dictatorship on the Italian model under prime minister Engelbert DOLLFUSS; his successor, Kurt von SCHUSCHNIGG, ceded Austria to the Nazis in the ANSCHLUSS of 1938, and the country was then incorporated into Germany until 1945. The republic was revived in 1945; it was led by highly controversial former UNITED NATIONS president Kurt WALDHEIM from 1986.

Autumn Harvest Uprisings (September 1927), unsuccessful armed rural revolts led by MAO ZEDONG in the Yangtse River valley that marked the beginning of the turn from the Communist strategy of urban revolution in China to the peasant-based strategy that would ultimately take the Chinese Communist party to power.

Axis Sally (Mildred Gillars; 1900–1988), American who became a Nazi broadcaster in Europe during World War II and was popular listening for American soldiers, who paid little attention to her message but rather liked her song selection, especially the German song "Lili Marlene." She was convicted of treason in 1949 and was imprisoned for 12 years.

Axis, The, the German–Japanese–Italian alliance that, with its lesser allies, fought the ALLIES in World War II. Benito MUSSOLINI supplied the name in a 1936 speech, calling his recently concluded secret treaty with HITLER an "axis" around which like-minded powers could circulate.

Ayub Khan, Mohammad (1907–1974), Pakistani officer in the British army, who saw service in Burma in World War II and became commander in chief of the Pakistani army in 1951. On October 7, 1960, he became chief martial law administrator when President Iskander Mirza took dictatorial power; on October 27 he took power from Mirza. He held power until March 1969, when growing economic and political problems, together with the growth of domestic opposition, forced his resignation. Then his army commander in chief, General Agha Mohammad Yahya Khan, became chief martial law administrator and took dictatorial power, and Ayub Khan retired from public life.

Azerbaijani-Armenian Civil War (1988–), in February 1988, a longstanding dispute between the Soviet republics of Armenia and Azerbaijan, over the Christian Armenian enclave of NAGORNO-KARABAGH, in largely Moslem Azerbaijan,

became an armed conflict. Armenia demanded sovereignty; nationalist Azerbaijanis responded with armed attacks on Armenian populations in Azerbaijan. In Sumgait, after at least 30 were killed, Soviet troops restored order. The dispute continued and grew, with large demonstrations in both republics. Soviet troops intervened again in November 1988 and August 1989, as Azerbaijani nationalists attacked Armenians, forced an estimated 100,000 from their homes, and blockaded Armenia, while a border war developed between the two republics. In January 1990, the conflict grew even further; characterizing it as very nearly a civil war, Soviet forces in divisional strength moved in, took Baku by force, and reimposed order, while negotiations proceeded.

B

Baader-Meinhof Gang (Red Army Faction), German Federal Republic anarchist-terrorist guerrilla group, organized primarily by Andreas Baader, that carried out a substantial series of bombings, robberies, and murders from 1968 to 1972. Baader was imprisoned in 1968 but escaped with the help of Ulrike Meinhof, a journalist, who then joined and worked with him until their capture in June 1972. In May 1976, Meinhof, then on trial, was found dead in her cell, having allegedly committed suicide; mass demonstrations charging police murder followed. In October 1977, Baader and two other group members, having been convicted and imprisoned, were found dead in prison, as well, also allegedly having committed suicide. The Red Army Faction continued its terrorist course.

Ba'ath Party (Arab Socialist Renaissance party), organization founded as part of a socialist, pan-Arab movement in the mid-1930s and formally organized into a political party in 1947, its first strength being in Syria, although Ba'ath groups were also organized in many other Arab countries. The Syrian Ba'ath party came to power in the coup of 1963; since 1970 it has been led by Hafez al-ASSAD. The Iraqi Ba'ath party, a rival group within the Ba'ath movement, came to power in the coup of 1968; since 1971 it has been led by Saddam HUSSEIN. Ba'ath groups continue to operate in Lebanon, Jordan, and other Arab countries but have achieved no major successes.

Badoglio, Pietro (1871–1956), Italian officer, who became chief of staff after World War I, was Benito MUSSOLINI'S chief of staff in 1925, and was a marshal of the Italian army from 1926. He was commander-in-chief of Italian forces in the ETHIOPIAN–ITALIAN WAR and again in 1940, but he lost his post after the major Italian defeat in Greece. In 1943 he succeeded Mussolini as Italian premier, signed an armistice with the Allies on September 3, 1943, and resigned in 1944.

Baghdad, Fall of (March 11, 1917), World War I taking of Baghdad, by British forces, which had retaken KUT (February 22–23), advancing along the Tigris River. Subsequently, British forces secured Mesopotamia.

Bahamas (Commonwealth of the Bahamas), until 1973 a British colony, with increasing self-government from 1964; it became an independent member of the COMMONWEALTH on July 10, 1973. The country was led by Prime Minister Lynden Oscar Pindling from 1967.

Bahrain, until 1971 a British protectorate; on August 15, 1971, it became an independent state, ruled by Sheikh Salman ibn Hamad Al Khalifa. Bahrain is closely associated with Saudi Arabia and the United States.

Baird, John Logie, (1888–1946), Scottish inventor, who in 1926 demonstrated the first practical TELEVISION in London and 2 years later made the first trans-Atlantic television transmission and demonstrated the first color television. Baird's system was a mechanical one, however, and though briefly used by the British Broadcasting Corporation (BBC) in 1936, it was soon replaced by an all-ELECTRONIC television system.

Baker, Howard (1925–   ), U.S. lawyer, Tennessee Republican senator 1966–85, minority leader of the Senate 1976–80, and majority leader 1980–85. An unsuccessful candidate for the Republican presidential nomination in 1980, he resigned from the Senate in 1984, planning to run again for the 1988 nomination. Instead, he agreed to succeed Donald REGAN as President Ronald REAGAN'S chief of staff in 1987, serving until July 1988.

Baker, James A., III (1930–   ), U.S. lawyer, from 1970 closely associated with George BUSH in Texas Republican politics. He was an undersecretary of commerce 1975–76, managed Bush's unsuccessful 1980 presidential campaign, and was Ronald REAGAN'S chief of staff 1981–85; he then swapped posts with Donald REGAN, becoming secretary of the treasury (1985–88). He resigned in August 1988 to manage Bush's successful presidential campaign and became secretary of state in the first Bush cabinet.

Baker* v. *Carr (1962), a landmark U.S. Supreme Court decision striking down discriminatory electoral apportionment practices, which forced massive reapportionment throughout the United States.

Bakke case (*Regents of the University of California* v. *Bakke*, 1978), a landmark U.S. Supreme Court decision requiring the admission to medical school of a qualified student who had been refused admission because of a quota system explicitly favoring certain minority students. The decision therefore invalidated key aspects of many educational special admissions programs throughout the United States.

Bakker-PTL scandal, the 1987 scandal that followed exposure of unbecoming sexual conduct on the part of the Reverend Jim BAKKER, a star television evangelist broadcasting on his own PTL (Praise The Lord) network. Bakker resigned his PTL position in March 1987 after being accused of having had sex with Jessica Hahn in 1980 and then buying Hahn's silence in 1985. The public accusations were generated, at least in part, by TV evangelist Jimmy SWAGGART, who was himself involved in a 1988

sexual scandal. Bakker passed PTL to another televangelist, Jerry FALWELL, later trying and failing to regain control. Falwell, after trying to reclaim the PTL enterprise, ultimately gave up, PTL then going into bankruptcy. In May 1988, Bakker was dismissed from his Assemblies of God ministry amid charges of bisexuality. Later in 1988 he and his wife, Tammy Faye Bakker, had little success in attempting to resume their religious broadcasting careers. On October 5, 1989, he was convicted on 24 counts of fraud and conspiracy, resulting in a 45-year jail sentence.

Balaguer, Joaquin (1907–   ), Dominican Republic lawyer and diplomat, who held a series of posts under dictator Rafael TRUJILLO, including that of president of the republic in 1960. After Trujillo's assassination he left the country, returned during the DOMINICAN REPUBLIC CIVIL WAR, and was subsequently elected to the presidency as the moderate candidate of the country's commercial and military elites. He defeated Juan BOSCH in 1966, remained president until 1978, and came back at the age of 78 to win the presidency again in 1985.

Balch, Emily Greene (1867–1961), U.S. social worker, teacher, and peace activist who worked with Jane ADDAMS at HULL HOUSE and worked and wrote on immigration and child welfare matters starting in the 1890s. A pacifist, she opposed U.S. participation in World War I, and for that opposition she lost her teaching position at Wellesley College in 1918. In 1919 she became a founder and first secretary of the WOMEN'S INTERNATIONAL LEAGUE FOR PEACE AND FREEDOM. Her work as a peace activist remained a primary concern for rest of her life; she was co-recipient of the Nobel Peace Prize in 1946.

Baldwin, James Arthur (1924–87), U.S. writer and Black civil rights leader, who powerfully attacked racism in such novels and essays as his semiautobiographical *Go Tell It on the Mountain* (1953), *Notes of a Native Son* (1955), and *The Fire Next Time* (1963).

Baldwin, Roger Nash (1884–1981), U.S. social worker, pacifist, and civil libertarian, director of the American Union Against Militarism during World War I, who was imprisoned during 1918 as a conscientious objector. In 1920 he was a founder of the AMERICAN CIVIL LIBERTIES UNION (ACLU) and was its first director, 1920–50, and then its chairman, 1950–55.

Baldwin, Stanley (1867–1947), three-time prime minister of Great Britain (1923; 1924–29; 1936–37), a Conservative MP, and then cabinet minister. With Bonar LAW he led his party out of the coalition with LLOYD GEORGE in 1922, was Law's chancellor of the exchequer, and became prime minister in 1923 after Law resigned due to illness. Defeated in January 1924, he came back as prime minister in November. He broke the GENERAL STRIKE of 1926, followed up with the repressive Trade Disputes Act, and survived in office until June 1929. He came back as prime minister once again, in June 1935, but, faced with international issues he found difficult, he did nothing while Italy invaded ETHIOPIA, Germany marched into the RHINELAND, and Germany and Italy rehearsed for World War II in the SPANISH CIVIL WAR. He did take a few small steps toward British rearmament in response to German and Italian aggression and also forced the abdication of EDWARD VIII—who chose Wallis SIMPSON over his crown—handling that matter smoothly. He retired in May 1937, to be succeeded by Neville CHAMBERLAIN.

Balfour, Arthur James (1848–1930), British diplomat and political leader, who was prime minister 1902–05 and whose 55-year-long public career included 48 years as a Conservative MP (1874–1922), several cabinet posts, and an important international role after World War I. He authored the BALFOUR DECLARATION, issued by the British government in 1917, while he was foreign secretary; it supported, with important qualifications, the formation of a Jewish homeland in Palestine.

Balfour Declaration (November 2, 1917), a letter issued by then British foreign secretary Arthur BALFOUR, stating that it was the policy of the British government to try to establish a Jewish homeland in Palestine, provided that nothing be done to harm the civil and religious rights of non-Jewish communities in Palestine or the rights and political status of Jews in other countries. This declaration became the official position of the ALLIES at the PARIS PEACE CONFERENCE of 1919, which resulted in the Treaty of VERSAILLES and the establishment of the British mandate over Palestine.

Balkan campaign of 1944–45 (October 1944–May 1945), series of late World War II engagements in which advancing Soviet forces took Belgrade on October 20, 1944, crossed the Danube in late November, and besieged Budapest, taking that city on February 13 and Vienna on April 15, then moving up the Danube Valley to meet the Americans.

Balkan League, the 1912 alliance of Bulgaria, Greece, and Serbia. Balkan League forces moving against the Turks began the 1912–13 BALKAN WARS.

Balkan Wars (1912–13), two wars involving Balkan countries, part of the run-up to World War I. Bulgaria, Greece, and Serbia formed the Balkan League in 1912; Montenegro also was associated with the League. The First Balkan War began on October 17, 1912, when Balkan League armies totaling 300,000–400,000 men attacked Turkish forces almost as large in Macedonia and Thrace, winning a decisive victory at Monastir, capturing Salonika, besieging Constantinople, and ultimately taking Adrianople and Yannina. Threatened with a general European war, the major powers forced both sides to make peace; at the Treaty of London, May 30, 1913, the new nation of Albania was created, and the Balkan League countries divided up almost all of what was left of European Turkey. But Bulgaria was dissatisfied and early in June began the Second Balkan War with surprise attacks on Serbia and Greece. In mid–July, Rumania and Turkey came into the war, against Bulgaria. Bulgaria was defeated and lost the gains made in the First Balkan War at the Treaty of Bucharest, August 10, 1913.

ballistic missile, self-powered, pilotless, flying vehicle, equipped with explosives, often nuclear, the bomb-carrying tip called a warhead. Those for long range (over 5,500 km) are INTERCONTINENTAL BALLISTIC MISSILES; those for medium range are INTERMEDIATE RANGE BALLISTIC MISSILES (IRBMs) or Intermediate-range Nuclear Missiles, the subject of the 1988 INF Treaty; those with multiple warheads are MULTIPLE INDEPENDENTLY TARGETABLE REENTRY VEHICLES (MIRVs); and those designed to intercept and destroy other ballistic missiles are ANTIBALLISTIC MISSILES (ABMs).

balloon angioplasty, non-surgical alternative to a CORONARY BYPASS operation, to deal with clogged arteries. The technique, developed in 1977 by Andreas R. Gruentzig, involves threading tubes into arteries and inflating "balloons" at the ends to compress the material clogging the arteries.

Baltic Campaign of 1944–45 (October 1944–May 1945), attack on German forces in Latvia by advancing Soviet armies, which soon pushed through to the Baltic and then moved forward into East Prussia and along the Baltic coast. By mid–April, Soviet forces had taken Danzig (Gdansk), Königsberg, and much of the Baltic coast, the German navy having evacuated much of the northern army and over a million civilians from those areas.

bamboo curtain, a COLD WAR term describing the isolation of the People's Republic of CHINA from much of the Western world, although inapplicable to its relationships with the countries of the THIRD WORLD and the Soviet bloc. The term fell into disuse during the late 1960s.

Banda, Hastings Kamuzu (1902–), Malawi political leader, who became head of his country's independence movement in 1958 on his return home from decades abroad. He became prime minister of newly independent Malawi in 1963 and president in 1966, having himself declared president-for-life of his one-party state in 1971. As president, he fostered a multiracial state, although maintaining such cordial relations with South Africa as to rouse the anger of neighboring Black African countries, which forced him in the late 1980s to take a somewhat harder line toward the South African government.

Bandaranaike, Sirimavo (Sirimavo Ratwatte; 1916–), Sri Lankan political leader, who became prime minister of Ceylon (Sri Lanka from 1972) and the world's first woman prime minister (1960–65; 1970–77), succeeding her assassinated husband, Solomon Bandaranaike (1899–1959). A socialist, she pursued a program of nationalization, although one not radical enough for the People's Liberation Front, which in 1971 conducted a brief, unsuccessful insurgency. In 1980, then out of power, she was expelled from parliament by her opponents.

Bandung Conference (April 1955), an international conference sponsored by President SUKARNO at Bandung, Indonesia, and attended by the representatives of 29 African and Asian nations, with observers from several other countries. The Bandung meeting prefigured the modern NONALIGNED MOVEMENT, focusing on common action against colonialism and racism within the context of a neutralist position regarding the COLD WAR.

Bangladesh (People's Republic of Bangladesh), until 1947 part of East Bengal in British colonial India. With the 1947 partition of India into India and Pakistan, largely Moslem East Bengal became part of Pakistan. In 1971 a 17-year struggle for autonomy, led by Mujibur RAHMAN, culminated in the BANGLADESH WAR OF INDEPENDENCE and the INDIA–PAKISTAN WAR OF 1971. On December 16, 1971, Bangladesh became an independent state, led by Prime Minister Rahman.

Bangladesh War of Independence (March–December 1971), conflict that resulted when the Awami League, led by Sheikh Mujibur RAHMAN, won the December 1970

Pakistani elections and the ruling military government of Pakistan refused to convene the new national assembly; in response, a massive civil disobedience campaign paralyzed East Pakistan. The government then outlawed the Awami League and undertook repressive action. Rahman declared East Pakistan independent on March 26, as an armed insurrection broke out. Insurgent forces were defeated by the Pakistani army within 6 weeks, with tens of thousands of insurgent dead and an estimated 6–10 million refugees fleeing to India. The insurgency continued as an Indian-supported guerrilla war from bases in India. On December 3, with the outbreak of the INDIA–PAKISTAN WAR OF 1971, strong Indian forces invaded East Pakistan, taking Dacca in 2 weeks, along with 90,000 Pakistani troops, and then installing the Bangladesh government-in-exile as the legitimate government of the new country. Rahman, who had been imprisoned in Pakistan since the March outbreak of the insurrection, returned early in 1972 to become first prime minister of Bangladesh.

bank holiday (1933), the temporary closing of all U.S. banks by President Franklin D. ROOSEVELT on March 6, 1933, the day after he took office, to forestall a developing banking system crisis. Bank reopenings began on March 13, after Roosevelt's first FIRESIDE CHAT, a radio address successfully reassuring the nation that the banking system was sound.

Banting, Frederick Grant (1891–1941), leader of the team that in 1921 discovered INSULIN and developed the basic treatment of diabetes.

Bao Dai (Nguyen Vinh Thuy; 1913–   ), the puppet ruler of Vietnam for the French (1926–40), the Japanese (1940–45), and the French again (1949–55), who was put aside by NGO DINH DIEM in 1955.

Barbados, until 1966, a British colony. The country became an independent state and member of the COMMONWEALTH on November 30, 1966. It was initially led by Errol

Walton BARROW, prime minister from 1961 to 1976.

Barbarossa, Operation, the code name of the German plan to invade the Soviet Union in 1941. The invasion began on June 22, 1941, on a front running from the Black Sea to the Baltic. By late July, the German central front armies had taken Minsk and Smolensk, with Soviet losses that included almost 400,000 prisoners, over 4,000 tanks, and thousands of artillery pieces. By late September the German southern armies also had taken Kiev and with it an estimated 600,000 more prisoners and much armor. By late October, Leningrad was besieged, Sevastopol was threatened, over half a million more prisoners had been taken, and the Germans were moving on Moscow, ultimately reaching within 15 miles of the city. But they went no farther; mud had slowed them down in late autumn, winter made the advance far more difficult, and the Soviets threw powerful new forces into the line in early December, then going on the offensive. Barbarossa had failed.

Barbie, Klaus (1913–   ), World War II Nazi war criminal, an SS officer in Holland 1940–41 and in France 1942–44. He committed war crimes against Dutch Jews in Holland and was SS commanding in officer in Lyon, France, there committing a series of major war crimes that earned him the name "Butcher of Lyon." He went into hiding after the war, then was employed by U.S. counterintelligence, 1947–51, and was assisted by the United States in his subsequent escape to South America, where he lived as Klaus Altmann until his capture in Bolivia in 1983. He was ultimately brought to trial in 1987, convicted of some of his major crimes, and sentenced to life imprisonment.

Barcelona riots (May 3–7, 1937), factional fighting between anarchist and Communist Spanish Republican forces in Barcelona; after 2 days of indecision the Republican government decisively intervened against the anarchists. The anarchist viewpoint, charging that the sequence of events was part of a Communist campaign to destroy all opposition within the republic, was put strongly in George ORWELL's *Homage to Catalonia*. An estimated 400–1,000 deaths and 2,000–4,000 other casualties resulted. Whatever the motives of the participants, the riots seriously weakened the Spanish Republic.

Barcelona, Fall of (January 26, 1939), collapse that signaled the effective end of the SPANISH CIVIL WAR. With the fall of Barcelona, large-scale Republican resistance in northern Spain ended; Madrid and Valencia surrendered in March, ending the war.

bar code, series of black and white stripes, representing BINARY DIGITS, to be read by a LASER scanner, with the encoded information processed by a computer. In 1973 the grocery industry of the United States first put the bar code to widespread use, calling it the Universal Product Code (UPC). Use of the bar code eliminated the need for repetitive keying of product information with its potential for errors; inventory tracking and price changing became far more efficient. By the 1980s bar codes were being used in a wide range of areas, including warehouses, hospitals, libraries, and the miltary.

Barco Vargas, Virgilio (1921–   ), Colombian public official and political leader, who held a long series of appointive and elective positions from 1943. In 1985 he became head of the Liberal party and president of Colombia. His presidency was marked by severe internal unrest, including a continuing left-wing insurgency, the emergence of right-wing DEATH SQUADS, the growing influence of the international drug cartels, and pressure from the army, which threatened to take control of an increasingly fragmented country.

Barkley, Alben William (1877–1956), U.S. lawyer, a Kentucky Democratic congressman (1913–27) and four-term senator (1927–49), who as majority leader of the Senate (1937–47) was a key NEW DEAL legislative figure. He was Harry S. TRUMAN's vice president (1949–53), playing a considerably larger legislative and advisory role than most vice-presidents before or since.

He was reelected to the senate in 1954, dying in office in 1956.

Barnard, Christiaan Neethling (1922–   ), South African surgeon who performed the first human HEART TRANSPLANT. Learning OPEN-HEART SURGERY techniques in America, Barnard introduced them to his homeland and went on to develop them further through operations on dogs; he also designed artificial heart valves. He made the first transplant of a human heart on December 3, 1967; the patient, Louis Washansky, died of pneumonia 18 days later, but Barnard had set the stage for further improvements.

Barrow, Clyde, U.S. murderer and armed robber of the early 1930s, with Bonnie PARKER partnered as "Bonnie and Clyde."

Barth, Karl (1886–1968), Swiss Protestant theologian, who formulated a "theology of crisis" to deal with the horrors of 20th-century wars, beginning with his 1919 *Epistle to the Romans*. A sharp critic of Nazism, he lost his professorial post at Bonn for refusing to take a loyalty oath to HITLER; he then transferred to Basel, where in 1934, with Martin NIEMÖLLER and others, he organized the Synod of Barmen, an anti-Nazi church coalition. After World War II he strongly urged reconciliation with Germany and criticized the IRON CURTAIN and the use of the ATOMIC BOMB.

Barthes, Roland (1915–80), French philosopher linked with STRUCTURALISM and a key figure in semiology, the study of cultural phenomena studied as signs, quite apart from their content.

Baruch, Bernard (1870–1965), U.S. stockbroker, who moved into public service during World War I, becoming chairman of the War Industries Board and then an economic advisor at the PARIS PEACE CONFERENCE. He continued to advise Amerian presidents of both parties informally on economic matters until the early 1960s, also becoming a popular figure who gained a good deal of media attention.

Barzani, Mustafa al- (1901–79), the leader of the KURDISH NATIONAL MOVEMENT in

Iraq from the 1930s until his death; he was the younger brother of Sheik Ahmad al-Barzani, head of the Barzanis, the leading clan in the Kurdish national movement. He led the armed forces of the short-lived (1945–46) Kurdish Republic in northern Iran, then fled to the Soviet Union, which had backed that government. He returned to Iraq in 1959, led the long (1960–70) Kurdish revolt in Iraq, and resumed that revolt in 1974; it continued after his death.

Bastogne, Battle of (December 19, 1944–January 2, 1945), attack during the Battle of the BULGE in which German forces surrounded the U.S. 82nd Airborne and 101st Airborne divisions holding Bastogne. The Americans held firm under attack by much superior forces until relieved by George PATTON's American Third Army on December 26. The combined American forces held Bastogne for another week while the Germans continued to attack; then general German withdrawal began. It was at Bastogne that U.S. general Anthony C. McAuliffe responded "Nuts!" to a German ultimatum to surrender.

Basutoland, the former name of LESOTHO (Kingdom of Lesotho), which was a British protectorate until becoming an independent nation on October 4, 1966.

Bataan Death March (April 1942), the long march, early in World War II, of captured and brutally mistreated U.S. and Philippine soldiers, many of them wounded and ill, to their prison camp after their surrender to the Japanese invaders of the Philippines.

Bates, Daisy Gatson (1922–   ), Little Rock, Arkansas, newspaper publisher and civil rights leader. As president of the Arkansas chapter of the NATIONAL ASSOCIATION FOR THE ADVANCEMENT OF COLORED PEOPLE (NAACP), in 1957 she led in the campaign to desegregate Little Rock Central High School.

bathyscape, submersible craft with a pressurized cabin, used for underwater observations; associated with a mother ship but (unlike the BATHYSPHERE) not linked to it by a vulnerable cable. First developed by

Auguste PICCARD in 1948, the bathyscape was improved upon by others in the 1950s, especially Jacques COUSTEAU, who added JET PROPULSION and helped create versions usable for long-term underwater stays. By 1965 Cousteau's aquanautic team had spent 23 days in a bathyscape below the Mediterranean, and in the same year a U.S. Navy team spent 45 days underwater off California in the *Sealab II* project.

bathysphere, nonnavigable, submersible craft suspended by a cable from a mother ship, used for underwater observations; developed in 1930 by U.S. zoologist William BEEBE and engineer Otis Barton. Because the cable could easily become entangled or snap, the bathysphere was dangerous for underwater observers and was largely replaced in the 1950s by the BATHYSCAPE.

Batista y Zaldivar, Fulgencio (1901–73), Cuban soldier, president of Cuba 1940–44 and dictator 1952–59, whose corrupt government was easily toppled by Fidel CASTRO'S guerrilla army when it came down from the Sierra Maestra in October 1958. Batista fled Cuba on January 1, 1959; Castro's forces entered Havana on January 8 without opposition.

Bavarian Communist Republic, short-lived Communist state set up in April 1919, which was quickly smashed by the right-wing German FREIKORPS, then growing in strength after its January defeat of the SPARTACIST rising in Berlin and the subsequent Freikorps assassinations of Rosa LUXEMBURG and Karl LIEBKNECHT.

Bay of Pigs invasion (April 17, 1961), amphibious landings at Cuba's Bahia de los Cochinos (Bay of Pigs) by an estimated 1,200–1,500 Cuban exiles armed, trained, and transported by the U.S. CENTRAL INTELLIGENCE AGENCY (CIA). President John F. KENNEDY, who otherwise approved the action, withheld the air cover promised by the CIA. A hoped-for Cuban insurrection against the government of Fidel CASTRO did not materialize, and the invasion force was easily defeated by Cuban forces, suffering approximately 90 battle deaths and the capture of the balance of the force, ultimately exchanged for food and medical supplies.

Beard, Charles Austin (1874–1948), U.S. historian, whose *Economic Interpretation of the Constitution* (1913) and subsequent works pioneered in the development of materialist interpretation of American history. He and Mary Ritter Beard, his wife, co-authored *The Rise of American Civilization* (1927), a full-scale and not entirely deterministic view of the entire sweep of American history.

beat generation, an avant-garde U.S. 1950s movement in literature and the arts, that focused on the theme of youthful alienation from the material culture of the post–World War II era, along with considerable stylistic innovation, as expressed in the work of such Beat leaders as Jack Kerouac and Allen Ginsberg. The movement had substantial impact on the developing social movements of the time, then merged with the much larger COUNTERCULTURE of the 1960s. Those enraged by the movement and its defiance of current conventions coined the derogatory term "beatniks" to describe those in the "beat" movement.

Beatles, The, George Harrison, John Lennon, Paul McCartney, and Ringo Starr, the four young singers from Liverpool, whose then-unconventional singing and personal styles revolutionized the popular music of their time and had a major impact on the social revolution, then in its formative stages, later called the COUNTERCULTURE. The Beatles began their joint career in Liverpool in 1958 and burst into popular consciousness in 1962.

Beauvoir, Simone de (1908–86), French writer, philosopher, and leading 20th-century feminist, whose book *The Second Sex* (1949) was a key work for the post–World War II feminist movement. She was a lifetime companion of Jean-Paul SARTRE.

Beaverbrook (Lord Beaverbrook, William Maxwell Aitken; 1879–1964), Canadian financier, who moved to London in 1910 and thereafter pursued twin and intertwined British careers as a politician and press baron. Before World War I he was a powerful supporter of Bonar LAW and a member of Parliment. During the war he helped topple the ASQUITH government and bring LLOYD GEORGE to power, becoming minister of information in 1918. Meanwhile, he began to acquire the major newspapers that were ultimately to make him a press baron, beginning with the purchase of the *Daily Express* in 1916. During World War II he served in CHURCHILL's cabinet until 1942 and thereafter did specific tasks on request, as his temperament made it difficult to fit him into a continuing working group. His last major direct political involvement was to play a very important role in developing strategy and tactics in Churchill's unsuccessful 1945 campaign.

Bechuanaland, the former name of BOTSWANA (REPUBLIC OF BOTSWANA), which was a British protectorate until September 30, 1966.

Beebe, Charles William (1877–1962), U.S. biologist, nature writer, and explorer long associated with the New York Zoological Gardens (Bronx Zoo), working in ornithology and tropical research. He also pioneered in exploring the depths of the world's oceans, in 1934 setting a record, with Otis Barton, for depth exploration off Bermuda in a BATHYSPHERE they had developed in 1930.

Beer Hall Putsch, the failed Nazi Bavarian coup of November 8–11, 1923, for which Adolf HITLER was jailed, and which first brought the NAZI PARTY to national attention in Germany.

BEF, the BRITISH EXPEDITIONARY FORCES, the British fighting forces in France during both world wars.

Begelman-Robertson case, a 1977 case in which actor Cliff Robertson was blacklisted for some years by the film industry because he had "blown the whistle" on David Begelman, Columbia Pictures executive, who had forged Robertson's name on a $10,000 check and cashed it himself. Ultimately, Begelman pleaded no contest to grand theft charges, which were later reduced to a misdemeanor, and continued to be a major film industry figure as president of Metro-Goldwyn–Mayer. Robertson eventually found work again.

Begin, Menachem (1913–   ), Polish Zionist leader, who was imprisoned by the Soviets early in World War II but released after the Nazi invasion of the Soviet Union, then finding his way to Palestine in 1942 as part of the Polish army in exile. A disciple of Zionist Revisionist Vladimir JABOTINSKY, he became leader of the terrorist IRGUN ZVAI LEUMI in 1943 and mounted a terror campaign against the British occupiers of Palestine, these tactics being in opposition to the policies of the main Zionist organizations of the time, including the World Zionist Organization and the HAGANAH, the Jewish army. After World War II the Irgun was temporarily allied with the Haganah; but it was effectively outlawed for a time after July 22, 1946, when, under the direct supervision of Menachim Begin and against strong Haganah protest, the Irgun bombed a British office wing in Jerusalem's KING DAVID HOTEL, killing 91 people, 17 of them Jews, and thereafter committed a series of major terrorist actions. After Israeli independence the new government attacked and sank an Irgun munitions ship off the Israeli coast and forced dissolution of Begin's separate Irgun military organization. In 1948 Begin founded the nationalist Herut party, leading it in opposition until 1967, when he joined the 1967–70 coalition government. He became LIKUD party prime minister of Israel, 1977–83. While prime minister, he negotiated the Israeli-Egyptian peace treaty in 1978—and with Anwar SADAT won the 1978 Nobel Peace Prize—while also engaging in the 1982 invasion of Lebanon. His resignation in 1983 resulted from ill health and also was widely reported to stem partly from the unpopularity of his Lebanon policy. He then entirely retired from public life.

behaviorism, school of psychology founded in 1913 by John B. WATSON that focuses on studying and shaping human actions, rather than on introspective analysis or "talking" therapy. Building on early experimental work by Russian physiologist Ivan PAVLOV and U.S. psychologist Edward Lee THORNDIKE, Watson attempted to make psychology a laboratory science. He posited that human behavior is not the result of instinct or heredity but of training (conditioning) and that experimental studies of observable and measurable responses to stimuli were the proper focus of psychology, not unobservable phenomena (feelings). One of behaviorism's best-known exponents from the late 1930s on was B. F. SKINNER, who taught that will and freedom are illusions and that behavior is wholly controlled by experience. From at least the 1960's some behaviorist approaches and results were given practical application, especially the idea of positive reinforcement for desired behavior. Skinner developed the idea of programmed instruction, using a "teaching machine" to organize learning in a more rigorous, efficient way; though the machine itself did not last, some of Skinner's approaches were taken on by modern education, especially when COMPUTERS arrived in the schools. Another practical application was behavior modification, which attempts to deal with problems not by analyzing why they occur but by changing the behavior itself, such as smoking.

Beijing Spring, media-generated term describing the CHINESE STUDENT DEMONSTRATIONS of 1989.

Beirut peacekeeping force bombings (October 23, 1983), the suicide bombings of the U.S. and French peacekeeping forces in Beirut, Lebanon, by Arab guerrillas, who drove trucks loaded with explosives into the barracks of both forces, killing 241 Americans and 58 French.

Belgian Congo, the former Belgian colony in central Africa, which became the independent nation of ZAIRE (REPUBLIC OF ZAIRE) on June 30, 1960.

Belgium, Battle of (May 10–28, 1940), invasion of Belgium early in World War II, starting when German ground forces struck across the Belgian frontier on May 10 while

German bombers carried out terror attacks on Belgian cities. Belgian, French, and British forces fell back to strong defensive positions, by May 15 facing the Germans on the Dyle Line. But by then German armies had taken Holland and were turning the Allied line from the north; meanwhile, German armies in France had broken through near Sedan in the ARDENNES and threatened from the south. The position was untenable; on May 27 the Belgian army surrendered, and by June 4 the British and French had completed the evacuation of Allied troops at DUNKIRK.

Belize, until 1981 a British colony. Belize became an independent state and member of the COMMONWEALTH on September 21, 1981, though remaining under British military protection because of the long-standing Belize–Guatemala border dispute, unresolved since 1940.

Belleau Wood, Battle of (May 30–June 17, 1918), the third U.S.World War I battle, in which the U.S. Second Division, spearheaded by its marine brigade, counterattacked German positions along the Marne, at Belleau Wood, Bouresches, and Vaux, thereby helping to limit German gains during the German AISNE offensive of 1918.

Bell X-1, type of U.S. jet flown by pilot Charles YEAGER when breaking the SOUND BARRIER in 1947.

Belsen (Bergen-Belsen), German CONCENTRATION CAMP on Lüneberg Heath in Germany, to which hundreds of thousands of prisoners from farther east were transferred late in the war as Soviet armies took Eastern Europe.

Ben Bella, Ahmed (1918–   ), Algerian officer, who saw service in the French army during World War II, then joined the Algerian independence movement and afterward co-founded the Special Organization, which prepared for armed action. He was arrested in 1952, escaped, and in 1954 was a key founder of the FLN (NATIONAL LIBERATION FRONT). He was captured by the French in 1956 and imprisoned until 1962, at the end of the ALGERIAN WAR OF INDE-

PENDENCE. In September 1962, Ben Bella became the first premier of independent Algeria. An Islamic socialist, he fostered Algerian state socialism, introduced authoritarian one-party rule in Algeria, and was a leading neutralist. In 1965 he was toppled and imprisoned by his long-time associate, Houari BOUMEDIENNE; he was released by the new government of Ben-Jedid CHADLI in 1980, and went into exile.

Benedict, Ruth (1887–1948), U.S. anthropologist, a leading figure in the study of preindustrial or "primitive" cultures. Her major work, *Patterns of Culture* (1934), posited cultural RELATIVITY and implied cultural equality among all peoples of the world. It greatly stimulated the development of comparative cultural studies, helped popularize such studies and the then relatively new science of anthropology, and was widely used to refute the racist theories disseminated by the NAZIS and their sympathizers.

Benes, Eduard (1884–1948), Czech independence movement leader, who from 1915 worked with Tomás MASARYK and was the first foreign minister of Czechoslovakia (1918–35), then succeeding Masaryk as Czech president. He resigned in 1938, after the MUNICH AGREEMENT, and headed the Czech government-in-exile in London from 1940. He became president again in 1945, resigned in 1948 after the Communist takeover of his country, and died shortly thereafter.

Bengal cyclones, a succession of cyclones out of the Bay of Bengal that for centuries have struck the low-lying islands and coastal lands of what is now Bangladesh, creating many of the worst natural disasters in history. In the 20th century one of the worst was the cyclone of of November 13, 1970, which killed an estimated 200,000–500,000 people. Major cyclone-caused disasters also were reported in 1942, 1960, 1963, 1965, 1977, and 1987.

Ben Gurion, David (David Green; 1886–1973), Polish-Israeli Zionist, who emigrated from Poland to Israel at the age of 20, there becoming a leader of the socialist sector of the Zionist movement. He joined the Jewish Legion, fighting with the British in World War I. In 1921 he became first secretary-general of the Palestine Jewish labor federation, the Histadrut, and in 1930 founded the united socialist party, the MAPAI. From 1935 through establishment of the state of Israel in 1948, he was chairman of both the Jewish Agency for Palestine and the World Zionist Organization, becoming the leader of the Israeli independence movement until and through the 1948 ISRAELI WAR OF INDEPENDENCE (FIRST ARAB–ISRAELI WAR). As leader he sharply opposed limitation of Jewish immigration into Palestine, fostered the development of the Jewish army, the HAGANAH, and its striking force, the PALMACH, and opposed the terrorist tactics of the IRGUN ZVAI LEUMI and the STERN GANG. Ben Gurion and his associates succeeded in developing worldwide support for Jewish national aspirations in Palestine, along with massive practical support from American and Western European Jewish communities. He was Israel's first prime minister (1949–53; 1955–63).

Benin (People's Republic of Benin), until independence on August 1, 1960, known as Dahomey, a French colony. A series of short-lived governments and military coups followed independence until the emergence in 1972 of then-major Ahmed Kerekou, who organized Dahomey into a one-party Marxist-oriented state, changed the name of the country to Benin in 1975, and continued to hold power.

Bennett, Floyd (1890–1928), U.S. aviator who, with Richard E. BYRD, was the first to fly over the NORTH POLE in 1926. He died of pneumonia before he could join Byrd on a flight over the SOUTH POLE.

Bentsen, Lloyd (1926–   ), U.S. lawyer and judge, a Texas Democrat, in the House of Representatives 1949–55 and in the Senate from 1970. He was the unsuccessful Democratic vice-presidential candidate in 1988; a moderate, his choice was widely thought to have supplied both geographical and ideological balance to the DUKAKIS candidacy.

Bergen-Belsen, alternate name for the BELSEN German concentration camp.

Berger, Victor Louis (1860–1929), U.S. socialist organizer and editor, who was a founder of the SOCIALIST PARTY in 1900 and in 1911 served one term in the House of Representatives, becoming the first socialist to sit in the House. He opposed U.S. participation in World War I, was indicted for sedition, and in 1918 was barred from serving his second term in the House because of the indictment. His conviction of sedition was voided by the Supreme Court in 1921; he then served three more congressional terms.

Beria, Lavrenti Pavlovich (1899–1953), the head of the Soviet secret police from 1938, a prime mover during the Soviet GREAT PURGE and MOSCOW TRIALS of the late 1930s, and thereafter chief secret police official as head of the ministry of internal affairs. He lost the power struggle that followed STALIN'S death in 1953 and was himself executed in December 1953.

Berkeley Free Speech Movement (1964–65), a U.S. college campus protest movement and a major event in the emergence of the 1960s NEW LEFT. The movement began as a dispute on the Berkeley campus of the University of California over a college administration ban on the distribution of political material originated off campus; it grew into a national series of protests touching on many issues, including campus recruitment by companies involved in VIETNAM WAR–connected production, war-related and government-funded research, and the war itself.

Berkman, Alexander (1870–1936), leading U.S. anarchist of the early 20th century and the long-time companion and lover of Emma GOLDMAN. In 1892 Berkman unsuccessfully tried to assassinate industrialist Henry Clay Frick, of the Carnegie Steel Company, after the violent Homestead Steel Strike. He served 14 years in prison for the attempt; from 1906 to 1919 he was, with Emma Goldman, the leading anarchist spokesperson of the time. In 1919, during the period of the PALMER RAIDS, both were deported to Soviet Union. Disillusioned with Soviet society, Berkman later left the Soviet Union, spent the rest of his life in Western Europe and finally committed suicide in 1936.

Berkowitz, David R., killer who wrote a series of highly publicized letters to newspapers, signed "SON OF SAM," while he was committing six murders and seven other assaults in a series of night attacks in New York City during 1976–77. Attempts to capitalize on his story led to passage of New York State's "Son of Sam" law, aimed at barring criminals from participating in profits derived from their crimes.

Berlin blockade and airlift (1948–49), blockade of West Berlin by Soviet forces, beginning on June 22, 1948, stopping all food, coal, and other necessary supplies from reaching the city. On June 26 a massive Allied airlift began; from then until September 30, 1949, more than 275,000 flights carried over 2,300,000 tons of supplies to the city. The blockade ended in May 1949; the airlift continued until stocks of supplies had been built up.

Berlin, fall of (April 22–May 2, 1945), late World War II collapse of the German capital as Soviet forces reached and surrounded Berlin in late April, while advancing U.S. troops paused on the Elbe River, and took the city in house-to-house fighting that ended on May 2. Adolf HITLER committed suicide in his command bunker on April 30, 1945.

Berlin Wall (1961), a wall dividing East and West Berlin, built overnight by the East German government on August 12, 1961, to close the East German border with West Berlin. It became one of the key symbols of the COLD WAR. In November 1989, massive political changes in East Germany began, negating the Wall and signalling the beginning of a new chapter in German history.

Bernadotte, Folke (1895–1948), Swedish diplomat who, while working with the Red Cross during World War II, carried Heinrich HIMMLER'S rejected peace proposal to the Allies and who in 1948, while

United Nations mediator in Palestine, was murdered by the STERN GANG.

Bernstein, Carl (1944–   ), U.S. journalist who, with his reporting partner Bob WOODWARD, covered the 1972 WATERGATE burglary story for the Washington *Post* and ultimately broke the major story that led to the resignation of Richard M. NIXON and the imprisonment of many of the Watergate conspirators.

Berri, Nabih (1937–   ), Lebanese lawyer, who became active in the AMAL Shiite militia in 1975, ultimately becoming chief Lebanese Shiite leader. In June 1985 he was active in negotiations leading to the release of American airplane hijacking hostages in Beirut.

Berrigan, Daniel (1921–   ), U.S. Catholic priest, who became a leading activist opponent of the VIETNAM WAR and who, with his brother Philip, (1923–   ), also a Catholic priest, was convicted in 1967 of pouring blood on Selective Service files in Baltimore. While awaiting sentencing in 1968, he poured napalm on draft cards in a Selective Service office in Catonsville, Maryland, for which he was again convicted, along with the rest of the CATONSVILLE NINE. Sentenced to prison, he fled; he was captured in 1970 and served 18 months in prison, later continuing his antiwar activities.

Besant, Annie (Annie Wood; 1847–1933), British suffragist, socialist, and mystic, active until 1893 in Great Britain. A theosophist from 1889, she lived in India from 1893 and was president of the Theosophical Society 1907–33. In India she founded the Central Hindu College at Benares in 1898 and became active in the nationalist movement. She became president of the CONGRESS PARTY in 1917, although opposed to civil disobedience. She lost her leadership as the party became committed to mass nonviolent action as developed by Mohatma GANDHI.

beta particles, one of the three products of natural RADIOACTIVITY, found to be speeded-up ELECTRONS; discovered and named by Ernest RUTHERFORD in the early 1900s.

beta rhythms, type of brain wave associated with wakeful alertness, first discovered by Hans Berger using his ELECTROENCEPHALOGRAPH (EEG).

Bethe, Hans Albrecht (1906–   ), German-Jewish-American physicist, who in 1939 proposed that the energy of the Sun and stars comes from NUCLEAR FUSION, work that won him the 1967 Nobel Prize for Physics and laid the foundation for the HYDROGEN BOMB. After early work in QUANTUM THEORY, Bethe left Germany at the 1933 rise of the NAZIS, settling in the United States; during World War II he headed the theoretical physics division at LOS ALAMOS, helping to create the ATOMIC BOMB. After the bombings of HIROSHIMA and NAGASAKI in 1945, however, he became a leading advocate of nuclear disarmament.

Bethune, Mary McLeod (1875–1955), U.S. teacher, college president (Bethune-Cookman College), and founder of the National Council of Negro Women (1935), who became a federal official and a presidential advisor on minority affairs in the 1930s and 1940s.

Bethune, Norman (1899–1939), Canadian doctor, who became a battlefront surgeon with Chinese Communist forces, 1937–39, and died at the front; he is regarded by Communist China as a major revolutionary hero.

Bettelheim, Bruno (1903–1990), Austrian-American psychologist and educator. Vienna-trained, Bettelheim was held in DACHAU and BUCHENWALD, 1938–39; he used what he learned about the effects of the camps on the prisoners in his later work. From 1944 to 1973 he was associated with the University of Chicago's Sonia Shankman Orthogenic School for severely disturbed children, adopting a strategy of total acceptance of the child's behavior and becoming widely known for his success with autistic children. Among his widely read books were *The Children of the Dream* (1969) and *The Uses of En-*

chantment: The Meaning and Importance of Fairy Tales (1976).

Bevan, Aneurin "Nye" (1897–1960), Welsh coal miner, trade unionist, socialist, British Labour MP 1929–60, and a leader of the left wing of his party from the mid-1930s until his death. He was minister of health in Clement ATTLEE'S post–World War II Labour government, during which time he established the NATIONAL HEALTH SERVICE. In the early 1950s he opposed Britain's increasingly strong links with the United States, promoted nuclear disarmament, and opposed the more moderate majority in his party; later he partially reconciled his differences, drawing somewhat closer to the party leadership. Bevan's wife was Jennie LEE.

Beveridge Plan, a 1942 report, developed under the leadership of British economist William Beveridge, that proposed the main outlines of the "cradle to the grave" social service network that largely came to being in Britain after World War II. Two of the plan's most important aspects were social security and NATIONAL HEALTH INSURANCE.

Bevin, Ernest (1881–1951), British laborer and Docker's Union official, who in 1921 merged 22 unions into the Transport and General Workers Union (TGWU), which he headed. He was CHURCHILL'S wartime coalition cabinet minister of labor and ATTLEE'S foreign secretary in the first post–World War II cabinet. In the latter position he welcomed the MARSHALL PLAN, brought Britain fully into the developing COLD WAR between the United States and the Soviet Union, and opposed the early establishment of Israel as an independent state.

Bhopal toxic cloud (December 3, 1984), a leak of lethal methyl isocyanate gas at Union Carbide plant in Bhopal, India, that caused a toxic cloud to spread over the city, killing over 3,500 people and injuring an estimated 200,000 more. In February 1989, after the Indian government had taken over prosecution of more than 500,000 compensation claims filed by its citizens, Union Carbide settled those claims for $470 million.

The case was reopened by the Indian government in early 1990.

Bhutto, Benazir (1943–   ), Pakistani political leader, daughter of Zulfikar Ali BHUTTO, and leader of the PAKISTAN PEOPLE'S PARTY. She returned from exile in July 1985 for the funeral of her brother and was arrested and returned to exile; in April 1986 she returned to lead the opposition to the rule of Mohammad ZIA UL-HAQ. She became the elected prime minister of Pakistan on December 2, 1988, after Zia's death in an August airplane crash.

Bhutto, Zulfikar Ali (1928–79), Pakistani lawyer and father of Benazir BHUTTO; he held several cabinet-level positions in the AYUB KHAN government beginning in 1958 but was dismissed as foreign minister in 1966. In 1967 he formed the PAKISTAN PEOPLE'S PARTY, which became a substantial opposition party, winning the majority of the West Pakistan and a minority of the East Pakistan parliamentary seats in the 1970 election. The election was voided, however, generating the sequence of events that during 1971 led to the BANGLADESH WAR OF INDEPENDENCE and the INDIA-PAKISTAN WAR OF 1971. On December 20, 1971, Bhutto took power as chief martial law administrator and in 1972 negotiated a peace settlement with India, recognized Bangladesh, initiated a new constitution, and became prime minister. His party won the March 1977 elections, but the election results were disputed by opposition parties; in July an army coup brought General Mohammad ZIA UL-HAQ to power. Bhutto was arrested, sentenced to death for an alleged 1974 political murder, and executed on April 4, 1979, despite worldwide protests.

Biafra famine (1967–69), massive famine, accompanied by resultant disease, that was generated by the NIGERIA–BIAFRA CIVIL WAR, taking the lives of an estimated 1 million Biafrans despite worldwide relief efforts. The Nigerian government's refusal for long periods to admit relief shipments contributed considerably to the scope of the disaster.

Bidault, Georges (1889–1983), French teacher who became an anti-APPEASEMENT political leader in the 1930s and led the French RESISTANCE 1943–44. He became foreign minister of the provisional government in 1944, in 1946 first prime minister of the Fourth Republic; and again prime minister, 1949–50, holding several other cabinet-level posts in the late 1940s and early 1950s. He was a leader of the insurgent opposition to Algerian independence, going into exile 1962–68.

Biden, Joseph Robinette, Jr. (1942–   ), U.S. lawyer and Democratic senator from Delaware from 1972. In 1976 he was chairman of the Senate Judiciary Committee, which rejected President Ronald REAGAN'S nomination of Judge Robert BORK to the Supreme Court. In September 1987 he withdrew from the Democratic presidential nomination race after the DUKAKIS staff had spread reports that Biden had plagiarized speeches from Neil KINNOCK and other political figures. In the wake of the affair, Dukakis campaign manager John Sasso resigned his post, returning to the campaign in 1988.

big bang theory, cosmological theory that the universe began with the explosion of a highly condensed "atom" containing all mass and has continuously expanded since then. First put forward in 1927 by Belgian priest Georges LEMAÎTRE and supported by eloquent physicists such as George GAMOW, the big bang theory stood in the shadow of the rival STEADY-STATE THEORY until the 1960s. Then RADIO ASTRONOMY discoveries began to confirm it, especially the 1965 detection of background cosmic MICROWAVE RADIATION consistent with a primordial "big bang" by Bell Laboratory scientists Arno A. Penzias and Robert W. Wilson, for which they were awarded the 1978 Nobel Prize for Physics.

Big Bertha, popular name for the battery of long-range siege guns, with a range of 75–80 miles, used by the Germans to bombard Paris March–August, 1918. The bombardment had no significant military effect, had some morale effect, and did not alter the course of World War I.

Big Brother is watching you, the totalitarian slogan penned by George ORWELL in *1984*, his 1949 novel warning of the dangers posed by the development of the bureaucratic state.

Bikini, depopulated Pacific atoll in the Marshall Islands, site of U.S. ATOMIC BOMB and later HYDROGEN BOMB tests from 1946 to 1958. In 1968 Bikini was declared safe, and its earlier inhabitants were allowed to return, only to be removed again in 1978 on reassessment of the medical hazards from FALLOUT.

Biko, Steve (1946–77), South African Black nationalist and an advocate of Black consciousness, who was a founder of the South African Students Organization in 1968, while still a medical student, and also of the Black People's Convention in 1972. In August 1977 he was arrested for alleged subversive activities; on September 12, 1977, he died while in the hands of the South African police in circumstances so questionable that his death was called murder by many, generating a worldwide protest and a nationwide student strike.

Billings, Warren K., U.S. labor leader convicted with Tom MOONEY of the 1916 Preparedness Day bombing in San Francisco; his life sentence was reduced, and he was released in in 1939.

binary system, 2-digit numerical system, as opposed to the standard 10-digit decimal system; adopted by John ATANASOFF for the ABC computer (built 1937–42) and widely used in modern DIGITAL COMPUTERS because the two binary digits (bits)—0 and 1—can correspond to "on" and "off" signals in a computer. The numbers 0, 1, 2, 3, 4, 5 in the decimal system would translate in the two-digit binary system to 0, 1, 10, 11, 100, 101, and so on.

Binet, Alfred (1857–1911), French psychologist, who developed the first formal tests of human intelligence, the score of which is the INTELLIGENCE QUOTIENT (IQ). Originally designed to test his own daughters, then

(with Théodore Simon) reoriented to test retarded children, the tests were revised in 1908 and 1911 to test normal children. That test was later adapted for American use by psychologist Lewis M. Terman at Stanford University, the result being the Stanford-Binet Intelligence Scale test.

Bingham, Hiram (1875–1956), U.S. explorer and politician, who in 1911 rediscovered the long-lost Inca stronghold, MACHU PICCHU, high in the Peruvian Andes.

biofeedback, assertion of some voluntary control over normally involuntary biological processes, such as heart rate and blood pressure, often guided by readings on devices such as ELECTROENCEPHALOGRAPHS. Though similar approaches were used earlier (as in yoga), biofeedback was first scientifically demonstrated in 1967 by Neal Miller and Jay Towill, who used PAVLOV's conditioning techniques to teach animals how to, for example, raise or lower their blood pressure.

biological clock, theoretical mechanism controlling internal biological cycles called BIORHYTHMS, that govern various functions and behavior in living things; in humans, including eating, sleeping, and sexual responses. The biological clock was first described and named in 1927 by U.S. psychobiologist Curt Paul Richter.

biological warfare, use of toxic biological agents in CHEMICAL AND BIOLOGICAL WARFARE.

Biological Warfare Ban Treaty, treaty supplementing the 1925 GENEVA PROTOCOL in attempting to ban use of CHEMICAL AND BIOLOGICAL WARFARE, ratified by the United Nations in 1972 and by the U.S. Senate in 1974, following President Richard NIXON's 1969 unilateral renunciation of biological weapons and first use of chemical weapons.

biorhythms, internal biological cycles seen in various functions and behavior in living things—in humans, including eating, sleeping, and sexual responses—governed by a kind of internal BIOLOGICAL CLOCK, regardless of external cues such as day or night. In humans, as in other beings, biorhythms affect many parts of life, effects heightened when modern technology runs counter to them, producing problems such as jet lag or decreased safety on a night shift.

Birenda Bir Bikram Shah Deva (1945–), Nepalese king (1972–), who succeeded to the throne after the death of his father, Mahendra Bir Bikram Shah Deva, and thereafter pursued a nonaligned course in world affairs, especially as regards the interests of Nepal's huge neighbors, China and India. Domestically, he sucessfully resisted the reintroduction of the short-lived democracy instituted by his father with the constitution of 1959 and then suppressed by his father in 1960.

Bir Hacheim, Battle of (May 28–June 13, 1942), World War II engagement in North Africa. After the Italian WESTERN DESERT CAMPAIGN disaster of 1941, the Germans sent General Erwin ROMMEL to North Africa, with substantial fresh German forces. In January 1942, his forces moved to the offensive in Libya; on May 28 they attacked and in a 2-week battle defeated the Allies and forced a long retreat back into Egypt.

Birkenau, alternate name for the AU-SCHWITZ-BIRKENAU German CONCENTRATION CAMP.

Birmingham civil rights campaign (April–September 1963), a campaign to desegregate public facilities and introduce fair employment practices in Birmingham, Alabama, which began with sit-ins at lunch counters and in other segregated public places and moved to substantial peaceful demonstrations, in a campaign led by Martin Luther KING, Jr. The city of Birmingham and its public safety commissioner, Eugene "Bull" CONNOR, responded with great violence, beating and jailing over 2,000 and using water hoses and police dogs against groups that included many children. The newsphoto of a police dog leaping at a Black child became one of the most celebrated photos of the period, enjoying worldwide circulation as a symbol of southern American justice. An agreement was ul-timately reached, desegregating many facilities in the downtown area, releasing those jailed, and setting up committees to further fair employment practices. On May 11 two bombings of CIVIL RIGHTS MOVEMENT headquarters led to Black rioting, and federal troops were sent to Birmingham to restore order. On September 15, while Sunday School was being conducted, the Sixteenth Street Baptist Church was bombed; four children were killed: Addie Mae Collins, Denis McNair, Carol Robertson, and Cynthia Wesley.

birth control clinic, institution for providing contraceptive information to individuals, focusing on planned, not accidental, parenthood. The first such clinic was founded in the 19th century in Amsterdam, but successors did not follow until 1916. Then Margaret SANGER, who had coined the phrase "birth control" 2 years earlier, founded the first such clinic in the United States; it was soon closed by the police, and Sanger was arrested, a permanent clinic opening only in 1923. The first birth control clinic in Britain was opened by Marie STOPES in 1921. Sanger, Stopes, and other birth control advocates were considerably hampered by legal restrictions. In the United States 19th-century Comstock Laws classified contraceptive information as obscene and therefore unlawful to send by mail. Not until Margaret Sanger won an appeal on her 1917 arrest were U.S. physicians able to give birth control information to their patients legally; and it was not until another ruling, in 1936, that they could provide or prescribe contraceptive devices. Other countries faced similar restrictions; in some countries, especially Catholic ones such as Ireland, contraceptive information was still not widely available as late as the 1980s. Meanwhile several new forms of contraceptives were introduced, for clinics to add to the traditional stock. A spermicide was developed in Britain in 1927; INTRAUTERINE DEVICES (IUDs) were used from the 1920s, often variations on cruder 19th-century devices and often with harmful side effects, as with the DALKON SHIELD;

and the BIRTH CONTROL PILL, introduced in 1955, had some side effects of its own. Birth control clinics also offered the options of sterilization for men or women or abortion. In many countries abortion became a main form of birth control in the 20th century. The Soviet Union, in 1920, was the first major country to make abortion available at the mother's request; many other countries followed, with various restrictions. In the United States, after the 1973 *ROE* v. *WADE* case, abortions became freely available and many birth control clinics began to double as abortion clinics. This brought them into conflict with people in the RIGHT TO LIFE movement, who in the 1980s staged emotional and often violent protests at clinics around the country. A "morning-after pill," developed in France in the 1980s, could make such questions moot.

birth control pill, drug of synthesized ESTROGEN and other HORMONES that interrupts a woman's monthly ovulation–menstruation cycle, preventing conception. The first such oral contraceptive was developed by research biologist Gregory PINCUS in 1951–55. Widely used, "the pill" was a major factor in the sexual revolution starting in the 1960s. By 1968 side effects such as increased susceptibility to blood clots became known, though longer-term studies into the 1980s also showed some beneficial side-effects.

Bishop, William Avery (1894–1956), Canadian pilot, who during World War I became a leading Allied ace, shooting down 72 German airplanes and winning the Victoria Cross. He was in commercial aviation during the interwar period, became a Canadian air vice marshal in 1936 and air marshal in 1938, and directed the Canadian air force during World War II.

Bismarck Sea, Battle of the (March 2–4, 1943), a series of Allied bomber and PT boat attacks on a Japanese convoy of eight destroyers and eight transports. All eight transports and four of the destroyers were sunk, with an estimated loss of 3,000 Japanese troops and with minor Allied losses.

Bismarck **sinking** (May 21–28, 1941), British sinking of the German battleship, the most heavily armed warship in the world. The *Bismarck* left port on May 21 and met pursuing British warships in Denmark Strait on May 24, there quickly sinking the battle cruiser *Hood* with a loss of almost 1,500 men and damaging the battleship PRINCE OF WALES. On May 26 British warships found the now-damaged *Bismarck* again, this time ultimately sinking the ship after a 2-day battle, with a loss of 2,300 men.

Bitberg dispute, controversy that developed when U.S. president Ronald REAGAN, on May 5, 1985, placed a wreath at the graves of German war dead in the Bitberg, West Germany, military cemetery, having placed a wreath at the BERGEN-BELSEN concentration camp memorial on the same day. He defended the Bitberg action as an act of reconciliation; those who attacked the action pointed out that the cemetery contained the graves of members of the WAFFEN SS, the organization that had primary DEATH CAMP responsibility.

Black, Hugo LaFayette (1886–1971), U.S. lawyer and Democratic Alabama senator (1927–37), who was appointed by Franklin D. ROOSEVELT to the Supreme Court in 1937 after some opposition because of his 1920s membership in the KU KLUX KLAN. During his 34 years on the Court he became one of its leading proponents of strict adherence to the Constitution, especially as to the protections afforded by the Bill of Rights, and of the separation of church and state; he was therefore often described as a liberal, never more so than during the height of the MCCARTHY period. However, his concern with strict adherence to the Constitution also led him take a number of positions that in political, rather than juridical, terms were thought conservative, as in his willingness to allow the federal barring of Japanese-Americans from the Pacific Coast states during World War II.

Black and Tans, a British military force operating as an occupation military police force in Ireland 1920–21, during the IRISH

CIVIL WAR, that committed a considerable body of atrocities against the civilian population while attempting to suppress the insurgency.

Black Book, a British World War I home front sensation; an entirely fictional list of tens of thousands of alleged perverts in high places, among them Prime Minister ASQUITH and his wife.

Black Dragon Society, a Japanese right-wing expansionist group, formed in 1901, that until the end of World War II pressed the Japanese government to aggressively expand Japan's area of control in northeast Asia.

Blackett, Patrick Maynard Stuart (1897–1974), British physicist, who made key early use of a much-improved Wilson CLOUD CHAMBER to study COSMIC RAYS, winning the 1948 Nobel Prize for Physics. Using the cloud chamber, in 1925 he took the first photographs of an atom disintegrating under bombardment and in 1935 confirmed with a physical demonstration Albert EINSTEIN's $E = MC^2$ equation. During World War II he strongly supported the development of RADAR and the ATOMIC BOMB, later speaking out against the dangers of nuclear warfare. His views on magnetism in ancient rocks supported the CONTINENTAL DRIFT theory.

Black Hand, the name supplied by the American press to an extortion scheme involving death threats, widely practiced in Italian-American communities early in the 20th century and mistakenly thought to be an alternative name for the Neapolitan criminal secret society, the Camorra.

Black Hand, the Serbian secret society "Unity or Death," which supplied guns and training to the Bosnian nationalists who assassinated archduke FRANCIS FERDINAND of Austria, thereby setting off the train of events leading directly to World War I.

black hole, theoretical late stage of STELLAR EVOLUTION for certain stars, a state of gravitational collapse in which space and time are curved and all light, energy, and matter are held by intense gravitation; first predict-

ed by German astronomer Karl Schwarzschild in 1907 from Albert EINSTEIN's general theory of relativity. The necessary mass required for a black hole was calculated in 1939 by J. Robert OPPENHEIMER.

blacklisting, placing people's names on government-generated and private lists as alleged "subversives," as was done to hundreds of thousands of Americans during the RED SCARE of the late 1940s and early 1950s. These listings were then used to destroy the livelihoods and careers of those listed, often without their knowledge of the listing and usually without any opportunity to defend themselves. The practice was especially widespread and damaging in the film and broadcasting industries, functioning to deprive thousands of their livelihoods, driving many to pursue their careers abroad or entirely out of their professions, and driving some to suicide. It began with the COLD WAR "internal security" programs of the TRUMAN administration and developed great momentum during the MCCARTHY period; it persisted in diminishing form throughout the balance of the 1950s and ended in the early 1960s.

Black Monday, October 19, 1987, the date of the 1987 U.S. stock market crash.

Blackmun, Harry Andrew (1908–   ), U.S. lawyer and law professor, who became an eighth Circuit U.S. Court of Appeals judge in 1959 and in 1970 was appointed by Richard M. NIXON to the Supreme Court. On the Court he remained a moderate-to-conservative influence in most matters, as originally expected, but pursued a strongly pro-civil rights course throughout his tenure.

Black Muslims (Nation of Islam), a religious organization espousing a form of the Moslem faith, stressing the importance of Black pride and education, along with Black separatism. It was founded in 1930 by W. D. Farah MUHAMMAD, led from 1934 by Elijah Muhammad, and was the organization from which MALCOLM X came.

Black Panther Party, a revolutionary Black activist organization founded by Huey

NEWTON and Bobby SEALE in Oakland, California, in October 1966 that advocated armed self-defense. Some of its members, including Eldridge CLEAVER, later advocated violent revolution. Members of the organization became involved in a series of armed confrontations with law enforcement authorities during the late 1960s and early 1970s, some of those confrontations resulting from violence directed against members of the group. Panther leaders Fred Hampton and Mark Clark were killed by attacking Chicago police in 1970. Eldridge Cleaver jumped bail, fled to sanctuary in Algeria, and later returned to the United States as a Christian convert. Huey Newton fled the country while retrial on a murder charge and later returned.

Black power, a largely undefined slogan put forward from 1966 by some of the Black activists associated with the STUDENT NON-VIOLENT COORDINATING COMMITTEE (SNCC) and the CONGRESS OF RACIAL EQUALITY (CORE) at a time when these elements of the CIVIL RIGHTS MOVEMENT were moving toward the tactics of violent confrontation and away from both nonviolence and biracial cooperation.

Black September, Palestinian Arab terrorist organization, that was responsible for the MUNICH OLYMPICS MURDERS of 1972 and has claimed responsibility for many other terrorist actions.

Blackshirts, Italian fascist paramilitary militia, from 1921 engaged in terrorist street fighting and in 1922 the vehicle used by BENITO MUSSOLINI to seize power in the march on Rome. Their black shirts were in emulation of the shirts worn by elite Italian combat troops during World War I, and during the fascist period they were worn by many in Italy as a symbol of fascist affiliation.

Black Sox scandal, the most notorious scandal in U.S. sports history, in which eight Chicago White Sox players were accused of conspiring to lose the 1919 World Series to the Cincinnati Reds. The series was indeed lost, and bribes were paid to some of the players. All eight were tried and acquitted in 1920 but also were barred from the game for the rest of their lives, public perception continuing to be that they had "thrown" the World Series.

Black Tuesday (October 29, 1929), the day of the most severe decline in market values during the U.S. stock market CRASH of October 1929, which precipitated the GREAT DEPRESSION of the 1930s.

Blagoveshchensk nuclear accident (1958), a major Soviet nuclear accident in the Ural Mountains, resulting in the contamination of hundreds of square miles of populated area; it was unreported for decades, and casualty figures are still unavailable.

Blair, Eric Arthur, the given name of British writer George ORWELL.

Blair House attack, the armed attack by Puerto Rican nationalists Oscar COLLAZO and Griselio Torresola, on November 1, 1950, at Washington, D. C.'s Blair House, in an attempt to assassinate President Harry TRUMAN.

Blalock, Alfred (1899–1964), U.S. surgeon, who in 1944 first performed the operation that corrected heart defects in BLUE BABIES, introducing a technique (developed with Helen TAUSSIG) that has since saved thousands of infants and helped pave the way for modern OPEN-HEART SURGERY. With C. R. Hanlon he developed another now-standard technique, that of correcting a reversal of the heart's major blood vessels. Earlier he had recognized that shock was linked to loss of blood or blood plasma and developed the basic approach of giving blood or plasma transfusions.

Blériot, Louis, French aviator, the first to fly over the English Channel, on July 25, 1909.

blimp, nonrigid type of DIRIGIBLE.

Blitz, The (November 1940–May 1941), the World War II terror bombing of London and other British cities by the German air force, that began as a prolonged series of attacks on London during the final phase of the Battle of BRITAIN; the attacks continued and were extended to other cities after the

Germans had lost that battle and Hitler had scrapped his invasion plans.

Blitzkrieg (lightning war), mobile warfare tactics first fully used in World War II by the German army, involving the used of armored formations led by massed TANKS to breach enemy defenses, achieve quick, deep penetration, and roll up opposing forces, often bypassing enemy fortifications, which would later be reduced at leisure. The technique had been proposed and experimented with by several countries during the interwar period, and both German and Soviet armored commanders used it during the SPANISH CIVIL WAR; but only the Germans used it early in World War II, and to great effect, in their conquests of Poland, France, Belgium, and Holland and their subsequent deep penetration of the Soviet Union. Later in the war the ALLIES followed suit in North Africa, the Soviet Union, and Western Europe.

blood bank, storage of blood or blood plasma, as in hospitals or by the Red Cross, for use as needed. The first known blood bank was formed in 1937 in Chicago. But it was Charles Richard DREW who in 1940 formulated plans for large-scale storage of blood plasma. After the discovery of the RHESUS (RH) FACTOR in 1940 allowed for testing for blood compatibility, blood banks became widespread, and tests were established to screen out blood that might carry disease or be otherwise unsuitable for transfusion. Blood banks saved many lives, notably during World War II. But in the 1980s the AIDS virus posed a threat to the safety of the blood bank system; numerous people who had blood transfusions during surgery or for hemophilia contracted AIDS before the danger was recognized and tests developed. Even so, some risk remained.

Blood Purge (June 29–30, 1934), the surprise SS attack on and mass murders of Ernst ROEHM and many other leaders and members of the Nazi STORM TROOPERS (SA), as well as of many Nazi sympathizers who had fallen into disfavor. The murders were ordered by Adolf HITLER to satisfy the demands of the army and the SS, who felt

the SA to be competitive. The date of the Blood Purge is called the NIGHT OF THE LONG KNIVES.

blood transfusions, introduction into a patient's body of blood from a donor, attempted with little success from the 18th century but made a practical reality in the 20th century with Karl LANDSTEINER'S discovery of blood groups in 1900–1902 and of the RHESUS (RH) FACTOR in 1940 and with the subsequent development of BLOOD BANKS.

blood, toil, tears, and sweat, statement by Winston CHURCHILL, speaking to Britain's House of Commons on May 13, 1940, for the first time as prime minister; from "I have nothing to offer but blood, toil, tears, and sweat."

Bloody Sunday (January 9,1905), the beginning of the RUSSIAN REVOLUTION OF 1905. At the Winter Palace in St. Petersburg, troops fired on a crowd of unarmed petitioners led by priest Georgy Gapon, killing over 100 and wounding hundreds more, and thereby setting off the massive countrywide mutinies and demonstrations that were the revolution.

blue babies, infants born with heart defects, such as blockage in the artery linking heart and lungs or a hole in the heart, causing insufficient oxygen intake and a resulting blue pallor (cyanosis), retardation, and premature death. U.S. pediatric cardiologist Helen TAUSSIG first diagnosed the cause of the problem and with her surgeon-colleague Alfred BLALOCK developed the operation that after 1944 saved thousands of such infants.

Blue Book, U.S. Air Force project (1948–69) to gather and evaluate information on sightings of UNIDENTIFIED FLYING OBJECTS.

Blue Division, the Spanish fascist division on the Russian front during World War II; ostensibly a volunteer unit, in reality it was sent by Francisco FRANCO'S government to assist its German allies, although Spain was formally a neutral country.

Blue Eagle, the symbol of the American Depression-era NATIONAL RECOVERY ADMIN-

ISTRATION (NRA), carrying a blue eagle and "NRA—We do our part." It was introduced in a massive national campaign conducted in 1933.

Bluford, Guion, Jr., first Black astronaut in space, launched aboard the U.S. SPACE SHUTTLE *CHALLENGER* on its third flight, August 30, 1983.

Blum, Léon (1872–1950), French political leader, the first socialist party leader and the first Jew to become French premier. A moderate socialist, he broke with the communists after the RUSSIAN REVOLUTION, founded a socialist newspaper, and in 1929 won a seat in the Chamber of Deputies. He became premier of the POPULAR FRONT coalition government in June 1936, then beginning a series of financial and labor reforms, but lost popular favor and resigned a year later, coming back briefly as premier in 1938. He opposed the MUNICH agreement and attempted to oppose VICHY after the fall of France in 1940 but was then indicted and tried by Vichy. The trial was suspended after the strong defense mounted by Blum and the other defendants, though he was held in jail for the rest of the war. He led a postwar delegation to the United States but otherwise retired from public life after the war.

Blunt, Anthony (1907–83), an eminent British art historian, museum director, and art adviser to the royal family, knighted in 1956. He had become a Soviet spy in the 1930s, with his Cambridge friends and espionage network colleagues, Kim PHILBY, Guy BURGESS, and Donald MACLEAN, working with them and others as Soviet spies within British intelligence during World War II. In 1964 his role was discovered; he then cooperated with British intelligence and was secretly pardoned, keeping all positions and honors. In 1979 his espionage became public knowledge; the resulting massive publicity caused him to lose his positions and honors, including his knighthood, although his repute as an art historian continued to be unassailable.

Blücher, Vasili Konstantinovich (1889–1938), a RUSSIAN CIVIL WAR partisan commander, who developed his forces into a Red Army division. He was Soviet military adviser to CHIANG KAI-SHEK, 1924–27, under the name "Galin" and later commander of the Soviet Far Eastern Army. He was executed in 1938 during the GREAT PURGE and posthumously rehabilitated in 1957.

Boas, Franz (1858–1942), German-American anthropologist, a leading figure in U.S. anthropology, whose work with the peoples of North America's northwest coast was a model for succeeding generations of anthropologists. His conclusions, teaching, and published work regarding the essential equality of all of the races of humankind provided an early and complete refutation of racist theories and were widely used to combat such Nazi theories in the 1930s and thereafter.

boat people, Vietnamese refugees attempting to flee by water to such nearby countries as Thailand, Malaysia, Indonesia, and the Philippines; a flow that began after the end of the VIETNAM WAR in numbers estimated to total as many as 1 million. Refugees fron other countries, attempting to flee by water, as from Cuba and Haiti, also have been called boat people.

Bock, Fedor von (1880–1945), German general in both world wars, who commanded German forces occupying Austria and Czechoslovakia during the interwar period and led major forces during the 1939 Polish and 1940 French campaigns in World War II. In 1941 he commanded German Group Center on the Russian Front but failed to take Moscow and was relieved of his command. In 1942 he commanded German armies moving toward STALINGRAD but was dismissed from command in July for not having moved forward as directly as Hitler thought he should.

Bodyguard, the Allied code name for the group of deceptions developed in 1942–44 to mislead the Germans as to the specifics of the coming invasion of Europe. In aggregate, the actions played an important role in spreading German defensive formations on the perimeter of Europe, and the last deception, code-named Fortitude, for a time helped to convince the Germans that the invasion was coming at the Pas de Calais, as they thought it should.

Boer War (1899–1902), conflict that began with the invasion of British South African territory by South African Republic and Orange Free State forces on October 12, 1899, with all major actions taking place between then and June 5, 1900. The Boers had early successes, winning battles at Stormberg, Magersfontein, and Colenso, and besieging Mafeking, Ladysmith, and Kimberley. In February 1900 the British moved to the offensive, taking Paardeberg and its Boer garrison and relieving Ladysmith. Then the British took Bloemfontein, capital of the Orange Free State, relieved Mafeking, and invaded the South African Republic, taking Johannesburg on May 31 and Pretoria on June 5. After that the Boers waged guerrrilla war against the British for almost 2 years, until their surrender on May 31, 1902. Ultimately, British forces numbering 450,000–500,000 men had defeated 80,000–90,000 Boers.

Boesky, Ivan, U.S. stock market figure of the early 1980s, a principal in the INSIDER TRADING SCANDAL of the late 1980s, who later agreed to gather information on his former associates and ultimately was imprisoned and heavily fined.

Bohr, Niels Henrik David (1885–1962), Danish physicist, who created the basic model of ATOMIC STRUCTURE. Building on Ernest RUTHERFORD'S model of the nuclear-centered atom, in 1913 Bohr posited that ELECTRONS circled the NUCLEUS in fixed concentric orbits, emitting energy in discrete units called quanta on moving from one orbit to another; for this model he won the 1922 Nobel Prize for Physics. A leading physicist working with NUCLEAR FISSION in the 1930s, Bohr was smuggled out of German-occupied Denmark during World War II. He then went to LOS ALAMOS, where he

played a major role in the development of the ATOMIC BOMB.

Bokassa, Jean Bédel (1921–   ), a former French army officer who became a colonel in the Central African army and on January 1, 1966, led a Central African Republic military coup that deposed President David Dacko. Bokassa then took dictatorial power in an 11-year tenure marked by wholesale murder, torture, and mutilation of opponents and even of schoolchildren, generating worldwide condemnation. On December 4, 1977, he had himself installed as Emperor Bokassa I; on September 20, 1979, he was deposed by the forces of David Dacko with French army help; he took refuge in Libya and then France. He was sentenced to death in absentia, returned home for unexplained reasons in October 1986, was again sentenced to death, and ultimately had his sentence commuted to life imprisonment.

Bolsheviks, the Russian revolutionary Marxist group led by Vladimir Illich LENIN, which began in 1903 as a dissident group within the Russian Social-Democratic Workers' Party, formed itself into a separate Russian Social-Democratic Workers' Party (Bolsheviks) in 1912, and in the OCTOBER REVOLUTION of 1917 took control of the RUSSIAN REVOLUTION. The term *bolshevik* means "majority," a label adopted by the group when, for a short time in 1903, it won votes on certain intraparty issues. In 1918 the party renamed itself the Russian Communist Party (Bolsheviks), in 1925 the All-Union Communist Party (Bolsheviks), and in 1952 the Communist Party of the Soviet Union, dropping the Bolshevik descriptor.

Bond, Julian (1940–   ), U.S. political leader, in 1960 a founder of the STUDENT NON-VIOLENT COORDINATING COMMITTEE (SNCC) and its communications director 1960–66. He was elected to the Georgia state legislature in 1965 but denied his seat because of his opposition to the VIETNAM WAR; he was seated after a Supreme Court decision in his favor.

Bonhoeffer, Dietrich (1906–45), German Protestant minister who became a leader of the German anti-Nazi resistance. He was arrested in 1943 and murdered in a Nazi CONCENTRATION CAMP in 1945, after having been accused of complicity in the 1944 army officers' plot to assassinate HITLER.

Bonnie and Clyde, Bonnie PARKER and Clyde BARROW, U.S. murderers and armed robbers of the 1930s, who became folk heroes.

Bonus Marchers, the "Bonus Army" of an estimated 20,000 American World War I veterans and their families, who in 1932, at the depth of the GREAT DEPRESSION, encamped in and around Washington, D. C., demanding immediate payment of the veterans' bonuses legislated in 1924 and by law payable in 1945. Congress refused the demand, but approximately 5,000 Bonus Marchers remained after Congress adjourned, many of them encamped at Anacostia Flats. In mid–July a clash between police and some of the veterans became violent, and the police killed two. President Herbert HOOVER then called out the army, which came in the person of Army Chief of Staff Douglas MACARTHUR at the head of the Third Cavalry, two infantry regiments, six tanks, and a machine gun detachment, all in full battle dress. MacArthur ordered the violent dispersal of the veterans, whom he regarded as a revolutionary mob, and the burning of their encampments; Hoover publicly approved, and in the eyes of the nation lost much of his remaining prestige as the great humanitarian who had organized the American war relief effort after World War I.

Bork, Robert Heron (1927–), U.S. lawyer, law professor 1962–73 and 1977–81, a strict constructionist and conservative legal theorist who was appointed U.S. solicitor-general in 1973 by president Richard M. NIXON. During the WATERGATE affair he acceded to Nixon's "SATURDAY NIGHT MASSACRE" request to fire Special Prosecutor Archibald Cox and Deputy Attorney General William Ruckelshaus, after Attorney General Elliot Richardson had refused to do so and had resigned. In 1982 Bork was a Ronald REAGAN appointee to the Court of Appeals. In July 1986 he was nominated as an associate justice of the Supreme Court by Reagan but was refused the nomination by the Senate after televised committee hearings and a major confirmation fight. In January 1988 he resigned from the Court of Appeals.

Borlaug, Norman (1914–), U.S. plant pathologist and agricultural scientist, who spurred the so-called GREEN REVOLUTION. After early work on plant diseases and pesticides, Borlaug worked in Mexico, 1944–60, under Rockefeller Foundation auspices, developing hardy, high-yield grains suitable to a wide range of climates. In the 1960s and 1970s these were planted in many undeveloped countries, significantly easing world hunger and earning him the 1970 Nobel Peace Prize.

Bormann, Martin (1900–), German Nazi administrator and chief personal assistant to Adolf HITLER, who since World War II has been widely—but inconclusively—reported to be living in South America.

Borodin, Mikhail Markovich (1884–1951), a Russian socialist organizer, in exile in the United States 1906–18, who returned to the Soviet Union after the OCTOBER REVOLUTION, then becoming a COMINTERN representative. He was chief Comintern advisor to SUN YAT-SEN and the KUOMINTANG 1923–27. After the Kuomintang-Communist split and the beginning of the CHINESE CIVIL WAR in 1927, he was recalled to the Soviet Union and worked as a Soviet official until 1949. He was arrested in STALIN'S anti-Jewish purge of 1949 and died a prisoner in Siberia.

Bosch Gaviño, Juan (1909–), Dominican Republic writer and socialist, a major opponent of dictator Rafael TRUJILLO, who lived in exile 1937–61 and returned to be elected president of his country in 1962. He was deposed in a 1963 military coup and in 1966 was defeated for the presidency by Joaquin BALAGUER after the 1965–66 DOMINICAN REPUBLIC CIVIL WAR. His party, the Dominican Revolutionary party, boycotted the 1970 and 1974 elections, and Bosch split away from it to form the Dominican Liberation party in 1974. He ran for the presidency and lost in 1978 and 1982.

Bose, Subhas Chandra (1897–1945), Indian nationalist leader, who generally favored armed insurrection against British rule in India, rather than the nonviolent approach fostered by Mahatma GANDHI and the main leadership of the CONGRESS PARTY. During World War II he fought beside the Japanese and Germans, heading the Indian National Army, which fought on the Japanese side in Southeast Asia. He died in an aircraft accident shortly after the end of the war.

Boskin, Michael Jay (1945–   ), U.S. economist and university professor, named chairman of the White House Council of Economic Advisors by President George BUSH on December 6, 1988.

Bosnia-Herzegovina, a province of the OTTOMAN EMPIRE, occupied by Austria-Hungary in 1878 and formally annexed in 1908, precipitating a Balkan crisis and threat of war between Serbia and Austria-Hungary that might draw Russia in on Serbia's side, leading to a general war. The dispute was part of the run-up to World War I. Bosnian members of the BLACK HAND assassinated Austro-Hungarian archduke FRANCIS FERDINAND at SARAJEVO in 1914 and set off World War I.

Boston Police Strike (September 1919), a strike by much of the Boston, Massachusetts, police department after suspensions because of moves toward union affiliation. Boston's mayor called out State Guard members living in Boston; Governor Calvin COOLIDGE then called out the balance of the State Guard and asked for a commitment of federal troops if necessary. The strike was broken. All of the strikers were dismissed, and Coolidge became a national hero, his handling of the strike making a great contribution to his presidential nomination and election in 1920.

Boston Strangler, media-developed name for mass murderer Albert H. DeSALVO.

Botha, Louis (1862–1919), South African farmer, who became a soldier and ultimately a guerrilla general during the BOER WAR. Going into politics, he became prime minister of the Transvaal (1907–10) and then first prime minister of the Union of South Africa (1910–19).

Botha, Pieter Willem (1916–   ), South African political leader, who rose through the ranks of the Afrikaner party, winning his first parliamentary seat in 1948. He moved with his party into the ruling NATIONAL PARTY in 1951, became defense minister in 1966, prime minister in 1978, and state president in 1984. After an illness he resigned his party leadership in early 1989. As leader of South Africa he used all available tools and institutions to foster the continuance of white rule, unhesitatingly using mass imprisonments, suppression of the press, and wide-scale police and army violence directed at demonstrators. Simultaneously, he promised to dismantle substantial portions of the system of APARTHEID and in some periods made such ameliorative moves as did not in substance alter the realities of South African racism.

Botswana (Republic of Botswana), until 1966 the British protectorate of Bechuanaland. On September 30, 1966, it became Botswana, an independent state and member of the COMMONWEALTH. A democracy, Botswana was led by president Seretse KHAMA from independence until his death in 1980.

Bouganville campaign (1943–44), World War II assault by American troops in the Solomon Islands, securing a substantial beachhead on the island of Bouganville in October and November 1943, then developing a naval base and airfields there. Japanese forces remaining on the island engaged in a long campaign to wipe out the beachhead but failed; the island was then secured by the Allies in a series of actions during 1944.

Boumedienne, Houari (Mohammed Boukharouba; 1927–78), Algerian teacher, who joined the FLN (NATIONAL LIBERATION FRONT) in 1954, fought as Oran regional guerrilla commander 1955–56, and was rebel army chief of staff 1960–62. After the Algerian-French agreement of 1962, he took his army into Algeria, backed Ahmed BEN BELLA'S new FLN government, and became defense minister and in 1963 deputy prime minister. In 1965 he toppled Ben Bella in a coup and imprisoned him. Boumedienne then ruled Algeria absolutely until his death of natural causes in 1978, eliminating all opposition and further developing state socialism, with emphasis on modernization and industrial and infrastructural development.

Bourbaki, Nicolas, pseudonym for a group of mathematicians, mostly French, who began publishing highly influential mathematical works in 1939.

Bourguiba, Habib (1903–   ), Tunisian lawyer, a founder of the Neo-Destour party in 1934; he was its leader and the leader of the Tunisian independence movement thereafter. Peaceful tactics gave way to guerrilla war after the arrests of Bourguiba and other leaders in 1952; in July 1955, France granted autonomy to Tunisia. Full independence was achieved in March 1956, with Bourguiba as first premier; he became first president of the new republic in March 1957 and led Tunisia until resigning under pressure in 1987. As president he was a democratic socialist who fostered economic, political, and social modernization, including considerable focus on the development of a government of laws, on civil liberties, and on the rights of women.

Boxer Protocol, the terms forced on China after the BOXER REBELLION, signed on September 7, 1901.

Boxer Rebellion (1900), conflict that started as a widespread antiforeign, anti-Manchu set of riots in 1899 and in 1900 became a joint Manchu–Boxer war against the foreign powers that had been attacking and exploiting China since the end of the Opium War in 1842. In June 1900, after an international force headed for Peking from Tientsin had been repulsed, Boxer forces entered Peking and began a 2-month-long siege of the foreign legations. On June 21 the Manchu dowager empress joined them, declaring war against the foreign powers. On August 4, a 20,000-strong international force started from Tientsin, lifting the siege on August 14, then burning and looting Peking. The punitive BOXER PROTOCOL, signed by the Chinese government and 11 foreign powers on September 7, 1901, provided for, among other things, huge indemnities, the execution of 10 high Chinese officials, and the garrisoning of the Peking legations, thereby greatly worsening the position of the Manchus and bringing the CHINESE REVOLUTION even closer.

Boyle, W. A. "Tony," former United Mine Workers president, who was convicted of arranging the December 31, 1959, murders of union opponent Joseph YABLONSKI and his family.

Bradley, Omar (1893–1981), U.S. officer who saw service in World War I, was a corps commander early in World War II, commanded the U.S. First Army during the NORMANDY invasion, and then commanded the U.S. Twelfth Army as it fought its way across Europe into Germany. During the postwar period he was U.S. Army chief of staff, first chairman of the Joint Chiefs of Staff, and a five-star general.

Bragg, William Henry (1862–1942) and **William Lawrence Bragg** (1890–1971), British physicists, father and Australian-born son, who were inspired by Max von LAUE'S work to make key developments in the field of X-RAY CRYSTALLOGRAPHY in the 1910s. They were the first to measure the wavelengths of X-RAYS, winning the 1915 Nobel Prize for Physics, the only father-and-son pair ever to do so.

brain death, absence of electrical activity in the brain, as measured on an ELECTROENCEPHALOGRAPH; first used as a clinical definition of death, instead of heart stoppage, by the French Academy of Medicine in 1966 and widely adopted since then. A person may be considered brain dead even though the heart is kept pumping and most organs functioning by means of various machines, such as respirators; that has led to complicated questions about a physician's responsibility to keep a patient alive by whatever means and a patient's RIGHT TO DIE.

brain trust, an informal group of advisors to Franklin Delano ROOSEVELT during and after the 1932 election campaign, some of whom were academics and therefore popularly called "brains." The academics in the group included Rexford G. Tugwell, Adolf A. Berle, Jr., and Raymond Moley; they had considerable influence on the specific proposals Roosevelt advanced to deal with the GREAT DEPRESSION, and on the legislation passed during the Roosevelt era, especially during the first HUNDRED DAYS.

Brandeis, Louis Dembitz (1856–1941), U.S. lawyer, who pursued a sharply liberal and independent political and legal course before being appointed by Woodrow WILSON to the Supreme Court in 1916; he was confirmed only after long hearings. The first Jewish Supreme Court Justice, Brandeis was one of the leading legal figures of his time, although in most instances a dissenter during his Court career.

Brandt, Willy (Carl Herbert Frahm; 1913–), German socialist and political leader, who was forced to flee Germany in 1933 and who worked as a journalist in Norway and in resistance movement activities during World War II. He returned to Germany in 1945, was in the West German assembly 1949–57, and was mayor of West Berlin 1957–66, in office when the BERLIN WALL was built in 1961. In 1964 he became chairman of the Social Democratic party; he was foreign minister 1966–69 and chancellor 1969–74, resigning when one of his aides was exposed as an East German spy, although Brandt had not known this. As chancellor he attempted a partial rapprochement with East Germany and the Soviet bloc, signing treaties with the Soviet Union and Poland while at the same time

developing closer ties with the EUROPEAN COMMUNITY and encouraging moves toward nuclear disarmament. He was awarded the 1971 Nobel Peace Prize.

Brauchitsch, Walther von (1881–1948), German officer, who saw service in both world wars, becoming commander-in-chief of the army in 1938 and directing the early German successes in World War II. Although he directed the invasion of the Soviet Union, he became convinced in late 1941 that German forces should be withdrawn from Moscow and so recommended to Adolf Hitler, who was enraged at the suggestion and relieved von Brauchitsch of his command. He died in 1948, a short while before he was to go on trial for alleged war crimes.

Braudel, Fernand (1902–85), French historian, a leading member of the *Annales* school, which studied societies and groups of societies as whole entities in an attempt to reach and understand deep and commonly experienced developmental trends throughout the world. His first major work, *The Mediterranean and the Mediterranean World in the Age of Philip I*, was written, without his notes and research materials, while a prisoner of war during World War II.

Braun, Eva (1912–45), German shop girl who became Adolf HITLER'S mistress and, at the end, his wife, just before their joint suicide in Berlin.

Braun, Wernher Magnus Maximilian von (1912–77), German-American ROCKET expert, who headed the German research teams at PEENEMÜNDE that developed the V-1 AND V-2 BOMBS used in the terror bombings of Great Britain, starting in June 1944. Escaping prosecution after the war, he instead became one of the key people in the development of U.S. MISSILE and space capabilities, helping to create INTERCONTINENTAL BALLISTIC MISSILES (ICBMs) in the early 1950s; using a modified V-2 rocket to help boost into orbit the first U.S. SATELLITE, *Explorer* 1, in 1958; and becoming an administrator of the NATIONAL AERO-

NAUTICS AND SPACE ADMINISTRATION (NASA) in 1970.

Brave New World (1932), an Aldous Huxley novel portraying a future "Utopia" in which an omnipresent bureaucratic state controls human development and social organization. The book was in particular an attack on the EUGENICS theories of the time, foreshadowing very real GENETIC ENGINEERING concerns later in the century.

Brawley, Tawana, a Black 15-year-old from Wappingers Falls, New York, who charged that on November 24, 1987, she had been kidnapped, raped, and otherwise mistreated by a group of six White men; she was found on November 28, wrapped in a plastic trash bag and with racist comments written on her body. The sensational nature of the charges, their racial content, and the public charges of racism and official coverup made by Brawley's advisors, including the Reverend Al Sharpton and lawyers Alton Maddox and C. Vernon Mason, fresh from their participation in the HOWARD BEACH case, brought massive, protracted publicity. After 7 months of grand jury hearings, at which Brawley refused to testify, the jury concluded in October 1988 that she had lied; investigations of possible misconduct by Brawley's advisers continued after the case had been closed by the jury.

Brazil circus fire (December 17, 1961), a deliberately set circus tent fire at Niterói, near Rio de Janeiro, Brazil, that killed 323 and injured an estimated 800 more; most of the dead and injured were children.

Bremer, Arthur Herman (1950–   ), man who shot and paralyzed Alabama governor George WALLACE in Laurel, Maryland, on May 15, 1972, and was subsequently sentenced to a prison term of 53 years.

Brennan, William Joseph, Jr. (1906–   ), U.S. lawyer, who was a New Jersey superior court judge 1949–50, appellate division judge 1950–52, and state supreme court judge 1952–56. He was appointed by president Dwight D. EISENHOWER to the U.S. Supreme Court in 1956. Brennan became a major liberal figure in his almost four de-

cades on the Court, often writing the majority decision during the 1960s, in such landmark decisions as NEW YORK TIMES COMPANY V. SULLIVAN and BAKER V. CARR. In his later years he became part of the Court's liberal minority.

Brereton, Lewis Hyde (1890–1967), U.S. aviator, who saw service in World War I and was commander of U.S. air forces in the Philippines at the outbreak of World War II. The bulk of his planes were caught and destroyed on the ground at CLARK FIELD on December 8, 1941. Later in the war he commanded Allied air forces in the European theater.

Brest-Litovsk, Treaty of (March 3, 1918), a treaty between the Soviet government and the CENTRAL POWERS, taking the Soviets out of World War I. Negotiated by Leon TROTSKY, the treaty provided for major losses of territory in western Russia and the Ukraine and demobilization of the Russian armies. It was clearly a ruse to gain time and was repudiated by the Soviet government immediately after Germany's defeat by the ALLIES, to be superseded by the treaties made at VERSAILLES and elsewhere following World War I.

Bretton Woods Conference (July 1944), major international planning meeting, held at Bretton Woods, New Hampshire, regarding post–World War II financial stabilization, at which the INTERNATIONAL BANK FOR RECONSTRUCTION AND DEVELOPMENT and the INTERNATIONAL MONETARY FUND were established.

Breuil, Henry Édouard Prosper (1877–1961), French archaeologist, paleontologist, and priest who specialized in Paleolithic art, such as that in the caves of Altamira and LASCAUX. Abbé Breuil copied the cave paintings, analyzed their style and color, and placed them in the context of known archeological finds, in the process deepening our understanding of prehistoric culture, notably in *Four Hundred Centuries of Cave Art* (1952).

Brezhnev, Leonid Ilyich (1906–82), Soviet metallurgist, who became a Communist party official in 1938 and was a political officer during World War II, rising to the rank of major general. After holding several party positions during the postwar period he became a Central Committee member in 1952. A Khrushchev supporter, he held several major positions during the Khrushchev period, including that of Soviet president, and was first secretary of his party when Khrushchev was ousted in October 1964; he succeeded as party leader. He shared "collective leadership" with Aleksei KOSYGIN during the balance of the 1960s and emerged as leader of both party and country in the early 1970s; he formally became both Communist party general secretary and Soviet president in 1977 and died in office. A conservative, he presided over the end of Khrushchev's period of THAW, reimposing tighter party control over dissidents but not going back to Stalinist mass repression, exile, and murder. Internationally, he pursued worldwide Soviet power aims while to some degree supporting DETENTE and arms limitation; in his time both superpowers continued their massive arms race. He bore the major responsibility for the ultimately failed Soviet invasion and occupation of AFGHANISTAN.

Brezhnev doctrine, the proposition that Soviet intervention in the affairs of any other Communist state is justified when communism is threatened in that state. This position was first published in a *Pravda* article on September 26, 1968, and argued by Leonid BREZHNEV speaking to a Polish Communist party congress on November 13, 1968. The doctrine was advanced to justify the August 1968 Soviet invasion of CZECHO-SLOVAKIA, and repudiated during the GORBACHEV era.

Briand, Aristide (1862–1932), French political leader, who in his socialist years founded *L'Humanité* (1904) with Jean JAURÈS and then went on to a public career that included 11 terms as premier of France (1909–10, 1915–17, 1921–22, and several times in the late 1920s). He was also foreign minister through many governments, from 1925 to 1932. He strongly supported the LEAGUE OF NATIONS from its inception; in the late 1920s he achieved the LOCARNO (1925) and KELLOGG-BRIAND (1928) pacts, and in the early 1930s he spoke out for European federation. He received a Nobel Peace Prize in 1926.

Bridges, Harry (1901–), Australian-born seaman, who became a U.S. labor leader, beginning with his work as an INDUSTRIAL WORKERS OF THE WORLD (IWW) organizer in the early 1920s. In 1933 he organized San Francisco longshoremen into a local of the International Longshoreman's Association (ILA), and in 1934 he led the longshoremen's strike that turned into the San Francisco general strike. In 1937 he led Pacific Coast ILA locals into the newly formed CONGRESS OF INDUSTRIAL ORGANIZATIONS (CIO) and became president of the new International Longshoremen's and Warehousemen's Union (ILWU), remaining the union's president until 1977, when he retired. Starting in 1938, the federal government tried for 17 years to deport him as an alleged Communist, in a series of ultimately unsuccessful legal actions.

brinkmanship, term describing the 1950s COLD WAR tactics of U.S. secretary of state John Foster DULLES, who spoke of having taken the United States to the "brink of war" with the Soviet Union on several occasions and viewed his willingness to do so as a necessary tactic. His views on the matter were highly controversial, his detractors calling them little short of madness in a nuclear age, his supporters regarding them as quite realistic.

Brink's robbery, highly publicized robbery occurring on January 17, 1950, at Brink's North Terminal Garage in Boston. The 11 robbers netted $2.7 million; all were later caught. In 1980 the theft and its aftermath were the subject of a film, *The Brink's Job*.

Britain, Battle of (August–October 1940), the early World War II air battle for control of the skies over Britain; part of Hitler's OPERATION SEA LION, which required air supremacy as an essential component of that invasion plan. British RADAR and resulting superior ability to concentrate response, coupled with stronger skills and motivation, overcame German numerical superiority. In late August and early September, however, concentrated German attacks on British airfields inflicted heavy damage on the British air force. But the Germans then changed their strategy, focusing on the terror bombing of London, wrecking much of that city, killing thousands of civilians—and probably saving Britain, for then the remaining British air strength was brought to bear over London. By the end of September the Germans were forced to halt daylight bombing and go over to night bombing alone. The Battle of Britain was won.

British Broadcasting Corporation (BBC), quasi-public British authority, designed to prevent "commercialization" of radio. Chartered in 1927, it was given a monopoly on RADIO and later TELEVISION broadcasting, under the early directorship of John REITH. It is widely known for its foreign language services, begun in 1938, though somewhat cut back in the leaner 1970s and 1980s. Private commercial firms began broadcasting in Britain in television in 1954 and in radio in 1972.

British Expeditionary Forces (BEF), in two world wars, the first major British fighting force in France. In World War I a British Expeditionary Force of approximately 100,000 men, the vanguard of millions more to come, saw its first major action at MONS on August 23, 1914. In World War II a British Expeditionary Force of approximately 400,000 men was in France in May 1940; over 200,000 British soldiers were evacuated from DUNKIRK, May 28–June 4, 1940, returning in force to Normandy on D-DAY, June 6, 1944.

British Somaliland, a former British African colony, that became part of independent SOMALIA in 1960.

British Togoland, the western portion of TOGOLAND, which became part of the new nation of GHANA on March 6, 1957.

British Union of Fascists, the British Nazi organization created and led by Oswald MOSLEY from 1932.

Brooke, Edward William (1919–   ), U.S. lawyer who in 1966 became the first Black elected U.S. senator in American history. He was Massachusetts attorney general 1963–66, and served in the U.S. senate 1967–79.

Browder, Earl Russell (1891–1973), U.S. socialist, Communist, and editor, who became a member of the Communist party in 1921, thereafter becoming a leading Communist during the 1920s, and working with the COMINTERN in China in the late 1920s. He was general secretary of the COMMUNIST PARTY OF THE UNITED STATES 1930–45 and that party's presidential candidate in 1936 and 1940, during the period in which the Soviet and other Communist parties around the world advocated a UNITED FRONT against fascism. He was imprisoned in 1940, during the period of the NAZI-SOVIET PACT, a period in which he and other Communists opposed support for the Allies in World War II. After the invasion of the Soviet Union he supported U.S. entry into the war and the American war effort, in 1944 initiating the temporary dissolution of his party and its replacement with the Communist Political Association. In 1946, as the COLD WAR was beginning, his party's position changed again, the Communist party was formed once more, and he was expelled for his most recent policies.

Brown, H. Rap (1943–   ), U.S. Black civil rights activist, who in 1967 succeeded Stokely CARMICHAL as chairman of the STUDENT NON-VIOLENT COORDINATING COMMITTEE (SNCC). He jumped bail while appealing a federal firearms conviction, was later wounded during an armed robbery, and was subsequently imprisoned.

Brown, Louise (1978–   ), world's first TEST-TUBE BABY, delivered by cesarean section on July 25, 1978, by British gynecologist-obstetrician Patrick STEPTOE, who had developed the procedure of IN VITRO FERTILIZATION.

Brown v. **Board of Education of Topeka** (1954), a landmark U.S. Supreme Court decision outlawing public school segregation; a unanimous opinion written by Chief Justice Earl WARREN. The Court's earlier *Plessy* v. *Ferguson* "separate but equal" doctrine was abandoned, and school segregation was declared unconstitutional, ushering in a new era in American education and providing powerful impetus to the CIVIL RIGHTS MOVEMENT.

Brownsville Raid (August 13, 1906), heavy gunfire from unidentified sources killed one white civilian and wounded another in Brownsville, Texas, on the night of August 13, 1906, after racial tension in the town following the stationing of Black soldiers in the area had caused incidents and the confining of the soldiers to barracks. Without any trial the soldiers of Company B were found collectively guilty by the U.S. Army, and all 167 soldiers were dismissed, on the direct order of President Theodore ROOSEVELT, for refusing to name those "guilty" of the shootings. A Congressional investigation in the early 1970s exonerated the soldiers of Company B.

Broz, Josip, the given name of Yugoslav Communist leader TITO.

Brunei, until 1984 a British protectorate. On January 1, 1984, it became an independent state, headed by Sultan Muda Hassanal Bolkiah, remaining by treaty under British military protection.

Brusilov Offensive (June 4–September 20, 1916), a powerful World War I Russian summer offensive that broke through Austrian lines in Poland but ultimately failed, as German reinforcements arrived. Casualties totaled an estimated 1 million on each side. The heavy Russian losses spurred Russian army disaffection and helped bring about the RUSSIAN REVOLUTION of 1917.

Bryan, William Jennings (1860–1925), U.S. lawyer, Nebraska Democratic congressman (1891–95), three-time unsuccessful candidate for the presidency (1896, 1900, and 1908), and the leading populist leader and orator of his time. His best-remembered address was the "cross of gold" speech at the Chicago Democratic Convention of 1896, which helped win him the nomination. He was defeated by William McKINLEY in 1896 and 1900 and by William Howard TAFT in 1908. He was Woodrow WILSON'S secretary of state (1913–15) but resigned in opposition to administration measures he saw as leading the United States into World War I. Late in his life he became a leading fundamentalist Christian speaker and writer and was active in the prosecution of the antievolution SCOPES TRIAL in Tennessee in the summer of 1925. He died 5 days after the trial's end.

bubble chamber, device filled with heated, pressurized liquid, used for tracking the path of subatomic PARTICLES and RADIATION, invented in 1952 by Donald GLASER. The bubble chamber was widely used by many scientists, such as Luis ALVAREZ, allowing more flexibility than the CLOUD CHAMBER.

Bucharest, Treaty of (1913), agreement ending the second of the two BALKAN WARS.

Buchenwald, a German CONCENTRATION CAMP near Weimar; one of the earliest of such camps, it was used from 1937 to imprison anti-Nazi Germans, German Jews, and other political prisoners and later to house a wide variety of prisoners from all over Europe. Buchenwald was especially notable for the inhuman medical experiments carried on there by Nazi doctors and other Nazi scientists.

Buckley, William, one of the American LEBANON HOSTAGES, the CIA station chief in Beirut, who was kidnapped on March 16, 1984. He was tortured and murdered by his captors during 1985 despite strong U.S. efforts to secure his release, which included some of the concessions leading to the IRAN-CONTRA AFFAIR.

Budenny, Semen Mikhailovich (1883–1973), leading Soviet cavalry general during the RUSSIAN CIVIL WAR and SOVIET-POLISH WAR, who later became a marshal of the Soviet Union and a member of the Soviet presidium. Having escaped the late 1930s purges that destroyed the main leadership of the Soviet armed forces, he was in 1941 the wholly ineffectual commander of the Soviet southwestern armies, losing Kiev and yielding an estimated 1 million prisoners to the advancing Germans.

Buffalo Creek Dam collapse (February 26, 1972), the collapse of a Pittston Coal Company slag heap in West Virginia that had been functioning as a dam, costing an estimated 125 lives and causing much property damage.

Bukharin, Nicolai Ivanovich (1888–1938), an early BOLSHEVIK writer and theoretician who closely collaborated with LENIN. In exile from 1911, he returned to Russia from America after the FEBRUARY REVOLUTION, was a leading Bolshevik throughout the RUSSIAN REVOLUTION and the civil war that followed, and was the second president of the COMINTERN. In the late 1920s he fell into disfavor with STALIN but regained favor in the mid-1930s. In 1937, during the GREAT PURGE, he was arrested and accused of treason. He was executed in 1938; 50 years later, in 1988, he was posthumously rehabilitated by the Soviet government.

Bulganin, Nikolai Aleksandrovich (1895–1975), Soviet official, a Communist from 1917, who worked for the CHEKA, as a factory manager, in the Moscow city administration, and in several other administrative positions during the interwar period, in 1939 becoming a full member of the Communist party central committee. He saw service as an army political administrator during World War II and became defense minister, a deputy premier, and a POLITBURO member in 1948. He was Soviet premier 1955–58, opposed Nikita KHRUSHCHEV after 1956, and lost all positions in the intraparty struggles of 1958, after which he retired.

Bulgaria (People's Republic of Bulgaria), until 1908, part of the Ottoman Empire, though from 1878 substantially autonomous, Bulgaria was a loser in the SECOND BALKAN WAR and in two World Wars, hav-

ing sided with Germany in both. The country was occupied by Soviet troops in 1944, and formally became a thoroughly orthodox one-party Communist state on December 4, 1947, led by Georgi DIMITROV. It was then part of the Communist bloc, led by Todor ZHIVKOV from 1954. In 1989, with the enormous changes generated in Eastern Europe in the GORBACHEV era, a Bulgarian pro-democracy movement arose, which swept Zhivkov out of office in November, developed powerful pro-democracy demonstrations in Sofia and other Bulgarian cities, and sought free elections.

Bulge, Battle of the (Battle of the Ardennes; December 1944–January 1945), the World War II German winter counteroffensive in the Ardennes, a surprise attack beginning on December 16, by 25 divisions, including 11 armored divisions, against much smaller U.S. forces. The German attack pushed the Americans back, surrounding some in the process, and at its peak it created a salient (bulge) 50 miles deep on the western front. But to the north, Allied forces held; and to the south, General George PATTON'S American Third Army turned and attacked, reaching besieged American troops at BASTOGNE on December 26. Severely damaged German forces began withdrawing from the salient in early January; by late January the salient had been wiped out. The Germans had used up much of their available reserve forces in the attack; after the Battle of the Bulge there was no real hope of stopping the Allied advance in the west.

Bull Moose Party, the popular name for the PROGRESSIVE PARTY, which unsuccessfully ran Theodore ROOSEVELT for the presidency in 1912. He proclaimed himself to be as strong as a "bull moose," hence the popular name of the party.

Bülow, Bernhard von (1849–1929), German chancellor 1900–09, who pursued German imperial aims and built German armed strength, in particular the German navy, in the period before World War I. In the process he alienated other possible strong European allies, assuring that the war, when it came, would be a two-front war for Germany.

Bunche, Ralph Johnson (1904–71), U.S. teacher, political scientist, and diplomat, who moved from the state department to the UNITED NATIONS in 1946, then became deputy to Folke BERNADOTTE, chief UN mediator for Palestine. After Bernadotte's assassination in 1948 by STERN GANG terrorists, he became chief mediator, concluding Arab–Israeli peace negotiations, becoming a world figure, and in 1950 gaining a Nobel Peace Prize for his work. From then on he carried out a series of major and often very difficult peacemaking missions on behalf of the UN throughout the world, from 1955 as a UN undersecretary and from 1967 until his retirement in 1971 as UN undersecretary-general. Simultaneously, he was one of the leading Black Americans of his time and a leader in many of the CIVIL RIGHTS struggles of the period, working closely with MARTIN LUTHER KING, JR., and other leaders of that movement.

Bundy, McGeorge (1919–   ), U.S. political scientist and university professor, an advisor to President John F. KENNEDY and special assistant for national security affairs 1961–66; he played a major role in developing U.S. interventionist foreign policy. He helped develop the 1961 BAY OF PIGS INVASION of Cuba, the 1965 DOMINICAN REPUBLIC INTERVENTION, and deepened U.S. involvement in the VIETNAM WAR. He later moderated his views on the Vietnam War, and during the 1980s favored increased U.S.–Soviet negotiation toward arms limitation. He was head of the Ford Foundation 1966–79.

Bundy, Theodore "Ted," U.S. mass murderer, executed in Florida on January 24, 1989, after having received death sentences for three 1978 Florida murders. Ex-law student Bundy had delayed execution of his sentence for a decade; in his final days he confessed to at least 16 other murders and was thought to have committed many more.

Burger, Warren Earl (1907–   ), U.S. lawyer, a judge on the U.S. Court of Appeals for the District of Columbia 1955–69, who was in 1969 appointed chief justice of the U.S. Supreme Court by president Richard M. NIXON, retiring in 1986. Burger introduced major administrative initiatives aimed at speeding the work of the Court, functioned as a critic of the legal profession during his tenure, and was a generally conservative influence on the Court, attempting to limit and in some instances reverse the course developed by the far more liberal WARREN court of the 1960s.

Burgess, Guy (1911–63), British journalist and spy, who was exposed in 1951 as actually having been a Soviet spy since his Cambridge days in the 1930s, along with his college friends and Soviet espionage network colleagues, Kim PHILBY, Anthony BLUNT, and Donald MACLEAN. He and Maclean escaped to the Soviet Union in 1951, thereafter continuing to work in Soviet intelligence.

Burkina Faso, until 1959, a French colony, which on August 5, 1960, became the independent Republic of UPPER VOLTA, then enduring a long series of military coups, punctuated by brief periods of democracy. The country's name was changed to Burkina Faso on August 4, 1984.

Burma (Socialist Republic of the Union of Burma), until 1937 part of British colonial India; then it was made a separate political entity but still under British rule. Burma was occupied by Japanese forces during World War II. It became an independent democratic state on January 4, 1948, led by prime minister U NU. In 1958 the country fell into the hands of military dictator Ne WIN, who developed a long one-party dictatorship.

Burma, Battle of (January–May 1942), early World War II campaign following the uncontested Japanese occupation of Thailand in December 1941; Japanese forces invaded Burma on January 12, 1942. They met and defeated defending British-led forces at Moulmein in late January and again on the Sittang River in late February. Chinese reinforcements arrived in mid–March, but a renewed Japanese offensive in late March drove the defenders back again, and after a series of engagements the Japanese took Mandalay on May 1, the main defense forces then retreating all the way to Imphal. There they prepared for the defense of India while much of the surviving Chinese force fled to Yunnan.

Burma, Liberation of (January–August 1945), retaking of Burma by the Allies in World War II. British forces commanded by General William SLIM crossed the Irrawaddy River in mid–January and in considerable force near Mandalay in mid–February, both crossings drawing strong Japanese counterattacks. Having drawn the Japanese, Slim's forces crossed the river farther south and then executed a planned encirclement, arriving behind the main Japanese force, taking Meiktila in early March and forcing the Japanese to turn to meet them. British troops on the Irrawaddy then took Mandalay and moved toward the main Japanese force. Caught between the two British forces, the damaged Japanese retreated. Rangoon was liberated in early May; the Japanese then retreated toward Thailand before the advancing British until the end of the war in August.

Burma Road, a 700-mile-long road built by the Chinese Republic during the Chinese–Japanese War, running from Lashio, Burma, to K'un-ming, China; from 1939 to 1942 it carried supplies arriving at the port of Rangoon and sent on by train to Lashio. It was cut in 1942 when advancing Japanese forces in Burma took Lashio but reopened in 1944, with some route changes, as the Stillwell Road, after General Joseph STILLWELL, then commander of Allied forces in the area.

Burmese Civil War (1948–   ), a four-decades-long group of concurrent and continuing insurgencies by ethnic minorities and Communist groups, such as the Karens, Shans, Kachins, and the Burmese Communist party. The Burmese government often contained but never fully ended these insurgencies.

Burmese Spring (March–September 1988), substantial March–April student demonstrations against the Ne WIN government that escalated into massive demonstrations involving hundreds of thousands of students and other Burmese in June and July. On July 23, Ne Win resigned, but major nationwide demonstrations continued against his successors, who had been identifed with his government and were widely thought to be still in his control. In late August, U NU initiated a united antigovernment organization, and on September 9 he announced the formation of a provisional government. But on September 18 the armed forces—headed by General Saw Maung, who had been closely associated with Ne Win—took control once again, banning protests and killing hundreds of demonstrators.

Burnham, Linden Forbes Sampson (1923–85), Guyanese lawyer, a founder of the People's Progressive Party in 1950, who broke away to form the People's National Congress in 1957. He became prime minister of GUYANA in 1964, first prime minister (1966–80), and then president (1980–85) of independent Guyana. He moved toward socialism after independence, from 1970 nationalizing many industries and expropriating many foreign holdings.

Burt, Cyril Lodowic (1883–1971), British psychologist, who played a key role in shaping the modern educational system in Britain. In his early years Burt developed many different types of tests, designed to identify students who needed special help and those who could benefit from more advanced education, and laid the groundwork for child guidance. He wrote key textbooks and served on several government committees, helping to frame the key Education Act of 1944. His published studies on twins, supporting his view that intelligence was largely inherited, were later found to be faked, a fact that tarnished his reputation.

Burton, Harold Hitz (1888–1964), U.S. lawyer, Republican mayor of Cleveland, Ohio, 1936–40 and U.S. senator from Ohio 1940–45, who was appointed to the U.S. Supreme Court in 1945 by President Harry S. TRU-

MAN. He took a generally conservative position on the Court, especially as regarded civil liberties matters, until his retirement in 1958.

Burundi (Republic of Burundi), until 1919 part of German East Africa. It was part of the British Ruanda–Urundi LEAGUE OF NATIONS mandate territory 1919–62, becoming an independent state on July 1, 1962.

Burundi massacres, the killing of an estimated 100,000–250,000 Hutus by the Tutsi-dominated Burundi armed forces, following the failed Hutu rebellion of 1965. There were also massacres of an estimated 5,000 or more Hutus by the Tutsi armed forces in August 1988, again after a failed Hutu rebellion.

Bush, George Herbert Walker (1924–), U.S. oil industry executive, congressman, UNITED NATIONS ambassador, CIA chief, vice-president, and 41st president of the United States from 1989. The son of Connecticut senator Prescott Bush, he moved to Texas in 1953, was a founder of Zapata Petroleum, and moved into Republican politics with an unsuccessful run for the senate in 1964. He served two terms as a congressman from Houston, lost another senate race in 1970, was UN ambassador 1970–72, U.S. liaison head in Peking 1974–76, and CIA director 1976–77. He made an unsuccessful run for the 1980 Republican presidential nomination, withdrew in favor of Ronald REAGAN, and became Reagan's vice-president 1980–88. As vice-president he traveled widely in support of administration aims and headed several government task forces, but he had little real impact on policy or the course of events. In 1988 he won the long campaign for the Republican presidential nomination and then defeated Democratic nominee, Michael DUKAKIS.

Bush, Vannevar (1890–1974), U.S. electrical engineer, who developed early forms of the ANALOG COMPUTER 1925–30. A professor and an inventor in a wide range of areas, Bush was head of the U.S. Office of Scientific Research and Development, from 1941 to 1945 overseeing the application of advanced technology to the military effort in World War II, including the development of the ATOMIC BOMB, RADAR, and ANTIBIOTICS such as SULFA DRUGS and PENICILLIN.

Bustamente, Alexander (1884–1977), Jamaican labor leader, founder of the Bustamente Industrial Trade Union and the Jamaica Labor party, the first prime minister of independent Jamaica 1962–67.

Buthelezi, Gatsha (1928–), South African Zulu tribal leader, chief minister of the Kwa-Zulu, who pursued a path of negotiation with the South African government toward formation of a multiracial government, in some periods directly opposing the AFRICAN NATIONAL CONGRESS. Activists of the INKATHA MOVEMENT, which he led, intermittently engaged in street fighting against others in South Africa's black communities during much of the 1980s.

buzz bomb, popular nickname for the ROCKET-powered V-1 BOMB used by Germany against Britain from June 1944.

Byrd, Richard Evelyn (1888–1957), U.S. naval aviator and explorer who, with co-pilot Floyd BENNETT, made the first flight over the NORTH POLE on May 9, 1926, though some, even as late as the 1980s, questioned whether or not he had actually reached the Pole. Byrd also made the first flight over the SOUTH POLE, with co-pilot Bernt Balchen, on November 29, 1929. During the next three decades, by then an admiral, he led several other expeditions to ANTARCTICA.

Byrnes, James Francis (1879–1972), U.S. lawyer, a South Carolina Democratic congressman (1911–25) and senator (1931–41), who in the 1930s became a strongly pro–NEW DEAL legislator. In 1940 Franklin D. ROOSEVELT appointed him to the Supreme Court; he resigned after 1 year to become head of the wartime Office of War Mobilization. He became Harry S. TRUMAN's secretary of state in July 1945, resigned in 1947, and later criticized Truman's domestic programs as too liberal. He was a prosegregation governor of South Carolina from 1951 to 1955.

C

Cabrini, Frances Xavier (1850–1917), Italian-born Catholic nun, popularly called Mother Cabrini, who from 1889 worked with poor immigrants, most of them of Italian origin, in the United States and later throughout the world, and helped develop a considerable body of Catholic institutions devoted to that work. She was declared a saint in 1946.

Cairo Conference (November–December 1943), actually a set of two conferences, occurring before and after the TEHRAN CONFERENCE. The first, involving Franklin ROOSEVELT, Winston CHURCHILL, and CHIANG KAI-SHEK (November 22–26), set forth a series of plans for the Pacific war. The Soviet Union was not represented at the conference, not then being at war with Japan. Then, after the four-power conference at Tehran (November 28–December 1), Roosevelt and Churchill met at Cairo again (December 3–7), to plan the coming invasion of Europe. Afterward, some of the agreements made with Chiang Kai-shek were not carried out by the western Allies.

Caldicott, Helen Broinowski (1938–), Australian pediatrician, who became an antinuclear activist after having been inspired by Nevil Shute's *On the Beach* (1957). While training in and practicing medicine in Australia and America, she sparked a 1970s campaign against France's atmospheric nuclear testing in the South Pacific. In the United States, she spurred the growth of Physicians for Social Responsibility from 1977 and later founded Women's Action for Nuclear Disarmament, becoming a full-time political activist from 1980, opposed to both nuclear weapons and nuclear power.

Cali explosion (August 7, 1956), explosion in a convoy of dynamite-laden trucks, parked overnight near the center of Cali, Colombia, killing at least 1,100 people, injuring many more, and destroying an estimated 2,000 buildings.

Callaghan, Leonard James (1912–), British trade unionist, in Parliament as a Labour member from 1945. He was Harold WILSON'S chancellor of the exchequer 1964–67, home secretary 1967–70, and foreign secretary 1974–76 and became prime minister after Wilson's 1976 resignation. His party lost the 1979 elections; he was replaced as prime minister by Conservative Margaret THATCHER. He resigned as Labour Party leader in 1980.

Calley, William L., Jr. (1943–), U.S. officer, found guilty of responsibility for the murders of Vietnamese civilians in the MY LAI MASSACRE during the VIETNAM WAR.

Calvin, Melvin (1911–), U.S. chemist, who discovered the sequence of chemical reactions involved in PHOTOSYNTHESIS. From 1937 working at the University of California at Berkeley, notably at the Lawrence Radiation Laboratory, he used a radioactive tracer to help him outline how plants use the green pigment CHLOROPHYLL and sunlight to transform carbon dioxide and water into vital nutrients, such as proteins, carbohydrates, and fats; the picture was completed 1945–57 and won him the 1961 Nobel Prize for Chemistry.

Cambodia, the former name of KAMPUCHEA; the change of name came on January 5, 1976, after KHMER ROUGE victory in the CAMBODIAN (KAMPUCHEAN) CIVIL WAR.

Cambodian (Kampuchean) Civil War (1969–75), a guerrilla insurgency by Communist KHMER ROUGE forces, at first directed against the neutralist government of Prince Norodom SIHANOUK and from 1970 against the pro-American government of LON NOL and throughout deeply intertwined with the parallel VIETNAM WAR. Despite U.S. military involvement, which included heavy bombing of Cambodian targets until August 1973 and a massive airlift to besieged Phnom Penh until March 1975, the Khmer Rouge won the civil war; Lon Nol fled into exile in early April, and Phnom Penh fell on April 16, 1975, ending the war. A second Civil War threatened to erupt after withdrawal of occupying Vietnamese troops in 1989.

Cambodian Holocaust (1975–78), the deaths of an estimated 2–3 million Cambodians at the hands of the KHMER ROUGE Cambodian government after the fall of the capital of Phnom Penh and the withdrawal of U. S. forces in April 1975. The HOLOCAUST, accompanied by a mass relocation of urban populations to the countryside, continued until the North Vietnamese occupation of Cambodia in 1978.

Cambodian incursion (April–June 1970), a U.S.–South Vietnamese invasion of Cambodia; invading forces were withdrawn after the invasion had generated powerful antiwar protests in the United States.

Cambodian secret bombing (1969–73), the heavy U.S. bombing of North Vietnamese and KHMER ROUGE forces in Cambodia, carried on for over 5 years and kept secret by the NIXON adminstration until exposed by the American press, then becoming a source of nationwide protest, which in turn increased administration concern with secrecy and "leaks" and contributed to the development of the WATERGATE scandal.

Cambrai, Battle of (November 20–December 3, 1917), British Third Army assault on the Hindenburg Line in World War I, led by 200 TANKS; the first such use of massed tanks in warfare. Although the British broke through German defenses, advancing 5 miles, many tanks were disabled by mechanical problems, and German counterattacks soon restabilized the front.

Cameroon (United Republic of Cameroon), until 1919 a German protectorate, then a joint French–British LEAGUE OF NATIONS interwar mandate territory and later a UNITED NATIONS mandate territory. It became an independent republic on October 1, 1961.

Campaign for Nuclear Disarmament (CND), British antinuclear peace organization that advocates unilateral British withdrawal from all activities related to nuclear, CHEMICAL, AND BIOLOGICAL WARFARE. It was founded in 1958; its first chairman was Bertrand RUSSELL. The CND was heavily involved in meetings, marches, and demonstrations in the late 1950s and early 1960s, becoming particularly well known for its periodic ALDERMASTON MARCHES. The organization lost strength during the balance of the 1960s and 1970s but became a powerful antinuclear organization again, beginning in 1979, around the issue of the deployment of U.S. Cruise missiles in the United Kingdom.

Camp David Accords (September 17, 1978), agreements between Anwar SADAT and Menachim BEGIN, sponsored and also signed by President Jimmy CARTER, that provided for Israeli withdrawal from the Sinai and for an Egyptian–Israeli peace treaty normalizing relations between the two nations. The accords stated a number of other plans to achieve a general settlement in the Middle East, including a plan to achieve some measure of WEST BANK autonomy. The peace treaty was signed on March 26, 1979, and Israel did withdraw from the Sinai, although none of the other stated plans bore fruit.

Camus, Albert (1913–60), Algerian-French writer, and a leading fighter-intellectual of the French RESISTANCE as editor of *Combat* during World War II. Close to Sartre and his EXISTENTIALIST circle in the immediate postwar period, he soon rejected Marxism and the Soviet model of socialism in favor of a continuing commitment to individual freedom and social justice, though he found it personally very difficult to openly favor Algerian independence.

Canal Zone, a 10-mile-wide strip of territory across the Isthmus of Panama between the Atlantic and Pacific oceans, within which was built the PANAMA CANAL. The Canal Zone was granted to the United States in the Panama–U.S. treaty of 1904, which was renegotiated in 1979.

Canaris, Wilhelm (1887–1945), German naval officer, who saw action in World War I and became head of the German armed forces intelligence but who secretly opposed HITLER, becoming an organizer of the anti-Hitler underground in the armed forces. He was arrested after the unsuccessful assassination attempt against Hitler in 1944 and was executed by the Gestapo in April 1945.

cancer, dread disease resulting from uncontrolled cellular growth, for which no cures but much knowledge and many therapies were developed in the 20th century. Widespread cancer research, using transplanted tumors in mice and rats, was begun in the first years of the 20th century. By 1915 scientists had created the first induced chemical cancers in animals, beginning a list of carcinogenic substances that has lengthened with the chemical explosion of the 20th century. In the interwar period many researchers began to connect cancers of the breasts and reproductive systems with ESTROGEN and other such STEROIDS; others found that various kinds of RADIATION also were carcinogenic. In the mid-1950s researchers established the link between lung cancer and tobacco smoking. In the same decade researchers found new evidence for the previously rejected idea that at least some cancers had a viral or immunological basis. In addition, evidence gradually accumulated that predisposition to cancer was, to some extent, hereditary and also influenced by diet, with excess calories and fats increasing cancer risk and fiber lowering it. Meanwhile, new treatments emerged. In addition to surgery, X-RAY radiation was used to good effect, especially after 1930. Chemotherapy was developed rapidly from the 1940s, with special success against Hodgkin's disease and leukemia and with HORMONES and steroids used especially for treating cancers of the reproductive system. At the same time, increasingly efficient diagnostic methods were being developed, among them the PAP SMEAR, the use of ULTRASOUND, and X-rays, as in mammography.

Cannon, Annie Jump (1863–1941), U.S. astronomer working at the Harvard Observatory, who directed and completed (1897–1924) a classificatory catalog of over 200,000 stars down to the 11th magnitude of brightness, discovering many new stars herself and providing an invaluable basis for much 20th-century astronomical research.

Cannon, Joseph Gurney ("Uncle Joe" Cannon, 1836–1926), U.S. lawyer, an Illinois Republican in the House of Representatives (1873–91, 1893–1913, 1915–23) and Speaker of the House (1903–11). As Speaker, the intensely conservative and dictatorial Cannon antagonized many from both parties; ultimately, in 1910, a bipartisan coalition led by progressive Nebraska Republican George NORRIS succeeded in changing House Speaker selection rules, breaking Cannon's power.

Cantigny, Battle of (May 28–29, 1918), the first U.S. World War I battle, in which the U.S. First Division attacked, took, and held the village of Cantigny against German counterattacks.

Canton, Fall of (October 21, 1938), the taking of the south China port of Canton after successful Japanese landings nearby, concluding the Japanese conquest of the China coast.

Canyon Lake Dam collapse (June 9, 1972), the collapse of a dam that flooded Rapid City, South Dakota, costing an estimated 200 lives and causing much property damage.

Cao Dai, Vietnamese religious group, some of whose members were employed by the CENTRAL INTELLIGENCE AGENCY (CIA) as anti-Communist mercenaries during the VIETNAM WAR.

Cape Canaveral (Cape Kennedy 1963–73), Florida launching site used by the NATIONAL AERONAUTICS AND SPACE ADMINISTRATION (NASA).

Cape Kennedy, Florida launching site used by the NATIONAL AERONAUTICS AND SPACE ADMINISTRATION (NASA); known as CAPE CANAVERAL before 1963 and after 1973.

Cape Verde Islands (Republic of Cape Verde), until 1975 a Portuguese colony; it became an independent nation on September 7, 1980, at that time looking forward to unification with GUINEA-BISSAU on the African mainland but dropping that plan in 1981.

capitalism, any economic system characterized primarily by private ownership, operation, and development of the means of production and distribution. In theory, capitalism implies unlimited economic and personal freedom; in practice, 20th-century capitalism has evolved as a set of mixed private–public forms, with government participation and control of significant portions of the economy the rule rather than the exception. The balancing of personal freedom and societal restraints has been a major process at work in all democratic societies, whether primarily capitalist- or socialist-oriented. In some instances, as in Germany, Italy, and Japan during the interwar period, capitalism and fascism were compatible; as with socialism, the other main economic form of the century, capitalism can exist in a considerable variety of political systems.

Capone, Alphonse (1899–1947), U.S. underworld leader and one of the most famous criminals of the 1920s, who at the peak of his power had murdered most of his rivals and had achieved considerable control of both police and the underworld in Chicago and some surrounding areas. His best known set of murders was the Chicago ST. VALENTINE'S DAY MASSACRE on February 14, 1929, in which his assassins, some of them posing as police officers, killed six members of an opposing gang and one bystander. Capone was later convicted of tax evasion and retired after his prison term, ultimately dying of syphilis.

Caporetto, Battle of (October 24–November 12, 1917), World War I battle in which German troops joined Austrian troops on the Isonzo River; both attacked and routed the Italian army, taking 275,000 prisoners while suffering small losses.

carbon 14, radioactive ISOTOPE of carbon used in RADIOCARBON DATING.

Cárdenas del Rio, Lázaro (1895–1970), Mexican soldier and political leader, who joined the MEXICAN REVOLUTION in 1913, becoming an army officer and in the early 1920s the youngest general in the Mexican army. He was elected governor of his home state of Michoacan in 1928, there initiating a series of reform programs, including redistribution of the land to the peasants and educational reforms. In 1930 he became head of the official party, the National Revolutionary Party, and was president of Mexico 1934–40. As president he sharply increased the pace of land redistribution and nationalization, initiated further educational reforms, and expropriated the foreign-owned oil companies, a move that was especially popular in Mexico. After his presidency he continued to be a major force on the left in Latin America.

Cardozo, Benjamin Nathan (1870–1938), U.S. lawyer, writer, scholar, and long-term member and chief justice of the New York Court of Appeals (1916–32); he was appointed to the Supreme Court by Herbert HOOVER in 1932.

Carlson, Chester Floyd (1906–68), U.S. inventor who developed XEROGRAPHY, an inexpensive dry (*xero* in Greek) process of copying. Carlson first developed the idea in 1938 and patented it in 1940, later licensing it to Xerox and other corporations.

Carlsson, Bernt (1938–88), Swedish diplomat, a close associate of Swedish premier Olaf PALME, and secretary-general of the

Socialist International 1970–76. He was UNITED NATIONS commissioner for Namibia 1987–88 and played a major role in negotiating the regional accords involving Namibia, Angola, Cuba, and South Africa. He was killed in the December 21, 1988, LOCKERBIE AIRPLANE BOMBING.

Carmichael, Stokely (1941–   ), U.S. Black civil rights activist, who became chairman of the STUDENT NON-VIOLENT COORDINATING COMMITTEE (SNCC) in 1966. He later became a Ugandan citizen with his wife, singer Miriam Makeba.

Carnarvon, George Edward Stanhope Molyneux Herbert (1866–1923), English archaeologist, who with Howard CARTER excavated widely in the Valley of the Kings in Luxor, Egypt, uncovering many tombs, the most famous being that of TUTANKHAMEN (King Tut) in 1922, which Carter later excavated.

Carnegie, Andrew (1835–1919), 19th-century U.S. industrialist, who built the Carnegie Steel Company while pursuing a parallel career as a philanthropist. In 1901 he sold his company to J. Pierpont MORGAN'S U. S. Steel Company and thereafter devoted substantially all of his time to philanthrophy, developing the Carnegie Endowment for International Peace in 1910 and the Carnegie Corporation in 1911, both models for future philanthropic organizations.

Carol II (1893–1953), dictatorial Rumanian king from 1930, who was replaced by fascist Ion ANTONESCU in 1940, Rumania then entering World War II on the side of the AXIS. Carol was exiled to Lisbon and never regained his throne.

Carol, Edna, and Hazel (August–October 1954), three successive Atlantic hurricanes that killed an estimated 300 people in the United States and Canada and caused approximately $700 million in property damage.

Carranza, Venustiano (1859–1920), Mexican landowner and revolutionary, who became governor of Coahuila, fought with Francisco MADERO against Porfirio Díaz in 1910–11, and in 1913 became leader of the insurrection against the rule of dictator Victoriano HUERTA, who was deposed in July 1914. The long civil war then continued; Carranza decisively came to power after the Battle of CELAYA in April 1915, in which his forces, led by General Alvaro OBREGÓN, defeated the army of Francisco (Pancho) VILLA. Obregon led a successful insurrection against Carranza in 1920; Carranza was killed by Obregón's forces in May 1920.

Carrel, Alexis (1873–1944), French surgeon, working in America 1905–44, who did key early work preparing the way for modern OPEN-HEART SURGERY and ORGAN TRANSPLANTS, winning him the 1912 Nobel Prize for Physiology or Medicine. At the turn of the century, with Charles Claude Guthrie, Carrel developed a method of suturing blood vessels and experimented with operations and transplants on animals. In 1914 he further refined his techniques by doing the first successful heart operation on a dog. During World War I, with Henry Dakin, he also introduced a widely used sterile solution for cleansing deep wounds. Afterward he worked on ways of growing living tissue, laying the basis for much medical and biochemical research, including that on CLONES. In 1936 he and Charles LINDBERGH designed a pumping machine—essentially, an external ARTIFICIAL HEART—to supply blood to a patient's organs, keeping them alive outside the body; further development of such machines made possible open-heart surgery and the use of artificial organs.

Carson, Rachel (1907–64), U.S. ecologist, teacher, and writer, whose pioneeering work on the adverse impacts of chemicals in the environment, especially as presented in her best-seller *The Silent Spring* (1962), had great influence on the development of worldwide ecological and GREEN movements.

Carter, Howard (1873–1939), English archaeologist, who with the Earl of CARNARVON excavated widely in the Valley of the Kings in Luxor, Egypt, uncovering many tombs, the most famous being that of TUT-ANKHAMEN (King Tut) in 1922, which he excavated after Carnarvon's death.

Carter, James Earl, Jr. (Jimmy Carter, 1924–   ), U.S. farmer, naval officer (1946–53), Democratic Georgia state legislator (1963–67), and governor of Georgia (1971–77), who became 39th president of the United States (1977–81) after defeating incumbent Gerald R. FORD in 1976. As president he initiated a good deal of new legislation but saw little of it become law, for his prestige and consequent political strength suffered greatly from a combination of unsolved domestic and foreign problems, including persistent inflation, recession, OPEC's OIL EMBARGO, and the IRAN HOSTAGE CRISIS. During his administration the CAMP DAVID ACCORDS were worked out in 1978, resulting in the Egyptian–Israeli Peace Treaty of 1979, and full Chinese-American diplomatic relations were restored; but relations with the Soviet Union worsened, especially after the Soviet invasion of Afghanistan, resulting in the U.S. boycott of the 1980 Moscow Olympics and the embargo on American grain shipments to the U.S.S.R. From November 1979 the Carter administration was preoccupied by the Iranian hostage crisis. He was defeated by Republican Ronald REAGAN in the 1980 presidential campaign.

Carver, George Washington (1864?–1943), U.S. agricultural chemist, who sparked the 20th-century change in crops in the American South. Born into slavery during the Civil War, Carver worked his way through school and college, becoming director of agricultural research at Alabama's Tuskegee Institute (1896–1943). There he experimented with crops that would, unlike cotton, enrich the soil, focusing especially on the peanut and the sweet potato and developing hundreds of uses for them. After 1914 reports of his research findings, farmers in the South—their cotton hard hit by boll weevils—began to follow his lead and revived their sagging fortunes.

Casablanca Conference (January 14–23, 1943), a meeting between Franklin ROOSEVELT and Winston CHURCHILL at which the unconditional surrender of the AXIS powers was first stated as an Allied war aim. The Atlantic antisubmarine battle, the strengthening of the Soviet supply line, the buildup to the Allied invasion of Europe, the bombing of Germany, and the coming invasion of Sicily were made top priorities, with the Pacific war continuing to take second place; but within those bounds the Americans were free to pursue the Pacific war as they chose. In practice, that meant strong prosecution of combined air, sea, and land operations in the Pacific, for by then American war production was capable of supplying much of what was needed for both wars.

Casement, Roger David (1864–1916), Irish Republican leader and former British diplomat, who sought German support and arms for an Irish revolution against Britain during World War I. The hoped-for arms did not materialize; he was captured in Ireland after embarking from a German submarine a few days before the EASTER RISING and was executed in London for treason on August 3, 1916.

Casey, William Joseph (1913–87), U.S. lawyer, who became a tax editor in the late 1930s, served in the OFFICE OF STRATEGIC SERVICES (OSS) during World War II, and in the postwar period became a well-known tax attorney and investor. He supported Richard M. NIXON during the 1968 presidential campaign, was head of the SECURITIES AND EXCHANGE COMMISSION 1971–72, and alternated appointive government positions with law practice during the rest of the 1970s. He managed the 1980 presidential campaign of Ronald REAGAN and became CENTRAL INTELLIGENCE AGENCY (CIA) director in 1981. In that position he undertook major covert operations throughout the world, encountering strong congressional opposition to some of those operations and to his freewheeling style. He was deeply involved in the IRAN-CONTRA AFFAIR, appearing four times before congressional committees before a developing illness hospitalized him in December 1986.

He never returned, resigning on February 2 and dying on May 6, 1987.

Cassino, a mountain monastery that in 1943–44 became a strong German defensive position on the GUSTAV LINE, the strongly held set of German positions running across Italy. Allied forces assaulted it three times in February–March 1944; it finally fell to Allied Polish troops on May 18, as part of a general breakthrough all along the Gustav Line.

Castro Ruz, Fidel (1926–   ), Cuban lawyer and revolutionary, who led the unsuccessful 26TH JULY MOVEMENT insurrection against the BATISTA government on July 26, 1953, was afterward imprisoned for 2 years, and moved to the United States after being freed in an amnesty. He returned to Cuba in December 1956, led the CUBAN REVOLUTION, and became Cuban ruler in January 1959. As relations with the United States worsened, notably after unsuccessful CIA-sponsored attempts on his life and the BAY OF PIGS invasion of 1961, Castro sought the sponsorship and military and economic aid of the Soviet Union. Declaring himself a Communist and consolidating his rule around the Communist Party, he welcomed the stationing of Soviet missiles in Cuba, which led to the CUBAN MISSILE CRISIS and the threat of nuclear war. He received massive Soviet aid and sent Cuban troops to fight beside Soviet-backed armies in Africa.

Castro Ruz, Raul Hector (1931–   ), Cuban revolutionary, brother of Fidel CASTRO, who fought beside his brother from the beginning of their revolutionary enterprise and became vice-premier and armed forces head after their victory.

cathode-ray tube (CRT), type of ELECTRON TUBE, used to create visual images; widely employed as a receiver or monitor for TELEVISION, RADAR, and COMPUTERS under various names such as visual display terminal (VDT). In 1906 Karl Braun discovered that by using a magnetic field he could change the path of ELECTRONS in a cathode-ray tube. Building on Albert EINSTEIN's 1905 theory of the PHOTOELECTRIC EFFECT, Russian scientist Boris Rosing suggested in 1907 that cathode-ray tubes could be used to convert electrical signals into patterns of light. Working independently, also in 1907, English inventor Alan Campbell Swinton suggested that a cathode-ray tube could act as both camera and receiver, and he outlined a method of electron-beam scanning that Vladimir ZWORYKIN later employed in creating his television.

Catonsville Nine, a group of anti-VIETNAM WAR activists, led by Catholic priests Daniel and Philip BERRIGAN, who in May 1968 set fire to draft cards in a Catonsville, Maryland, draft board office; some members of the group were later imprisoned for the action. Their trial was subsequently dramatized as *The Trial of the Catonsville Nine.*

CAT scan (computerized axial tomography), medical diagnostic device that links a high-speed X-RAY machine with a COMPUTER so that a series of pictures at different planes are combined to give the doctor a computer-simulated three-dimensional view. The first CAT scan machine was introduced in Britain in 1971; it was developed by South African–American Allan MacLeod Cormack and British physicist Godfrey N. Hounsfield, who shared the 1979 Nobel Prize for Physiology or Medicine for their invention. The CAT scan reflects differences in ELECTRON density in body tissues, as oppposed to the NMR IMAGER, which measures PROTON density.

Catt, Carrie Chapman (1859–1947), a leading U.S. women's suffrage activist of the early 20th century, who as president of the National American Woman Suffrage Association led the fight for the adoption of the 19TH AMENDMENT in 1920. In 1919 she led in the organization of the LEAGUE OF WOMEN VOTERS and also was active in many other domestic reform and international disarmament causes.

Causa, La (The Cause), the slogan developed by Cesar CHAVEZ while turning the grape growers' strike and boycott of 1965–70 into a nationwide movement.

Cavell, Edith Louisa (1865–1915), British nurse, who was executed by the Germans on October 12, 1915, after having confessed to being part of an Allied underground organization in Belgium; her execution became a *cause célèbre*, and she was posthumously recognized as a major World War I British heroine.

CB warfare, shorthand name for CHEMICAL AND BIOLOGICAL WARFARE.

CCC, the initials of the CIVILIAN CONSERVATIONS CORPS, by which this U.S. NEW DEAL federal agency was best known.

Ceausescu, Nicolae (1918–1989), Rumanian Communist leader, active in the 1930s, who rose during the post–World War II period, becoming a member of the Rumanian politburo in 1955, succeeding Gheorghe GHEORGHIU-DEJ as party secretary-general in 1965 and becoming president in 1967. He continued and extended Gheorghiu-Dej's independent policies, differing with the Soviet Union and other Soviet-bloc states on many major international issues and maintaining diplomatic relations with China, Israel, Egypt, and many Western nations. He also took a far more conservative Marxist position on such matters as economic reform and human rights, encountering severe economic problems and increasing internal dissension. Ceausescu was deposed by the December 1989 RUMANIAN REVOLUTION. On December 22, he and his wife, Elena Ceausescu, were captured, and on December 25 were executed by the new National Salvation Front government.

Celaya, Battle of (April 1915), a battle between the Mexican government forces of Venustiano CARRANZA, led by general Alvaro OBREGON, and revolutionary forces led by Francisco (Pancho) VILLA. The battle was won by the government forces, Villa then retreating into northern Mexico.

Central African Republic, until 1960 a French colony, part of French Equatorial Africa, becoming an independent state on August 13, 1960. The Central African Republic's first president, David Dacko, quickly created a one-party state. He was deposed by the forces of Jean-Bedel BOKASSA on January 1, 1966; Bokassa then turned the country into a corrupt and murderous police state. He abolished the republic in 1976 and created the Central African Empire, with himself as emperor, on December 4, 1976. Bokassa was deposed by Dacko, with French army assistance, on September 20–21, 1979, and the republic was formally reestablished. Dacko's democratic government lasted only until the army takeover of July 21, 1982, which was followed by reestablishment of a one-party state led by general Andre-Dieudonne Kolingba.

Central Intelligence Agency (CIA), U.S. federal espionage, foreign intelligence, and covert action organization that from its authorization by the National Security Act of 1947 played a wide and varied role in furthering U.S. COLD WAR objectives. In several major situations it greatly expanded its role, sometimes going far beyond legal bounds, and also becoming involved in espionage and surveillance directed at domestic dissenters. It succeeded the World War II OFFICE OF STRATEGIC SERVICES (OSS), using the personnel of that agency as its nucleus. Operating out of headquarters in Langley, Virginia, on a large, wholly secret budget, for more than four decades the CIA has functioned as the chief federal intelligence advisory organization while at the same time mounting hundreds of covert operations. Some of the best known of these were participation in the toppling of the Iranian and Guatemalan governments in the early 1950s; the failed BAY OF PIGS Cuban invasion of 1961, coupled with unsuccessful attempts to assassinate Fidel CASTRO; the massive Southeast Asian covert operation of the 1960s and early 1970s, with its "secret army" and the operation of a war in Laos; aid to the army coup that toppled the ALLENDE government in Chile; and involvement in domestic espionage directed against dissenters during the VIETNAM WAR, as exposed in the PENTAGON PAPERS case and in subsequent Congressional investigations. CIA activities were closely scrutinized and considerably curbed during the late 1970s, though the agency regained some of its former status and free-wheeling capability during the Reagan years. CIA officials denied any agency participation in the WATERGATE and IRAN–CONTRA scandals, although CIA director WILLIAM J. CASEY was widely accused of deep implication in the Iran–Contra scandal.

Central Park Nuclear Freeze meeting (June 12, 1982), the largest American antinuclear weapons demonstration, in support of a nuclear freeze; attendance estimates varied greatly, most being in the 500,000–1 million range.

Central Powers, during WORLD WAR I, Germany, Austria-Hungary, Turkey, and Bulgaria.

cesium clock, type of ATOMIC CLOCK using the oscillations of cesium 133 as a standard.

Chaco War (1932–35), a conflict between Bolivia and Paraguay over control of the Chaco region, in which Bolivia sought an outlet to the sea via the Paraguay River. Early Paraguayan successes were reversed by strengthened Bolivian forces, which had won much of the region by June 1932; however, greatly augmented Paraguayan forces won the war by June 1935. The Treaty of Buenos Aires (July 1938) awarded most of the Chaco to Paraguay but did give Bolivia its desired outlet to the sea.

Chad (Republic of Chad), region that became a French protectorate in 1900, part of French Equatorial Africa in 1910, and on August 11, 1960 an independent state, led by President N'Garta (François) Tombalbaye, who quickly turned the new nation into a one-party state and by 1966 was facing the beginnings of the long insurgency that led to civil war. Tombalbaye's assassination during a 1975 military coup began the CHAD CIVIL WAR.

Chad Civil War (1975–87) a long civil war with roots in the traditional conflict between northern Moslems and the Blacks of Chad's south, many of them Christians. The war was fueled by Libyan support of the north-ern forces, with consequent support of the southern forces by France, the area's former colonial occupier, and by many black African nations. Libyan forces intervened after assassination of Chad's President Tombalbaye in 1975 during a coup attempt. French, Libyan, and Chadian forces engaged in a sporadic, sometimes major series of clashes during the next 5 years. Mediation and the supply of peacekeeping forces by neighboring African nations, especially during 1980, promised but ultimately failed to bring peace. During the early 1980s ORGANIZATION OF AFRICAN UNITY peacekeeping units and French forces brought temporary halts to the fighting, and in 1984 Libya and France agreed to pull their forces out of Chad. Peace did not come; guerrilla war continued, and Libyan-backed forces mounted strong attacks in the south early in 1986. The southern forces struck back, however, successfully moving north; on March 22, 1987, they captured the Libyan air base at Ouadi Doum and then the major Libyan base at Faya-Largeau with its estimated $1 billion worth of weapons and supplies. Chadian forces then invaded southern Libya as well, in all severely damaging the power and prestige of Muammar al-QADDAFI and paving the way for the negotiated truce that followed.

Chadli, Ben-Jedid (1929–   ), Algerian officer, who joined the FLN (NATIONAL LIBERATION FRONT) in 1955, became a general staff officer of the FLN army in Tunis in 1961, and was Oran regional commander of the Algerian army 1963–68. In 1979 he succeeded Houari BOUMEDIENNE as president of Algeria (1979–   ) and head of the FLN, continuing but somewhat moderating Algeria's socialist course in an attempt to solve deepening economic problems. He continued Algeria's one-party, authoritarian rule but with some moderation, as evidenced by his release of Ahmed BEN BELLA from his 15-year imprisonment.

chain reaction (nuclear), self-sustaining process of NUCLEAR FISSION, in which—once a sufficient amount, or CRITICAL MASS, of fuel is available—extra NEUTRONS from earlier fission reactions induce other fission reactions; first suggested as a possibility by Frédéric JOLIOT-CURIE and others in 1939 and achieved by Enrico FERMI'S research team in 1942 as part of the MANHATTAN PROJECT. In an ATOMIC BOMB this chain of reactions builds rapidly to an explosion, but in a NUCLEAR REACTOR it is controlled, with rods to absorb extra neutrons and supply a steady flow of energy.

Chalk River chain reaction (December 2, 1952), a major nuclear accident at Canada's experimental Chalk River reactor: a chain reaction created 1 million gallons of radioactive water inside the reactor. On May 23, 1958, a defective fuel rod in the same plant overheated, creating a second nuclear accident.

Challenger, second of the U.S. SPACE SHUTTLES, launched first on April 4, 1983, which in 1986 exploded on takeoff, killing all seven aboard. Its early flights were successful, carrying into space the first American woman astronaut, Sally RIDE, on its second flight on June 18, 1983, and the first Black astronaut, Guion BLUFORD, Jr., on its third flight on August 30, 1983. On its fourth flight, begun February 3, 1984, two astronauts took the first untethered SPACE WALK. But its fifth flight—launched at CAPE CANAVERAL, Florida, at 11:38 AM on a cold January 28, 1986, as millions of people watched on their television sets—ended in disaster. About 1 minute after lift-off, a fuel tank fire started; and only a few seconds later, at 73 seconds after lift-off, the spacecraft went down in flames, its pieces falling 60,000 feet into the Atlantic. The seven people aboard died; they had no available exit and probably would have had no time to use one in any case. They were Francis R. Scobee, flight commander; Michael J. Smith, pilot; Gregory B. Jarvis, engineer; Ronald E. McNair, physicist; Ellison S. Onizuka, aeronautical engineer; Judith A. Resnick, engineer; and S. Christa MCAULIFFE, a high school social studies teacher, whose role was to have been the teaching of science by television from space. Previous tests had shown that the seals (O-rings) join-

ing the rockets on the sides of the shuttle might fail, even in much warmer weather than that January day, and there had been seal problems in earlier flights. The predictability of the failure was dramatically demonstrated for the investigating commission by physicist Richard FEYNMAN, who simply placed an O-ring in a glass of ice water and showed the resulting inelasticity. But NASA had elected to take a chance with the lives of the astronauts and proceeded with the launching, for it was committed to a rush schedule. The result was a disaster that claimed seven lives and set back the American space program for years.

Chamberlain, Neville (1869–1940), British Conservative MP, who became prime minister in 1937 after a political career in which he was concerned mainly with internal British matters. He ignored the advice of his own foreign office, entirely underestimated HITLER'S intentions, and embarked on a policy of APPEASEMENT. Thinking that he could reason with Hitler, he agreed to the dismemberment of Czechoslovakia at the MUNICH conference of 1938, that great milestone on the road to World War II. He is best remembered for Munich and for his "PEACE FOR OUR TIME" quote afterward. He changed his views after the Nazis went on to take the rest of Czechoslovakia; he pledged British support to Poland and took Britain to war in September 1939. He remained as wartime prime minister although he had lost the confidence of his people, resigning only after the Germans had moved into the Low Countries in May 1940.

Chambers, Whittaker (1901–61), U.S. writer and editor, who claimed to have been an American Communist from 1925 and a Soviet spy in the United States from 1932 to 1938; he was a *Time* magazine editor from 1939 to 1948. In 1948, in testimony before the HOUSE UN-AMERICAN ACTIVITIES COMMITTEE (HUAC), he accused Alger HISS of having been a spy; and in 1949 and 1950 he was chief witness against Hiss in two perjury trials, the second of which resulted in the conviction of Hiss. Chambers was later an editor of the *National Review.*

Chamoun, Camille (1900–87), Lebanese lawyer, who became a member of parliament in 1934, served in several cabinet-level and ambassadorial posts during the 1930s and 1940s, and in 1952 became president of Lebanon after leading a coup against the government of Bishara al-Khouri. A pro-Western moderate and leader of the Maronite Christian community, he appealed to the West for help when a Pan-Arab–Christian Left coalition revolted in 1958; the United States responded with marine and army units, totaling over 14,000 men. Chamoun left the presidency as part of the peace agreement ending the civil war, agreeing not to run again when his term ended in 1958. He later held several other government positions but exerted little influence on the later course of events in his country.

Chandrasekhar, Subrahmanyan (1910–), Indian-American astronomer, who in 1931 identified the size, known as the Chandrasekhar limit, above which a star in a late stage of STELLAR EVOLUTION may explode in a nova or SUPERNOVA.

Chaney, James, young civil rights worker, who with Andrew GOODMAN and Michael SCHWERNER was murdered in Neshoba County, Mississippi, in June 1964, in the MISSISSIPPI CIVIL RIGHTS MURDERS.

Chang Hsueh-liang (1898–), Manchurian warlord, son of warlord CHANG TSO-LIN, who after the Japanese invasion of Manchuria, was driven into northwest China by the Japanese because he pledged loyalty to the Nationalists. At Sian (now Xian), in 1936, he arrested CHIANG KAI-SHEK, who was there to personally lead an anti-Communist offensive, and he did not let Chiang go free until he had pledged a united front with the Communists against the Japanese. Chang went back to Nanking with Chiang, was arrested there, and spent the next quarter century under house arrest on the mainland and in Taiwan.

Ch'angsha, Battle of (July 1930), the key battle in the failed attempt by Communist guerrillas to take several cities in central China; following this defeat the Communist insurgents fled into the mountains of western Kiangsi and there set up the KIANGSI SOVIET.

Chang Tso-lin (1873–1928), Manchurian warlord, 1913–28. He expanded his area of control in north China in the mid-1920s but was defeated by KUOMINTANG forces in 1927. He was assassinated in 1928, reportedly by Japanese seeking a pretext to take Manchuria. His son, CHANG HSUEH-LIANG, then took control of his forces.

Chao Tzu-yang, the old-style name of Chinese Communist Premier ZHAO Ziyang.

Chappaquiddick incident (July 1969), accident in which U.S. Senator Edward M. KENNEDY drove his car off a bridge at Chappaquiddick Island, near Martha's Vineyard, Massachusetts, and for 9 hours failed to report the accident, even though his passenger, Mary Jo Kopechne, had drowned. There was no criminal liability, but the resulting adverse publicity destroyed Kennedy's presidential hopes, even though Massachusetts voters continued to elect him to the Senate.

Chateau-Thierry, Battle of (May 30–June 17, 1918), the second U.S. World War I battle, in which the U.S. Second and Third Divisions moved into the battle line at the Marne during the German AISNE offensive of 1918 and pushed German forces back over the Marne.

Chavez, Cesar Estrada (1927–), U.S. farm worker, who in the 1950s worked to develop political action organizations among California's agricultural poor, in the early 1960s switching his attention to union organization. He led the United Farm Workers Organizing Committee in the long strike against table-grape growers, 1965–70, ultimately developing a national boycott. He embarked on a series of hunger strikes and turned the action into La CAUSA (The Cause), around which many other trade unions and their sympathizers rallied. During the 1970s and 1980s Chavez attempted, with mixed success, to apply the same kinds of tactics to the development of other farm labor organizing efforts in and beyond California.

Cheka, the Soviet secret police organization from December 1917. Somewhat reorganized, it became the GPU in 1922 and the OGPU in 1923. As the OGPU—from the mid-1920s in the control of Joseph STA-LIN—it became the chief instrument of internal repression and was directly responsible for the killing and internal exile of millions of Soviet citizens.

Chelyabinsk railroad disaster (June 3, 1989), the worst railroad disaster in history, claiming an estimated 600–650 lives. Two passenger trains going in opposite directions but side by side on the Soviet Trans-Siberian railway, and carrying a total of 1,200 passengers, were engulfed in flames from an exploding gas pipeline beside the railway. It was thought that sparks from the passing trains had ignited an accumulation of gases from the leaking pipeline. Many of the dead were schoolchildren traveling to summer camps.

chemical and biological warfare (CB warfare), use of poisonous gases or biological agents in a military context; although both are centuries old, they were first employed on a large scale at the 1915 battle of YPRES. Toxic gases were used in World War I by both sides, the Germans often introducing new ones. Gases such as chlorine, phosgene, and, by 1917, mustard produced widespread casualties, often affecting lungs, eyes, and skin, though killing a relatively small percentage of those affected. Poison gases also were used by Italy in the ETHIO-PIAN–ITALIAN WAR; by Japan in the CHI-NESE–JAPANESE WAR, leading into World War II; probably by both sides in the IRAN-IRAQ WAR; and possibly in the AFGHAN CIVIL WAR. Tear gases, designed to incapacitate temporarily but not to harm, have been widely used by police forces throughout the world, especially for riot control. Use of biological agents to infect enemies is less efficient and less reliable than chemical agents and therefore less widespread. Both chemical and biological agents are used against plants and animals, to cut down on the food supply, or on forest or jungle shelter—most notably, the U.S. use of AGENT ORANGE in Vietnam. Attempts to ban use of chemical and biological weapons include the 1925 GENEVA PROTOCOL and the 1972 BIO-LOGICAL WARFARE BAN TREATY.

chemical origin of life, theory that life originated from a non-living chemical stew energized by lightning and producing the building blocks of life: amino acids that form DNA. The idea of such a chemical evolution of life was first put forward, and demonstrated in the laboratory, in the 1950s by Harold UREY and Stanley Miller. Though later much refined by others, the basic view came to be widely accepted.

chemical warfare, use of toxic chemical agents in CHEMICAL AND BIOLOGICAL WAR-FARE.

Cheney, Richard Bruce (1941–), U.S. political leader, presidential assistant 1974–76, and Wyoming Republican congressman 1978–89, who was named and swiftly confirmed as secretary of defense in March 1989, after the nomination of John TOWER was rejected by the Senate.

Chengchow offensive (June, 1938), a Japanese offensive drowned by the Chinese destruction of the YELLOW RIVER DIKES; the offensive was halted, although it was resumed 2 months later.

Chennault, Claire (1890–1958), U.S. Air Force officer, who came out of retirement in 1937 to become CHIANG KAI-SHEK's air adviser. In 1941 he organized the FLYING TIGERS (American Volunteer Group) to fly American planes lend-leased to China, and he was U. S. Army Air Force commander in China 1942–45.

Ch'en Tu-hsiu (1879–1942), Chinese scholar and teacher, whose thinking played a substantial role in the development of the MAY FOURTH MOVEMENT and who was a founder of the COMMUNIST PARTY OF CHI-NA, becoming its first chairman in 1920. He was removed from that post by orders of the COMINTERN after the KUOMINTANG—Communist split of 1927 and the beginning of the CHINESE CIVIL WAR. He then became a dissenting voice in his party, was expelled from the Communist Party in 1930, and was imprisoned by the Chinese government from 1932 to 1937, after which he left public life.

Chernenko, Konstantin Ustinovich (1911–85), Soviet Communist Party official, who became associated with Leonid BREZHNEV in the early 1950s and thereafter rose with him, becoming chief of party personnel in 1965, a member of the Central Committee in 1971, secretary of that committee in 1976, and a member of the Politburo in 1977. In February 1984, after a brief tenure by Yuri ANDROPOV, he succeeded Brezhnev as general secretary of the Communist Party of the Soviet Union and leader of his country, functioning from then until his death in 1985 essentially as a caretaker acting on behalf of the conservative elements in the Soviet bureaucracy. He slowed the reforms started during the Andropov period and held off the new generation, led by Mikhail GORBACHEV, which took control immediately after his death.

Chernobyl meltdown (April 28–May 1, 1986) a core meltdown, explosion, and fire at the Soviet Union's Chernobyl, Pripyat, nuclear plant, near Kiev in the Ukraine, which emitted a massive radioactive cloud. It was first noted over Sweden, then throughout Europe, and ultimately throughout the northern hemisphere. At least nine people were killed immediately, and widespread environmental contamination was reported, with probable adverse effects on the lives and environment of hundreds of thousands more alleged, but still to be definitively reported.

Chernyakovsky, Ivan (1906–45), Soviet general, who saw service throughout World War II and in 1944–45 commanded a powerful group of Soviet armies that retook much of western Russia and Poland and ultimately moved into Germany; he was killed in battle in February 1945.

Chessman, Caryl (1921–60), robber and sex offender convicted in California in 1948 and sentenced to death in the gas chamber.

Between then and May 2, 1960, the date of his execution, he generated and led a worldwide campaign for clemency, writing four books and winning several stays of execution.

Chetniks, Yugoslav guerrilla forces led by General Draja MIHAJLOVIC during World War II and affiliated with the Yugoslav government-in-exile headquartered in London. During and after the war the Chetniks came into conflict with the Partisan forces led by Josip Broz (TITO), who accused them of fighting on the German side; after 1943 they were supported by the Allies. Following the war many Chetniks went into exile; some, including Mihajlovic, were executed by the Yugoslav government.

Chiang Ch'ing, the old-style name of Chinese leader JIANG QING, the wife of MAO ZEDONG, who was in 1981 convicted of being the leader of the GANG OF FOUR.

Chiang Ching-kuo (1910–88), son of CHIANG KAI-SHEK, who was a student in the Soviet Union when his father broke with the Communists in 1927 and who averred that he had been held in the Soviet Union until the CHINESE CIVIL WAR truce of 1937. Thereafter closely associated with his father's government, he fled to Taiwan in 1949 and ultimately became chairman of the KUOMINTANG, later prime minister, and then president of the Republic of China.

Chiang Kai-shek (1887–1975), Chinese soldier, who became president and leader of the Republic of China during the CHINESE CIVIL WAR (1927–49) and the SINO-JAPANESE WAR (1937–45). A soldier who trained in China and Japan, he fought in the CHINESE REVOLUTION OF 1911. He joined the KUOMINTANG in 1918, was sent to the Soviet Union in 1923 for training, and became head of the WHAMPOA MILITARY ACADEMY in 1924. He became military commander of the Kuomintang in 1926, after SUN YAT-SEN'S death, led the NORTHERN EXPEDITION, and broke with his Communist allies in 1927, beginning the civil war. That same year he married Mei-ling SOONG. He remained military commander during the years that followed, although he was not in complete control of the Kuomintang until 1937. During the Sino-Japanese war he became virtual dictator of Republican China and commanded all Allied forces in China during World War II. He prosecuted and lost the remainder of the civil war, then fled to Taiwan, where he continued to rule.

Chiang Kai-shek, Madame, the name by which Mei-ling SOONG, the wife of CHIANG KAI-SHEK, is best known.

Chicago Democratic National Convention (1968), the convention that nominated Hubert H. HUMPHREY for the presidency while thousands of anti–VIETNAM WAR demonstrators violently clashed with the Chicago police outside the convention hall. Opposition Democrats and newscasters were assaulted by Chicago mayor Richard J. Daley's security operatives inside the hall, and leading Democrats verbally assailed Daley. All of this happened in the full glare of national and international television coverage, doing irretrievable harm to the Democratic presidential campaign. The long trial of the CHICAGO SEVEN followed.

Chicago Seven, the seven defendants at the September 1969–February 1970 Chicago trial that grew out of the antiwar protest demonstrations at the CHICAGO DEMOCRATIC NATIONAL CONVENTION of 1968. The defendants, Abbie HOFFMAN, Jerry RUBIN, Tom HAYDEN, David DELLINGER, Rennie Davis, John Froines, and Lee Weiner, were all found not guilty of conspiracy charges, though five were convicted of lesser charges. Judge Julius Hoffman issued more than 100 contempt citations against the defendants and their lawyers. In 1972 the convictions and most of the contempt citations were reversed, and Judge Hoffman was censured for his prejudicial behavior.

Chifley, Joseph Benedict (1885–1951), Australian trade unionist, a Labour member of parliament (1928–31; 1940–51), who became minister for postwar reconstruction and redevelopment (1942–45) and prime minister (1945–49). As Labour prime minister of Australia's first post–World War II

government he successfully initiated several major social welfare programs but was less successful in attempts to substantially nationalize the country's financial system.

Childe, Vere Gordon (1892–1957), Australian-British archeologist who, in syntheses such as *The Dawn of European Civilzation* (1925), laid down the broad outlines of cultural development in Europe and western Asia, notably in the third and second millennia B.C., which others have since filled out and modified, in the process helping to set his field in a firmer context within the social and natural sciences.

Chilean coup of 1973 (September 11, 1973), the seizure of power by the forces of General Augusto PINOCHET, which encountered little armed opposition. During or after the brief battle around the presidential palace Chilean president Salvador ALLENDE Gossens was killed; Pinochet's forces claimed that he had committed suicide, though his murder was widely reported. The coup concluded 3 years of increasingly sharp contention between right and left forces in the country, with considerable assistance to the right provided by the U.S. CENTRAL INTELLIGENCE AGENCY (CIA), including assistance in the preparation of the coup. The new military government imposed martial law and embarked on a long reign of terror in which tens of thousands of its opponents were imprisoned, tortured, and murdered, including such cultural figures as folksinger Victor Jara; more precise and reliable estimates of the numbers of state terrorism victims in Chile are not yet available.

Chin, Larry Wu-tai, a spy for China for over three decades, most of them spent as a CENTRAL INTELLIGENCE AGENCY (CIA) employee; he was arrested in 1985. Convicted of espionage, he died in his prison cell, possibly a suicide, early in 1986.

China, until 1912 ruled by the Manchu dynasty, followed by the REPUBLIC OF CHINA, led by SUN YAT-SEN, briefly by YUAN SHIH-K'AI, and from 1926 by CHIANG KAI-SHEK, who took it into the long CHINESE CIVIL WAR in 1927. After the Communist victory in 1949, the Republican government moved to the island of Taiwan (Formosa). On October 1, 1949, the republic was succeeded on the mainland by the PEOPLE'S REPUBLIC OF CHINA, led by MAO ZEDONG, 1949–74, and from 1977 by DENG XIAOPING, who introduced wide and deep economic and political reforms, greatly changing the course of modern Chinese history. The CHINESE STUDENT DEMONSTRATIONS OF 1989, culminating in the TIENANMEN SQUARE MASSACRE, once again sharply changed the course of modern Chinese history.

Chindits, small British forces engaged in long-range ground raids into Japanese-held Burma, beginning in February 1943; the raids were of limited military value but of some morale value to the Allies in a difficult period of World War II.

Chinese Civil War (1927–49), the 22-year struggle between the COMMUNIST PARTY OF CHINA and the KUOMINTANG, interrupted in part by the long SINO-JAPANESE WAR (1937–45), which eventuated in the Communist victory of 1949 and the establishment of the PEOPLE'S REPUBLIC OF CHINA. Until 1927 the Communists worked within the Kuomintang, which was closely advised by the Soviet Union. In 1927 the Kuomintang, then led by CHIANG KAI-SHEK and in the process of taking north China, decided to break with the Communists, in April turning on and massacring 5,000–6,000 Communists and their allies while taking Shanghai. This SHANGHAI MASSACRE was the real beginning of the civil war and was soon followed by the first major clash of the war, at NANCHANG; the defeated Communists, led by ZHU DE, then fled to the Chingkang Mountains of western Kiangsi, where they were joined by MAO ZEDONG and the other survivors of the AUTUMN HARVEST UPRISINGS. Kuomintang main forces completed their conquest of the north, defeating the northern warlords in April 1928 in a series of battles involving a total of approximately 1 million men and then taking Peking. In 1930 Communist forces attempted to take several central Chinese cities; they lost the Battle of CH'ANGSHA, fled into the

mountains, and during the next 4 years formed and developed the KIANGSI SOVIET Republic. But in a series of campaigns, the last of them organized by German military advisers, Kuomintang troops defeated Communist forces, which then embarked on the LONG MARCH north to Shensi. Chiang planned a renewed series of attacks in 1936 but was captured in the SIAN INCIDENT and ultimately did not pursue his campaign. When the Japanese attacked China in 1937, the Communists and the Kuomintang began a long, very uneasy truce, punctuated by many armed clashes, most notably the Kuomintang attack on allied Communist troops in ANHWEI, in 1941. In 1943 Nationalist forces blockaded Communist-held north China, and in 1944–45 Japanese forces heavily attacked the Nationalists while sharply limiting their attacks on Communist forces. In August 1945 Communist forces moved into formerly Japanese-held portions of north China. Nationalist forces were airlifted into north China by American planes, and in September 53,000 American marines occupied strategic areas, including Peking. By mid–November, full-scale civil war had resumed, and in early 1946 General George C. MARSHALL's peace mission failed. During 1946 Nationalist troops took much of Manchuria and north China, but in July 1946 American supplies were stopped, and by January 1947 all but a few American marines had been withdrawn. During 1947 Communist armies went on the offensive in Manchuria and north China. From May 1948 through January 1949 Communist troops won a series of major battles, destroying Nationalist armies at MUKDEN in Manchuria, in the Yellow River valley, and finally in the decisive battle of SUCHOW, in which defending Nationalist armies lost an estimated 250,000 men, half of their effective forces. Peking fell on January 22, Nanking on April 22, and the rest of China's major cities during that summer and autumn while the remaining Nationalist armies disintegrated. In December 1949 the Nationalist government fled to Formosa, later renamed Taiwan, ending the long civil war.

Chinese Revolution of 1911, the series of uprisings against the Ch'ing (Manchu) dynasty that began at Wuchang, in central China, on October 10, 1911, and then spread throughout China. The Manchu government recalled general YUAN SHIH-K'AI, but he made peace with the revolutionaries rather than fighting for the Manchus. SUN YAT-SEN, who had been abroad raising money and support for the revolution, hurried home from the United States and was elected provisional president of the new Republic of China, but he felt that his forces were too weak to govern; he negotiated with YUAN, who became first president of the new republic on March 10, after the child emperor HSÜAN T'UNG (later Henry P'U YI) had abdicated.

Chinese–Indian border war of 1962, conflict in which Chinese frontier troops invaded and took disputed territory from India during October and November 1962, declaring a cease-fire on November 21, when their objectives had been achieved.

Chinese student demonstrations of 1989, a series of major demonstrations in the spring of 1989, which began as student demonstrations in Beijing and soon spread to other Chinese cities and included other portions of the population, most notably teachers and journalists. The demonstrations began as a tribute to reformer HU YAOBANG on his death and became massive prodemocratic demonstrations involving millions, centering on the long student occupation of Beijing's TIANANMEN SQUARE. The demonstrations generated a national crisis and a struggle for dominance between the liberal and conservative wings of the Chinese Communist movement. The conservative faction, led by LI PENG with the backing of DENG XIAOPING, ultimately gained power, ousting the liberals led by ZHAO ZIYANG. A massacre followed in and around Tiananmen Square on June 4, 1989, in which hundreds and perhaps thousands of Chinese citizens were killed by the Chinese

army. Mass arrests and country-wide repression of dissidents then ensued.

Chirac, Jacques (1932–   ), French conservative political leader, who held several adminstrative posts before and after entering the national assembly in 1967. He was premier 1974–76 and 1986–88.

chiropractic, nontraditional form of treatment involving mechanical manipulations and adjustments of the body's skeletal system, on the assumption (outlined in 1953) that disease results from interference with the body's nerve impulses; from the Greek words *cheir* (hand) and *praktikos*. Though the approach and first school were developed in the U.S. Midwest by Canadian-American Daniel David Palmer in the 1890s, it was not until the early 20th century, under the direction of Palmer's son Bartlett, that chiropractic became firmly rooted. Early chiropractors were often subject to arrest for practicing medicine without a license; in 1968 HEW reported to Congress that chiropractic had no scientific research to support its claims and was ineligible for Medicare. Even so, chiropractors have gradually become more widely accepted by the general public and by the 1980s were to be found throughout the United States and in many other countries.

Chisholm, Shirley Anita St. Hill (1924–   ), U.S. social worker, New York Democratic state legislator (1964–68), and the first Black woman member of the House of Representatives (1969–83). In 1972 she was an unsuccessful candidate for the Democratic presidential nomination.

Chissano, Joaquim Alberto (1939–   ), Mozambiqe guerrilla general, a longtime FRELIMO leader who became president of Mozambique on November 3, 1986, succeeding Samora MACHEL. As president he pursued the long civil war against RENAMO and other guerrilla groups while attempting to bring peace through negotiations that included South Africa within the context of a developing set of regional peace initiatives.

chlorofluorocarbons (CFCs), also called chlorofluoromethanes (CFMs) or Freons, chemicals used as spray propellants and refrigerants, implicated as early as 1974 in depletion of the OZONE LAYER.

chlorophyll, green pigment in plant tissue vital to the process of PHOTOSYNTHESIS, by which plants create vital nutrients; first discovered in the 19th century. German scientist Richard Willstatter detailed the structure of chlorophyll (1905–13), for which he won the 1915 Nobel Prize for Chemistry, and by 1957 Melvin CALVIN had worked out its precise role in photosynthesis.

cholesterol, fatty, crystalline substance in the body, found in many foods but especially in eggs and meats. High cholesterol has been linked with heart disease, particularly if caused by deposits in the arteries, and also with formation of gallstones, spurring massive anticholesterol campaigns, especially in the United States, from the 1970s on.

Chomsky, Noam (1928–   ), U.S. linguistics scholar, who posited the view that underlying grammatical forms are innate. His controversial theory, first expressed in *Syntactic Structures* (1957), proposed that a series of "transformational" rules provided an underlying "generative" grammar, from which specific human languages resulted. From the mid-1960s Chomsky also wrote and spoke widely on political issues of the left, especially against the VIETNAM WAR.

Chou En-lai, the old-style name of Chinese leader ZHOU ENLAI.

Choukoutien Cave (Zhoukoudian), site near Peking (Beijing), China, where early human fossil remains, popularly called PEKING MAN, were found in 1927.

Christian X (1870–1947), king of Denmark (1912–47) and of Iceland (1920–44), who defied German authority and refused to cooperate with occupation forces after the 1940 conquest of Denmark. Although held by the Germans from 1943 to 1945, he remained a major symbol of Danish resistance throughout the war.

Christian General, the popular name of FENG YU-HSIANG, a leading north China warlord in the 1920s, who was defeated by the KUOMINTANG IN 1930.

Chungking fire (September 2, 1949), a dock fire that spread into the city at Chungking, China; 1,700 people died.

Churchill, Winston Leonard Spencer (1874–1965), son of Lord Randolph Churchill and American Jennie Jerome. He was an army officer who ultimately became British prime minister, after a long and checkered political career, and led his country through World War II. He also was a writer, historian, and one of the most quotable speakers of the century. His early career included military service in India and Egypt, and a period as a war correspondent during the BOER WAR. He became a Conservative MP in 1901, switched to the Liberals in 1904, and rose quickly to the cabinet level in politics, becoming First Lord of the Admiralty (1911–15). He was largely responsible for the British fiasco at GALLIPOLI and the Dardanelles in 1915, and was thereafter dropped from the wartime cabinet, coming back into LLOYD GEORGE's cabinet in 1919. From 1917, he was deeply concerned about the threat that he felt the BOLSHEVIK Revolution posed. He went back to the Conservatives in the 1920s, becoming chancellor of the exchequer in the Baldwin cabinet (1924–29), and in that position he pursued policies that were widely blamed for the GENERAL STRIKE of 1926 and held contributory to the GREAT DEPRESSION that began in 1929. Leaving office in 1929, he spent 10 years as a writer and speaker, during the 1930s joining his concern regarding bolshevism with deep concern about the rise of HITLER and the intentions of Germany. In 1939 he became Admiralty Lord again, and on May 10, 1940, as Western Europe was falling to the Nazis, he became prime minister, leading a wartime coalition cabinet. He played a huge role in rallying his country, bringing the United States into the war, and leading the ALLIES to victory over the AXIS powers, in conjunction with Franklin D. ROOSEVELT. His party lost the election of July 1945; he then turned to writing *The Second World War* and later his *History of* *the English Speaking Peoples*, and to speaking: his "IRON CURTAIN" speech signaled the beginning of the COLD WAR and reflected the profoundly anti-Communist views he had always continued to hold. He was prime minister again from October 26, 1951, to April 5, 1953, and an MP until 1964, in that year completing an extraordinary political career then as old as the century.

Chu Teh, the old-style name of Chinese leader ZHU DE.

CIA, the initials of the CENTRAL INTELLIGENCE AGENCY.

Ciano, Galeazzo (1903–44), Italian fascist, a lawyer who married Benito MUSSOLINI's daughter Edda in 1930. Ciano led a bomber squadron in the ETHIOPIAN–ITALIAN WAR, by 1936 was MUSSOLINI'S foreign minister, and became very rich during his years in power. He turned against his father-in-law in 1943, joining the rest of the Fascist Grand Council in stripping Mussolini of power and imprisoning him, but then fled to Germany to escape charges of financial misconduct. He participated in the Italian puppet government set up by the Germans, was captured in northern Italy, and was executed for treason in January 1944.

Cicippio, Joseph James, one of the American LEBANON HOSTAGES, comptroller of American University of Beirut, who was kidnapped on September 12, 1986.

CIO, Initials of the CONGRESS OF INDUSTRIAL ORGANIZATIONS, by which the organization was best known.

Ciudad Juarez, Battle of (May 1911), the decisive action of the MEXICAN REVOLUTION, in which rebel forces operating in Chihuahua in support of Francisco MADERO defeated the the government forces of Porforio DIAZ, who soon resigned.

Civilian Conservation Corps (CCC), a massive U.S. NEW DEAL self-help unemployment-relief program (1933–42), in which young men lived in work camps, were cared for and minimally paid, and were employed in a wide variety of conservation projects.

Civil Rights Act of 1964, the most important U.S. civil rights legislation since the post–Civil War Reconstruction period, which included equal voting standards for all, outlawed racial exclusion from and segregation within public places, withheld federal funds from discriminating educational institutions, outlawed union and employer racial discrimination, and provided for effective enforcement of these and the other provisions of the Act.

Civil Rights Act of 1968, law that outlawed discriminatory practices in the purchase, sale, and rental of homes; these open housing provisions, although effective in some areas, were only partly effective in areas in which community pressures continued to exclude Blacks and other minority groups.

civil rights movement, an interracial, interfaith U.S. movement and set of related campaigns that began with the tremendous impetus supplied by the Supreme Court's school desegregation decision in *Brown* v. *Board of Education* in 1954 and the MONTGOMERY BUS BOYCOTT led by Martin Luther KING, Jr., and Ralph ABERNATHY in 1955. A long, ultimately successful campaign to desegregate southern schools and colleges followed the *Brown* decision, in several instances involving the intervention of federal troops, as in the integration of the Little Rock, Arkansas, schools in 1957 and the forced admission of James MEREDITH to the University of Mississippi in 1962. Beginning in 1960 and 1961, sit-ins and FREEDOM RIDES, supported by new civil rights laws and the willingness of John F. KENNEDY and Lyndon B. JOHNSON to enforce those laws, began to desegregate public facilities in the American South. In the same period a series of civil rights campaigns and demonstrations—as at BIRMINGHAM, Alabama, in 1963; the MARCH ON WASHINGTON, D.C., in 1963, the occasion of Martin Luther King's I HAVE A DREAM speech; and SELMA, Alabama in 1965—focused world attention on the problem. At the same time an increasingly strong group of organizations, including the SOUTHERN CHRISTIAN LEADERSHIP CONFERENCE (SCLC), STUDENT NON-VIOLENT COORDINATING COMMITTEE (SNCC), CONGRESS OF RACIAL

EQUALITY (CORE), and BLACK PANTHER PARTY, continued to campaign for civil rights. The CIVIL RIGHTS ACT of 1964, TWENTY-FOURTH AMENDMENT TO THE CONSTITUTION (1964), VOTING RIGHTS ACT OF 1965, and CIVIL RIGHTS ACT OF 1968 responded to many of the demands of the civil rights movement, and the election of Black officeholders throughout the South signaled massive changes in southern life, though many of the deepest questions raised by the civil rights movement remained unresolved.

Civil Works Administration (CWA), a U.S. federal NEW DEAL agency administered by Harry HOPKINS, operating in the winter of 1933–34, that provided temporary work on public projects for 4 million unemployed workers and was a model for the later WORKS PROGRESS ADMINISTRATION (WPA).

Clark, Mark Wayne (1896–1984), U.S. officer, who saw service in World War I, worked as Dwight D. EISENHOWER's deputy commander to prepare the 1942 Allied North African invasion, and then commanded the American Fifth Army during the Italian campaign. He headed U.S. occupation forces in Austria until 1947 and commanded United Nations forces in Korea as that war was winding down, from May 1952 through July 1953.

Clark, Ramsay (1927–   ), U.S. lawyer, son of Tom C. CLARK, in the justice department from 1961 and U.S. attorney general 1967–69. Clark was a strong advocate of individual and civil rights and played a key role in enforcing civil rights laws during the late 1960s.

Clark, Tom Campbell (1899–1977), U.S. lawyer, in the justice department from 1937, U.S. attorney general 1945–49, and associate justice of the Supreme Court 1949–67. He resigned in 1967 to avoid any conflict of interest that might arise from the appointment of his son, Ramsay CLARK, as U.S. attorney general.

Clark Field attack (December 8, 1941), destruction of the main U.S. air strength in the Philippines on the ground at Clark Field, near Manila, by Japanese planes attacking from Formosa, despite knowledge of the PEARL HARBOR disaster only the day before.

Cleaver, Eldridge (1935–   ), U.S. radical civil rights activist, whose book, *Soul On Ice* (1968), written in prison, was one of the key Black-consciousness works of the 1960s. He was the presidential candidate of the Peace and Freedom party in 1968 and a leader of the BLACK PANTHER PARTY. After participating in a 1968 gun battle between some members of the Black Panthers and police in Oakland, California, he fled the United States. He returned to the United States as a "born again" Christian in 1975, then touring the country as a conservative religious spokesperson.

Clemenceau, Georges Eugene Benjamin ("The Tiger"; 1841–1929), French doctor, journalist and political leader, twice premier of France (1906–09 and 1917–20), a leader of the parliamentary opposition during the last three decades of the 19th century and of the campaign to vindicate Alfred Dreyfus. As premier and thereafter, he was a strong supporter of the French military buildup prior to World War I. He became wartime premier in November 1917, at the age of 76, and then played a central role in the winning of the war, at the PARIS PEACE CONFERENCE of 1919, and in the shaping of the Treaty of VERSAILLES.

Cleveland natural gas explosion (October 20, 1944), explosion of a liquefied natural gas storage facility at Cleveland, Ohio. The massive resulting fire destroyed 50 city blocks and an estimated 300 buiildings. At least 125 people were killed in the explosion and fire.

Clifford, Clark McAdams (1906–   ), U.S. lawyer and diplomat, legal counsel to President Harry S. TRUMAN, 1946–50; a troubleshooter and key Southeast Asia presidential advisor for Presidents John F. KENNEDY and Lyndon B. JOHNSON before becoming secretary of state in 1968. At first a strong supporter of the VIETNAM WAR, Clifford played a key role in Johnson's decision to stop the bombing of North Vietnam and to begin the long American disengagement

Clippers, airplanes built by Igor SIKORSKY and put into South American, trans-Atlantic, and trans-Pacific service by Pan American Airways in the late 1930s.

clone, in biology, one or more organisms that are genetically identical, produced from a single ancestor, asexually, rather than receiving half of their genetic heritage from each of two parents. Cloning has long been used in botany and in the laboratory, where cloning of tissues (plant or animal) provides uniform matter for researchers to work with. But with the rise of GENETIC ENGINEERING interest began to focus on cloning larger organisms. Public interest was spurred in the 1970s by the appearance of popular books and articles claiming that a human had been cloned. No such achievement was confirmed, but in 1980 Chinese scientists produced a clone of a fish. The following year Swiss scientist Karl Illmensee cloned several mice, the first known cloned mammals; in the same year American researchers Allan Wilson and Russell Higuchi first cloned genes from an extinct species, the zebra-like quagga.

clone, in computer science, a machine built to be virtually identical in operation with a mainstream "name brand" computer; Compaq produced the first clone of the IBM PERSONAL COMPUTER in 1982.

Cloquet forest fire (October 21, 1918), a forest fire that destroyed Cloquet, Minnesota, and 25 neighboring towns, killing 559 people and destroying over more than 2,000 square miles of forest.

cloud chamber, device for detecting atomic PARTICLES, using supersaturated air through which RADIATION and subatomic particles leave a track that can be observed and photographed. The cloud chamber was invented by Charles WILSON in 1911 and (with improvements by others) was for decades a basic tool of nuclear physicists. A variation called the BUBBLE CHAMBER was developed in 1952 by Donald GLASER.

Clubb, Oliver Edmund (1901–89), U.S. diplomat, writer, and teacher, in the U.S. foreign service 1928–52. He was sent to Beijing in 1928 and during the next two decades became an "old China hand," spending much of his diplomatic career in East Asia and leaving Beijing in 1950. In 1951, at the height of the MCCARTHY period, he was accused of being pro-Communist and was suspended from his post as head of the state department's China section by a departmental loyalty review board, a suspension that was lifted on appeal in 1952. But his diplomatic career was over; he was transferred internally to a dead-end job and soon resigned. In later years he became an author, focusing on East Asian matters, and taught at the Columbia University East Asian Institute.

Club of Rome, international group on world economic problems that commissioned the Massachusetts Institute of Technology to write the 1972 report, THE LIMITS OF GROWTH, on the dangers of unchecked economic expansion.

CND, the initials of the CAMPAIGN FOR NUCLEAR DISARMAMENT, a leading British antinuclear organization.

Coalbrook mine disaster (January 21, 1960), death by methane poisoning of 417 coal miners trapped by rock falls in a mine at Coalbrook; South Africa's worst mine disaster.

Cocoanut Grove fire (November 28, 1942), conflagration in a Boston nightclub with inadequate exits, making it impossible for most to escape when flames erupted; smoke, fire, and panic killed 491 people.

Coffin, William Sloane, Jr. (1924–   ), U.S. minister who became Yale University chaplain in 1958, and was active in the CIVIL RIGHTS MOVEMENT and the anti–VIETNAM WAR campaign in the 1960s. He was convicted of conspiring to counsel draft evasion in 1968; the conviction was reversed in 1969.

Cohn, Roy Marcus (1927–86), U.S. lawyer, an assistant government prosecutor in the 1951 ROSENBERG case, part of the prosecution staff in the unsuccessful 1952 perjury prosecution of Owen LATTIMORE, and chief counsel of the Senate investigations committee of Joseph R. MCCARTHY, 1953–54. Cohn's activities in the last position helped bring the epithet MCCARTHYISM into the language. He was discredited, with McCarthy, after the 1954 ARMY-MCCARTHY HEARINGS, and went into private practice. Cohn became a powerful, extremely controversial New York lawyer, who survived many tax audits and three federal prosecutions on a variety of charges, ultimately being disbarred on June 23, 1986, shortly before his death on August 2, 1986.

Cohn-Bendit, Daniel "Danny the Red" (1945–   ), 1960's French-German left-wing political activist, a leader of the March 1968 student demonstrations at the University of Paris. During the 1980s he was active in the German GREEN MOVEMENT.

Cointelpro, U.S. FEDERAL BUREAU OF INVESTIGATION (FBI) domestic counterintelligence program, initiated by J. Edgar HOOVER in 1956 and continuing into the early 1970s, in which the FBI engaged in massive illegal operations as a matter of policy, including harassment of political dissidents, illegal wiretapping, burglary, kidnapping, the provocation of illegal acts by dissidents, and the attempted disruption of dissident groups through the spread of disinformation. Some of these FBI activities were exposed in the 1976 report of the Senate Select Committee on Intelligence, in the atmosphere engendered by the WATERGATE SCANDAL.

cold fusion, NUCLEAR FUSION achieved at room temperatures, as claimed (but not confirmed) by researchers in 1989.

cold war (1945–   ), more than four decades of sharp, continuing conflict, short of shooting war, between the United States and the Soviet Union, the world's two nuclear superpowers, each possessed of the power to destroy the other many times over and much of the world in the process. The cold war generated a massive, continuing arms race between the two powers, and a contin-

uing covert war between their vastly expanded espionage organizations, and greatly enhanced many civil and regional wars among factions and states influenced by the superpowers. It also brought the world to the brink of nuclear holocaust on several occasions, most notably during the CUBAN MISSILE CRISIS of 1962. During the early 1970s and again in the late 1980s both nations evinced a desire to reduce tensions, negotiating nuclear arms limitation and regional conflict agreements. In the GORBACHEV era the war came to an end, though not without great concern on both sides and throughout the world as to its possible revival.

Collazo, Oscar, and Griselio Torresola, Puerto Rican nationalists who on November 1, 1950, tried to shoot their way into Blair House in Washington, DC, and assassinate President Harry S. TRUMAN. Terresola and a guard were killed; Collazo was wounded and sentenced to life imprisonment; his sentence was commuted in 1979.

Collingwood school fire (March 8, 1908), a fire at the Collingwood Elementary School, in Cleveland, Ohio, killing 173 children and 2 teachers; the flames had blocked the main exit, and the rear windows and doors were locked.

Collins, Michael (1890–1922), Irish Republican leader who was head of IRISH REPUBLICAN ARMY intelligence during the IRISH WAR OF INDEPENDENCE, a main Irish representative during the negotiations that in 1921 ended the war and partitioned Ireland, and commander of the Irish Free State forces during the IRISH CIVIL WAR. He was ambushed and killed near the end of the civil war, on August 22, 1922.

Colombian Civil War (1947–58), a rural guerrilla war between liberals and conservatives, with government forces on the side of the conservatives, in which an estimated 200,000–300,000 people died; generally called La VIOLENCIA. After it ended, low-level insurgency continued, and during the 1980s grew into a substantial, multifaceted guerrilla insurgency complicated by some guerrilla links with the MEDELLÍN CARTEL and other drug-related organizations.

Colombo Plan, a major development aid plan for Asia and the Pacific conceived at a meeting of COMMONWEALTH foreign ministers at Colombo, Sri Lanka, in 1950 and later joined by Japan and the United States as aid providers and by many other nations as aid recipients. The aid totals more than $5 billion per year in grants, loans, goods, technical help, training, drug abuse advice, and a miscellany of other assistance. Japan is by far the largest contributor; their aid is more than the total contributions of all other countries.

Colossus, all-ELECTRONIC, special-purpose DIGITAL COMPUTER built in 1943 by Alan TURING to break the German codes, notably those from the ENIGMA machine.

Columbia, first of the U.S. SPACE SHUTTLES, launched initially on April 12, 1981 and first reused in November 1981; in 1982, on its fifth flight, it launched the first SATELLITE from a shuttle.

Columbia University sit-ins, the student demonstrations of April 1968, in which protestors occupied five Columbia University campus buildings for 6 days, until finally evicted by New York City police at the request of the college administration. Hundreds of arrests were made, and the campus was closed for the balance of the semester.

COMECON, the initials of the COUNCIL FOR MUTUAL ECONOMIC ASSISTANCE, a multinational Soviet-bloc mutual economic assistance group.

Cominform (Communist Information Bureau), international organization formed in 1947 by the Communist parties of the Soviet Union, Yugoslavia, Italy, France, Poland, Czechoslovakia, Hungary, Rumania, and Bulgaria, which from 1947 until the death of Joseph STALIN in 1953 was a major instrument of Soviet domination of the Communist parties of Europe, except for Yugoslavia; in 1948 TITO refused to conform, taking Yugoslavia on an independent path. Yugoslavia was then expelled from the Cominform. After Stalin's death the Cominform was little used, and was dissolved in 1956.

Comintern, an alternate name for the COMMUNIST INTERNATIONAL, founded by LENIN in 1919.

Common Market, an informal name for the EUROPEAN ECONOMIC COMMUNITY (EEC).

Commonwealth, The, a 46-nation association that evolved as the British Empire dissolved. Although its existence was never formally declared, the British Commonwealth of Nations, which later came to be called the Commonwealth, was tacitly recognized by Britain's Statute of Westminster (1931), which established equality among those autonomous former British colonies still affirming their loyalty to Britain and its royal house. After World War II, Britain's former colonies joined the Commonwealth in substantial numbers, as new, developing countries.

communism, as a 19th-century theoretical term, a construct advocating absolute economic and political equality, advocated by Karl Marx and Friedrich Engels as well as by anarchist Peter Kropotkin. In the 20th century, communism, as put forward by V. I. LENIN, had the egalitarian "from each according to his ability, to each according to his needs" goal, the road to that goal consisting of the development of a Communist Party led by a revolutionary elite, which would seize power and then rule in authoritarian fashion for the good of those ruled and with the aim of developing a Communist state. To that end, Lenin and his associates developed the BOLSHEVIK party, seized power in the OCTOBER REVOLUTION, and held it during the RUSSIAN CIVIL WAR. In the wake of the Russian Revolution, existing socialist movements split all over the world, with competing democratic socialist and Soviet-oriented authoritarian Communist parties emerging, as in Germany, the United States, and France; in other countries, such as China, the new parties has no such existing base. That split greatly helped the rise of fascism in Germany and the development of World War II. The worldwide Communist party network continued to be Soviet-oriented, successfully suppressing and removing dissidents, until the first major breakaway, that of the COMMUNIST PARTY OF CHINA during and after the LONG MARCH of 1934–35. The second major breakaway was that of Yugoslavia, in 1948, which was in essence a refusal to become part of a set of Eastern European Soviet-dominated nations. After STALIN'S death in 1953 and KHRUSHCHEV'S SECRET SPEECH of 1956, many of the world's Communist parties outside Eastern Europe began to pursue independent paths. In Western Europe that movement was EUROCOMMUNISM; In Eastern Europe, however, attempts to pursue separate national paths were repressed until the GORBACHEV era. In the mid-1980s communism, led by Mikhail Gorbachev, began to reexamine and redefine itself, moving away from repressive authoritarianism and centralized, wholly controlled economies, a movement very much in process and flux in the late 1980s, and bringing massive changes in the Soviet Union and Eastern Europe. In February 1990, the Central Committee of the Communist Party of the Soviet Union renounced its guaranteed leading role, and with it the heart of Leninist doctrine.

Communist International (Comintern, or Third International; 1919–43), the international organization of the world's Communist parties, initiated by LENIN in 1919 as an alternative to the socialist SECOND INTERNATIONAL. The organization functioned essentially as an instrument of Soviet Communist Party policy during its life span, supporting Soviet attacks on western Socialist parties in the 1920s and early 1930s, moving over to a UNITED FRONT policy against fascism in the mid-1930s, to a neutralist position vis-à-vis fascism during the period of the NAZI–SOVIET PACT, and finally to full support of the ALLIES in World War II, after the German invasion of the Soviet Union.

Communist Party of China (CCP), organization founded by CH'EN TU-HSIU and LI TA-CHAO, Peking University librarians, in May 1920. Its First Congress was in Shanghai in July 1921 and was a meeting of 11–13 people, among them MAO ZEDONG and Soviet advisor MARING. Ch'en was elected party chairman. In its early years, with its Soviet advisers, the CCP supported the KUOMINTANG. The two parties split after the SHANGHAI MASSACRE of 1927, which initiated the 22-year CHINESE CIVIL WAR, with a period of partial truce and united front during the SINO-JAPANESE WAR (1937–45). The CCP, led by MAO ZEDONG, achieved power in 1949, thereafter remaining the ruling power in the PEOPLE'S REPUBLIC OF CHINA.

Communist Party of the Soviet Union, since 1952, the name of the ruling party in the Soviet Union, originally (in 1912) called the Russian Social-Democratic Workers Party (BOLSHEVIKS)

Communist Party of the United States, political organization formed in 1919 as two dissident American Communist parties split from the Socialist Party; the two splinters united into a single Communist Party in 1920, which was led by William Z. FOSTER 1921–30 and 1945–57, and by Earl BROWDER, 1930–45. A weak organization wielding very little influence during the 1920s and early 1930s, the Communist Party achieved some strength and as many as 100,000 members during the UNITED FRONT period of the late 1930s, many of its members becoming effective mass-production industries labor organizers, some of its intellectual adherents and activists becoming influential in the anti-fascist movements of the time, and some of its members going abroad as "premature anti-fascists" to fight on the Republican side in the SPANISH CIVIL WAR. But with the NAZI–SOVIET PACT of 1939 the American Communist Party suddenly "flip-flopped," becoming isolationist and then losing many of its most devoted members. Then it flip-flopped again, supporting U.S. intervention once Germany had invaded the Soviet Union. In 1943, on a Soviet initiative, the organization disbanded and formed the Communist Political Association. It flip-flopped again at war's end, reforming and mirroring Soviet political positions as the COLD WAR began. The organization was severely damaged and then effectively outlawed during the early post–World War II period as the anti-Communist hysteria of the time mounted and its leaders continued to insist on adherence to every detail of Soviet policy. The coup de grace, however, was administered by the Soviets, when Nikita KHRUSHCHEV'S 1956 secret speech to a Soviet Communist party congress revealed many of the crimes of the STALIN era. Believing themselves to have been betrayed, most of the remaining American Communists left their party, which afterward survived only as one small, left-wing splinter group among many.

Comoro Islands (Federal Islamic Republic of the Comoros), part of the group of French island colonies in the Indian Ocean, until independence was achieved on July 6, 1975. France retained control of the nearby island of Mayette, triggering a continuing dispute with the new Comoros government. Considerable turbulence followed independence; in 1978, with French mercenary assistance, the one-party government led by Ahmed Abdallah Abderemane emerged.

compact disc (CD), thin metal disc on which sounds, encoded as digits, appear as millions of tiny indentations, to be read by the LASER beam in a CD player and then translated by an amplifier back into sounds; a striking result of miniaturization in COMPUTERS. Introduced by Philips and Sony in 1982, CDs quickly took over much of the market from TAPE RECORDINGS and long-playing records. In the United States alone, 700,000 CD players were sold in the first 3 years, plus 15 million compact discs. By 1990 record publishers were redoing major portions of their libraries onto CDs, and some ceased publishing records altogether. Related technology had produced the videodisc in the late 1970s, which failed initially as a consumer product but retained potential in business and education for storage of massive amounts of information.

Compton, Arthur Holly (1892–62), U.S. physicist who developed the idea of the PHOTON. In 1923 he found that some X-RAYS reflected from matter increased their wavelength, (later called the Compton effect). His explanation of the effect involved the idea of light as a particle, or photon, a key contribution to QUANTUM THEORY, inspiring Louis DE BROGLIE'S work on WAVE-PARTICLE DUALITY and winning Compton the 1927 Nobel Prize for Physics. Later he focused on study of COSMIC RAYS, during World War II heading the effort to synthesize PLUTONIUM for the MANHATTAN PROJECT'S ATOMIC BOMBS.

computer, powerful electronic calculating device, the two types being DIGITAL COMPUTERS, operating with discrete values such as numbers and using the BINARY SYSTEM for calculation, with electronic on-off switches; and the less common ANALOG COMPUTERS, operating with continuous values, such as with changing temperatures. Before the late 1930s computers were mechanical, the most sophisticated being the MARK I and Vannevar BUSH's analog machines. The first all-electronic computer was the ATANASOFF-BERRY COMPUTER (ABC), built 1937–42, followed by Alan TURING's COLOSSUS, developed in Britain in 1943 for breaking German codes. The ENIAC, long regarded as the first all-electronic, general-purpose digital computer, also developed originally for military purposes, was built 1942–46. The ENIAC needed to be rewired for each new task, but John von NEUMANN made the revolutionary suggestion that programs might be stored in the computer, with instructions coded as numbers. In 1951, the first computer became available for commercial use: the UNIVAC I, built by the ENIAC creators, which also introduced storage of data on MAGNETIC TAPE. By 1956 COMPUTER LANGUAGES were being developed to ease the task of programming—instructing the machine. Early computers, sometimes called "electronic brains," were massive, extremely expensive affairs made of heat-producing VACUUM TUBES and electrical wires, or circuits, mounted on boards. By the late 1950s TRANSISTORS were replacing the cumbersome vacuum tubes, leading to a smaller "second generation" of computers and beginning the drive toward miniaturization. By the 1960s ever-smaller multiple transistors were being built into smaller computer boards, and wires were being replaced by integrated circuits soldered onto the boards. The resulting third generation of computers was made more flexible by the 1970 introduction of removable "floppy disks" for information storage. The following year saw the arrival of the MICROPROCESSOR CHIP: a computer's entire central processing unit, once a massive affair, was placed on a single chip of silicon, which replaced the computer board. Such innovations led to the PERSONAL COMPUTER (PC), designed and priced for small-scale home and business use, introduced in 1975. After that, small but increasingly capacious computers—some with hundreds of thousands of circuits on a single chip and far more powerful than the early ENIAC—proliferated in homes and businesses. Special-purpose computers were inserted into a wide range of other machines, such as cars and telephones; and tiny, hand-size computers also were available for personal use, starting with Hewlett-Packard's 1974 programmable pocket calculator. The same period saw the arrival of prepackaged application programs that the computer user could simply plug into the computer. By the 1980s computers had spread so quickly into schools and homes that many parents and grandparents were seen as "computer illiterate," whereas preschoolers took computers as a fact of life. The PCs grew so quickly in power and speed that by the late 1980s they were capturing much of the middle-range business and scientific market; instead of a number of terminals connected to a massive mainframe computer, the more usual pattern became a series of smaller computers connected to each other in a network. But miniaturization also allowed the building of supercomputers, enormously powerful machines able to perform hundreds of millions of operations per second, often used for heavy scientific, industrial, and military ap-

plications. As John von Neumann's early MANIAC had aided the development of the HYDROGEN BOMB by swiftly doing calculations that would have taken scientists years to do manually, so computers were basic to areas such as space exploration, RADIO ASTRONOMY, and ROBOTICS. These computers, using very large scale integrated (VSLI) circuits, were the fourth generation of computers. From 1982 Japanese computer scientists were working on a so-called fifth generation, incorporating aspects of ARTIFICIAL INTELLIGENCE, including the ability to communicate with people in everyday language and to translate one language to another.

computerized axial tomography, formal name of the device used in a CAT SCAN.

computer language, special sets of coded instructions, in words rather than numbers, used in programming COMPUTERS. From 1947 computers had stored programs containing instructions in "machine language," that is, using numerical codes written in the BINARY SYSTEM. But in 1956 an IBM team led by John Backus developed a computer programming language, FORTRAN (**For**mula **Tran**slator), which made the process of instructing the computer much easier. In 1959 COBOL, a programming language designed for business use, was introduced by Grace Murray Hopper. In the mid-1960's computers became more widespread, John Kemeny and Thomas Kurtz created a popularly oriented language, BASIC (**B**eginners **A**ll-purpose **S**ymbolic **In**struction **C**ode). But from 1979 prepackaged "plug-in" programs designed to do specific kinds of activities were on sale, especially for PERSONAL COMPUTERS, freeing the general user of the necessity of personally programming the computer.

comsat, a condensed name for **com**munications **SAT**ellite; as in Comsat, the U.S. organization participating in INTELSAT.

concentration camps (death camps), detention and sometimes murder camps holding large numbers of people. Detention camps are by no means a 20th-century invention, and in the 20th century many nations have operated large-scale camps, sometimes as temporary holding sites and very often as mass prisons. But "concentration camp" and the synonymous "death camp" acquired a very special meaning during the Nazi era, describing the mass prisons run by the Germans in which an estimated 10–15 million died, at least 6 million of them the Jews of the genocidal JEWISH HOLOCAUST. Some estimates of Nazi concentration camp deaths run as high as 26 million. Millions of those who died were directly murdered, mostly in the crematoria run by the Germans in many of the camps. Some of the most notorious German camps were those at BELSEN, BUCHENWALD, and DACHAU in Germany and at AUSCHWITZ, MAIDENEK, and TREBLINKA in Poland. Other 20th-century concentration camps that have been places of mass murder, include the Turkish camps in the Syrian desert used to genocidally murder an estimated 1–1.5 million victims of the ARMENIAN HOLOCAUST.

Concorde, world's first regularly scheduled SUPERSONIC airliner, a joint Anglo-French venture that went into service in 1976.

Condon Report, 1969 review of sightings of UNIDENTIFIED FLYING OBJECTS, prepared by Edward U. Condon.

Condor Legion, a German air force group supporting the Nationalists in the SPANISH CIVIL WAR. Germany sent an estimated 100 airplanes, including bombers, in a rehearsal for World War II.

Congo (People's Republic of the Congo), until 1958 the French Middle Congo colony, becoming autonomous as the Republic of the Congo in 1958 and a fully independent state on August 15, 1960. In 1963 the country became a one-party state and in 1969 added "People's" to its name.

Congo (Zaire) Civil War (1960–67), conflict that began with Congolese independence on June 30, 1960, with immediate army rebellions and secessionist movements. The most important of them was secession of the province of Katanga on July 11, led by Moïse TSHOMBE and supported by Belgian

troops and industrial interests. President Joseph KASAVUBU asked for and received a UNITED NATIONS peacekeeping force, which stayed until 1964, ultimately numbering 20,000. Prime Minister Patrice LUMUMBA sought Soviet help in 1960, was dismissed by Kasavubu, and fled from a coup led by army commander Joseph MOBUTU. Lumumba set up a rival government in Stanleyville but was captured and then, in 1961, murdered while in prison in Katanga. The UN force fought Tshombe in Katanga; on September 17, 1960, UN Secretary-General Dag HAMMARSKJÖLD died in a plane crash over the Congo while en route to negotiate a ceasefire with Tshombe. UN forces took Katanga in 1963, Tshombe fleeing abroad, and withdrew from the Congo in 1964, although other insurgencies continued. Kasavubu brought back Tshombe as his prime minister in 1964, used Belgian troops and mercenaries against insurgents, and dismissed Tshombe in 1965 for alleged electoral fraud. He was himself dismissed on November 25, 1965, with Mobutu openly taking power and creating a one-party state. In 1967 his government survived a mercenary revolt and an attempted exile force invasion from Rwanda.

Congress of Industrial Organizations (CIO), a U.S. labor organization that began in 1935 as a group of AMERICAN FEDERATION OF LABOR (AFL) unions seeking to organize American industrial workers into industry-wide unions that included both the skilled and unskilled, a radical departure from the craft union philosophy of the AFL. The Committee for Industrial Organizations, led by John L. LEWIS, was formed in 1935; with the help of favorable NEW DEAL labor legislation, it successfully organized unions in several mass-production industries, most notably the automobile and steel industries. Its organizing efforts gained great impetus from the successful automobile industry SIT-DOWN STRIKES of 1936 led by Walter REUTHER, while Philip MURRAY led the steelworkers, and Sidney HILLMAN of the Amalgamated Clothing Workers organized the CIO's very active

Political Action Committee. Led successively by Lewis, Murray, and Reuther, the CIO soon rivaled the AFL in membership and power. During the post–World War II period, however, the CIO split over COLD WAR political matters, expelling 11 of its affiliated unions during 1949–50 as Communist-dominated while in the same period losing much of its ability to organize the unorganized, in a more conservative political climate. Walter REUTHER led the CIO into a merged AFL-CIO in 1955, though he and his United Automobile Workers (UAW) left the merged federation in 1968.

Congress of Racial Equality (CORE), U.S. civil rights organization founded in Chicago in 1942 by James Farmer, it used such tactics of nonviolent confrontation as desegregating biracial sit-ins and FREEDOM RIDES to great effect during the 1960s. Floyd McKissick became CORE chairman in 1966, the organization thereafter becoming much less nonviolent, often joining the STUDENT NON-VIOLENT COORDINATING COMMITTEE (SNCC) and the BLACK PANTHERS in violent confrontations.

Congress party (Indian National Congress), Indian majority party, the socialist party of Mahatma GANDHI, Jawaharlal NEHRU, Indira GANDHI, and Rajiv GANDHI. Formed in 1885 as a movement to win greater Indian representation in the British-Indian political process, the party strongly protested the partition of Bengal in 1905 and demanded home rule in 1906 and full self-determination for India in 1918. It became the main vehicle of the Indian independence movement in the 1920s, identifying with the SAT-YAGRAHA civil disobedience movement of Mahatma GANDHI and in 1929, under the leadership of Jawaharlal NEHRU, beginning to call for full Indian independence. Its entire leadership was imprisoned during World War II after pressing in 1942 for immediate British withdrawal from India. During the postwar period the party emerged to lead India to independence, with Nehru as India's first prime minister. During the leadership of Indira Gandhi there were major party splits in 1969 and

1978, with the party ultimately coalescing around her once again, as the Indian National Congress—Indira, later led by her son, Prime Minister Rajiv Gandhi.

Connally, John Bowden (1917–), U.S. lawyer, who became secretary of the navy in 1961 and was Texas governor 1962–68; on November 22, 1963, he was seriously wounded during the assassination of President John F. Kennedy. He was secretary of the treasury 1971–72 and an unsuccessful Republican presidential candidate in 1980.

Connolly, James (1868–1916), Irish Republican leader, a socialist, leader of the 1913 Dublin general strike, an organizer of the IRISH CITIZEN ARMY, and as its leader one of the organizers of the EASTER RISING. He was executed in Dublin on May 12, 1916.

Connor, Eugene "Bull," Birmingham, Alabama, police commissioner during the 1963 civil rights campaign led by Martin Luther KING, Jr. in that city. Connor became a symbol of southern racism; the newsphoto of one of his police dogs attacking a child aroused worldwide revulsion and condemnation.

Conservative Party, in Britain, for most of the 19th century, the Tory party of Peel and Disraeli. In the early 20th century it was until 1922 the Conservative and Unionist Party, for its alliance with 19th-century Liberals who had split with their party on the issue of Irish Home Rule. After 1922, it became the sometimes reformist-minded Conservative party of BALDWIN, CHAMBERLAIN, CHURCHILL, EDEN, MACMILLAN, HEATH, and Margaret THATCHER, who has been viewed by many other leaders of her party as far more conservative than any of the other post–World War II leaders of the party.

conspicuous consumption, phrase coined by U.S. economist Thorstein VEBLEN, in his book, *The Theory of the Leisure Class* (1899), both phrase and book sharply criticizing what he saw as the conscienceless overconsumption and overdisplay of the American rich of his time. The phrase was seen as apt and went into the language.

containment, the U.S. post–World War II attempt to hold the Communist countries to their existing borders, a key strategy in the COLD WAR. It was first put into practice in the TRUMAN DOCTRINE of 1947, which was quickly followed by the MARSHALL PLAN, in 1948.

continental drift, geological theory that the continents move around the Earth, having some 200 million years ago been one huge continent now called Pangaea. Though jigsaw-like correspondences between the old and new worlds had long been remarked, Alfred WEGENER first formally proposed the continental drift theory in 1912. It was treated with skepticism and downright ridicule until the 1950s, when new geological evidence and later the theoretical mechanism of PLATE TECTONICS began to support it.

contraceptive pill, alternate name for birth control pill.

Contras U.S.-supported Nicaraguan guerrilla armies fighting on against the SANDINISTA government after the defeat of the SOMOZA government during the NICARAGUAN CIVIL WAR. As U.S. support was withdrawn, the Contra position became untenable, and the cease-fire of March 1988 effectively ended the war. Supply of the Contras was a key motor behind the events in the IRAN-CONTRA AFFAIR. Low-level Contra military operations continued during 1989 and early 1990.

Cooley, Denton Arthur (1920–   ), U.S. cardiologist who did key work in early OPEN-HEART SURGERY, in 1955 developing a widely used heart-lung bypass machine. An assistant to Alfred BLALOCK at the first BLUE BABY operation in 1944, he performed many operations to cure congenital heart defects in infants. He also implanted the first artificial heart in a patient, in 1969, replacing it with a human heart after 5 days, but the patient, Haskell Karp, died a day later.

Coolidge, Calvin (1872–1933), U.S. lawyer, a Republican Massachusetts state senator (1912–15), lieutenant governor (1916–19), and governor (1919–21), who as governor broke the BOSTON POLICE STRIKE, thereby achieving national prominence. He became vice-president in 1921 and succeeded to the presidency on the death of Warren G. HARDING on August 2, 1923, as the 30th president of the United States. He defeated Democrat John W. DAVIS and Progressive Robert M. LAFOLLETTE for the presidency in 1924, then served a full term. His presidential years were clouded by the TEAPOT DOME and other scandals, and by the continuing investigations and prosecutions they generated, although he was not personally involved. As president, he exerted little impact on the course of his times, allowing the economic overheating that characterized the boom of the late 1920s to proceed unchecked, continuing immigration restriction, and limiting his domestic efforts to relatively minor administrative and regulatory matters. His attempts to foster international peace and disarmament helped bring about the KELLOGG-BRIAND PACT of 1928 and the DAWES PLAN regarding German war reparations, both of which seemed major accomplishments at the time but were soon overtaken by events abroad.

Coral Sea, Battle of the (May 7–8, 1942), the first U.S.–Japanese aircraft carrier battle of the Pacific in World War II, in which the failure of the seemingly successful Japanese attack at PEARL HARBOR began to appear. In terms of losses the battle was inconclusive; of two American carriers the *Lexington* was sunk and the *Yorktown* damaged, and of two Japanese carriers, the *Shoho* was sunk. Thereafter, both fleets broke off the action. But the Japanese could not then go forward, aborting their planned landings at Port Moresby.

CORE, the initials of the CONGRESS OF RACIAL EQUALITY, a leading CIVIL RIGHTS MOVEMENT organization of the 1960s.

Cori, Carl Ferdinand (1896–1984) and **Gerty Theresa Radnitz Cori** (1896–1957), Czech-American husband-and-wife medical biochemists, who worked out the series of chemical reactions by which the body metabolizes carbohydrates. The Cori cycle, by which glycogen is converted ultimately into lactic acid and energy, was the work for which they shared the 1947 Nobel Prize for Physiology or Medicine with Bernardo A. Houssay.

Corona, Juan, U.S. mass murderer, a Mexican labor contractor in Yuba County, California, who was convicted of murdering 25 Mexican migrant workers 1970–71. In 1973 he was sentenced to 25 consecutive life terms of imprisonment.

coronary bypass, operation performed using open-heart surgery in which an unclogged blood vessel "harvested" from the leg is placed in a patient's heart to reroute blood from a clogged artery. Based on earlier work in surgical opening of blocked heart arteries, notably by Michael DE BAKEY in 1964, the coronary bypass was first performed by U.S. surgeon Rene Favalaro in 1967. Coronary bypasses were widely performed for decades, although partly supplanted from 1977 by BALLOON ANGIOPLASTY.

Coronel, Battle of (November 1, 1914), the World War I sinking of two British cruisers by a German squadron off Coronel on the west coast of Chile.

Corregidor, siege of (April–May 1942), early World War II successful assault by Japanese forces on the island fortress off Bataan peninsula in the Philippines. After a siege that lasted almost a month, Corregidor's defenses were almost destroyed by heavy bombardment, and its defenders had almost run out of food, water, and munitions.

cortisone, type of vital HORMONE produced by the adrenal glands just above the kidneys. After much work on animals by many scientists, Frank A. Hartman first posited correctly that Addison's disease was caused by lack of cortisone (1927). In 1935 American biochemist Edward Calvin Kendall isolated cortisone, and the following year Polish-Swiss chemist Tadeusz Reichstein worked out its structure. But cortisone did not have a major impact on society until 1948, when U.S. physician Philip Showalter Hench first used it successfully to treat

rheumatoid arthritis, for which he shared the 1950 Nobel Prize for Physiology or Medicine with Kendall and Reichstein. Since it became commercially available in 1949, cortisone has been used to treat a wide range of ailments; as a STEROID it has been subject to abuse in some quarters.

Cosa Nostra (Our Thing), an alternative name for the U.S. MAFIA.

cosmic rays, RADIATION from outer space, first detected during balloon flights in 1911 by Victor Hess and named by Robert A. MILLIKAN. Before these discoveries scientists believed all radiation came from earth.

Cote D'Ivore (Ivory Coast), a French colony until autonomy was granted in 1958. On August 7, 1960, the country became an independent state, led by President Felix HOUPHOET-BOIGNY, national leader from 1944. He presided over a one-party state thereafter.

Coughlin, Charles Edward (1891–1979), Detroit Catholic priest who became a national figure as a pro-fascist, anti-Semitic broadcaster in the 1930s. His publication *Social Justice* was ultimately denied mailing privileges by application of the Espionage Act, and the Catholic Church silenced him in 1942 with World War II in progress.

Council For Mutual Economic Assistance (COMECON), an international mutual economic assistance organization established in 1949 by the Soviet Union and its Eastern European allies, which since then has expanded to include Cuba and Vietnam, with some participation by several other countries, including Yugoslavia, Mexico, Finland, Iraq, and several third world countries such as Nicaragua and Laos.

Council of Europe, an international body established by 11 Western European nations in 1949; by 1989, a 21-nation organization composed of a Parliamentary Assembly and several specialized bodies. It is particularly active in the area of human rights: the European Court of Human Rights and the European Commission of Human Rights were established in 1953 under the terms of the European Convention for the Protection of Human Rights and Fundamental Freedoms.

counterculture, the radical, "antiestablishment" youth culture of the 1960s and early 1970s, which focused on alternative lifestyles, new musical modes, and sometimes on HALLUCINOGENIC and other mood-altering drugs and stressed the value of a simple, very personally oriented life. Its most radical exponents, the HIPPIES, sought the simplest possible lives, away from modern industrial society, often retreating into rural communes and such urban enclaves as San Francisco's Haight-Ashbury district and New York City's East Village.

Courant, Richard (1888–1972), German-American mathematician who, from 1934 to 1958, raised to world-class caliber New York University's Courant Institute of Mathematical Sciences, so named on his retirement. A student of David HILBERT, Courant was a key figure in applied mathematics, influencing two generations of mathematicians—in Germany before the rise of the Nazis and then in America.

Cousteau, Jacques-Yves (1910–), French sea explorer and environmentalist, who became internationally famous for his pioneering underwater photographs, television pictures, and films. While working with the French Navy, 1930–57, Cousteau and Émil Gagnan developed (1943) the AQUALUNG used by underwater divers, also called SCUBA GEAR (for self-contained underwater breathing apparatus). In 1948 Cousteau helped test Auguste PICCARD's BATHYSCAPE, later developing a jet-propelled version of it and making other innovations that led to long-term underwater stays and enhanced knowledge of the underwater world. Associated with Monaco's Museum of Oceanography from 1957, Cousteau led many expeditions, which spawned not only films but also books, including *The Silent World* (1953) and *The Living Sea* (1963), both written with others.

Covenant of the League of Nations, the document establishing the LEAGUE OF NATIONS; it was signed at the PARIS PEACE CONFERENCE OF 1919 and ultimately by 63 nations, though never by the United States.

Coventry, British Midlands city that was very heavily bombed 1940–41, as part of the German terrorist bombing campaign. The city thereafter became a symbol of British resistance to the Nazis; it was completely rebuilt after the war. Long after the war it was learned that the British had been forewarned of heavy attacks on Coventry (German codename MOONLIGHT SONATA) planned for November 14–15, 1940, but dared not display any foreknowledge because that might risk disclosing the existence of crucial ULTRA information gained from the breaking of the ENIGMA code.

Cox, Archibald (1912–), U.S. lawyer, Harvard Law School professor 1946–61 and 1965–76, and U.S. solicitor-general 1961–65, who was the WATERGATE special prosecutor in 1973. In that position he played a major role in the exposure and resignation of president Richard M. NIXON and in the successful prosecution of many of Nixon's associates. He was fired in the SATURDAY NIGHT MASSACRE.

Cox, James Middleton (1870–1957), U.S. journalist, Democratic Ohio congressman (1909–13), and twice governor (1913–15, 1917–21), a liberal who became his party's unsuccessful nominee for the presidency in 1920; his vice-presidential candidate was Franklin Delano ROOSEVELT. He campaigned as a supporter of Woodrow WILSON's programs and ideals, including U.S. membership in the LEAGUE OF NATIONS, and was defeated by Warren G. HARDING in a landslide. He then finished his term as Ohio governor and left public life.

Crash, the, popular name for the precipitous U.S. stock market decline of late October 1929 that triggered the GREAT DEPRESSION of the 1930s, the worst day being BLACK TUESDAY, October 29.

Crash of 1987, the U.S. stock market crash of October 19, 1987, BLACK MONDAY, in which the Dow Jones industrial average declined 508.32 points in a single day, or 22.6%, on a volume of 604.33 million shares; both decline and volume were single-day records. In August the Dow had reached 2722; by the end of the trading day, October 19, it had declined to 1738, a total loss of 983 points. Stocks in other world markets followed suit, but no further large decline or substantial recession followed. Instead, the stock markets soon rebounded.

Crater, Joseph Force (1889–1937), New York supreme court justice who disappeared on August 6, 1930, and was subsequently the subject of a grand jury investigation and an enormous amount of media speculation for many years. He was never seen again.

creationism, belief that humans were specially created by God, rather than evolving, as Darwin suggested; an old idea strongly revived among fundamentalist Christians in the 20th century. The 1925 SCOPES TRIAL was an early attempt to ban the teaching of evolution in schools. From the 1920s, creationists pressured local schools, with some success, to stop teaching evolution. Periodically, notably from the 1960s, creationists have tried to gather scientific support for their view, advancing an alternative view they call creation science and lobbying to have that view taught as equal with evolution in science classes. By the 1980s they were succeeding in many parts of the United States and in some other places as well.

credit cards, plastic cards with preprinted magnetic strips offered by banks and businesses, often associated with credit lines, and used in place of cash or checks to pay for goods and services; a basic ingredient in the envisioned checkless society. Available since the 1950s but with major growth in the late 1960s, bank credit cards also allow individuals to do ELECTRONIC BANKING. Because counterfeit and stolen cards became a problem, some firms replaced magnetic strips with more personalized data, such as a digitized fingerprint or a photograph, especially one produced by a HOLOGRAPH process.

Crerar, Henry Duncan Graham (1888–1965), Canadian general who in 1945 commanded Canadian and other Allied forces pushing into southern Germany.

Crete, invasion of (May 20–31, 1941), World War II taking of the Mediterranean island by a heavy German airborne assault, the first major assault of its kind in the history of warfare. German parachute troops encountered strong British and Greek resistance, but with complete control of the air they were able to win the battle. Some of the defenders were ultimately evacuated by sea.

Crick, Francis Harry Compton (1916–   ), British molecular biologist and co-discoverer (with James D. WATSON) of the DOUBLE HELIX form taken by the DNA molecule, the substance that carries and duplicates basic hereditary information. He shared the 1962 Nobel Prize for Physiology or Medicine with Watson and Maurice WILKINS.

Cripps, Stafford (1889–1952), British lawyer, who in 1930 became solicitor general in Ramsey MACDONALD's cabinet, later breaking with MacDonald. He became an MP in 1931 and was a leading anti-fascist and radical socialist throughout the 1930s. He was expelled from the Labour Party in 1939 for advocating a popular front with the Communists, and readmitted in 1945. Cripps was Churchill's ambassador to the Soviet Union in 1940; he was in Churchill's cabinet from 1942 and was a leading member of ATTLEE'S cabinet and of the Labour party during the post–World War II period, resigning as chancellor of the exchequer in 1950 due to illness.

critical mass, sufficient amount of fuel, such as URANIUM 235 (U-235), to support a self-sustaining CHAIN REACTION in NUCLEAR FISSION, first achieved in 1942 by Enrico FERMI.

Croatia, at the turn of the century, part of Hungary, within Austria-Hungary. The region became part of Yugoslavia after World War I; Croatian nationalists undertook worldwide terrorist operations during the interwar period. During World War II a fascist puppet government ruled Croatia;

afterward the region became part of the Yugoslavia again, and worldwide Croatian terrorist operations resumed.

Croce, Benedetto (1866–1952), Italian historian and humanist philosopher, one of the most respected intellectuals in Italian life from the 1890s until his death. Although at first somewhat equivocal regarding the rise of Italian fascism, he soon came to oppose it fully, but because of his standing he was not imprisoned. He participated in the negotiations leading to the resignation of the king and the establishment of democracy in post–World War II Italy and was a member of the Italian government in 1944.

Croix de feu (Cross of Fire), a French monarchist, fascist veterans' organization of the interwar period that, with smaller French fascist organizations, engaged in demonstrations and street fighting, some of it anti-Jewish, especially in the early 1930s. After such organizations were outlawed in 1936, its influence and membership declined; it did not reappear after World War II.

Cronkite, Walter Leland, Jr. (1916–   ), U.S. journalist and broadcaster; as a political reporter for CBS 1950–62 and chief anchor 1962–81, he covered and interpreted most of the main stories of three decades, becoming in the process the best known TELEVISION newscaster of his time and a powerful free press advocate and much sought-after source of media coverage.

Crossbow, Operation, a series of World War II Allied bombing raids on missile launching sites in Western Europe during late 1943 and early 1944.

Cross of Gold, speech by William Jennings BRYAN to the Chicago Democratic Convention of 1896 that helped secure his nomination. It became a populist rallying slogan in that campaign and during the early years of the 20th century. The phrase was taken from "You shall not crucify mankind on a cross of gold."

CRT, popular shorthand for CATHODE-RAY TUBE, a type of ELECTRON TUBE used as the viewing monitor used in TELEVISION, COMPUTERS, and RADAR.

Crystal Night (*Kristallnacht*, November 9–10, 1938), night named after the broken glass that littered the streets of cities, towns, and villages throughout Germany, when the windows of Jewish-owned businesses, homes, and synagogues were smashed in a massive Nazi pogrom that left many dead, an estimated 30,000 Jews imprisoned, and thousands of structures destroyed.

Ctesiphon, Battle of (November 22–26, 1915), World War I battle in which British forces in Mesopotamia moved up the Tigris River in the spring of 1915 toward Kut, Ctesiphon, and Baghdad. They took Kut in late September, then advanced and met superior Turkish forces at strongly defended Ctesiphon. The Turks won the battle, the British suffering 4,600 casualties out of a total force of 11,000 and then retreating to Kut.

Cuba (Republic of Cuba), after the Spanish-American War and the American occupation formally an independent nation from 1902 but a de facto U.S. protectorate until 1934. On January 1, 1959, after the victory of the CUBAN REVOLUTION led by Fidel CASTRO, Cuba became a one-party socialist state, declaring itself a Communist state in 1961.

Cuban Missile Crisis (October 22–November 2, 1962), a major threat of nuclear war between the United States and the Soviet Union arising from a Soviet military build-up in Cuba that included missile sites and the arrival of Soviet bombers able to carry nuclear weapons. On October 22, U.S. president John F. KENNEDY, in a nationally televised address, announced a blockade of Cuba, demanded the removal of such offensive weapons from the island, and declared that any nuclear attack originating in Cuba, on any Western Hemisphere nation, would be considered a Soviet attack on the United States that would set off nuclear war. The United States then prepared to invade Cuba. On October 23 the Soviet government alerted its armed forces. Premier Nikita

KHRUSHCHEV and President Kennedy then negotiated Soviet withdrawal, which was unconditional; Kennedy announced the end of the crisis on December 2, with Soviet dismantling of the missile launching sites and withdrawal of bombers in progress.

Cuban occupations, occupation of Cuba by U.S. troops, from the end of the Spanish-American War in 1898 until May 1902, leaving under the terms of the Cuban–Amercan Treaty of 1903, which made Cuba an American protectorate. The U.S. base at Guantánamo was acquired at this time. From 1906 to 1909, U.S. troops occupied Cuba once again, to prevent an impending revolution and to maintain Cuba's status as a protectorate. In 1917, U.S. troops landed again, this time staying briefly to quell an insurrection in progress.

Cuban Revolution (1956–59), a guerrilla insurgency led by Fidel CASTRO against the government of dictator Fulgencio BATISTA, which began with the return by sea of a small group led by Castro on December 2, 1956. After an initial defeat, the remnants of the group fled to the Sierra Maestra, grew in the course of conducting a 2-year guerrilla insurgency, and came down out of the mountains as a small guerrilla army in October 1958. Castro's forces then took Cuba, against very light resistance, entering Havana on January 8, 1959, then taking power and ultimately turning Cuba into a Communist state.

cult of personality, phrase coined by Soviet premier Nikita KHRUSHCHEV to describe the public glorification of Joseph STALIN, in his speech to the 20th Congress of the Communist Party of the Soviet Union, in February 1956

Cultural Revolution (Great Proletarian Cultural Revolution), the 1966 campaign and massive set of purges initiated by MAO ZEDONG, in which he attempted to decisively change China into an entirely egalitarian society, to that end developing the RED GUARDS, and initiating their disastrous attack on Chinese society and culture.

Cunningham, Andrew Browne (1883–1963), British admiral who saw service in World War I, and was Mediterranean fleet commander at the outbreak of World War II. His naval air arm sank three Italian battleships at TARANTO and scored other victories over the numerically superior Italian fleet early in the war, fought a losing battle against superior German airpower thereafter, and from the 1943 Allied invasion of North Africa controlled the Mediterranean. He later became First Sea Lord.

Cuomo, Mario (1932–   ), U.S. lawyer, New York State secretary of state 1975–79, lieutenant-governor 1979–82, and governor from 1982. A leader of the liberal wing of the Democratic party, Cuomo seemed by far the strongest contender for the presidential nomination of his party in 1988 but refused to run.

Curie, Irène, original name of Irène JOLIOT-CURIE, daughter of Marie and Pierre CURIE.

Curie, Marie Sklodowska (1867–1934), Polish-French chemist who was the only person to receive two Nobel prizes in science. Much of her early work on RADIOACTIVITY was done in the 19th century with her husband Pierre Curie (1859–1906); they and Antoine Henri Becquerel shared the Nobel Prize for Physics in 1903, the year she completed her doctoral dissertation. After Pierre's accidental death in 1906 she took his professorship at the Sorbonne, the first woman to teach there, and 5 years later was awarded the 1911 Nobel Prize for Chemistry for discovering two new elements, radium and polonium. She continued to explore radioactivity, especially its applications to medicine, until she died of leukemia (as later did her daughter, Irène JOLIOT-CURIE), presumably caused by her long-term exposure to radioactivity.

Curtin, John Joseph (1885–1945), Australian Labour journalist, who became a Labour member of parliament (1928–31, 1934–45), party leader (1934–45), and wartime prime minister (1941–45). He led his country through World War II while laying the groundwork for the social welfare and socialist programs fostered by his party in the postwar period.

Curtis, Charles (1860–1936) U.S. lawyer, Kansas Republican congressman (1892–1906), senator (1907–13, 1915–29), and Herbert HOOVER'S vice-president (1929–33).

Curtiss, Glenn Hammond (1878–1930), aviator-mechanic, who in 1911 developed the first practical seaplane and invented the aileron, a key device for AIRPLANE stability. Before turning to aeronautics Curtiss put engines on bicycles and set a land speed record on the resulting motorcycle. He became a celebrity in 1908 when he won a *Scientific American* prize for making the first public flight of more than a kilometer in his self-designed airplane, the *June Bug,* and in 1910 he won a $10,000 prize for a daring flight from Albany to New York City. He opened the first flying school in 1909, and his factories made hundreds of military airplanes for use in World War I. His NC-4 "flying boat," built for the Navy, made the first trans-Atlantic crossing in 1919. For a time in bitter litigation with the Wright brothers, the two sides later joined to form a single company.

Curzon, George Nathaniel (1859–1925), British aristocrat, who became greatly interested in east and south Asia in the late 1890s, writing three books on his travels. He then moved into diplomacy, becoming undersecretary of state for India in 1891 and viceroy of India 1898–1905, until a dispute with his commander-in-chief in India, Lord KITCHENER, forced his resignation. As viceroy he played a major role in developing further British penetration into China, Tibet, and Central Asia, also making it possible for archeologist Aurel STEIN and others to rediscover earlier civilizations and to take away massive numbers of artworks. He was part of the ASQUITH and LLOYD GEORGE cabinets during World War I and foreign secretary to Lloyd George 1919–23, in that position influencing the postwar settlements in Europe and the Middle East.

Curzon Line, the provisional Polish eastern frontier declared by the Allies in 1919; the border was not accepted by Poland, which fought for and won much more territory to the east during the SOVIET–POLISH WAR of 1920.

Cushing, Harvey Williams (1869–1939), U.S. neurosurgeon who pioneered in the study of the pituitary gland. In a key 1912 work on the pituitary he identified a previously unknown disorder, now called Cushing's disease. A professor and surgeon long associated with Harvard, he did extensive work on brain tumors and developed new techniques for brain and spinal cord surgery.

cybernetics, comparative study of communications systems in living organisms and machines, aimed at better understanding and control of both, especially through the use of FEEDBACK. The term was coined by Norbert WEINER in 1948 from the Greek for "the science of steering ships."

cyclotron, first of the circular, rather than linear, ACCELERATORS; invented by U.S. physicist Ernest O. LAWRENCE in 1930, it used electromagnetic fields to speed up atomic PARTICLES.

Cyprus, long a part of the Ottoman Empire, then a British colony during World War I, remaining so until formation of the independent REPUBLIC OF CYPRUS on March 13, 1960, led by Archbishop MAKARIOS III. Greek–Turkish communal conflicts led to informal but firm partition of the island in 1967. The 1974 Turkish invasion of the island in support of Cypriot Turks led to establishment of the TURKISH REPUBLIC OF NORTHERN CYPRUS.

Cyprus, Turkish invasion of (1974), seizure of much of northern Cyprus by Turkish armed forces, effectively partitioning Cyprus between its majority Greek and minority Turkish populations; the partition continued.

Cyprus Civil War (1963–64), the escalation of long-standing low-level guerrilla conflict between the Greek majority and the Turkish minority on Cyprus into full-scale civil war in late December 1963. In late March 1965, the UNITED NATIONS responded with a peacekeeping force, but Turkish air attacks in early August nearly brought about war between Greece and Turkey, which was averted by a UN-arranged cease-fire.

Cyrankiewicz, Josef (1911–89), Polish socialist and underground newspaper editor early in World War II, imprisoned by the Nazis 1941–45. He became secretary-general of the Communist Socialist Party in 1945 and was prime minister 1947–52 and 1954–70, though at no time exercising substantial power in Poland.

Czech coup of 1948 (February 1948), Communist takeover of the democratic Czech government; it was directed by Klement GOTTWALD and took the form of a government reorganization. President Eduard BENES resigned; Foreign Minister Jan MASARYK stayed on for a few weeks and then died in a fall from a window of the foreign ministry.

Czech Legion, military force operating in eastern Russia and Siberia during the RUSSIAN CIVIL WAR, composed of 40,000–70,000 former Czech and Slovak prisoners of war who were being repatriated through Vladivostock in the spring of 1918 but were blocked by BOLSHEVIK forces. They formed themselves into an army, took substantial portions of the Trans-Siberian Railroad, and supported White forces against the Bolsheviks.

Czechoslovakia (Czechoslovak Socialist Republic), until independence in 1918 part of the Austro-Hungarian Empire, then a republic led by Tomás MASARYK. The country fell to Nazi Germany in 1938 after the MUNICH AGREEMENT. In 1945 the republic was reestablished but lasted only 3 years. In 1948 a one-party Soviet-bloc Communist state was established, which was challenged sharply only in 1968, when Alexander DUBCEK led a reform government, triggering a Soviet invasion. In late 1989, the massive changes of the GORBACHEV era swept through Eastern Europe, and Czech democracy reemerged, as a bloodless revolution swept away the Communist government. On November 17, student protesters were attacked by riot police in Prague; by November 23 Alexander DUBCEK was addressing mass meetings of hundreds of thousands of pro-democracy protesters in Prague. On December 28, Dubcek became chairman of the newly democratic Czech parliament. On December 29, dissident playwright Vaclav HAVEL became the first non-Communist president of Czechoslavakia since 1948.

Czechoslovakia, Soviet invasion of (August 1968), occupation of Czechoslovakia by an estimated 400,000 Soviet and Soviet-allied troops, beginning on August 20, 1968. The action ended the PRAGUE SPRING, an attempt by Alexander DUBCEK and his associates to liberalize Czech society.

Czolgosz, Leon (1873–1901), assassin of U.S. president William MCKINLEY at the Buffalo Pan-American Exposition on September 6, 1901. An anarchist who stated that he had killed McKinley for political reasons, Czolgosz was executed on October 29, 1901.

D

Dahomey, the former name of BENIN (People's Republic of Benin), which was a French colony until August 1, 1960.

Daladier, Édouard (1884–1970), French teacher and socialist, in parliament from 1919, who served in many French cabinets during the 1920s and 1930s and was French premier January–October 1933 and January–February 1934. He was premier once again from 1938 to 1940, and in September 1938 signed the MUNICH AGREEMENT, which allowed the destruction of Czechoslovakia by the Germans and was a major step toward World War II. He was imprisoned by the VICHY government and the Germans during World War II, then from 1946 to 1958 was back in parliament.

Dalai Lama, Fourteenth (1935–   ), Tibetan religious and political ruler from 1940 until he fled to India in 1959, following a Tibetan insurrection against Chinese rule; from that time he was head of the Tibetan exile community in northern India. He was awarded the Nobel Peace Prize in 1989.

Dalkon Shield, type of INTRAUTERINE DEVICE (IUD) for contraception, implanted in an estimated 5 million women 1971–74, that greatly enhanced the possibility of pelvic infection, with resultant miscarriages, birth defects, chronic illness, infertility, and sometimes death. The A. H. Robins Company, which had manufactured and distributed the Dalkon Shield, became the target of many thousands of lawsuits filed by women who had been damaged. Ultimately, a major trust fund was set up to settle these monetary claims, with Robins and its insurer contributing to the fund, though money could in no way compensate for much of the dam-

age that had been done to the women, children, and families involved.

Dalmatia, at the turn of the century, part of Austria-Hungary. After Austrian defeat in World War I, Dalmatia was divided between Italy and Yugoslavia, was occupied by German forces during World War II, and became part of Yugoslavia again after the war.

Dan, Takuma (1858–1932), key Japanese ZAIBATSU leader, head of Mitsui, whose murder by Japanese nationalist assassins in 1932 was a milestone on the road to Japanese militarism and World War II.

Danbury Hatters' case (*Loewe* v. *Lawlor*, 1908), a landmark U.S. Supreme Court decision that outlawed a national boycott organized against a Danbury, Connecticut, hat manufacturer by the United Hatters of North America, as a conspiracy in restraint of trade.

Daniel, Yuli (1925–89), Soviet dissident of the early 1960s, a writer and poet whose work satirized and criticized the repressive aspects of Soviet society. Despite worldwide protests he and his colleague, Andrei Sinyavsky, were imprisoned 1966–70 for their dissidence. Their trial signaled the end of the Soviet "thaw" of the period.

Danilof, Nicholas, a *US News & World Report* correspondent who had been arrested in Moscow and who, in an arrangement by the United States and the Soviet Union in 1986, was exchanged for Gennadi F. ZAKHAROV, a UNITED NATIONS employee, who had been arrested and charged as a spy in New York.

D'Annunzio, Gabriele (1863–1938), Italian writer, nationalist, and then fascist, who saw service in World War I and led the small private army that took disputed Fiume in 1919. In 1921 the Italian army ejected his forces from Fiume. Thereafter, he became a fascist, strongly and publicly supporting MUSSOLINI until his death.

Danny the Red, the popular name of 1960s left student leader Daniel COHN-BENDIT.

Danzig (Gdansk), the Polish city on the Baltic that had long been occupied by Germany prior to World War I and became a free city during the interwar period that followed. It was a source of continuing German–Polish tension; a March 1939 attempt to annex Danzig and the POLISH CORRIDOR was blocked by Great Britain. With the September 1939 invasion of Poland, continuing British guarantees of Polish independence brought the onset of World War II.

D'Aquino, Iva Ikuko Toguri, the real name of World War II Japanese propagandist TOKYO ROSE.

Darkness at Noon, influential 1940 novel by ex-Communist Arthur Koestler that exposed STALIN's GREAT PURGE trials, portraying the experience through the eyes of an old Bolshevik enmeshed in the political charade of a forced confession.

Darlan, Jean François (1881–1942), naval officer who commanded the French fleet during World War II and collaborated with the Nazis after the fall of France. He held several positions in the VICHY government, including naval minister and commander in chief of all French forces. He was in Algiers when Allied forces landed in North Africa in 1942. He then negotiated an arrangement with General Dwight D. EISENHOWER, in command of the invasion force, by which Darlan called for French forces to lay down their arms throughout North Africa in return for being named head of government in French North Africa. He was assassinated on December 24, 1942.

Darrow, Clarence Seward (1857–1938), leading labor lawyer of the early 1900s and later defense attorney in some of the best-known cases of the century. As a labor lawyer he defended Eugene V. DEBS during the Pullman STRIKE of 1894. In 1907 he cleared IWW leader William "Big Bill" HAYWOOD of a charge of murder and later represented the MCNAMARA brothers, who pleaded guilty to the 1910 LOS ANGELES TIMES BOMBING. Darrow's labor clients blamed him for causing the McNamaras to plead guilty, and labor then abandoned him to fight charges of jury tampering on his own, refusing to pay his fee, and causing him in turn to refuse future labor clients. In 1924 he defended LEOPOLD AND LOEB and in 1925 was attorney for the defense in the SCOPES TRIAL (the "monkey trial") in Tennessee, the defense and case for which he is best known. Spencer Tracy portrayed Darrow in the 1960 film *Inherit the Wind*.

Dart, Raymond A. (1893–1988), Australian–South African anatomist and physical anthropologist, who in 1924 discovered the first fossilized early human skull in South Africa, naming its species *Australopithecus africanus*, and who used his anatomical knowledge to postulate that the being walked on two legs, not four. Dart's theories that his species was a "missing link" between humans and apes and the corollary that humans developed in Africa, were at first greeted with scorn, but they inspired numerous fossil hunters, such as Louis and MARY LEAKEY, in the years after World War II.

date that will live in infamy, a, phrase from U. S. president Franklin Delano ROOSEVELT's address to Congress on December 8, 1941, after the Japanese attack on PEARL HARBOR; from "Yesterday, December 7, 1941—a date that will live in infamy—the United States of America was suddenly and deliberately attacked by naval and air forces of the Empire of Japan."

Daud Khan, Sardar Mohammad (1909–78), Afghan officer, a member of the royal house, who became defense minister 1946–53, premier 1953–63, and leader of the revolution that toppled the monarchy in 1973, then becoming president of the new Afghan republic. He was assassinated in 1978 when a left-led military coup overthrew his government.

Daugherty, Harry Micajah (1860–1941), U.S. lawyer, Ohio state legislator (1890–1894), and manager of Warren G. HARDING'S successful 1920 campaign for the presidency, who in 1921 became U.S. attorney general and was widely charged with complicity in the TEAPOT DOME and other Harding administration scandals. He was never successfully impeached, survived two court trials, and continued to maintain his innocence of all charges.

Davis, Angela (1944–   ), former professor of philosophy at the University of California, Black militant, and Communist, who was indicted for murder, conspiracy, and kidnapping for allegedly supplying the guns used by Jonathan Jackson during the 1970 shootings at the Marin County, California, courthouse, in which Judge Harold Haley and two inmates were killed and District Attorney Gary Thomas paralyzed. Davis became a fugitive, was later captured in New York City, and was then held without bail in California; a worldwide "Free Angela" movement eventually forced local authorities to grant bail. She was acquitted on all of the counts in the indictment.

Davis, Benjamin Oliver (1877–1970), U.S. officer, who saw service in the Philippines during the Spanish-American War, spent much of the interwar period as a military science teacher, and in 1940 became the first Black general in the U.S. army. He saw European service in World War II as army race relations advisor.

Davis, John William (1873–1955), U.S. lawyer, West Virginia Democratic congressman (1911–13), solicitor-general and diplomat during the administrations of Woodrow WILSON, and unsuccessful Democratic presidential candidate who was defeated by Calvin COOLIDGE in 1924.

Dawes, Charles Gates (1865–1951), U.S. lawyer and banker, who was President William MCKINLEY'S comptroller of the currency, chief purchasing agent for the U.S. Army in France during World War I, and budget director in the HARDING administration. He worked out the DAWES PLAN regarding German reparations in 1924 and won a Nobel Peace Prize for it in 1925. He was Calvin COOLIDGE'S vice president (1925–29).

Dawes Plan (1924), a plan that resulted in the temporary stabilization of the German economy by arranging a package of international loans to Germany, amounting to almost 17 billion gold marks, which enabled the German government to comply with the reparations provisions of the Treaty of VERSAILLES; named after Charles Gates DAWES, U.S. banker, who was vice president 1925–29.

Dawn Man, alternate name for *Eoanthropus dawsoni*, popularly called PILTDOWN MAN, early human-like fossil remains found in 1911–12 but proved fraudulent in the 1950s.

Day, Dorothy (1897–1980), U.S. journalist and socialist, who became a Catholic in 1927 and in 1932 became part of a Catholic settlement house movement. She was cofounder of the pacifist and later antinuclear *Catholic Worker*, which became identified with her views and the many causes she espoused for the rest of her life. In later years it became a forum for those seeking change within the Catholic Church.

Dayan, Moshe (1915–81), Israeli officer, who saw service in the HAGANAH and with the British army during World War II. He was a Haganah officer during the ISRAELI WAR OF INDEPENDENCE (FIRST ARAB-ISRAELI WAR), commanding Israeli forces during the losing battle for Jerusalem. He was chief of staff 1953–58, commanding Israeli forces during the SINAI–SUEZ WAR (SECOND ARAB-ISRAELI WAR) of 1956. Going into politics, he became a MAPAI party agriculture minister 1959–64, was defense minister 1967–74, and foreign minister 1977–79. He then resigned, differing with Menachim BEGIN'S harsh treatment of the Palestinian population of the WEST BANK.

D-Day (June 6, 1944), the date of the Allied NORMANDY invasion in World War II.

DDT (dichlorodiphenyltrichloroethane), powerful, widely used insecticide banned in the 1970s; best known of many environmental chemicals whose promise was later found to have a darker side. Known from the 19th century, DDT was discovered in 1939 to be a powerful insecticide, by Swiss chemist Paul Müller, who won the 1948 Nobel Prize for Physiology or Medicine. Widely used by Allied armies in World War II and then by the general public, especially in agriculture, by the 1960s DDT was found to concentrate in the environment's food chains, proving toxic to many living things, especially thinning the shells of birds' eggs and leaving some species in danger of extinction; as a result DDT was banned by many countries, by the United States starting in 1972.

Dead Sea Scrolls, ancient leather-and-papyrus writings found in desert caves overlooking the Dead Sea in modern Israel; the first group was found in Qumran Cave in 1947 by some young shepherds. Most date from the first century B.C. to the mid-first century A.D., a few to the third century B.C. All are rare documents and include copies of books of the Bible centuries older than any previously known. They are of immense value to religious and secular scholars in shaping their view of the pivotal history of the time.

Dean, John Wesley III (1938–), U.S. lawyer, a figure in the WATERGATE scandal, who was counsel to president Richard M. NIXON 1970–73. In 1973 he became a key Senate Watergate committee witness, charging Nixon and other conspirators with complicity in the affair. In October 1973, he pleaded guilty to conspiracy charges, ultimately serving 4 months in prison, and was disbarred. He wrote two books on Watergate: *Blind Ambition* (1976) and *Lost Honor* (1983).

death camps, a synonym for the German CONCENTRATION CAMPS.

Death's Head Battalion, a section of the German SS, that provided the CONCENTRATION CAMP personnel who committed mass murder during the Nazi era.

death squads, bands of assassins, often operating as paramilitary units, and often with covert government support, whose role is to terrorize political opponents, as in Argentina during the DIRTY WAR period of the late 1970s and early 1980s and in El Salvador during the 1980s civil war. The term is a recent one; the technique is not.

Deaver, Michael K. (1938–), U.S. political figure, a personal assistant to Ronald REAGAN 1967–85, who became a lobbyist after leaving the White House in May 1985. In 1987 he was convicted of perjury in connection with his lobbying activities, and in 1988, after losing his Supreme Court appeal on the validity of the applicable lobbying law, he received a suspended sentence, was fined $100,000, and was barred from lobbying for 3 years.

De Bakey, Michael Ellis (1908–), U.S. surgeon, who in 1967 first implanted an ARTIFICIAL HEART in a patient, using it to aid the patient's own heart for 4 days. De Bakey earlier contributed to the heart-lung machine—an external artificial heart—that allowed modern OPEN-HEART SURGERY. In the mid-1950s he also pioneered in the use of artificial tubes to replace damaged human blood vessels, and in 1964 in the surgical opening of a blocked aorta, leading to the CORONARY BYPASS procedure.

De Broglie, Louis Victor Pierre Raymond (1892–1987), French physicist, who first posited the wave nature of particles in 1923 and won the 1929 Nobel Prize for Physics. Inspired by early work in QUANTUM THEORY and by Arthur Holly COMPTON's assumption that light—long thought to be a wave—had particle-like qualities, his theory was confirmed in 1927 by experimental measurements that established WAVE-PARTICLE DUALITY.

Debs, Eugene Victor (1855–1926), U.S. railroad worker, who became a labor leader and the leading American socialist of his time. In 1893 he organized the American Railway Union, the first major industrial union in the United States, which was destroyed in the course of the Pullman Strike of 1894. Debs became a socialist while in jail after that strike. He was Social-Democratic presidential candidate in 1900, led in the organization of the SOCIALIST PARTY in 1901, and was Socialist presidential candidate in 1904, 1908, 1912, and 1920, receiving over 900,000 votes in the elections of 1912 and 1920, the 1912 total being more than 6% of the total vote. He strongly opposed U.S. participation in World War I and was imprisoned for that opposition in 1918, receiving a ten-year sentence that was commuted in 1921. He thereafter continued to work as a socialist writer and leader.

Decline of the West, a thesis positing democracy as decadent in historical terms and urging Germans to end the democracy of the WIEMAR REPUBLIC in favor of authoritarianism; it was advanced by Oswald SPENGLER in his 1922 book of that name. The attack and theory helped pave the way for German fascism.

Deep Sea Drilling Project (DSDP), organized effort to take core samples from seabeds worldwide, using pipes punched deep into the earth. The U.S. drilling ship *GLOMAR CHALLENGER* (1968–83) supplied geological information on the development and resources of the Earth.

Deep Throat, Bob Woodward's informant on the WATERGATE scandal, one of the chief characters in Woodward and Carl BERNSTEIN's book *All the President's Men* (1974), about their uncovering of the scandal. Nicknamed after a popular pornographic film of the period, Deep Throat was someone who apparently had access to extremely confidential information up to the highest levels of the White House. Again and again, he (or she) led Woodward and Bernstein further into the unfolding Watergate story, though never completely revealing every aspect. At first Woodward and Deep Throat communicated by telephone. Later, as the scandal deepened, Deep Throat became alarmed, would not use the telephone, and met with Woodward in secluded places, including the garage featured in the Robert Redford-Dustin Hoffman film of the book, with Hal Holbrook playing Deep Throat. The identity of Deep

Throat has never been revealed, though years later guesses continue to abound.

De Forest, Lee (1873–1961), electrical engineer and inventor, who developed the triode ELECTRON TUBE, basic to the growth of ELECTRONICS. A pioneer of WIRELESS telegraphy and early RADIO, De Forest made contributions both to radio engineering and to its public popularity. After World War I he developed a sound system for motion pictures, demonstrating it first in 1923, though it was put into effect much later. He also worked in many other areas, including TELEVISION and RADAR.

De Gasperi, Alcide (1881–1954), Italian political leader, who successfully worked for the reunification of his native Trento with Italy and entered the Italian Chamber of Deputies in 1921. From 1922 he opposed fascism as leader of the Popular party, was imprisoned twice, and from 1931 worked in the Vatican Library. During World War II he organized the illegal Christian Democratic party and was premier 1945–53, the years of renascent Italian democracy. In that position he built a series of center coalitions, moved Italy toward the European Coal and Steel Community, the forerunner of the EUROPEAN COMMUNITY, and took the Western side in the cold war, opposing communism and refusing to include the Italian Communist party and other far left forces in the Italian government.

De Gaulle, Charles André Joseph Marie (1890–1970), French officer, who saw service in World War I, became a war prisoner at VERDUN, and continued his army career during the interwar period while writing several books on military matters. A tank force colonel at the beginning of World War II, he quickly became a brigadier general and member of the French cabinet. Fleeing to Great Britain rather than surrender in 1940, he there organized the FREE FRENCH movement. In 1943 and 1944 he emerged as leader of the French government-in-exile, and on August 25, 1944, led the parade that celebrated the LIBERATION OF PARIS. He headed the first postwar provisional government of France but resigned in January 1946 when overruled as taking an antidemocratic view on matters relating to the form of the coming Fourth Republic. He then retired from public life, having failed in an attempt to rally support in 1947. On June 1, 1958, at the height of the civil disturbances generated by the ALGERIAN WAR OF INDEPENDENCE, and with civil war threatening France, he became premier, developing a new constitution. In September the constitution was accepted; in January 1959 he became president of the Fifth Republic. He then took several steps to stablilize the French economy, including devaluation of the franc. Internationally, he took a sharply independent course, fostering the development of French atomic weapons, expelling NATO forces, opposing British COMMON MARKET entry, and in several other ways moving away from Great Britain and the United States. During 1960 and 1961 he suppressed French civil and military insurrections in Algeria and in 1962 agreed to Algerian independence; in the same period he began the liquidation of all former French colonial arrangements in Africa. Economic problems and widespread student demonstrations preceded his resignation in January 1969.

Deir Yasin, small Palestinian Arab village near Jerusalem. On April 9, 1948, during the ISRAELI WAR OF INDEPENDENCE (FIRST ARAB–ISRAELI WAR), IRGUN ZVAI LEUMI and STERN GANG units attacked Deir Yasin, killing all 254 of its inhabitants, most of them noncombatant men, women, and children.

De Leon, Daniel (1852–1914), U.S. orthodox Marxist, who became a leader of the Socialist Labor Party in the 1890s and joined William D. HAYWOOD and Eugene V. DEBS in founding the INDUSTRIAL WORKERS OF THE WORLD (IWW) in 1905; he left in 1908 in a doctrinal dispute.

Dellinger, David (1915–   ), U.S. pacifist and peace activist, who became a leading opponent of the VIETNAM WAR; beginning in 1965 he helped to organize what became massive antiwar demonstrations. He was convicted with the rest of the CHICAGO SEVEN after the CHICAGO DEMOCRATIC CONVENTION of 1968; the conviction was later reversed.

Demara, Ferdinand, U.S. man dubbed by the media as the "Great Imposter" who, during the 1940s and 1950s, falsely posed as a professional in a considerable body of occupations, many of them requiring great skill and some requiring certification. He posed, for example, as a surgeon, a psychology professor, a cancer researcher, and a clergyman, apparently practicing all or most of his professions rather competently; but he was often caught and in several instances imprisoned.

Demjanjuk, John, TREBLINKA concentration camp guard known as "Ivan the Terrible," who was extradited from the United States to Israel in 1986, charged with DEATH CAMP crimes, and sentenced to death by an Israeli court on April 25, 1988.

Democratic party, one of the two major U.S. political parties, formally adopting the name in 1840. During the 20th century, the party has been in power 40 of 89 years, during the presidencies of Woodrow WILSON, Franklin D. ROOSEVELT, Harry S. TRUMAN, John F. KENNEDY, Lyndon B. JOHNSON, and Jimmy CARTER. It has been a party of shifting coalitions. By far the most successful of these was the Roosevelt coalition, which joined emerging ethnic and labor groups to existing big city machines, the then-solid Democratic South, and a national liberal constituency within the context of the GREAT DEPRESSION and World War II. After the 1950s that coalition eroded, with suburbanization, the growth of a prosperous middle class, and population shifts; it also splintered over the issues raised by the CIVIL RIGHTS MOVEMENT and the VIETNAM WAR. A new set of political alignments developed with Black enfranchisement, coupled with the emergence of a new conservatism; the "solid" Democratic South then became an almost-solid Republican South, and the net result was Republican occupancy of the White House 1968–76 and 1980–90.

Democratic People's Republic of Korea, the portion of Korea above the 38th parallel that became an independent state on September 9, 1948. Continuing tension between the two Korean states led in 1950 to the KOREAN WAR, involving the United States, the UN, and China; it was followed by a decades-long stalemate between the two Koreas.

democratic centralism, the wholly misleading term used by LENIN to describe the main feature of Communist Party discipline in his era: the concerted, undeviating execution of all party decisions by members, however those decisions were derived and without regard to personal agreement with those decisions.

dendrochronology, system of dating based on tree rings—the wood laid down by annual growth—which vary year by year according to conditions and form a distinctive pattern; a technique developed and named about 1920 by Andrew Ellicott DOUGLASS. Starting with living trees, scientists could work their way backward, matching the tree-ring patterns from trees of varying age, well over 3,000 years, a technique of great use in archaeology as well as forestry.

Deng Xiaoping (T'eng Hsiao-ping; 1904–), leader of the PEOPLE'S REPUBLIC OF CHINA who became a Communist while in France in the 1920s and was a Communist Party instructor and political commissar during the the CHINESE CIVIL WAR. In 1934 he made the LONG MARCH north with MAO ZEDONG and the other leaders of Chinese communism. After 1949 he continued to rise in the Chinese government, was purged during the CULTURAL REVOLUTION of the late 1960s, and was then rehabilitated in 1973. He and ZHOU ENLAI then led the moderates in China, but he was purged again in 1976 after Zhou's death. When JIANG QING and what came to be known as the GANG OF FOUR lost power after Mao's death in 1976, Deng was once again rehabilitated. He moved into effective leadership of China and from that position of strength directed the country into its modern course, which included a major opening to the west

during the 1970s, normalization of relations with the Soviet Union (as signaled by the GORBACHEV visit of 1989) and extensive economic reforms. He also fostered much increased freedom of expression in China but resisted the liberalization of Chinese political institutions, taking the conservative side in the crisis generated by the CHINESE STUDENT DEMONSTRATIONS of 1989.

Denikin, Anton (1872–1947), Czarist army officer and general of the White armies fighting in the Don region during the RUSSIAN CIVIL WAR; his forces were defeated by late 1919, and he went into exile.

Dennis v. United States (1951), a landmark U.S. Supreme Court decision, sustaining as constitutional the conviction of 11 Communist Party leaders under the conspiracy provisions of the SMITH ACT and effectively outlawing the Communist party. A major MCCARTHY period decision, for some years it greatly diminished First Amendment free speech guarantees.

DES (diethylstilbestrol), synthetic ESTROGEN; from 1940 prescribed for many pregnant mothers to prevent miscarriage. It was banned by the FDA in 1971 after evidence emerged that the daughters of those mothers later tended to develop otherwise rare cancers of the reproductive organs.

DeSalvo, Albert H. (1933–73), killer known as the Boston Strangler, who sexually assaulted and then strangled 13 women from June 1962 through January 1964; he ultimately confessed to the crimes. He was murdered in his jail cell in 1973.

desaparacios (the disappeareds), the estimated 40,000 Argentinians murdered by the DEATH SQUADS during the DIRTY WAR conducted by Argentina's military government 1976–82.

Desert Fox, The, the popular name of World War II German general Erwin ROMMEL.

Desert One (April 24–25, 1980), code name for the aborted U.S. armed forces attempt to rescue the American hostages held by Iran during the IRAN HOSTAGE CRISIS; helicopter breakdowns in sandstorms caused cancellation of the operation, and eight lives were lost in an airplane collision.

de-Stalinization, the several processes involved in ending the unrestrained secret police reign of terror that was a main feature of Soviet life from the early 1930s until the death of Joseph STALIN in 1953. In 1956, with KHRUSHCHEV'S SECRET SPEECH, the attack on Stalin, his methods, and some of his old associates became explicit, as Nikita Khrushchev sought to destroy the Stalinist CULT OF PERSONALITY.

Destroyers for bases swap (September 1940), World War II American-British agreement by which the United States supplied Britain with 50 American destroyers in return for bases on British territories in the Western Hemisphere; in reality, a gift of badly needed destroyers to Britain, then engaged in the Battle of the ATLANTIC.

détente, the long-term attempt to relax the Soviet-American COLD WAR tensions that nearly brought the world to nuclear war during the CUBAN MISSILE CRISIS of 1962. The approach dates from 1962; the use of the term détente to describe it was most pronounced in the early 1970s, a period of thaw in Soviet-American relations, thought at the time to be leading to the end of the cold war. President Richard M. NIXON and Secretary of State Henry KISSINGER adopted the concept as basic U.S. policy and with U.S.S.R. premier Leonid BREZHNEV fostered it in a series of three NIXON-BREZHNEV SUMMITS.

deterrence, a nuclear age theory postulating that the way to avoid massive nuclear war between the United States and the Soviet Union is to maintain so strong a nuclear arsenal as to make general nuclear war too costly to seriously contemplate; it is the major theory governing the development of the superpower nuclear arsenals in the modern period.

deuterium, ISOTOPE of hydrogen, with twice the mass of ordinary hydrogen, like TRITIUM a form of heavy hydrogen; discovered by Harold C. UREY in 1931. Deuterium was soon being used as a radioactive tracer in the study of biochemical reactions in living tissue. Later it was used as an energy source in the HYDROGEN BOMB or in a NUCLEAR FUSION generator and also in HEAVY WATER—water made with high proportions of deuterium replacing regular hydrogen—used in NUCLEAR REACTORS.

De Valera, Eamon (1881–1975), Irish Republican leader, who became first president of the Irish Republic in April 1919 while in prison. He escaped from prison and spent the balance of the IRISH WAR OF INDEPENDENCE raising money and support abroad. He and his supporters did not accept the peace of 1921, with its partition of Ireland, but lost the resulting IRISH CIVIL WAR to the Irish Free State forces led by Michael COLLINS. He was then jailed for a year, but in 1926 accepted the settlement and founded the Fianna Fail party, becoming Irish prime minister in 1932. He held that post for 21 of the next 27 years.

Dewey, John (1859–1952), U.S. philosopher and educator, advocate of "democracy in education," the title of his seminal book, published in 1916. His views, most often called "instrumentalist," developed in part from the pragmatism of William JAMES and provided the basis for much 20th-century teaching practice, which stressed the educational value of practical experience while rejecting the rote learning and and other authoritarian classrooom practices of an earlier day. His thinking also provided much of the basis for the "progressive education" and "vocational training" movements, both of which he sharply criticized for too often dispensing with what he considered the essential cultural and historical elements necessary for liberal education in a democracy.

Dewey, Thomas Edmund (1902–71), U.S. lawyer, prosecutor, three-term governor of New York (1942–54), and twice unsuccessful Republican presidential candidate (1944 and 1948). In 1935, while an assistant U.S. attorney for the southern district of New York, he became nationally recognized as a successful prosecutor of organized crime and municipal corruption. He was elected

Manhattan district attorney in 1937, nearly won the Republican presidential nomination in 1940, and won his first gubernatorial election in 1942. But he was defeated for the presidency by Franklin Delano ROOSEVELT, who won his fourth term in 1944, and again by Harry S. TRUMAN in 1948 in a very close election—so close that many newspapers erroneously announced Dewey's victory on the night of the election.

Diamond Sutra, oldest full printed book known, dating from 868 A.D., sealed in a cave near China's old Silk Road in the 11th century, rediscovered by a Chinese monk in about 1904, and taken out of China shortly thereafter by Marc Aurel STEIN.

Diamond v. *Chakrabarty,* key case establishing that genetically engineered biological organisms could be patented under U.S. federal law. The subject was a microbe, *Pseudomoma originosa,* genetically engineered by a General Electric employee, Ananda M. Chakrabarty, from four different strains of bacteria; it was intended to break down crude oil. The parties to the case changed several times, but in 1980 the Supreme Court ruled that GE could patent the microbe. GENETIC ENGINEERING firms rejoiced while critics warned that Aldous Huxley's *BRAVE NEW WORLD* had finally arrived.

Díaz, Porforio (1830–1915), Mexican lawyer, who fought in the Mexican-American war and became a revolutionary general in the army of Benito Juárez. Díaz took power by force in 1876 and ruled Mexico until 1911. In those years he brought increased economic development to Mexico, often at the expense of the Mexican peasantry and urban poor. In 1908 he announced a new era of democracy for Mexico and in 1910 allowed Franciso MADERO to run against him for the presidency; but when threatened with defeat he arrested Madero and thousands of his supporters and had himself declared victor in the election. Madero fled to Texas, from there organizing the armed revolt that in May 1911 forced Diaz to resign.

Diefenbaker, John George (1895–1979), Canadian lawyer, in parliament 1940–79, who became Conservative party leader in 1956 and was prime minister 1957–63, losing his party leadership in 1967. In office he encountered substantial economic problems and a growing French-Canadian separatist movement, and for a time resisted U.S. pressure to arm Canada-based MISSILES with nuclear warheads.

Diem, Ngo Dinh (1901–63), Vietnamese political leader, who became South Vietnamese prime minister in 1954, in the last BAO DAI government, and then president of South Vietnam in 1955. He then became military dictator of the country, with his brother, Ngo Dinh Nhu, functioning as head of his secret police. After a series of internal conflicts, the last of them with Buddhist organizations, a group of generals, operating with U.S. approval, deposed him on November 1, 1963. He and his brother were killed on November 2.

Dien Bien Phu, Siege of (March–May 1954), the decisive battle of the FRENCH-VIETNAMESE WAR, in which this heavily fortified Laos-Vietnam border town, with a French garrison of 16,000, was successfully besieged by the North Vietnamese army. The French had seriously underestimated the relative strengths of the two forces, trapping their own forces in a position that could be supplied only by air and could not be relieved by available French forces. After surrender of the remaining French forces, the French agreed to withdraw from Vietnam.

Dieppe Raid (August 19, 1942), a World War II cross-Channel raid by almost 6,000 Canadian and British troops. The attack failed, with more than 3,000 casualties and the loss of much equipment, as the invading force was quickly repelled by German shore defense units.

Dies, Martin, Jr. (1901–72), U.S. congressman, who in 1938 organized the first HOUSE COMMITTEE TO INVESTIGATE UN-AMERICAN ACTIVITIES (HUAC), which during his tenure as its head was known as the Dies Committee. Dies and his committee strongly attacked President Franklin Delano ROOSEVELT, the NEW DEAL, THE CONGRESS OF INDUSTRIAL ORGANIZATIONS (CIO), and a host of other individuals and organizations as pro-Communist. In this he was warmly supported by some of those most vigorously opposed to New Deal social programs and to the principle of labor organization, and he was simultaneously sharply attacked by very substantial forces drawn from throughout the political spectrum, who described his tactics as those of the witchhunt.

digital computer, type of COMPUTER that deals in discrete variables, such as numbers or on-off signals; in contrast to ANALOG COMPUTERS, which work with continuous variables, such as temperature or voltage. The first fully electronic DIGITAL COMPUTER was the ATANASOFF-BERRY COMPUTER (ABC), built 1937–42. An electromechanical computer, the MARK I, was built in the United States 1939–44. In 1943 a British team headed by Alan TURING built the all-electronic COLOSSUS, designed to break German codes. In the United States, the ENIAC, long regarded the first fully electronic computer in America, was built 1942–46. Most 20th century computers are of the digital type.

Dillinger, John Herbert (1903–34), U.S. midwestern murderer and bank robber of the early 1930s, whose jailbreaks, gun battles, and series of confrontations with a publicity-seeking FEDERAL BUREAU OF INVESTIGATION brought him national publicity as "Public Enemy Number One." He was killed by FBI agents in Chicago on July 22, l934.

Dimitrov, Georgi Mikhailovich (1882–1949), Bulgarian Communist organizer, who in 1933 was accused by the Nazis of responsibility for the REICHSTAG FIRE and won his release after a trial that generated worldwide attention. He headed the COMINTERN 1934–43, signaling a major Communist strategic turn in 1935 in his UNITED FRONT speech. He took power in Bulgaria

after Soviet occupation in 1945 and was prime minister 1946–49.

dioxin, family of highly poisonous, carcinogenic compounds, one of which (2,3,7,8-tetrachlorodibenzo-P-dioxin, or 2,3,7,8-TCDD) is considered to be one of the most dangerous of chemicals in TOXIC WASTE DUMPS. Dioxin was a key constituent of the herbicide code-named AGENT ORANGE, employed as a defoliant by the U.S. Army in the VIETNAM WAR. It also figured in numerous cases of toxic chemical waste problems, notably at LOVE CANAL, TIMES BEACH, Missouri, and in SEVESO, Italy.

diphtheria, widespread, much-feared childhood disease for which the SCHICK TEST was developed in 1913.

Dirac, Paul Adrien Maurice (1902–84), British mathematical physicist, who first predicted the existence of ANTIMATTER. Inspired by Louis DE BROGLIE'S work on the wave properties of fundamental particles like ELECTRONS, from the late 1920s Dirac worked to develop the mathematical implications and underpinnings of wave mechanics in QUANTUM THEORY. In 1928 his work led him to suggest that the electron had a twin with an opposite charge, this positron (originally called an antielectron) being discovered in 1932 by U.S. physicist Carl D. Anderson. Dirac shared the 1933 Nobel Prize for Physics with Erwin SCHRÖDINGER, with whom he worked at the Dublin Institute for Advanced Studies from 1940.

dirigible, cigar-shaped, balloon-like airship filled with a lighter-than-air gas, either hydrogen (very light but highly flammable) or helium (nonflammable but not as light). The first rigid dirigible was built by German Count Ferdinand von ZEPPELIN in 1900; dirigibles were sometimes called zeppelins in his honor. The British *R34* dirigible crossed the Atlantic in 1919; the German *Graf Zeppelin* circled the globe 10 years later. From 1932 to 1937, the *Graf Zeppelin* and the *Hindenburg* were in regular trans-Atlantic service from Frankfurt-am-Main, Germany, to the U.S. and Brazil. But in 1937 the hydrogen-filled *Hindenburg* exploded on being moored at Lakehurst, New Jersey, killing 36 people. This disaster and a general vulnerability to storms effectively ended dirigible development, though nonrigid, helium-filled dirigibles called blimps remained in small-scale use.

dirty tricks campaign, a series of actions directed against political opponents of U.S. president Richard M. NIXON, organized by Donald Segretti, who was employed by Nixon's subordinates; part of the series of related scandals exposed as the WATERGATE affair unfolded.

dirty war (1976–82), a campaign of state terrorism, carried out by Argentina's military government against all opponents of the regime, which resulted in the murders of tens of thousands of Argentinian citizens, called the DESAPARACIOS (the disappeareds), some estimates running as high as 40,000. Upon restoration of democracy in 1983 the new government moved to prosecute some of those responsible for the mass murders.

disappeareds, the, English translation of the term DESAPARACIOS, referring to the many Argentinians murdered by the government 1976–82.

Dixiecrats, Southern Democrats who bolted their party in 1948, refusing to accept the civil rights plank in the Democratic platform that year and running their own candidates, J. Strom Thurmond and Fielding Wright, for the presidency and vice-presidency. The Thurmond-Wright ticket won 39 electoral votes and polled over 1.1 million votes but failed to stop the election of Harry S. TRUMAN to the presidency.

Djibouti (Republic of Djibouti), until the achievement of national independence on June 27, 1977, a French colony, known until 1967 as French Somaliland and as the Territory of the Afars and Issas 1967–77. The new country was from the beginning a one-party state, led by president Hassan Gouled Aptidon.

Djilas, Milovan (1911–   ), Yugoslav lawyer, writer, World War II partisan fighter, and Communist leader who was closely associated with TITO during and after World War II. In 1954 he became Yugoslavia's best-known dissenter and then became a world figure with publication of *The New Class* (1957), which was followed by other highly critical works; he was imprisoned 1956–61 and 1962–66.

DMZ (Demilitarized Zone), a 5-mile-wide buffer zone between North and South Vietnam, established by the French-North Vietnamese GENEVA ACCORDS of 1954. It became a front line and the site of a series of battles during the VIETNAM WAR.

DNA (deoxyribonucleic acid) **and RNA** (ribonucleic acid), molecules that make up GENES and carry basic hereditary information, first discovered and explored chemically in 1909 by Phoebus Aaron Theodor Levene. Erwin SCHRÖDINGER, in his 1944 work, *What Is Life?*, outlined how a set of chemical codes might determine genetic inheritance, inspiring further work on the structure of DNA. Building on earlier studies of DNA by British researchers Maurice WILKINS and Rosalind FRANKLIN, using X-RAY CRYSTALLOGRAPHY, an unorthodox pair of molecular biologists—American James WATSON and British Francis CRICK—worked at Cambridge University's Cavendish Laboratory in the early 1950s, seeking to clarify the molecular structure of the gene, especially how it replicated itself. In 1953 they found their answer: the DNA was made up of two strands of paired molecules in a twisting, ladder-like form called a DOUBLE HELIX. The DNA passes on "instructions" to RNA, which reproduces itself by duplicating the paired molecules, an understanding worked out in the 1960s by various scientists, including Jacques MONOD. DNA and RNA are the very stuff of life and represent the "genetic code" that determines the characteristics of living beings, as was confirmed by Charles Yanofsky's research team in 1967. In that year other researchers demonstrated that the same basic DNA code is used by Earth's various forms of life, and a team headed by Arthur Kornberg succeeded in synthesizing active DNA. Meanwhile others (including Crick) continued to work out the actual codes being used and to identify GENETIC MARKERS, parts of a DNA molecule linked with a specific genetic disease or defect. GENETIC ENGINEERING developed in 1973; strands of DNA are "cut and pasted" into new forms, the result being RECOMBINANT DNA.

doctor's plot (1953), the arrest of nine Soviet doctors in January 1953, six of them Jewish, who were collectively charged with and confessed to the murder of Communist Party leader Andrei ZHDANOV in 1948 and also confessed to conspiracy to murder many other Soviet leaders. Nikita KHRUSHCHEV, in his 1956 SECRET SPEECH, called the "plot" a plan by Joseph STALIN to begin a massive new Soviet purge with strongly anti-Semitic features. Stalin soon died, however; his secret police chief, Lavrenti BERIA, declared that the doctors' confessions had been elicited by torture and were false. Two doctors died in prison; the others were released. Beria was arrested in June 1953 and executed.

Doctor Zhivago (1957), a Boris PASTERNAK novel celebrating the triumph of the individual artist's will to be free over the coercive power of the Soviet state. The book took as its period the years before and during World War I, followed by the RUSSIAN REVOLUTION and CIVIL WAR. The work, banned in the Soviet Union, was published abroad, becoming a best-seller in many languages and achieving wide underground circulation in the Soviet Union. Pasternak was awarded the 1958 Nobel Prize for Literature but was forced to refuse it. In 1965 the book was adapted for film by David Lean.

Doenitz, Karl (1891–1980), German naval officer, who became a submarine commander in World War I, and who in 1936 became commander of the submarine section of the German fleet. During World War II he commanded the German submarine campaign, and became naval commander-in-chief in January 1943. After the death of Adolf HITLER, Doenitz claimed for a week to be German chancellor and unsuccessfully tried to negotiate peace with the Allies, surrendering unconditionally on

May 7, 1945. He was sentenced to a 10-year term of imprisonment after his conviction at the NUREMBERG WAR CRIMES TRIALS in 1946.

Dole, Elizabeth Hanford (1936–   ), U.S. lawyer and Republican political leader, a member of the Federal Trade Commission 1973–80, transportation secretary 1983–87, and labor secretary from 1989. She is the wife of Republican senate leader Robert DOLE.

Dole, Robert Joseph (1923–   ), U.S. lawyer, Kansas Republican congressman 1961–69, and senator from 1969. Dole was chairman of the Republican National Committee 1971–73 and Senate minority leader from 1985. A longtime and powerful Republican leader, Dole was his party's vice-presidential candidate in the lost 1976 presidential campaign, sought the presidential nomination in 1980 and 1988, and was for a time in 1988 the frontrunner. He is married to Elizabeth Hanford DOLE.

Dollfuss, Engelbert (1892–1934), Austrian politician, who became chancellor in 1932 and ended Austrian democracy in 1934, outlawing all parties but his own and forcibly suppressing the Social Democratic protests that followed, killing and jailing many of the protesters. With Italian fascist support he resisted German annexation pressures but was assassinated by Austrian Nazis during a failed coup attempt on July 25, 1934.

Dominica (Commonwealth of Dominica), until 1978, a British colony, with internal autonomy from 1967 and full independence and COMMONWEALTH membership from November 3, 1978.

Dominican Republic Civil War (1965–66), conflict that started with a revolt in late April 1965 against the military government that had come to power in the coup that toppled the elected government of Juan BOSCH in 1963. Although the aim of the revolt was to restore constitutional government, accusations of Communist influence on the rebel forces led President Lyndon JOHNSON to intervene against the revolutionaries, sending in a U.S. force within a few days. American troops numbered almost 21,000 by late May. As ORGANIZATION OF AMERICAN STATES (OAS) peacekeeping forces began to arrive, some American troops were withdrawn. Fighting continued after establishment of a provisional government in August 1965 and came to an end after the election of June 1966, in which Joaquin BALAGUER defeated Juan BOSCH; constitutional government was then restored.

Dominican Republic interventions, actions in the Dominican Republic, beginning in 1905 with a U.S. takeover and administration of Dominican Republic customs duties and with American investment and presence thereafter increasing. U.S. forces openly occupied the country 1916–24. In 1965 President Lyndon B. JOHNSON sent U.S. forces to intervene once again, during the DOMINICAN REPUBLIC CIVIL WAR.

domino theory, the belief of some Americans that the loss of South Vietnam to the North Vietnamese Communist government would inevitably lead to Communist conquest of the other countries of Southeast Asia; the belief was not borne out by subsequent developments.

Dona Paz **sinking** (December 20, 1987), sinking of the inter-island ferry *Dona Paz* after it collided with the oil tanker *Victor* in Philippine waters. At least 1,750 on the overcrowded ferry were killed, and the death toll may have been as high as 3,000, as passenger lists were far from complete. It was the 20th century's worst peacetime maritime disaster.

Donovan, William Joseph "Wild Bill" (1883–1959), U.S. lawyer and army officer, who saw service in Mexico and in World War I. In the mid-1930s, at Franklin Delano ROOSEVELT'S request, he began to plan the intelligence organization that in 1942 became the World War II OFFICE OF STRATEGIC SERVICES (OSS), the forerunner of the CENTRAL INTELLIGENCE AGENCY (CIA). He operated as the freewheeling head of the OSS during World War II.

Dooley, Thomas Anthony (1927–61), U.S. physician, who devoted his life to improving medical care in Southeast Asia. Treating Vietnamese refugees first in 1954 while a U.S. Navy medical officer, Dooley organized camps and medical services in Haiphong, as detailed in *Deliver Us from Evil* (1956). As a private citizen Dooley (with Peter D. Comanduras) founded an international organization for medical aid, called Medico. Using royalties from his books and contributions to Medico, he founded hospitals and medical missions in various parts of Cambodia, Laos, and Vietnam until felled by cancer.

Doolittle raid (April 18, 1942), the bombing of Japanese cities, including Tokyo, by carrier-based B-25 bombers led by Lieutenant Colonel James Doolittle; a largely symbolic action, aimed at building Allied morale during the most difficult days of World War II in the Pacific.

Dorpat, Treaty of (October 1920), recognized the independence of Finland and Estonia after their respective wars of independence.

double helix, twisting, ladder-like form, made up of two strands of paired molecules; the basic structure of DNA, discovered by Francis CRICK and James WATSON in 1953.

Douglas, Helen Gahagan (1900–80), U.S. actress, a Broadway star in the early 1920s, who appeared in movies during the 1930s and went into California politics as a liberal Democrat in the late 1930s. She was a California congresswoman 1945–50, giving up her seat to run for the Senate against Richard M. NIXON in 1950. Nixon successfully attacked her liberal record, strongly implying that Douglas was a Communist, tactics that worked extremely well during the McCARTHY period. Nixon won the election; Douglas did not again run for public office. She was married to actor Melvyn Douglas.

Douglas, William Orville (1898–1980), U.S. lawyer, law professor, author, and chairman of the SECURITIES AND EXCHANGE COMMISSION 1937–39. He was appointed to the Supreme Court by Franklin D. ROOSEVELT in 1939. During his 36 years on the Court, he strongly defended the Bill of Rights, became one of the Court's leading liberals, and continued to write and travel extensively, until a stroke in 1974 diminished his physical capacity and ultimately caused his retirement in 1975.

Douglass, Andrew Ellicott (1867–1962), U.S. astronomer who, while studying sunspot activity in the American Southwest at the turn of the century, found that tree rings—the wood laid down by annual growth—varied year to year, developing a distinctive pattern. By 1920 he had turned this knowledge into a dating system, dubbed DENDROCHRONOLOGY.

Dowager Empress, Western name for T'SU HSI, the last Manchu ruler of China, who was regent until 1908 and whose conservative policies did much to create the conditions for the CHINESE REVOLUTION OF 1911.

Dresden raids (February 13–14, 1945), Allied bombing attacks on Dresden, Germany, which created firestorms that destroyed much of the city, with an estimated 100,000 deaths and hundreds of thousands of other casualties.

Drew, Charles Richard (1904–50), U.S. physician, who in 1940 first formulated plans for large-scale storage of blood plasma in BLOOD BANKS. At the start of World War II, Drew supervised the blood plasma programs first for Britain, for which blood was collected in America, and then for the United States, directing the American Red Cross's blood donor program from 1941. Ironically, he was at first barred by the Red Cross from donating blood himself, because he was Black; that policy was changed at the protest of Drew and others, though blood from Blacks was still kept separate, apparently at the request of the armed forces. As a result, Drew resigned in protest, to become a teacher.

Drexel, Burnham, Lambert case, charges of multiple, massive securities law violations, brought against Drexel, Burnham, Lambert in September 1988, after a 2-year federal investigation, assisted by convicted stock manipulator Ivan BOESKY; most violations were in connection with its "junk bond" operations, which were headed by Michael MILKEN. Subsequently, Drexel was charged with a series of felony securities frauds; in December 1988, Drexel and the government tentatively agreed to a settlement of all charges, with Drexel paying $650 million and firing Milken, who was later charged on his own.

Druse Rebellion (1925–27), a revolt against French rule by the Druse people of southern Syria, which began in July 1925. The Druses quickly took control of the south and by December had forced the French out of Damascus as well. But French forces armed with modern weapons, including tanks and airplanes, ultimately defeated the Druses. The war ended in June 1927.

Duarte, José Napoleon (1926–90), Salvadoran engineer, a founder of the Christian Democratic party in 1960. Losing in an attempt to take power after a stolen presidential election, he went into exile in 1972, returning after the military coup of 1979, and from 1980 led moderate forces in his country. Strongly supported by the United States, Duarte led the governing junta during the early 1980s and was elected president by those voting in 1984; the insurgents boycotted the election. During the late 1980s, in failing health, he repeatedly attempted to negotiate an end to the El SALVADOR CIVIL WAR but without success.

Dubcek, Alexander (1921–   ), Slovak Communist party leader, a World War II resistance fighter who became a Communist official in 1949, head of the Slovak Communist party in the late 1950s, and first secretary of the Czech Communist party in January 1968. He initiated the PRAGUE SPRING, a series of democratic reforms that were not to be seen again in the Soviet-bloc countries until the GORBACHEV era. After the SOVIET INVASION OF CZECHOSLOVAKIA in August he stayed on as party first secretary but with no real power; he was replaced by Gustav HUSAK in 1969 and was expelled from his party in 1970. In November 1989, he reemerged as one of the leaders of a newly democratic Czechoslovakia. On December 28, 1989, Dubcek was unanimously elected chairman of the Czech parliament.

Dubinsky, David (1892–1982), U.S. garment worker, who became an officer and in 1932 president of the International Ladies Garment Workers Union (ILGWU). He was a key labor member of Franklin Delano ROOSEVELT'S NEW DEAL coalition in the 1930s; a socialist and anti-Communist, he was also in the 1930s a key initiator of New York's Liberal party after a split in the earlier American Labor Party, and in the 1950s he was a founder of AMERICANS FOR DEMOCRATIC ACTION (ADA).

Du Bois, William Edward Burghardt (1868–1963), U.S. teacher, historian, writer, and Black leader, whose *Souls of Black Folk* (1903) was a seminal work in the development of the Black American freedom movement in the 20th century and whose life and work made him one of the foremost Black leaders of the 20th century. He founded the NIAGARA MOVEMENT in 1905 and went with it into the NATIONAL ASSOCIATION FOR THE ADVANCEMENT OF COLORED PEOPLE (NAACP) in 1909, becoming editor of the NAACP's journal, *The Crisis*. He simultaneously became internationally active in the worldwide anti-colonial and PAN-AFRICAN movements of the time. He continued to write throughout his life, exerting a powerful influence on Blacks in America and throughout what came to be known as the THIRD WORLD.

Dubos, René Jules (1901–82), French-American bacteriologist and ecologist, working for over 40 years at the Rockefeller Institute. In 1939 he became the first to seek and find naturally occurring ANTIBIOTICS in the soil. Dubos early became interested in the relationship of humans to their environment, especially how disease results from environmental changes, such as chemical pollution and RADIATION. His ideas on ecology and humanity were expressed in a series of influential books, notably the Pulit-

zer Prize–winning *So Human an Animal* (1968).

Duclos, Jacques (1896–1975), French Communist leader, a founder of his party in 1920 and its head as general secretary 1931–64. He was in the Chamber of Deputies 1926–40 and its vice-president 1936–39, during the Popular Front period. But he fled into hiding in 1939, refusing to support his government during World War II, until the German invasion of the Soviet Union; then he directed Communist RESISTANCE forces inside France. After the war he was in the Chamber of Deputies 1945–58 and the senate 1959–75. He was an unsuccessful candidate for the presidency in 1969. Throughout his career he was an entirely orthodox Communist, supporting the Soviet Union in all matters, though sometimes uncomfortably in periods of relative liberalization.

Dukakis, Michael Stanley (1933–   ), U.S. lawyer, Democratic governor of Massachusetts (1973–77, 1983–   ), who in 1988 was his party's candidate for the presidency, losing to George BUSH, in a campaign notable for its namecalling and "negative" advertising.

Dulles, John Foster (1888–1959), U.S. lawyer and diplomat, who became a leading international lawyer during the interwar period, was active in the formation of the UNITED NATIONS, and was a U.S. delegate to the UN 1946–50. He briefly filled an unexpired Senate term (1949–51) and negotiated the final peace treaty with Japan in 1951. As president Dwight D. EISENHOWER'S secretary of state, 1953–59, Dulles helped to intensify the COLD WAR then in progress, favoring what he described as the necessary diplomatic art of taking his country to the "brink" of war, and developing the doctrine of "massive retaliation," meaning the use of atomic war as a legitimate instrument of national policy.

Dumbarton Oaks Conference (August–October 1944), meeting held at the Dumbarton Oaks estate in Washington, DC, at which representatives of the United States,

Great Britain, the Soviet Union, and the Republic of China planned the structure and main procedures of the UNITED NATIONS.

Dung, Van Tien (1915–   ), North Vietnamese officer, who was a divisional commander during the siege of DIEN BIEN PHU in 1954 and in 1975 commander of the North Vietnamese offensive against the South Vietnamese that ended the VIETNAM WAR; he later became North Vietnamese defense minister.

Dunkirk (May 28–June 4, 1940), the evacuation to Britain of Allied troops, by an improvised flotilla protected by the British navy and air force, after the lost Battle of FLANDERS early in World War II. Those evacuated included 220,000 British troops, much of the BRITISH EXPEDITIONARY FORCE in France; an estimated 130,000 French troops; and a small number of Belgian troops. The evacuation was greatly helped by the German failure to mount a strong ground attack on the remaining Allied beachhead as the evacuation proceeded, relying instead on their air force, which failed to halt or even seriously impede the evacuation.

Dupont Plaza fire (December 31, 1986), a fire that killed 97 people at the Dupont Plaza hotel, in San Juan, Puerto Rico. Subsequent investigation revealed arson by a few dissident union members during a labor dispute.

Dust Bowl, a portion of the south central United States, including parts of Oklahoma, west Texas, Kansas, and several other states, that suffered from both a long drought and the GREAT DEPRESSION during the period 1933–39. The land had been used for grain cultivation during the 1920s and early 1930s but fell into disuse and was not reseeded during the early years of the Depression; its topsoil blew away when the long drought came. More than half of its people were forced to leave, becoming penniless, mostly California-bound migrants, the "Okies" of John Steinbeck's *Grapes of Wrath*. In the early 1940s widespread reseeding reclaimed the land for farming.

Duvalier, François "Papa Doc" (1907–71), Haitian dictator, a physician and public health official before becoming a presidential candidate. After winning the presidential election of 1957 he set out upon a path of ruthless suppression of all opposition. In the process he developed the TONTON MACOUTES, a terrorist secret police. He had himself declared president-for-life in 1964 and arranged a dynastic succession—his son, Jean-Claude ("Baby Doc"), succeeding him as president—an arrangement that lasted until Jean-Claude fled the country in February 1986 during the HAITIAN REVOLUTION.

Dzerzhinsky, Felix Edmundovich (1877–1926), Polish Social Democrat who became a BOLSHEVIK. He organized the Soviet secret police after the RUSSIAN REVOLUTION, and as head of the CHEKA, the OGPU, and the NKVD, was responsible for all national security matters.

E

Eagleton, Thomas Francis (1929–   ), U.S. lawyer, Missouri attorney-general 1961–65, Democratic lieutenant governor 1965–68, and U.S. senator from 1968. In 1972 he was the Democratic nominee for the vice-presidency on the McGovern ticket but was asked to withdraw, and did, after disclosure of earlier nervous exhaustion problems, which had on two occasions been treated with electric SHOCK THERAPY. McGovern's indecision on the matter, first supporting and then rejecting Eagleton, seriously harmed his presidential campaign.

Eanes, António Ramalho (1935–   ), Portuguese officer and socialist, who led antiguerrilla units in Guinea, Mozambique, and Angola before joining the PORTUGUESE ARMED FORCES MOVEMENT in toppling the Portuguese dictatorship in 1974. In 1975 he played a key role in defeating a left-wing coup attempt, then became army chief of staff. He was president of Portugal from 1976 to 1986.

Earhart, Amelia Mary (1897–1937), U.S. aviator, who set several early solo flight records and was the leading woman flier of her time. On July 2, 1937, while over the central Pacific in the course of a round-the-world flight, she reported trouble. Radio contact was then lost, and she and her co-pilot, Fred Noonan, were not heard from again. Considerable speculation then developed as to whether she might have been shot down by the Japanese in the course of a reconnaissance flight, but no data was ever brought forward.

Earle, Willie (1922–47), Black accused of murder and lynched in Pickens County, South Carolina, in 1947. Although 26 mob members admitted participation in the lynching and were prosecuted, all were acquitted.

Early Bird (*Intelsat 1*), first communications SATELLITE for commercial purposes, launched on April 6, 1965, as part of the INTELSAT system.

East African campaign (January–April 1941), series of World War II engagements in East Africa. In late January 1941 British troops moving out of Kenya and the Sudan attacked substantially more numerous Italian troops in Eritrea, Ethiopia, and Somaliland. By late March the British had taken Somaliland, and in April they had taken Addis Ababa, in the process capturing an estimated 50,000 Italian prisoners with less than 500 casualties. On May 18 the remnants of the Italian army in Eritrea surrendered.

Easter offensive (March 1972), a substantial but ultimately failed North Vietnamese offensive during the VIETNAM WAR, in which South Vietnamese forces, supported by U.S. air power, repelled the North Vietnamese with heavy losses.

Easter Rising (April 24–29, 1916), an armed insurrection against British rule, in Dublin, Ireland, in which 1,500–2,000 lightly armed rebels engaged approximately 5,000 British regulars equipped with artillery. The rebels, led by Patrick PEARSE of the IRISH VOLUNTEERS and James CONNOLLY of the IRISH CITIZEN ARMY, surrendered after taking and holding a few buildings in Dublin for several days; they had failed to take their main objective, Dublin Castle. The rising was limited to Dublin; hoped-for German arms had not materialized. Roger CASEMENT, who had tried to secure the German arms, was arrested on embarkation from a German submarine 3 days before the Rising and was sent to to London, where he was later executed for treason. Fifteen leaders of the Rising, including Pearse and Connolly, were executed in Dublin. But their executions made them martyrs, and the Irish Republican political arm, SINN FEIN, won the elections of 1918 and declared the independence of the Irish Republic on January 21, 1919, beginning the successful armed insurrection that was IRISH WAR OF INDEPENDENCE.

East Indies, Battle of the (January–March 1942), taking of the Dutch East Indies (Indonesia) by Japanese invasion fleets early in World War II. The only serious Dutch resistance occurred on Java in late March and early February, but outnumbered Dutch troops without air support soon surrendered to much stronger Japanese forces.

Eastland **sinking** (June 24, 1915), the sinking of the American Great Lakes excursion ship *Eastland* while still at its Chicago dock and full of passengers, with a loss of over 800 people.

East Pakistan, the mostly Moslem eastern region of Bengal, from 1947 part of PAKISTAN, and from 1971 independent as BANGLADESH.

Eaton, Cyrus Stephen (1883–1979), Canadian-American financier and industrialist, who founded the Republic Steel Corporation in 1930 and during the post–World War II period became a leading advocate of nuclear disarmament and reduced Soviet–U.S. tensions. In 1957 he organized and sponsored the annual Pugwash Conference, which brought together leading intellectuals from both sides in the COLD WAR, in a continuing attempt to find areas of agreement and possible cooperation.

Eban, Abba (Aubrey Solomon; 1915–   ), South African–Israeli diplomat, who was Israeli UNITED NATIONS representative 1949–59 and ambassador to the United States 1950–59, holding Israeli cabinet-level positions 1959–74. He was foreign minister

1966–74 during the SIX-DAY WAR (THIRD ARAB–ISRAELI WAR) of 1967 and the YOM KIPPUR WAR (FOURTH ARAB–ISRAELI WAR; OCTOBER WAR) of 1973.

Ebert, Friedrich (1871–1925), German socialist, who became leader of the German Social Democratic Party in 1913, supported the German government during World War I, and formed a government after the abdication of Emperor Wilhelm II during the GERMAN REVOLUTION of 1918. He cooperated with the German general staff during that revolution, setting up the right-wing FREIKORPS, which unsuccessfully attempted to take power in the KAPP PUTSCH of 1920. Ebert became first president of the WEIMAR REPUBLIC.

Ebro, Battle of the (July–August 1938), the most decisive battle of the SPANISH CIVIL WAR, in which the Republican army of the north repulsed a Nationalist offensive aimed at Barcelona, but then went on the offensive, suffered major losses, and was fatally weakened. The next Nationalist offensive, in December and January, took Barcelona.

EC, the initials of the multinational EUROPEAN COMMUNITY.

Echo, world's first communications SATELLITE, launched in August 1960.

ECSC, the initials of the EUROPEAN COAL AND STEEL COMMUNITY, which was the earliest part of what later became the EUROPEAN COMMUNITY.

ECT, popular shorthand for electroconvulsive therapy, a type of SHOCK TREATMENT, developed in Italy in 1937.

Eddington, Arthur Stanley (1882–1944), British astrophysicist, who in 1924 discovered that the luminosity of a star is directly related to its mass, work basic to the theory of STELLAR EVOLUTION. He also discovered that stars are gaseous, with their energy traveling to the surface not by convection but by radiation, and he helped to confirm Albert EINSTEIN'S theory of RELATIVITY with observations at a 1919 total solar eclipse, doing later work aimed at developing a UNIFIED FIELD THEORY.

Eden, Sir Anthony (1897–1977), British diplomat, who was three times foreign secretary (1935–38; 1941–45; 1951–54), and prime minister 1955–57. He was a Conservative MP from 1923 and in 1926 began his long career in foreign affairs as a parliamentary secretary in the foreign office. In the early 1930s he strongly supported the LEAGUE OF NATIONS, and as foreign secretary he opposed Neville CHAMBERLAIN'S APPEASEMENT policies, resigning on that issue in February 1938. He went back into the government when war came in September 1939 and was WINSTON CHURCHILL'S wartime foreign secretary from December 1940 to July 1945. He came back as foreign secretary with Churchill in 1951 and became prime minister on Churchill's retirement in 1955. He fell from power after what was widely regarded in Britain as his mishandling of the SUEZ CRISIS of 1956, then retiring to write his memoirs.

Edward VII (Albert Edward, 1841–1910), son of Victoria and Albert, who gave his name to the Edwardian era and was king of Great Britain and Ireland, 1901–10. As the Prince of Wales he led an almost wholly social life—his mother blocked his participation in affairs of state—and figured in some of the society scandals of his time. As king he had very little impact on the course of events in Europe, though he supported Britain's naval buildup and the formation of the alliances with France and Russia that Britain would take into World War I.

Edward VIII (Edward Albert Christian George Andrew Patrick David, 1894–1972), British king in January 1936 after the death of his father, GEORGE V. Before that he had been a rather socially conscious prince of Wales, although his main functions had been largely ceremonial. In November 1936 he informed Prime Minister Stanley BALDWIN of his desire to marry American divorcee Wallis SIMPSON, setting off the ABDICATION CRISIS, which resulted in his relinquishing the throne in December. His brother, GEORGE VI, who succeeded him, then named him duke of Windsor, and it was as the duke and duchess of Windsor that he and wife spent the rest of their lives.

Edwards Air Force Base, California site often used by the NATIONAL AERONAUTICS AND SPACE ADMINISTRATION (NASA) as a landing site for the SPACE SHUTTLE.

EEC, the initials of the multinational EUROPEAN ECONOMIC COMMUNITY, which is part of the EUROPEAN COMMUNITY.

EEOC, the initials of the EQUAL EMPLOYMENT OPPORTUNITY COMMISSION, a U.S. federal agency concerned with the elimination of discrimination in the workplace.

E = mc², Albert EINSTEIN'S famous statement of the interconvertibility of mass and energy, specifically that energy equals mass times the speed of light squared; it was first expounded as part of his 1905 special theory of RELATIVITY.

EFTA, the initials of the multinational EUROPEAN FREE TRADE ASSOCIATION.

Egypt (Arab Republic of Egypt), a British protectorate until establishment of the republic in 1952, though it formally became independent in 1922. Under the leadership of Gamal Abdel NASSER, Egypt became an Arab socialist state, ultimately breaking all ties with Great Britain after British withdrawal from the canal area during the SUEZ CRISIS of 1956. During the brief 1958–61 formal union with Syria, Egypt-Syria was renamed the United Arab Republic, taking its present name in 1971.

Egyptian Revolution (June 23, 1952), an officers' coup, led by Colonel Gamal Abdel NASSER, which overthrew the Egyptian monarchy, dethroned FAROUK I, who went into exile, and established the Egyptian republic. The first premier of the new republic was General Mohammed Naguib, who was succeeded by Nasser in 1954.

Ehrlich, Paul (1854–1915), German bacteriologist who, after widely productive work in finding serums to treat a variety of diseases (for which he shared the 1908 Nobel Prize for Physiology or Medicine), developed in 1910 an arsenic treatment for the dreaded SYPHILIS, a medicine soon dubbed the "magic bullet."

Ehrlichmann, John Daniel (1925–), U.S. lawyer, and a campaign aide to Richard M. NIXON during the 1960s who became chief domestic political adviser to President Nixon in 1969. In 1970–71 he was heavily involved in the PENTAGON PAPERS and WATERGATE scandals. He resigned from his White House post on April 30, 1973, and in 1974 was convicted on charges connected with both sets of scandals. Subsequently imprisoned for 18 months, he wrote political novels before and after his imprisonment.

Eichmann, Adolf (1906–62), German SS official instrumental in capturing Jews and sending them to Nazi CONCENTRATION CAMPS. He escaped to South America after the war, was captured in Buenos Aires by Israeli agents in 1960, and was tried and hanged in Israel on May 31, 1962.

Eighteenth Amendment (1919), the amendment to the U.S. Constitution that brought about PROHIBITION.

Einstein, Albert (1879–1955), German-Swiss-American physicist, who developed the revolutionary concept of RELATIVITY. An indifferent student, excellent only in mathematics, Einstein was an astonishingly original theoretician. In 1905, the year he earned his Ph.D. and while still working at the Swiss Patent Office, he made three major contributions to physics. First, he explained the PHOTOELECTRIC EFFECT, in the process incorporating Max PLANCK's previously little-regarded ideas of QUANTUM THEORY; this effect is central to, among other things, TELEVISION and RADAR. Second, he provided a mathematical explanation of Brownian motion, long-observed movement of particles suspended in water, making clear for the first time that it was the result of molecules striking each other randomly. Third, and most important, he posited a new view of the universe, one in which all motion was viewed as relative to a particular frame of reference, the idea popularly known as RELATIVITY. In this paper, called the Special Theory of Relativity because it dealt only with certain types of motion, Einstein worked out his famous equation stating the interconvertibility of mass and energy, $E = mc^2$, specifically that energy equals mass times the speed of light squared, an idea soon supported by experiment. Another result of Einstein's theory was that the distinction between space and time disappeared, both existing on a single SPACE-TIME CONTINUUM. Few immediately recognized the power of these ideas, but in 1913 Max PLANCK found Einstein a scientific position in Berlin, where 2 years later he published a wider version of his theory, popularly called the General Theory of Relativity. In it he pointed out some ways in which the theory could be tested: by looking for a RED SHIFT in star light, found in 1920, and by looking for bending of light by a gravitational field, observed during a 1919 solar eclipse. His work earned him the 1921 Nobel Prize for Physics. By then famous, Einstein left Germany after Hitler's rise, in 1933, taking up residence at the Institute for Advanced Studies in Princeton, New Jersey, where he vainly sought to develop a UNIFIED FIELD THEORY combining both gravitation and electromagnetic phenomena. Understanding the implications of NUCLEAR FISSION and the dangers of Hitler's developing the technology first, Einstein sent a letter (drafted by Leo SZILARD) to President Franklin ROOSEVELT urging the funding of a project to develop an ATOMIC BOMB. The result was the MANHATTAN PROJECT and ultimately HIROSHIMA and NAGASAKI, which led him after war's end to press for banning of nuclear arms.

Eisenhower, Dwight David (1890–1969), U.S. Army officer, who became Supreme Commander of Allied forces in Europe during World War II and 34th president of the United States (1953–61). A colonel at the outbreak of war in 1941, he came to the attention of army chief of staff George MARSHALL, who promoted him twice, and in June 1942 he became American European theater commander. He commanded all Allied forces in the North African landings of 1942 and in the Sicilian and Italian invasions of 1943, leaving the Italian campaign to take command of the coming NORMANDY invasion. He also commanded Allied forces in the Western European theater, from Normandy to the German surrender, and was made a five-star general during the European campaign. After heading occupation forces and then becoming army chief of staff, he resigned in 1948 to become president of Columbia University, going back into the military as Allied European commander in 1950. He won a closely contested Republican nomination from Senator Robert A. TAFT in 1952 and went on to defeat Democrat Adlai STEVENSON in 1952 and 1956. As president he was a moderate in both domestic and foreign affairs. At home he resisted, but did not confront, further witchhunting by Senator Joseph MC-CARTHY and others, encouraging the opposition that ultimately destroyed McCarthy at the ARMY–MCCARTHY HEARINGS of 1954. He resisted desegregation activity as well, although meeting defiance of federal law at Little Rock, Arkansas, by sending troops to enforce a court order. He also resisted federal spending, focusing on a balanced budget and initiating very little new legislation. Abroad, he was a good deal more active, bringing the KOREAN WAR to an end, attempting to develop arms control agreements with the Soviets, and refusing to join Great Britain and France in their seizure of the SUEZ Canal in 1956, while at the same time sending Marines to Lebanon in 1957 and maintaining a strong anti-Communist posture throughout his years in office. Before leavng office, he publicly voiced strong misgivings about the development of a powerful "MILITARY-INDUSTRIAL COMPLEX" in the United States.

Eisenhower Doctrine, a statement of U.S. commitment to supply economic and military aid, including direct military support, to Middle Eastern countries faced by "overt armed aggression from any nation controlled by international communism." It was issued in January 5, 1957, signaling greater U.S. involvement in the Middle East after the SUEZ CRISIS of 1956, and was supported by a Congressional resolution in March 9, 1957.

El Alamein, Battle of (October 23–November 4, 1942), a decisive British victory in North Africa, in which superior British forces led by General Bernard MONTGOMERY ultimately routed overextended German-Italian forces commanded by General Erwin ROMMEL, which had pursued the British into Egypt after their spring victories at BIR HACHEIM and TOBRUK.

electrocardiograph (ECG or EKG), device for measuring the electrical activity of the heart and detecting aberrations, developed in 1900–03 by Dutch physiologist Willem Einthoven, for which he won the 1924 Nobel Prize for Physiology or Medicine.

electroconvulsive therapy (ECT), type of SHOCK TREATMENT, developed in Italy in 1937.

electroencephalograph (EEG), device for measuring the electrical activity of the brain and detecting aberrations, developed 1924–29 by German psychiatrist Hans Berger. Using his machine, Berger and others discovered that the brain has several different types of waves: alpha waves, associated with dream-sleep or relaxation; beta waves of higher frequency and lower voltage, associated with wakeful alertness and physiological stress; and delta waves of higher voltage and lower frequency, associated with deep sleep and also with some problems, such as strokes or tumors. Modern BIOFEEDBACK techniques help people deliberately modify their brain waves, allowing some control in mild cases of epilepsy. Absence of electrical activity in the brain is called BRAIN DEATH.

electron, negatively charged PARTICLE circling the NUCLEUS in an atom. Though named, described, and discovered by Joseph THOMSON in 1895, the electron's properties were elucidated and exploited in the 20th century. In the 1920s various scientists learned how to measure an electron's charge; Ernest RUTHERFORD, Niels BOHR, and others described its place in ATOMIC STRUCTURE; Wolfgang PAULI found that only one electron can occupy a single, specific state; and Louis DE BROGLIE found that electrons sometimes acted like waves as well as particles. Meanwhile, others put the electron's properties to practical use, most notably, from 1904, developing the ELECTRON TUBE, which formed the basis for the whole 20th-century explosion in ELECTRONICS, and employing the PHOTOELECTRIC EFFECT in later developing TELEVISION and RADAR.

electronic banking, transfer of funds using COMPUTER ELECTRONICS, rather than physical transfer of paper checks; for some, the beginning of a checkless society. Automation of check clearing among major banks was pioneered in Britain in 1968, beginning in New York City 2 years later; an international automated check-clearing system, centered in Europe, was begun in 1977. On the personal level, electronic banking has meant the proliferation of automated teller machines (ATMs)—not only in banks but also in supermarkets, airports, and other high-traffic places around the world—from which, on presentation of a valid CREDIT CARD and a personal identification number (PIN), a person can obtain cash from specified accounts. Individuals can also link their home computers with some banks, doing all their banking over telephone lines.

electronics, branch of applied physics dealing with the behavior of ELECTRONS in a wide range of devices, including COMPUTERS, TELEVISION, and RADIO; the term itself emerged in the 1920s. Early electronic devices relied on cumbersome, heat-producing VACUUM TUBES, but after 1948 they began to be replaced by TRANSISTORS, which form the basis of solid-state electronics, so-called because the electrons move through solid metal crystals, rather than through a vacuum. The age of microelectronics began in the 1960s as ever-smaller multiple transistors began to be built into integrated circuits on MICROPROCESSOR CHIPS.

electron microscope, magnifying device in which electron beams are focused on a screen, much as light is focused by a normal lens but with far greater magnifying power. Based on work by many scientists in the 1920s, the first practical electron micro-

scope was developed in 1928–33 by Max Knoll and Ernst Ruska, but the model most widely adopted was made in 1937–40 by Canadian-American physicist James Hillier and Albert Prebus, working under Vladimir ZWORYKIN. Widely used since 1934 in the study of bacteria, VIRUSES, and living molecules, the electron microscope was also from 1941 used in chemistry and industry, as in analyzing the strength of metals. By the 1980s scientists were even able to photograph DNA directly using this powerful instrument.

electron tube, sealed tube in which ELECTRONS float relatively freely, either in a vacuum or in gas; vacuum tubes (in Britain called valves) were the mostly widely used, providing the working "guts" of RADIO, TELEVISION, RADAR, and COMPUTERS. Drawing on some 19th-century observations by Thomas Edison, in 1904 British electrical engineer John Ambrose Fleming developed a diode, a tube with two electrodes—a cathode and an anode—able to detect signals from electromagnetic RADIATION, such as RADIO WAVES. In 1907 American electrical engineer Lee DE FOREST added a mesh grid to control the movement of electrons, making a three-element electron tube, or triode, which he called an audion; this allowed for generation, detection, and amplification of electrical signals. Many vacuum tubes are photoelectric-tubes, converting light signals to electrical impulses, or vice versa; perhaps the best known is the CATHODE-RAY TUBE. Other vacuum tubes store electrical signals, creating an image of electrical charges on a screen; these are the basic units of electronic memory, used in radar and in early computers until replaced by TRANSISTORS beginning in the 1950s.

Elixir Sulfanilamide, drug that killed at least 73 people in the United States in 1937, sparking passage of the 1938 federal Food, Drug, and Cosmetic Act that set up the FOOD AND DRUG ADMINISTRATION (FDA).

Elizabeth II (Elizabeth Alexandra Mary, 1926–   ), queen of the United Kingdom from 1952, head of the COMMONWEALTH, married to Philip Mountbatten and mother of Prince Charles (1948–   ), Princess Anne (1956–   ), Prince Andrew (1960–   ), and Prince Edward (1964–   ), a highly visible symbol of the continuing Commonwealth relationships among the now-independent nations of the former British empire.

Ellis Island, the main U.S. immigration station during the first quarter of the 20th century, in upper New York harbor, also known the world over in its time as the "Island of Tears." Through the Great Hall at Ellis Island passed over 10 million immigrants, most of them from southern and eastern Europe, in some periods at the rate of 10,000 a day. Immigration was heavy from 1900 to 1914, slowed to a trickle during World War I, and became heavy again from 1919 until the advent of the sharply restrictive American immigration laws of the early 1920s. During the post–World War I RED SCARE, it was used as a detention center, holding, among others, anarchists Emma GOLDMAN and Alexander BERKMAN, before they were deported to the Soviet Union. During World War II, it was again used as a detention center. The Ellis Island immigration station was completed in 1892, burned to the ground the day after its opening, and was then completely rebuilt, reopening in December 1900. Originally a 3-acre facility, built on little more than a sandbar, by the 1920s it was a large set of buildings built on 27 acres of landfill, complete with two hospitals, dormitories, a power plant, and other structures. In 1954 the entire station was abandoned but has since been restored, and is now an American national shrine.

Ellis, Henry Havelock (1859–1939), British physician, whose seven-volume *Studies in the Psychology of Sex* (1897–1928) opened discussion of a previously forbidden subject. Though for years judicially branded a "filthy publication," available only to physicians, Ellis's work had considerable effect on the growth of sex education and BIRTH CONTROL in the 20th century.

Ellsberg, Daniel (1931–   ), U.S. military advisor with top secret clearance, who be-

came an anti–VIETNAM WAR activist and took the top secret PENTAGON PAPERS to the *New York Times,* which published them beginning in June 1969, a June 30 Supreme Court decision upholding the newspaper's right to publish. Ellsberg was prosecuted, but proof of government wiretapping and burglary caused withdrawal of all charges after mistrials had been declared.

Ellsworth, Lincoln (1880–1951), U.S. explorer and engineer, who was one of the first people to fly over both the NORTH and SOUTH POLES, the former with Roald AMUNDSEN and Umberto NOBILE in a dirigible in 1926, the latter with Herbert Hollick-Kenyon in 1935. From a wealthy family, Ellsworth funded and led many other expeditions, notably to the Peruvian Andes and to the North Pole region by submarine in 1931. He was the first to fly over vast regions of ANTARCTICA 1933–39; a large area of Antartica was named for him.

El Niño (1982–83), periodic shift in the winds and ocean currents in the Pacific Ocean that had devastating effects from late 1982 to late 1983, the worst such occurrence in the century, possibly intensified by the early 1982 eruption of a Mexican volcano, El Chicón. As normal east-west winds dropped, warm Pacific water pushed up against South America's western coast, killing much of the marine life used to cooler waters and thereby starving many larger animals in the food chain. Torrential rains brought floods and mudslides to South America and parts of North America; meanwhile terrible droughts struck Australia, the Philippines, and parts of India and Africa.

El Salvador Civil War (1979–   ), a guerrilla insurgency that during the 1980s grew to control much of the countryside, with the guerrillas receiving some military supplies from Nicaragua and the Salvador army receiving massive military assistance from the United States. The moderate Salvador government, led by José Napoleon DUARTE and strongly supported by the United States, was unable to contain either the rebels or the army-sponsored DEATH

SQUADS that from the mid-1970s attempted to suppress opposition by means of wholesale murder. Early civil war death squad victims included Catholic Archbishop Oscar Arnulfo Romero and seven Americans, three of them nuns. Later victims included 6 Jesuit priests, murdered by a uniformed death squad in November, 1989.

Emergency Farm Mortgage Act, a U.S. NEW DEAL law enacted during the first HUNDRED DAYS of the ROOSEVELT administration, providing for massive refinancing for farm mortgages, which saved large numbers of family farms and helped stabilize the farm-related operations of the financial industries.

Empire State bomber crash (July 28, 1945), crash of a B-25 bomber into the Empire State Building, in New York City, killing 13 people, setting six floors of the building on fire, and showering the surrounding streets with airplane fragments. Casualties were light because it was a Saturday morning; on a workday a major disaster would have resulted.

Empress of Ireland **sinking** (May 29, 1914), sinking of the Canadian Pacific liner *Empress of Ireland* in the St. Lawrence River after it collided with a Norwegian coalship; 1,024 people died.

energy crisis, the oil shortage that occurred in many industrial countries during the period October 1973–March 1974, resulting from the OIL EMBARGO imposed by the ORGANIZATION OF PETROLEUM EXPORTING COUNTRIES (OPEC), after Israeli victory in the 1973 YOM KIPPUR WAR (FOURTH ARAB–ISRAELI WAR), and until disengagement of the combatants had been negotiated.

Energy Research and Development Administration (ERDA), U.S. agency designed, with the Nuclear Regulatory Commission (NRC), to replace the ATOMIC ENERGY COMMISSION (AEC) from 1975.

Engel v. *Vitale* (1962), a landmark U.S. Supreme Court decision invalidating a compulsory New York school prayer as a violation of religious freedom.

ENIAC (**E**lectronic **N**umerical **I**ntegrator **a**nd **C**alculator), long regarded as the first fully electronic DIGITAL COMPUTER until recognition of the earlier ATANASOFF-BERRY COMPUTER (ABC). The ENIAC was unveiled in 1946 by John William Mauchly and John Presper Eckert at the University of Pennsylvania. Construction had begun in 1942, at the request of the Department of War, for calculation of ballistics data. Though 80 × 8 × 3 feet and employing 18,000 vacuum-style ELECTRON TUBES, the machine had far less capacity than a PERSONAL COMPUTER of the 1980s and had to be rewired for each new task. As part of a later patent suit brought by ENIAC licensees, a federal judge in 1973 ruled that ENIAC's patent was invalid, much of its substance deriving from the work of John V. ATANASOFF. Mauchly and Eckert later built UNIVAC, the first commercially available computer, in 1951.

Enigma, German radio code transmitter during World War II. It was secretly reproduced by the Allies and its codes broken early in the war, notably through the work of Alan TURING, supplying the Allies with the ULTRA information that was so important throughout the war.

Eniwetok, depopulated Pacific atoll in the Marshall Islands, site of the first successful test of a HYDROGEN BOMB, on November 1, 1952, and of other U.S. atomic tests from 1948 to 1956.

Eniwetok, Battle of (February 17–21, 1944), a short, very sharp World War II battle for Eniwetok and Parry Island, in which the 2,000 Japanese defenders chose to fight to the death and were destroyed by much stronger U.S. forces; American casualties included a few hundred dead.

Enola Gay, the name of the U.S. B-29 bomber that dropped the first atomic bomb on HIROSHIMA, on August 6, 1945.

Enosis (Union with Greece), the goal of the Greek Cypriot majority, led by Archbishop MAKARIOS III from 1950. It was formally dropped on achievement of the independence of Cyprus in 1959 but has remained the goal of many Greek Cypriots.

Entebbe rescue (July 4, 1976), the successful effort to release 98 hostages taken by terrorists in an Air France hijacking on June 27, 1976. The hijackers had flown to Libya and then to Entebbe, Uganda, where they were welcomed by Idi AMIN. There they separated out and held 98 Jewish passengers. The Israeli government began negotiations with the hijackers through Amin but then mounted a surprise rescue operation; airborne Israeli commandos took the hostages back by force at the Entebbe airport, and flew them out, with the loss of three lives.

Entente Cordiale, the Anglo-French agreement of April 8, 1904, settling British and French spheres of influence in Egypt and Morocco and several other colonial disputes between the two countries; part of the settling of the European powers into the two rival systems that ultimately went into World War I.

Environmental Protection Agency (EPA), U.S. federal agency created by the National Environmental Protection Act of 1970, and responsible for administering the web of environmental safeguards set up by that law and subsequent laws aimed at protecting the environment.

Eoanthropus dawsoni, scientific name for Piltdown Man, early human-like fossil remains found in 1911–12, but proved fraudulent in the 1950s.

Epinephrine, alternate name for ADRENALINE.

Equal Employment Opportunity Commission (EEOC), a U.S. federal agency created by the CIVIL RIGHTS ACT OF 1964 to monitor and encourage compliance with legal prohibition of discrimination by employers and unions. The agency has no enforcement powers of its own but can bring suit in federal court in an attempt to force compliance.

Equal Rights Amendment (ERA), a proposed amendment to the U.S. Constitution, pushed through Congress in its modern form by the NATIONAL ORGANIZATION FOR WOMEN (NOW) and other interested groups in 1971 and 1972; but it did not secure ratification by a sufficient number of states. It read: "Equality of rights under the law shall not be denied or abridged by the United States or by any state on account of sex."

equal-time provision, requirement by the FEDERAL COMMUNICATIONS COMMISSION (FCC) that a U.S. radio or television station must grant the same amount of air time to all political candidates in an election if any one is allowed time.

Equatorial Guinea (Republic of Equatorial Guinea), until 1968 a Spanish colony, although it was granted internal autonomy in 1964. Independence came on October 12, 1968; with it came the presidency of Francisco Macías (later known as Macie Nguema Biyuogo Negue Ndong), who took absolute power in 1969, murderously repressed all opposition, and had himself declared president-for-life in 1972. He was deposed in 1979 and later executed. Although the country remained a one-party state, the new government, led by Macie's nephew, Teodoro Obiang Nguema Mbasogo, was far more moderate than the one it replaced.

Equity Funding fraud, a U.S. 1973 financial scandal in which key executives of the Equity Funding Corporation, an insurance and other financial services company, were shown to have created billions of dollars worth of false insurance policies in the preceding 4 years and then sold the false policies to reinsurance companies. The scandal bankrupted the company, cost the reinsurance companies $1.75 billion, and made billions of dollars worth of company stock nearly worthless.

ERA, the initials of the proposed EQUAL RIGHTS AMENDMENT.

Erikson, Erik Homburger (1902–   ), German-born Danish-American psychoanalyst, who introduced the idea of an "identity crisis." Trained and analyzed in Vienna by Anna Freud, and with experience in MONTESSORI teaching, Erikson emigrated to the United States in 1933, working as a child psychoanalyst. Building on Sigmund Freud's theories, he drew on cross-cultural studies among Native American cultures to develop a view of various stages of life development, each containing a crisis to be resolved, as outlined in several books, notably *Childhood and Society* (1950).

Eritrea, disputed East African region, annexed by HAILE SELASSIE I with United Nations support, and later the focus of the ETHIOPIAN–ERITREAN WAR.

Erlander, Tage (1901–85), Swedish Social Democratic party leader, in parliament from 1932 and premier 1946–69, a period in which he played a major role in developing the modern Swedish welfare state, while maintaining Sweden's traditional nonaligned position in international affairs.

Ervin, Samuel James, Jr. (1896–1985), U.S. lawyer and a North Carolina judge before becoming a Democratic U.S. senator 1954–75. In 1973–74, he was Senate head of the WATERGATE committee, in that position successfully resisting the executive privilege claims of president Richard M. NIXON and playing a major role in the events that led to the Nixon resignation.

ESM fraud, 1980's securities fraud, in which Florida-based ESM Government Securities defrauded institutional customers all over the United States, including many banks and municipalities, promising high returns that were in reality paid out of new incoming investment purchases. When the fraud was exposed in 1985, hundreds of millions of dollars of government securities supposedly held by ESM for customers were missing and probably nonexistent. The fraud caused a run on those Ohio savings and loan associations that were not federally insured, many of them ESM customers who had suffered huge losses, providing final evidence to Americans that the only reasonably safe government financial guarantee at the time was the federal guarantee.

ESP, popular shorthand for EXTRASENSORY PERCEPTION, a term coined by Joseph RHINE.

Estes, Billy Sol (1925–   ), swindler, prominent Texas citizen, and supporter of president Lyndon JOHNSON; in 1966 he was convicted of selling interests in nonexistent fertilizer tanks and again in 1979 for using nonexistent collateral to borrow money.

Estonia, from 1721, a Russian Baltic province, which won its freedom in the ESTONIAN WAR OF INDEPENDENCE (1918), but was reoccupied by the Soviet Union in 1940, as provided in the NAZI-SOVIET PACT. During the GORBACHEV era, powerful independence movements arose in all three Baltic Soviet Republics; in early 1990, the issues had not yet been resolved.

Estonian War of Independence (1918), conflict that developed as part of the RUSSIAN CIVIL WAR. After the armistice of November 11, 1918, German troops withdrew from Estonia, which had declared its independence after the Treaty of BREST-LITOVSK in 1917. Soviet forces entered the former Russian Baltic province but were repelled by Estonian troops aided by the British Baltic squadron. Independence was formally recognized by the Treaty of Dorpat in October 1920.

estrogen, female sex HORMONE first identified in the 1920s. Synthetic forms of estrogen and other hormones were used by Gregory PINCUS in his 1951–55 development of a BIRTH CONTROL PILL, which interrupted a woman's monthly ovulation-menstruation cycle, so preventing conception. By 1965 researchers had discovered that estrogen given to women after menopause helped prevent the bone-weakening disease osteoporosis, as well as hardening of the arteries, or atherosclerosis.

Ethiopian–Eritrean famine of 1984–85, a famine accompanied by epidemic disease, resulting from severe drought, and complicated by long periods of refusal by the combatants in the ETHIOPIAN–ERITREAN war to admit aid shipments; an estimated 1 million died.

Ethiopian-Eritrean War (1962–   ), conflict that began in 1962, when Ethiopia abolished the autonomy Eritrea had been granted within its federation with Ethiopia, established in 1952. The result was an Eritrean separatist guerrilla war that by 1965 had grown into a long-term, major conflict in the region. After the overthrow of Haile SELASSIE in 1974, the war grew even more intense, as the new Soviet-backed military government of Ethiopia made repeated, unsuccessful attempts to smash the long insurgency. Ethiopian efforts weakened during the SOMALI–ETHIOPIAN WAR of 1977–78. Renewed major Ethiopian attacks, beginning in the summer of 1978, had no more success than before, the insurgents retreating to the countryside and later returning to occupy most of Eritrea. During the 1980s the decades-long war was a stalemate, with an estimated 1–2 million civilian victims, most of the casualties resulting from drought, famine, disease, and in some periods the refusal of the combatants to allow delivery of foreign famine relief and medical supplies.

Ethopian–Italian War (October 1935–May 1936), Italian invasion of Ethiopia, without declaring war, in pursuit of long-cherished Italian fascist imperial ambitions; the Italian troops quickly scored easy victories over ill-equipped Ethiopian forces. THE LEAGUE OF NATIONS declared Italy an aggressor and voted some sanctions but failed even to attempt to block the oil supplies that were vital to further Italian advances or to stop Italian passage through the Suez Canal. Italian forces paused in November, resumed their offensive in May, heavily bombing defenseless civilian and military targets and ending the war by taking Addis Ababa. Italy occupied Ethiopia until early 1941, when Allied East African forces liberated the country, restoring HAILE SELASSIE I (Ras Tafari) to the throne.

eugenics, planned improvement of the genetic makeup of the human population, drawing on breeding programs developed with plants and animals; so-called positive eugenics involves the fostering of desirable genes, whereas negative eugenics involves suppressing undesirable genes and is often used by racists or xenophobes for their own ends, sometimes to disastrous effect. Dating back at least to Plato, the idea of eugenics began to spread widely in the early 20th century, with pseudoscientific ideas about racial and criminal "types." British biologist Francis Galton, who coined the term "eugenics" (meaning well-born) in 1883, sparked the founding of eugenics societies, as in Great Britain in 1907 and the United States in 1926. Eugenists believed in the superiority of Whites, especially those of "Nordic" background, over other races and of the "higher" over the "lower" classes, despite the lack of supporting scientific evidence and the patent subjectivity of the classifications. They also took the INTELLIGENCE QUOTIENT derived by testing to be a measure of genetic heritage, rather than of learning from the environment. Eugenics views were used to restrict non-Northern European immigration to the United States, especially after 1924. They also resulted in the passage of sterilization laws in the mid-1930s, notably in Germany, the Scandinavian countries, and in over half of the states in the United States. Whole classes of people, especially those labeled as feeble-minded, insane, criminal, or epileptic, were subject to voluntary or compulsory sterilization. Such laws were unevenly applied; in the United States most heavily in the South and in California, which alone had almost 10,000 sterilizations by 1935. Though such laws remained on the books for decades, often fed by racist attitudes, the ideas of eugenics were sharply questioned in the scientific community from the mid-1930s in both America and Europe, particularly by figures such as Franz BOAS and Ashley MONTAGU. Regardless, the Nazis took the ideas of eugenics to support their view of a German "master race," the end result being not only sterilization, as under the NUREMBERG LAWS, but also the deaths of millions of people, especially in the JEWISH HOLOCAUST. Revulsion against the Nazi actions discredited the eugenics movement after World War II. But advances in biology and medicine from the 1950s have, in fact, made "selective breeding" and genetic counseling of humans relatively wide-spread—the key difference being that the individual, not the state or any self-appointed group, is generally making the choices. Using AMNIOCENTESIS, since 1952 parents have been able to learn about their fetus's genetic makeup, and if problems are found, they can decide on an abortion or medical treatment. Artificial insemination and IN VITRO FERTILIZATION are common approaches to infertility, with sperm sometimes coming from SPERM BANKS containing the semen of men regarded as "superior." And since 1973 GENETIC ENGINEERING has offered the prospect of altering human makeup deliberately or even of producing CLONES.

Euratom, an alternate name for the EUROPEAN ATOMIC ENERGY COMMUNITY.

Eurocommunism, the post-STALIN approach taken by many of the leaders of the Communist parties of Western Europe, especially after Nikita KHRUSHCHEV'S 1956 SECRET SPEECH, which called for the development of many different national paths toward socialism and communism, rather than unquestioning adherence to the Soviet model. During the 1970s Eurocommunism became the dominant Communist Party doctrine in Western Europe; during the GORBACHEV era, the doctrine was also adopted in practice by the Communist Parties of Eastern Europe.

European Atomic Energy Community (Euratom), a component part of the EUROPEAN COMMUNITY (EC), established in 1958, by the terms of the 1957 Treaty of Rome. Euratom then moved to develop a common nuclear industries market and to foster the peaceful and safe uses of atomic energy; it also became involved in Community-wide nuclear and other scientific research projects.

European Coal and Steel Community (ECSC), the earliest component part of the EUROPEAN COMMUNITY (EC); it was established in 1952 by the terms of the Paris Treaty of 1951, then moved to develop a coal and steel common market as proposed

by the SCHUMAN PLAN and served as a model for the later EUROPEAN ECONOMIC COMMUNITY (EEC).

European Community (EC), a supranational organization of 12 European nations, including Belgium, Denmark, France, Federal Republic of Germany, Greece, Ireland, Italy, Luxembourg, Netherlands, Portugal, Spain, and the United Kingdom, which since its formation as a six-nation organization in 1967 has grown toward a substantial economic union of all of the major and many of the smaller European states. The EC has merged the functions of the EUROPEAN ECONOMIC COMMUNITY (EEC, or COMMON MARKET), the EUROPEAN COAL AND STEEL COMMUNITY (ECSC), and the European Atomic Energy Community (EURATOM). The European Community has become a powerful economic and therefore political force, organizing and supervising such matters as trading and subsidy arrangements within its own borders and negotiating worldwide agreements on behalf of its members, and from the late 1980s moving toward a planned economic union of its members scheduled for 1992. The EC includes the European Parliament and the European Court of Justice.

European Economic Community (EEC), a component part of the EUROPEAN COMMUNITY (EC), established in 1958 by the terms of the 1957 Treaty of Rome. It established a Community-wide customs union in 1968, was joined by Great Britain in 1972 and thereafter by several smaller European nations, has developed worldwide trading relationships on behalf of the EC as a unified entity, and has continued to move toward a complete economic union while preserving the separate national sovereignties of its members.

European Free Trade Association (EFTA), an international organization established in 1960, then led by Great Britain, as a counterbalance to the recently formed EUROPEAN ECONOMIC COMMUNITY (EEC). Great Britain later joined the EUROPEAN COMMUNITY (EC), as did some other EFTA members. In the 1980s, EFTA and the EC formed a common free trading area, and developed many other areas of mutuality.

euthanasia, suicide or murder for the sake of providing an "easy death" (the word's literal meaning) for an individual, especially someone incurably ill and in great pain; an old question taken up with renewed force in the 20th century because medical technology can extend life far beyond previously normal bounds. Where the RIGHT TO DIE implies the ability to choose to end life-supporting medical assistance, euthanasia goes further, encompassing the individual's right to commit suicide or request someone else to kill them for their benefit. Though the official medical position, as stated by the World Medical Association in 1950, remained that euthanasia is unethical, some individual physicians have engaged in mercy killing at the request of the patient or family, leading to considerable debate on the question in the professional journals, especially in the 1980s, with the advent of AIDS. Sometimes family members have performed mercy killings themselves, posing difficult questions for juries considering murder charges, the decision often resting on consideration of the murderer's motives.

Evans, Arthur John (1851–1941), English archaeologist, long associated with Oxford's Ashmolean Museum, who from 1894–1919 led excavations at Crete, especially at Cnossus, uncovering striking finds from the Minoan and later Mycenean civilizations.

Everest, Mount, world's highest mountain, target of numerous 20th-century expeditions. The first mountaineers to reach the top were Edmund HILLARY and Tenzing NORGAY on May 29, 1953.

Evers, James Charles (1922–   ), U.S. civil rights leader and elected official, who in 1963 left his business in Chicago to take up the role of his murdered brother, Medgar EVERS, becoming Mississippi state chairman of the NATIONAL ASSOCIATION FOR THE ADVANCEMENT OF COLORED PEOPLE (NAACP). He became mayor of Fayette, Mississippi, in 1969, the first Black mayor of a southern racially mixed town since the period of Reconstruction following the Civil War. He was also a leader of the MISSISSIPPI FREEDOM DEMOCRATIC PARTY and was its gubernatorial candidate in 1972.

Evers, Medgar Wiley (1925–63), U.S. political leader, a Mississippi lawyer and Black civil rights leader, who was state chairman of the NATIONAL ASSOCIATION FOR THE ADVANCEMENT OF COLORED PEOPLE (NAACP) when he was murdered at his home in Jackson, Mississippi, in 1963.

Evita, the popular name of Maria Eva Duarte PERON, partner and prime mover in the Argentinian dictatorship of her husband, Juan PERON.

exclusion principle, theory that within an atom only one ELECTRON could occupy a specific, single state; developed by Wolfgang PAULI in 1925.

existentialism, a theory of personal freedom positing that life has no meaning beyond direct personal engagement and commitment based on personal experience, free of the limiting influences of society. It was developed in the 19th century by Søren Kierkegaard and others, developed further in the 20th century by such philosophers as Karl JASPERS and Martin Heidegger, and became a post–World War II artistic and social movement led most notably by Jean Paul SARTRE and Albert CAMUS.

Explorer, series of U.S. satellites, including America's first artificial satellite, launched on January 31, 1958, following the Soviet Union's SPUTNIK FLIGHT. *Explorer 4* (boosted in part by a modified V-2 ROCKET) discovered the Van Allen Belts, two wide bands of radiation circling Earth, earlier predicted by James VAN ALLEN; *Explorer 6,* launched August 7, 1959, transmitted the first TELEVISION picture of Earth from space; and later Explorer satellites collected and transmitted cosmic data from above the Earth's atmosphere.

extra-sensory perception (ESP), term coined in the early 20th century by Joseph RHINE for the acquisition of information without using the known senses. The umbrella term generally includes telepathy, clairvoyance, precognition, and often psychokinesis. Though subjected to substantial laboratory research, the existence of ESP remains, so far at least, unproved.

Exxon Valdez, the Exxon oil company tanker that was the source of a massive oil spill in Prince William Sound, off Alaska, on March 24, 1989. An estimated 250,000 barrels of oil were discharged into the sea; it was the largest U.S. oil tanker spill to date, and it caused a series of related ecological disasters, some of them many hundreds of miles away.

F

Fabian Society, a gradualist British socialist educational and propaganda organization formed in 1884 that exercised great formative and continuing influence on the development of the Labour party; its key members were Beatrice WEBB, Sidney WEBB, and Bernard SHAW.

Fairbanks, Charles Warren (1852–1918), U.S. lawyer and conservative Republican senator from Ohio (1897–1905), and Theodore ROOSEVELT'S vice-president for one term (1905–09), having been chosen to balance the ticket. In 1916 he was vice-presidential candidate in the losing Charles Evans HUGHES campaign.

Fair Deal, a slogan put forward by U.S. president Harry S. TRUMAN in his 1949 annual message to Congress, describing his domestic program, which he regarded as an extension of Franklin D. ROOSEVELT'S liberal NEW DEAL program; it included a broad range of labor, welfare, and civil rights legislation, little of which was enacted during his administration.

Fair Employment Practices Commission (FEPC), a U.S. Federal commission set up by executive order in 1941, created by President Franklin Delano ROOSEVELT in response to a threat by A. Philip RANDOLPH to lead a march on Washington for fair employment practices. The commission had some success during World War II, although its practical accomplishments were rather limited. However, it was the first federal government organization solely and directly concerned with discrimination in the workplace, and as such it was a trailblazer. During the postwar period, states began to follow suit, and during the 1960s many far more effective federal and state laws and enforcement organizations came into being.

Faisal (1883–1933), son of HUSSEIN IBN ALI and first king of Iraq. He commanded the Arab desert army during the ARAB REVOLT of 1916 and in subsequent guerrilla warfare against the Turks, collaborating closely with T. E. LAWRENCE. He became king of Syria in 1918 but in 1920 was deposed by the French, who then controlled Syria. In 1921, with British sponsorship, he became king of Iraq and in 1932 became king of an independent Iraq. His son and grandson ruled after him, until his grandson, Faisal II, was killed during the rebellion of 1958.

Falange, the Spanish fascist party, a mixture of earlier fascist and right-wing Catholic elements united behind Francisco FRANCO and, from April 1937 until his consolidation of power after the end of the SPANISH CIVIL WAR, his chief ideological base in Spanish life. Falange influence diminished after the defeat of German and Italian fascism, although its members continued to hold key positions in fascist Spain.

Falkenhayn, Erich von (1861–1922), German World War I general who replaced Helmuth von MOLTKE as head of the German general staff after the first German offensive was stopped at the Battle of the MARNE. He was replaced by General Paul von HINDENBURG after the failure of the long, costly German effort to take VERDUN.

Falkland Islands, Battle of (December 8, 1914), the World War I sinking of four German cruisers by superior British forces off the Falklands.

Falklands War (1982), British-Argentine war, which began on April 2, 1982, when Argentine troops occupied the Falklands (which they claimed as the Malvinas), disputed territory occupied by Britain since 1833. The small British garrison on the Falklands surrendered, but on April 5 a British task force set off to retake the islands. Using U.S. bases and assistance in the South Atlantic, British forces reached the Falklands and began a series of island-hopping invasions in late April; they were substantially reinforced in May and completed their campaign with Argentine surrender on June 14. British losses included a destroyer, the *Sheffield,* and three other ships; Argentine air, sea, and land losses were considerably heavier, including the loss of a cruiser, the *General Belgrano.* In the wake of the lost war, the Argentine government collapsed.

Falwell, Jerry (1933–), U.S. fundamentalist Protestant minister and television evangelist, founder of the *Old Time Gospel Hour,* who in 1979 founded the conservative MORAL MAJORITY political organization, becoming an influential political figure on the right, and strongly supporting Ronald REAGAN throughout the 1980s. In 1987 he took control of Jim Bakker's PTL evangelistic empire at Bakker's request after the BAKKER-PTL SCANDAL broke. Later he relinquished control and let PTL drift into bankruptcy after Bakker attempted to regain control by accusing Falwell of holding PTL against Bakker's wishes.

fallout, tiny radioactive particles remaining after a nuclear explosion, as of an ATOMIC BOMB or NUCLEAR REACTOR, or from natural sources, some remaining locally, but some transported by wind currents far over the Earth's surface. Fallout particles such as strontium 90, potassium 40, carbon 14, and iodine 131, gradually lose their RADIOACTIVITY, but only over weeks or years; meanwhile, they concentrate in the environment, particularly affecting animals at the end of food chains, such as mammals and birds, and causing substantial health hazards. Concern over the effects of fallout sparked the building of fallout shelters, a short-lived fad of the early 1960s and spurred many attempts at control of nuclear technology, especially atmospheric testing, starting with the 1963 NUCLEAR TEST BAN TREATY.

Fanfani, Amintore (1908–), Italian author, historian, and economist, who entered parliament as a Christian Democrat in 1946, served at the cabinet level in many governments, was prime minister four times between 1954 and 1983, and was president of the senate twice. He was president of the United Nations General Assembly 1965–66.

Fanon, Franz Omar (1925–61), Martiniquan Black psychiatrist, writer, and Marxist revolutionary, who left medicine while working in Algeria, to become editor of the Algerian National Front (FLN) newspaper during the ALGERIAN WAR OF INDEPENDENCE. He subsequently became a major THIRD WORLD revolutionary theoretician, advocating violent revolution, and relying on a peasant base for revolution, as put forward in his best known work, *The Wretched of the Earth* (1961).

FAO, the initials of the FOOD AND AGRICULTURE ORGANIZATION, a UNITED NATIONS special agency.

Farley, James Aloysius (1888–1976), U.S. Democratic politician, who played a key role in developing the presidential campaigns of Franklin Delano ROOSEVELT in 1932 and 1936 and was postmaster-general during the first two Roosevelt administrations. He split with Roosevelt in 1940 on the issue of the third term, thereafter playing little part in national affairs.

Farmer, James Leonard (1920–), U.S. pacifist and civil rights leader, who in the early 1940s was active in the FELLOWSHIP OF RECONCILIATION and in 1942 founded the CONGRESS OF RACIAL EQUALITY (CORE), which in the 1960s became a major civil rights organization. From 1961 to 1966 he was national director of CORE, in a period that included the CORE-organized FREEDOM RIDES and a series of other demonstrations throughout the South.

Farmers Home Administration (FHA), U.S. federal agency originating in the 1930s farm relief and financing programs of the NEW DEAL; it makes direct loans and guarantees private loans to farmers and farm-related enterprises.

Farouk I (1920–65), the last Egyptian king (1936–52), whose country was effectively, though not formally, dominated by Great Britain before and during World War II. He was the ineffective and increasingly corrupt ruler of Egypt as it moved toward independence in the postwar period. In July 1952 the monarchy was overthrown and a republic established after a coup led by General Mohammed Naguib and Colonel Gamal Abdul NASSER. Farouk went into exile, dying in Rome.

fascism, a system of totalitarian state control that used prejudice, and the short-term economic benefits of militarism to fan nationalism, as exemplified by the fascist regimes in Germany and Italy, which were directly responsible for the murder of tens of millions before and during World War II; the underlying basis for the NAZI PARTY and the FASCIST PARTY.

Fascist Party, the Italian political party formed by Benito MUSSOLINI in 1921, from 1922 until 1943 the ruling party in that country. Its program was an incoherent amalgam of authoritarianism and social reform, relying heavily on calls for order, increased employment, and anticommunism. In practice the party was essentially a vehicle for the development of Mussolini's dictatorship. The concept and slogans of FASCISM were thereafter similarly used in Germany, Spain, Portugal, Austria, and to some extent in Japan and several other countries in Europe and South America. The German variety added a virulent racism that resulted in the death of tens of millions of victims.

Fatah (al-Fatah; Palestine Liberation Movement), Palestinian Arab organization established in 1958; led by Yasir ARAFAT, it began guerrilla operations against Israel in 1964. It joined and became the central organization of the PALESTINE LIBERATION ORGANIZATION in 1969, its leadership and

organization paralleling that of the PLO, with Arafat heading both. Although several harder-line groups have split off as Fatah and the PLO have come to be perceived as moderate, it continues to be the most important of the organizations affiliated with the PLO.

FBI, the initials of the FEDERAL BUREAU OF INVESTIGATION, by which this U.S. federal agency is best known.

FCC, the initials of the FEDERAL COMMUNICATIONS COMMISSION, a U.S. agency set up by the Communications Act of 1934 to regulate use of radio airwaves.

FDA, the initials of the FOOD AND DRUG ADMINISTRATION, set up in 1931.

FDIC, the initials of the FEDERAL DEPOSIT INSURANCE CORPORATION, the U.S. federal agency that insures most deposits in federally chartered commercial banks.

February Rebellion (Japan; February 26–28, 1936), the revolt in Tokyo of a group of young right-wing Japanese army officers leading 1,400 soldiers of the army's First Division, resulting in the assassinations of many leading government officials. The revolt was suppressed by army and navy forces, and many of the rebels were later executed, but it was nonetheless a major step on the road toward the victory of Japanese militarism and the onset of World War II.

February Revolution (January–March 1917), the insurrection that ended the Romanov dynasty in Russia. It began in January with a series of strikes, demonstrations, and army mutinies in many parts of Russia. The czar's government was unable to reestablish control, because army units sent to restore order either refused to leave their barracks or joined the revolutionaries, as did many soldiers returning from the front. By early February, NICHOLAS II could no longer govern; he resigned on March 15, and the new PROVISIONAL GOVERNMENT took over control of the country.

fedayeen, a general term for guerrilla fighters in the Arab world but in the long Arab–Israeli conflict, especially describing PALES-

TINE LIBERATION ORGANIZATION (PLO) commando groups.

Federal Bureau of Investigation (FBI), U.S. federal investigative agency, formally attached to the Department of Justice, but with a substanially independent life of its own. It was established in 1908, as the Bureau of Investigation and was reorganized and greatly expanded during the directorship of J. Edgar HOOVER (1924–72). The organization became highly visible and expanded its operations during the 1930s, while conducting a well-publicized campaign against the "most wanted" criminals of the period; it expanded even further as a counterintelligence organization during World War II. It continued to expand as an antisubversive organization during the MC-CARTHY period, then and thereafter engaging in massive abuses of authority, as revealed during the WATERGATE investigations of the early 1970s; these included harassment of a wide range of political dissenters, among them Martin Luther KING, Jr. and tampering with Watergate evidence. Such abuses were in the main curbed by later FBI directors, but charges of the harassment of dissenters have periodically recurred, as did charges of harassment of minority groups employed by the organization.

Federal Communications Commission (FCC), U.S. agency set up by the Communications Act of 1934 to regulate use of RADIO airwaves. Among other things, the FCC controlled licensing of radio and TELEVISION stations, allocation of frequency bands for transmission, limitation on monopolistic networks in any one market, and types of commercials and programming allowed; for example, lotteries, fraud, and obscenity are forbidden. The FCC also required that stations carry a certain amount of public interest programming.

Federal Deposit Insurance Corporation (FDIC), U.S. federal agency, established by the Federal Reserve Act of 1933, guaranteeing deposits in federally chartered commercial banks up to statutory limits, thereby also protecting the banking system from the kind of large-scale bank insolvency that occurred in the early years of the GREAT DEPRESSION. The FDIC is also involved in bank regulation, and in settling the affairs of insolvent banks at the lowest possible cost to the federal government; in the 1980s, as the American banking system suffered massive insolvencies, this became a substantial federal budget factor. Its companion organization, the FEDERAL SAVINGS AND LOAN INSURANCE CORPORATION (FSLIC), performs the same function for federally chartered savings and loan associations, and in the 1980s was even more heavily involved in merging insolvent savings and loan associations and paying their insured depositors.

Federal Emergency Relief Administration (FERA), a new deal agency created during the first HUNDRED DAYS of the ROOSEVELT administration, through which Harry HOPKINS quickly distributed approximately $500 million to the states, most of it used in direct relief payments to the destitute.

Federal Republic of Germany, those portions of Germany occupied by the Western Allies after World War II, popularly known as West Germany, which became an independent democratic state on May 23, 1949, partially effecting the formal partition of Germany. Partition was formally concluded on October 7, 1949, with the establishment of the GERMAN DEMOCRATIC REPUBLIC.

Federal Reserve System, the U.S. central banking system, established by law in 1913 and activated in 1914. The system consists of 12 regional banks engaged collectively in a considerable variety of credit control, bank regulation, balance of trade, and national debt financing activities.

Federal Savings and Loan Insurance Corporation (FSLIC), a U.S. federal agency that guarantees deposits in federally chartered savings and loan associations, as does the FEDERAL DEPOSIT INSURANCE CORPORATION (FDIC) for federally chartered commercial banks; during the 1980s, savings and loan insolvencies imposed a drain amounting to tens of billions of dollars on the U.S. treasury, with much more to come.

Federal Trade Commission (FTC), a U.S. federal regulatory agency, since 1914 charged with enforcing antitrust legislation and prohibiting practices that are in restraint of trade. Originally a major antitrust instrument, it became much less effective during the 1920s, resuming its antitrust course during the NEW DEAL era with the appointment of Thurman Arnold as head of the Antitrust Division of the FTC, a course that substantially continued, although shifting somewhat with the tenor of the times.

feedback, self-regulation by a living or machine system using information from previous output or experience, often aimed at maintaining an equilibrium, called HOMEOSTASIS. Use of the feedback concept in relation to machine systems grew from the 1930s and was clarified by Norbert WIENER, who saw feedback as key to his theory of CYBERNETICS. The development of sophisticated ROBOTS and ARTIFICIAL INTELLIGENCE—both holy grails of modern science—depends on feedback, especially the ability for a machine to "learn" from experience and modify its workings to meet changing conditions. Wiener and many others also explored how feedback mechanisms work in living systems. In humans self-regulation is called BIOFEEDBACK and since 1967 been developed as a deliberate self-control technique.

Feminine Mystique, The (1963), a key feminist work by Betty FRIEDAN that had powerful impact on the development of the modern American women's movment.

Feng Yu-hsiang (1882–1948), Chinese warlord, also known as the Christian General, who commanded substantial forces in northern China, taking Peking in 1924 but failing to hold it. He allied himself with CHIANG KAI-SHEK in 1927, took Peking again with warlord allies in 1928, broke with Chiang in 1929, and was defeated by Chiang's KUOMINTANG armies in 1930.

FEPC, the initials of the trailblazing World War II U.S. federal FAIR EMPLOYMENT PRACTICES COMMISSION.

Fermi, Enrico (1901–54), Italian-American nuclear physicist, who achieved the first controlled nuclear CHAIN REACTION, heralding the beginning of the atomic age. After early work in mathematics and theoretical atomic physics, he experimented with using NEUTRONS to bombard elements, work for which he received the 1938 Nobel Prize for Physics, afterward fleeing from Sweden to the United States with his Jewish wife and children, instead of returning to fascist Italy. On learning that three German scientists in 1939 had repeated his experiment with URANIUM, producing NUCLEAR FISSION, he (and others) urged that the United States develop an ATOMIC BOMB before the Germans could do so. In 1942 he created the first chain reaction in the world's first NUCLEAR REACTOR in the then-small MANHATTAN PROJECT, working in a University of Chicago squash court. The project then moved to LOS ALAMOS, and Fermi moved with it. After the war he advised the ATOMIC ENERGY COMMISSION (AEC).

Fermi reactor meltdown (October 5, 1966), the partial meltdown of the core of the Enrico Fermi breeder reactor at Detroit, Michigan, causing plant shutdown and considerable contamination of the plant but without direct casualties or other serious consequences. It was later knowledgably reported to have been an extremely close call for Detroit and its millions of inhabitants.

Fernald environmental contamination, secret release of radioactive uranium waste from the Fernald nuclear weapons plant, near Cincinnati, Ohio, into the Great Miami River, into the air, and into the ground, via waste pits that were known to be leaking. In the autumn of 1988, the U.S. government admitted that the releases had been going on for decades, part of a pattern of secrecy and breakdown throughout the U.S. nuclear weapons production system.

Ferraro, Geraldine Anne (1935–   ), U.S. lawyer, prosecutor, and New York Democratic Congresswoman (1979–84) who became Democratic vice presidential candidate on the MONDALE ticket in 1984 and was the first woman to be a major-party candidate for that office. She ran a strong campaign as a liberal, although her candidacy was somewhat damaged by charges of "guilt by association" with her husband, who was attacked for allegedly unethical business activities.

Feynman, Richard Phillips (1918–88), U.S. physicist, who in the late 1940s developed quantum electrodynamics to describe the behavior of ELECTRONS with mathematical precision, a major contribution to the underpinnings of QUANTUM THEORY. For his work he shared the 1965 Nobel Prize for Physics with Julian S. Schwinger and Shinichiro Tomonaga, who worked independently. During World War II he worked on the ATOMIC BOMB and later, with Murray GELL-MANN, explored the possible existence of QUARKS. He is best-known to the public as a member of the commission exploring the 1986 *CHALLENGER* disaster, for showing with a simple glass of ice water how the craft's O-ring seals could become brittle and fail.

FHA, the initials of the FARMERS HOME ADMINISTRATION, by which this federal agency has been best known since its formation during the GREAT DEPRESSION.

fifth column, a phrase indicating subversion, introduced by Spanish fascist general Queipo de Llano during the SPANISH CIVIL WAR. He described the advance on Madrid as proceeding in five columns—four of them military and one composed of sympathizers within the city itself.

Figueres Ferrer, José (1906–   ), Costa Rican political leader and socialist, who in 1948 led a successful insurrection after a presidential election was stolen from Otilio Ulate Blanco; he served as president of the interim government until Blanco took office in 1949. Figueres was elected president twice (1953–58; 1970–74), and in that post

he continued to develop the social welfare program of the socialist National Liberation party, which he founded in 1948 and which is also the party of Oscar ARIAS SANCHEZ.

Fiji, until 1970, a British colony; it became an independent state and member of the COMMONWEALTH on October 10, 1970. A period of turbulence began with the election of April 1987; it was generated by ethnic conflicts, mainly between native Fijians and Indian-Fijians. A more stable period began with the army coup of September 25, 1987. A republic was established on October 7, 1987. Commonwealth status was withdrawn on October 16, 1987.

final solution, the NAZI code name for the German plan to murder all of Europe's Jews, a plan put into effect during 1941 and carried on uninterruptedly thereafter, resulting in GENOCIDE: the JEWISH HOLOCAUST.

Finland (Republic of Finland), until the December 6, 1917, declaration of independence part of the Russian Empire. Independence was won in the FINNISH CIVIL WAR of 1918, Finland becoming a republic on October 14, 1920.

Finland Station, a Leningrad railway station, at which Vladimir Illich LENIN arrived on April 16, 1917, on returning from exile in Switzerland after a voyage across Europe under German safe conduct.

Finnish campaign of 1944 (July–September 1944), series of engagements following Soviet forces' breach of the Mannerheim Line in June 1944. By early September the Finns were defeated; the Soviet–Finnish armistice of September 4, 1944, took Finland out of World War II.

Finnish-Soviet War (November 1939–March 1940), Soviet invasion of Finland, starting on November 30, 1939. After the successful German invasion of Poland in September 1939 and the subsequent Soviet–German partition of Poland, the Soviet Union demanded military bases from Finland. Finland refused; the invasion resulted. In heavy early fighting, the Finns held the Soviets on all fronts, inflicting large losses in the fighting at the MANNERHEIM Line. In December and early January the Soviets lost most of two divisions in heavy fighting at Suomussalmi, with small Finnish losses. But in February 1940 a powerful new Soviet offensive breached the Mannerheim Line, and by early March the Finns had been defeated, then granting essentially the same bases that had been originally demanded by the Soviet Union.

Finnish War of Independence (1918), conflict that developed as part of the RUSSIAN CIVIL WAR. On December 6, 1917, after the OCTOBER REVOLUTION, the Finnish parliament declared Finland's independence. In January 1918, Finnish White Guard forces led by Baron Carl Gustav MANNERHEIM were at war with BOLSHEVIK and Finnish Red Guard forces. In April 1918 German intervention took the White Guard to victory; independence was formally recognized by the Treaty of Dorpat, in October 1920.

fireside chats, a series of radio addresses to the nation by Franklin D. ROOSEVELT during his long presidency, taking up those matters he considered of considerable importance. The first of these was the address of Sunday evening, March 12, 1933, in which he assured his listeners that the country's banking system was sound and asked them to leave their money in the banks and redeposit more when the banks, which had been closed by his BANK HOLIDAY order, began to reopen on March 13.

First Arab–Israeli War (May 1948–January 1949), an alternate name for the ISRAELI WAR OF INDEPENDENCE.

First Balkan War (1912–13), the first of the two BALKAN WARS, in which the nations of the Balkan League defeated Turkey; part of the run-up to World War I.

First World War (1914–18), alternate name for WORLD WAR I, the major international conflict of the early 20th century.

Fisher, Andrew (1862–1928), Australian coal miner, labor leader, and socialist, who became a Labour member of the Queensland parliament in the 1890s and of the Australian parliament 1901–15. He was

three-time prime minister (1908–09, 1910–13, 1914–15), and in that position fostered economic development, social welfare, and later Australian participation in World War I.

Fiume Coup, an episode beginning in September 1919 when Italian nationalists led by Gabriele D'ANNUNZIO seized the Adriatic coast city of Fiume, then disputed by Yugoslavia and Italy. Italian troops attacked and expelled the nationalist group in December 1920. Fiume's status was settled for some years by the 1920 Treaty of RAPALLO.

five-year plans, three Soviet interwar economic plans (1928–32, 1933–37, 1938–42) aimed at developing Soviet heavy industry and collectivizing Soviet agriculture, although the second put slightly more emphasis on consumer goods than the first; and the third, executed just before and during World War II, was in essence a wartime plan. The first FIVE-YEAR PLAN was intertwined with and part of the justification for the massive Stalinist attack on all internal opposition, and on the KULAKS, who were the family farmers of the Soviet Union, an attack that was to cost an estimated 20 million Soviet lives during the interwar period.

Flanders, Battle of (May 10–June 4, 1940), successful World War II German invasion and conquest of Belgium, Holland, and northern France, which began on May 10; by May 15, Belgium and Holland had both fallen, and the Germans had broken through near Sedan and split the Allied armies in the ARDENNES, the key action of the war in the west. The German army then easily drove to the sea, forcing Belgian surrender and the British evacuation from DUNKIRK, which was completed by June 4. Then the Germans turned to what were essentially mopping up operations in France, which surrendered on June 21.

Fleming, Alexander (1881–1955), Scottish bacteriologist who, in the course of his search for another antibacterial substance, accidentally discovered PENICILLIN in 1928, making a contribution to medicine that would save millions of lives; he shared the

1945 Nobel Prize for Physiology and Medicine.

Fletcher, Frank Jack (1885–1973), U.S. admiral, who saw action in Mexico and during World War I, and commanded task forces in the Battle of the CORAL SEA and the Battle of MIDWAY.

FLN (National Liberation Front), Algerian revolutionary organization formed in November 1954 and the main force in the ALGERIAN WAR OF INDEPENDENCE. The FLN was socialist, pan-Arab, and neutralist; with independence in July 1962, the FLN became the sole official state party of Algeria.

flower children, a popular term describing many of the young people of the U.S. 1960s COUNTERCULTURE, whose orientation to a rural, communal, nonviolent, alternative set of life-styles appealed to some, threatened others, and made them highly controversial in a culture that celebrated and simultaneously attacked cultural diversity.

Floyd, Charles Arthur "Pretty Boy" (1904–34), U.S. midwestern murderer and bank robber of the early 1930's who was at one time designated "Public Enemy Number One" by the FEDERAL BUREAU OF INVESTIGATION. He was killed by FBI agents in 1934.

fluoridation, addition of fluorides to the water supply, aiming to reduce the number of dental cavities, first introduced in the United States in 1945. At first a *cause célèbre* in many communities, it was widely adopted, especially after 1967, when a 20-year study in Evanston, Illinois, showed that fluoridation dramatically decreased dental decay.

Flyer I, name of the Wright brothers' craft in the first successful AIRPLANE flight in 1903, later often called *Kitty Hawk.*

flying saucer, popular designation for an UNIDENTIFIED FLYING OBJECT.

Flynn, Elizabeth Gurley (1890–1964), U.S. Marxist revolutionary, who became an INDUSTRIAL WORKERS OF THE WORLD (IWW) leader in 1908–09, was a founding member of the AMERICAN CIVIL LIBERTIES UNION (ACLU) in 1920, became a leader of the

COMMUNIST PARTY OF THE UNITED STATES in the mid-1930s, and was imprisoned for more than two years for being a Communist, 1955–57, becoming chairman of the Communist party in 1961. She had been expelled from the ACLU executive board in 1940 because she was a Communist and was posthumously rehabilitated by the ACLU in 1976.

FNLA, initials of the NATIONAL FRONT FOR THE LIBERATION OF ANGOLA, by which the organization is best known.

Foch, Ferdinand (1851–1929), French World War I general whose Ninth Army played a key role in throwing back the advancing German armies at the first Battle of the MARNE. In 1917 he became French chief of staff.

Food and Agriculture Organization (FAO), a UNITED NATIONS special agency established in 1945 to foster rural economic development and improve the conditions of rural life throughout the world. Since then it has played a major role in bringing modern farming techniques and tools to the THIRD WORLD, providing relief to areas stricken by drought and other natural and man-made calamities, and developing a wide range of educational activities aimed at improving the quality of rural life.

Food and Drug Administration (FDA), U.S. federal agency charged with protecting the public health, in such areas as foods, drugs, and product safety. Set up in 1931, its operations were greatly expanded by the 1938 Federal Food, Drug, and Cosmetic Act, after at least 73 people died in 1937 from taking a drug called ELIXIR SULFANILAMIDE. That act was amended in 1962, after the THALIDOMIDE tragedies of 1961, to tighten rules regarding testing of possible new drugs (rules later to come under criticism during the AIDS crisis) and in 1966 to require that patients be informed when they are being given an experimental drug.

Ford, Gerald Rudolph (1913–   ), U.S. lawyer, a Republican Michigan congressman (1949–73) and minority leader of the House (1965–73), who was appointed to the vice presidency in 1973 after the resignation of Vice President Spiro AGNEW. He became the 38th president of the United States (1974–77) on August 9, 1974, succeeding Richard M. NIXON, who had resigned to avoid impeachment because of his role in the WATERGATE scandal. He then appointed Nelson ROCKEFELLER to the vice-presidency, with congressional approval. On September 8, 1974, Ford pardoned former president Nixon for all possible federal offenses committed during Nixon's presidency. As president, and as a fiscally conservative Republican facing economic problems at home and a Democratic Congress, he proposed little new legislation, focusing instead on spending control. As the first post-Watergate president he initiated major changes and curbs on the national security agencies. Abroad, he pursued the OPENING TO CHINA begun by Richard Nixon and encouraged Egyptian–Israeli and other Middle Eastern negotiations but had little success in the area of U.S.–U.S.S.R. relations. He won the closely contested Republican presidential nomination in 1976, defeating Ronald REAGAN, but lost the election to Democrat Jimmy CARTER.

Ford, Henry (1863–1947), U.S. mechanic, who became an innovative automobile developer and major industrialist, paying higher minimum wages than his competitors and developing a profit-sharing program. At the same time he strongly resisted unionization, being in 1941 the last of the major automobile manufacturers to become unionized. His revolutionary moving assembly line, introduced in 1913, influenced factories worldwide. Ford was also the most prominent anti-Jewish bigot of the 1920s, who refused to moderate his position even though a committee headed by Presidents WILSON and TAFT asked him to do so, and whose *Dearborn Independent* printed an uninterrupted series of anti-Semitic articles until 1927, when threatened boycotts and lawsuits forced his public apology.

Forrestal, James Vincent (1892–1949), U.S. investment banker, who joined the administration of Franklin D. ROOSEVELT in 1940 and became undersecretary and then secretary of the navy. He became secretary of defense in 1947, resigned under political pressure in March 1949, and committed suicide in May 1949.

***Forrestal* explosion** (July 29, 1967), explosion of the *U.S.S. Forrestal*, in the South China Sea, off South Vietnam, killing 134 people.

Fortas, Abe (1910–82), U.S. lawyer and law professor, who held several federal government posts 1937–46, then becoming a prominent Washington lawyer. He was appointed to the Supreme Court by Lyndon B. JOHNSON in 1965 and was nominated by Johnson to succeed Chief Justice Earl WARREN in 1968, but the latter appointment was successfully resisted by Senate conservatives. In 1969 charges of possibly irregular, though not illegal, financial conduct caused him to resign from the Court, the first such resignation in history.

Fosdick, Harry Emerson (1878–1969), U.S. Protestant minister and educator, professor at Union Theological Seminary 1908–46, pastor of Riverside Church 1926–46, and one of the leading liberal ministers of his time. Fosdick took the modernist position in attempting to reconcile Christianity, social justice, and science, and in practical terms he became a leading political liberal on such issues as racial discrimination and planned parenthood.

Fossey, Dian (1932–85), U.S. primatologist, known for her studies of mountain gorillas in east central Africa. Like Jane GOODALL encouraged by Louis LEAKEY, she worked first in 1966 in Zaire (then the Congo), and from 1967 at the Karisoke Research Centre in Rwanda's Virungas Mountains, where the local people called her *Nyiramachabelli*, meaning "the old lady who lives in the forest without a man." But her singleminded concern for the mountain gorillas led her into direct conflict with some in Rwanda who desired the land occupied by the endangered species. Her 1983 book, *Gorillas in the Mist*, inspired the 1987 book and 1988 movie about her life and work.

fossil fuels, burnable substances such as oil, coal, or natural gas, formed from ancient plants deposited in previous ages and latterly put to human use. Gas by-products of burning such fuels are implicated in major ecological effects, such as ACID RAIN and in long-term global changes such as the GREENHOUSE EFFECT. The 1970s OIL EMBARGO temporarily spurred efforts to find other, cleaner energy sources, such as SOLAR POWER and synthetic fuels, but the oil glut of the 1980s caused funding for such efforts to drop to almost nothing.

Foster, William Zebulon (1881–1961), U.S. industrial worker, who became a socialist, an organizer for the INDUSTRIAL WORKERS OF THE WORLD (IWW), founder of the Syndicalist League of North America in 1912, and leader of the AMERICAN FEDERATION OF LABOR (AFL) great steel strike of 1919, which failed to organize the basic steel industry. In 1920 he initiated the Trade Union Educational League and in 1921 joined and became a leading member of the Communist Party; he was its presidential candidate in 1924, 1928, and 1932. After his old friend and associate, Earl BROWDER, was removed from Communist Party leadership in 1945, Foster became chairman of his party. He was indicted with other Communist leaders in 1948 but was excused from the SMITH ACT TRIALS because of poor health, continuing as party chairman until 1957.

Foucault, Michel (1926–84), French philosopher linked with STRUCTURALISM, who tried to find a historical sequence of basic thought structures. He explored the relationship between society and social deviance, especially in people regarded as insane or criminal, in works such as *Madness and Civilization* (1961) and *The Archaeology of Knowledge* (1969).

Four Freedoms, freedom of speech and expression, freedom of worship, freedom from want, and freedom from fear of war; these slogans were originated by Franklin Delano ROOSEVELT in his January 6, 1941, State of the Union speech and became key popular slogans during and immediately after World War II.

Fourteen Points, a peace and post-World War I redevelopment program put forward by U.S. president Woodrow WILSON on January 8, 1918, which became the basis of the American position at the PARIS PEACE CONFERENCE of 1919 and which included a proposal for the formation of a LEAGUE OF NATIONS. That proposal was adopted and embodied in the Treaty of VERSAILLES, as were his and other proposals for the creation of several new European nations. But the U.S. Senate was unwilling to authorize American participation in the League of Nations; it refused to ratify the Treaty of Versailles and in 1921 made a separate peace.

Fourth Arab–Israeli War (October 6–24, 1973), an alternate name for the YOM KIPPUR WAR, also called the OCTOBER WAR.

France (French Republic), until the fall of France in 1940, a country governed by the Third Republic, formed in 1870. During World War II, the puppet VICHY GOVERNMENT existed during the period of the German occupation. The Fourth Republic governed 1947–58, until the crisis generated by the ALGERIAN WAR OF INDEPENDENCE. The Fifth Republic was formed under the leadership of Charles DE GAULLE, in 1958.

France, Battle of (June 5–25, 1940), conflict early in World War II after the Battle of FLANDERS, which ended with the evacuation at DUNKIRK. As the German army moved south against remaining French forces, they smashed them in a week, the French government fleeing from Paris to Bordeaux. Paris was declared an open city on June 13; the Germans marched in on June 14. France surrendered on June 21, effective June 25.

Francis Ferdinand of Austria (1863–1914), archduke and heir to the Austro-Hungarian throne who was assassinated with his wife at SARAJEVO, on June 28, 1914, setting off WORLD WAR I.

Franco, Francisco (1892–1975), Spanish soldier, who became a general in the 1920s, was sent to commands abroad in 1931 and 1936 by two Spanish Republican governments, and came back in 1936 to lead the winning Nationalists in the SPANISH CIVIL WAR. From 1939 to 1975, he reigned as dictator of fascist Spain. He maintained official neutrality during World War II while informally cooperating with Germany and Italy for much of the war; the Spanish BLUE DIVISION fought on the Russian front beside its Nazi allies.

Frank, Hans (1900–46), Nazi party official, justice minister, and governor of much of Poland during World War II. Frank was convicted of war crimes at the NUREMBERG TRIALS and executed in 1946.

Frank, Leo (1884–1915), Brooklyn-born Jew who was accused and convicted of the rape and murder of 14-year-old Mary Phagan in Atlanta, Georgia, April 26, 1913. Active in Atlanta's Jewish community, Frank was tried and convicted in an anti-Jewish climate that precluded the possibility of a fair trial. A worldwide campaign for his release and new evidence discovered by detective William J. Burns brought commutation of his death sentence in June 1915. On August 17, 1915, a lynch mob removed him from jail without opposition from prison guards, and later that day he was lynched by the mob in Marietta, Georgia.

Frankfurter, Felix (1882–1965), U.S. lawyer and Harvard law professor 1914–39, who was also active as an advisor to government, a founder of the AMERICAN CIVIL LIBERTIES UNION, and a legal writer; in 1939 he was appointed to the Supreme Court by Franklin Delano ROOSEVELT. He became, somewhat to the surprise of many, one of the leading conservative members of the Court, advocating judicial restraint, rather than activism in pursuing social and political goals.

Franklin, Rosalind (1920–58), British biochemist, whose work in X-RAY CRYSTALLOGRAPHY, along with Maurice WILKINS, produced key photographs that aided

James WATSON and Francis CRICK in uncovering the DOUBLE HELIX structure of DNA, though she died before she could share in their 1962 Nobel Prize.

Fraser, Malcolm (1930–), Australian rancher, in parliament from 1955, who became Liberal Party leader in 1975 and was prime minister of the Liberal–National Country coalition government 1975–83. In that position he leaned strongly toward the United States and substantially reversed the somewhat more neutralist policies of the previous Labour government. Worsening economic problems helped bring Labour back into office in 1983.

Fraser, Peter (1884–1950), New Zealand trade unionist and socialist, a Labour party founder who was imprisoned for his opposition to involvement in World War I, became a member of parliament in 1918, and rose to become prime minister 1940–49. He took his country through World War II, which he did not oppose, and into the postwar period.

Frazer, James George (1854–1941), British anthropologist and classical scholar, whose *Golden Bough,* published in brief in 1890 but expanded into 12 volumes in 1907–15, was a seminal work on religion, magic, and folklore, drawn on by scholars from his own and many other fields.

Free French, the London-based French government-in-exile led by Charles DE GAULLE from June 1940. With Allied support, the Free French began to develop small military forces in Britain and in the French central African colonies, developing further strength when the Allies took North Africa and many former VICHY French soldiers joined the Allied forces. As the invasion of Europe approached, substantial resistance forces grew in France, and the Free French became the Committee of National Liberation and then the French provisional government, De Gaulle entering Paris as its leader on August 26, 1944, one day after the Allied liberation of the city.

Freedom of Information Act, a 1966 U.S. law, requiring increased disclosure of information held by the federal government and providing a procedure for legal challenge of government secrecy claims, although it continued to protect much information from public disclosure.

freedom rides, a nonviolent interracial campaign to desegregate public transportation and related facilities in the American South, originally organized by the CONGRESS OF RACIAL EQUALITY (CORE) in May 1961. The campaign, featuring the use of segregated facilities by Blacks, often as part of interracial groups, was met by violence in many parts of the South and was ultimately federally enforced.

Freedom 7, U.S. MERCURY spacecraft that first put an American into space; flown on a suborbital flight on May 5, 1961, by Alan SHEPARD.

Frei Montalva, Eduardo (1911–82), Chilean Catholic liberal political leader, a founder of the Christian Democratic party, and president of Chile 1964–70, who inaugurated a series of major land, industrial, and financial reforms during his presidency. He could not run again in 1970, given Chile's one-term presidency, and was succeeded by Salvador ALLENDE. After the military coup of 1973 and Allende's death, Frei strongly opposed the new military government of Augusto PINOCHET and its reign of terror.

Freikorps (Free Corps), the right-wing German militia developed by the German general staff in alliance with the new socialist government during the GERMAN REVOLUTION of 1918. In 1920 a government attempt to control the Freikorps led to its attempted KAPP PUTSCH, and its dissolution after the coup failed.

Frelimo (National Liberation Front), the Mozambique ruling party was founded by Eduardo MONDLANE in 1962 as a united front against Portuguese rule. It fought and won the long MOZAMBIQUE WAR OF INDEPENDENCE (1964–74) and became the Marxist governing party of that single-party state in 1975.

French Army mutinies (April–May 1917), World War I army revolt that followed the failed NIVELLE OFFENSIVE in Champagne and took much of the French army out of its trenches on the Western Front for most of May. Tens of thousands of arrests were made; 55 mutineers were shot.

French Equatorial Africa, four former French colonies, all of which became overseas territories in 1946 and independent nations in 1960. CHAD and GABON retained their names. Middle Congo became the Republic of the CONGO; Ubangi-Shari became the CENTRAL AFRICAN REPUBLIC.

French Somaliland, the former name of DJIBOUTI (Republic of Djibouti), which became the Territory of the AFARS AND ISSAS in 1966, and Djibouti in 1977.

French Togoland, the eastern portion of TOGOLAND, which became the independent nation of TOGO on April 17, 1960.

Freon, alternate name for CHLOROFLUORO-CARBONS, implicated from at least 1974 in depletion of the OZONE LAYER.

Freud, Sigmund (1856–1939), Viennese neurologist who founded PSYCHOANALYSIS. Early work with hysteria and hypnosis and analysis of his own dreams and childhood development led to Freud's key studies, *The Interpretation of Dreams* (1900) and *The Psychopathology of Everyday Life* (1904). From explorations of the influence of sexual life and fantasies on the development of neuroses, Freud developed a general theory of the personality (involving the unconscious primitive id, the conscious ego, and its "conscience," the superego) and the therapeutic approach of psychoanalysis. Though highly controversial in his lifetime, Freud's work attracted some key followers, including his daughter Anna (1895–1982); through them his ideas and the techniques of psychoanalysis spread widely, especially in the United States after World War II, influencing not only modern psychology but much popular thinking.

Frick, Wilhelm (1887–1946), Nazi party official, interior minister, and governor of much of Czechoslovakia during World War II. Frick was convicted of war crimes at the NUREMBERG TRIALS and executed in 1946.

Friedan, Betty Naomi (1921–   ), U.S. feminist activist and writer, whose book *The Feminine Mystique* (1963), had substantial impact on the development of the modern American women's movement. In 1966 she was a founder of the NATIONAL ORGANIZATION FOR WOMEN (NOW), and was its president until 1970, thereafter continuing to work as a writer and activist.

Friedman, Milton (1912–   ), U.S. economist, whose monetarist and laissez-faire economic theories deeply influenced the thinking of such politically and economically conservative leaders as Richard M. NIXON, Margaret THATCHER, and Ronald REAGAN in the United States, Britain, and other industrially developed countries from the mid-1960s. His opposition to government economic intervention brought him to advocate such measures as unlimited free trade, deregulation of many industries, divestiture of publicly owned institutions, and the destruction of existing government-funded social service networks. He was awarded the 1976 Nobel Prize for ECONOMICS.

Friendship 7, U.S. MERCURY spacecraft that put the first American into orbit around the Earth; flown on a 5-hour, 3-orbit flight on February 20, 1962, by John GLENN.

Frolinat (Chad National Liberation Front), an insurgent movement formed in northern CHAD in 1966 to oppose the southern-based government of François Tombalbaye (N'Garta) and the French military force still occupying northern Chad in support of the year-old government of independent Chad. Frolinat remained a major insurgent force until 1976, then began a long process of breakup into opposing factions, and thereafter became an "umbrella" term for many northern-based insurgent groupings, each of them claiming to be the leading force in the insurgent movement.

Fromm, Erich (1900–80), German-American psychoanalyst and social critic, who focused on the cultural, rather than biological, factors in the shaping of the individual. A student, professor, and practitioner of PSY-CHOANALYSIS in Germany, Fromm emigrated to the United States in 1934 after the rise of the Nazis, gradually moving away from the strict views of FREUD to a wider consideration of the individual in society. His popular writings, such as *Escape From Freedom* (1941), reflected his feelings as a humanist, pacifist, and critic of the dangers for humans in a technological society.

Fromme, Lynette Alice "Squeaky," follower of Charles MANSON who tried to shoot president Gerald R. FORD in Sacramento, California, on September 5, 1975, but did not fire; she was immediately captured and subsequently sentenced to life imprisonment.

Frontiers, Battles of the (August 14–23, 1914), a group of major World War I battles fought by the Franco-British and German armies along the Franco-Belgian and Franco-German borders. In Alsace-Lorraine, when the French attacked, the Germans first fell back, as provided by the SCHLIEFFEN PLAN, and then counterattacked, completely stopping the French advance. In the Ardennes region, the French attacked, but the Germans held firm, according to plan. To the west and north, the main German forces attacked through Belgium, aiming to sweep around Paris and enfold the French and British armies, also as provided by the Schlieffen Plan. In southern Belgium, at the Sambre River, part of the main German force quickly overran the French Fifth Army, forcing its retreat. A little further west, at Mons, the BRITISH EXPEDITIONARY FORCE was forced to retreat, fighting and retreating again at Le Cateau, on the French side of the border, while the French managed to slow the German advance at Guise. The Germans then turned toward Paris and the first Battle of the MARNE, one of the decisive battles of the 20th century.

Front-Line States, term for Angola, Botswana, Mozambique, Tanzania, and Mozambique; together they are seen by the nations of Black Africa as those countries directly confronting the segregationist South African government.

FSLIC, the FEDERAL SAVINGS AND LOAN INSURANCE CORPORATION, the U.S. federal agency that insures most deposits in federally chartered savings and loan associations.

Fuchs, Klaus (1911–88), German-British atomic physicist, who worked on the development of the ATOMIC BOMB at LOS ALAMOS 1944–45, then returned to Britain to head the physics department at the Harwell atomic energy installation. He was a Soviet spy from 1943 and passed atomic information to the Soviet Union. He was exposed in 1950, confessed, and was imprisoned until 1959, thereafter continuing to work on NUCLEAR ENERGY in East Germany and the Soviet Union.

Fugard, Athol (1932–   ), South African playwright and novelist, a White who in such plays as *Boesman and Lena, Sizwe Bansi Is Dead,* and *Master Harold ... & the Boys* powerfully attacked the system of APARTHEID, and the racism from which it springs.

Fulbright, James William (1905–   ), U.S. lawyer, an Arkansas Democratic congressman 1943–45 and senator 1945–75. In 1945, he sponsored the Fulbright Act, initiating the educational interchange program that bears his name. He headed the Senate Banking and Currency committee 1955–59 and the Foreign Affairs Committee 1959–75, from that vantage point opposing such adventures as the BAY OF PIGS INVASION and the developing American Vietnam intervention during the 1960s; he was a leading opponent of the VIETNAM WAR.

Fuller, Melville Weston (1833–1910), U.S. lawyer and state legislator, who in 1888 became chief justice of the United States, a position he held until 1910. A moderate conservative, his main role was that of administrator, rather than judicial leader.

Fuller, Richard Buckminster (1895–1983), designer and inventor who popularized the GEODESIC DOME. After an apprenticeship in a family construction firm, in 1927 the largely self-trained Fuller began to develop his unorthodox designs for inexpensive houses, cars, and other items. Though his early corporations had little commercial success, in 1954 he formed a new corporation to sell his geodesic dome, a structure composed of lightweight metal tetrahedrons, using his characteristic small amount of material to maximum effect. Easily erected and solidly built, these domes attracted wide attention, and were used, for example, to house people and equipment along the Arctic Distant Early Warning (DEW) line. Fuller's unconventional approach brought him great attention and popularity late in life, especially in the 1960s.

G

Gabon (Gabonese Republic), earlier part of French Equatorial Africa, becoming an independent state on August 17, 1960. The new country's first president was Léon M'ba, who was succeeded after his death in 1968 by Vice-President Albert-Bernard (later El Hadj Omar) Bongo. Under Bongo, Gabon became a one-party state.

Gacy, John Wayne, U.S. mass murderer, who killed 33 boys and young men during 1972–78, at his suburban home in Knollwood Park, near Chicago; he was convicted of the murders in 1980.

Gagarin, Yuri Alekseyevich (1934–68), Soviet pilot who became the world's first astronaut; on April 12, 1961, in the spacecraft *VOSTOK I*, he made the first space flight, orbiting the Earth once. He died in an air accident in 1968.

Gaitskell, Hugh (1906–63), British economist and moderate socialist, who became a Labour MP in 1945, joined the ATTLEE government in 1947 as fuel and power minister, became chancellor of the exchequer in 1950, and succeeded Attlee as leader of the Labour party in 1955.

Galbraith, John Kenneth (1908–), Canadian-American economist, writer, and social critic, whose thinking was greatly influenced by that of John Maynard KEYNES. A leading liberal, he was an advisor to John F. KENNEDY and was ambassador to India 1961–63. After the late 1960s his continuing advocacy of government economic and social intervention, as well as his opposition to the dominant laissez-faire and monetarist theories of such conservative presidents as Richard M. NIXON and Ronald REAGAN placed him outside the corridors of power, although his continuing stream of writings continued to greatly influence liberal thinking. His book THE AFFLUENT SOCIETY (1958) sharply criticized American overconsumption habits of the day, the sardonic phrase then moving into the language.

Galen, pseudonym adopted by Vasili BLÜCHER during 1924–27, when he was Soviet military advisor to CHIANG KAI-SHEK.

Gallipoli expedition (February 1915–January 1916), a long, ultimately failed British-French attack on Turkish forces in the Dardanelles and the Gallipoli Peninsula. The British fleet lost three battleships while attacking Turkish shore fortifications in the Dardanelles, and three more battleships were disabled; three more were lost later in the campaign. The expeditionary force was pinned down on its small beachheads for months. There were a little over 500,000 casualties, half of them Allied, half Turkish.

Gallup, George Horace (1901–84), U.S. statistician and public-opinion analyst who was a key figure in the development of scientifically based public opinion polls. In 1935 he founded the American Institute of Public Opinion, which conducted Gallup Polls on the main political and social issues of the day while also doing polls for market research and advertising. He expanded to Britain in 1936 and later to some 30 other countries as well, especially after World War II.

Galveston hurricane (September 8, 1900), a Gulf Coast hurricane that destroyed much of Galveston, Texas, killing an estimated 6,000 people and causing tremendous physical damage.

Gambia (Republic of the Gambia), until 1963, a British colony; after gaining internal autonomy in 1963 it became an independent state and COMMONWEALTH member on February 18, 1965. The country has been led by President Dawda Kairaba Jawara since 1962. On February 1, 1982, Gambia joined its much larger neighbor, Senegal, in the confederation of SENEGAMBIA.

Gamelin, Maurice Gustave (1872–1958), French officer, who saw action in World War I, commanded the French army from 1935, and was one of the chief architects of the Allied defensive strategy during the PHONY WAR period. His failure in command contributed to the success of the German attack on France and its allies in the spring of 1940. In late May, too late to undo the damage, he was relieved of command.

game theory, mathematical analysis of conflict situations, taking as a model parlor games as if played for money, with each player trying to maximize gain and minimize loss, the result of the conflict for each person in various situations being the "payoff." First suggested in 1921 and explored by French mathematician Émile Borel, game theory was actually formulated in 1926 by John von NEUMANN, later working with German-American economist Oskar Morgenstern; their classic work is *Theory of Games and Economic Behavior* (1944). Game theory had wide application, notably in economics, politics, and military situations.

gamma rays, type of low-frequency RADIATION and one of the three products of natural RADIOACTIVITY; discovered in 1900 by French physicist Paul Villard and quickly found by Ernest RUTHERFORD to be similar to X-RAYS, but with a shorter wavelength.

Gamow, George (1904–68), Russian-American physicist, who was a leading exponent of the BIG BANG THEORY of the universe's origin. In America from 1934, Gamow expanded on Hans BETHE's ideas to show that as a star uses up its hydrogen fuel it becomes hotter, not cooler. In 1954, he was the first to suggest that nucleic acids in DNA worked in groups of units as a genetic code.

He also wrote many widely popular books, notably *One, Two, Three . . . Infinity* (1947).

Gandhi, Indira (1917–84), Indian political leader, the daughter and political heir of Jawaharlal NEHRU, who was active in the CONGRESS PARTY from her youth. She succeeded Lal Bahadur Shastri as prime minister after his death in January 1966. Her party split in 1969, but her faction won a decisive majority in the 1971 elections, returning her to power. Her party declared a state of emergency in June 1975, in response to a powerful campaign to remove her from parliament for alleged electoral fraud. She then arrested hundreds of opposition leaders, curbed press freedom, and ruled by decree until the parliamentary elections of 1977, in which her party was defeated by the Janata party. In January 1978, she and her followers split from the Congress party to form the Indian National party–Indira; in November, she was reelected to parliament, but was refused her seat and imprisoned for the balance of that parliamentary term (1 week). She became prime minister again when her party secured a huge majority in the 1980 elections. During the early 1980s, she faced mounting internal violence, including a major campaign for Sikh autonomy in the Punjab, which climaxed in the June 1984 Indian army assault on the Sikh GOLDEN TEMPLE in Amritsar. On October 31, 1984, she was assassinated by two Sikh members of her personal guard and was succeeded by her son, Rajiv GANDHI.

Gandhi, Mohandas Karamchand "Mahatma" (1869–1948), Indian barrister, who became the Mahatma (Great Soul) to hundreds of millions of Indians. He was the spiritual and political leader of the Indian independence movement, a worldwide symbol of commitment to the poor and suffering, and the foremost advocate and practitioner of nonviolence, in the form he called SATYAGRAHA, during the first half of the 20th century. Born in India, and trained as a barrister in London, he took a job in South Africa in 1893; there, after suffering racist indignities, he entered public life, organizing the Natal Indian Congress in 1894 and in 1906 beginning the first satyagraha campaign, which ended in 1913 with substantial gains. In 1914 he went home to India, practiced law, and in February 1919 emerged as the leader of India's first satyagraha campaign, which swept India, and which he ended temporarily after the violence that began with the AMRITSAR MASSACRE. At the head of the CONGRESS PARTY he led a huge satyagraha movement in 1920–22 and was imprisoned from 1922 to 1924. He lost much influence as the independence movement fragmented in the mid-1920s but emerged again to lead the massive salt tax satyagraha campaign of 1930. In 1932, imprisoned again by the British, he fasted, beginning his long campaign on behalf of the Untouchables, whom he called Harijans (children of God). During the mid-1930s he focused on multiple campaigns for the Indian poor and oppressed. In 1942 he and the other leaders of the Congress Party called on the British to leave India and were imprisoned; he was released in 1942 because of ill health the others remaining in prison until the end of World War II. After the war, in the run-up to Indian independence, he unsuccessfully opposed the PARTITION OF INDIA, and then attempted to stop the rioting and mass murder that accompanied partition. He was assassinated by a Hindu extremist in New Delhi, on January 30, 1948.

Gandhi, Rajiv (1944–   ), Indian engineer and pilot, son of Indira GANDHI and grandson of Jawaharlal NEHRU, who succeeded his mother as Indian prime minister after her assassination in October 1984. He had entered political life after the death of his brother, Sanjay, who had been groomed as his mother's political heir before his death in a 1980 airplane crash, becoming a member of parliament in 1981 and general secretary of the Congress party–Indira in 1983. As prime minister he faced continuing Sikh terrorism in the Punjab as well as continuing armed insurgency and communal violence in several other northern provinces. In 1987 his government directly

intervened in Sri Lanka, in an attempt to end the long SRI LANKAN CIVIL WAR. In 1989 he and Benazir BHUTTO began an attempt to normalize always-sensitive India-Pakistan relations. He resigned in November 1989, after failing to win enough seats to form a government, and was succeeded by National Front leader V.P. SINGH.

Gang of Four, JIANG QING, Zhang Chunqiao, Wang Hongwen, and Yao Wenhuan, Chinese CULTURAL REVOLUTION leaders who were accused of attempting to take power in China after Mao's death. All were arrested in October 1976 and subsequently convicted of a considerable series of crimes against the state. Jiang had, until the death of her husband, MAO ZEDONG, wielded immense power in China, much of it by inference in his name. Her arrest, as leader of the Gang of Four, signaled the victory of far more moderate forces, and a turn away from Maoism in China.

Garner, John Nance (1868–1967), U.S. lawyer, journalist, and 15-term Texas congressman (1903–33). "Cactus Jack" Garner was Speaker of the House of Representatives before becoming Franklin D. ROOSEVELT's vice-president (1933–41). A conservative, he was chosen to balance the Roosevelt ticket; he broke with Roosevelt in 1937 and was an unsuccessful candidate for the Democratic nomination in 1940, thereafter retiring.

Garvey, Marcus Mosiah (1887–1940), Jamaican Black nationalist and PAN-AFRICAN leader, who became leader of the American "Back to Africa" movement. He founded the Universal Negro Improvement Association (UNIA) in Jamaica in 1914, and in 1916 transferred his main activities to New York, where he founded the widely circulated newspaper *Negro World*. In 1919 he founded the Black Star shipping line and in 1920 became provisional president of the African Republic at a New York UNIA convention, in that period becoming a major force in the American Black community. In 1923 he was convicted of stock fraud in connection with his failing Black Star line, began a 5-year prison term in 1925 and was deported to Jamaica in 1927 after his sentence had been commuted, his movement and influence then sharply declining.

GATT, the initials of the GENERAL AGREE-MENT ON TARIFFS AND TRADE, a multinational trade regulation organization.

Gay Liberation, a U.S. movement for homosexual equal rights, that began after the June 1969 police raid on the Stonewall Inn in New York City, and quickly grew into a national movement, with large numbers of male and female gays openly declaring their sexual preferences and coming "out of the closet" demanding equal legal and social rights. In spite of a conservative countermovement, the Gay Liberation movement made considerable social and some legal progress, though it was greatly damaged in the 1980s by the enormous medical and social impact of the AIDS epidemic.

Gaza, Battles of (1917), three World War I battles, in which British forces tried to take Gaza, finally succeeding. Their first attempt, on March 26, failed, with almost 4,000 casualties. Their second, on April 17, was a direct attack on well-fortified Turkish positions; it also failed, with over 6,000 casualties. Their third, on October 31, took the form of a successful attack on Beersheba, followed by a move toward now-vulnerable Gaza, which was then evacuated by the Turks. The British pursued the retreating Turks, taking Jerusalem on December 9.

Gaza Strip, a 25-mile-long section of Mediterranean shore, 4–9 miles deep, in southwestern Palestine, centered on the Arab town of Gaza. It has been disputed territory ever since the 1948 ISRAELI WAR OF INDE-PENDENCE (FIRST ARAB–ISRAELI WAR), occupied by Egypt 1948–56, by Israel 1956–57, by Egypt again until 1967, and by Israel from 1967. Its population of over 500,000, most of them Palestinian refugees and the children of refugees, became deeply involved in the INTIFADA, beginning in 1988, although largely dependent on wages earned at low-paying jobs in Israel.

Gdansk Lenin Shipyard strike (August 1980), the strike of 17,000 workers at the Gdansk Lenin Shipyard on August 14, 1980, which led to a series of related strikes on the Baltic coast and then throughout Poland. The Gdansk strikes were settled by the Gdansk Agreement of August 30, negotiated by a committee headed by Lech WALESA; it led in turn to the formation of SOLIDARI-TY, on September 22.

Geiger, Johannes Wilhelm (1882–1945), German physicist, who in 1913 developed a device to record energized subatomic particles, or RADIATION, now called a Geiger counter. Earlier, as an assistant to Ernest RUTHERFORD, he worked on the experiments that led to the nucleus-centered theory of ATOMIC STRUCTURE. During World War II he participated in Germany's unsuccessful attempt to develop an ATOMIC BOMB.

Gell-Mann, Murray (1929–   ), U.S. physicist, who in 1946 discovered an unusual quality of certain subatomic PARTICLES, which in 1953 he (and others) labeled STRANGENESS, and in 1961 developed a schematic for classifying elementary particles, for which he was awarded the 1969 Nobel Prize for Physics. In 1964, with Richard FEYNMAN, he also proposed the idea that QUARKS were the basic building blocks of matter, a theory reached independently by George Zweig.

Gemayel, Amin (1942–   ), Lebanese lawyer and Maronite Christian leader, oldest son of Pierre GEMAYEL; he became president of Lebanon in 1982 after the assassination of his brother, president-elect Bashir GEMAYEL. A moderate, he had little impact on the warring Lebanese militias, the Syrians, the Israelis, and the course of events in his country.

Gemayel, Bashir (1947–82), Lebanese Maronite Christian leader, son of Pierre GEMAYEL; he became PHALANGE militia commander in 1976 and destroyed competing Christian militias as well as Muslim and leftist civil war adversaries. Gemayel opposed Syrian intervention, covertly welcomed Israeli intervention, and sought to establish a Christian Lebanon, if necessary partitioning the country to achieve his goal. In August 1982 he became president-elect of Lebanon; he was assassinated on September 14 and was then succeeded by his brother, Amin GEMAYEL.

Gemayel, Pierre (1905–84), Lebanese Maronite Christian leader, who founded the PHALANGE party in 1936, then becoming and remaining a powerful force in Lebanese politics until his death; father of Amin GEMAYEL and Bashir GEMAYEL. He was a member of parliament (1960–84), but his chief strength was as leader of his party and its militia during the LEBANESE CIVIL WAR of 1958 and the LEBANESE WARS of the 1970s and 1980s.

Gemini, series of U.S. spacecraft that flew missions from 1965 to 1966, after the MERCURY and before the APOLLO programs. In 1965 *Gemini 3* flew the U.S.'s first two-man space crew, Virgil GRISSOM and John Young; in the same year *Gemini 6* and *7* accomplished the first rendezvous in space; in 1966 *Gemini 8* participated in the first dual launch of spacecraft, and docking in space with an unpiloted craft.

gene, unit of inheritance, a term proposed in 1909 by W. L. Johannsen for something discovered only a year later by Thomas Hunt MORGAN. Morgan found that genes were lined up in rows on chromosomes and that certain characteristics were linked by appearing near each other on the same chromosome, called sex-linked if they were on the chromosome that determined the individual's sex. Such information allowed the drafting of the first chromosome "map" in 1912. In 1927 Hermann J. Muller discovered that X-RAYS could cause mutations in genes, study of which revealed that genes were made up of more basic material, later found to be DNA. A single gene was isolated for the first time in 1969 by Jonathan Beckwith and other researchers.

General Agreement on Tariffs and Trade (GATT), a multinational trade-regulation organization set up after the signing of the 1947 General Agreement on Tariffs and Trade, with almost 100 member nations.

GATT has since functioned as a vehicle for scores of interim meetings and for eight major rounds of trade and tariff negotiations, the eighth, or "Uruguay Round" still being in progress. The "KENNEDY ROUND" of the mid-1960s took substantial steps to reduce tariffs and trade barriers; developing trade imbalances, competitive pressures, and economic slowdown impeded development thereafter.

General Belgrano, the Argentinian cruiser sunk by British torpedoes on May 2, 1982, during the FALKLANDS WAR.

***General Slocum* fire** (June 15, 1904), fire on the excursion steamer *General Slocum* in the East River, off Manhattan, caused by a combination of incompetent seamanship, unavailable lifeboats, and defective lifejackets. The fire ultimately caused the death of 1,031 people, even though help was never more than a few hundred yards away. Had the captain steered for shore, the disaster would have been averted.

General Strike, British (May 4–12, 1926), a nationwide strike called by the British Trades Union Congress in support of the miners' union, which struck because of employer demands for longer hours and lower pay. BALDWIN's Conservative government responded by using troops and large numbers of temporary police and volunteers to keep essential services and food supplies available, and succeeded in breaking the general strike, which was called off after 9 days. The miners' strike continued until August, the miners charging that the rest of the trade union movement had betrayed them.

genetic engineering, deliberate manipulation of DNA, the hereditary material in GENES, for scientific purposes. Short segments of DNA are "cut and pasted"—that is, separated and recombined differently—to produce useful products, to eliminate defects, or to isolate GENETIC MARKERS for study; the spliced segments are called RECOMBINANT DNA. From at least the 1940s, researchers had found that some life forms, such as bacteria, exchanged genetic material. Then in 1953 Francis CRICK and James WATSON worked out the DOUBLE HELIX structure of DNA; in 1969 Jonathan Beckwith and others isolated the first gene; and in 1970 a team led by Har Gobind Khorana first synthesized a gene directly from chemicals. Meanwhile, in 1968 Werner Arber discovered that bacteria produce substances called restriction enzymes, that naturally split genes; the first such enzyme was found in 1970 by Hamilton Othanel Smith. Actual genetic engineering appeared in 1973 with Stanley Cohen and Herbert Boyer's use of restriction enzymes to split and transfer genes from the *Escherichia coli* bacteria. Public concern over genetic engineering and the possibility of altered life forms escaping to overrun the environment brought pressure on the scientific community from 1974 to create stringent guidelines for researchers to follow; these were relaxed somewhat after 1980, but several scientists who had failed to get proper clearance had their experiments stopped. Even early on, the technique bore valuable fruit. As early as 1976 the first commercial genetic engineering firm, Genentech, was founded near San Francisco, California. Six years later the U.S. FOOD AND DRUG ADMINISTRATION approved the first genetically engineered commercial product, human INSULIN produced by bacteria (chosen partly because they reproduce so rapidly). By 1981 interferon, synthesized by genetically altered bacteria, was being used with cancer patients, and Genentech was offering the first genetically engineered vaccine, against hoof-and-mouth disease. The courts quickly became involved in ruling on these new forms of life. In 1980 the Supreme Court ruled in *DIAMOND* v. *CHAKRABARTY* that genetically engineered biological organisms could be patented under federal law; at the time of the ruling, more than 100 other such patents were pending. The first field trials of genetically engineered organisms were held in 1986, earlier trials having been halted in court. The following year the U.S. Patent and Trademark Office ruled that patents applied to all genetically engineered ani-

mals, and the first vertebrate—a genetically engineered mouse—was patented in 1988.

genetic fingerprint, repetitive sequences of DNA taken from a person's body fluids or tissue that, when analyzed, yield a unique pattern, akin to the BAR CODE used on supermarket products. The technique, developed in 1984 by Alec Jeffreys, can identify individuals and confirm or rule out family relationships between people. Even as the technique was being refined, genetic fingerprinting was introduced in U.S. and British courts, the first conviction based on genetic fingerprinting occurring in 1987 in Britain. By 1989 California and other states were planning computerized data bases of genetic information on people convicted of violent crimes, though the efficacy and acceptability of the test remained to be determined through longer-term scientific analysis and courtroom use.

genetic marker, part of a DNA molecule linked with a specific genetic disease or defect. From the early 1970s various scientists realized that techniques being developed in GENETIC ENGINEERING could be used in a deliberate search for such markers. The first ones, for Duchenne muscular dystrophy and Huntington's disease, were found in 1983. Once found, a marker can be used to tell individuals whether or not they carry the gene for the disease, and are likely to develop it later in life or pass it on to their children. The marker also can be isolated and analyzed to see precisely what results from a defective gene—in Duchenne muscular dystrophy, a protein essential to muscles is not produced. Such information also opens the door to correction by genetic engineering. From the mid-1980s major efforts were being made to make a map showing the location of all of the genes—some millions of them—carried by humans.

Geneva Accords on Vietnam (July 1954), an agreement between France and North Vietnam ending the FRENCH–VIETNAMESE WAR and partitioning the country into North and South Vietnam, reached at the multinational Geneva Conference. A similar conference in 1961 agreed to the neutrality of Laos.

Geneva Conventions, series of international treaties regarding the treatment of various groups in wartime, the first treaty in 1864 covering medical treatment and personnel. It was followed by updates and expansions in the 20th century, notably in 1906 to include maritime warfare, in 1929 to cover prisoners of war, and in 1949 to cover civilians and civil wars. The treaties have been accepted by many countries as standards of civilized behavior but often are disregarded in practice.

Geneva Protocol, 1925 treaty banning use of CHEMICAL AND BIOLOGICAL WARFARE, much violated around the world and not ratified by the U.S. Senate until 1974, following President Richard NIXON's 1969 unilateral renunciation of biological weapons and first use of chemical weapons.

Geneva summit (July 1955), the first postwar superpower summit, a week-long meeting between U.S. president Dwight D. EISENHOWER and U.S.S.R. premier Nikita KHRUSHCHEV. No specific agreements occurred, although a long dialogue began, expressed at the time as the "spirit of Geneva," or the willingness to seek peaceful solutions.

Geneva summit (November 1985), the first meeting between U.S. president Ronald REAGAN and U.S. premier Mikhail GORBACHEV, at which they began the series of discussions that would in 1987 and 1988 eventuate in the INF TREATY, substantial reductions of regional conflicts in many parts of the world, and a great thaw and change in American–Soviet relations.

genocide, commission of acts intended to wholly or partly destroy any national, ethnic, racial, or religious group. Such acts have often occurred, before and during the 20th century; but the Nazi murder of millions of Jews in the HOLOCAUST generated demands to make genocide an international crime, and it was so defined by the UNITED NATIONS genocide convention of 1948. However, no prosecutions for genocide have eventuated since, although charges of genocide, a few of them quite clearly well founded, have been abundant in the latter half of the 20th century.

Genovese murder (March 13, 1964), a killing on a New York City street that attracted widespread attention, for scores of people in the surrounding area heard Kitty Genovese's cries for help over a period of more than 35 minutes; they did nothing to help her, not even calling the police.

Gentlemen's Agreement (1907), an informal agreement between President Theodore ROOSEVELT and the Japanese government by which the Japanese agreed to restrict emigration to the United States in return for the rescission of xenophobic anti-Japanese laws and regulations in the U.S. West Coast states.

geodesic dome, solidly built, easily erected structure composed of lightweight metal tetrahedrons, designed by R. Buckminster FULLER. It gained great attention at the 1967 Montreal Exposition and was later used to house people and equipment along the Arctic Distant Early Warning (DEW) line.

George V (George Frederick Ernest Albert, 1865–1936), king of Great Britain 1910–36, through World War I and the onset of the Great Depression. He was the son of EDWARD VII, and the father of EDWARD VIII, who became the duke of Windsor, and of GEORGE VI. Like most of the other British constitutional monarchs of the century, he was largely a symbol, rather than a figure of intrinsic power.

George VI (Albert Frederick Arthur George, 1895–1952), king of Great Britain, 1936–52, and father of ELIZABETH II. George VI and his wife, Elizabeth Bowes-Lyon, later popularly dubbed the "Queen Mum," were important symbols to the British people during the very difficult early years of World War II.

geothermal energy, hot water or steam produced by the Earth and put to human use, either directly for heating or indirectly to create electricity by driving a turbine; most accessible in volcanic or earthquake areas where molten rock is relatively close to the surface and hot springs and geysers abound. The first known modern use was in Italy, where in 1907 Prince Piero Conti used naturally occurring steam to drive a steam engine hooked to a generator, producing electricity for local use; the first electrical plant for converting geothermal energy was built nearby in 1913. Since the 1950's several nations, such as Iceland and New Zealand, have made effective use of geothermal energy; the California electrical plant, The Geysers, started in 1960, was by the 1980s the largest geothermal plant in the world. Even so, this free energy source has been little tapped.

germ warfare, popular name for use of toxic biological agents in CHEMICAL AND BIOLOGICAL WARFARE.

German Democratic Republic, the Soviet occupation zone after World War II, popularly known as East Germany, officially becoming a Soviet-bloc communist state on October 7, 1949. This concluded the formal partition of Germany, which had been partially effected by the establishment of the FEDERAL REPUBLIC OF GERMANY on May 23, 1949. In late 1989, the massive changes of the GORBACHEV era swept through eastern and central Europe; the hardline East German government, led by Erich HONECKER, at first strongly resisted change, but was swept away. In September, a tide of young emigrants flowed out of East Germany, through newly free Hungary. Simultaneously, massive pro-democracy demonstrations, involving hundreds of thousands, erupted in Leipzig, and soon spread to East Berlin, Dresden, and other cities. Honecker was deposed on October 18. On November 9, the government announced a policy of free travel and emigration to the West, negating the BERLIN WALL and opening a new chapter in German and European history. Pro-democracy demonstrations continued, as East Germans reached for free elections, to be held in early 1990.

German High Seas Fleet Mutiny (October 29, 1918), World War I uprising, in which German sailors ended the possibility of another major sea battle against the British fleet by seizing command of their own ships, almost 2 weeks before the Allied–German armistice of November 11, 1918.

German Revolution of 1918, uprising that began with a sailors' revolt at the Kiel naval base in early November and soon spread throughout Germany, with Workers' and Soldiers' Councils, along Soviet lines, spreading throughout the country. Emperor Wilhelm II abdicated on November 9 and fled the country, his government ceding power to Social Democrat Friedrich EBERT. On the night of November 10, Ebert and the German general staff allied themselves against the growing power of the left, developing a militia, the FREIKORPS, which on January 5, 1919 smashed the SPARTACIST revolt in Berlin and then went on to smash the armed forces of the left throughout the country. Ebert's government established the WEIMAR REPUBLIC, which was to last until the advent of the THIRD REICH in 1933.

German-American Bund, U.S. NAZI organization of the 1930s, that under the leadership of Fritz Kuhn and with the financial assistance of the German government, attempted to build Nazi support among German-Americans. It reached a membership of an estimated 10,000–20,000, conducted some anti-Jewish street actions, and disseminated a considerable volume of pro-Nazi propaganda, before the entry of the United States into World War II ended the effective life of the organization.

Germany, at the beginning of the 20th century, was the German Empire, a major power engaged in the long contest for supremacy that led to World War I. After the loss of that war, pursuant to the Treaty of VERSAILLES, Germany lost its overseas possessions and a good deal of its prewar territory while being forced to pay heavy war reparations. The GERMAN REVOLUTION OF 1918 and the subsequent SPARTACIST REVOLT ushered in the short-lived WEIMAR REPUBLIC, to be succeeded in 1933 by the THIRD REICH of Adolf HITLER. Hitler's Germany saw rearmament, internal repression, CONCENTRATION CAMPS, GENO-

CIDE, attacks on neighboring countries, and finally World War II, ending in unconditional surrender. Following World War II, Germany lost all territories gained during the Nazi period and was dismembered, first into Allied occupation zones and then into the GERMAN DEMOCRATIC REPUBLIC and the FEDERAL REPUBLIC OF GERMANY.

Gesell, Arnold Lucius (1880–1961), U.S. child psychologist and physician best known for his Gesell Development Schedules, stages of development against which individual children could be measured. His many books on normal child growth, drawing on his experience at the Yale Clinic of Child Development, made him enormously influential.

Gestapo, the Nazi secret police portion of the SS; as such, Gestapo operatives were above whatever law still existed in Nazi Germany, being answerable only to Heinrich HIMMLER and through him to Adolf HITLER.

Getty, J. Paul, III, the 17-year-old grandson of oil billionaire and art collector J. Paul Getty, who was kidnapped in southern Italy on July 10, 1973, and released on December 15, 1973, after payment of a $2.8 million ransom.

Ghana (Republic of Ghana), formerly the GOLD COAST and BRITISH TOGOLAND. Until independence in 1957, the Gold Coast was a British colony. Togoland was a German protectorate in 1900; in 1922 it was split between France and Great Britain, British (West) Togoland becoming a LEAGUE OF NATIONS mandate territory and a UNITED NATIONS mandate territory after World War II until 1957. Ghana's independence movement, led by Kwame NKRUMAH, won independence and COMMONWEALTH membership on March 6, 1957. Nkrumah became first prime minister and in 1960 first president of the new nation, then establishing personal control in a one-party state until deposed in 1966.

Gheorghiu-Dej, Gheorghe (1901–65), Rumanian Communist leader, imprisoned 1933–44, who became secretary-general of his party in 1945 and premier of Rumania in 1952. At first a hard-line Stalinist, he sharply moved away from Soviet control in the early 1960s, a policy continued by his successor, Nicolae CEAUSESCU.

Giap, Vo Nguyen (1912–   ), North Vietnamese officer, who commanded his country's forces at the siege of DIEN BIEN PHU in 1954, soon becoming defense minister and army commander-in-chief and then commanding the North Vietnamese army during the VIETNAM WAR.

GI Bill of Rights (GI Bill; 1944), a U.S. law providing educational benefits, home and business loans, unemployment benefits, and a miscellany of other benefits to returned veterans after World War II; it became a major postwar readjustment, education, and home-building tool.

Gideon v. *Wainwright* (1963), a landmark U.S. Supreme Court decision establishing the right of indigent defendants in state court criminal cases to have counsel, thus furthering the ideal of equality of all before the law.

Gierek, Edward (1913–   ), Polish miner who lived in Western Europe during the interwar period, becoming a World War II resistance leader in Belgium. He returned to Poland in 1948, became a Communist Party leader, and during the crisis generated by the riots of 1970 succeeded Wladislaw GOMULKA as party head and leader of his country. He resigned in 1980 during the crisis generated by the GDANSK LENIN SHIPYARD and other strikes, which led to the formation of SOLIDARITY.

Gilbert Islands, the former name of KIRIBATI (Republic of Kiribati), until July 12, 1979, a British colony.

Gilbert (September 12–14, 1988), a massive Caribbean hurricane that caused enormous damage and left an estimated 500,000 homeless in Jamaica, caused much damage in the Cayman Islands, and killed at least 200 people and left an estimated 100,000 homeless in Mexico.

Gillars, Mildred, the real name of Nazi broadcaster AXIS SALLY.

Gilmore, Gary Mark (1940–77), convicted Utah murderer, who was the first to be executed after reinstatement of the death penalty by the U.S. Supreme Court after a decade in which no such executions had been carried out in the United States. His death was described in Norman Mailer's *Executioner's Song.*

Giraud, Henri-Honoré (1879–1949), French officer who saw service in World War I and the RIF WAR and was captured by the Germans while commanding the French Ninth Army during the Battle of FRANCE, May 1940. He escaped from the Nazis in 1942, became head of government and head of the French army in French North Africa after the assassination of François DARLAN, and in 1943 shared leadership of the Committee of National Liberation with Charles DE GAULLE. He lost a power struggle against De Gaulle in 1944.

Giscard d'Estaing, Valéry (1926–   ), French administrator and conservative political leader, who entered the national assembly as a Gaullist in 1956, held several cabinet-level economic positions, and was president of France from 1974 to 1981, when he was defeated by socialist François MITTERAND.

Gjöa, Roald AMUNDSEN's sloop, used on the first voyage along the NORTHWEST PASSAGE, north of North America, in 1903–06.

Glaser, Donald Arthur (1926–   ), U.S. physicist, who in 1952 invented the BUBBLE CHAMBER, an improvement on Charles WILSON's CLOUD CHAMBER, used to track the path of subatomic PARTICLES and RADIATION. He won the 1960 Nobel Prize for Physics.

glasnost, a Soviet political slogan introduced by Mikhail GORBACHEV, literally meaning "openness" and describing Gorbachev-era Soviet policies favoring greater freedom of expression, including criticism of Soviet bureaucracy. In a more general sense glasnost came to be synonymous with increased democracy in the Soviet Union and throughout the Communist world. Glasnost and PERESTROIKA were the main early themes of the Gorbachev era.

Glass, Charles, one of the American LEBANON HOSTAGES, an ABC-TV news correspondent, who was kidnapped on June 17, 1987. He escaped on August 18, 1987.

Glassboro summit (June 1967), a 2-day meeting at Glassboro, New Jersey, between U.S. president Lyndon B. JOHNSON and U.S.S.R. premier Aleksei N. KOSYGIN, that resulted in some progress toward a nuclear nonproliferation treaty.

Glenn, John Herschel, Jr. (1921–   ), U.S. aviator and astronaut who, on February 20, 1962, in the MERCURY spacecraft *FRIENDSHIP 7,* became the first American to orbit the Earth. He had earlier been a much-decorated pilot in World War II and Korea, then a test pilot and a trainee astronaut (1959–62). In 1974 he became a Democratic senator from Ohio and was later an unsuccessful candidate for the presidential nomination.

global village, interconnected world culture that, according to Marshall MCLUHAN, resulted from the 20th-century rise of the ELECTRONIC media, especially TELEVISION.

Glomar Challenger, U.S. drilling ship that took cores, samples from pipes punched deep into the Earth, from the world's seabed as part of the DEEP SEA DRILLING PROJECT (1968–83), notably in the Red Sea, the Galápagos Rift, and the Falkland Plateau, searching for information about the geological evolution of the Earth, giving much supporting evidence for the theory of PLATE TECTONICS, and locating likely sites for oil deposits.

Glubb, John Bagot (Glubb Pasha; 1897–1986), British officer, who saw service in World War I and in Iraq (1920–26), then leaving the British army but continuing to live in the Middle East. From 1931 to 1956, he served with the Jordanian army, commanding the ARAB LEGION (1939–56) and building it into a fighting force effective enough to defeat the Israelis at Jerusalem and on the WEST BANK during the FIRST ARAB-ISRAELI WAR (ISRAELI WAR OF INDE-

PENDENCE), the only Arab force to do so. In 1956, as anti-British feeling built up in the Arab world, he was dismissed by King HUSSEIN of Jordan.

gluons, subatomic PARTICLES that bind together, or "glue," other subatomic particles called QUARKS; first observed by Hamburg physicists in 1979.

Glushko, Valentin (1908–89), U.S.S.R. engineer, who created the ROCKETS that in 1957 boosted into orbit SPUTNIK, the world's first artificial SATELLITE, and that same year launched the Soviet Union's first INTERCONTINENTAL BALLISTIC MISSILE (ICBM). As early as 1929 Glushko had developed the first electric rocket and the first Soviet liquid-propellant rocket. From 1932 he worked closely with Sergei KOROLEV, chief designer of Soviet rockets and spacecraft, whom he succeeded in 1974. He built MIR, which in 1987 became the first permanently manned space station.

Goddard, Robert Hutchings (1882–1945), U.S. physicist, who became one of the world's foremost rocketry pioneers, starting before World War I. In 1919 he published his classic monograph *A Method of Reaching Extreme Altitudes*, which predicted the coming of space flight. Seven years later, on March 16, 1926, he launched the first liquid-propellant rocket. Later recognized as a key figure in the history of space flight, his work was ignored and often ridiculed during his lifetime, although German rocket researchers knew and used it, ultimately in the development of the V-2 ROCKET missiles of World War II.

Gödel, Kurt (1906–78), Austrian-American mathematician who, building on but also undercutting the work of Bertrand RUSSELL and Alfred North WHITEHEAD, demonstrated in 1931 that certainty in any mathematical system is impossible, for some axioms will always remain unprovable. His work, called Gödel's Proof, or the incompletability theorem, effectively ended the modern search for certainty in mathematics, as Werner HEISENBERG'S UNCERTAINTY PRINCIPLE had done in physics. From 1938

Gödel worked in the United States at the Institute for Advanced Study in Princeton, New Jersey.

Goebbels, Joseph (1897–1945), a failed writer who joined the NAZI PARTY in 1924, became a party journal editor in 1925, and Berlin party leader in 1926. Within 2 years, he was chief Nazi propagandist, and in 1933 he became Nazi propaganda minister, in that position becoming chief Nazi bookburner. His influence waned during the early years of World War II, but he was needed again after the tide turned against Germany in 1943. He committed suicide, killing his wife and six children as well, on May 1, 1945.

Goering, Hermann (1893–1946), German World War I flying corps officer, who joined the NAZI PARTY in 1922 and who was severely wounded during the failed BEER HALL PUTSCH of 1923, then fleeing abroad until 1927. He returned to Germany to become a Reichstag deputy in 1928 and in 1932 its Nazi president. During the years of power he was second only to HITLER, who in 1939 declared Goering to be his successor. He also became very rich and a major art "collector," before and during the war, his wealth coming from Jews and others in Germany and from confiscation in the conquered nations. In the early years of the war he was head of the Luftwaffe. Afterward, he was adjudged a major war criminal at the NUREMBERG TRIALS and sentenced to death. He committed suicide in his cell on October 15, 1946.

Goethals, George Washington (1858–1928), officer in the U.S. Army Corps of Engineers who oversaw the construction of the PANAMA CANAL. Having gained experience in building several major canals in the 19th century, Goethals was appointed by President Theodore ROOSEVELT in 1907 to take over construction of the Panama Canal, after an earlier French effort had failed. With the help of William GORGAS's successful anti–YELLOW FEVER campaign, Goethals completed the job in 1913, months ahead of schedule, and was appointed first governor of the CANAL ZONE. He served as U.S. quartermaster general in World War I.

Goetz, Bernhard, the media-dubbed "subway vigilante," who found himself in a threatening situation on a New York City subway in December 1984, drew his illegally carried weapon, shot four young Black men, and then gave himself up to the police. One of the young men was paralyzed permanently. The action generated years of legal actions, accompanied by an often acrimonious national debate on the questions of vigilante action, gun control, self-defense, and discrimination. In the end Goetz was found guilty of carrying a concealed and loaded weapon and was acquitted of assault and attempted murder.

Goldberg, Arthur Joseph (1908–89), U.S. labor lawyer, who from the late 1930s through 1961 represented several major labor organizations, including the CONGRESS OF INDUSTRIAL ORGANIZATIONS (CIO) and the AFL-CIO. He became John F. KENNEDY's secretary of labor in 1961, and a Supreme Court justice in 1962, resigning in 1965 to become U.S. representative to the UNITED NATIONS 1965–68.

Gold Coast, former name for the West African British colony that on March 6, 1957, became part of the new nation of GHANA, led by Kwame NKRUMAH.

Golden Bough, the seminal work on religion, magic, and folklore, published in brief in 1890 but expanded to 12 volumes in 1907–15, by James FRAZER.

Golden Temple assault (June 5–6, 1984), an attack by the Indian army on Sikh extremists, led by fundamentalist Jarnail Singh Bhindranwale, who were using the Sikh temple as the headquarters of their terrorist operations in the Punjab. Bhindranwale and an estimated 1,000 of his followers were killed in the attack. Sikh separatist violence continued in the Punjab. One direct result was the assassination of Indian prime minister Indira GANDHI by two of her Sikh bodyguards on October 31, 1984, an action that further inflamed Hindu–Sikh enmities and generated massive anti-Sikh riots in India in which thousands of Sikhs were killed.

Goldmark, Peter Carl (1906–77), Hungarian-American engineer, who made major contributions to the TELEVISION and recording industries. Working with CBS laboratories from 1936, Goldmark developed a method of producing color television in 1940 that became the industry standard in a decade. He also invented the long-playing record, in 1948, and in the 1950s he developed the scanning device that was used on the LUNAR ORBITER to send pictures from the Moon. Later Goldmark made key contributions to the development of video-cassette recording.

Goldwater, Barry Morris (1909–   ), U.S. department store owner, who was elected to the Phoenix, Arizona, city council in 1949 and went on to become a five-term Arizona Republican Senator (1953–65, 1969–87). A conservative, he defeated Nelson ROCKEFELLER for his party's presidential nomination in 1964 but lost the election by a wide margin to Lyndon B. JOHNSON; in 1969 he resumed his career in the Senate.

Gompers, Samuel (1850–1924), U.S. labor leader, who in 1886 founded and became first president of the AMERICAN FEDERATION OF LABOR (AFL) and was its president until his death in 1924, except for the year 1895. He developed the AFL as a group of affiliated craft unions representing their skilled-worker members on economic matters, and strongly resisted industrial unionism and the organization of the unskilled; he also favored immigration restriction. He and the AFL advocated "pure and simple" unionism, rather than the highly political unionism of the INDUSTRIAL WORKERS OF THE WORLD (IWW) and opposed the SOCIALIST PARTY or the development of a labor party, as was the pattern in many other countries. This set of views established the dominant economic pattern in U.S. trade unionism, until formation of the CONGRESS OF INDUSTRIAL ORGANIZATIONS (CIO) in the mid-1930s, and it remained the dominant pattern as regards political affiliations.

Gomulka, Wladyslaw (1905–82), Polish Communist Party leader, a World War II resistance fighter, who in 1945 became first secretary of his party and a deputy premier. An advocate of a "Polish road to socialism," he was removed from all party posts in 1949, during the antinationalist purges in Eastern Europe that followed the YUGOSLAV–SOVIET BREAK of 1948, and was imprisoned 1951–55. In 1956, during the POLISH OCTOBER, he was returned to power, then embarked on a more liberal, anticollectivist course. But it was not enough; unrest redeveloped in the mid-1960s as conservatism returned to power in the Soviet Union and made itself felt in Poland. Gomulka's government encouraged endemic Polish anti-Semitism in an attempt to distract its opponents and also moved directly against dissenters, but it could not curb the unrest; Gomulka was replaced by the more conservative Edward GIEREK in 1970.

Gonzalez Marquez, Felipe (1942–   ), Spanish socialist leader and labor lawyer, who became a leader of the Spanish Socialist Workers Party while it was still illegal and prime minister after his party's 1982 electoral victory. In office he followed a moderate and democratic socialist course domestically, took Spain into the EUROPEAN COMMON MARKET in 1986, and made major contributions to the development of renascent Spanish democracy.

Goodall, Jane Van Lawick- (1934–   ), British ethologist, famed for her studies of chimpanzees in East Africa. Inspired by early work with Louis LEAKEY, Goodall worked from 1960 at the Gombe Stream Game Reserve in Tanzania (then Tanganyika), closely observing the primates in their natural habitat, gaining their confidence and coming to know them individually. Among other things, she learned that chimpanzees are not strict vegetarians and that they can make simple tools. From 1962 Dutch wildlife photographer Hugo Van Lawick, later her husband, took many of the photographs and documentary films that made her famous worldwide.

Goodman, Andrew, young civil rights worker, who with James CHANEY and Michael SCHWERNER was murdered in Neshoba County, Mississippi, in June 1964, in the MISSISSIPPI CIVIL RIGHTS MURDERS.

Goodman, Robert, U.S. Air Force lieutenant, shot down on December 4, 1983, while attacking Syrian positions in Lebanon's Bekaa Valley. Two planes were shot down; one crew escaped capture, but Goodman's navigator was killed, and he was captured. He was released by President Hafez ASSAD of Syria, on January 3, 1984, after a direct appeal from Jesse JACKSON.

Good Neighbor Policy, the Latin American foreign policy of the United States as expressed by Franklin D. ROOSEVELT in 1933, eschewing U.S. dominance over its Latin American neighbors. It resulted in abrogation of the PLATT AMENDMENT in 1934, completion of the American withdrawal from Haiti in 1935, and the end of Panama's protectorate status by the treaty of 1936.

Gorbachev, Mikhail Sergeyevich (1931–   ), Soviet political leader, who swiftly rose in party and government, becoming a Central Committee member in 1971, agriculture minister 1978–85, a member of the Politburo in 1980, and general secretary of his party and leader of the Soviet Union in March 1985. In the last position he put into play a massive set of internal reforms, including major attempts to decentralize the Soviet economic system and introduce many elements of a market economy, positive encouragement of open discussion and criticism, and a restructuring of his country's political system, though it is still considerably short of Western-style democracy. Internationally, his initiatives did a great deal to move the Soviet Union and the United States toward ending decades of COLD WAR. He initiated a series of meetings with U.S. president Ronald REAGAN, in which the major arms cuts of the 1987 INF TREATY and a series of moves aimed at ending regional conflicts were developed, and in early 1989 he completed the withdrawal of Soviet forces from Afghanistan. In May 1989, after 30 years of antagonism, he visited and normalized relations with China. During 1989 and 1990, his initiatives brought about massive political changes in Eastern Europe, including free elections and a non-communist government in Poland, neutralization of the BERLIN WALL, new governments in Czechoslovakia, East Germany, Hungary, and Bulgaria, and the RUMANIAN REVOLUTION. In early 1990, he caused the Central Committee of the Communist Party of the Soviet Union to renounce the guaranteed leading role of the Communist Party, until then the central tenet of Leninism.

Gordimer, Nadine (1923–　　), South African writer, most noted for her short stories; a White whose work shows South Africans and their society as tremendously damaged by racism and its offspring, APARTHEID.

Gorgas, William Crawford (1854–1920), U.S. physician, who supervised the mosquito control program in Panama, 1904–14, allowing the PANAMA CANAL to be constructed without widespread YELLOW FEVER deaths. In Havana, Cuba, in 1900, in the wake of the Spanish-American War, Walter REED recognized that mosquitoes were causing yellow fever. Gorgas then developed a mosquito-eradication campaign, which he later applied to Panama. As surgeon general of the army, he organized the mobilization of medical resources for World War I.

Gorky, Maxim (Aleksey Maximovich Pyeshkov; 1868–1936) Soviet writer and revolutionary; with such works as *The Lower Depths* (1902), and *Mother* (1907), he established himself as a major writer and helped develop the revolutionary movement in the period before the RUSSIAN REVOLUTION. He became an active revolutionary in the late 1880s, was imprisoned after the 1905 revolution, and went into exile abroad, returning to Russia in 1913. After the establishment of the Soviet government, as a leading Communist and sometime friend of Lenin he saved many intellectuals from persecution, while himself becoming active in Soviet cultural affairs. He was abroad 1921–31, in apparent disagreement with the gov-

ernment, and returned to the Soviet Union in 1929, then becoming first president of the government-dominated Union of Soviet Writers. He died in 1936, possibly of natural causes and possibly assassinated by the STALIN government, which was then moving into the GREAT PURGE period.

Gorlice–Tarnow Breakthrough (May-December 1915), World War I push in which German and Austrian armies in Poland broke through on the Russian-Polish front, ultimately advancing 300 miles against collapsing Russian forces and taking Przemysl, Lemberg, Warsaw, Brest-Litovsk, Grodno, and Vilna, though autumn rains and Russian resistance finally stopped their advance.

Gossamer Albatross, aircraft used to make the first human-powered flight across the English Channel, in 1979, with 26-year-old California biologist Bryan Allen pedaling to work the propeller in the craft's tail.

Gottwald, Klement (1896–1953), Czech Communist party leader, a founder of his party in 1921 and a leading Czech Communist of the interwar period. Returning home after spending World War II in the Soviet Union, he was deputy premier and then premier before the CZECH COUP OF 1948 and became the first Communist president of Czechoslovakia. His rule came at the end of the STALIN era and included the 1952 SLANSKY SHOW TRIALS and executions.

Gowon, Yakubu (1934–　　), Nigerian officer, who took power in July 1966 after a series of coups and countercoups, mainly by northern Moslems, that had resulted in the killing of two former prime ministers and a massacre of southern Christian and animist Ibos. Gowon, a Christian, led the Nigerian government during the ensuing NIGERIA–BIAFRA CIVIL WAR (1967–70), in which an estimated 1.5–2 million died. He was overthrown by a coup in 1975 while he was abroad and went into exile.

Graf Spee, German pocket battleship active in the South Atlantic early in World War II; it was badly damaged at the December 1939

Battle of the RIVER PLATE and was shortly thereafter sunk by its captain outside the harbor of Montevideo, Uruguay.

Graham, William Franklin "Billy" (1918–), U.S. fundamentalist Protestant minister, a radio and television evangelist and political conservative who from the late 1940s conducted Christian evangelical crusades throughout the world, preaching directly to millions and broadcasting to hundreds of millions more, including audiences in the Soviet Union.

grain embargo, the 1980 embargo on all grain shipments from the United States to the Soviet Union imposed by U.S. president Jimmy CARTER in early 1980 after the late 1979 Soviet invasion of AFGHANISTAN. It was lifted by President Ronald REAGAN in April 1981.

Gramm-Rudman Act, U.S. law passed in December 1986, requiring the automatic across-the-board cutting of most budget items, including defense and most domestic programs, when specified budgetary goals are not met; an attempt to reduce the enormous national debt increases of the REAGAN era, with the stated goal of producing a balanced budget by 1991.

Gramsci, Antonio (1891–1937), Italian socialist theoretician, who led the left wing of the Socialist Party into the Italian Communist Party in 1921. His party was outlawed by the fascists, and he was imprisoned (1926–37), being released to die soon after.

Grand Mosque incident (July 31, 1987), battle at Mecca's Grand Mosque, between thousands of pro-KHOMEINI Iranian pilgrims and Saudi Arabian police, resulting in the deaths of hundreds of pilgrims, many of them innocent bystanders.

Grand Mufti of Jerusalem, Palestinian Arab leader Haj Amin al HUSSEINI.

grand unification theory (GUT), alternate name for UNIFIED FIELD THEORY.

Great Depression, the sharp worldwide decline in trade, production, employment, and financial stability that began with the U.S. stock market CRASH of October 1929. The effects of the crash were greatly en-

hanced by the American SMOOT-HAWLEY TARIFF and other protective tariff walls thrown up by many nations. The Great Depression grew into a massive crisis that fed the growth of fascism and militarism and for a time threatened the governmental and social systems of the United States and the other major Western democracies. Economic revival and amelioration of the social consequences of the Depression began with Franklin Delano ROOSEVELT'S NEW DEAL in 1933. With the New Deal came the beginning of a social service safety net in the United States, the unionization of the mass production industries, and the will to ultimately defeat German fascism and Japanese militarism in World War II. The American economy rebounded considerably 1933–37, seriously sagged again in 1937, picked up again with the advent of the European war in 1939, and went into overdrive to meet war production needs after December 1941.

Great Idaho Fire (August 10–21, 1910), a massive forest fire that burned out of control in Idaho's Bitterroot Mountains despite the efforts of several thousands of firefighters, including federal troops. It burned out over 3 million acres, killing eight people; it was one of a series of major fires throughout western North America that summer.

Great Imposter, the media-generated name of Ferdinand DEMARA, who posed as a professional in many occupations.

Great Leap Forward, the massive, failed nationwide industrialization campaign initiated by MAO ZEDONG in 1958 and 1959. The campaign featured the development of large, labor-intensive rural and urban communes that owned all of the land and means of production and used ideological exhortation rather than economic incentives. One of the chief objectives of the campaign was the nationwide production of such low-quality industrial products as the steel produced in backyard furnaces, which could not be used in modern industry. The campaign enormously damaged the fragile Chinese economy; within 2 years it was seen to be a failure and was abandoned in 1960 and 1961.

Great Purge (1934–39), a long, nationwide series of show trials and executions, resulting in the killing of tens of thousands of the key people in the Soviet Union's main elites; it was begun by Joseph STALIN, who used as a pretext the assassination of Leningrad Communist party leader Sergei KIROV in 1934. In the course of the purge the nation lost most of its top military leaders, including Marshal Mikhail TUKHACHEVSKY, and most of the Soviet officer corps; some were reclaimed from labor camps when the Germans struck in 1940. It also lost most of its leading Communists, including such old allies and colleagues of Stalin as Lev KAMENEV, Grigori ZINOVIEV, and Nicolai BUKHARIN, along with many thousands of lower level Communist officials throughout the country.

Great Society, a slogan put forward by U.S. president Lyndon B. JOHNSON in his Madison Square Garden speech of October 31, 1964, as a basis for the wide range of social welfare legislation he then initiated, including the introduction of MEDICARE and MEDICAID, increased aid to education, subsidized housing, and a series of WAR ON POVERTY programs.

Great War (1914–18), alternate name for WORLD WAR I, the major international conflict of the early 20th century.

Greece, invasion of (October 1940–April 1941), World War II attack on Greece, starting with Italian forces moving out of Albania on October 28, 1940, and being immediately defeated. A Greek offensive in late November moved into Albania, with heavy Italian losses. But on April 6, 1941, German forces entered this part of the war, attacking Yugoslavia and Greece. They took both countries in the same month; Yugoslavia fell in 11 days, Greece in 17 days, the Greek army surrendering on April 23 with over 50,000 casualties and over 250,000 prisoners taken. The British had sent four divisions to Greece in March; of these, 43,000 were evacuated by sea (April 24–27), and there were 12,000 British casualties.

Greek Civil War (1946–49), conflict following World War II. Greek Communist forces, operating out of Albania, Bulgaria, and Yugoslavia, took much of northern Greece and made substantial gains throughout the country, beginning in May 1946. In March 1947 the United States, pursuant to the TRUMAN DOCTRINE, began supplying large quantities of military assistance to the Greek government, and both Great Britain and the United States sent military advisers. In early 1948 the government's army began to regain lost ground, going over to the offensive as Yugoslav aid to the insurgents dried up after the YUGOSLAV–SOVIET BREAK in mid-1948. In the summer of 1949 Greek army forces took Mount Grammos, essentially ending the war, although guerrilla war continued through mid-October. This was the first major armed conflict of the COLD WAR.

Greek colonels' coup, the Greek military coup of April 21, 1967, which brought a 7-year-long military government to power, led by army colonels George PAPADAPOULOS and Stylianos Pattakos. Their repressive government was known as the "Greek Colonels government."

Greek–Turkish War (1920–22), conflict following World War I. Greek forces established a base at Smyrna in 1919, a city they then acquired the right to administer by the terms of the 1920 Treaty of SÈVRES. In late 1920 the Greeks moved east out of Smyrna in an attempt to conquer much of western Turkey, and from then until August 1921 they fought a series of battles with Turkish forces led by Mustapha Kemal (later ATATÜRK) as they moved east to Sakkaria. After an inconclusive battle at Sakkaria, in late August the somewhat overextended Greeks withdrew; they were then smashed by a strong Turkish counteroffensive, and fled back to Smyrna. The Turks took the city, massacring tens of thousands of Greek soldiers and civilians. In victory, Kemal deposed the last Ottoman Caliph, forced replacement of the Treaty of Sèvres with the much more favorable Treaty of LAUSANNE, and established the Turkish Republic with himself as first president.

Green, William (1873–1952), U.S. coal miner, who became a United Mine Workers official in 1900, thereafter pursuing a career as a trade union leader. In 1924, he succeeded Samuel GOMPERS as president of the AMERICAN FEDERATION OF LABOR (AFL) and held that position until his death, undeviatingly pursuing craft union economic aims, opposing the formation of the CONGRESS OF INDUSTRIAL ORGANIZATIONS (CIO) in the 1930s, and resisting labor union political affiliation.

Greenham Common, the site of a U.S. Air Force base in Great Britain, and of periodic antinuclear encampments organized by British peace movement women in the early 1980s to protest the deployment of U.S. nuclear arms in Great Britain.

greenhouse effect, warming of the Earth's atmosphere as human activities, especially the burning of FOSSIL FUELS, increase carbon dioxide in the air. This then traps INFRARED RADIATION from the Sun, much as a greenhouse's glass covering does. The idea was first suggested in 1938 by British engineer G. S. Callendar. By the mid-1960s there were clear warnings of such global warming, with its major potential long-term effects, including melting of ice caps and rising of the world's sea level, but little counter-action was taken.

Greenlease kidnapping, the September 28, 1953, kidnapping-murder of 6-year-old Bobby Greenlease by Bonnie Brown HEADY and Carl Austin HALL; both were executed on December 18, 1953.

Green movement, in a narrowly political sense the development of several European political parties concerned in their early stages of development primarily with environmental matters, which began in the late 1970s, and emerged most visibly with organization of the West German GREEN PARTY in 1980. Later such parties tended to widen their concerns to include a wide range of other political issues, many of them only remotely connected with ecological matters. In a wider sense the Green movement has meant the emergence of enormous concern about environmental damage, especially in the developed countries; with that concern came great media attention, the formation and strengthening of hundreds of environmental organizations, expressions of concern by public officials, and some concerted international action.

Green Party (the Greens), German Federal Republic political party and movement organized in 1980 largely on a ecological preservation–antinuclear platform. The party achieved some parliamentary representation but was influential far beyond its parliamentary strength, mounting major demonstrations throughout the Republic and generating the formation of similarly oriented parties in other European countries as part of a wider GREEN MOVEMENT.

green revolution, development and planting in undeveloped countries of hardy, high-yield grains, suitable to a wide range of climates, to ease chronic hunger. From 1944 U.S. agricultural scientist Norman BORLAUG worked in Mexico, under Rockefeller Foundation auspices, to develop just such types of crops, which were later planted widely in other undeveloped countries in the mid-1960s and after. Though heavily dependent on irrigation and pesticides, these grains largely ended actual food shortages in many countries, but significant distribution problems remained, frustrating early hopes of an easy solution to social problems.

Greenspan, Alan (1926–   ), U.S. economist and consultant, who advised presidents NIXON and FORD on economic matters and was appointed to succeed Paul Volcker as chairman of the Federal Reserve Board in June 1987. An advocate of free market competition, his main concern during his early period at the Federal Reserve was the control of incipient inflation through manipulation of interest rates and money supply.

Gregg v. *Georgia* (1976), a landmark U.S. Supreme Court decision clearly reinstating the right of states to enforce capital punishment laws; after this decision, the killing of prisoners by law was resumed in the United States.

Grenada, until 1974 a British colony, although internal autonomy was granted in 1967. Independence and COMMONWEALTH membership came on February 7, 1974. The new government, led by prime minister Eric M. Gairy, was deposed by an opposition coup in March 1979, which set up a Marxist-oriented state led by Maurice Bishop. In October 13, 1983, Bishop was arrested by his internal opposition and was killed on October 19. On October 25, U.S. forces invaded and quickly took the country in the brief GRENADA WAR, reestablishing democratic rule.

Grenada War (October 1983), small-scale U.S. invasion of Marxist-dominated Grenada, halting construction of a Cuban base on the island. Invading U.S. forces, supplemented by token forces from other Caribbean countries, took Grenada in less than 3 days, defeating Grenadan forces and a party of Cuban combat engineers. A new government was then installed.

Grew, Joseph Clark (1880–1965), U.S. career diplomat, who became ambassador to Japan in 1932 and throughout the late 1930s repeatedly warned of impending Japanese–American armed conflict, specifically warning of a possible attack on PEARL HARBOR early in 1941. He and his staff were interned in Japan until late 1944.

Grey, Edward, British foreign secretary, 1905–16, who was largely responsible for building the series of alliances that constituted the Allied side during the run-up to World War I, taking Great Britain to war; known for his comment that the "LAMPS ARE GOING OUT ALL OVER EUROPE."

Grissom, Virgil I. "Gus" (1926–67), U.S. astronaut, who made the second suborbital MERCURY space flight on July 21, 1961, and made a three-orbit flight in a GEMINI spacecraft with John Young on March 23, 1965;

he was killed on January 27, 1967, along with Edward H. White II and Roger B. Chaffee, when fire broke out in their APOLLO spacecraft during a countdown rehearsal.

Griswold v. *Connecticut* (1965), a landmark U.S. Supreme Court decision, stating that the right to privacy included the right of Planned Parenthood counselors to provide contraceptive information to married couples, and the right of those couples to receive and act on that advice without the interference of government.

Grivas, George (1898–1974), Greek Cypriot soldier, a World War II resistance fighter, who led Cypriot guerrilla forces from 1955 until the achievement of independence for Cyprus in 1959. He continued to favor union with Greece, however, and took part in guerrilla warfare against the Cypriot government, until his death.

Gromyko, Andrei Andreyevich (1909–1989), Soviet economist and diplomat, who was ambassador to the United States 1943–46, UNITED NATIONS delegation head 1946–48, and ambassador to Great Britain 1952–53. A deputy foreign minister from 1946, he was foreign minister 1957–85, functioning for most of the COLD WAR as his country's notably grim-visaged chief diplomat and during the early 1980s as a major foreign policymaker as well. As leadership passed to new hands during the GORBACHEV era, in 1985 Gromyko moved into the then largely ceremonial position of Soviet president, retiring in 1988.

Groves, Leslie Richard (1896–1970), U.S. Army general, who from 1942 headed the Manhattan District of the Army Corps of Engineers, better known as the MANHATTAN PROJECT, assigned to produce an ATOMIC BOMB.

Guadalcanal, Battle of (August 1942–February 1943), fighting following U.S. landings on the Japanese-held island of Guadalcanal, beginning on August 7, 1942, with the Americans capturing the airport, which they named Henderson Field. Both sides skirmished and built their strength until mid-September, the Japanese then attacking the airfield and losing a division-size engagement at Bloody Ridge. In late October heavy Japanese assaults again failed to take the airfield, and both sides continued their buildups. On January 10, U.S. forces, by then much stronger, went on the offensive, driving the Japanese from the island by early February; the remaining Japanese were evacuated by sea.

Guam, Battle of (December 10, 1941), early World War II attack on the small Guam garrison by Japanese forces, which took the island.

Guam, Battle of (July–August, 1944), World War II amphibious landings in late July, followed by a 2-week hand-to-hand battle for the Pacific island by its Japanese defenders and much stronger U.S. Marine and army units. Most of the island's 10,000 defenders chose to fight to the death, rather than surrender.

Guatemala City earthquake (February 4, 1976), an earthquake that destroyed much of the capital city and many other populated places in central Guatemala, killing an estimated 20,000–25,000 people.

Guatemalan Civil War (June 1954–   ), conflict that began with the overthrow of the elected government of President Jacobo ARBENZ by forces led by Carlos Castillo Armas and aided by the United States, which charged the Arbenz government with being Communist-influenced. Thirty-five years of low-level guerrilla warfare followed, as did left-wing assassinations and right-wing DEATH SQUAD massacres.

Guderian, Heinz (1888–1954), German officer, who saw service in World War I and became chief German TANK corps commander and a major advocate of BLITZKRIEG tactics during the interwar period. His armored divisions led the attack on Poland in 1939, and in 1940 made the decisive breakthrough at Sedan that led to the fall of France. He was not as successful on the Russian front, being relieved of his command in 1941, coming back after the defeat at STA-

LINGRAD, and again being relieved early in 1945.

Guernica bombing (1937), the heavy German bombing of the nonmilitary objective that was the defenseless city of Guernica, in northern Spain during the SPANISH CIVIL WAR, an act that provoked worldwide protest, inspired Pablo Picasso's *Guernica* painting, and was seen by many as a terrible augury of much that was yet to come—and did.

Guevara, Che (Ernesto Guevara de la Serna; 1928–67), Latin-American revolutionary, born in Argentina, who in 1955 joined Fidel CASTRO in Mexico, went to Cuba with Castro in 1956, and became a key guerrilla leader during the CUBAN REVOLUTION. A Marxist, he played a major role in developing the ideology of the revolution, his work on guerrilla warfare becoming required reading for leftist revolutionaries in many countries. He also held many cabinet-level posts in the new Cuban government. In 1966, seeking to foster revolution throughout Latin America, he left Cuba and developed a small guerrilla movement in Bolivia, but was killed after being captured by the Bolivian government.

guided missile, ROCKET containing one or more explosive warheads, often nuclear, and capable of being directed toward a target after launching, rather than having a preset path. The idea of an "aerial torpedo" was conceived by turn-of-the-century Swedish scientist Wilhelm Unge, coming to pass with the World War II V-2 BOMBS and later the even more deadly INTERCONTINENTAL BALLISTIC MISSILES (ICBMs).

Guinea (Republic of Guinea), until 1958 a French colony. On October 2, 1958, after the emergence of a powerful independence movement, led by Ahmed Sékou TOURÉ, Guinea became an independent state, with Touré as its first president; he remained president of his one-party state until his death on March 25, 1984.

Guinea-Bissau (Republic of Guinea-Bissau), until 1974, a Portuguese colony known as Portuguese Guinea. It gained independence on September 10, 1974, after a long guerrilla war led by Amilcar Cabral, who was assassinated in 1973; his brother, Luis de Almeida Cabral, became the first president of Guinea-Bissau. Luis Cabral was deposed by the military coup of November 14, 1980, which brought President Joao Bernardo Viera to power.

Guise, Battle of (August 29, 1914), engagement after the World War I Battles of the FRONTIERS, in which French forces retreating south before the German advance counterattacked at Guise and held the Germans back for 36 hours, but were then forced to resume their retreat.

Gulf War, an alternate name for the IRAN-IRAQ WAR of 1980–88.

Gustav Line, the German defensive line running across Italy south of Rome during the Italian campaign of 1943–44. The Germans held the line until May 1944; Allied troops then broke through, to link up with Allied forces moving out of the ANZIO beachhead north of the line.

GUT, acronym for **g**rand **u**nification **t**heory, an alternate name for UNIFIED FIELD THEORY.

Guyana (Cooperative Republic of Guyana), until 1966, a British colony; it became an independent state and COMMONWEALTH member on May 26, 1966, and was led from 1966 until his death in 1985 by Forbes BURNHAM.

H

Haakon VII (1872–1957), king of Norway (1905–57), who during World War II led his country's London-based government-in-exile, serving as a focus for continuing Norwegian resistance.

Habash, George (1925–   ), Palestinian Christian doctor, a founder in the 1950s of the Arab Nationalist Movement organization and in 1969 of the POPULAR FRONT FOR THE LIBERATION OF PALESTINE (PFLP), a Marxist-oriented guerrilla organization deeply involved in terrorist operations. Although long an opponent of the mainstream PALESTINE LIBERATION ORGANIZATION (PLO) and of Yasir ARAFAT, Habash brought his organization back into the PLO in 1987, after several years of estrangement. In 1988 he publicly disavowed further acts of terrorism, though still being accused by the Israelis and others of continuing complicity on terrorist acts.

Haganah, originally a paramilitary organization formed by Palestinian Jews in 1920; it grew into an underground army during the 1920s and 1930s, from 1937 engaging in a covert guerrilla war with Palestinian Arab paramilitary forces. During World War II, some Haganah soldiers fought as individuals with British forces, and others fought in their own PALMACH commando units with the British. The Haganah opposed the terrorist tactics of the IRGUN ZVAI LEUMI, led by Menachim BEGIN, and the STERN GANG. During the ISRAELI WAR OF INDEPENDENCE (FIRST ARAB–ISRAELI WAR), the Haganah became the nucleus of what became the Israeli army, afterward forcing the terrorist groups to disband and either join the Israeli armed forces as individuals or go into civilian life.

Haig, Alexander Meigs, Jr. (1924–   ), U.S. officer, who saw service in Vietnam, became a military adviser to Henry KISSINGER in 1968, an assistant and key VIETNAM WAR adviser to Richard M. NIXON during the concluding years of the war, and chief of Nixon's White House staff 1973–74. He was commander of the NORTH ATLANTIC TREATY ORGANIZATION (NATO) 1975–79. He was Ronald REAGAN'S secretary of state 1981–82, and an unsuccessful candidate for the Republican presidential nomination in 1988.

Haig, Douglas (1861–1928), British general and later field marshal, who commanded British forces in France from 1915 until the end of World War I. He has been strongly criticized for causing enormous British losses by sending British infantry against entrenched German machine gun positions at the first Battle of the SOMME in 1916, and at the Third Battle of YPRES, also called PASSCHENDAELE, in 1917. On the Somme, the British gained 8 miles and suffered an estimated 420,000 casualties. At Passchendaele, the British advanced 5 miles and suffered an estimated 320,000 casualties.

Haight-Ashbury, the San Francisco neighborhood that became a COUNTERCULTURE center and symbol in the 1960s.

Haile Selassie I (Ras Tafari; 1892–1975), Ethiopian political leader, who became regent (1916–28), king (1928–30), and emperor (1930–74). He was a reformer who took Ethiopia into the League of Nations, abolished slavery, and began a many-faceted national modernization program. Italian forces invaded his country in 1935, and took Addis Ababa in May 1936. He appealed to the LEAGUE OF NATIONS unsuccessfully in June, then went into exile until Allied forces liberated Ethiopia in 1941. During the postwar period he continued to develop reform programs, also annexing Eritrea with United Nations support. But severe economic and social problems in the early 1970s made him vulnerable to an army coup in September 1974, followed by house arrest until his death in August 1975.

Haiphong, a major North Vietnamese port city that was heavily bombed by U.S. forces, 1965–68, during the VIETNAM WAR. Haiphong harbor was also mined by U.S. forces, at the time a highly controversial NIXON administration decision.

Haitian Revolution (November 1985–February 1986), the sequence of events and pressures that toppled the weak Jean-Claude Duvalier regime, including major demonstrations, student boycotts, and intense U.S. and French pressure. Duvalier fled the country on February 7, ushering in two years of ultimately unsuccessful attempts to bring democracy to Haiti, which ended for a time with the military coup of June 1988.

Hakim, Albert, U.S. businessman who, with his partner, retired general Richard V. SECORD, became a figure in the IRAN–CONTRA AFFAIR, allegedly being deeply involved in the arms-for-hostages and Nicaraguan Contra arms supply arrangements; in March 1988 he was indicted in connection with the scandal.

Hakodate fire (March 22, 1934), a fire that destroyed the city of Hakodate, Japan, killing an estimated 1,500 people and injuring at least 1,000.

Haldane, John Burdon Sanderson (1897–1964), British geneticist, who did key work in population genetics and evolution; also a writer whose works, such as *Science and Ethics* (1928), influenced other scientists and a wider audience. Disenchanted both with Marxism after LYSENKO'S rise and with British politics, he became a citizen of India after 1957.

Haldeman, Harry Robbins "Bob" (1926–), U.S. political administrator, a campaign aide to Richard NIXON during the 1960s, and Nixon's 1968 campaign manager. He was White House chief of staff 1969–73, later became heavily involved in the WATERGATE SCANDAL, and resigned his White House post on April 30, 1973. In 1974 he was convicted on Watergate-connected charges and was subsequently imprisoned for 18 months.

Halder, Franz (1884–1972), German staff officer, who saw service in World War I and was chief of the German general staff 1938–42, being dismissed by Hitler after predicting the Russian counteroffensive at STALINGRAD. He was arrested and imprisoned after the failed 1944 army plot to assassinate Hitler and spent the balance of the war in a CONCENTRATION CAMP.

half-life, length of time it takes for half of a given amount of a RADIOACTIVE element to decay; recognized and named by Ernest RUTHERFORD in the early 1900s. In the atomic age, half-life has become a crucial figure in calculating when waste products from NUCLEAR REACTORS or FALLOUT from nuclear explosions will no longer be dangerous to living beings. It is also used in RADIOCARBON DATING to show the age of rocks or archaeological artifacts.

Halifax (Lord Halifax, Edward Wood; 1881–1959), British Conservative MP 1910–25, who was viceroy of India 1925–31, succeeded Anthony EDEN as CHAMBERLAIN'S foreign minister in 1938, and was closely associated with Chamberlain's APPEASEMENT policy. He was Chamberlain's preferred successor but was passed over in favor of Winston CHURCHILL. He was ambassador to the United States 1941–46.

Halifax Harbor explosion (December 6, 1917), an explosion aboard a munitions ship on fire in the Canadian harbor of Halifax, Nova Scotia, that touched off munition stocks on shore, killing more than 1,600 people, injuring approximately 6,000 more, and leveling much of the harbor area.

Hall, Carl Austin, and Bonnie HEADY, the kidnap-murderers of 6-year-old Bobby Greenlease, at Kansas City, Missouri, on September 28, 1953.

Hall, Fawn, U.S. government employee, secretary to Oliver NORTH, who became a figure in the IRAN–CONTRA AFFAIR and who testified at the 1988–1989 trial of Oliver NORTH that she had helped him shred and conceal government documents.

Halley's Comet, one of the brightest periodic comets, named for Edmond Halley who, after its 1682 sighting, predicted its regular return; the comet generated enormous popular interest on its arrival in 1910 and again in 1986, when both the United States and the Soviet Union sent missions to pass through the comet's tail, the Soviet probe making the closest approach.

Hall-Mills case, the killing of the Reverend Edward Wheeler Hall and Mrs. Eleanor Mills, whose bodies were found on September 16, 1922, at New Brunswick, New Jersey; both had been murdered. Love letters from Mrs. Mills to Mr. Hall were scattered about their bodies, and these were widely reprinted and discussed in the press. No indictments occurred until 1926, when, after the *New York Daily Mirror* claimed discovery of a new witness, Hall's wife, Mrs. Frances Stevens Hall, and her two brothers were indicted for the murders. After a trial that received a great deal of press coverage, the defendants were quickly acquitted.

hallucinogenic drugs, mind-altering drugs such as LSD or mescaline, often called psychedelic (mind-manifesting) drugs. From the mid-1950s many professionals, especially in psychology and psychiatry, explored such drugs, some seeking a natural biochemical cause for mental disorders such as schizophrenia, others hoping to expand the mind's possibilities through drugs. But by the mid-1960s, as the dangers of such drugs became clear, their use was restricted, though many in the COUNTERCULTURE continued to obtain them on the black market.

Halsey, William Frederick, Jr. (1882–1959), U.S. naval officer, who saw service in World War I, became a pilot and aircraft carrier commander during the interwar period, and was a vice-admiral at sea commanding the carrier *Enterprise* when PEARL HARBOR was attacked. He became South Pacific commander late in 1942, supervising the island-hopping American invasion campaign across the central Pacific until mid-1944, and then going back to sea as commander of the Third Fleet, which played a major role in the invasion of the Philippines and the air attack on the Japanese mainland.

Hamaguchi Osachi (1870–1931), Japanese political leader, who became Japanese prime minister in 1929; he was shot by a rightist in 1930 and later died.

Hamburg bombings, a series of World War II Allied raids in 1943–44, some of which produced firestorms and leveled much of Hamburg, killing an estimated 50,000 Germans.

Hamburger Hill, Battle of (May 1969), a costly U.S. VIETNAM WAR assault on mountain positions near the Laotian border, in which American forces in regimental strength eventually dislodged North Vietnamese forces, which retreated into Laos. To Vietnam War opponents, the assault, which was highly publicized in the American media, seemed a waste of lives and symbolic of American involvement in the war; to those supporting the war the assault seemed a heroic victory.

Hamer, Fannie Lou (1917–77), U.S. political leader, a Mississippi sharecropper who became a leading southern Black activist in the 1960s CIVIL RIGHTS MOVEMENT and a co-founder of the MISSISSIPPI FREEDOM DEMOCRATIC PARTY, which challenged southern Democratic party racist practices at the 1964 Democratic National Convention, successfully challenged the seating of the regular state delegates at the 1968 convention, and was seated at the 1972 convention.

Hammarskjöld, Dag (1905–61), Swedish diplomat, political economist, and career government official, who was head of the Swedish UNITED NATIONS delegation 1952–53, and second secretary-general of the UN 1953–61. He played a major role in concluding the SUEZ CRISIS of 1956, with creation of the first UN Emergency Force to keep peace in the area. He mediated in Lebanon during the late 1950s, and created substantial UN peacekeeping forces in the Congo during 1960–61. He died in an airplane crash while on his way to attempt to negotiate peace in the Congo, and was awarded a posthumous Nobel Peace Prize in 1961.

Hands Across America (May 25, 1986), U.S. privately sponsored relief project aimed at raising money for the poor and homeless in the United States, in which an estimated 6 million people linked hands to form a human chain across the United States, from Long Beach, California, to New York City.

Hankow, Fall of (October 25, 1938), the fall of the provisional Chinese capital to advancing Japanese troops, after heavy fighting along the Yangtze River, forcing removal of the Chinese capital to Chungking.

Hanoi Christmas bombing (December 18–19, 1972), the heavy bombing of Hanoi ordered by Richard M. NIXON during the last stages of U.S. involvement in the VIETNAM WAR.

Hansson, Per Albin (1885–1946), Swedish Social Democratic leader, in parliament from 1918 and premier 1932–46, who led his country through the GREAT DEPRESSION and kept it out of World War II; he also played a major early role in developing the Swedish welfare state.

Hara, Takashi (Hara Kei; 1856–1921), a Japanese journalist who became a leading politician. He was president of the Seiyūkai party from 1914 and a representative of Japan's industrialists. He became Japanese prime minister in 1918 and was assassinated by a rightist in 1921.

Harappä, center (with Mohenjo-daro) of a major Bronze Age civilization in the Indus Valley, now in Pakistan, dating from about 2500 to 1500 B.C., rediscovered and excavated from the 1920s by British archaeologist Mortimer WHEELER.

Hardie, James Keir (1856–1915), British socialist, labor leader, and key ally of the WOMAN SUFFRAGE movement. He was a coal miner while still a child, became a miners' union organizer and labor newspaper editor, founded the Scottish Labour party, became an MP in 1892, and was a founder of the Independent Labour party in 1893 and the Labour Representation Committee in 1900. In 1906 that committee became the LABOUR PARTY, and he became the first leader of Labour in the House of Commons. He unsuccessfully opposed support of World War I in the Socialist International and in his own party.

Harding, Warren Gamaliel (1865–1923), U.S. journalist, an Ohio Republican state legislator (1899–1903), lieutenant governor (1903–1903), U.S. senator from Ohio (1915–21), and 29th president of the United States (1921–23), a Republican whose "return to normalcy" campaign of 1920 brought him victory over Democrat James M. COX. Although Harding was not personally involved, his brief presidency was chiefly notable for the speed with which his associates, led by Harry M. DAUGHERTY, developed the web of corrupt relationships and practices that were ultimately to result in the TEAPOT DOME and other scandals that surfaced during the COOLIDGE administration. His administration did sharply restrict immigration, responding and helping to generate the wave of nativism and isolationism that swept the United States after World War I. He died of a heart condition in San Francisco, on August 2, 1923, and was succeeded in office by his vice-president, Calvin COOLIDGE.

Harijans (Children of God), Mohatma GANDHI'S name for India's Untouchables caste.

Harlan, John Marshall (1899–1971), U.S. lawyer and judge, appointed to the Supreme Court by Dwight D. EISENHOWER in 1954, thereafter becoming a conservative and strict constructionist opposed to the activist tendency of the majority in the WARREN court.

Harriman, William Averell (1891–1986), U.S. diplomat and New Deal Democrat, who was a World War II special representative of President Franklin Delano Roosevelt to the Soviet Union and Great Britain, ambassador to the Soviet Union 1943–46, briefly ambassador to Great Britain in 1946, and secretary of commerce in the first TRUMAN administration. Thereafter he held a series of diplomatic positions, among others those of chief negotiator of the 1963 NUCLEAR TEST BAN TREATY. He was also governor of New York 1955–59.

Harris, Barbara Clementine (1931–   ), U.S. Episcopal priest, a Black woman who, on February 11, 1989, in Boston, was consecrated as the first woman bishop of the Episcopal Church, also becoming the first woman bishop of the worldwide Anglican communion. Bishop Harris was ordained in 1980 after a career in public relations and considerable participation in the CIVIL RIGHTS MOVEMENT.

Harris, Louis (1921–   ), U.S. public-opinion analyst who, from the 1950s, developed more sophisticated polls that attempted to look beyond the simply yes-no responses of earlier polls. After work with Elmo ROPER's polling firm, Harris established his own in 1956, becoming a key consultant to John F. Kennedy during his 1960 presidential campaign. In the 1960s he worked with the Columbia Broadcasting System (CBS), developing a sophisticated system that used COMPUTERS to analyze survey data.

Hart, Brooke (1911–33), young woman kidnapped and murdered by John Holmes and Thomas Thurmond at San Jose, California, November 9, 1933. Her murderers were soon captured and on November 24 were lynched by a mob of more than 10,000 after the local sheriff's request for troops was ignored by Governor James Rolfe, whose subsequent statements indicated support for the lynch mob. No members of the mob were ever indicted.

Hart, Gary (1937–   ), U.S. lawyer, a liberal activist of the 1960s, who in 1968 helped organize the presidential campaign of Robert KENNEDY, and in 1972 was chief organizer of the McGOVERN presidential campaign. He was a two-term senator from Colorado 1974–86, and a major contender for the 1988 Democratic presidential nomination until being accused of engaging in an extramarital affair with Donna Rice, an accusation followed by enormous media attention. He denied the charges, but was forced to abandon his presidential nomination campaign.

Hartford Circus fire (July 9, 1944), a small fire in the "Big Top" tent housing the Ringling Brothers–Barnum and Bailey Circus that suddenly spread to the entire, wholly unfireproofed tent, bringing it down in flames on the thousands inside; 168 people died and many others were injured in the fire and accompanying panic.

Harvey, Donald, U.S. mass murderer, a Middletown, Ohio, hospital orderly who in 1988 confessed to the murders of 24 hospitalized people, most of them by poisoning, and may have killed as many as 30 more.

Hatem, George (Ma Haide; 1910–88), U.S. public health doctor, who practiced in Shanghai, China, from 1933, visited Yenan with writer Edgar SNOW in 1936, and stayed on as a Red Army doctor, becoming a Communist in 1937. After the Communist victory in 1949, Hatem, known and greatly respected throughout China as MA HAIDE, became a leading Chinese public health organizer, especially active in the fight against venereal disease, and a world figure in public health.

Hatfield, Mark Odum (1922–   ), U.S. political scientist and university professor, in the Oregon state legislature 1951–56, Oregon secretary of state 1957–59, governor 1959–67, and long-term senator, from 1967. A leading liberal Republican, Hatfield was an outspoken critic of the VIETNAM WAR and a co-sponsor of the antiwar Mc-

Govern-Hatfield amendment. In the 1980s he was a leading proponent of bilateral nuclear disarmament.

Hauptmann, Bruno Richard, kidnapper and murderer of 20-month-old Charles A. Lindbergh, Jr., on March 1, 1932. Hauptmann was convicted of the murder and executed on April 3, 1936.

Havel, Vaclav (1936–), Czech writer and political leader, a playwright and essayist, who in 1977 became a leader of Charter 77, a leading Czech human rights organization. He spent much of the next decade in prison, and his plays were banned. On December 29, 1989, with the quick, bloodless revolution that toppled his country's Communist government, he became the first non-Communist president of Czechoslovakia since 1948.

Have you no sense of decency, sir, at long last? Have you left no sense of decency? rhetorical query by Joseph Nye WELCH, U.S. Army attorney at the ARMY-MCCARTHY HEARINGS of 1954, to Senator Joseph R. MCCARTHY.

Haw-Haw, Lord (William Joyce; 1906–46), British fascist who became a Nazi broadcaster during World War II. Joyce was executed for treason after the war.

Hawke, Bob (1929–), Australian economist and trade union official, who was president of the Australian Council of Trade Unions 1970–80, became a Labour member of parliament in 1980, and prime minister in 1983, then pursued an independent and antinuclear path in foreign affairs while enjoying considerable economic success at home, although he encountered some damaging political scandals in the late 1980s.

Hawking, Stephen William (1942–), British physicist, who made major theoretical insights into the nature of BLACK HOLES, attempted to develop a QUANTUM THEORY of gravity, and strongly supported the BIG BANG THEORY of the universe's origin. Despite being badly disabled from age 20 by amytrophic lateral sclerosis, he communicated widely through his writings, most no-

tably in the surprise best-seller *A Brief History of Time* (1988).

Hawkins, Gerald Stanley (1928–), British astronomer, who in 1963 suggested that Stonehenge was a gigantic ancient observatory, aligned with solar and lunar eclipses when it was built, a view outlined in *Stonehenge Decoded* (1965). Controversial at the time, Hawkins's view gained credence as other such early observatories were found around the world, forming the basis for the new specialty of paleoastronomy.

Haya de la Torre, Victor Raúl (1895–1979), Peruvian liberal political leader, founder of the American Popular Revolutionary Alliance (APRA) while in Mexican exile in 1924, and a major figure in Peruvian and Latin American politics. He returned from exile to run unsuccessfully for the presidency in 1931, moving into guerrilla warfare against the government after charging electoral fraud. After imprisonment, release, a new set of disputes, and the outlawing of APRA, he went underground, emerging with the legalization of APRA in 1945. In 1949, with APRA once again outlawed, he took refuge in Lima's Colombian embassy and stayed there until 1954, when he was allowed to go into Mexican exile once again. He returned to Peru with the restoration of democracy in 1957, won the presidential election of 1962, and was denied the presidency by the Peruvian military; he then lost the election of 1963. He died in 1979; in 1985, his party did take power, with the election of Alan García Pérez to the presidency.

Hayden, Thomas Emmett (1940–), U.S. civil rights and peace activist, president of the STUDENTS FOR A DEMOCRATIC SOCIETY (SDS) 1962–63, and a leading anti–VIETNAM WAR activist. He was convicted as one of the CHICAGO SEVEN after the CHICAGO DEMOCRATIC NATIONAL CONVENTION violence of 1968 and was later freed. He later became a California state legislator.

Hayek, Freidrich August von (1899–), Austrian-born economist, who opposed government intervention in economic, political, and social matters, and whose popular book, *The Road to Serfdom* (1944), was influential in developing conservative political thinking. He shared a Nobel Prize in economics with Gunnar MYRDAL in 1974.

Haynesworth, Clement Furman (1912–), U.S. lawyer and judge, a conservative who was in August 1969, nominated to the Supreme Court by president Richard M. NIXON. After a major nomination battle, the Haynesworth nomination was defeated 55–45 in the Senate.

Haywood, William Dudley "Big Bill" (1869–1928), leader of the Western Federation of Miners in the late 19th and early 20th centuries, a founder of the INDUSTRIAL WORKERS OF THE WORLD (IWW) in 1905, and its leader until his death. In 1906 he was accused, with two others, of directing confessed murderer Harry Orchard to kill former governor of Idaho Frank Steunenberg, but he was acquitted of the charge in 1907 after a notable defense by Clarence DARROW. Haywood opposed American participation in World War I and was convicted of sedition in 1918. Free on bail, he fled to the Soviet Union in 1921 and died there in 1928.

H-bomb, popular shorthand for the HYDROGEN BOMB, first developed in the United States in 1952.

He kept us out of war, the 1916 reelection slogan of U.S. president Woodrow WILSON.

Heady, Bonnie Brown, and **Carl Austin Hall,** the kidnap-murderers of 6-year-old Bobby Greenlease, at Kansas City, Missouri, on September 28, 1953. Hall murdered the child after the kidnapping; then he and Heady demanded and secured a $600,000 ransom, of which half was eventually recovered. They were executed on December 18, 1953.

Hearst, Patricia "Patty" (1954–), daughter of publisher Randolph Hearst and granddaughter of William Randolph HEARST, who was kidnapped in San Francisco on February 5, 1974, by members of the SYMBIONESE LIBERATION ARMY (SLA), in a case that then and later attracted world-wide attention. On April 15, Hearst participated in a San Francisco bank robbery. On May 17, six SLA members died in a gun battle with police. Hearst then went into hiding, was captured in 1975, and was subsequently sentenced to 7 years imprisonment for her role in the bank robbery. Her sentence was later commuted to 22 months.

Hearst, William Randolph (1863–1951), U.S. entrepreneur and journalist, who bought the New York *Morning Journal* in 1895, built it into a commercially successful mass circulation daily, and used it as the base of a major publishing enterprise, which included print and broadcast media. He promoted U.S. initiation of the Spanish-American War, opposed U.S. participation in both World Wars, and opposed the LEAGUE OF NATIONS. He served two terms as a New York Democratic congressman 1903–1907 but was defeated in several other electoral campaigns. He also collected substantial numbers of artworks, from 1927 housing most of them in or near his castle at San Simeon, California. His career was memorialized in the Orson Welles film, *Citizen Kane* (1941).

Heart of Atlanta Motel, Inc.* v. *United States (1964), a landmark U.S. Supreme Court case outlawing discrimination in facilities serving interstate travelers.

heart transplant, replacement of a diseased human heart with a donor's healthy heart, the first being performed by surgeon Christiaan BARNARD in 1967 on Louis Washansky; a type of organ TRANSPLANT, made possible by the development of OPEN-HEART SURGERY.

Heath, Edward Richard George (1916–), British political leader, who saw service in World War II, became a Conservative member of Parliament in 1950, leader of his party in 1965, and prime minister in a surprise victory over Harold WILSON in 1970. As prime minister, he successfully led Britain into the EUROPEAN COMMUNITY in 1973 but was unable to cope with Britain's continuing economic and corollary labor problems, and was unseated in 1974 by

Harold Wilson's Liberal-Labour coalition. He lost his party leadership in 1975 to Margaret THATCHER.

Heaviside layer, alternate name for the IONOSPHERE, which enhances the quality of radio transmission, predicted in 1902 and found in 1924.

heavy water (deuterium oxide), water made with a high proportion of DEUTERIUM (a heavy ISOTOPE of hydrogen) replacing ordinary hydrogen; heavy water is used in some NUCLEAR REACTORS.

Hedin, Sven (1865–1952), Swedish explorer who traveled widely in Central Asia from the 1890s to the 1930s, mapping areas unknown and uncharted by Europeans and rediscovering many long-abandoned sites along the route of the old Silk Road. Much of Hedin's wide-ranging work in geology, botany, ethnography, and archaeology went unregarded after midcentury, because of his support for the Nazis in World War II.

Heisenberg, Werner Karl (1901–1976), German physicist, who in 1927 posited the UNCERTAINTY PRINCIPLE, the revolutionary view that the position and the momentum of a body cannot both be calculated at the same time with full accuracy; the more accurate the one measurement, the less accurate the other. His theory won him the 1932 Nobel Prize for Physics. In earlier work on nuclear theory with Niels BOHR, in 1925, he developed matrix algebra to help form a mathematical basis for QUANTUM THEORY. Heisenberg was in charge of the German effort to build an ATOMIC BOMB during World War II, but some early calculation errors and the bombing of the laboratories slowed the project.

helicopter, aircraft lifted by one or more horizontal rotors, as opposed to AIRPLANES, which are driven by vertical propellers or JET PROPULSION. Many Europeans and Americans experimented with such craft in the years just after the Wright brothers first flew. From 1907, several crude helicopters—including one by Igor SIKORSKY—were built, some rising inches or feet off the ground before crashing. In 1923 Spanish

engineer Juan de la Cierva developed a craft called an autogiro; by the 1930s dozens were in small-scale service in Europe and the Americas. The Germans, too, developed a practical helicopter in 1937, reaching a record altitude of 11,700 feet by 1938. Then in 1939 Russian-American engineer Igor Sikorsky developed a practical workhorse helicopter. Sikorsky's design proved the model for post-war helicopters. They were widely used in the KOREAN WAR for transportation and evacuation, and again in the VIETNAM WAR, becoming an offensive weapon as well, with the addition of guns and ROCKETS. Helicopters also saw widescale local use for traffic reports and disaster surveys.

Helsinki Accords, the human rights provisions of the agreement generated by the Conference on Security and Cooperation in Europe, signed on August 1, 1975, by all of the nations of Europe except Albania and including the Soviet Union, and by the United States and Canada. The accords generally supported the concepts of civil liberties and freedom of expression, but had no binding power on the signatories, which became very clear in the years immediately following.

Henry Street Settlement, a pioneer American settlement house on New York City's lower East Side, organized in 1893 by nurse Lillian WALD; it was her home for 40 years.

Henson, Matthew Alexander (1866–1955), U.S. explorer, who accompanied Robert Edwin PEARY on several polar expeditions, including the successful one to the NORTH POLE in 1909; he was the first Black man to reach the site.

Hepburn Act U.S. federal law granting the Interstate Commerce Commission (ICC) the right to regulate interstate railroad freight rates, thereby greatly increasing the power of the ICC. The law was strongly supported by President Theodore ROOSEVELT, as an important part of his trust-regulation strategy.

Herero-Hottentot Rising (1904–1908), a long insurrection in German Southwest Africa (later NAMIBIA), ultimately defeated by the Germans.

Hertzog, James (1866–1942), South African farmer and deeply committed segregationist, who became a general during the BOER WAR and opposed British-Boer cooperation and reconciliation after the war, as fostered by Louis BOTHA and Jan Christian SMUTS. He founded the NATIONAL PARTY in 1914, opposed South African entry into World War I, and defeated Smuts to become National party prime minister (1924–39). He was a coalition prime minister 1933–39, losing office and leaving politics after he unsuccessfully opposed South African entry into World War II.

Hertzsprung-Russell diagram, key diagram in modern STELLAR EVOLUTION theory, relating brightness and stellar types, based on ideas developed independently by Danish astronomer Ejnar Hertzsprung in 1911 and U.S. astronomer Henry Norris Russell, who in 1913 put them into diagram form.

Herzl, Theodor (1860–1904), Hungarian lawyer and writer, who became the chief organizer of ZIONISM. He convened the founding meeting and became first president of the Congress of Zionist Organizations at Basel, Switzerland, in 1897, and led the Zionist movement until his death.

Hess, Rudolph (1894–1987), German Nazi, who went to prison with Adolf HITLER after the BEER HALL PUTSCH of 1923, and then became Hitler's private secretary. During the years of power, he became deputy party leader and kept Hitler's confidence, but had little actual power. In May 1941 he flew to Britain, parachuted to earth, and proposed peace and a British-German alliance against the Soviet Union. He was held as a war prisoner, tried and convicted of war crimes at NUREMBERG in 1946, and spent the rest of his life in Spandau Prison.

Heydrich, Reinhard (1904–42), Nazi GESTAPO head and JEWISH HOLOCAUST organizer, who was known throughout Europe as "Heydrich the Hangman." He was assassinated in Czechoslovakia, being wounded in May and dying in June 1942. The Gesta-

po charged that the village of LIDICE, near Prague, had sheltered his killers. In reprisal, on June 10, 1942, the Gestapo murdered or sent to concentration camps the 1,200 people of Lidice, and destroyed the village.

Heyerdahl, Thor (1914–   ), Norwegian ethnologist and explorer, who believed that cultural similarities in widely separated lands sprang not from independent parallel development but from cultural infusions from distant lands. In support of these hypotheses regarding pre-Columbian civilizations in South America, Heyerdahl crossed the Pacific (1947) on a balsa-wood raft, as related in his best-selling book *Kon-Tiki* (1948), and also crossed the Atlantic in an early-Egyptian-style reed boat (1969–70), named *Ra II*.

Hezbollah (Hizb-Allah; Party of God), in Lebanon, an Iranian-influenced Shiite Moslem Lebanese militia using guerrilla and terrorist tactics, often against such targets as airliners, foreign legations and embassies, and foreign nationals taken as hostages; in the late 1980s it was an increasingly strong force in the LEBANESE WARS.

Hezbollah (Party of God), in Iran, a paramilitary force operating as an adjunct of the Islamic Republican party, the party of Ayatollah KHOMEINI until he dissolved it in 1987.

Higgins, William Richard, one of the LEBANON HOSTAGES, a U.S. lieutenant colonel and head of the UNITED NATIONS truce supervision team, kidnapped on February 17, 1988. He was murdered by his captors on or before July 31, 1989. They claimed his killing to be in retaliation for the July 28, 1989 Israeli kidnapping of Sheikh Abdul Karim Obeid, but he may have been killed at an earlier date.

Hilbert, David (1862–43) German mathematician, who in a 1900 speech spelled out 23 unsolved mathematical problems, challenging his colleagues to break out into new areas of study. Hilbert himself made wide-ranging contributions to mathematics, as in his formulation of modern algebraic number theory. His work on space of infinite dimensions, called Hilbert space, helped form the mathematical underpinnings of QUANTUM THEORY.

Hill, James Jerome (1838–1916), U.S. railroad financier and operator, who built a railroad system from the Midwest to the Pacific late in the 19th century. In the early 1900s, he and J. Pierpont MORGAN won a battle for control of that system and other major U.S. railroads, setting up the Northern Securities Company, a holding company that they controlled, and in which their former antagonists held minority interests. In 1904, in the landmark NORTHERN SECURITIES antitrust case, the Supreme Court forced dissolution of the company.

Hill, Joe (1879–1915), Swedish immigrant born Joel Hägglund, Americanized to Joseph Hillstrom, memorialized in the song "Joe Hill." He was an INDUSTRIAL WORKERS OF THE WORLD (IWW) activist and popular labor songwriter of the early 20th century, whose songs included "Casey Jones." He was executed for murder in Utah in 1915, on evidence widely thought to be insufficient.

Hillary, Edmund Percival (1919–   ), New Zealand–born explorer and later ambassador who, with Tenzing NORGAY, was the first to reach the top of Mt. Everest, the world's highest mountain, on May 29, 1953. During the INTERNATIONAL GEOPHYSICAL YEAR (1957–58), Hillary led what was only the third party to reach the SOUTH POLE, after Roald AMUNDSEN and Robert SCOTT, arriving by tractor on January 4, 1958.

Hillman, Sidney (1887–1946), U.S. garment worker, who in 1914 became the first president of the Amalgamated Clothing Workers of America, a position he held until his death. His union pioneered in such areas as the provision of banking services and cooperative housing for members, and in winning adoption of the 40-hour week. He was an initiator of the CONGRESS OF INDUSTRIAL ORGANIZATIONS (CIO) in the mid-1930s, and during World War II held several key labor-related government posts.

A Democrat, he was close to Franklin Delano ROOSEVELT and one his key labor supporters.

Hillquit, Morris (1869–1933), U.S. lawyer, who became a key theoretician, writer, defense counsel, and spokesman for the socialist movement, from late in the 19th century through the early 1930s. He opposed American participation in World War I and defended many of those accused of sedition for opposing that war. He was an unsuccessful socialist congressional candidate five times and twice an unsuccessful candidate for the New York mayoralty.

Hills, Carla Anderson (1934–   ), U.S. lawyer, and secretary of the Department of Housing and Urban Development 1975–77; she was named U.S. trade representative by president George BUSH on December 6, 1988.

Himmler, Heinrich (1900–45), Nazi Party leader, who was from 1929 head of the SS and who, after HITLER'S rise to power in 1933, created the GESTAPO, the Nazi secret police, and at the same time began the CONCENTRATION CAMP system. He directly operated the camps in which an estimated 10–26 million, 6 million of them Jews, were murdered by the Nazis. He also developed the large SS military organization that fought in World War II, the WAFFEN SS. He committed suicide on May 23, 1945.

Hinckley, John W. (1955–   ), young man who shot President Ronald REAGAN and wounded three others in Washington, DC, on March 30, 1981; in August 1981 he was acquitted as insane at the time of the shootings and was institutionalized.

Hindenburg, hydrogen-filled zeppelin, a German DIRIGIBLE, in regular trans-Atlantic service 1932–37. It burst into flame while landing in Lakehurst, New Jersey, on May 6, 1937, killing 36 people, an event reported by eyewitnesses on radio with great impact.

Hindenburg, Paul von (1847–1934), Prussian general, who stopped the Russian advance into East Prussia early in World War I, winning major victories at TANNENBERG and the first Battle of the MASURIAN LAKES. He became commander-in-chief on the Eastern Front and in 1916 chief of the German general staff; for the balance of the war he was largely responsible for running Germany as well as the armed forces. He remained chief of the general staff after the war, became president of the WEIMAR REPUBLIC in 1925, and ultimately brought the NAZIS into his government in 1933, effecting an easy way for HITLER to take power in Germany.

Hindenburg Line, a strong German defensive line in World War I, approximately 20 miles behind its 1914–17 Western Front Line, to which the German army withdrew February 23–April 5, 1917.

Hindenburg Line Offensive (September 27–November 11, 1918), World War I push in which British forces stormed and breached the HINDENBURG LINE; joined by Belgian forces, they took Ypres and moved ahead in Flanders. The offensive stopped only with the Armistice on November 11, 1918.

Hine, Lewis Wickes (1874–1940), U.S. photographer, whose portrayals of the immigrant experience, from arrival at ELLIS ISLAND to working life in America, coupled with his portrayals of child labor, made a deep impact on the development of social reform movements in the United States. In retrospect, his work is in aggregate also a major work in American social history.

hippies, the most radical exponents of the COUNTERCULTURE of the 1960s and early 1970s, who stressed the virtue of personal simplicity and attempted to retreat from modern industrial culture, often into rural communes, though sometimes into such urban enclaves as San Francisco's Haight-Ashbury district and New York City's East Village.

Hirohito (1901–89), emperor of Japan from 1926. He was a revered figure but essentially a figurehead, who was unable to stop Japan's militarists from beginning World War II, although he had doubts about the wisdom of the course taken. Traditionally silent, he announced Japan's World War II surrender in a radio address, and after the war made himself considerably more visible.

Hiroshima, site on Japan's Honshu Island where the ATOMIC BOMB was first used in warfare. At 8:15 A.M. on August 6, 1945, the *Enola Gay*, a B-29 bomber of the U.S. Air Force, dropped the bomb, one of two atomic bombs then in existence, on Hiroshima, at the time a city of 350,000 people and a relatively undamaged minor military target. The bombing was conceived as a demonstration of the killing power of the atomic weapon, and an attempt to force Japan to surrender unconditionally. The bomb struck the center of the city, immediately or shortly thereafter killing an estimated 70,000–80,000 people, injuring an equal number, and destroying or seriously damaging almost all of the city's structures. An estimated 75,000–125,000 more people later died of RADIATION, CANCER, and other bomb-related injuries, most of them within a few years of the bombing; victims and their children are still dying today from the bomb's effects. The city was rebuilt after the war, away from the radiation-damaged area; it is also now a Japanese national peace park. Since Hiroshima, the existence of the atomic weapon has cast a shadow over every life on the planet and on the possibility of human survival; in that sense, it seems quite proper to describe it as the most significant event of the 20th century.

Hiss, Alger (1904–   ), U.S. lawyer, who held several federal government positions in the early 1930s; in 1936 he moved into diplomacy and during World War II became active in developing plans and meetings in preparation for the formation of the UNITED NATIONS. He was president of the Carnegie Endowment for International Peace 1946–1949. In August 1948 he was accused by Whittaker CHAMBERS, testifying before the HOUSE COMMITTEE ON UN-AMERICAN ACTIVITIES (HUAC), of having been a Communist spy, and the HISS-CHAMBERS case gained enormous national and international attention. The case was one of the centerpieces of the witchhunt of the period and helped make the career of then-congressman and HUAC memberer Richard M. NIXON. Ultimately, in 1950, Hiss was convicted of perjury, and was imprisoned for almost 4 years. Afterward, Hiss continued to maintain his innocence, but was no longer able to participate in public life.

Hiss–Chambers Case (1949–1950), the perjury trials of Alger HISS, who had been accused by Whittaker CHAMBERS of having stolen top-secret state department files while a federal government employee in the 1930s and of having given Chambers documents to hide for him in 1937 and 1938. Some of these documents were the PUMPKIN PAPERS, rolls of microfilm Chambers stated he had hidden in a hollow pumpkin on his farm in Maryland. Hiss denied the allegations and was charged with perjury; the first trial ended in a hung jury, the second in conviction and imprisonment.

Hitler, Adolf (1889–1945), World War I corporal who became German dictator, took the world into World War II, and became by far humanity's greatest mass murderer. Hitler joined the Workers' party in 1920, became leader of what had by then become the NAZI PARTY in 1921, conducted the failed Munich BEER HALL PUTSCH of 1923 (writing *MEIN KAMPF* during his resulting jail term), and was until the late 1920s leader of a minor party. He picked up popular, army, and business support beginning in the late 1920s, took power in 1933, and immediately began the process of turning Germany into a fully totalitarian, fully armed state, in the process murdering tens of thousands of his opponents. After achieving power he became an extremely successful international adventurer, bluffing his way into a series of bloodless conquests, as in the RHINELAND, in AUSTRIA, and at MUNICH. Ultimately, he took his country, his allies, and the world into war—and finally, into the same kind of two-front war that had brought Germany defeat in World War I. During his 12 years in power he was directly responsible for the deaths of tens of millions of people, including at least 10 million

(and perhaps as many as 26 million) who were murdered in German CONCENTRATION CAMPS, 6 million of them the Jews of the HOLOCAUST, the others Poles, Russians, and innocents drawn from many other nations. Until very near the end his army, party, and the great mass of the German people fully supported him; the only internal challenge he faced was the aborted army OFFICERS' PLOT to assassinate him, coming in July 1944, when the war was clearly lost. He committed suicide in Berlin on April 30, 1945, with his mistress-turned-wife, Eva BRAUN.

Hitler diaries fraud, cause célèbre that erupted on April 22, 1983, when the West German magazine *Stern* announced discovery of 60 volumes of the diaries of Adolf HITLER, for which it had paid $3.7 million to Nazi memorabilia dealer Konrad Kujau, as arranged by *Stern* reporter Gerd Heideman. On April 23, British scholar Hugh Trevor-Roper vouched for the authenticity of the memoirs, a position he moderated somewhat two days later, as great skepticism was voiced from many quarters. Meanwhile, the Sunday *Times* of London paid $400,000 for the right to print excerpts. By May 6, tests had proved the purported diaries to be false. Kujau admitted the forgeries. Heideman was fired. The *Times* demanded its money back. Heads rolled in the *Stern* executive suite.

HIV (human immunodeficiency virus), organism that causes the deadly disease AIDS.

Hizb-Allah (Hezbollah; Party of God), Iranian-influenced Shiite Moslem Lebanese militia, using guerrilla and terrorist tactics, often against such targets as airliners, foreign legations and embassies, and foreign nationals taken as hostages; in the late 1980s an increasingly strong force in the LEBANESE WARS,

Hoa Hao, Buddhist Vietnamese religious group, some of whose members were employed by the CENTRAL INTELLIGENCE AGENCY (CIA) as anti-Communist mercenaries during the VIETNAM WAR.

Ho Chi Minh ("He who enlightens," originally Nguyen That Thanh; 1890–1969), Vietnamese leader who lived in Western Europe in his youth, joining the French Socialist Party in 1917 and becoming a founder of the French Communist Party in 1920. He studied in Moscow in the early 1920s, and from 1924 was a COMINTERN agent in China and southeast Asia. In 1941, he organized the League for the Independence of Vietnam (VIETMINH), which controlled large sections of northern Indochina at the end of World War II, and he became the first president of the Democratic Republic of Vietnam in Sepember 1945. From 1946 to 1954, his forces fought and won the long FRENCH–VIETNAMESE WAR, and they were engaged in the VIETNAM WAR when he died.

Ho Chi Minh Trail, the North Vietnamese route through Laos and Cambodia used for supply and troop transport from 1959; it was a major military route during the VIETNAM WAR.

Hodgkin, Dorothy Crowfoot (1910–   ), Egypt-born British chemist, who used X-RAY CRYSTALLOGRAPHY, along with a computer for analysis of the complex results, to detail the structure of large organic molecules, including pepsin, PENICILLIN, INSULIN, and VITAMIN B_{12}, work for which she won the 1964 Nobel Prize for Chemistry.

Hoffa, James Riddle (1913–1975?), U.S. worker who became a Detroit labor leader and then national head of the International Brotherhood of Teamsters, becoming president of the union in 1957. His union was charged with corruption and expelled from the AFL-CIO in 1957, but it continued to grow—and to grow even more corrupt—under his leadership. He was convicted of jury tampering, mail fraud, and financial malfeasance in office during the 1960s, sentenced to a total of 13 years imprisonment, and was in prison for almost 5 years, 1967–71. His sentence was then commuted by President Richard M. NIXON. On July 30, 1975, he disappeared and is thought to have been kidnapped and murdered.

Hoffman, Abbie (1936–89), a leading figure of the 1960s U.S. counterculture. He was a founder and leader of the Youth International Party (YIP) and became known as a "YIPPIE" leader. He was indicted and convicted as one of the CHICAGO SEVEN after the CHICAGO DEMOCRATIC CONVENTION riots of 1968, but was later acquitted. He went into hiding in 1973, rather than face a drug charge, giving himself up in 1980.

HOLC, the initials of the HOME OWNERS LOAN CORPORATION, a NEW DEAL federal agency of the 1930s.

Holland, Battle of (May 10–14, 1940), a quick German victory in Holland early in World War II, accomplished by a combination of ground forces striking across the border; airborne troop landings that destroyed interior communications, took the Rhine estuary bridges, and neutralized key defenses; and terror bombings. The Dutch breached their own dikes, but flooding did not stop the German advance; nor did French forces, which were easily driven back. The Dutch government fled to Britain, and Dutch armed forces surrendered on May 14.

Hollywood Ten, 10 U.S. film directors and screenwriters who refused to testify before the HOUSE UN-AMERICAN ACTIVITIES COMMITTEE in 1947, claiming the protection of the First Amendment; they were cited for contempt, jailed for 1-year terms, and thereafter blacklisted by the film industry. In later years several of the writers worked under pseudonyms, some winning major film industry awards. Later still, long after the anti-Communist hysteria of the MCCARTHY period had subsided, several were rehabilitated, and worked openly again in the industry that had expelled them.

Holmes, Oliver Wendell (1841–1935), U.S. lawyer, the son of 19th-century writer-physician Oliver Wendell Holmes; he saw service in the Civil War, became a scholar, writer, and philosopher in the law, a justice and chief justice of the Massachusetts

Supreme Court, and in 1902 was appointed to the Supreme Court by Theodore ROOSEVELT. During the next 30 years, he became a major figure in the history of the Court and the Court's much-quoted "Great Dissenter."

Holocaust, a term applied in the 20th century to three enormous sets of mass murders: the JEWISH HOLOCAUST, in which an estimated 6 million Jews died at the hands of a German Nazi government bent on committing GENOCIDE; the ARMENIAN HOLOCAUST, in which an estimated 1.5 million Armenians died at the hands of the Turkish government before and during World War I; and the CAMBODIAN (KAMPUCHEAN) HOLOCAUST, in which an estimated 3 million Cambodians died at the hands of their own government.

holography, technique of producing three-dimensional photographs or illustrations of objects; conceived of in 1947 by Hungarian-British physicist Dennis Gabor but not made practical until the 1960s development of the LASER. Because holographs are difficult to reproduce, and therefore to counterfeit, they were increasingly used on CREDIT CARDS and other sensitive materials.

Holyoake, Keith Jacka (1904–83), New Zealand farmer, National Party member of parliament (1932–38; 1943–72), and prime minister briefly in 1957 and again 1960–72. A conservative, he supported the VIETNAM WAR and fostered New Zealand participation in regional military alliances.

homeostasis, ability of an organism to establish a physiological equilibrium, as through the mechanism of FEEDBACK or, when deliberately manipulated, BIOFEEDBACK; a term coined in 1926 by American physiologist Walter Bradford Cannon. Others later applied the idea of homeostasis to institutions and societies as social organisms.

Home Owners Loan Corporation (HOLC), a U.S. NEW DEAL agency created during the first HUNDRED DAYS of the Franklin ROOSEVELT administration; it made direct federal loans to more than 1 million home-owners, saving many of them from foreclosure and helping to stabilize the home mortgage operations of the financial industries.

Homma, Masaharu (1887–1946), the general who commanded Japanese invasion forces in the Philippines 1941–42. In 1946 he was convicted and executed for the crimes committed by his troops against war prisoners, including those during the BATAAN DEATH MARCH.

Honecker, Erich (1912–   ), East German communist and antifascist activist, who was imprisoned by the Nazis 1935–45, then rose in the postwar period to become a member of the Socialist Unity party secretariat in 1958. He succeeded Walter ULBRICHT as party secretary-general and East German leader in 1971, in that position continuing to develop his country's industrial system within the context of a one-party Soviet-oriented state. He resigned under pressure, on October 18, 1989, as massive political changes rocked East Germany.

Hong Kong, Battle of (December 8–25, 1941), attack by Japanese forces across the Chinese border on December 8; after an ultimatum was rejected by British defenders, air and artillery assaults on the island began. Japanese troops began to land on December 18, and by December 25 they had overcome the British garrison, which surrendered.

Honkeido mine explosion (April 26, 1942), an explosion in a coal mine in Honkeiko, Manchuria, that killed at least 1,549 in the world's worst mine disaster to date.

Hoover, Herbert Clark (1874–1964), U.S. engineer, active as chairman of several war relief organizations during and after World War I, who became secretary of commerce (1920–27), and 31st president of the United States (1929–1933). A Republican, he defeated Democrat Alfred E. SMITH in 1928. As president, his major domestic work was the passage of the SMOOT-HAWLEY TARIFF, in June 1930, thereby erecting major tariff barriers that did much to accelerate the world's slide into the GREAT DEPRESSION, which had begun with the CRASH of October 1929. He also initiated the RECONSTRUCTION FINANCE CORPORATION in 1932, in a modest and wholly unsuccessful attempt to reverse the impact of the economic downturn by supplying government money to large institutions to stimulate economic growth. He was opposed to directly helping the ever-increasing masses of unemployed who had by the early 1930s become highly visible throughout the United States, and acquiesced when troops led by Douglas MACARTHUR evicted the BONUS MARCHERS from their squatters' camp near Washington, in July 1932, the camp burning down during the eviction, an action widely blamed on the president. He was defeated by Franklin Delano ROOSEVELT in 1932, then retiring to private life until being asked to serve on several federal advisory groups after World War II.

Hoover, J. Edgar (1895–1972), director of the FEDERAL BUREAU OF INVESTIGATION 1924–72. Early in his career, as a special assistant to U.S. Attorney General A. Mitchell PALMER, Hoover participated in the organization and execution of the PALMER RAIDS. In the 1930s he directed the FBI's highly publicized internal war against criminals, dubbed "public enemies." In the 1940s and 1950s he was a leading American anti-Communist, and in the 1960s he expanded his role to include surveillance and sometimes harassment of anti–VIETNAM WAR dissidents and of such civil rights leaders as Martin Luther KING, Jr.

Hoovervilles, the shanty towns that were thrown up all over the United States by the unemployed and homeless during the early years of the GREAT DEPRESSION of the 1930s, before Franklin Delano ROOSEVELT'S NEW DEAL programs began to take hold.

Hopkins, Harry Lloyd (1890–1946), U.S. social worker, who in 1931 became New York governor Franklin Delano ROOSEVELT'S state emergency relief administrator, and a member of Roosevelt's inner circle. In 1933, he followed Roosevelt to Washington to become head of the FEDER-

AL EMERGENCY RELIEF ADMINISTRATION and later organizer of the WORKS PROGRESS ADMINISTRATION (WPA). He became secretary of commerce in 1938 and was a key organizer of Roosevelt's 1940 presidential campaign, but in 1941 resigned his cabinet post because of illness. During World War II, he continued to advise Roosevelt, taking on many missions abroad and attending all of Roosevelt's wartime conferences with Allied leaders.

hormones, group of substances that influence or control organs or tissues, especially in such vital areas as growth, metabolism, and reproduction; usually secreted in the body by endocrine glands. Though some such substances were known from the 19th century, they were first recognized as a group and named hormones (Greek for "I excite") in 1904 by British physiologist Ernest Starling. Among the best known of these chemical messengers are INSULIN, ADRENALINE, THYROXINE, CORTISONE, ESTROGEN, and TESTOSTERONE, many of which have been synthesized for use as medications, sometimes with the aid of GENETIC ENGINEERING.

Horney, Karen Danielsen (1885–1952), German-American neo-Freudian psychoanalyst, who broke with the Freudians over the issue of sexual primacy. A student and professor of PSYCHOANALYSIS in Germany, Horney emigrated to the United States in 1932. After publishing her views that environmental factors were more important than sexual urges in the formation of neuroses, and rejecting many of FREUD'S views on women's sexuality, especially the idea of penis envy, she was in 1941 expelled by the New York Psychoanalytic Institute, thereafter founding her own Association for the Advancement of Psychoanalysis.

Horthy, Miklós (1868–1957), Hungarian naval officer, whose forces defeated the Communist Béla KUN government in 1919; Horthy then took over the country as regent but did not allow the king to return, instead becoming dictator of Hungary 1920–44. He was an ally of Adolf HITLER before and during World War II, pulling away from Hitler in 1944 when it became clear that the war was being lost. He was then imprisoned by the Germans, imprisoned and then released by the Americans, and went into exile.

Horton, William (Willie), an imprisoned murderer who, while on furlough under a Massachusetts weekend furlough program committed rape and murder. The incident became an issue in the 1988 presidential campaign, when George BUSH used it to attack his opponent, Massachusetts Governor Michael DUKAKIS.

hospice movement, approach to treating terminally ill patients that focuses on maximizing patients' comfort and dignity, often allowing them to die in their own homes or in a homelike shelter called a hospice, rather than in an impersonal hospital setting. Inspired by medieval hospices, and in reaction to technological intervention that sometimes extended suffering, rather than relieving it, medical workers in midcentury Britain began experimenting with giving pain-killing and life-enhancing drugs according to need, notably at London's St. Joseph's Hospice from 1958. In 1967, St. Christopher's, a teaching and research hospice, opened in London, inspiring others there and abroad, as at New Haven, Connecticut, and Montreal, Quebec, from 1974, and the movement spread widely.

Hot Line Agreement (1963), a U.S.–U.S.S.R. agreement to set up a direct link between the leaders of the two superpowers, to reduce the risk of nuclear war; the need for such a direct link had become apparent during the CUBAN MISSILE CRISIS.

Houphoüt-Boigny, Felix (1905–   ), Ivory Coast political leader, an organizer of the Ivory Coast Democratic Party in 1945, who represented the Ivory Coast in the French National Assembly 1946–59. In 1959, he became the first prime minister and in 1960 the first president of his country, which became a single-party, Western-oriented state with close ties to France.

House, Edward Mandell (1858–1938), U.S. political adviser, active in Texas politics 1892–1902; an honorary Texas colonel, he was known as "Colonel House" after 1892. He became a key confidante and adviser to President Woodrow WILSON in 1912, and was Wilson's most important foreign policy advisor throughout World War I. House was one of those who drafted Wilson's FOURTEEN POINTS and was Wilson's chief negotiator at the PARIS PEACE CONFERENCE of 1919. Wilson became convinced that House was compromising away the American position, and broke with him on conclusion of the conference, refusing to see him thereafter.

House Un-American Activities Committee (HUAC), the Communist-hunting committee of the House of Representatives, successor to the DIES COMMITTEE of the 1930s. HUAC achieved a considerable U.S. following and worldwide notoriety during the late 1940s and early 1950s, losing its power as the anti-Communist hysteria of the MCCARTHY period subsided. Its chief early victory was in the case of the HOLLYWOOD TEN, which was followed by a long series of public investigations of the entertainment and other industries, and resulted in massive BLACKLISTING. The committee was somewhat eclipsed by the more spectacular witchhunting activities of Senator Joseph MCCARTHY in the early 1950s.

hovercraft (hydrofoil), type of AIR-CUSHION VEHICLE (ACV) designed to travel over water on a self-generated air cushion. Conceived of in 1870, the hovercraft was first developed as a practical design in 1955 by British engineer Christopher Cockerell, making its maiden voyage across the English Channel in 1959 and going into regular commercial service there in 1968.

Howard Beach case (December 21, 1987), incident in which a group of young white racists attacked, beat, and pursued two Black Americans at Howard Beach, a neighborhood in Queens, New York, on the night of December 21, 1987. One of the Black men, Michael Griffith, died after being hit by a vehicle while fleeing on foot on the Belt Parkway. After a highly publicized trial, Scott Kern, Jason Ladone, Jon Lester, and

Michael Pirone were convicted on charges stemming from the attack.

Howe, Louis McHenry (1870–1936), U.S. journalist, who became Franklin Delano ROOSEVELT'S key political adviser in 1911, and was his personal assistant 1915–35. With Eleanor ROOSEVELT, Howe saw Franklin Roosevelt through polio in 1921, brought him back into political life, and then went with him to Albany and Washington.

Hoxha, Enver (1908–1985), Albanian teacher, World War II resistance leader, a founder of the Albanian Communist party in 1941, and from 1944 through his death in 1985 leader of the Albanian Communist party and government. A hardline Stalinist, Hoxha opposed DETENTE and closer Soviet bloc-Yugoslav relations, breaking with Nikita KHRUSHCHEV in 1957 and with the Soviet Union in 1961. He then moved Albania into a close relationship with China, breaking with China in 1977, as that country moved toward detente with the United States.

Hoyle, Fred (1915–   ), British astronomer and writer who was one of the main exponents of the STEADY STATE THEORY of the universe and whose writings brought new concepts in astronomy to a wide audience.

Hsüan T'ung (Henry P'u Yi; 1906–1967), the last Manchu (Ch'ing) emperor of China, who reigned from 1908 and abdicated on February 12, 1912. He became Japanese puppet ruler of Manchuria (Manchukuo) in 1934, was held by the Soviet Union 1945–50, and was then returned to the PEOPLE'S REPUBLIC OF CHINA, where the Chinese imprisoned and in 1959 pardoned him. He was the subject of the 1987 film, *The Last Emperor.*

HTLV (human T-lymphotropic virus), alternate name for the organism that causes the deadly disease AIDS.

Hua Guofeng (Hua Kuo-feng; 1920–   ), Chinese Communist leader, who became premier in 1976 succeeding CHOU EN-LAI. Although long a Maoist, he approved of the action taken against the GANG OF FOUR, at the same time attempting once again to purge DENG XIAOPING and other reformers. However, he was within a year sharing power with Deng and was forced out of power in 1980 as the reform movement took full power in China.

Hua Kuo-feng, the old-style name of Chinese leader HUA Guofeng.

Hubbard, Lafayette Ronald (1911–1986), U.S. writer and founder of the Church of Scientology (1952), which used an "auditor," a device something like a lie detector, to help its members increase control over their minds. Although the church itself came under attack from many quarters, including the FBI, Hubbard's science fiction works and his *Dianetics: The Modern Science of Mental Health* (1950), the "bible" of Scientology, attracted wide audiences.

Hubble, Edwin Powell (1889–1953), U.S. astronomer who did key work at California's Mt. Wilson Observatory, identifying many nebulas—"cloudy" masses of stars—as other galaxies and positing that the universe is constantly expanding, based on his analysis of the RED SHIFT in star light. Hubble's law, stated in 1929, indicated a constant relationship between the speed at which a galaxy is receding from Earth and its distance from us; that relationship was labeled "Hubble's constant," and is basic to much of 20th-century astronomy.

Hué, Battle of (January–March 1968), a regimental-strength engagement and long house-to-house series of battles between attacking North Vietnamese and defending U.S. forces, causing many civilian casualties and much damage to the city of Hué before the North Vietnamese retreated; the North Vietnamese assault was part of the TET OFFENSIVE.

Huerta, Victoriano (1854–1916), Mexican officer who became a general in the army of Porforio DÍAZ, was commander of the Mexico City garrison during the presidency of Francisco MADERO, and led a successful coup in February 1913, his forces then assassinating Madero and his vice-president,

Pino Suárez. Huerta ruled as a dictator until July 1914, then fleed the country. In exile, he sought to regain power, attempting to organize a revolt while operating out of Texas, much as Madero had done in 1910. Arrested and then released by the U.S. authorities, he died of illness in El Paso, in January 1916.

Hughes, Charles Evans (1862–1948), U.S. lawyer, a Republican governor of New York (1907–1910), appointed to the Supreme Court in 1910 by William Howard TAFT. Hughes resigned in 1916 to become Republican presidential candidate and was then defeated by Woodrow WILSON. He was Warren G. HARDING'S secretary of state 1921–25, and was appointed chief justice of the United States by Herbert HOOVER in 1930, retiring in 1941. He opposed and helped defeat Franklin D. ROOSEVELT'S attempt to "pack" the Supreme Court with his supporters in 1937.

Hukbalahap insurgency (1946–1954), a post-World War II rural insurgency in the Philippines, developed by previously anti-Japanese, Communist-led guerrilla forces demanding land reform; in the late 1940s they held much of central Luzon. Government forces led by defense minister Ramón MAGSAYSAY, with American military supplies, defeated the insurgency, which effectively ended in the spring of 1954. Some guerrillas fought on, however, providing experience and leadership for the new Communist-led insurgency that developed in the mid-1960s and still continues.

Hull, Cordell (1871–1955), U.S. lawyer, a Tennessee Democratic congressman 1907–21; 1923–31), and senator (1931–33), who was Franklin D. ROOSEVELT'S secretary of state (1933–44), resigning because of illness and winning a Nobel Peace Prize in 1945. As secretary of state, he developed the GOOD NEIGHBOR POLICY toward Latin America, while facing growing German and Japanese threats to world peace. During World War II he played a substantial role in developing the UNITED NATIONS; Franklin Roosevelt called him "the father of the United Nations."

Hull House, a pioneeering Chicago settlement house founded in 1889 by Jane ADDAMS and a group of co-workers; it served as an incubator for the American social work movement and a training ground for two generations of social workers. The house was named after its first owner, Charles Hull.

human immunodeficiency virus (HIV), organism that causes the deadly disease AIDS.

human T-lymphotropic virus (HTLV), alternate name for the organism that causes the deadly disease AIDS.

Hump, The, the late 1942 airlift route over the Himalayas taken by American planes flying supplies from India to Kunming in Nationalist-held China.

Humphrey, Hubert Horatio (1911–78), U.S. teacher, Democratic-Farmer-Labor mayor of Minneapolis (1945–49) and four-term Minnesota Democratic senator from Minnesota (1949–65, 1971–78). He was Lyndon JOHNSON'S vice president, 1965–69, and was defeated for the presidency by Richard M. NIXON in 1968. On domestic issues he was a liberal in the Senate, strongly advocating CIVIL RIGHTS and health care legislation, though as vice president he strongly supported the VIETNAM WAR. His 1968 presidential campaign was seriously damaged by the street fighting outside the CHICAGO DEMOCRATIC CONVENTION hall, between antiwar protesters and the Chicago police, and by the coercive tactics employed by Chicago Mayor Richard J. DALEY'S people inside the hall.

Hundred Days, the first 100 days of Franklin Delano ROOSEVELT'S presidency; actually the 104 days between the special congressional session opening March 9, 1933, and its adjournment on June 16, 1933, in which an extraordinary body of legislation was enacted; in aggregate, it constituted Roosevelt's NEW DEAL approach to the huge problems of the GREAT DEPRESSION. These new laws established the FEDERAL EMERGENCY RELIEF ADMINISTRATION, the CIVILIAN CONSERVATION CORPS, and the PUBLIC WORKS ADMINISTRATION;

provided for farm and home mortgage refinancing and loans to small business and farmers; and included passage of the AGRICULTURAL ADJUSTMENT ACT and the NATIONAL INDUSTRIAL RECOVERY ACT, both highly stimulative in that period, though both later ruled unconstitutional.

Hundred Flowers Campaign, the brief 1956–57 Chinese Communist encouragement of moderate dissent sparked by a quotation by MAO ZEDONG that began "Let a hundred flowers bloom, and a hundred schools of thought contend." Dissent did appear and grew very swiftly, triggering an equally swift reaction that imprisoned and otherwise penalized many intellectuals who had dissented.

Hungarian Revolution (1956), unrest that began to grow in Hungary during the spring and summer of 1956, as it did throughout the Soviet bloc, following the February KHRUSHCHEV SECRET SPEECH. Although prime minister Mátyas RAKOSI resigned in July, the unrest broke into open revolution in Budapest on October 23. Soviet troops began to leave Hungary, hoping to avoid armed conflict. On October 24, a new government was formed, headed by reformer Imre NAGY, with reformer János KÁDÁR heading the Communist Party. The new government immediately instituted major democratic reforms, released Cardinal MINDZENTY, and announced Hungary's neutrality and coming withdrawal from the WARSAW PACT. On November 1, Kádár broke with the Nagy government, leaving Budapest to form a new government. On November 4, Soviet forces returned in strength, quickly defeated the lightly armed revolutionaries, and took the country, an estimated 100,000–200,000 Hungarians then fleeing to the west. Nagy was soon executed; Kádár led the country for 32 years, with Soviet advice and support.

Hungary (Republic of Hungary), until the end of World War I part of the Austro-Hungarian Empire, then becoming an independent state. The Communist revolution of 1919 briefly brought the BELA KUN government to power; it was followed by the Fascist HORTHY government, allied with Germany in World War II. The democratic postwar Hungarian Republic lasted from February 1, 1946, until the spring of 1947, then was supplanted by the one-party Communist government that formally became the People's Republic on August 20, 1949. The Communist government was seriously challenged only in 1956 by the failed HUNGARIAN REVOLUTION. During the GORBACHEV era Hungary fully participated in the wave of changes and reevaluations sweeping the Communist world. In October 1989, as part of a large body of constitutional changes, the country became The Republic of Hungary, dropping the People's Republic from its name. The Communist Party transformed itself into a social democratic party, opposition parties were legalized, and Hungary moved toward democratic elections in 1990.

Huntley, Chet (1911–1974), U.S. journalist and television broadcaster who with David Brinkley co-anchored the NBC Huntley-Brinkley Report 1956–70, covering and interpreting the news in the most widely viewed newscast of the period.

Husák, Gustav (1913–   ), Czechoslovakian lawyer, a Slovak Communist leader in the 1930s and a World War II resistance fighter. Imprisoned by his own party 1951–60 and then rehabilitated. Husák was a deputy premier in Alexander DUBCEK'S government during the PRAGUE SPRING, and then succeeded Dubcek as first secretary of the Czech Communist party in 1969, staying on to liquidate the reforms he had helped initiate. He remained a conservative until his 1987 retirement, which was occasioned in part by his difficulty in adjusting to the reforms of the GORBACHEV era, which were strikingly similar to those of the Prague Spring.

Hussein I (1935–   ), king of Jordan, succeeding to the throne in 1953 after his father had been declared mentally incompetent to rule. Although a moderate who generally sought peace with Israel, he took his country into the SINAI–SUEZ WAR (THIRD ARAB–ISRAELI WAR) of 1967 and

was defeated, Israel then occupying Jerusalem and the WEST BANK, although Jordan
continued to claim sovereignty. In 1970 his
forces fought, defeated, and expelled the
substantial PALESTINE LIBERATION ORGAN-
IZATION (PLO) guerrilla army fighting from
Jordan across the Israeli border. He healed
the breach with the PLO during the early
1980s and continued to press for removal of
Israeli occupation forces from the West
Bank and Gaza Strip. In 1988, as the IN-
TIFADA (uprising) grew on the West Bank,
he gave up all responsibility for the area,
paving the way for the assertion of a Palestinian state.

Hussein Ibn Ali (1853–1931), leader of the
ARAB REVOLT of 1916, king of the Hejaz,
sharif of Mecca, and father of FAISAL I of
Iraq and ABDULLAH IBN HUSSEIN of Transjordan. Under pressure from IBN SAUD, he
abdicated in 1924.

Hussein, Saddam (1937–   ), Iraqi
BA'ATH PARTY activist who was a leader of
the Ba'ath coup of 1968; by 1971 he had become de facto leader of Iraq, and in 1979
formally became Iraqi president. He is
Iraq's sole leader, having repressed all political opposition. In his early years in power
he attempted to conciliate Iraq's Kurdish
population but later faced a renewed full-
scale Kurdish insurgency, which continues.
In 1980, his armed forces attacked Iran, beginning the IRAN–IRAQ WAR. In the course
of that war his forces initiated the widescale
use of chemical weapons. After its conclusion his forces moved against the Kurds,
who had been allied with the Iranians, again
using CHEMICAL WARFARE, killing
thousands and driving hundreds of
thousands of into exile.

Husseini, Haj Amin al (1893–1974), Palestinian Arab leader who, as a Turkish army
officer early in World War I, joined the AR-
AB REVOLT led by FAISAL and was a member of the British governing body for
Palestine and a leading Arab nationalist
during the immediate post–World War I
period. In 1921 the British appointed him
Grand Mufti of Jerusalem; in 1922 he was
elected head of Palestine's Supreme Muslim

Council. During the 1920s and 1930s he became the leading Palestinian Arab nationalist, resisting British occupation of and
increasing Jewish migration into Palestine.
In 1936 he founded and became chairman
of the Arab Higher Committee, and played
a major role in initiating the PALESTINIAN
GENERAL STRIKE AND REVOLT of 1936–39.
In 1937 the British outlawed his committee
and dissolved the Supreme Muslim Council;
Husseini then left Palestine, continuing to
lead the revolt from other Arab countries.
During World War II he worked for the
Nazis, spending much of the war in Germany. In 1946, the ARAB LEAGUE reconstituted the Arab Higher Committee; he became
its president and worked to organize the
Arabs of Palestine for the approaching civil
war, but never regained the preeminent position he had occupied before the war. After
the Arab defeat in 1948 he steadily lost influence, although continuing to be a historical figure in the Arab world.

Huxley, Julian Sorell (1887–1975), British
biologist and writer, grandson of biologist
and early Darwin supporter Thomas Henry
Huxley, and brother of novelist and visiona-
ry Aldous Huxley. He worked variously in
zoology, ecology, ethology, and genetics,
and his widely read written works fused beliefs in evolution and humanism; so it was
fitting that from 1946 to 1948 he served as
the first director general of UNESCO (United
Nations Educational, Scientific, and Cultural Organization).

Hu Yaobang (Hu Yao-pang; 1915–89), a
protege and ally of Deng XIAOPING who
joined the Chinese Communist party in the
late 1933, was a political officer during the
CHINESE CIVIL WAR, and was a Communist
official after the war. He was purged with
Deng in the mid-1960s, came back to power
with him and became chairman of the Communist party in 1981. He was the leading
Chinese democratic reformer of his time,
falling from power in the conservative back-
lash that followed the student demonstrations of 1986. His death generated the
massive prodemocratic CHINESE STUDENT
DEMONSTRATIONS of 1989.

Hu Yao-pang, the old-style name of Chinese leader HU YAOBANG.

Hwai Hai, Battle of (November 1948–January 1949), a CHINESE CIVIL WAR battle involving an estimated 1 million combatants, in which the attacking Central Plains and East China Communist field armies destroyed the Nationalist Seventh Army Group and routed the Second Army Group, with Nationalist losses of an estimated 250,000 men. It was the last major battle of the war; on January 22, 1949, Peking fell.

Hyatt Regency walkway collapse (July 17, 1981), collapse of two interior suspended walkways over the atrium lobby of the Hyatt Regency hotel in Kansas City, one atop the other falling on the crowded dance floor below; 113 people were killed and 186 more were injured, many of them seriously.

hydrofoil, alternate name for a HOVERCRAFT, a type of AIR-CUSHION VEHICLE developed in 1955 by Christopher Cockerell.

hydrogen bomb (H-bomb), explosive device using an ATOMIC BOMB to trigger NUCLEAR FUSION, producing much heat and therefore called a thermonuclear device. Enrico FERMI and Edward TELLER recognized the possibility of building what they called a "Super" as early as 1942, but the idea received little funding until 1949 when the Soviet Union exploded its first atomic bomb. Then properly funded, Teller led the project to build the H-bomb, aided by the calculating power of the MANIAC COMPUTER developed by John von NEUMANN. They successfully tested the bomb first at ENIWETOK on November 1, 1952, and two years later at BIKINI. After the Russians built their own H-bomb in 1953 and the British in 1957, the ARMS RACE moved to a new level, increasing pressure for controlling, reducing, or eliminating nuclear weapons.

I

Iacocca, Lee Anthony (1924–   ), U.S. engineer, who became president of the Ford Motor Company, 1970–78, moving in 1978 to become president and later chairman of Chrysler Corporation, and a leading spokesperson for corporate interests. He also spoke for the concept of a multiethnic, immigrant-built United States during his chairmanship of the drive to restore ELLIS ISLAND and the Statue of Liberty in the mid-1980s.

Ia Drang, Battle of (October–November 1965), regimental-strength engagement between North Vietnamese and U.S. army units in the Ia Drang valley, near the Vietnam–Cambodia border, and the first major battle between large U.S. and North Vietnamese army units of the VIETNAM WAR.

IAEA, the initials of the INTERNATIONAL ATOMIC ENERGY AGENCY.

Ibarruri, Dolores ("La Pasionaria;" 1895–1989), Spanish Communist Party leader, a founder of her party in 1920, and in parliament 1936–39. A powerful speaker, she became one of the key symbols of the Republic during the SPANISH CIVIL WAR. The war lost, she fled to the Soviet Union, returning to Spain and a seat in parliament after the death of Francisco FRANCO.

Ibn Saud (Abd al-Aziz Ibn Saud; 1880–1953), Saudi Arabian king, who took control of the Nejd district of Arabia in the period 1902–06 and had taken much of eastern Arabia by 1913. During World War I he was formally but passively allied with the British against the Turks after 1915. He won control of western Arabia (the Hejaz) in 1925 after a long civil war with the Hashemite forces of HUSSEIN IBN ALI. He became king of the new nation of Saudi Arabia in 1932 and granted the first Arabian oil concession to Standard Oil in 1933, thereafter becoming the first of the wealthy oil potentates of the Middle East.

IBRD, the initials of the INTERNATIONAL BANK FOR RECONSTRUCTION AND DEVELOPMENT, a multinational investment bank and UNITED NATIONS agency that is part of the WORLD BANK.

ICBM, popular shorthand for the INTERCONTINENTAL BALLISTIC MISSILE, first developed in 1954.

Iceland (Republic of Iceland), until 1918 an island country ruled by Denmark; Iceland achieved internal autonomy in 1918 and became an independent state on June 17, 1944, after the World War II Allied occupation.

Ickes, Harold LeClaire (1874–1952), U.S. lawyer and political leader, a Republican who supported Theodore ROOSEVELT'S BULL MOOSE PARTY and Robert LA FOLLETTE'S PROGRESSIVE PARTY. In 1933 he became Franklin Delano ROOSEVELT'S strongly conservationist secretary of the interior and head of the PUBLIC WORKS ADMINISTRATION. Strong-willed and outspoken, he was sharply criticized by business interests desiring to exploit federal lands and responded in kind. He resigned in 1946 after a difference of opinion with President Harry S. TRUMAN.

IDA, the initials of the INTERNATIONAL DEVELOPMENT ASSOCIATION, a UNITED NATIONS agency engaged in long-term international lending to developing nations; part of the WORLD BANK.

Idaho Falls nuclear explosion (January 3, 1961), an explosion at the Idaho Falls, Idaho, nuclear reactor that killed three people; until the KERR-MCGEE nuclear accident of 1986, these were the only reported direct deaths due to nuclear accident in the United States.

IFC, the initials of the INTERNATIONAL FINANCE CORPORATION, a multinational investment bank and UNITED NATIONS agency; part of the WORLD BANK.

If I turn traitor to the cause I now pledge, may this hand wither from the arm I now raise, pledge taken by 3,000 Jewish-American and Italian-American women garment workers on the eve of the waistmakers' strike of 1909–10.

I have a dream, the celebrated phrase in the speech by Martin Luther KING, Jr., at the MARCH ON WASHINGTON, August 28, 1963.

I have sinned!, announcement by the Reverend Jimmy SWAGGART, tearfully addressing a national television audience on February 21, 1988, after having been accused of unbecoming sexual conduct.

Il Duce (The Leader), a popular alternate name for Benito MUSSOLINI.

IMF, the initials of the INTERNATIONAL MONETARY FUND, a multinational banking fund and UN agency.

Inchon landings (September 15, 1950), surprise divisional-strength amphibious landings of UNITED NATIONS forces at INCHON on the east coast of Korea, near Seoul, during the second phase of the KOREAN WAR. UN forces quickly broke through North Korean defenses, and UN defensive forces to the south broke out to meet them at and retake Seoul. Combined UN forces then pursued North Korean forces north toward the 38th Parallel and the Yalu River boundary with the PEOPLE'S REPUBLIC OF CHINA.

India (Republic of India), until 1947 part of British India, which also dominated many minor, nominally independent states on the subcontinent. After the long struggle for independence led by Mohandas K. GHANDI, Jawaharlal NEHRU, and their associates, British India was split into the new nations

of India and PAKISTAN, in the disastrous PARTITION OF INDIA; the minor states, including Kashmir, were thereafter sources of dispute, sometimes leading to war. Indian independence came on August 15, 1947.

India, Japanese invasion of (March–September 1944), World War II attack across the Chindwin River by Japanese forces in early March, besieging Imphal and Kohima. Kohima was relieved in late April and Imphal in late June, the Japanese then retreating with heavy losses.

India, partition of (August 15, 1947), the division of what had been British-ruled India into the new nations of India and Pakistan, on August 15, 1947. The transfer of power itself occurred without incident, but was accompanied by huge internal migrations and an immense wave of communal rioting and mass murder, as the Hindu-Moslem riots that had been mounting during 1946 and 1947 peaked. Estimates vary widely; in the 6 weeks following the partition, at least 10 million and as many as 18 million people migrated between the two countries. At least 500,000 and probably closer to 1 million died in that period.

Indian National Congress, the formal name of India's CONGRESS PARTY.

India–Pakistan War of 1965 (May–September 1965), conflict in which a successful Pakistani military action in the Rann of Kutch encouraged division-strength Pakistani armored attack across the Kashmir cease-fire line on September 1, 1965; it was accompanied by air strikes on Indian airfields. On September 6, Indian forces attacked in the Punjab, threatening Lahore. The UNITED NATIONS mediated a cease-fire and withdrawal on September 27, and at Tashkent on January 19, 1966, the parties agreed to withdraw and fully end hostilities.

India–Pakistan War of 1971 (December 1971), conflict that began on December 3, with a major, unsuccessful Pakistani air attack on Indian airfields, and only slightly more successful ground attacks in Kashmir. India had received an estimated 6 million refugees from East Pakistan after the beginning of the BANGLADESH WAR OF INDEPENDENCE in March, was supporting Bangladesh insurgent forces, and was prepared for a Pakistani attack. Major Indian forces immediately invaded East Pakistan, and by December 15 they were successfully counterattacking in Kashmir. The Indians took Dacca on December 16 and with it over 90,000 Pakistani prisoners; independent Bangladesh effectively came into being on that day. Fighting ended with the cease-fire of December 17, with peace agreements following in July and August.

Indochina War (1946–54), conflict that began as guerrilla warfare, in December 1946, between France and the Democratic Republic of Vietnam, the French attempting to hold Indochina as part of the French Union and the Vietnamese, led by HO CHI MINH, demanding full independence. In 1949 the French recognized the BAO DAI government of Vietnam, but insurgent forces continued to gain strength, linking up with the PATHET LAO and KHMER ROUGE (Laotian and Cambodian Communist forces) during 1950–51. In May 1954 the French suffered a crushing defeat at DIEN BIEN PHU; in July 1954 at Geneva, a cease-fire agreement provided for withdrawal of French troops from Vietnam and division of the country into North and South Vietnam. The balance of the long VIETNAMESE CIVIL WAR and VIETNAM WAR lay ahead.

Indochina, occupation of (September, 1940), taking and occupation of what was then French Indochina by Japanese troops, starting on September 22, 1940; from Indochina, Japanese forces moved into southern China and prepared for the coming invasion of the rest of southeast Asia.

Indonesia (Republic of Indonesia), until 1949 the Netherlands colony of the Netherlands East Indies. Occupied by Japanese forces during World War II, independence movement leaders set up an independent republic on August 17, 1945, and then fought a 4-year war against the Dutch, which was settled by Dutch withdrawal and recognition of Indonesia in December 1949.

The first president of the new nation was SUKARNO (1949–66), who was succeeded by the more conservative SUHARTO (1966–).

Indonesian political massacres (October 1965–January 1966), the mass murders of an estimated 200,000–300,000 Communists, other dissidents, and bystanders by the Indonesian army and village militia, following an unsuccessful coup attempt by the Communist party of Indonesia. Tens of thousands of others were arrested, many of whom were later executed in prison, and 25,000–30,000 were released in 1979.

Indonesian War of Independence (1945–49), conflict that began in October 1945, as Dutch and British troops occupied Indonesia, ignoring SUKARNO'S declaration of Indonesian independence of August 17, 1945. Surabaya fell in November, although guerrilla fighting continued. In November 1946, the Cheribon Agreement provided for the establishment of the Republic of Indonesia within a larger United States of Indonesia, but with a continuing Dutch presence. Meanwhile, the guerrilla war continued, along with concurrent Islamic insurgency against both the Dutch and the Republic. During 1947 and 1948, Dutch forces consolidated their hold on Indonesia, taking the republican capital of Jogjakarta in December 1948. But UNITED NATIONS intervention, coupled with continuing guerrilla insurgency, ultimately caused the Dutch to withdraw from Indonesia; a cease-fire ended hostilities on May 7, 1949, and the Republic of Indonesia came into being on August 15, 1950.

Industrial Workers of the World (IWW), a U.S. syndicalist labor organization, founded in 1905 by Western Federation of Miners leader William D. HAYWOOD, socialist leader Eugene V. DEBS, and Socialist Labor Party leader Daniel DE LEON as an industrial, rather than an AFL-style craft union. It eschewed political action, instead advocating direct industrial action, and it was violence-prone, which turned away the Western Federation of Miners in 1907, De Leon in 1908, and later Debs as well. Haywood, accused of hiring out the murder of Governor Frank Steunenberg of Idaho, was defended by Clarence DARROW and acquitted in 1907. The most notable victory of the IWW was the LAWRENCE TEXTILE STRIKE of 1912; its most notable defeat, the Passaic textile strike of 1913. But win or lose, the organization never developed staying power, instead attempting to build all of its actions into violent revolutionary confrontations. The organization did build its membership up to an estimated 50,000–100,000 by 1917, but its opposition to World War I led to heavy government attack, coupled with a good deal of illegal violence directed against its members. In November 1917, its entire leadership was arrested; hundreds were ultimately convicted of sedition, including Haywood, who fled to the Soviet Union and died there in 1928. The organization was never again a force on the American scene, though many of its members, such as Elizabeth Gurley FLYNN, went into the COMMUNIST PARTY OF THE UNITED STATES.

influenza pandemic (1918–19), the greatest natural disaster of the 20th century, in which an estimated 25–50 million people died as the result of a largely untreatable pandemic that ultimately affected most of the world's inhabited areas, often spread by and among soldiers and sailors. Probably originating in Asia, the VIRUS was first identified in the United States at Fort Riley, Kansas, but was named "Spanish flu" for its severity in Spain. In some places, such as the United States, people wore surgical masks and many public institutions, shops, and businesses closed down for a time. In the 1957–58 ASIAN FLU pandemic, many more people became ill, but the disease was less lethal, mostly because ANTIBIOTICS had been developed to treat secondary infection.

infrared, type of high-frequency RADIATION beyond the red end of the visible part of the electromagnetic spectrum; the form of most heat produced by the Sun or lamps. Discovered in 1800, infrared radiation was put to wide use only in the 20th century, as in heat-seeking MISSILES, thermal photo-

graphs made in the dark or in fog, infrared analysis of cosmic objects in RADIO ASTRONOMY, and thermal imaging in medicine.

INF Treaty (Intermediate Nuclear Forces Treaty), agreement to destroy all Soviet and American INTERMEDIATE RANGE NUCLEAR MISSILES, signed by U.S. president Ronald REAGAN and U.S.S.R. premier Mikhail GORBACHEV at the WASHINGTON SUMMIT, on December 8, 1987, the first agreement to destroy a whole class of nuclear weapons. The treaty was subsequently ratified by the U.S. Senate and the Supreme Soviet, the formal treaty documents being exchanged by the two leaders at the MOSCOW SUMMIT, on June 1, 1988.

Inkatha movement, South African Zulu organization, led by Chief Gatsha BUTHELEZI, which pursued a declared path of negotiation toward the formation of a multiracial government. During the 1980s, Inkatha activists were often accused of attacks on other South African Black groups, often in pursuit of Zulu tribal goals. In response, Inkatha declared in 1988 that other Blacks might join if they so desired.

Inönü, Ismet (1884–1973), Turkish officer, who saw service in the Balkans in World War I, then joining ATATÜRK (Mustapha Kemal) in the seizure of power and in the GREEK–TURKISH WAR, he became first prime minister of the Turkish republic. He succeeded Atatürk as president (1938–50), moved further and further away from authoritarianism during the postwar period, was prime minister again, 1961–65, of a left-leaning democratic coalition, and after 1965 was out of power.

Inouye, Daniel Ken (1924–   ), U.S. lawyer, Democratic majority leader of the Hawaiian territorial House of Representatives and the Hawaiian territorial Senate; on the winning of Hawaiian statehood in 1959 he became simultaneously the first Hawaiian and the first Japanese-American congressman. A senator from Hawaii from 1962, he served on the Senate WATERGATE committee and was chairman of the Senate IRAN–CONTRA committee.

insider trading scandal, 1980s U.S. stock market scandal involving the illegal use of inside information for profit. Several rather low-level brokerage firm employees were charged in 1986, many of them pleading guilty. The best known of these was Drexel Burnham Lambert employee Dennis Levine. Wealthy stock market figure Ivan BOESKY also was charged, winning some clemency by gathering information for the government on others, although also imprisoned and heavily fined. The set of related cases generated by the scandal continued into the late 1980s, with considerable focus upon Drexel Burnham Lambert and some of its key personnel.

insulin, vital HORMONE excreted by the pancreas, lack of which produces diabetes; first deduced and named in 1909 but finally extracted in 1921 by Canadian physician Frederick Grant BANTING and Charles Best. They first successfully treated a diabetic patient with an insulin injection in 1922. For this discovery, Banting and John J. R. Macleod, in whose laboratory he had worked, won the 1923 Nobel Prize for Physiology or Medicine, though Best was not so honored. In 1955 Frederick Sanger established the structure of insulin, winning the 1958 Nobel Prize for Chemistry. The hormone was finally synthesized in the mid-1960s, and in 1982 the FDA approved the marketing of insulin made by bacteria, the first product of GENETIC ENGINEERING offered commercially.

Insull, Samuel (1860–1938), U.S. midwestern utility magnate of the 1920s, whose companies failed in 1932, with huge losses by small investors. On the verge of indictment, he fled to Europe but was ultimately forced to return to the United States, where he was tried and acquitted, his situation and case providing a focus for those who felt it necessary to regulate utilities and securities much more closely, and subsequently did so.

intelligence quotient (IQ), score on the intelligence test developed in the early 20th century by Alfred BINET and later adapted for American use at Stanford University, as the Stanford-Binet Intelligence Scale test. That and other IQ tests were at first regarded as neutral and applicable to all. Some believers in EUGENICS even regarded the IQ as measuring genetically determined ability, rather than ability determined in any way by cultural exposure; Arthur JENSEN was a modern spokesman for that point of view. But by midcentury many critics were questioning what intelligence tests actually "measured" and whether they favored some groups in society over others. Scores were treated with more caution, and some tests were modified so that measurement of intellectual ability was less affected by cultural background.

Intelsat (**Int**ernational **Tel**ecommunications **Sat**ellite Consortium), worldwide SATELLITE communications system, founded as an 18-nation joint venture in 1964; by the 1980s it had grown to more than 100 countries, the U.S. arm being COMSAT (***Com***munications ***Sat***ellite Corporation). A worldwide satellite communications system was visualized as early as 1945 by A. C. Clark in *Wireless World*, but the first satellite to relay trans-Atlantic signals was *TELSTAR 1*, launched from Cape Canaveral on July 10, 1962. The first Intelsat satellite, *EARLY BIRD* (*Intelsat 1*), was launched in 1965.

intercontinental ballistic missile (ICBM), long-range (over 5,500 km) BALLISTIC MISSILE equipped with one or more nuclear warheads, developed in the United States in 1954, largely by imported German scientists, many of whom had worked on the V-1 AND V-2 BOMBS during World War II. Russian teams, headed by Valentin GLUSHKO, developed an ICBM in 1957. Medium-range versions are called INTERMEDIATE RANGE BALLISTIC MISSILES (IRBMs) or (as in connection with the 1988 INF TREATY) intermediate range nuclear missiles. The two are the major means by which the United States and the Soviet Union are capable of destroying each other and much of humanity. In 1963, during the COLD WAR, the United States set up an extensive "early warning" radar system in Greenland, England, and Alaska for detecting ICBMs.

interferon, protein produced naturally in the body to fight VIRUSES; first discovered in 1957 by Alick Isaacs and Jean Lindemann. Interferon was one of the first substances produced by bacteria altered through GENETIC ENGINEERING in 1980, and has been used to combat conditions such as herpes infections, warts, and tumors.

Intermediate Nuclear Forces Treaty, the full name of the 1987 REAGAN–GORBACHEV INF TREATY, in which the superpowers for the first time agreed to destroy a whole class of nuclear weapons.

intermediate range ballistic missile (IRBM), medium-range version of the INTERCONTINENTAL BALLISTIC MISSILE (ICBM). This kind of MISSILE, which directly threatened Europe, was the main subject of the 1987 INF TREATY, being defined as those with a range of 500–5,000 kilometers, or 300–3400 miles.

International Atomic Energy Agency (IAEA), a multinational independent agency loosely associated with the UNITED NATIONS, established in 1957 to foster the peaceful uses of ATOMIC ENERGY while guarding against the development of atomic warfare capability. The IAEA has developed activity in regard to nuclear safety but has had little or no impact on the development of nuclear weapons and their proliferation.

International Bank for Reconstruction and Development (IBRD), a multinational investment bank established by the BRETTON WOODS CONFERENCE of 1944, that became a UNITED NATIONS agency in 1947. The IBRD makes long-term loans and provides several kinds of specialized technical and other assistance to foster the industrial development of the less developed nations of the world. The IBRD, the INTERNATIONAL DEVELOPMENT ASSOCIATION (IDA), and the INTERNATIONAL FINANCE CORPORATION (IFC) are together often informally called the WORLD BANK.

International Brigades, military units composed of an estimated 40,000 volunteers from 53 countries who fought on the Republican side in the SPANISH CIVIL WAR, suffering an estimated 12,000–15,000 dead and many thousands of other casualties. Organized by the COMINTERN, an estimated 60% of brigade members were Communists and 40% were non-Communists. The first groups arrived in October 1936, and the first brigade units went into battle in early November at the seige of Madrid. During 1937 the number of volunteers entering the brigades abroad dropped sharply, and by the end of the war they were manned largely by Spanish soldiers. The last major action in which foreign brigade members participated was the Battle of the EBRO in 1938, and the foreigners were withdrawn in November 1938. From the beginning of the war, there were other foreigners fighting on the Loyalist side in Spain as well, including some hundreds who fought in the anarchist POUM.

International Court of Justice, the Geneva-based predecessor of the WORLD COURT; it was established as the Permanent Court of International Justice in the COVENANT OF THE LEAGUE OF NATIONS in 1919.

International Criminal Police Organization (INTERPOL), a worldwide international crime information center organized in 1923; most of the nations of the world are members, including the nations of the Communist world, which began to join in the late 1980s.

International Development Association (IDA), a UNITED NATIONS agency established in 1960 that extends long-term credits to the world's poorer countries, mainly for such infrastructural developments as schools, roads, dams, power facilities, and industrial plants, and also for the development of rural productivity. The IDA, the INTERNATIONAL BANK FOR RECONSTRUCTION AND DEVELOPMENT (IBRD), and the INTERNATIONAL FINANCE CORPORATION (IFC), are together often informally called the WORLD BANK.

International Fellowship of Reconciliation (IFOR), an international peace-fostering, nonviolent religious organization, founded in 1919, that works, with other peace groups, to promote further education on peace-connected issues throughout the world; members have included Martin Luther KING JR., and Mohandas GANDHI.

International Finance Corporation (IFC), a multinational investment bank established in 1956 that became a UNITED NATIONS agency in 1957; it makes loans, invests in, and provides technical and other forms of assistance to private and mixed private-public business organizations in developing nations. The IFC, the INTERNATIONAL BANK FOR RECONSTRUCTION AND DEVELOPMENT (IBRD), and the INTERNATIONAL DEVELOPMENT ASSOCIATION (IDA) are together often informally called the WORLD BANK.

International Geophysical Year (IGY), 18-month period from July 1957 to December 1958, during which more than 70 nations and some 30,000 scientists cooperated in research on the Earth and the universe. New information about the Earth's crust, especially under the oceans, gave support to the theory of PLATE TECTONICS. SATELLITES launched during the IGY discovered the VAN ALLEN BELTS and the charged particles that cause auroras. Work at ANTARCTICA proved so fruitful that agreement was later reached to set aside the continent as an unmilitarized area for scientific research. Among the other areas that benefited from the IGY cooperation were climatology, COSMIC RAYS, and the nature of the Earth's magnetic field.

International Labor Organization (ILO), a body established as part of the COVENANT OF THE LEAGUE OF NATIONS in 1919; in 1946 it became a UN agency. From its headquarters in Geneva it has since its establishment organized conferences, attempted to set recommended international work standards, run a publication program, and engaged in a variety of other research and educational activities.

International Monetary Fund (IMF), a multinational banking fund established by the BRETTON WOODS CONFERENCE of 1944; it became a UNITED NATIONS agency in 1947. The IMF attempts to maintain international exchange stability and to help members correct international balance of payment problems by extending credit, often demanding that creditor nations adopt difficult internal austerity programs as a credit condition. During the 1970s and 1980s, as world economic imbalances mounted, and huge THIRD WORLD debts became a worldwide debt crisis, the IMF reorganized itself and raised its capital limits again and again, with only marginally effective results and with increasing pressure from lenders to stiffen loan requirements and from borrowers to loosen them.

International Overseas Services (IOS) scandal, the 1970–72 failure of Bernard Cornfeld's large Swiss-based group of mutual funds, which had for over a decade guaranteed unrealistically high rates of return to gullible small investors while funding the expensive life-style of Cornfeld and many of his associates. Finally alerted to the highly questionable financial practices of IOS, many investors cashed in what was left of their investments in 1970, precipitating a crisis. Financier Robert Vesco then bought control of IOS from Cornfeld, looted over $224 million of the remaining assets, and ultimately avoided extradition on fraud and bribery charges, buying refuge in Costa Rica, and in the 1980s finding refuge in Cuba, in return for unspecified services to the Cuban government.

International Telecommunications Satellite Organization, full formal name of the worldwide SATELLITE communications system, INTELSAT, founded in 1964.

INTERPOL, an acronym for the INTERNATIONAL CRIMINAL POLICE ORGANIZATION.

Intifada (Uprising), the Palestinian uprising on the WEST BANK of the Jordan river and the GAZA STRIP, beginning in 1988, that focused world attention on the two-decades-long Israeli occupation of and the national aspirations of the Palestinian populations of both areas. In the course of the Intifada, hundreds of Palestinians were killed and thousands injured, most of them teenagers. Jordan withdrew from the West Bank, a Palestinian state was proclaimed, and the PALESTINE LIBERATION ORGANIZATION (PLO) sought a more moderate identity, as its leaders attempted to pursue negotiations with Israel toward the establishment of a Palestinian state.

intrauterine device (IUD), full name of the common contraceptive implant, such as the DALKON SHIELD.

Intrepid, the World War II code name of British intelligence organizer William STEPHENSON.

Inukai Tsuyohi (1855–1932), Japanese political leader who became prime minister in 1931 and who resisted the developing military control of Japan and the occupation of Manchuria. He was assassinated by a group of naval officers in 1932, his assassination essentially ending Japanese democracy in that period and ushering in the period of military control that took Japan into the war with China and World War II, ending with Japan's defeat in 1945.

in vitro fertilization, joining of a human egg and sperm in an artificial setting outside of the body, the fertilized egg later being implanted into the womb for normal childbirth; in vitro (New Latin for "in glass") refers to the test-tube setting for the fertilization. The technique, developed by British gynecologist-obstetrician Patrick STEPTOE, was first used successfully in late 1977, with the resulting fully normal TEST-TUBE BABY, Louise BROWN, being delivered by cesarean section on July 25, 1978. In vitro fertilization has since been widely used by infertile couples, despite some controversy about the proper limits of human intervention in life processes; the first U.S. clinic opened in 1980.

ionosphere, electrically charged layer of air in the upper atmosphere, from about 30–400 miles up, that reflects RADIO waves, aiding long-distance transmission. In 1902 British mathematician Oliver Heaviside and American electrical engineer Arthur E. Kennelly independently predicted the existence of such a layer, then called the HEAVISIDE or KENNELLY-HEAVISIDE LAYER; it was confirmed in 1924 by Edward Appleton and M. F. Barett. Daily and seasonal variations in the degree of ionization affect the quality of radio transmission; transmission at night is more powerful, because the ionosphere is ionized—that is, electrically charged—by sunlight.

Iowa gun turret explosion (April 19, 1989), an explosion within a 16-inch armored gun turret of the battleship *U.S.S. Iowa* that left 47 sailors dead, all of them in the five top levels of the turret; only those on the sealed sixth level of the turret survived.

I pledge you, I pledge myself, a new deal for the American people, comment by Franklin Delano ROOSEVELT, in his acceptance speech to the Democratic nominating convention of 1932.

IQ, popular shorthand for INTELLIGENCE QUOTIENT score and intelligence test developed in the early 20th century by Alfred BINET.

Iran, an independent state at the beginning of the 20th century, but one that had long experienced Russian and British imperial penetration, losing substantial portions of its territory to Russia in the 19th century, and granting major economic concessions to British interests. Iranian nationalists forced a constitution on the Russian-supported shah in 1906, precipitating a series of coups and countercoups that resulted in Russian occupation of much of northern Iran by 1914. During World War I, Iran was neutral but still a battleground for Turkish and Allied forces. After the war, Iran was an independent state, from 1921 led by Reza Khan PAHLEVI, who became the first Pahlevi shah (1926–41). At the same time, it was heavily penetrated by British oil interests. Early in World War II the shah resisted Allied use of Iran and was forced to resign in favor of his young son, Muhammed Reza PAHLEVI. During the early 1950s, the crisis precipitated by the nationalization of Iran's oil industry was ultimately resolved by the American-supported army coup that toppled the MOSSADEGH government and returned the shah to power. In 1979, the shah was deposed in the IRANIAN REVOLUTION, which brought the Islamic Republic of Ayatollah Ruhollah KHOMEINI to power and with it the triumph of Islamic fundamentalism, the IRAN HOSTAGE CRISIS, the IRAN–IRAQ WAR, the IRAN–CONTRA AFFAIR, the *SATANIC VERSES* murder incitements, and a major increase in hostage-taking and international terrorism. With the death of Khomeini, on June 3, 1989, a new chapter in Iranian history began.

Iran–Contra Affair (1985–   ), a REAGAN administration attempt to trade the sale of arms to Iran for American hostages held in Lebanon, coupled with a plan to use the profits derived from such arms sales to buy and send arms to the Nicaraguan CONTRAS. The exposure of both plans created a massive U.S. political scandal, as the first was entirely opposite to the stated no-negotiation-with-terrorists policy of the United States, and the second was widely perceived to contravene the spirit and probably the letter of Congressional restrictions on military aid to the Contras. With Israeli involvement, and the participation of White House staff members Oliver NORTH, Robert MCFARLANE, John POINDEXTER, CIA chief William CASEY, and others inside and outside the White House, at least 2,000 TOW missiles were shipped to Iran during 1985 and 1986 while covert Contra supply operations continued. Some newspaper stories hinted at the arms-for-hostages scandal during 1986. The covert Contra supply operation was exposed after the confession of pilot Eugene Hasenfus, shot down on a covert mission over Nicaragua on October 5, 1986. The arms-for-hostages story was broken by the Beirut newspaper *Al Shiraa* on November 3, 1986. The complex set of scandals then unfolded, amid a series of conflicting statements from President Reagan and other administration officials, much of it during 41 days of televised Congressional committee hearings. Both operations were discontinued, the Reagan administration was greatly discredited, the

Contra aid cause was destroyed, and the release of one hostage may have been assisted, although other hostages were taken during the period. On November 25, 1986, Lieutenant Colonel North was dismissed from his White House National Security Council post, and Admiral Poindexter resigned as national security advisor. CIA director Casey died before giving testimony in the case. In March 1988, North, Poindexter, businessman Albert HAKIM, and retired general Richard V. SECORD were indicted in connection with the scandal. After a long jury trial, North was convicted on three felony counts in May 1989; he planned to appeal the conviction. Other Iran–Contra trials were still in process.

Iran hostage crisis, international crisis that began with the Iranian seizure of 66 American hostages at the U.S. embassy in Tehran on November 4, 1979. Although 14 were subsequently released, 52 hostages were held for 444 days while the Iranian government attempted to force concessions of several kinds from the United States. Although Iran did not succeed in forcing return of the former shah, Mohammed Reza PAHLEVI, the ultimate settlement included the release of frozen Iranian assets, with direct payment of almost $3 billion, and the establishment of an international court to hear Iranian and United States claims. UNITED NATIONS and WORLD COURT condemnations of the Iranian action were fruitless, as was an aborted American armed forces hostage rescue operation mounted on April 24, 1980. The hostage crisis was a major factor in the defeat of Jimmy CARTER in the 1980 presidential elections, the hostages being released on the day he was succeeded in office by Ronald REAGAN, January 20, 1981.

Iranian Revolution, the overthrow of the government of Shah Mohammed Reza PAHLEVI of Iran, who fled his country on January 16, 1979, after a mounting series of strikes and demonstrations during 1978, coupled with loss of army support, had made it impossible to continue to rule. Before leaving he appointed National Front leader Shahpur Bakhtiar premier of Iran, but Bakhtiar's government was not viable. Ayatollah Ruhollah KHOMEINI returned from exile in France on February 1; his fundamentalist forces and their allies seized power on February 11, Bakhtiar then resigning and Khomeini taking over effective control of the country. Later that year (December 2–3) Khomeini was formally named religious and de facto secular leader of the Shiite Islamic state. In June 1981, he removed the secular and somewhat more moderate Iranian president, Abol Hasan Bani-Sadr, who subsequently became leader of an exile organization, and Iran became in practice an entirely Islamic fundamentalist state.

Iran–Iraq War (Persian Gulf War; 1980–88), an immensely costly, inconclusive World War I–style war of attrition that cost more than 1 million lives. The war began in September 1980, with Iraq abrogating a 1975 treaty and claiming the whole Shatt al-Arab waterway between Iraq and Iran. Iraqi forces took some Iranian territory in late 1980, capturing Khorramshahr; Iranian forces gained supremacy in 1981 and 1982. Iraq sought peace in June 1982, but Iran forced continuation of the war and invaded Iraq. After mid-1982 the war was essentially a stalemate; the "human wave" infantry attacks of the Iranian army, often using untrained volunteers and levies, achieved some very limited successes while causing enormous losses, but they failed to substantially breach the Iraqi defense lines. Throughout the war there was also a second front, as the long Kurdish insurgency in northern Iraq continued, now supported by Iran. By 1984 Iraq was using chemical weapons and continued to do so; in 1985 both sides began missile attacks on enemy cities. In an attempt to free the American hostages in Lebanon, the United States became deeply involved in supplying arms to Iran, beginning in 1985, a set of actions resulting in the IRAN–CONTRA AFFAIR. Both Iraq and Iran mined and attacked neutral tankers in the Persian Gulf; in 1987 an Iraqi attack on the *U.S.S. STARK* triggered major

U.S. naval involvement against Iran, with American ships escorting tankers, and several engagements between Iranian and American forces in the Gulf. In July 1988 the *U.S.S. VINCENNES* mistakenly attacked an Iranian passenger plane over the Gulf, killing 290 people. On August 20, 1988, after peace efforts mediated by UNITED NATIONS secretary general Javier PEREZ DE CUELLAR, a cease-fire began, followed by peace negotiations in Geneva. The Iraqi army then moved strong forces against the Kurdish insurgents and civilian population, using both conventional and CHEMICAL WARFARE to kill tens of thousands, most of them civilians, and driving hundreds of thousands of Kurds across the Turkish and Iranian borders as refugees.

Iraq (Republic of Iraq), until 1918 part of the Ottoman Empire. It became a LEAGUE OF NATIONS British-administered mandate territory after World War I, formally becoming an independent state in 1932. However, Iraq was in reality a British protectorate until after World War II, and heavily British-influenced until the 1958 nationalist coup led by Abdul Karim KASSEM, which declared Iraq a republic. After the 1968 military coup, Iraq became an Arab Islamic Socialist state led by the BA'ATH PARTY.

Ireland (Republic of Ireland), until 1921 part of the United Kingdom, winning its freedom in December 1921, after the EASTER RISING of 1916 and the IRISH CIVIL WAR of 1919–21, ending with the north-south partition of Ireland. The country was the Irish Free State, 1922–37, then became a republic.

Irgun Zvai Leumi (National Military Organization), a militant underground Jewish fighting force of the mid-20th century, engaged in armed action against the British occupiers of Palestine and against Palestinian Arabs, with the aim of creating a Jewish state throughout the areas that are now Israel, the WEST BANK, and Jordan. The Irgun was formed in Jerusalem in 1931, and was originally led by ex-HAGANAH army commander Avraham Tehomi. In

1936 it became part of the Revisionist movement, led by Vladimir JABOTINSKY. After 1943 it was led by Menachim BEGIN, later to become the premier of Israel (1977–83). During the 1930s and early 1940s the Irgun freely used assassination and other acts of terrorism as weapons of war, and was condemned for doing so by the leaders of the Haganah and the World Zionist Organization. It also worked to bring Jews illegally into Palestine after immigration was limited in 1939, thereby helping to save some European Jews from the JEWISH HOLOCAUST. After the end of World War II, the open battle for the creation of the state of Israel allied the Irgun Zvai Leumi with the Haganah, which was the main Jewish army, and with the STERN GANG, a small, even more terrrorist-oriented group than the Irgun. But the terrorist tactics of the Irgun and the Stern Gang greatly embarrassed the main Jewish leadership. On July 22, 1946, under the direct supervision of Menachim Begin and against strong Haganah protest, the Irgun blew up British administrative offices in a wing of the KING DAVID HOTEL in Jerusalem, killing 91 people, 17 of them Jews. On October 31, 1946, the Irgun blew up the British Embassy in Rome. The Irgun also took British hostages, in one instance hanging two British army sergeants in reprisal for the execution of Irgun activists. And on April 9, 1948, during the ISRAELI WAR OF INDEPENDENCE (FIRST ARAB–ISRAELI WAR), which established Israel, Irgun units attacked the small Arab village of DEIR YASIN, outside Jerusalem, killing all 254 of its inhabitants, most of them noncombatants. The Irgun was disbanded on September 21, 1948, most of its members then joining the Israeli army. Menachim Begin and his followers went on into Israeli political life, first in the Herut party and later in the Likud (Unity) party, which brought Begin to power in 1977.

Irish Citizen Army, a small Irish Republican military group, numbering a few hundred men, organized by socialists James CONNOLLY and James Larkin after the Dublin General Strike of 1913. It participated in the EASTER RISING of 1916.

Irish Civil War (1921–22), a brief civil war between the provisional government of the new Irish Free State and IRISH REPUBLICAN ARMY elements that refused to accept the peace settlement following the IRISH WAR OF INDEPENDENCE. Although the Irish government won the war, IRISH REPUBLICAN ARMY (IRA) elements continue their decades-old guerrilla war against the existence of Northern Ireland or any British presence in Ireland.

Irish Republican Army (IRA), the military arm of the Irish Republic during the IRISH WAR OF INDEPENDENCE (1919–21), growing from the IRISH VOLUNTEERS, the main Irish force during the EASTER RISING. Large elements of the IRA refused to accept the treaty ending the war of independence and partitioning Ireland into the Irish Free State and Northern Ireland, but they lost the ensuing IRISH CIVIL WAR. However, some elements of the IRA to this day continue a policy of armed opposition to the existence of Northern Ireland and to any British presence in Ireland, conducting a now decades-long guerrilla war that has extended to other parts of Great Britain, and to British installations in many parts of the world.

Irish Volunteers, an Irish republican military organization founded in 1913 under the leadership of Patrick PEARSE. It was the main force in the EASTER RISING of 1916, and from it grew the IRISH REPUBLICAN ARMY.

Irish War of Independence (1919–21), war that resulted after the executions of the leaders of the EASTER RISING (Dublin, 1916) had made them martyrs. The Irish Republican political arm, SINN FEIN, won the elections of 1918, declaring the independence of the Irish Republic on January 21, 1919, with Eamon DE VALERA its first president. The British did not accept Irish independence, nor did the large Protestant population of Northern Ireland and the Protestant military organization, the

ULSTER VOLUNTEERS. The IRISH REPUBLI-
CAN ARMY then conducted a 3-year guerrilla war for independence, which ended with
the truce of July 11, 1921, and the subsequent agreement to a partition of Ireland,
between the 26 counties of the Irish Free
State (which in 1937 became the Republic of
Ireland) and the six counties of Northern
Ireland. De Valera, who had spent the war
abroad, raising money and support for the
revolution, did not accept partition; he and
his supporters then unsuccessfully engaged
the new Irish provisional government, led
by Michael COLLINS, in the brief IRISH CIV-
IL WAR.

iron curtain, phrase coined by Winston
CHURCHILL to describe the Soviet–Western
schism then growing into the COLD WAR,
during a March 5, 1946, speech at Westminster College, Fulton, Missouri.

Iron Triangle, a Viet Cong guerrilla base
area on the northern approaches to Saigon,
the scene of many unsuccessful U.S.–South
Vietnamese anti-guerrilla raids and campaigns during the VIETNAM WAR.

Iroquois Theater fire (December 30, 1903),
a backstage fire during a crowded matinee
at Chicago's Iroquois Theater, then featuring comedian Eddie Foy in *Mr. Bluebeard*,
that caused heavy smoke and then panic.
Within 15 minutes, 602 had died, in spite of
Foy's valiant attempt to quiet the crowd and
organize an orderly evacuation of the building.

Irving, Clifford, U.S. novelist who created a
false autobiography of wealthy recluse
Howard Hughes, after having very easily
convinced his McGraw-Hill editors that his
entirely imaginary relationship with Hughes
was real. Late in 1971 the fraud was discovered, drawing a great deal of media attention. Irving, his wife Edith, and co-author
Richard Suskind all pleaded guilty and received light sentences.

Ishizaka, Taizo (1886–1975), Japanese
business leader, chairman of the Federation
of Economic Organizations 1956–68, and
chairman of Toshiba Electric Company.

Islamic Holy War (Islamic Jihad), Shiite
Moslem Lebanese militia, that during the
LEBANESE WARS claimed responsibility for
many acts of terrorism, including the 1985
ATHENS-BEIRUT AIRPORT HIJACKING.

isolationism, the belief that U.S. interests
would best be served by an insular approach
to world affairs, fed by geographic position
and an often strong strain of antiforeign bias in the United States. In the 20th century,
isolationism was particularly strong during
the interwar period, first directly after
World War I, when the LEAGUE OF NA-
TIONS was rejected and xenophobic immigration restriction adopted, and then
during the 1930s, when "isolationism" became a movement that opposed U.S. support for the European democracies in the
run-up to World War II, and until PEARL
HARBOR opposed U.S. entry into the war.

Isonzo, Battles of (June, 1915–September,
1917), a series of World War I Italian attacks on Austrian border fortifications in
mountainous terrain along the Isonzo River, the equivalent of the Western Front's
TRENCH WARFARE. All of the attacks failed,
with hundreds of thousands of casualties on
both sides.

isotopes, variant forms of an element whose
atoms have the same number of PROTONS
and ELECTRONS but a different number of
NEUTRONS, so that they occupy the same
place on chemistry's period table but behave
somewhat differently because of the different mass in their NUCLEUS. Frederick SOD-
DY recognized such variant forms in 1913,
calling them isotopes (Greek for "same
place"); his theory of isotopes was confirmed in 1919 by British chemist Francis
William Aston, who was able to measure the
proportion of different isotopes in an element. RADIOACTIVE isotopes, or radioisotopes, are widely used in medicine, as in the
treatment of CANCER or as tracers in the
body as an aid to diagnosis.

Israel (State of Israel), until 1918 part of the
Ottoman Empire. After World War I the
area that later became Israel then became
part of the British-administered LEAGUE OF

NATIONS Palestine mandate territory, and from the early 1920s it was beset by increasingly serious Arab-Jewish conflicts. The British withdrew on May 14, 1948; on that day Israeli independence was declared, and then established during the subsequent ISRAELI WAR OF INDEPENDENCE (FIRST ARAB-ISRAELI WAR) and the partition of Palestine, which was followed by over four decades of Arab-Israeli conflict.

Israeli War of Independence (First Arab-Israeli War; May 1948-January 1949), conflict starting in January 1948 as the British army prepared to leave Palestine, pursuant to the UNITED NATIONS Palestine partition decision of 1947, with civil war breaking out in Palestine. After hard fighting, by early May massive Palestinian Arab evacuations of Haifa, Jaffa, and other cities were well under way, as well as evacuations of rural populations throughout the country, spurred partly by fears raised after the April 9 massacre at DEIR YASIN by the IRGUN ZVAI LEUMI and STERN GANG. On May 14, the British left Palestine, and the Israeli state was proclaimed; on that day and the next, Syrian, Lebanese, Iraqi, Jordanian, and Egyptian forces invaded Israel, joining Palestinian Arab forces already at war. A chaotic war on several fronts followed, punctuated by two truces, June 11-July 9 and July 18-October 15. The Israeli forces steadily grew in strength as the war progressed, ultimately heavily outnumbering the combined Arab expeditionary forces and being far better led throughout the war. The sole exception was that of the Transjordanian ARAB LEGION, which effectively fought the Israelis in and around Jerusalem, taking and holding much of the city. UN mediation efforts effectively ended with the Stern Gang assassination of UN mediator Folke BERNADOTTE on September 17. The war ended on January 7, 1949, with an Israeli-Egyptian ceasefire agreement. No peace treaties resulted, 500,000-1,000,000 Palestinian Arab refugees had fled, and guerrilla warfare continued while terrorism grew. The stage had been set for at least four more decades of Arab-Israeli conflicts, which were to include three more wars, interventions, armed strikes and counterstrikes, and continuing insurgencies.

Italian Somaliland, the name of a former Italian African colony that became part of independent SOMALIA in 1960.

Italo-Turkish War (1911-12), conflict that began with the Italian declaration of war, on September 29, 1911. Italian forces then invaded and occupied Libya, Rhodes, and the Dodecanese Islands, all against weak Turkish resistance; Italy was ceded these territories by the Treaty of Ouchy, on October 15, 1912.

Italy, invasion of (September-October 1943), World War II attack on Italy, after the fall of Sicily to the Allies, in August 1943. The invasion of Italy began on September 3, as British troops crossed from Sicily to Calabria against light opposition and began to move north. On September 9, British troops also landed at Taranto, and major American and British landings were made at Salerno. The Salerno landings were strongly resisted, and for a time it seemed that the Allied troops would be pushed off their small beachheads. The beachheads were reinforced and held until relieved by British troops moving up from the south. The combined Allied forces then moved north; by mid-November they had taken all of southern Italy, and faced German GUSTAV LINE defences running across the country from sea to sea.

IUD (intrauterine device), coil or loop, often of metal or plastic, implanted in a woman's uterus; an old form of contraceptive device, always with some attendant hazards, especially disastrous with the DALKON SHIELD.

Ivan the Terrible, JOHN DEMJANJUK, TREBLINKA DEATH CAMP guard, sentenced to death in Israel on April 25, 1988.

Ivory Coast, English version of the name for COTE D'IVORE, a former French colony independent from 1960.

Iwasaki, Koyota (1879-1945), Japanese Mitsubishi family business leader who led the Mitsubishi Company from 1916 to 1945, and was a leading armaments maker through the end of World War II, then being forced to formally leave the business world by the Occupation authorities.

Iwo Jima, Battle of (February 19–March 16, 1945), an extremely costly engagement on the small Pacific island late in World War II. The U.S. Marine assault on heavily fortified Japanese positions, most of them underground, began with amphibious landings under heavy fire on February 19. Mount Suribachi was taken 5 days later, and Iwo Jima was secured in mid-March. Almost all of the estimated 22,000–25,000 Japanese defenders fought to the death; there were almost 25,000 American casualties, and almost 7,000 of those died.

IWW, the initials of the INDUSTRIAL WORKERS OF THE WORLD, by which this U.S. syndicalist labor organization was best known.

J

Jabotinsky, Vladimir (1880–1940), Russian-Jewish journalist who became an active Zionist after the KISHINEV POGROMS of 1903, and fought in the Jewish Legion on the side of the British in Palestine during World War I. In 1925 Jabotinsky founded the Zionist Revisionist movement, which called for armed struggle, and the development of a terrorist campaign against the British occupiers of Palestine, in opposition to the main strategy of the world Zionist movement, which urged restraint. His views were adopted by the terrorist IRGUN ZVAI LEUMI and by its militant leaders, including Menachim BEGIN, who led the organization from 1943 and was later premier of Israel 1977–83.

Jackson, Jesse Louis (1941–   ), U.S. Black leader, active in the CIVIL RIGHTS MOVEMENT of the 1960s, in the CONGRESS OF RACIAL EQUALITY (CORE), and as an associate of Martin Luther KING, JR., in the SOUTHERN CHRISTIAN LEADERSHIP CONFERENCE. In 1967 he was a founder of Operation Breadbasket, and in 1971 he founded PUSH (People United to Save Humanity). In 1983–84 he sought the Democratic presidential nomination, mounted a substantial registration campaign, and emerged as the first major Black contender for the presidency, although failing to move far beyond a Black constituency. In 1987–88 he ran again, this time building a substantial Democratic liberal coalition around his candidacy while mounting another strong registration drive; he ran second to Michael DUKAKIS in the Democratic primaries. He then emerged as one of the most important Black leaders since Martin Lu-

ther King, Jr., and simultaneously as a major liberal Democratic party leader, whose address to his party's convention was by far the most notable speech at that convention.

Jackson, Robert Houghwout (1892–1954), U.S. lawyer, who served in a succession of federal government legal positions, beginning in 1934, and was U.S. attorney-general 1940–41. In 1941 he was appointed to the Supreme Court by Franklin D. ROOSEVELT and was a moderate on the Court. He was chief U.S. prosecutor at the NUREMBERG TRIALS 1945–46.

Jacobsen, David one of the American LEBANON HOSTAGES, a director of the American University, who was kidnapped on May 28, 1985, and released on November 2, 1986.

Jadar, Battle of (August 12–21, 1914), World War I battle in which invading Austrian forces 200,000 strong retreated back across the Drina River after defeat in this first major Austro-Serbian battle of World War I.

Jallianwallah Bagh, site of the April 13, 1919, AMRITSAR MASSACRE of unarmed Indian demonstrators by the British.

Jamaica, until 1962, a British colony, becoming an independent state and COMMONWEALTH member on August 6, 1962; its first prime minister was Alexander BUSTAMENTE.

James, William (1842–1910), U.S. physician, psychologist, and philosopher, elder brother of novelist Henry James. Much of his teaching at Harvard, and his classic 12-volume *Principles of Psychology*, in which he introduced the "stream of consciousness," belong to the 19th century, but two key works marked the early 20th century. *The Varieties of Religious Experience* (1902) took the novel approach of treating people's religious feelings as real, as shown by their effect on the individual's behavior. His *Pragmatism* (1907) inveighed against absolutes, arguing that truth and goodness are to be found not in theory, but in results that seem good, and not harmful.

Jansky, Karl Guthe (1905–50), U.S. radio engineer at Bell Labs who, while searching for ways to decrease static on transoceanic telephone calls in 1931, discovered RADIO waves produced by objects outside the solar system, laying the basis for modern RADIO ASTRONOMY.

Japan, until its loss of World War II in 1945, an imperial power, ruled by a line of divine, though in practice not absolute, monarchs, the last of them being HIROHITO. After Japan's unconditional surrender the country lost its imperial gains and was occupied, 1945–52, during that period becoming a constitutional monarchy and experiencing major structural changes, then emerging as a major economic power.

Japanese-American World War II internment, World War II removal of 110,000 U.S. Pacific coast Japanese-Americans from their homes to ten CONCENTRATION CAMPS, established by President Franklin D. ROOSEVELT'S Executive Order 9066 of February 19, 1942. Many were forced to sell their farms, businesses, homes, and personal possessions at ruinous distress prices. In 1976 President Gerald FORD publicly apologized on behalf of the United States to those so held. In 1988 those internees still alive were voted tax-free payments of $20,000 each, with a further apology from President Ronald REAGAN.

Japanese–Soviet Border War (May–September 1939), an undeclared war over disputed territory on the Manchuria–Outer Mongolia border, involving division-strength Japanese and Soviet forces. Soviet forces ultimately occupied the disputed territory.

Jaruzelski, Wojciech (1923–   ), Polish soldier, who fought beside Soviet forces on the Eastern Front during World War II; he became an officer during the postwar period, army chief of staff 1965–68, and defense minister 1968–83. In 1981, during the crisis generated by the government's confrontation with SOLIDARITY, he took power with Soviet sponsorship, in October 1981 becoming first secretary of the Polish Communist Party. In December 1981 he declared martial law and arrested many dissident leaders, including Lech WALESA. He formally became prime minister in 1983, resigning in 1985 to become chairman of the Council of State, retaining his Communist party and real state leadership throughout the period. In late 1987, with the loosening of Soviet control that came in the Gorbachev era, Jaruzelski began a broad liberalization program, including the initiation of the talks that ultimately resulted in the 1989 legalization of SOLIDARITY.

Jaspers, Karl (1883–1969), German clinical psychiatrist and philosopher, whose views on individual freedom much influenced the development of 20th-century EXISTENTIALISM. Jaspers rejected schools of thought and abstract theory, preferring to focus on the individual's attempt to understand concrete reality. An anti-Nazi, after the war Jaspers focused on wide moral questions, including the collective guilt of the German people for World War II and the need for the country's de-Nazification and regeneration.

Jaurès, Jean (1859–1914), French socialist leader who was also a leader of the SECOND INTERNATIONAL and who opposed socialist participation in the coming European war, pressing for French-German reconciliation in the period before World War I. He was assassinated by a French nationalist on July 31, 1914. Some have thought that he might have been able to prevent French socialist support of the French government during World War I, encouraging opposition to the war by other socialist parties.

Java Sea, Battle of the (February 27, 1942), World War II engagement in which Japanese air and naval forces sank most of a small combined Dutch-American battle fleet; two Allied cruisers and five destroyers survived. The Japanese invasion and conquest of the East Indies then moved ahead uncontested.

Jeans, James Hopwood (1877–1946), British mathematician and astronomer, who first put forward the STEADY STATE THEORY of the universe in 1928.

Jenco, Reverend Martin one of the American LEBANON HOSTAGES, head of Catholic Relief Services in Lebanon, who was kidnapped on January 8, 1985, and released on July 26, 1985.

Jensen, Arthur R. (1923–   ), U.S. educational psychologist, who aroused great controversy when—in 1969, in the midst of a CIVIL RIGHTS MOVEMENT—he claimed that Blacks achieve lower INTELLIGENCE QUOTIENT scores than Whites because they are genetically inferior, an extreme form of the old argument that heredity, rather than environment, is the key to human differences.

Jericho, ancient city in modern Jordan, excavated 1952–58 by Kathleen KENYON and found to be perhaps 9,000 or more years old.

jet, AIRPLANE driven by JET PROPULSION, forward motion from rearward discharge of fluids and gases produced by burning fuels, using air from the atmosphere. British engineer Frank Whittle obtained the first patent for a turbojet engine in 1930, but it was not tested until 1937, and the first British flight was not until 1941. Working independently from a 1935 design, German engineers had the first turbojet-powered flight in 1939, the craft being a Heinkel HE 178. In World War II a German MESSERSCHMIDT jet first saw action in 1944; the British Glostor Meteor was first used in 1945. An American jet, the Bell X-1, piloted by Charles YEAGER, broke the SOUND BARRIER in 1947. Jets were put into commercial service in 1952, starting with a BOAC De Havilland DH 106 Comet. The Boeing 707 was introduced in 1954, making nonstop trans-Atlantic flights by 1958; this workhorse passenger jet was in use for decades, alongside smaller jets, which, from the 1960s, were widely used for short hauls. Larger craft, like the "jumbo"

747, operated from the late 1960s and faster jets, notably SUPERSONIC TRANSPORT, operated from 1976.

jet propulsion, forward motion in response to rearward discharge of fluid or gases, especially from burning fuels, the main kind of propulsion used in ROCKETS, MISSILES, and JETS, first envisioned in 1909 by French engineer René Lorin.

jet stream, strong air currents 7 to 8 miles above the Earth, first discovered by high-flying bomber pilots during World War II; an aid or a drag to modern JETS, depending on their direction.

Jewish Holocaust the murder of an estimated 6 million Jews during the years 1933–45, and especially after 1940, by a German Nazi government bent on committing GENOCIDE. Some of the mass murders occurred in and after battle, as in the Battle of the WARSAW GHETTO, and in the executions by the Germans of captured Jewish partisans and frontline fighters on the Polish and Russian fronts during World War II. The great majority of the mass murders, however, occurred in CONCENTRATION CAMPS, such as those set up by the Germans at BELSEN, BUCHENWALD, and DACHAU in Germany and at AUSCHWITZ, MAIDENEK, and TREBLINKA in Poland. Estimates vary greatly as to how many people of all nationalities were murdered, but it is clear that at least 6 million Jews were among the 10 million—according to some estimates, as many as 26 million people—who died in these camps, many millions of them in crematoria run by the Germans. The camps were set up and run by the German government, by order of Adolf HITLER, and under the direct supervision of the head of the SS (Schutzstaffel), Heinrich HIMMLER.

Jiang Qing (Chiang Ch'ing; Luan Shumeng; on stage, Lan P'ing; 1914–   ), Chinese actress who became the third wife of MAO ZEDONG during the YENAN period of 1930s. She became an increasingly powerful figure in Chinese cultural affairs before and during the CULTURAL REVOLUTION, but after Mao's death she lost much of her power and was ultimately convicted in 1981 of being the leader of the GANG OF FOUR.

jihad, an Islamic holy war; such holy wars have been declared very often in the late 20th century, on many occasions by very small splinter groups with little or no ability to move masses of Moslems to concerted military action.

Jinnah, Mohammad Ali (1876–1948), Indian Moslem lawyer, who became the founder of Pakistan. Early in his career he espoused Moslem–Hindu and MOSLEM LEAGUE–CONGRESS PARTY cooperation in the Indian independence movement, but he began to move away from the Congress Party in the 1920s, as it became a mass movement, leaving political life in the early 1930s. In the mid-1930s he began to successfully organize the MOSLEM LEAGUE into a mass movement, in 1940 he called for a separate Islamic state of Pakistan, and after World War II, with bitter Moslem-Hindu communal violence growing, he won agreement from reluctant Congress party leaders for a two-country solution. He was the first governor-general of Pakistan.

Jodl, Alfred (1890–1946), German officer who saw service in World War I and during World War II was a key military planner. He signed the German surrender at Reims on May 7, 1945, was convicted of war crimes at the NUREMBERG TRIALS, and was executed in 1946.

Joffre, Joseph (1852–1931), French World War I general who commanded the French armies during the first Battle of the MARNE, and who was French commander-in-chief from December 1915 through December 1916.

Johanson, Donald Carl (1943–   ), U.S. physical anthropologist working in eastern Africa, who discovered an almost complete primitive skeleton, which he made famous in his book *Lucy: The Beginnings of Human Kind* (1982). His interpretations of his finds, such as those of the apparent family of skeletons he believed represented a new human-like species, often brought him into disagreement and controversy with Richard LEAKEY.

John XXIII, Pope (Angelo Giuseppe Roncali; 1881–1963), Italian priest, ordained in1904, and pope 1958–63. In the 54 years before becoming Pope he performed a wide variety of functions, including those of World War I chaplain, Vatican diplomatic representative during the interwar period, and papal nuncio to France after World War II. He became a cardinal and patriarch of Venice in 1953. During his tenure as pope he made an enormous impact on the Roman Catholic Church, ushering in a new period of ecumenical participation, social concern, and activism in the cause of world peace. He issued a series of notable encyclicals, including *Pacem in Terris,* and initiated VATICAN II, widely described as the most important Catholic Church meeting in hundreds of years.

John Birch Society, an ultraconservative U.S. political organization, founded by Robert Welch in 1958, that advocated a series of extremist positions on the issues of its time and charged several American presidents, among others, with being Communist agents. It attracted a considerable following in the early 1960s, estimated to be in the 100,000-member range, and temporarily managed to ban some books and win a few local elections; but its extremism ultimately made it an embarrassment to those it supported.

John Paul I, Pope (Albino Luciani; 1912–78), Italian priest, ordained in 1934 and pope from August 26, 1978 to September 18, 1978, then dying suddenly of a heart attack. He had been a priest, teacher, bishop, and cardinal before his brief tenure as pope.

John Paul II, Pope (Karol Wojtyla, 1920–), Roman Catholic pope who became a priest in 1946, archbishop of Kraków in 1964, and pope in 1978, the first-ever Polish pope and the first non-Italian pope in four centuries. A generally conservative leader, he insisted on adherence to his church's traditional positions on such issues as abortion and the politicalization of the clergy. He has stressed the development of his church's influence in the THIRD WORLD.

Johnson, Lyndon Baines (1908–73), U.S. teacher, and a Texas Democratic congressman (1937–49) and senator (1949–61), who became John F. KENNEDY'S vice president in 1961 and succeeded to the presidency after Kennedy's assassination in Dallas, on November 22, 1963. He defeated Republican Barry GOLDWATER in 1964 and did not run for a second full term in 1968. As president he initiated a great deal of social legislation, much of it around the unifying slogan, the GREAT SOCIETY, and including the establishment of MEDICARE, the CIVIL RIGHT ACTS of 1964 and 1965, national aid to education, a substantial series of new and expanded antipoverty programs, and the establishment of two new federal departments: Housing and Urban Development and Transportation. Abroad, he greatly expanded the role of the United States in the VIETNAM WAR, including the bombing of North Vietnam and clandestine operations in Laos and Cambodia. At the same time, he refused to sanction a full-scale invasion of North Vietnam. On March 31, 1968, he announced that he would not seek reelection, at the same time revealing new peace initiatives, which did not succeed. His vice-president, Hubert H. HUMPHREY, became Democratic candidate for the presidency in 1968, after a bitter Democratic national convention in Chicago, and was defeated by Richard M. NIXON.

Johnson, Philip Cortelyou (1906–   ), U.S. architect, a leading exponent of the International Style and then of the post-Modernist style. His home, the Glass Box (1949) in New Canaan, Connecticut, and his Seagram Building (1958) in New York, built in collaboration with MIES VAN DER ROHE, were seminal influences in the development of modern architecture, as were such later buildings as the New York State Theater (1964) and the American Telephone and Telegraph Building (1978), both in New York City.

Johnson, Virginia Eshelman (1925–   ), U.S. psychologist and sex researcher working with William MASTERS.

Johnson Space Center, site of the NATIONAL AERONAUTICS AND SPACE ADMINISTRATION (NASA)'s mission control for space flights, founded 1961; originally called the NASA Spacecraft Center, but renamed in 1973.

Joliot-Curie, Irène (1897–1956) and **Jean Frédéric Joliot-Curie** (1900–58), French physicists who met as young assistants to Irène's mother, Marie CURIE. In 1934 the Joliot-Curies were the first to induce artifical RADIOACTIVITY, bombarding one element and causing its transformation into another, with the release of particles; their work won them the 1935 Nobel Prize for Chemistry. In 1939, Frédéric was the first to recognize the possibility of a CHAIN REACTION in the NUCLEAR FISSION of URANIUM, but the Joliot-Curies' work was short-circuited by World War II, during which they hid their store of uranium and smuggled out of the country their store of precious HEAVY WATER. They remained behind to work in the French RESISTANCE. Afterward, Frédéric helped build the first French NUCLEAR REACTOR, completed in 1948. Partly in reaction to the Nazis during World War II, the Joliot-Curies became Communists and during the COLD WAR were removed from sensitive political positions. Irène died of leukemia, as had her mother, probably because of their work with RADIATION.

Jonathan, Leabua (1914–   ), Basuto chief, head of the Basutoland National Party, who became the first prime minister of Lesotho in 1966, when the British protectorate of Basutoland became independent Lesotho. He became ruler of Lesotho in 1970, suspending the constitution and imprisoning opposition party leaders after his party had suffered electoral losses; he ruled his country absolutely until being overthrown by an army coup in 1986. Although his Black African country was entirely surrounded by South Africa, he sharply and publicly opposed APARTHEID, giving sanctuary to thousands of South African refugees, among them some AFRICAN NATIONAL CONGRESS (ANC) members and activists. In 1982 South African troops attacked alleged ANC groups in Lesotho; in 1986 South Africa began an economic blockade of Lesotho, which was lifted after Jonathan was deposed and South African refugees accused of being ANC activists were deported to Zimbabwe.

Jones, James Warren "Jim", PEOPLE'S TEMPLE cult leader, who was responsible for the deaths of over 900 people in the JONESTOWN mass suicides and murders of 1978.

Jones, Mary Harris "Mother Jones" (1830–1930), U.S. teacher, who became active in the Knights of Labor in the early 1870s and spent the rest of her life as a trade union organizer and speaker. She was 70 years old as the 20th century began, and continued to be active in most of the major American strikes of the first two decades of the century, up to and including the great STEEL STRIKE of 1919.

Jonestown, a Guyana settlement to which James Warren "Jim" JONES and approximately 1,000 of his followers in the PEOPLE'S TEMPLE cult fled, when the cult's practices were in 1976 exposed in San Francisco. In November 1978, U.S. Congressman Leo Ryan and a party of investigators and newspeople went to Jonestown, in response to charges that some there were being held against their will. As they were boarding an airplane home, Ryan, three newspeople, and a defecting cultist were murdered by Jones' followers; ten others were wounded. Jones then induced most of his followers to commit suicide, giving them cyanide-laced drinks. Those who refused to do so were murdered. Jones committed suicide; 913 cult members died, only a few escaped.

Jordan (Hashemite Kingdom of Jordan), until 1920, part of the Ottoman Empire. After World War I, it became part of the British-administered LEAGUE OF NATIONS mandate territory of Transjordan. Full independence came on May 25, 1946, although some British influence remained

until the mid-1950s. Jordan lost the WEST BANK (of the Jordan River) territories during the 1967 war with Israel, formally giving up its claims and obligations regarding those territories in 1988 as the INTIFADA developed.

Jordan, Barbara (1936–   ), U.S. lawyer, law professor, and civil rights leader, who became the first Black Texas state legislator (1966–72) since Reconstruction, a Democratic Texas congresswoman (1973–79), and the keynote speaker at the 1976 Democratic NATIONAL CONVENTION.

Jordan, Vernon Eulion, Jr. (1935–   ), U.S. lawyer, active in the CIVIL RIGHTS MOVEMENT from the early 1960s, as Georgia field secretary for the NATIONAL ASSOCIATION FOR THE ADVANCEMENT OF COLORED PEOPLE (NAACP) 1961–63, Southern Regional Council voter education project director 1964–68, head of the United Negro College Fund 1980–81, and head of the Urban League 1972–81. On May 29, 1980, Jordan was shot and seriously wounded in an unsolved assassination attempt.

Jorgenson, Christine (born George Jorgensen, 1926–89), pioneer U.S. transsexual who, after a series of HORMONE injections and operations (1950–52), given by a medical team in Copenhagen, Denmark, headed by Dr. Christian Hamburger, accomplished an early, highly publicized successful SEX CHANGE, to the great dismay of many in her homeland. She later became a popular entertainer.

Joyce, William, the name of Nazi broadcaster Lord HAW HAW.

Juan Carlos (Juan Carlos Alfonso Victor Maria; 1938–   ), king of Spain, who was named by Francisco FRANCO as successor to the throne in 1969, becoming king after Franco's death in 1975. His grandfather, Alfonso XIII, had been deposed in 1931; Spain had no king from 1931–75. A constitutional monarch, Juan Carlos strongly supported the return of Spanish democracy and played a key role in putting down the attempted right-wing military coup of 1981.

July Days, a series of major Russian demonstrations led by the BOLSHEVIKS, in July 1917, aimed at overthrowing the PROVISIONAL GOVERNMENT. After the demonstrations failed, some of the Bolshevik leaders went into hiding and others were arrested.

Jumblat, Kamal (1917–77), leader of the Druse Moslems in Lebanon and of the Druse militia, who organized and led the Progressive Socialist party from 1949. He joined Camille CHAMOUN in toppling the Bishra government, which they had both supported, in the coup of 1952, and then broke with Chamoun in 1958, becoming one of the organizers of the revolutionary coalition in the LEBANESE CIVIL WAR of 1958, thereafter holding cabinet-level posts in several governments. He supported PALESTINE LIBERATION ORGANIZATION (PLO) operations in Lebanon and was a leader of the left during the LEBANESE WARS, until his assassination in March 1977. He was the father of Walid JUMBLAT.

Jumblat, Walid (1949–   ), son of Kamal JUMBLAT, who succeeded to the leadership of the Lebanese Druse community after the 1977 assassination of his father; he essentially continued his father's policy of coalition with antigovernment forces and alliance with Syria.

June Bug, AIRPLANE designed and flown by Glenn Hammond CURTISS in 1908, and winning a *Scientific American* prize for making the first public flight of more than a kilometer.

Jung, Carl Gustav (1875–1961), Swiss psychiatrist and key 20th-century psychoanalyst. Pioneering in word-association tests, Jung was an early disciple of PSYCHOANALY-SIS from 1907 to 1912, before breaking with FREUD over the primacy of sexual instincts and youthful experiences. In his own school of analytic psychology, Jung strove to encompass the whole development of adult life, with potential crises, notably at midlife. He reached out to mythology and religion, Eastern and Western, finding patients' dreams often paralleling archetypal cultural images, regarding these as perhaps drawn from a "collective unconscious," or pool of myth and symbol common to all cultures.

Jungle, The (1906), the pioneer U.S. muckraking novel by Upton SINCLAIR, which, by focusing public attention on appalling conditions in Chicago's meatpacking industry, greatly helped passage of the PURE FOOD AND DRUG LAWS, including the Pure Food and Drug Act (1906), the Meat Inspection Act (1906), and the Pure Food, Drug, and Cosmetic Act (1908).

Jupiter, planetary target of space probes, such as the U.S. *PIONEER 10* spacecraft, which flew within 81,000 miles of the planet in 1973, exploring its magnetic field and its moons, and *VOYAGERS 1* and 2, which flew by in 1979, revealing a turbulent atmosphere and possible volcanic activity on Jupiter's moon Io.

Jutland, Battle of (May 31–June 1, 1916), the only major sea battle of World War I, between the British Grand Fleet and the German High Seas Fleet. The British fleet, led by 28 modern dreadnoughts, and the German fleet, led by 16 dreadnoughts, fought to a draw, neither side losing any of its dreadnoughts. The German fleet ultimately fled home, not to emerge again for the rest of the war.

K

Kádár, János (1912–89), Hungarian Communist organizer during the 1930s, who became interior minister 1948–50, was imprisoned by his government 1950–54 and then rehabilitated, and joined in the HUNGARIAN REVOLUTION of 1956, becoming first secretary of the Hungarian Communist party on October 25, 1956. Less than a week later he broke with Imre NAGY, leaving Budapest to set up a Soviet-oriented government. He became prime minister after the revolution had been crushed, was prime minister until 1958 and again 1961–65, and remained general secretary of his party until 1988, when the new wave of liberalization characterizing the GORBACHEV era forced him into retirement.

Kahn, Herman, U.S. physicist and nuclear strategist who, in his highly controversial books, notably *On Thermonuclear War* (1960) and *Thinking About the Unthinkable* (1962), accepted nuclear war as probable, feeling it would not end civilization; his critics thought that he thereby made nuclear war more likely.

Kaiser, the, WILHELM II, German emperor 1888–1918 and World War I leader of the Central European alliance, who was deposed by the GERMAN REVOLUTION of 1918.

Kaiser, Henry John (1882–1967), U.S. industrialist, whose contracting firm built some major 20th-century structures, such as the Boulder (now Hoover) Dam (1936) and the Grand Coulee Dam (1942). During World War II Kaiser had a chain of shipyards, building many of the famous Liberty ships; he turned also to car-building after the war. In 1942, he also pioneered with a nonprofit organization to provide health care for his workers, widely known as the Kaiser-Permanente Plan, model for later health maintenance organizations (HMOs).

Kaltenbrunner, Ernst (1903–46), Austrian Nazi who became an SS general, head of the GESTAPO and, military intelligence, and who was personally responsible for wide-scale mass murders, including those of millions of Jews and of large numbers of prisoners of war. He was captured soon after the war, convicted of war crimes at the NUREMBERG TRIALS, and executed.

Kamenev, Lev Borisovich (1883–1936), a leading BOLSHEVIK and close associate of Grigori ZINOVIEV, who in the early 1920s joined with Joseph STALIN to defeat Leon TROTSKY (whose sister was married to Kamenev), but in the mid-20s opposed Stalin's takeover of the Soviet Union. For this he was expelled from the Communist party and lost his official positions; but later he was rehabilitated, after recanting. He was executed in 1936, a victim of the first major show trials of the GREAT PURGE. In June 1989, during the GORBACHEV era, he was once again rehabilitated, this time posthumously.

Kamikazes, Japanese suicide pilots who crashed their planes directly into military targets, destroying their aircraft and themselves in the process. Large numbers of kamikazes died during the retaking of the Philippines in 1944, and an estimated 2,000–4,000 kamikazes died thereafter, many of them during the Battle of OKINAWA.

Kammerer, Paul (1880–1926), Austrian biologist, who figured in a notorious case in which he claimed from 1918 to have experimentally proven the inheritance of acquired characteristics. However, other scientists—held off for years—found in 1926 that his experimental specimens of the midwife toad had been colored with India ink. Kammerer committed suicide a short time later.

Kampuchea (Cambodia), until 1953, a French protectorate that had been occupied by Japanese forces during World War II and was granted some degree of autonomy by the French after World War II. Independence came on November 9, 1953, and was made firm by French withdrawal with the end of the INDOCHINA WAR in 1954. After the KHMER ROUGE victory in the CAMBODIAN (KAMPUCHEAN) CIVIL WAR, Cambodia was renamed Democratic Kampuchea on January 5, 1976. With the Vietnamese invasion of 1978 came the formation of the competing People's Republic of Kampuchea, and a long guerrilla war that in 1989–1990 threatened to become another full-scale civil war.

Kampuchea–Vietnam War (December 1978–   ), invasion and occupation of Kampuchea by Vietnamese forces after a series of border clashes. The Vietnamese took the capital of Phnom Penh and ultimately drove POL POT'S forces to the Kampuchea–Thailand border. A long occupation and accompanying guerrilla war followed; in 1988 Vietnam pulled some of its forces out of Kampuchea, stating intentions to pull out the balance within 2 years, and claimed completion of a troop pullout on September 26, 1989, although Chinese and opposing guerilla sources claimed otherwise.

Kansu earthquake (December 16, 1920), an earthquake in south central China that caused an estimated 150,000–200,000 deaths.

Kao Kang (1902–55), Chinese Communist political leader who lost a top-level Communist party internal struggle in the mid-1950s and committed suicide shortly before he was about to be denounced by his party.

Kapitza, Peter Leonidovich (1894–1984), Soviet physicist, who worked in Britain from 1921 on magnetic fields and low-temperature physics with Ernest RUTHERFORD until 1934, when he was not allowed to leave the U.S.S.R. after a visit. He continued his work in the Soviet Union, but was persona non grata 1946–55 for refusing to work on development of nuclear weapons; he later joined in the space effort but continued to support freedom of communication, defending dissenters like Andrei SAKHAROV. Kapitza shared the 1978 Nobel Prize for Physics for his work on helium at temperatures approaching absolute zero.

Kapp Putsch (1920) the German FREIKORPS coup led by Wolfgang Kapp, which for a short time took control of the German government but was defeated by a general strike and withdrawal of some army support.

Karamanlis, Constantine (1907–   ), Greek lawyer, in parliament 1935–67, who was premier 1955–63, and again in 1974–80; in the latter period he helped to restore and stablilize Greek democracy after 7 years of military government. He was president 1980–85.

Karmal, Babrak (1929–   ), Afghan political leader, a member of parliament 1965–73, who headed the more moderate, Soviet-influenced wing of the People's Democratic Party and became a vice-president of Afghanistan after the coup of 1978. He was exiled to Czechoslovakia by the more radical wing of the party, which controlled the country after the coup. After Soviet intervention in 1979 and the execution of former vice-president Hafizullah Amin, who had seized power from President Nur Mohammed Taraki, Babrak was installed by the Soviets as Afghan president. He resigned from all posts in 1986, as the AFGHAN–SOVIET WAR continued.

Kármán, Theodore von (1881–1963), Hungarian-American aeronautical engineer and physicist, who played a major role in the development of aerodynamic theory and practice in the development of SUPERSONIC flight and ROCKETS, heading a practical research and development program at the

California Institute of Technology from 1930.

Kasavubu, Joseph (1910–69), Congolese nationalist, an experienced administrator who became coalition president of the first Congo (Zaire) government, with Patrice LUMUMBA as premier, after independence from Belgium had been secured, effective June 30, 1960. He remained president of the Congo until 1965, steering a shifting political course. He dismissed Lumumba in 1960, and authorized the UNITED NATIONS peacekeeping force intervention that put down Moïse TSHOMBE'S Belgian-supported 1960–63 Katanga secession. He recalled Tshombe as his prime minister in 1964, after departure of the UN force, and then used Belgian troops to suppress several insurgencies, dismissing Tshombe for electoral fraud in 1965. On November 25, 1965, army commander-in-chief General Joseph MOBUTU, who had held a great deal of power since his brief open assumption of power in September 1960, openly took power again; Kasavubu then left public life.

Kashmir War (1947–49), an undeclared war between India and Pakistan that began in October 1947, with Moslem insurgency developing after the Hindu ruler of Kashmir decided to join Kashmir to India, following the August partition of British-ruled India and the emergence of independent India and Pakistan. After the rebellion Moslem irregulars and then Pakistani army forces moved into Kashmir, fighting Indian forces sent to put down the revolt and take the province for India. On January 1, 1949, the UNITED NATIONS mediated a truce and an informal partition of Kashmir along the existing battlefront.

Kassem, Abdul Karim (1914–63), Iraqi general who led the republican revolution of 1958 and became first premier of the Iraqi republic. He was killed during an army coup in 1963.

Kasserine Pass, Battle of (February 14–22, 1943), a surprise attack by German armored units on Allied troops in Tunisia, that caused heavy American casualties and impeded Allied offensive plans, but gained no great advantage for weakening Axis forces in North Africa.

Katyn Massacre (spring 1940), the mass murder of an estimated 10,000 Polish soldiers and officers at Katyn Forest early in World War II, a crime widely attributed to the Soviets but which the Soviets blamed on the Nazis throughout the postwar period. In 1988 the Polish government placed blame for the massacre on the Soviets.

Kaunda, Kenneth David (1924–   ), Zambian teacher and nationalist leader, who in 1958 led the breakaway movement from his country's African National Congress that formed the majority United National Independence party. In 1963, when Northern Rhodesia and Nyasaland were granted autonomy by Great Britain, pulling away from then white-ruled Southern Rhodesia, Kuanda became first prime minister of Northern Rhodesia, and in 1964 first president of the Republic of Zambia. After being democratically reelected in 1968, he set up a one-party state in 1973, and from then on ruled Zambia. Throughout his presidency, he was deeply involved in bringing world pressure to bear on South African racism, increasingly provided haven for AFRICAN NATIONAL CONGRESS (ANC) exiles and guerrilla groups, and participated in efforts to solve such regional problems as the insurgencies in Zimbabwe, Angola, and Mozambique. In the 1980s he faced difficult economic problems at home, some of them stemming from the disruption of normal trading patterns in the region caused by the multiple wars and continuing insurgencies in the area.

Kaysone Phomvihane (1920–   ), Laotian nationalist and Communist, who commanded PATHET LAO forces during the LAOTIAN CIVIL WAR, and became secretary-general of the Laotian Communist party (the People's Party of Laos, after 1975 the ruling Laos People's Revolutionary Party). In December 1975, after Pathet Lao victory, he became first prime minister of the Laos People's Democratic Republic.

Kefauver, Carey Estes (1903–63), U.S. lawyer, Tennessee Democratic congressman (1939–49), and senator (1949–63), who was a NEW DEAL supporter in the 1930s and 1940s, and in the 1950s was the leading Senate investigator of organized crime and other monopolistic practices and groups. His 1950–51 KEFAUVER COMMITTEE hearings on organized crime made him a national figure, but he was not able to win the Democratic presidential nomination he sought in 1952 and 1956.

Kefauver Committee, a U.S. Senate committee led by Senator Estes Kefauver of Tennessee that investigated organized crime in the United States in a series of nationally televised hearings during 1950 and 1951, and heightened public awareness of MAFIA operations, although no indictments resulted.

Keitel, Wilhelm (1882–1946), German officer, who became head of the Nazi high command in 1938, and functioned as HITLER's chief staff adviser throughout World War II. He was found guilty of war crimes at the NUREMBERG TRIALS, and was executed on October 16, 1946.

Keller, Helen Adams (1880–1968), U.S. writer and speaker, who was made blind, deaf, and mute by illness when 19 months old, and who, with the aid of her teacher and companion, Annie Sullivan, became the world's leading advocate of aid for the blind and other physically handicapped people, and the main developer of the the American Foundation for the Blind.

Kellogg, Frank Billings (1856–1937), U.S. lawyer, who was the federal prosecutor in the STANDARD OIL case (1906–11) and other early major antitrust cases. He was Republican senator from Minnesota (1916–22), ambassador to Great Britain, and secretary of state during the COOLIDGE administration. With French foreign minister Aristide BRIAND, Kellogg initiated the KELLOGG-BRIAND PACT, by which the United States, France, and 60 other nations stated their intention to attempt to cease using war as a means of settling international disputes.

The treaty was ratified by the Senate, and Kellogg won a Nobel Peace Prize in 1929; the rise of fascism and militarism soon altered international circumstances.

Kellogg-Briand Pact (Pact of Paris; August 27, 1928), a treaty stating joint intent to attempt to halt the use of war as a means of settling international disputes, which was ultimately signed by 62 nations, but was never an effective tool for disarmament and against war. The rise of fascism and militarism in Germany, Japan, and Italy made far stronger practical measures necessary; when these were not forthcoming, the run-up to World War II began.

Kemal, Mustapha (1881–1938), Turkish national leader who in 1933 renamed himself ATATÜRK.

Kemp, Jack French (1935–   ), U.S. political leader, in his early years a professional football player, a New York Republican congressman 1971–88, and an unsuccessful candidate for the 1988 Republican presidential nomination. On December 19, 1988, President-elect George BUSH named him housing and urban development secretary.

Kendi, Ruhollah, the given name of Ruhollah KHOMEINI.

Kennan, George Frost (1904–   ), U.S. State Department specialist on Soviet affairs, in Moscow 1933–35 and 1944–46. In 1947, then in Washington, writing in the magazine *Foreign Affairs* as Mr. X, he authored the policy of CONTAINMENT, which became the basic COLD WAR policy of the United States and its allies. He was back in Moscow as American ambassador from 1952–53. By the mid-50s Kennan had greatly moderated his views, becoming sharply opposed to continuing U.S. COLD WAR policies, the VIETNAM WAR, and the continuing nuclear arms race.

Kennedy, Anthony McLeod (1936–   ), U.S. lawyer, who served on the Ninth Circuit U.S. Court of Appeals 1975–88, after having been recommended by then-California governor Ronald REAGAN. In 1988 President Reagan nominated him to the Supreme Court, after the unsuccessful fight to confirm nominee Robert BORK. Kennedy was quickly confirmed by the Senate.

Kennedy, Edward Moore "Ted" (1932–), U.S. political leader, the younger brother of John F. KENNEDY and Robert F. KENNEDY and the son of Joseph P. KENNEDY; a Democratic senator from Massachusetts from 1962. He entered the senate while both of his brothers were still alive; after the 1968 assassination of his brother, Robert, he would most probably have been his party's presidential nominee in 1972. However, he was involved in the CHAPPAQUIDDICK incident of July 1969, leaving the scene of an accidental death, and the resulting national furor destroyed his presidential possibilities then and into the late 1980s. A liberal, Kennedy was a strong advocate in such areas as social legislation, nuclear arms limitation, and civil rights.

Kennedy, John Fitzgerald (1917–63), U.S. political leader, a Massachusetts Democratic congressman (1947–53) and two-term senator (1953–61), who became the 35th president of the United States (1961–63), and was assassinated while in office. In 1960 he defeated Republican Richard M. NIXON by a very narrow margin in a presidential campaign that included, for the first time, a series of live TELEVISION debates between the candidates. He was the first American Roman Catholic president. As president he was heavily involved in foreign affairs, including the failed BAY OF PIGS Cuban invasion of April 1961, the BERLIN WALL crisis that began late in 1962, and the CUBAN MISSILE CRISIS of October 1962, which came close to causing nuclear war between the United States and the Soviet Union. He also negotiated the NUCLEAR TEST BAN TREATY of 1963, initiated the PEACE CORPS, and attempted to develop new ties with Latin America in the ALLIANCE FOR PROGRESS. Domestically, many new programs were discussed, but few were accomplished, as he faced a largely hostile Congress, though he strongly supported the developing national campaigns for CIVIL RIGHTS that characterized the period. On November 22, 1963, in Dallas, Texas, he was assassinated by Lee Harvey OSWALD, and was then succeeded by his vice president, Lyndon B. JOHNSON. On November 24, Oswald was himself assassinated by Jack RUBY. Although the WARREN COMMISSION, headed by Supreme Court chief justice Earl WARREN, declared Oswald the sole assassin, and found no conspiracy to assassinate the president, controversy continued to surround the assassination and its aftermath.

Kennedy, Joseph Patrick (1888–1969), U.S. financier and father of John, Robert, and Edward KENNEDY; he became a successful investor in the 1920s, held onto his gains after the CRASH OF 1929, and became Franklin D. ROOSEVELT'S head of the new SECURITIES AND EXCHANGE COMMISSION in 1934. In that position, he investigated many of his former securities industry colleagues and began to develop effective financial regulation. He was ambassador to Great Britain 1937–40.

Kennedy, Robert Francis (1925–68), U.S. lawyer, a brother of President John F. KENNEDY and Senator Edward M. KENNEDY, and a son of Joseph P. KENNEDY. He worked as a Justice Department and then Senate committee lawyer 1952–60, with major focus on labor union corruption, James HOFFA, and the Teamsters' Union. He managed his brother's 1960 presidential campaign and became U.S. attorney general 1961–64, keeping that post in the JOHNSON administration after his brother's assassination. A liberal Democrat, he was a New York senator 1965–68. In 1968 he campaigned for his party's presidential nomination; but his campaign and life were cut short in Los Angeles, on June 5, 1968, when he was shot by Sirhan Sirhan and died the next day.

Kennedy Round, the 1963–67 set of negotiations organized by the GENERAL AGREEMENT ON TARIFFS AND TRADE (GATT), which succeeded in substantially reducing international tariff and trade barriers.

Kennelly-Heaviside layer, alternate name for the IONOSPHERE, which enhances the quality of RADIO transmission, predicted in 1902 and found in 1924.

Kent State killings (May 4, 1970), attack on unarmed students by Ohio National Guard troops, called out during anti–VIETNAM WAR demonstrations at Kent State University, killing 4 and wounding 10. Massive national protests followed, further strengthening the U.S. antiwar movement. There were no convictions at a later trial of the National Guard members who had opened fire.

Kenya (Republic of Kenya), until 1963, a British colony. During the post–World War II period, a powerful independence movement arose, led by Jomo KENYATTA, that generated the unsuccessful 1952–56 MAU MAU UPRISING. Independence came on December 12, 1963; Jomo Kenyatta was Kenya's first prime minister, and was Kenya's first president on establishment of the republic in 1964.

Kenyatta, Jomo (1890–1978), Kenyan political leader and anthropologist, who became the leading figure in his country's national movement and a major figure in 20th-century African and worldwide anticolonial movements. A Kikuyu, he was secretary of and in 1929 represented the Kikuyu Central Association in London. He returned to London in 1931 to study anthropology at the London School of Economics with Bronislaw MALINOWSKI, among others. One product of that period was Kenyatta's classic work, *Facing Mount Kenya*. He returned to Kenya in 1946 as head of the Kenya African Union and leader of the Kenyan independence movement. Although arrested by the British in 1952, charged with leading the MAU MAU UPRISING, and imprisoned for the next 9 years, he remained leader of the national movement and became head of the Kenya African National Union (KANU) in 1960. He was released in 1961, became prime minister in 1963, and in 1964 became the first president of the Republic of Kenya, holding that position until his death. As president, he built Kenya into a multitribal, economically viable, largely democratic state, though

one with substantial and continuing economic and intratribal problems that surfaced more easily when Kenyatta's guidance and enormous prestige were removed.

Kenyon, Kathleen Mary (1906–78), British archeologist, who worked on many sites but was best known for her excavation (1952–58) of Jericho, in modern Jordan, which is one of the oldest cities known, dating back perhaps 9,000 years.

Kerensky, Alexander Fyodorovich (1881–1970), a Russian lawyer and SOCIALIST REVOLUTIONARY PARTY leader, who was a member of the executive committee of the PETROGRAD SOVIET OF WORKERS AND SOLDIERS DEPUTIES and then successively minister of justice, minister of war, and premier of the short-lived PROVISIONAL GOVERNMENT of Russia after the FEBRUARY REVOLUTION of 1917. As war minister he unsuccessfully attempted to continue World War I on the Eastern Front and to resist the kinds of massive changes demanded by the BOLSHEVIKS and other forces on the left. Ultimately, his government had little support and was easily overthrown by a Bolshevik-led rebellion in Leningrad (then Petrograd), on October 24, 1917, the date of the OCTOBER REVOLUTION. Kerensky spent the rest of his life as an emigre, in western Europe and the United States.

Kerensky Offensive (July 1, 1917), the only substantial Russian World War I action after the RUSSIAN REVOLUTION, in which Russian armies attacked and scored early sucesses against Austro-German forces in Galicia. Reinforced German forces counter-attacked on July 6, and smashed the Russian armies, which soon disintegrated. The Germans did not push farther into Russia.

Kerner Commission Report (National Advisory Commission on Civil Disorders), a U.S. commission appointed by President Lyndon JOHNSON and headed by Illinois governor Otto Kerner, that studied the causes of the 1966–68 U.S. race riots, such as that at WATTS. The commission reported on March 2, 1968, placing major blame for the riots on pervasive white racism and adverse social conditions, and recommending a series of major reforms.

Kerr-McGee nuclear accident (January 6, 1986), bursting of a container of nuclear material at the Kerr-McGee facility in Gore, Oklahoma, killing 1 person and hospitalizing 100. The only previously reported U.S. nuclear accident directly causing death was the IDAHO FALLS NUCLEAR EXPLOSION of 1961.

Kesselring, Albert (1885–1960), German officer, who saw service in World War I, became German air force chief of staff in 1936, and during World War II commanded air forces during the invasion of Poland, the Battle of FRANCE, the Battle of BRITAIN, and in the Mediterranean, where he ultimately became commander of all AXIS forces, conducting the long retreat through Italy. At the end of the war he was German commander on the Western Front. After the war, he was tried for the murders of prisoners of war and was imprisoned as a war criminal, but was released in 1952.

Keynes, John Maynard (1883–1946), British economist whose major work, *The General Theory of Employment, Interest, and Money* (1935), was seen by many during the GREAT DEPRESSION and thereafter to provide a theoretical basis for widespread and continuing government economic intervention, with the aim of creating full employment and prosperity.

KGB (Committee of State Security), the main Soviet espionage and counter-espionage organization from 1954; it was also responsible for some aspects of internal security, though its predecessors, including the CHEKA of the OCTOBER REVOLUTION and the NKVD of the GREAT PURGE of the 1930s, were more deeply concerned with internal secret police functions.

Khama, Seretse (1921–80), hereditary chief of the Bamanwato people, the largest group in Botswana, then Bechuanaland; he studied law in Great Britain, gave up his hereditary chieftaincy in a dispute, and returned home in 1956 to become his country's leading advocate of independence. Khama be-

came the first president of Botswana (1966–80). He was a builder of multiracial democracy, who opposed racism in South Africa while attempting to continue peaceful trading and political relations with his much stronger neighbor.

Khe Sanh, Siege of (January–April, 1968), an attack by North Vietnamese forces on the U.S. Marine base at Khe Sanh near the Vietnam–Laos border as part of the TET OFFENSIVE. The siege was lifted in April; the base was abandoned in July, generating substantial criticism of the original decision to defend it.

Khmer Rouge (Red Khmers), the army of the Communist party of Kampuchea, winner of the CAMBODIAN CIVIL WAR. Since then, the term "Khmer Rouge" has often been used as a synonym for the Communist government of Kampuchea, and later for the main Kampuchean guerrilla force fighting the Vietnamese army during the KAMPUCHEA–VIETNAM WAR, although the military organization itself was dissolved in 1981.

Khomeini, Ruhollah (Ruhollah Kendi; 1900–89), Iranian Shiite Islamic religious leader (ayatollah), who led demonstrations against the westernizing policies of Shah Mohammed Reza PAHLEVI in 1963, and was subsequently exiled. He led Iranian Islamic fundamentalist forces from exile in France until his return to Iran on February 1, 1979. He then became undisputed religious and political leader of Iran, reversing the course of modernization and westernization pursued by the Pahlevi shahs, and ultimately destroying all internal opposition in a prolonged reign of terror. In power, he fostered both international terrorism and Islamic fundamentalist movements throughout the world, and pursued sharply anti-Western and in particular anti-American policies, including the actions that generated the HOSTAGE CRISIS of 1979–80. After Iran's heavy losses in the IRAN–IRAQ WAR of the 1980s his regime made some attempts to normalize relationships with many Western countries, but in 1989 Khomeini's open call for the murder of author Salman RUSHDIE made such normalization impossible.

Khrushchev, Nikita Sergeyevich (1894–1971), Soviet Communist Party official, who fought in the RUSSIAN CIVIL WAR and rose in the party hierarchy during the 1930s, becoming Ukrainian party leader in 1938, a Politburo member in 1939, and Central Committee secretary in 1949. After STALIN'S death in 1953, he took over effective control of his party and in 1955 took over national leadership after a successful power struggle that toppled Georgi MALENKOV. In 1955 he and U.S. president Dwight D. EISENHOWER met in GENEVA, at the first postwar summit meeting between the heads of the two superpowers. Khrushchev's extraordinary 1956 SECRET SPEECH, attacking the crimes of Joseph STALIN, had an immense impact on Communists all over the world, causing massive splits and defections, and ushered in the THAW within the Soviet Union. He survived early internal opposition, expelled Malenkov and others from the Central Committee in 1957, and consolidated power as Soviet premier in 1958. Internationally, he operated rather erratically, fostering DETENTE and improved relations with Yugoslavia while at the same time becoming involved in several dangerous COLD WAR moves. In 1961, facing and testing a young American president, John F. KENNEDY, Khrushchev became involved in a major crisis over the building of the BERLIN WALL. In 1962 the world came very close to humanity-destroying nuclear war at the time of the CUBAN MISSILE CRISIS. Khrushchev was forced to withdraw Soviet missiles from Cuba, a grave blow to Soviet prestige at the time. That blow and serious internal economic problems led to his loss of power and forced retirement in October 1964.

Khrushchev's secret speech, a February 1956 address by Nikita KHRUSHCHEV to the 20th Congress of the Soviet Communist party, in which he attacked the police state and long reign of terror developed by Joseph STALIN from the early 1930s, exposing many of the multifold crimes of the Stalin era. Khrushchev's extraordinary speech had an immense impact on Communists all over the world, causing massive splits and defections, and ushered in the THAW within the Soviet Union.

Kiangsi Soviet (1931–34), the Kiangsi Soviet Republic, organized by the Chinese Communists in their rural Kiangsi base area. At its peak it governed approximately 4 million people and mustered a 200,000-strong army. It was ultimately destroyed by KUOMINTANG offensives; the Communist army then fled north through mountainous areas in the LONG MARCH.

kidney transplant, replacement of a diseased kidney with a healthy one from a donor; first attempted in the early 1900s, sometimes using a pig or dog kidney, but first performed successfully in 1954 by a Harvard medical team led by Joseph E. Murray. Kidney TRANSPLANTS continued to be performed even though an "artificial kidney" dialysis machine was developed in 1943 by Dutch physician Willem Johan Kolff.

Kiel Mutiny (November 1918), the rebellion of German sailors at the Kiel naval base, which began the GERMAN REVOLUTION of 1918.

Kilburn, Peter, one of the American LEBANON HOSTAGES, an American University librarian, who was kidnapped on December 3, 1984, and murdered by his captors on April 17, 1986.

Kill Devil Hills, sand dunes near Kitty Hawk, North Carolina, from which the WRIGHT brothers made the first engine-powered AIRPLANE flight in 1903.

Kim Il Sung (Kim Sung Chu; 1912–   ), Korean Communist Party activist from 1931 who was an anti-Japanese guerrilla leader during World War II. He became head of the North Korean provisional government 1946–48 and was prime minister and effectively dictator of the Democratic People's Republic of Korea from 1948. In that period he took his country into the KOREAN WAR, after that war continuing to mount a cold war against South Korea, with some tentative moves toward normalization of relations occurring only in the late 1980s. From the mid-50s he developed around himself a massive cult of personality.

Kimmel, Husband Edward (1882–1968), U.S. naval officer, who saw service in World War I and was commander of the Pacific Fleet at PEARL HARBOR on December 7, 1941. He was relieved at the end of December, faced a board of inquiry, retired in 1942, and was cleared of dereliction of duty in 1946.

King, Ernest Joseph (1878–1956), U.S. naval officer, who became commander of the Atlantic fleet in February 1941, and in the early days of World War II became both U.S. fleet commander-in-chief and chief of naval operations. In those capacities he was chief American naval officer throughout the war, fighting a two-front war and winning on both, with what was ultimately by far the largest navy in the world. He was also a key advisor to Franklin Delano ROOSEVELT, and was present at all of the major conferences of Allied leaders throughout the war. He became a five-star admiral in December 1944.

King, Martin Luther, Jr., (1929–68), the major U.S. Black leader of the 20th century, a Protestant minister whose policy of nonviolent confrontation became the basic approach of the successful CIVIL RIGHTS MOVEMENT of the 1950s and 1960s, and who personally led many of the major campaigns and demonstrations of that movement. He became a national figure through his leadership of the landmark MONTGOMERY BUS BOYCOTT of 1955–56. In 1957 he was a founder and first president of the SOUTHERN CHRISTIAN LEADERSHIP CONFERENCE (SCLC), and from that position developed the major series of campaigns and confrontations that ultimately broke the southern system of white supremacy. These included the actions at BIRMINGHAM and SELMA, Alabama, and at Albany, Georgia, and also included the MARCH on WASHINGTON civil rights demonstration of August 28, 1963, with his "I HAVE A DREAM" speech

as its centerpiece. In 1964 he was awarded the Nobel Peace Prize. He continued his civil rights work through the mid-60s, extending it into the north, joining economic issues with civil rights issues and also opposing the war in Vietnam. He was assassinated by James Earl RAY in Memphis, Tennessee, on April 4, 1968.

King, William Lyon Mackenzie (1874–1950), Canadian economist, reformer, Liberal leader, and three-time prime minister (1921–26, 1926–30, 1935–48), who began his government service in 1900 as a labor department deputy prime minister, appointed by his mentor, Prime Minister Wilfrid LAURIER. He entered parliament for the first time 1908–11 and then became a labor mediator in the United States. In 1919 he entered parliament again, also succeeding Laurier as Liberal party leader. During his long leadership of party and country, he moved Canada toward economic and political independence from Great Britain. He did not strongly oppose the rise of fascism during the interwar period but after 1937 developed a close personal and political relationship with Franklin D. ROOSEVELT, moving into a close Canadian-U.S. alliance after the Nazi victories of 1940. After World War II he also guarded against dependence upon the United States. During his final years in power, he began to build what would become Canada's very substantial social service support network.

King David Hotel bombing (July 22, 1946), bombing of the British office wing of Jerusalem's King David Hotel by the IRGUN ZVAI LEUMI, under the direct supervision of Menachim BEGIN, killing 91 people, 17 of them Jews. The HAGANAH had denounced the proposed bombing in advance; afterward the Irgun and Begin were sharply criticized by the main Jewish organizations of the time.

King Tut, popular name for TUTANKHAMEN, Egyptian pharaoh (1361–52 B.C.) whose tomb was excavated in 1922 by English archeologist Howard CARTER and much caught the public fancy.

Kinnock, Neil Gordon (1942–), British LABOUR PARTY leader, in parliament from 1970, a member of the national executive committee of his party from 1978 and leader of the party and the parliamentary opposition from 1983. A moderate socialist, he took the Labour party on a course designed to capture the independent center in British politics. A superb speaker, he was paid the supreme compliment of emulation by U.S. senator Joseph BIDEN, who appropriated some of Kinnock's lines during the 1988 presidential nomination campaign, then was forced to leave the presidential race after the appropriation was discovered.

Kinsey, Alfred Charles (1894–1956), U.S. sex researcher who directed the Institute for Sex Research at Indiana University from 1942. His pioneering works, *Sexual Behavior in the Human Male* (1948), popularly called the "Kinsey Report," and *Sexual Behavior in the Human Female* (1953), drew on personal interviews, rather than on first-hand observation, as in the later MASTERS and JOHNSON works. Though badly dated, Kinsey's work was still being referred to more than 35 years later, no comparable work having taken its place.

Kiribati (Republic of Kiribati), until 1979, the British Gilbert Islands colony; independence and COMMONWEALTH membership came on July 12, 1979.

Kirkland, Joseph Lane (1922–), U.S. labor leader who was an assistant to George MEANY and secretary-treasurer of the AMERICAN FEDERATION OF LABOR-CONGRESS OF INDUSTRIAL ORGANIZATIONS (AFL-CIO), before succeeding Meany in the presidency of the organization in 1979.

Kirkley, Howard Leslie (1911–89), British pacifist and international relief worker, who became active in post–World War II European relief work, and then chairman of the then–small Oxford Committee for Famine Relief in 1951. He spent the next 23 years (1951–74) in developing Oxfam into a major international relief organization, also moving Oxfam into long-term Third World self-development projects. He remained active as secretary-emeritus of Oxfam and in other relief organizations after his retirement.

Kirov, Sergei Mironovich (1886–1934), Leningrad Communist Party leader, whose assassination in 1934 was used by Joseph STALIN as a pretext for beginning the GREAT PURGE of the late 1930s. The Kirov assassination was in all probability ordered by Stalin, though the evidence adduced to support this view is not yet entirely conclusive.

Kishi, Nobusuki (1896–), Japanese government official, who in the late 1930s was involved in industrial matters in occupied Manchuria, and during World War II was responsible for directing much of Japan's wartime production; brother of Eisaku SATO. Afterward adjudged a war criminal, he was imprisoned from 1945 to 1948, resumed his political career as a member of the Diet in 1953, and was prime minister from 1957 to 1960, resigning after forcing through a United States–Japanese treaty, against powerful opposition.

Kishinev pogroms, a series of Russian anti-Jewish attacks, which began in the spring of 1903 at Kishinev in Bessarabia (Moldavian SSR). The first attacks killed hundreds and caused major property damage; subsequent widespread attacks killed an estimated 50,000 Jews. The pogroms were the first major Russian anti-Jewish attacks since 1881; they were the proximate cause of massive Jewish migrations to the United States and Palestine, and enormously strengthened both the internal Russian revolutionary movement and the ZIONIST movement.

Kissinger, Henry Alfred (1923–), U.S. teacher, author, and consultant, who became president Richard M. NIXON's national security assistant in 1968, soon becoming Nixon's key foreign affairs advisor as well. Kissinger negotiated the end of U.S. involvement in the VIETNAM WAR, with mutual prisoner exchange, in January 1973. He and LE DUC THO, the North Vietnamese negotiator, shared a Nobel

Peace Prize for this in 1973, which he accepted and Le Duc Tho declined. He became secretary of state in 1973 and continued in that position during the FORD administration after the WATERGATE-inspired resignation of President Nixon, in those years engaging in SHUTTLE DIPLOMACY, an attempt to personally mediate Arab–Israeli differences in the Middle East.

Kitchener, Horatio Herbert (1850–1916), British general, who became a national hero in 1898, after his victory over Sudanese forces at the Battle of Omdurman. He was chief of staff and then commander of British South African forces during the BOER WAR, held several colonial posts, and then became secretary of state for war when World War I began in 1914. He helped turn the small peacetime British army into a large wartime army, although in constant conflict with others in the cabinet. Kitchener was killed in 1916, on his way to Russia, when the cruiser *Hampshire* was sunk by a mine off the Orkney Islands.

Kitty Hawk, North Carolina town, near which the WRIGHT brothers made the first engine-powered AIRPLANE flight in 1903, at Kill Devil Hills.

Klein, Melanie Reizes (1882–1960), Austrian-British psychoanalyst who pioneered in child PSYCHOANALYSIS. Interested in the field because of her own psychoanalysis in 1912, Klein used "play therapy"—observation of infants at play—to uncover the emotional states of her very young patients. She moved to England in 1926, and there developed a following; later she also worked with troubled adults.

Kleist, Paul Ludwig Ewald von (1881–1954), German officer, who saw service in World War I and became a general during the interwar period. He commanded the PANZER army group that broke through at Sedan during the Battle of FRANCE, and Panzer armies in Yugoslavia and in the Soviet Union. He played a key role in the captures of Kiev, SEVASTOPOL, and Rostov but ultimately fell back before Soviet armies after the defeat at STALINGRAD, and was re-

lieved of command in March 1944. He was imprisoned for war crimes in Yugoslavia after the war, and then in the Soviet Union, where he died in prison.

Kluge, Hans Günther von (1882–1944), German officer, who saw service in World War I, was an army commander during the invasions of Poland and France and on the Russian front, and was Western Front commander July–August, 1944. He was relieved of command by Adolf HITLER, who suspected him of being involved in the July 1944 assassination attempt; shortly afterward he committed suicide.

Knudsen, William (1879–1948), Danish-American industrial manager, who moved ahead in the automobile industry to ultimately become head of General Motors (1937–40) and was during World War II head of arms production in the war department (1942–45).

Koestler, Arthur (1905–83), Hungarian-British writer, a Communist 1932–38, whose best known work was DARKNESS AT NOON, an anti-Communist novel based on the MOSCOW TRIALS of the 1930s. He and his wife committed suicide together in 1983, while he was ill.

Kohl, Helmut (1930–   ). West German Christian Democratic party leader in the RHINELAND from 1956, deputy national chairman of his party 1969–73, and party chairman from 1973. In 1976 he became leader of the opposition in the federal parliament and in 1982 chancellor of the Federal Republic of Germany. As chancellor, he developed a somewhat independent course in international affairs during the late 1980s, responding to internal pressure to remove nuclear MISSILES while also remaining in the Western alliance. Domestically, he cut German social safety net spending, as economic problems developed in the mid-80s.

Kolchak, Alexander Vasilievich (1874–1920), Czarist admiral of the Black Sea Fleet and commander of White armies fighting in Siberia during the RUSSIAN CIVIL WAR; his forces were defeated by 1920, and he was captured and executed that year by the BOLSHEVIKS.

Kolmogorov, Andrey Nikolayevich (1903–), Soviet mathematician, who largely shaped 20th-century mathematics in the Soviet Union. His own work spread widely in areas such as probability theory, topology, CYBERNETICS, and information theory. Through his textbooks and influence on school curricula, he influenced decades of Soviet mathematicians.

Kolubra, Battle of (December 3–9, 1914), World War I battle, in which Austrian forces invading Serbia had taken Belgrade and were pursuing the Serbian army in difficult terrain; but the Serbs counterattacked, driving the Austrians back and recapturing Belgrade.

Konev, Ivan Stepanovich (1897–1973), Soviet officer who saw service in World War I, fought in the Red Army during the RUSSIAN CIVIL WAR, and became an army commander in the autumn of 1941, playing a major role in the defense of MOSCOW and the subsequent Soviet counteroffensive. Armies under his command fought at the Battle of KURSK and thereafter fought their way into Germany, ultimately taking Berlin. After the war he held a series of key government positions, including those of defense minister, commander of the WARSAW PACT armies, and member of the Communist party Central Committee.

Konoe, Fumimaro (1891–1945), Japanese political leader, who was prime minister (1937–39; 1940–41) during the invasion of China and the run-up to World War II. He committed suicide in 1945, while awaiting trial as a war criminal.

Kon–Tiki, balsa-wood raft sailed across the Pacific in 1947 by Norwegian explorer Thor HEYERDAHL, and the title of his 1948 bestseller about the voyage.

Korea, at the beginning of the 20th century, a Chinese protectorate. It was taken by Japan in 1910 and held until the end of World War II, then divided into U.S. and Soviet occupation zones that later became independent nations. The REPUBLIC OF KO-REA became an independent state on August 15, 1948. The DEMOCRATIC PEOPLE'S REPUBLIC OF KOREA became an independent state on September 9, 1948.

Koreagate, 1970s South Korean government influence-buying operation in the United States, run by businessman Tongsun Park, who made substantial payments to many U.S. congressmen in an apparently rather successful effort to buy their support for Korean national aims. After a major investigation, accompanied by much media attention and headed by WATERGATE prosecutor Leon Jaworski, one Congressman, Richard T. Hanna, pleaded guilty; one other was indicted but not convicted; and three more were reprimanded by Congress.

Korean Air Lines Flight 007 (August 30, 1983), the Korean civilian airliner that was shot down by Soviet interceptor planes, after straying into Soviet air space near Soviet Sakhalin Island bases from the Sea of Japan. All 269 people on board were killed.

Korean War (1950–53), a civil war between North Korea and South Korea, with quick intervention on the side of South Korea by United States and other, much smaller UNITED NATIONS forces, and later intervention on the side of North Korea by PEOPLE'S REPUBLIC OF CHINA forces. North Korean and Chinese casualty figures are unavailable; estimates indicate 1 million South Korean civilian casualties, 300,000 South Korean military casualties, and 150,000 UN (including U.S.) casualties. The war began on June 25, 1950, with a surprise attack by the North Koreans driving toward Seoul against much weaker Republic of Korea (ROK) forces. The UN condemned the invasion, calling for an immediate ceasefire. On June 27, President Harry S. TRUMAN ordered General Douglas MACARTHUR to give air and sea support to ROK forces, and on June 30 ordered in U.S. ground forces, which began to move in from Japan. In August and September, UN forces established a defensive line across the Korean peninsula, holding it with difficulty. On September 15, UN forces effected division-strength amphibious landings at IN-CHON, 150 miles north of the defensive line, while the defensive forces to the south broke out to meet them at and retake Seoul. Combined UN forces then pursued North Korean forces north, taking Pyongyang on October 20 and moving across the 38th Parallel toward the Yalu River boundary with the People's Republic of China, which had threatened to come into the war if the 38th Parallel were crossed. Having completely underestimated Chinese intentions and strength, MacArthur continued to move north toward the Yalu; on November 25 his forces were struck by a Chinese Red Army main force of 18 divisions, numbering an estimated 180,000 men, with ready combat reserves of 100,000 more men in nearby Manchuria. UN forces were driven back with heavy losses, western forces ultimately developing a defensive line north of Seoul in mid-December, and eastern forces of more than 100,000 troops being evacuated from Hungnam by sea, along with a similar number of civilians. On January 1, 1951, an estimated 500,000 Chinese and North Korean troops resumed their offensive, taking Seoul on January 4, but then stalling and retreating in February and March; UN forces retook Seoul on March 14. MacArthur was dismissed by President Truman on April 11, when MacArthur publicly attacked the U.S. limited-war policy, demanding the right to bomb Chinese bases in Manchuria, which Truman refused to do. During April and May, UN forces withstood a further Chinese–North Korean offensive and then counterattacked, driving north and in June consolidating a new front north of Seoul, which became a truce line when negotiations began in July 1951. Negotiations broke down in August, and limited war resumed; armistice negotiations began at Panmunjon on November 12. Fighting resumed in June 1953; final negotiations began in July, and an armistice was concluded on July 27, 1953, with the battle line becoming the North Korea–South Korea boundary line.

Korematsu v. United States (1944), a landmark U.S. Supreme Court decision, up-

holding the 1942 federal Executive Order removing large numbers of Japanese-Americans from their West Coast homes and placing them in CONCENTRATION CAMPS, the rationale of the Court majority at the time being wartime necessity caused by security considerations. The Court minority called the action overt racism, and that view in the long run prevailed. President Gerald R. FORD rescinded the Executive Order and apologized for the action in 1972; reparations were voted by Congress in 1988.

Kornilov Affair, an attempted coup by Russian general Lavr Kornilov, the PROVISIONAL GOVERNMENT'S chief of staff, in August 1917. In support of the KERENSKY government, Kornilov ordered his troops to march on Petrograd and destroy the growing power of the PETROGRAD SOVIET. But RED GUARD and revolutionary armed forces units in the city mobilized to meet Kornilov's forces, while Kornilov's troops refused to move in force against the capital. The failure of the coup greatly strengthened the BOLSHEVIK position in the weeks before the OCTOBER REVOLUTION.

Korolev, Sergei (1906–66), Soviet aeronautical engineer, who became chief Soviet ROCKET fuel and spacecraft designer and a leading figure in humanity's exploration of space, beginning his work on liquid rocket fuel in the early 1930s. Korolev designed the VOSTOK series of spacecraft, the first of which carried Yuri GAGARIN on the first manned orbit of Earth on April 12, 1961; he also designed the first Soviet space SATELLITES and space probes to the MOON and planets.

Korsun, Battle of (January–February 1944), encirclement and partial destruction of German forces on the Dnieper River by major Russian forces during the Soviet winter offensive of 1944; the remainder of the Germans fought their way out of the encirclement.

Kosygin, Alexei (1904–80), Soviet industrial manager who became a Communist official in 1938, a member of his party's Central Committee in 1939, and then held a succession of party and government posts, becoming a deputy prime minister in 1940 and a Politburo member in 1948. He was out of power briefly in 1953, made a comeback in the mid-50s, supported Khrushchev in the intra-party dispute of 1957, emerged as chief of Gosplan and therefore chief Soviet economic planner in 1959, and as first deputy prime minister in 1964. He and Leonid BREZHNEV shared power in the "collective" leadership that succeeded Khrushchev, Kosygin being responsible for internal economic matters. But Kosygin lost power in the late 1960s and early 1970s, Brezhnev then becoming undisputed leader of the Soviet Union. After his 1976 heart attack, Kosygin's duties were taken over by others, although his formal resignation came in 1980, shortly before his death.

Krebs, Hans Adolf (1900–81), German-British biochemist who in 1937 discovered a sequence of chemical reactions, called the Krebs or citric acid cycle, by which cells obtain energy for use in the body. For his work in outlining basic metabolic reactions, he shared the 1953 Nobel Prize for Physiology or Medicine. He also discovered the urea cycle, the series of chemical reactions by which the liver produces urine.

Kreuger, Ivar "The Match King" (1880–1932), Swedish industrialist, who started with his family's match-producing business in 1907, and built a worldwide match production empire. His enterprise fell apart in the early years of the GREAT DEPRESSION; it then became clear that he also had been engaged in massive financial misconduct during his years of financial and industrial eminence. Kreuger committed suicide in 1932.

Kreisky, Bruno (1911–   ), Austrian socialist leader and diplomat, who was foreign minister 1959–66 and chancellor 1970–83, in the latter position continuing Austria's role as a waystation and haven for refugees from Soviet-bloc countries and attempting to expand government social service activities.

Kristallnacht, the German word for CRYSTAL NIGHT, the Nazi pogrom of November 9–10, 1938.

Kronstadt Rebellion (March 1921), a rebellion against the BOLSHEVIK government by previously sympathetic sailors of the Baltic Fleet, based at the Kronstadt naval base, near Leningrad. These were Bolshevik supporters, who had joined in the OCTOBER REVOLUTION of 1917, and although their rebellion was quickly suppressed by army units personally led by Leon TROTSKY and General Mikhail TUKHACHEVSKY, it significantly contributed to LENIN'S decision to end WAR COMMUNISM and institute his NEW ECONOMIC POLICY.

Krupp family, the RUHR-based steelmaking family that became chief armaments supplier to the Prussian army in the latter third of the 19th century, and continued to perform that function for the German army during World Wars I and II. From 1931, even before HITLER'S rise to power, the Krupps were closely tied to the Nazis, the family's oldest son, Alfred, becoming a BLACKSHIRT (SS) in 1931. The Krupps used slave laborers out of CONCENTRATION CAMPS during World War II; Alfred Krupp was convicted of having done so after the war and sent to prison for it, the family's holdings being confiscated. But a year later, he was pardoned by the American occupation authorities, the Krupps' properties were restored, and the Krupps went on to become West Germany's steelmakers once again, after promising that they would not produce any more war materials.

Krupskaya, Nadezhda (1869–1939), Russian revolutionary, who married Vladimir LENIN in 1898 while they were both in Siberian exile, and later worked with him to develop the BOLSHEVIK party. After the RUSSIAN REVOLUTION, she worked on social welfare and eduational matters, but had little impact on subsequent Soviet development.

Kubitschek, Juscelino (1902–1976), Brazilian doctor, who entered politics in the early 1930s, served in several posts during the

VARGAS dictatorship, and was elected to the presidency (1955–61) after Vargas' 1954 suicide. Kubitschek took Brazil on an expansive and inflationary course, building Brasilia, embarking upon massive public works projects, and amassing a large national debt. He had planned to run again in 1965 but was barred from doing so by the military coup of 1964. The military rulers of the country then continued essentially on the economic course he had charted and came very close to bankrupting Brazil, while at the same time sharply restricting Brazilian democracy.

Kubler-Ross, Elisabeth (1926–   ), Swiss-American psychiatrist, who pioneered in focusing on the care of terminally ill patients and the need to help and support their families and friends, writing widely influential works, notably *On Death and Dying* (1969).

Kuhn, Thomas Samuel (1922–   ), U.S. historian and sociologist of the development of scientific knowledge. In works such as *The Structure of Scientific Revolutions* (1962), he introduced the idea of a paradigm—a shared body of experimental approaches and interpretations, such as that stemming from the work of Newton or EINSTEIN—within which scientists work, and with which their results must be reconciled, suggesting that revolutionary science occurs when results force a crisis of confidence in the paradigm, causing it to be overthrown.

Ku Klux Klan (KKK), originally a secret racist and terrorist organization formed after the Civil War in the former Confederate states, which used murder and intimidation to destroy Black gains during Reconstruction. Starting in 1915, the KKK reorganized and became a national racist, anti-immigrant, antidissident organization, achieving a membership of 1.5–4 million members and considerable political power, especially in the South and Midwest. It lost most of its power during the Depression and World War II, reviving again as a group of small, loosely organized terrorist splinter organizations from the 1950s through the 1980s.

kulaks, Russian family farmers, former peasants, who had been encouraged to become small landowners by the Czarist government land reforms of the early 1900s. In the late 1920s, when Joseph STALIN'S first FIVE-YEAR PLAN forcibly collectivized Soviet agriculture, he ordered the "liquidation" of the kulaks. The resulting purges and accompanying famines resulted in the deaths of an estimated 10–20 million Soviet citizens.

Kun, Béla (1886–1939), Hungarian Communist, who led the short-lived Hungarian Socialist Republic (March–August 1919). He had been a Social Democrat before World War I, was captured by the Russians during that war while serving in the Austrian army, and became a BOLSHEVIK while in Russia, then working with LENIN. In 1918 he returned to Hungary and was soon jailed, but came out of prison to become leader of Hungary. His Red Army had early successes against Rumanian and Czech forces, but he was ultimately forced to flee when Rumanian forces occupied Budapest. He later became a leader of the COMMUNIST INTERNATIONAL but was executed in the Soviet Union in 1939, as part of the Soviet GREAT PURGE of the period.

Küng, Hans (1928–   ), Swiss theologian, who in 1970 became the first major Roman Catholic thinker to reject the idea of the pope's infallibility, in his work *Infallible? An Inquiry*. Earlier noted for his ecumenical work under Pope JOHN XXIII, Küng came into conflict with Pope JOHN PAUL II over the church's suppression of dissent, then was censured by the Vatican and forbidden to teach under Roman Catholic auspices.

Kuomintang, the Chinese political party founded by SUN YAT-SEN in 1914, and reorganized with Soviet advisers and on the BOLSHEVIK Party model beginning in 1922. During the NORTHERN EXPEDITION of 1926, CHIANG KAI-SHEK rose to leadership of the party, split with its Communist component and his Soviet advisers, and in 1927 began the CHINESE CIVIL WAR, with the SHANGHAI MASSACRE. From 1929 until 1949, the Kuomintang was the ruling party of the Republic of China, ultimately losing mainland China to the Communists in 1949, and then fleeing to Taiwan, where it has continued to govern and claim legitimacy as the governing party of China.

Kurdish national movement, nationalist movement by Kurdish peoples, promised autonomy, after four centuries of Ottoman rule, by the Treaty of SÈVRES (1920) following World War I, a promise broken when the Treaty of LAUSANNE (1923) superseded Sèvres. Since then, Kurdish minorities in Turkey, Iraq, and Iran have aspired to autonomy, often moving into armed rebellion. There were Kurdish uprisings in Turkey and Iraq in the 1920s and 1930s, those in Iraq led by Mustafa al-BARZANI. After World War II, Barzani led in the formation of a Kurdish republic in northern Iran, with Soviet backing, but Kurdish forces were defeated by the Iranians in 1946, and the republic was dissolved. Barzani returned to Iraq after the revolution of 1958 and led a long rebellion against the Iraqi government (1960–70), ultimately securing guarantees of Kurdish autonomy. He then led his people in renewed rebellion, after breakdown of that agreement in 1974; their long guerrilla war continues today. Iran's KHOMEINI government suppressed Iran's Kurds on coming to power, but during the IRAN–IRAQ WAR of the 1980s supported the Iraqi Kurdish insurgents. On conclusion of the Iran–Iraq War, the Iraqis moved large forces against the Kurds, using both conventional armaments and CHEMICAL WARFARE, their chemical weapons causing large numbers of civilian casualties. Hundreds of thousands of Kurds fled across the Turkish and Iranian borders.

Kursk, Battle of (July 1943), the failed last World War II German offensive on the Eastern Front, which had hardly started before it encountered a powerful Soviet counteroffensive. Kursk was primarily a huge TANK battle, the largest known, in which large masses of Soviet armor and anti-tank weapons won over a German concentration that included 17 mechanized divisions, the Germans then retreating.

Kurusu, Saburo (1886–1954), Japanese diplomat who had held many posts during three decades in the foreign office, including that of ambassador to Nazi Germany, before coming to the United States as a negotiator in November 1941. He was with U.S. Secretary of State Cordell HULL when the PEARL HARBOR attack occurred.

Kut, Siege of (December 7, 1915–April 29, 1916), World War I Turkish siege of Kut, in Mesopotamia, to which British forces had retreated after their defeat at CTESIPHON in November 1916. After relief forces failed to get through, 8,000 British and Indian troops ultimately surrendered to the Turks.

Kuwait (state of Kuwait), until 1961 a British protectorate, becoming independent on June 19, 1961. An oil-rich and very small country, Kuwait continued to rely on external military guarantees after independence, at first from Great Britain and later from other countries in the ARAB LEAGUE. During the IRAN–IRAQ WAR Kuwait became an Iranian target, as it leaned toward Iraq, and ultimately accepted naval and air support from the United States.

Kwajalein, Battle of (January–February 1944), World War II movement of large U.S. naval forces into the Marshall Islands, in late January and early February 1944. U.S. Army and Marine forces made an amphibious assault on Kwajalein atoll on February 1, while Marine units attacked other islands in the group; in a week Kwajalein had been taken and almost all of its 8,000 defenders killed when they refused to surrender. American casualties were under 1,500 men in all, including less than 400 dead.

Kwangtung Army, the Japanese Manchurian army, which in 1931 manufactured the MUKDEN INCIDENT and then seized Manchuria without the prior approval of the Japanese government, which later ratified the action.

Ky, Nguyen Cao (1930–   ), South Vietnamese officer and aviator, head of the armed forces group that seized power in

1965. He was prime minister of South Vietnam 1966–67 and vice-president 1967–71.

Kyshtym nuclear explosion (winter 1957–58), a massive explosion of buried nuclear wastes at a Soviet nuclear waste disposal site near Kyshtym in the Ural Mountains, creating a radioactive cloud that contaminated an estimated 400 square miles, killing and damaging an unknown number of people, though whole villages were later reported to have been destroyed. The event was reported outside the Soviet Union in 1976 but was not acknowledged by the Soviet government.

L

Labour Party, British moderate socialist party formally organized in 1906, succeeding the Labour Representation Committee, which was formed in February 1900 by several British socialist organizations, including the FABIAN SOCIETY, the Independent Labour party, and the trade union movement. The first Labour prime minister was Ramsay MACDONALD in 1924, and again in 1929. The party achieved full power with an overwheming victory in 1945, thereafter creating the NATIONAL HEALTH SERVICE, introducing other welfare reforms, nationalizing several basic industries, and beginning to dismantle the British Empire. It was the governing party under Harold WILSON and James CALLAGHAN during several periods in the 1960s and 1970s but encountered serious difficulties in the late 1970s and throughout the 1980s, because of a series of splits along ideological lines within the party.

laetrile, controversial drug manufactured from apricot pits, and touted as a treatment for CANCER. Branded by the U.S. National Cancer Institute in 1981 as "ineffective" for that purpose, it was still used in Mexico and elsewhere. Desperate cancer victims sometimes traveled internationally to seek laetrile treatment.

La Follette, Robert Marion (1855–1925), U.S. lawyer, Wisconsin Republican congressman (1885–91), governor (1900–06), senator (1906–25), and presidential nominee of the PROGRESSIVE PARTY IN 1924. A reformer, his views often sharply varied from those of his party; after 1912 he sometimes broke party lines on reform matters, but could not support Woodrow WILSON on

U.S. participation in World War I. In 1924, he was active in exposing the TEAPOT DOME scandal. Although he received 5 million votes in the 1924 elections, he won only his home state of Wisconsin, and his new party did not again seriously challenge the two major parties.

La Guardia, Fiorello Henry (1882–1947), U.S. consular official, interpreter at ELLIS ISLAND, and lawyer, who became a reform New York Republican congressman (1917–19, 1923–33). While a young consular official at Fiume, Italy (1903–06), he initiated medical inspections of emigrants departing for America, an innovation later adopted by many governments, saving thousands of poor immigrants from being turned back at ELLIS ISLAND; with treatment in Europe, many were later able to emigrate to the United States. In 1933 he became reform mayor of New York City on an antimachine, anticorruption fusion ticket, and during the next 12 years successfully and colorfully fought municipal corruption, developed social and public works programs, and became by far the best-loved mayor of his city. He was director of the UNITED NATIONS RELIEF AND REHABILITATION ADMINISTRATION (UNRRA) in 1946.

Lagunillas oil refinery fire (November 14, 1939), a fire that began in an oil refinery, then spread to the nearby town of Lagunillas, near Lake Maracaibo, Venezuela, destroying the town and killing more than 500 people.

Laika, first dog in space, launched into orbit in 1957 aboard the U.S.S.R.'s *Sputnik 2.*

Laing, Ronald David (1927–1989), Scottish psychiatrist, who pioneered in the communal treatment of schizophrenic patients. In his *Divided Self* (1960), and *The Politics of Experience* (1967), he proposed that schizophrenia was an individual's defense against a society gone mad. He proposed that schizophrenic and other mentally disturbed people should live together in small, homelike, sheltered, and supervised communes. Though his theory of schizophrenia remained controversial, his success with communal living for the mentally ill, pioneered in London from 1965, led to its adoption in many countries, including the United States.

Lake Naroch, Battle of (March 18, 1916), an unsuccessful World War I Russian attack on German forces, resulting in approximately 100,000 Russian and 20,000 German casualties.

Lake Nios toxic cloud (August 21, 1986), a cloud of toxic gas rising from Lake Nios, Cameroon, a lake within a volcanic crater, that killed an estimated 1,700 people and injured an estimated 500 more.

Lake Okeechobee flood (September 16–17, 1928), flood that killed an estimated 2,000–2,500 people, when a Caribbean hurricane struck this central Florida lake, causing it to flood surrounding low-lying areas.

Lame Duck Amendment, the TWENTIETH AMENDMENT to the U.S. Constitution, which moved the presidential and vice-presidential inauguration dates from March 4 to January 20; it also provided for the new Congress to take office on January 3.

lamps are going out all over Europe, comment by Edward GREY, British foreign secretary at the beginning of World War I; from "the lamps are going out all over Europe; we shall not see them lit again in our lifetime."

Land, Edwin Herbert (1909–   ), U.S. inventor, who in the early 1930s discovered how to use tiny crystals embedded in PLASTIC to polarize light, as in safety glass, founding the Polaroid Corporation in 1937 to market his invention; the name became famous in 1947 when Land invented the Polaroid Land Camera, which produces photographs within the camera itself and turns out a print in seconds.

Landon, Alfred Mossman (1887–1987), U.S. businessman, Republican governor of Kansas 1933–36, and the Republican nominee for the presidency in 1936. He was defeated by Franklin Delano ROOSEVELT, winnng only Maine and Vermont.

Landsteiner, Karl (1868–1943), Austrian-American pathologist and physiologist, who in 1900–02 recognized that blood comes in various types; he labeled the main ones A, B, O, and AB. This discovery allowed blood transfusions to be made much more safely, and it won him the 1930 Nobel Prize for Physiology or Medicine. Some disastrous reactions still occurred, however, and in 1940, with Alexander S. Wiener, Landsteiner discovered that one cause was the RHESUS (RH) FACTOR.

Lange, David Russell (1942–   ), New Zealand lawyer and socialist who became a Labour member of parliament in 1976, party leader in 1983, and prime minister in 1984. In 1985, he refused admission to a U.S. warship after demanding but not receiving certification that it was not carrying nuclear arms, and in 1987 he led in the parliament's decision to declare New Zealand waters a nuclear-free zone, developing a major dispute with the United States on the issue. In 1985 New Zealand arrested and convicted French agents who had sunk the Greenpeace antinuclear ship *RAINBOW WARRIOR* in Auckland harbor, later releasing them after French payment of $7 million in compensation.

Lan P'ing, stage name of Chinese leader JI-ANG QING, the wife of MAO ZEDONG; in 1981 she was convicted of being the leader of the GANG OF FOUR.

L'Anse aux Meadows, Viking settlement in northern Newfoundland, dating to the 11th century A.D., rediscovered in 1960 by Helge Ingstad and George Decker. Its discovery confirmed that Norse colonists had indeed reached and, at least for a time, had settled in North America.

Laos (Lao People's Democratic Republic), until 1953 a French protectorate, which was granted some degree of autonomy by the French after World War II. Independence came on October 23, 1953, and was made firm by French withdrawal with the end of the INDOCHINA WAR in 1954. After the PATHET LAO victory in the LAOTIAN CIVIL WAR came formal establishment of the People's Democratic Republic, on December 2, 1975.

Laotian Civil War (1950–73), a long insurrection by Communist PATHET LAO forces, supported by the VIETMINH (later the government of Vietnam), the Soviet Union, and China. From 1950 to 1954 it was a low-level factional struggle set into the LAOTIAN WAR OF INDEPENDENCE against the French. After 1954 it was a low-level continuing Pathet Lao insurgency, which burst into full-scale guerrilla civil war after the Kong Le military coup of 1960. Pathet Lao victories soon drew American threats to intervene. When an April 1961 cease-fire did not hold, there were U.S. naval movements toward the area, and American troops were sent to neighboring Thailand. In July 1962 an internationally mediated peace agreement reached in Geneva temporarily ended the war, with Prince SOUVANNA PHOUMA and Prince SOUPHANOUVONG both serving in the 1960–62 coalition government. War broke out again in 1962, side by side with the developing VIETNAM WAR. North Vietnam used Laotian supply routes and bases, and North Vietnamese troops fought beside Pathet Lao forces; the United States supplied the Laotian armed forces and in the 1970s provided air combat support. With American withdrawal from Vietnam, Pathet Lao victory became certain. A cease-fire went into effect in February 1973, followed by a coalition government and in May 1975 by Pathet Lao occupation of Vientiane. In December 1975 the Laotian People's Democratic Republic was formally established.

Largo Caballero, Francisco (1869–1946), Spanish socialist who became prime minister of the Spanish Republic in September 1936, 2 months after the outbreak of the SPANISH CIVIL WAR. He resigned in May 1937 after the anarchist-Communist factional fighting in Barcelona.

La Rouche, Lyndon, Jr., a political extremist who had during his career veered both left and right, and a four-time right-wing presidential candidate. In December 1988 La Rouche and six associates were convicted of mail fraud and conspiracy relating to $30 million of "loans." He was sentenced to 15 years imprisonment.

Lascaux, cave in France's Dordogne Valley, discovered in 1940 by four boys looking for a dog, that has some of the finest prehistoric paintings ever found, dating from about 16,000 years ago. They were closed to the public in 1963 after the paintings began to deteriorate, but photographs and copies, like those made by Abbé BREUIL, remain to record their magnificence.

laser (light amplification by stimulated emission of radiation), device that produces an intense, concentrated beam of light, similar in concept to the MASER but with many more applications. As early as 1917, Albert EINSTEIN had seen that molecules stimulated in a certain way would emit light of a single color, but no practical action was taken until the 1950s, when several scientists in the U.S. and U.S.S.R. independently developed the idea of a laser. The first working laser was built in 1960 by U.S. physicist Theodore Harold Maiman. Since then lasers have been used in many ways: for high-resolution mapping, for HOLOGRAPHY, for industrial welding and cutting (even through diamonds), in long-distance fiber-optic networks, and in biological research. Probably their best-known uses have been in medicine: because they can be focused so accurately, lasers have been used for everything from cleaning out clogged arteries to welding together a damaged retina, from making an incision to sealing a leaking blood vessel.

Lateran Treaty (1929), agreement between the Vatican and the Italian government of Benito MUSSOLINI by which the Vatican recognized Mussolini's government and the government recognized the sovereignty of the Vatican and the establishment of Catholicism as a state religion, superior to all other religions in Italy.

Lattimore, Owen (1900–89), U.S. scholar and author, expert on east and central Asia, editor of *Pacific Affairs* 1934–41, director of the Page School of International Relations at Johns Hopkins 1939–50, and U.S. diplomat in China during World War II. In 1950 he was falsely accused of being a Soviet spy by Senator Joseph MCCARTHY, but was exonerated by a Senate committee. He detailed the experience in his book *Ordeal by Slander* (1950). In 1952 he was indicted for perjury; all charges against him were withdrawn in 1955.

Latvia, from the late 18th century, a Russian Baltic province, which won its freedom in the LATVIAN WAR OF INDEPENDENCE (1918–20), but was reoccupied by the Soviet Union in 1940, as provided in the NAZI-SOVIET PACT. During the GORBACHEV era, powerful independence movements arose in all three Baltic Soviet Republics; in early 1990, the issues had not yet been resolved.

Latvian War of Independence (1918–20), conflict that developed as part of the RUSSIAN CIVIL WAR. Latvia declared its independence on November 18, 1918; in response, Soviet troops entered the former Russian Baltic province and took Riga in January. Combined German and Latvian forces fought against the Soviets and each other until January 1920. The Germans left the country in November 1919, in accordance with the terms of the Treaty of VERSAILLES, and the Russians left in January 1920. Independence was formally recognized by the Treaty of RIGA in August 1920.

Laue, Max Theodor Felix von (1879–1960), German physicist who developed the technique of X-RAY CRYSTALLOGRAPHY, in the process discovering in 1912 that X-rays were a form of electromagnetic RADIATION. He won the 1914 Nobel Prize for Physics.

Laurier, Wilfrid (1841–1919), Canadian lawyer, in parliament from 1874, who was Canada's first French-Canadian prime minister and was also Liberal party leader 1896–1911. He was an advocate of some separation of Canadian and British interests in world affairs and of multiethnic cooperation in Canada. He lost power in 1911 largely on the issue of the Canadian–U.S. reciprocity treaty, which brought Canada closer to the United States. He also lost Liberal party multiethnic unity in 1917 on the issue of conscription during World War I, which most French Canadians opposed and most British Canadians favored. His party returned to power 2 years after his death, led by his protégé, William Mackenzie KING.

Lausanne, Treaty of (July 24, 1923), the Turkish peace treaty following World War I. The Turks, led by Mustapha KEMAL (who later became ATATÜRK), refused to accept the much more severe Treaty of SÈVRES, which had been signed by a Turkish delegation on August 10, 1920. At Sèvres, Turkey had been dismembered, with much loss of territory to Greece and Italy; several new nations, including Armenia and eventually Kurdistan, had been created, and the Dardanelles had been internationalized. At Lausanne, the Turks kept much more of their territory, including Turkish Armenia and Turkish Kurdistan; by the terms of a separate Straits Convention they agreed to keep the Dardanelles open except in time of war, but kept control of the straits.

Laval, Pierre (1883–1945), French political leader, who was a socialist defense lawyer (1909) and member of the Chamber of Deputies 1914–19, leaving the Socialist Party after electoral defeat. He was a rightist French premier in 1931 and again in 1935, in those years urging close cooperation with fascist Italy, and was out of office from 1936 to 1940. As a member of PETAIN'S government in 1940, he was largely responsible for the establishment of the collaborationist VICHY government, though out of the government for a time in 1940–42. He then headed the Vichy government until the liberation of France, fled to Spain, and returned to France to stand trial for treason in

1945. He was convicted, and was executed on October 15, 1945.

Law, Andrew Bonar (1858–1923), a long-time British Conservative party leader (1911–21; 1922–23), who served at cabinet level in the ASQUITH and LLOYD GEORGE World War I governments, and was Conservative prime minister for 7 months in 1922 and 1923.

Lawrence, Ernest Orlando (1901–58), U.S. physicist, who in 1928 developed the CYCLOTRON, using electromagnetic fields to accelerate atomic PARTICLES, and won the 1939 Nobel Prize for Physics. With successively more powerful versions of this "atom smasher," at the University of California at Berkeley, Lawrence developed methods to separate out fissionable URANIUM and also to produce PLUTONIUM, both for use in early ATOMIC BOMBS. He identified and produced radioactive ISOTOPES, many later used as tracers in medical and biological research, and laid the foundations for modern particle physics.

Lawrence, Thomas Edward "Lawrence of Arabia" (1888–1935), a British officer who became adviser to FAISAL during the ARAB REVOLT and Arab-British World War I alliance. He worked with Faisal to develop guerrilla strategy, participated in a successful attack on Aqaba, and organized consistent Arab raids on the vital Hejaz railway. Press coverage made him an almost mythical figure. In the early 1920s he was a British political adviser in the Middle East, but disillusion soon caused him to retire from his work in that area. His book, *The Seven Pillars of Wisdom*, on his desert years with the Arabs, was published in 1926.

Lawrence of Arabia popular name for Thomas Edward (T. E.) LAWRENCE.

Lawrence textile strike (1912), a successful strike by an estimated 20,000 textile workers in Lawrence, Massachusetts, most of them recent immigrants. The strike, which was led by the INDUSTRIAL WORKERS OF THE WORLD (IWW), gained widespread labor and liberal support and provided the

IWW with a temporary surge of acceptance and growth.

League of Arab States an alternate name for the ARAB LEAGUE.

League of Nations (1920–46), the international peacekeeping and collective security organization called for in U.S. president Woodrow WILSON'S FOURTEEN POINTS, which was established by the PARIS PEACE CONFERENCE in 1919 and acknowledged in the Treaty of VERSAILLES and other treaties following World War I. Its enabling document was the COVENANT OF THE LEAGUE OF NATIONS; 63 nations signed that Covenant during the life of the organization; the United States did not. During the 1930s there were key withdrawals of fascist nations, including the Japanese withdrawal after the League had condemned Japan's invasion of Manchuria and withdrawals by Germany and Italy. From 1920 to 1922, the League set up supervision by other countries of former German and Turkish territories, such as the British mandate in Palestine and the Japanese mandates over several Pacific island groups, and was theoretically responsible for supervision of those mandates; in fact, it had little to do with them once established. The League also included the INTERNATIONAL LABOR ORGANIZATION and the Permanent Court of International Justice, which in 1945 became the WORLD COURT; both were, in practice, separate organizations. Throughout its life, the League attempted to promote international peace and disarmament, and did play a significant role in the settlement of some small disputes. But it had very little effect on the course of major events; by the mid-1930s it was clear the that major powers had entirely bypassed the League, and were heading for war.

Leakey, Louis Seymour Bazett (1903–72), **Mary Douglas Nicol Leakey** (1913–   ), and **Richard Erskine Frere Leakey** (1944–   ), British anthropologists and paleontologists, husband and wife, and the middle of their three sons, who did key work at Olduvai Gorge, in Tanzania, and at other East African locations. Beginning in 1959,

Mary and Louis Leakey discovered hominid remains as much as 2 million years old, indicating that humanity's beginnings were far earlier than had previously been thought. They also encouraged the work of primatologists, notably Jane GOODALL and Dian FOSSEY. Mary Leakey, continuing to work in East Africa after her husband's death in 1972, made further discoveries indicating the possibility of even earlier origins. From 1968, Richard Leakey did similar work in Kenya, writing popular works about anthropology, and sometimes coming into conflict with Donald JOHANSON over interpretation of fossil finds.

Lebanese Civil War of 1958, conflict that began in May, with rebellion against the pro-Western government of Camille CHAMOUN by a coalition of Pan-Arab and Christian Left forces. By June, there was factional streetfighting in Beirut. Chamoun appealed for Western help; on July 15 the United States sent marine and army units, which grew to a force of over 14,000. The insurrection ended with a compromise peace settlement, with Chamoun agreeing not to run for the presidency after the end of his term in 1958. All U.S. troops were withdrawn by late October.

Lebanese Wars (1975–   ), conflict that began in earnest in 1975, after the progressive destabilization of Lebanon from 1967, with increased Palestinian commando activity in southern Lebanon, and the beginning of Israeli armed response across the Lebanese border. In 1971 Jordan expelled the PALESTINE LIBERATION ORGANIZATION (PLO); Yasir ARAFAT then moved PLO headquarters to Lebanon, and both guerrilla activity and Israeli response increased dramatically. In April 1975, heavy fighting between PHALANGE Christian militia and PLO forces began in Beirut, and soon drew in other Christian and Moslem militias, becoming a full-scale civil war in 1975–76. Direct Syrian army intervention began in April 1976, and a cease-fire, to be enforced by a joint Arab states force, which became in fact a Syrian force, went into effect in October and November. However, heavy fight-

ing continued in the south, sporadic fighting continued throughout the country, and PLO forces continued to raid across the Israeli border. In March 1978 Israeli forces invaded southern Lebanon, withdrawing in June after formation of a Christian Lebanese buffer zone abutting the Israeli border. In the same period, factional fighting broke out throughout the country, which continued, with scores of militias in fluid, ever-changing alliances engaged in a civil war without fixed boundaries or fronts. This factional fighing destroyed much of Beirut and an estimated 80% of the country's industrial capacity, cost tens of thousands of dead, and left hundreds of thousands homeless. In June 1982, the Israelis invaded Lebanon, quickly drove to Beirut, drove Syrian forces into the Bekaa valley, and encircled and besieged PLO and Syrian forces in West Beirut. In August, negotiations mediated by the United States led to PLO and Syrian withdrawal from Beirut, under the protection of a multinational peacekeeping force, which then left Beirut, returned in September, and remained in Beirut until early 1984. The Israelis withdrew from Beirut in 1983 and from southern Lebanon in 1985, though still maintaining a Christian-dominated buffer zone on their border. Their position in Lebanon and international standing were severely damaged by their probable complicity in the Phalangist massacres of September 1982, at Beirut's SABRA AND CHATILLA Palestinian refugee camps. The civil war continued: In September and October 1983 U.S. marine and naval forces at Beirut were drawn into fighting between the Druse militia and Lebanese army forces. In October 1983 the remaining PLO forces in Lebanon were besieged by Syrian-backed Lebanese forces at Tripoli, and were evacuated by sea. From 1983 rival militias fought for control of small areas of Beirut, of the Palestinian refugee camps, of Tripoli, of southern Lebanon, and of the Chouf mountains north of Beirut, while support and intervention from abroad continued to help fuel the fire that consumed the country. In the spring of 1989, the war intensified, as the Lebanese army, led by General Michel Aoun, attempted to expel Syrian forces. Beirut was reduced to rubble, and an estimated 1 million more refugees left the city. A truce was effected in late September, and on November 5 Rene Moawad was elected president by the Lebanese parliament, after an agreement had been reached by some Moslem and Christian factions. But hardline Christian and Moslem forces did not accept the new government; Maowad was assassinated on November 22, replaced by another moderate, and the civil war went on, with no end in sight.

Lebanon (Republic of Lebanon), until 1918 part of the Ottoman Empire. During the interwar period Lebanon was a French-administered LEAGUE OF NATIONS mandate territory. Formation of an independent republic was announced on November 26, 1941, but actual independence was achieved upon French withdrawal in 1946. After independence, with governments carefully balanced between Christians and Moslems, Lebanon became a prosperous Middle Eastern financial and resort center. In the mid-1950s, existing balances began to break down, a process resulting in the civil war of 1958. In the mid-1960s, Lebanon began to be drawn into the ongoing Arab–Israeli conflict; in 1975, the long, disastrous LEBANESE WARS began.

Lebanon hostages, scores of people who from early 1984 were kidnapped, some murdered and most held as possible bargaining counters, by Moslem extremist groups in Lebanon. The hostages included British Anglican church hostage negotiator Terry Waite, kidnapped January 20, 1987, and the following Americans, in the order in which they were kidnapped: Jeremy LEVIN, CNN bureau chief, taken March 7, 1984, escaped February 14, 1986; William BUCKLEY, CIA station chief in Beirut, taken March 16, 1984, murdered during 1985; Rev. Benjamin WEIR, taken May 6, 1984, released September 14, 1985; Peter KILBURN, American University librarian, taken December 3, 1984, murdered April 17,

1986; Rev. Martin JENCO, head of Catholic Relief Services, taken January 8, 1985, released July 26, 1986; Terry ANDERSON, Associated Press Middle East correspondent, taken March 15, 1985; David JACOBSEN, director of American University, taken May 28, 1985, released November 2, 1986; Thomas SUTHERLAND, American University agriculture dean, taken June 9, 1985; Frank REED, director of the Lebanese International School, taken September 9, 1986; Joseph James CICIPPIO, American University comptroller, taken September 12, 1986; Edward Austin TRACY, writer, taken October 21, 1986; Charles GLASS, ABC-TV news correspondent, taken June 17, 1987, escaped August 18, 1987; Robert POLHILL, American University professor, taken January 24, 1988; Alann STEEN, American University professor, taken January 24, 1988; Jesse TURNER, American University professor, taken January 24, 1988; Mithileshwar SINGH, American University professor, taken January 24, 1988, released October 3, 1988; William HIGGINS, UNITED NATIONS truce supervision team head and U.S. lieutenant colonel, taken February 17, 1988. During the late 1980s hostage release negotiations proceeded in several countries, including Great Britain, Germany, and the United States, in the United States greatly contributing to the development of the IRAN-CONTRA AFFAIR. Higgins was murdered by his captors on or before July 31, 1989. They announced the murder on July 31, after Sheikh Abdul Karim Obeid had been abducted by Israeli commandos on July 18, but HIGGINS may have been murdered earlier. They did not carry out their announced intention to murder Cicippio and negotiations continued.

lebensraum (living space), the Nazi slogan and justification for the invasion of its eastern neighbors, allegedly in search of land and resources for Germany's farmers and industrial machine.

Le Cateau, Battle of (August 26–27, 1914), engagement after the World War I Battles of the FRONTIERS, in which British forces falling back before German armies sweeping south and west through Belgium made a stand, but after a daylong battle could not hold their positions and resumed their retreat.

Leclerc, Jacques Philippe (1902–47), French general who saw service in Africa during the interwar period, was wounded and captured during the Battle of FRANCE, and escaped to join the FREE FRENCH in London. In 1942 he led Free French forces in Central Africa; his forces then crossed the Sahara to join Allied forces in North Africa. His Second Armored Division fought in the invasion of NORMANDY; at its head, he entered Paris to take the German surrender of the city.

Lee, Jennie (1904–1988), British socialist and Labour party leader, who became the youngest member of parliament at the age of 24; she was in parliament 1928–31 and 1945–70. Throughout the post-World War II period, and until his death in 1960, she and her husband, Aneurin BEVAN, were major figures on the left in the Labour party. In 1964 she became arts minister and in 1967 chairperson of her party.

Legionnaire's disease (Legionellosis), dangerous type of pneumonia first discovered when over 180 American Legion members contracted it while attending a July 1976 convention in Philadelphia; 29 of them died. Researchers later identified the bacillus (*Legionella pneumophilia*) that caused Legionnaire's disease and—through analysis of stored samples from previous mysterious outbreaks—found that it had been around for decades at least, often harbored in ventilation systems or water tanks.

Lehi, an alternate name for the terrorist STERN GANG.

Lehman, Herbert Henry (1878–1963), U.S. investment banker, a liberal Democrat, and lieutenant governor of New York 1929–33; in 1933 he succeeded Franklin Delano ROOSEVELT as New York's governor, serving four terms. As governor, he introduced a series of reforms and public works much like those of Roosevelt's NEW DEAL, and he strongly supported Roosevelt through the

years of depression and war. In 1943 he became first director of the UNITED NATIONS RELIEF AND REHABILITATION ADMINISTRATION (UNRRA). He was a senator from New York 1949–56, throughout the MCCARTHY period, and was one of the few in the Senate who consistently opposed McCarthy and his witchhunting colleagues. After his retirement he joined Eleanor ROOSEVELT and other New York reformers in finally breaking the power of the New York City Tammany machine.

Lemaître, Georges Édouard (1894–1966), Belgian priest and astronomer who first suggested the BIG BANG THEORY of the universe's origin in 1927.

Lend-Lease, a World War II aid program authorized by the U.S. Lend-Lease Act of 1941, by which President ROOSEVELT was enabled to supply huge amounts of war materials to the ALLIES, first to Britain and then to the Soviet Union and scores of other allied countries.

Lenin, Vladimir Illich (Vladimir Illich Ulyanov; 1870–1924), chief organizer, theoretician, and leader of the BOLSHEVIK party and of the OCTOBER REVOLUTION of 1917, and head of the Soviet Union through the RUSSIAN CIVIL WAR and the early years of Soviet power; therefore, the father of the Russian Revolution and of the Soviet Union. Simultaneously, he was the leading theoretician and organizer of the world Communist movement in the 20th century and the founder of the COMMUNIST INTERNATIONAL. His brother, Alexander Ulyanov, was executed for plotting to assassinate the czar in 1887. Lenin became a Marxist while still a student, became an active member of the Russian Social-Democratic Party in 1895, and was exiled to Siberia from 1895 to 1900, in this period beginning to produce theoretical work. In 1903 he split with the majority of his party, forming its BOLSHEVIK wing. From 1907 to 1917 he led the Bolsheviks from abroad, in 1912 leading in the formation of the Russian Social-Democratic Party (Bolshevik). He opposed Russian participation in World War I, and in April 1917 returned from abroad, passing through German-held territory with a safe-conduct from German authorities eager to help him take Russia out of the war. Once again in Russia, he quickly built his party, tried and failed to set off a revolution in July, and went into hiding; but by November 7 he was able to lead the Bolsheviks to power. From then until his death in 1924 he ruled his country, through the RUSSIAN CIVIL WAR and the NEW ECONOMIC POLICY, and led the world Communist movement as well. He was physically weakened by wounds suffered during an assassination attempt in 1918, and from May 1922 was beset by a series of major illnesses.

Leningrad, Siege of (September 1941–January 1944), World War II siege of the Russian city and its 2.5 million people, beginning September 8, 1941. From then until relief of the city in 1944 only very small quantities of supplies reached the city across Lake Ladoga. Estimates of loss of life within Leningrad during the period vary widely; probably 750,000–1,000,000 died during the seige, in prolonged trench and blockhouse combat, and of illness and famine.

Lennon murder (December 8, 1980), the killing of former BEATLE John Lennon outside his home in New York City, by deranged Mark David Chapman.

Leonov, Aleksei Archipovich (1934–   ), U.S.S.R. cosmonaut who made the first SPACE WALK while on the *VOSKHOD 2* flight in March 1965.

Leopold and Loeb, 19-year-old Nathan Leopold and 18-year-old Richard Loeb, Chicago children of privilege and "thrill killers," who on May 22, 1924, murdered 14-year-old Robert Franks in Chicago. They were saved from execution by Clarence DARROW, who made a pioneering insanity plea on their behalf. Loeb was murdered in prison; Leopold was ultimately paroled in 1958.

Lesotho (Kingdom of Lesotho), until 1966 Basutoland, a Basotho (Basuto) enclave and British protectorate surrounded by South African territory. Independence and COM-MONWEALTH membership came on October 4, 1966.

Let a hundred flowers bloom, and a hundred schools of thought contend, the MAO ZEDONG quotation that generated the short-lived HUNDRED FLOWERS CAMPAIGN of 1956–57.

Letelier assassination (September 21, 1976), the Washington, DC murder of Orlando Letelier del Solar, a former official in Chile's ALLENDE government and a prominent opponent of General Augusto PINOCHET'S military dictatorship. It was widely thought to have been the work of Chilean agents. A sharp break in U.S.–Chilean relations followed Chilean refusal to extradite the former head of the Chilean secret police and two other officers, all charged in the case, and refusal even to investigate the charges in Chile.

Lévesque, René (1922–87), Canadian journalist and newscaster who became leader of the QUEBEC SEPARATIST MOVEMENT. He entered the Quebec parliament in 1960 as a Liberal, was a founder of the PARTI QUÉBECOIS in 1968, and was Quebec premier 1976–85. He left his party and premiership when his party, having failed to win majority support for separation from Canada, formally gave up separatism, as least as a current goal.

Levin, Jeremy, one of the American LEBANON HOSTAGES, CNN bureau chief, who was kidnapped on March 7, 1984, and escaped on February 14, 1986.

Lévi-Strauss, Claude Gustave (1908–   ), French anthropologist, who applied the principles of STRUCTURALISM to the study of preindustrial or "primitive" societies, postulating a single universal set of understandable principles governing the development of human behavior and societies. He has been variously described as a structural anthropologist, social anthropologist, and philosopher-anthropologist.

Lewis, John Llewellyn (1880–1969), U.S. coal miner who became a local and then a national leader of the United Mine Workers (UMW) and the AMERICAN FEDERATION OF

LABOR (AFL), and who in 1920 became president of the UMW. In 1935 he was a founder of the Committee for Industrial Organization, a group of AFL unions determined to organize industrial unions, including the unskilled. Expelled by the AFL, these unions formed the CONGRESS OF INDUSTRIAL ORGANIZATIONS (CIO); Lewis was its first president, and its leader in the massive and successful organizing efforts of the late 1930s. Lewis broke with Franklin ROOSEVELT in 1940, and with the CIO in 1942; he and his union remained independent thereafter, except for a brief reaffiliation with the AFL in 1946–47. He led his union in a series of major strikes during World War II and in the early postwar period. He survived a postwar mine seizure by the federal government that ended one strike, two federal injunctions, contempt of court citations, and large resulting fines, winning massive pay increases and pension and welfare benefits for his members. He stayed on to administer those benefits after his retirement in 1960.

Ley, Robert (1890–1945), head of the Nazi German Labor Front; he committed suicide in prison while awaiting trial for war crimes in 1945.

Leyte, Battle of (October–December 1944), major World War II U.S. landings on the Pacific island of Leyte, beginning October 22, 1944, against light resistance; at the end of the first day more than 100,000 men were ashore and beginning to move inland. In late October and early December, reinforced Japanese forces impeded the American advance, but by late December the island had been taken.

Leyte Gulf, Battle of (October 24–25, 1944), the largest naval battle of the Pacific in World War II, occurring side by side with the American invasion of LEYTE, the first step in the liberation of the Philippines. On October 24 the main remaining forces of the Japanese navy attacked huge U.S. naval concentrations in Leyte Gulf. A series of connected engagements followed, in which the Japanese lost 4 aircraft carriers, an estimated 500 airplanes, 3 battleships, and

many other vessels, effectively crippling the Japanese navy for the balance of the war. American losses were relatively light, in no way damaging the capability of the U.S. Navy.

Liaquat, Ali Khan (1895–1951), Indian Moslem lawyer who became active in the MOSLEM LEAGUE in the early 1920s, becoming a powerful figure as the League developed into the main Moslem Indian independence organization. He became first prime minister of Pakistan in 1947, remaining in that post until his assassination in October 1951.

Libby, Willard Frank (1908–80), U.S. chemist, who in 1947 developed the technique of RADIOCARBON DATING, for which he won the 1960 Nobel Prize in Chemistry. During World War II he had worked on the MANHATTAN PROJECT, at Columbia University helping to develop a gaseous method for isolating fissionable URANIUM ISOTOPES for the ATOMIC BOMB, later serving on the ATOMIC ENERGY COMMISSION (1954–59).

Liberal party, in Britain in the 19th century, the mildly reformist party of Russell, Palmerston, and Gladstone; in the early 20th century, the party of ASQUITH and LLOYD GEORGE, whose long feud enormously damaged the party. Thereafter it was a steadily diminishing force in British politics.

Liberty Bell 7, U.S. MERCURY spacecraft that put the second American into space, flown on a suborbital flight on July 21, 1961, by Virgil (Gus) GRISSOM.

Libya (Socialist People's Libyan Arab Jamahiriya), until 1912 part of the Ottoman Empire, then becoming an Italian colony until the end of World War II. Independence came on December 24, 1951, with the establishment of a monarchy; on September 1, 1969, Muammar al-QADDAFI took power in a military coup, announcing the formation of a republic, in actuality a one-party state.

Lidice (Czechoslovakia), site of a German atrocity during World War II. On June 10, 1942, the village was destroyed, and its 1200 people were murdered by the GESTAPO in reprisal for the assassination of Gestapo chief Reinhard HEYDRICH. After the war the village became a Czech national shrine.

Lie, Trygve Halvdan (1896–1968), Norwegian lawyer and government official who headed the Norwegian delegation to the founding SAN FRANCISCO CONFERENCE of the UNITED NATIONS, and was first secretary-general of the UN 1946–53. During his tenure, he faced a series of major postwar crises, including the Israeli independence movement and the beginning of the long series of Arab–Israeli conflicts, the partition of India and the conflicts that followed, a crisis in Iran, and the war in Korea, with its UN participation on the side of South Korea. In 1953 he resigned because of determined Soviet opposition to continuing tenure, returning to Norway.

Liebknecht, Karl (1871–1919), leading young socialist before World War I, who strongly opposed that war and was imprisoned 1916–18 for his opposition. The son of German Socialist Wilhelm Liebknecht, he was a founder of the Sparticist League and on his release in 1918 was a founder of the Communist party of Germany. He and Rosa LUXEMBURG led the armed SPARTACIST revolt of January 1919, were captured after failure of the revolt, and were murdered by right-wing FREIKORPS troops on January 15, 1919.

Liège, Belgian fortress that fell to the Germans on August 16, 1914, in their first victory of World War I.

Ligachev, Yegor Kuzmich (1920–   ), Soviet engineer and Communist party official, who became a member of his party's Central Committee in 1976, its secretariat in 1983, and its Politburo in 1985, at the beginning of the GORBACHEV era. A conservative, he was until mid-1988 sharply critical of Gorbachev's reform program and a potential competitor for national leadership. He lost strength in 1988, and was sidetracked within the Politburo.

Likud (Unity Party), Israeli hard-line nationalist party formed in 1973, which came

to power under the leadership of Menachim BEGIN in 1977; Begin was succeeded by Yitzhak SHAMIR in 1983.

Li Li-san (1896–1967), early Chinese Communist leader who was in 1928 leader of the COMMUNIST PARTY OF CHINA, but whose Soviet-directed policies resulted in the unsuccessful attempt to take CH'ANG-SHA and other central Chinese cities in 1930 and the subsequent flight into the mountains of western Kiangsi. He was sent to the Soviet Union in 1930, staying there until 1945 and then returning to China.

Limits of Growth, The, 1972 report, prepared by Dennis L. Meadows of the Massachusetts Institute of Technology for the CLUB OF ROME, that warned of the dangers of unchecked economic expansion, waste, pollution, and population growth. Using computer modeling, the report developed a cautionary scenario in which rapidly increasing industrial expansion and rising population could deplete natural resources, leading to a disastrous decline in ability to provide food and services for the world's population.

Lin Biao (1907–71), Chinese Communist soldier who led Red troops throughout the CHINESE CIVIL WAR and the SINO-JAPANESE WAR, and was in the final years of the civil war Communist army commander in Manchuria. In the late 1950s and 1960s, from 1959 as minister of defense, he was closely associated with MAO ZEDONG's CULTURAL REVOLUTION, and as vice-chairman of the Communist party in 1969 he was Mao's heir apparent. He died in a 1971 plane crash; the Chinese government later stated that he had been fleeing China after an unsuccessful attempt to take power.

Lindbergh, Charles Augustus (1902–74), U.S. aviator, who on May 20–21, 1927, made the first solo flight across the Atlantic, from New York to Paris, in his airplane *The Spirit of St. Louis*, instantly becoming one of the major celebrities of the century. In 1932, the kidnapping and murder of his and Anne Morrow Lindbergh's 20-month-old son, Charles, Jr., for which Bruno

HAUPTMANN was convicted, provided unwanted celebrity of a different kind. In 1936, with Alexis CARREL, he developed a pump, popularly called the Lindbergh machine, to supply blood to organs, keeping them alive outside the body; this laid the groundwork for OPEN-HEART SURGERY, organ TRANSPLANTS, and ARTIFICIAL HEARTS. During the 1930s, Lindbergh publicly expressed sympathy for the Nazi government of Germany and received a Nazi medal in 1938. In 1939 he became a leading spokesman for the isolationist AMERICA FIRST COMMITTEE, and was attacked for his pro-Nazi and anti-Semitic speeches by President Franklin D. ROOSEVELT and others. After the United States entered World War II, however, he fully supported the war effort, flying in combat.

Lindbergh kidnapping, the taking of 20-month-old Charles A. Lindbergh, Jr., from his home in Hopewell, New Jersey, on March 1, 1932. The kidnapper left a note demanding a ransom of $50,000, which was paid. Yet the kidnapper murdered the child; the body was found on May 12. Bruno Richard HAUPTMANN was convicted of the murder and was executed on April 3, 1936. From beginning to end, and long after, the case generated enormous worldwide publicity. It also generated the Lindbergh Law, in June 1932, which makes the transport of a kidnapped person across state lines a federal offense, thereby justifying the intervention of the Federal Bureau of Investigation.

linear accelerator, type of ACCELERATOR, in contrast to a circular accelerator, or CYCLOTRON.

L'Innovation department store fire (May 22, 1967), a massive fire that destroyed L'Innovation department store in Brussels, Belgium, killing 322 people.

Lin Piao, the old-style name of Chinese leader LIN BIAO.

Lion of Kashmir, the popular name for Sheikh Mohammad Abdullah, Kashmiri independence leader.

Li Peng (1928–   ), Chinese political leader, from childhood a protégé of ZHOU ENLAI; he rose slowly and steadily through the Chinese party bureaucracy until reaching cabinet level as vice-minister of power in 1979, then becoming power minister in 1981. He became a Politburo member in 1985 and succeeded ZHAO ZIYANG as prime minister in 1987, Zhao remaining head of the Communist party. In the late 1980s, he emerged as a leader of the conservative wing of Chinese communism, defeating Zhao Ziyang and the liberal wing of his party in the spring of 1989, during the crisis generated by the CHINESE STUDENT DEMONSTRATIONS OF 1989.

Lippman, Walter (1889–1974), U.S. journalist, editor, writer, and political philosopher, who became a highly influential political analyst and widely read columnist through his syndicated "Today and Tomorrow" column in the *New York Herald Tribune* (1931–67), and through his many books. An independent, he strongly supported and was an adviser to Woodrow WILSON during and after World War I. He later criticized many NEW DEAL programs and opposed MCCARTHYISM, and the wars in Korea and Vietnam.

Li Ta-chao (1888–1927), Peking University librarian and Marxist theoretician who became, with CH'EN TU-HSIU, co-founder of the COMMUNIST PARTY OF CHINA and who deeply influenced the thinking of MAO ZEDONG and other Chinese Communist leaders. He was killed by order of warlord CHANG TSO-LIN after being taken from the Soviet embassy in Peking.

Lithuania, from the late 18th century, split between Russia and Prussia, the major portion of the country becoming a Russian Baltic province. Lithuania won its freedom in the LITHUANIAN WAR OF INDEPENDENCE (1918–20), but was reoccupied by the Soviet Union in 1940, as provided in the NAZI-SOVIET PACT. During the GORBACHEV era, powerful independence movements arose in all three Baltic Soviet Republics; in early 1990, the issues had not yet been resolved.

Lithuanian War of Independence (1918–20), conflict that developed as part of the RUSSIAN CIVIL WAR and the SOVIET–POLISH WAR. Lithuania declared its independence on February 16, 1918; in response Soviet troops entered the former Russian Baltic province but were expelled by the occupying German army. After the World War I armistice German troops withdrew, and Soviet troops reentered the country; in January they occupyied Vilna, claimed by Poland, which drew Poland into the war. Independence was formally recognized by the Treaty of Moscow in July 1920.

Little Entente, a mutual assistance alliance, from 1920 through the mid-1930s, among Yugoslavia, Czechoslovakia, and Rumania, informally affiliated with France. After HITLER'S accession to power in Germany the entente weakened, as Yugoslavia and Rumania sought accommodation with Germany and Italy. The alliance failed completely in 1937, when Yugoslavia and Rumania refused to support Czechoslovakia against German aggression.

Little Steel Massacre (Memorial Day Massacre), the killing of 10 striking steelworkers by Chicago police on Memorial Day 1937, during the Little Steel strike of that year. Although United States Steel and several other major steel companies had recognized the steelworkers' union earlier in the year, Republic Steel and several smaller companies did not; they defeated the union in the resulting strike, thereby successfully resisting organization until 1941.

Litvinov, Maksim Maksimovich (1876–1951), Soviet diplomat, an old BOLSHEVIK who was first Soviet representative to Great Britain, and became foreign minister in 1930. Throughout the 1930s, he tried to develop collective security agreements against the growing threat of Nazi Germany. He was dismissed in 1939, possibly because he was Jewish and the Soviets were in the process of concluding the NAZI–SOVIET PACT. He was reactivated during World II, and was Soviet ambassador to the United States from 1941 to 1943.

Liu Shao-chi, the old-style name of Chinese leader LIU SHAOQI.

Liu Shaoqi (Liu Shao-chi; 1899–1969), leading Chinese Communist theoretician who became chairman of the PEOPLE'S REPUBLIC OF CHINA in 1959 and was therefore MAO ZEDONG'S heir apparent. However, he was attacked by Mao's followers during the CULTURAL REVOLUTION, lost all of his official positions in 1968, and died in prison a year later. He was posthumously rehabilitated during the DENG era.

Liuzzo, Viola Gregg, Detroit civil rights activist shot and killed in Selma, Alabama, on March 25, 1965, while participating in a voter registration drive. Three KU KLUX KLAN members were later imprisoned for conspiring in her murder.

Live Aid, the July 13, 1985, telethon for African relief, with marathon concerts in London and New York. It had been preceded by a 6-month campaign for African relief that began with the writing and taping of the Michael Jackson/Lionel Ritchie song "We Are the World," which became a best-seller. All profits went to the relief fund, including those from a record album and from the concerts, which were seen by more than one billion people throughout the world.

Lleras Camargo, Alberto (1906–   ), Colombian political leader, twice president of Colombia (1945–46; 1958–62), who in his second presidency finally ended LA VIOLENCIA with an imaginative Liberal–Conservative alternate presidency agreement. He was the first secretary-general of the ORGANIZATION OF AMERICAN STATES (OAS) 1948–54.

Lloyd George, David (1863–1945), British solicitor and Welsh Liberal party leader, in Parliament 1890–1945, who served in several cabinet-level posts before and during the early years of World War I and became wartime coalition prime minister in 1916. As prime minister, he played a major role in winning the war, at the PARIS PEACE CONFERENCE of 1919, and in 1921 negotiations to end the IRISH WAR OF INDEPENDENCE.

Locarno, Treaty of (October 5–16, 1925), a group of related treaties signed by France, Great Britain, Germany, and several other European countries, guaranteeing that German borders with Belgum and France would remain as set by the Treaty of VERSAILLES, and pledging continued demilitarization of the RHINELAND. The Locarno treaties were abrogated by Germany on reoccupation of the Rhineland in 1936.

Lochner v. *New York* (1905), a landmark U.S. Supreme Court decision invalidating a New York law that limited bakers' to a 10-hour day and a 60-hour week, as a violation of the Fourteenth Amendment's federal guarantee of freedom of contract.

Lockerbie aircraft bombing (December 21, 1988), detonation of an explosive device aboard a Pan Am 747 jet bound for the United States, killing all 259 people aboard. The plane's remnants fell on the town of Lockerbie, Scotland, killing at least 11 others on the ground. Islamic extremists claimed "credit" for the action.

Lockheed scandal, the 1975 international scandal that broke when a congressional investigation revealed that the U.S. Lockheed Corporation had, for at least 17 years, been routinely and massively bribing influential figures in many countries to gain their support for aircraft purchases. Although the investigation was widely publicized in the United States, no indictments resulted. Massive scandals did result in several other countries, the most notable leading to the forced resignation and later conviction of Japanese prime minister Kakuei TANAKA.

Lodge, Henry Cabot (1850–1924), U.S. diplomat, political leader, and author, a Massachusetts Republican congressman (1887–93) and senator (1893–1924). Lodge was a conservative who favored American entry into World War I, while opposing the domestic reforms and international policies of the WILSON administration. After World War I he successfully led the opposition to U.S. membership in the LEAGUE OF NATIONS, and played a major role in the nomi-

nation of Warren G. HARDING and the defeat of Woodrow Wilson in 1920.

Lodge, Henry Cabot (1902–85), U.S. political leader, the grandson of Senator Henry Cabot LODGE. He was a Massachusetts Republican senator (1937–43; 1947–53), losing his seat to John F. KENNEDY. He was U.S. ambassador to the UNITED NATIONS (1953–60), and in 1960 was unsuccessful Republican vice-presidential candidate on the NIXON ticket. He became ambassador to South Vietnam in 1963, left to try unsuccessfully for the Republican presidential nomination in 1964, became South Vietnam ambassador again (1965–67), ambassador to the Federal Republic of Germany in 1968, and chief Vietnam peace negotiator during 1969.

Lodz, Battle of (November 11–25, 1914), World War I battle in which Russian armies in western Poland, moving toward Silesia and East Prussia, were stopped by smaller German forces, with Russian casualties totaling an estimated 90,000–100,000 men. After Lodz, the Russians withdrew from Silesia, back into Russian-occupied Poland.

Loewe v. *Lawlor* (1908), a landmark U.S. Supreme Court case better known as the DANBURY HATTERS' CASE.

Lombardo Toledano, Vicente (1894–1968), Mexican labor leader, a Marxist who founded the Confederation of Mexican Workers (CTM) in 1936 and led it until 1941 and who closely collaborated with President Lazaro CARDENAS during 1934–40 in developing Mexico's radical reforms of that period. He was a founder of the International Confederation of Latin American Workers in 1936 and of the Popular Party in 1948, which in 1960 became the Popular Socialist party; and an unsuccessful presidential candidate in 1952.

London, Treaty of (1913), agreement ending the first of the two BALKAN WARS.

Long, Huey Pierce (1893–1935), governor and political boss of Louisiana in the late 1920s and early 1930s, who was assassinated at Baton Rouge, Louisiana, on September 8, 1935, by Dr. Carl Weiss; Weiss was then killed by Long's bodyguards. Long was a powerful Southern politician who had consolidated his hold on Louisiana after successfully fighting impeachment charges in 1929, and had developed presidential ambitions. His political machine survived him, making his brother, Earl Long, governor of Louisiana three times between 1939 and 1960.

Long March, the very difficult long retreat of the Chinese Communist armies after their defeat by KUOMINTANG forces in Kiangsi in 1934. Their route led west and then north through mountain country to Shensi, a distance of 2,500–3,000 miles; but they were in battle with Kuomintang forces much of the way and reportedly marched 6,000 miles during the course of the entire action. Most of the leaders of the COMMUNIST government that took power in 1949 made the march, including MAO ZEDONG, ZHOU ENLAI, and ZHU DE. Of the approximately 200,000 who began the march, an estimated 30,000–50,000 completed it.

Longo, Luigi (1900–80), Italian Communist leader, a founder of the Italian Communist party in 1921 and a leading Communist of the interwar period, who fought in the SPANISH CIVIL WAR with the INTERNATIONAL BRIGADES. He spent the early years of World War II in an Italian prison, and led partisan units in northern Italy late in the war. During the postwar period he was second to Palmiro TOGLIATTI in the Italian Communist party, and party leader 1964–72, a period in which he advocated a course independent of the Soviet Union.

Lon Nol (1913–85), Cambodian administrator and officer, prime minister (1966–67; 1969–70), who deposed Prince Norodom SIHANOUK as head of state in 1970, and set up a republic with himself at its head. Despite U.S. military support, his forces lost the CAMBODIAN CIVIL WAR to the KHMER ROUGE Communist army; in April 1975 he fled into exile.

Lorenz, Konrad Zacharias (1903–89), Austrian zoologist and psychiatrist; in the 1930s, he and Nikolaas TINBERGEN founded ethology, the scientific study of animal behavior, for which they (and Karl von Frisch) shared the 1973 Nobel Prize for Physiology or Medicine. He made famous the process called imprinting, by which newborn animals show patterns of behavior determined by their genetic makeup and earliest experiences, demonstrated when his favorite greylag geese responded to Lorenz as children to a parent. His *On Aggression* (1966) expressed the controversial view that some human behavior, such as aggression, is inherited.

Lorraine, Battle of (August 14–20, 1914), one of the World War I Battles of the FRONTIERS, in which French forces, in their first major offensive of the war, pushed into Alsace-Lorraine with initial success, but were thrown back by the Germany army.

Los Alamos, U.S. national laboratory in New Mexico, where the first ATOMIC BOMBS were designed and built, 1942–45, as part of the MANHATTAN PROJECT.

Los Angeles Times bombing (October 1, 1910), explosion at the *Los Angeles Times*, killing 21 *Times* employees and injuring many more. Union leaders John J. and James B. MCNAMARA were charged with the crime, along with a confederate who testified against them. Labor saw the case as an attack on the whole labor movement, and a worldwide campaign was begun to free the McNamaras, with Clarence DARROW hired to defend them. Harrison Gray Otis, *Times* publisher, brought in detective William J. Burns, who claimed to find conclusive evidence against the McNamaras. Darrow saw the case as hopeless and pleaded his clients guilty in an attempt to save their lives; the attempt succeeded, James McNamara getting a life sentence and John McNamara a 15-year sentence. But the labor movement was outraged, refused to pay Darrow's fee, and refused to support Darrow when he was then twice charged with attempted bribery of jurors. Darrow was exonerated on both charges.

Love Canal, site near Niagara Falls, New York, found in the late 1970s to have been poisoned by decades of TOXIC WASTE DUMP-ING, including DIOXIN, by local chemical plants; health and environmental problems multiplied in the area and most of its residents were forced to move away to preserve what remained of their health. After considerable resistance from federal agencies and lawsuits against the Hooker Chemical Company, Occidental Petroleum (which had acquired Hooker) in 1983 settled long-standing lawsuits, compensating current and former residents of the area. During the 1980s New York State razed most of the structures in the area. The question of possible chemical contamination of much of the Niagara Falls area, as alleged by some, remained to be fully addressed.

Lowell, Percival (1855–1916), U.S. astronomer, member of the Massachusetts Lowell family and founder of the Lowell Observatory in Flagstaff, Arizona, who in 1905 predicted the existence of an unknown planet beyond Neptune. It was discovered in 1930 by U.S. astronomer Clyde William TOMBAUGH, and named PLUTO.

loyalty oaths, a U.S. COLD WAR phenomenon, most evident from 1947, when President Harry S. TRUMAN required a loyalty check of all federal employees and the firing of any deemed subversive. During the following decade such a disclaimer of Communist affiliation was required of many millions of Americans as a condition of securing or keeping employment, trade union position, and/or passports, as well as in a number of other connections. During the period of national revulsion against MC-CARTHYISM, beginning in the mid-1950s, the loyalty oath practice diminished, although in some areas remaining officially in force for decades.

LSD (lysergic acid diethylamide), HALLUCI-NOGENIC DRUG popular in the 1960s, its PSYCHEDELIC properties first discovered in 1943 by a Swiss chemist who accidentally ingested some. Over the next two decades many health professionals explored the use of LSD, searching for a natural biochemical cause of schizophrenia. But by the mid-1960s it was clear that in some people LSD could lead to severe panic, permanent psychosis, or even suicide. In 1967 LSD was found to cause genetic damage, increasing the rate of chromosome-breaking in users. As a result, from then on LSD was largely a restricted drug, though still sought on the black market.

Luan Shu-meng, alternate, old-style name of Chinese leader JIANG QING, the wife of MAO ZEDONG, who was in 1981 convicted of being the leader of the GANG OF FOUR.

Luce, Henry Robinson (1898–1967), U.S. magazine publisher, who with Briton Hadden in 1923 founded *Time* magazine, thereafter using that very successful publication as a base for his wholly-owned Time, Inc., and initiating several other high-circulation magazines, such as *Life* and *Fortune*. He later controlled several other communications companies. A political conservative, he was particularly active as a leading anti-Communist during the MCCARTHY period.

Luciano, Charles "Lucky" (1897–1962), a leader of organized crime in the United States during the 1930s, and a chief organizer of the national crime syndicate controlled by the MAFIA. He was successfully prosecuted by District Attorney Thomas E. Dewey in 1936, but his 30–50 year sentence was commuted in 1946 for service to the United States during World War II; he was then deported to Italy.

Ludendorff, Erich (1865–1937), Prussian general, active in German preparation for World War I. His forces scored the first major German victory of the war, taking the fortress of Liège, Belgium, on August 14, 1914. He spent most of the war on the Eastern Front, as General Paul von HINDEN-BURG's chief of staff. In 1916, when von Hindenburg became chief of the German general staff, Ludendorff became his quartermaster general. He was an early supporter of Adolf HITLER, but later backed away somewhat.

Lufthansa robbery (December 11, 1978), the robbery at the Lufthansa Airlines cargo warehouse at New York City's Kennedy Airport; the largest robbery in U.S. history, realizing $5.85 million. The robbery remains largely unsolved.

Lujan, Manuel Jr. (1928–   ), U.S. political leader, a long-term New Mexico Republican congressman 1969–89, who on December 22, 1988, was named secretary of the interior by President George BUSH.

Luminous Path, an alternate name for the Peruvian SHINING PATH guerrilla army.

Lumumba, Patrice (1925–61), Congolese nationalist who founded the Congolese National Movement in 1958, and who on June 30, 1960 became coalition prime minister of the first independent Congo (Zaire) government. When insurrection immediately developed, including the Belgian-supported Katanga secession, he sought help from the Soviet Union and was dismissed by President Joseph KASAVUBU. He fled after a military coup led by General Joseph MOBUTU, but was imprisoned and then murdered in January 1961 by the secessionist Katanga government led by Moîse TSHOMBE.

Lunar Orbiter, series of U.S. unmanned spacecraft exploring for possible landing sites on the MOON in the 1960s, preparatory to the APOLLO flights.

lunatic fringe, phrase coined by U.S. president Theodore ROOSEVELT in his *Autobiography* (1913); from "the lunatic fringe in all reform movements."

Lunik, series of U.S.S.R. satellites launched toward the Moon, starting in 1959. *Lunik 2,* the first to reach the Moon, made a "hard" or crash landing on September 14, 1959; *Lunik 3,* launched on October 4, 1959, first photographed the Moon's far side on a flyby; *Lunik 9* made a soft landing on the Moon on February 3, 1966; *Lunik 10* first orbited the Moon on April 4, 1966; and *Lunik 19,* launched September 12, 1970, landed a remote-controlled roving vehicle on the Moon's surface.

***Lusitania,* sinking of** (May 7, 1915), World War I attack in which the British liner *Lusitania* was torpedoed without warning by a German U-20 submarine off the Irish coast; 1,198 died, 128 of them Americans. The British successfully denied that the ship was carrying munitions as well as passengers; the sinking aroused great anger in the United States and contributed to later American entry into World War I.

Luthuli, Albert John (1898–1967), South African Zulu chief, teacher, and leader of the South African nonviolence movement, who, after many years of work in the AFRICAN NATIONAL CONGRESS, became its president in 1952. He was unsuccessfully prosecuted for treason by the South African government in 1956, generating a worldwide protest, and was in his later years placed in internal exile. One of the world's leading advocates of nonviolence, he received the Nobel Peace Prize in 1960.

Luxemburg, Rosa (1871–1919), Polish socialist activist and theoretician who became a founder of the Polish Social Democratic party, the Polish Communist party, the German Spartacist League, and the Communist party of Germany. She was active in Warsaw during the RUSSIAN REVOLUTION of 1905 and was afterward imprisoned; she was imprisoned again in Germany in 1916, for opposing World War I. With Karl LIEBKNECHT, she led the failed SPARTICIST revolt of January 1919; when captured, they were both murdered by right-wing FREIKORPS troops on January 15, 1919.

Lyme disease, tick-borne bacterial disease that can cause arthritis and serious neurological and cardiological problems. Though its effects were known in Europe from the 19th century and in the United States from at least the mid-1960s, it was not recognized as a disease until 1976, when Allen Steere and a Yale medical team were alerted by a mother in Lyme, Connecticut, to the unusual incidence of arthritis in a nearby wooded area. The bacteria responsible, *Borrelia burgdorferi,* carried by deer ticks, was isolated 6 years later by Willy Burgdorfer. Lyme disease responds to various ANTIBIOTICS, but is often mistaken for flu and untreated. By the 1980s the disease had spread to most parts of the United States, occurring in epidemic proportions in the Northeast.

Lynd, Robert Staughton (1892–1970), and **Helen Merrell Lynd** (1894–1982), U.S. sociologists who did classic studies of middle-class America, described in their books *Middletown* (1929) and *Middletown in Transition* (1937); these were based on Muncie, Indiana, but passed into popular culture as an anthropological portrait of middle America in general.

Lys Offensive (April 9–29, 1918), the second of five major German offensives in 1918, all of them aimed at winning World War I with the help of the Eastern Front troops freed by Soviet withdrawal from the war. German forces attacked British armies in Flanders, seeking to break through to take the Channel ports, but failed in the attempt.

Lysenko, Trofim Denisovich (1898–1976), Soviet agriculturalist and geneticist who fiercely supported the Lamarckian view of the inheritance of acquired characteristics against the scientifically supported view of inheritance put forward by Gregor Mendel and Thomas Hunt MORGAN. In 1929 Lysenko purported to have found a way to modify plants so that the changes would be passed on to later generations. When other scientists could not reproduce his supposed results, he attacked GENETICS and geneticists, denying that the GENE existed and taking refuge in political oratory. From 1935, with support from STALIN, Lysenko gradually purged from Soviet scientific research all of those who disagreed with him, sidetracking Soviet genetics and agricultural science onto a dead-end path for over 20 years; he lost power only after 1956, though remaining director of the Institute of Genetics until 1965. During this time not only did the Russians lose the benefits of possible biological research but farmers were required to plant crops according to his nonscientific methods, making Lysenko responsible to a large degree for the failure of the U.S.S.R.'s farmlands to feed its people.

Lytton Commission, the LEAGUE OF NATIONS commission that declared Japan an aggressor nation after its invasion of Manchuria in 1931. Japan withdrew from the League of Nations and continue to hold Manchuria until the end of World War II.

M

MacArthur, Douglas (1880–1964), U.S. army officer, son of General Arthur MacArthur, who saw service as a divisional commander in World War I and during the interwar period was army chief of staff (1930–35). In 1932 he commanded the military forces that violently ejected the war veteran BONUS MARCHERS from their Washington, DC, encampment at Anacostia Flats. He resigned from the U.S. Army in 1937 while American commander in the Philippines, staying on to command Philippine army forces. Rejoining the U.S. Army, he became Philippines combined forces commander in July 1941. His forces unsuccessfully opposed the Japanese invasion of the Philippines during World War II, and he was evacuated in February 1942, becoming commander for the Allied Southwest Pacific. He led Allied forces retaking the Philippines in 1944–45, became a five-star general, and personally took the formal Japanese surrender in Tokyo harbor on September 2, 1945. After serving as Allied commander of postwar Japanese occupation forces, he was named commander of UNITED NATIONS forces at the outbreak of the KOREAN WAR. By November 1950 his forces had reached the YALU River, the border between North Korea and China, there to be met by a major Chinese counterattack and the entry of China into the war. President Harry TRUMAN refused MacArthur's call for the bombing of China, and MacArthur publicly disagreed; as a result he was dismissed from command in April 1951. Although he then became a major focus of political opposition, he did not attempt to move into elected office; instead he retired from public life.

McAuliffe, Anthony (1898–1975), U.S. officer who commanded the 101st Airborne Division, besieged at BASTOGNE during the Battle of the BULGE in December 1944. On December 22 his classic response to a German surrender ultimatum was "NUTS!"

McAuliffe, Sharon Christa, Concord, New Hampshire, social studies teacher selected to be the first teacher in space; she died with six astronauts in the *CHALLENGER* explosion, on January 28, 1986.

MacBride, Seán (1904–88), Irish Republican leader, the only son of Maud Gonne and John MacBride, a Republican soldier executed after the EASTER RISING. While still a youth, he fought in the IRISH WAR OF INDEPENDENCE and the IRISH CIVIL WAR, becoming a leader of the outlawed Irish Republican Army (IRA) in the late 1920s. In the late 1930s he left the IRA and practiced law, in part as an IRA defense lawyer. He organized a new party and went into electoral politics after World War II; he became Irish foreign minister in the 1948 coalition government, but left Irish politics in 1957 after a series of defeats. In 1963 he became secretary-general of the International Commission of Jurists, a human rights organization, from then on focusing on human rights and disarmament questions. In 1974 he received the Nobel Peace Prize; in 1977, the Lenin Peace Prize.

McCarran Internal Security Act (1950), U.S. law requiring registration of all Communist and Communist-front groups and their members; it denied passports and government or defense industry employment to members of such groups, prohibited similarly affiliated aliens from gaining admittance and citizenship, and empowered the federal government to set up detention camps in case of war. President Harry S. TRUMAN vetoed the bill; it was passed over his veto during the anti-Communist hysteria of the MCCARTHY period.

McCarthy, Eugene Joseph (1916–   ), U.S. teacher and poet, a Minnesota Democratic congressman (1949–59) and senator (1959–71). A VIETNAM WAR opponent, he campaigned for the Democratic presidential nomination in 1967–68, ultimately losing the nomination to Hubert H. HUMPHREY at the violence-filled CHICAGO DEMOCRATIC CONVENTION OF 1968. His independent presidential candidacy of 1976 had little impact.

McCarthy, Joseph Raymond (1908–57), U.S. lawyer and Wisconsin senator (1947–57). From February 1950 through April 1954 McCarthy was the leading witchhunter of his time, his name ultimately supplying a new pejorative word to the English language: "MCCARTHYISM." He began his brief but powerful assault on American democracy on February 9, 1950, with a speech falsely charging that there were 205 card-carrying Communists in the state department, and continued in the same vein thereafter. His career essentially ended at the televised ARMY-MCCARTHY HEARINGS of April 1954, in which U.S. Army attorney Joseph WELCH effectively exposed and ruined McCarthy. But for more than 3 years McCarthy and such assistants as Roy COHN enjoyed huge influence and great popular support, attacking and vilifying a wide range of imagined subversives and traitors, in the process ruining a good many careers and tainting the "McCarthy period" in U.S. history. He was censured by the Senate in December 1954.

McCarthyism, synonym for witchhunting aimed at alleged subversives during the 1950s, named after Senator Joseph MCCARTHY; later the term kept that meaning, while also becoming an epithet aimed at anyone engaged in the reckless public vilification of others.

McCloy, John Jay (1895–1989), U.S. lawyer, an assistant secretary of war 1941–45, president of the International Bank for Reconstruction and Development 1947–49, and U.S. high commissioner for Germany 1949–52. As high commissioner, he played a major COLD WAR role in preserving and encouraging the rebuilding of West German industry, and in encouraging West German rearmament. He was chairman of the Chase Manhattan Bank from 1953 to 1960, and continued to advise several successive American presidents on foreign policy matters through the 1970s.

MacDonald, James Ramsay (1866–1937), moderate British socialist who was active in organizing the Labour Representation Committee in 1900, was elected to Parliament in 1906 as the committee formed itself into the Labour party, and became leader of his party in 1911. He lost his leadership and much of his support, and in 1918 his seat in the House of Commons, for supposedly not supporting World War I strongly enough. He was reelected in 1922 and became the first Labour prime minister, for 10 months in 1924. In 1929 he again became Labour prime minister but faced a loss of power in August 1931, given the tremendous economic problems of the GREAT DEPRESSION. To hold power he then converted his government into a coalition government dominated by Conservatives—much against the wishes of most of those in the Labour party, who viewed him as a traitor—continuing in office until 1935.

MacDonald murders (February 17, 1970), the killings of Colette MacDonald and her two daughters, in which army doctor and Green Beret captain Jeffrey MacDonald was slightly injured, in their Fort Bragg, North Carolina, home. MacDonald claimed that intruders had committed the murders and that his injuries were the result of his struggle with them. He was not believed, was court-martialed by the U.S. Army later that year, then exonerated and honorably discharged. But Colette MacDonald's stepfather, at first his defender, later came to believe him guilty and had the case reopened. MacDonald was indicted in 1975, convicted of murder in 1979, and sentenced to three consecutive life-imprisonment terms.

McDonald's Restaurant massacre (July 18, 1984), the killing of 21 people, most of them children, at a San Ysidro, California, McDonald's Restaurant, the worst mass murder on a single day in U.S. history. The killer was James Oliver Huberty, a security guard who had been fired. The restaurant was quickly razed and left as a memorial to the dead.

McDougall, William (1871–1938), English-American psychologist, whose views on EUGENICS—notably the supposed superiority of the "Nordic race"—as expressed in his 1921 work *Is America Safe for Democracy?*, caused a firestorm of criticism, as did his belief in the inheritance of acquired characteristics. He had earlier done key work in psychophysics, proposing that intellectual operations are carried out through a network of neural circuits.

McFarlane, Robert Carl (1937–   ), U.S. naval officer, military assistant to Henry KISSINGER in the White House, 1973–75; special assistant to the president for national security affairs in the White House, 1975–77; and on the staff of the Senate Armed Services Committee, 1979–81, after his resignation from the Marine Corps. In 1981 he became a state department counselor and then deputy assistant for national security affairs in the White House; he succeeded William Clark as national security adviser in October 1983, resigning in December 1985 after implication in the IRAN–CONTRA AFFAIR. In March 1988 he pleaded guilty to having withheld information from House and Senate Iran–Contra investigation committees, and during 1989 was a witness at subsequent related trials.

McGovern, George Stanley (1922–   ), U.S. political leader, South Dakota congressman 1957–61, and head of John F. KENNEDY'S Food for Peace program, 1961–62. Elected to the Senate in 1962, he soon became an opponent of the VIETNAM WAR and a leader of the liberal wing of the Democratic party. He won his party's presidential nomination in 1972, suffering a serious early blow when he decided to drop his running mate, Senator Thomas EAGLETON, because of previously undisclosed potential psychiatric problems; he went on to lose in what became a NIXON landslide, winning only Massachusetts and the District of Columbia. He lost his Senate seat in the 1980 election, and unsuccessfully sought his party's 1984 presidential nomination.

McKinley, William (1843–1901), U.S. lawyer, an Ohio Republican congressman (1877–91), and twice governor of Ohio (1892–96), who became the 25th president of the United States (1897–1901), the first American president of the 20th century. In 1896 and again in 1900 he defeated Democrat William Jennings BRYAN for the presidency. During his first term he led the United States into the Spanish-American War, followed by the occupation of Cuba and the Philippines and the annexation of Puerto Rico. His adminstration then faced a major insurrection in the Philippines led by Emile AGUINALDO. He also sent U.S. troops into China during the BOXER REBELLION; they participated in the relief of the besieged foreign legations in Peking. A fiscal conservative, McKinley was largely responsible for establishing stronger tariff barriers, and in 1900 he succeeded in placing the United States on the gold standard, rather than the more expansionist silver or silver-and-gold standard favored by the Democrats. Early in his second term, on September 6, 1901, he was shot by anarchist Leon CZOLGOSZ in Buffalo, New York. He died in that city on September 14, and was succeeded by his vice-president, Theodore ROOSEVELT.

McKissick, Floyd (1922–   ), U.S. lawyer and civil rights leader who was national chairman of the CONGRESS OF RACIAL EQUALITY (CORE), 1966–68, in that period favoring a move away from nonviolence and calling for BLACK POWER.

Maclean, Donald (1913–83), British diplomat and spy, who was exposed in 1951 as actually having been a Soviet spy since his Cambridge days in the 1930s, along with his college friends and Soviet espionage network colleagues Kim PHILBY and Guy BURGESS. Burgess and Maclean escaped to the Soviet Union in 1951, thereafter continuing to work in Soviet intelligence.

McLuhan, Herbert Marshall (1911–80), Canadian literary professor and communications theorist, who posited that the rise of the ELECTRONIC media, especially TELEVISION, had transformed a previously atomized world culture into one great interconnected "global village," and that the printed word in book form would gradually disappear. His views on television were made popular by his 1967 book (with Quentin Fiore), *The Medium Is the Message.*

Macmillan, Maurice Harold (1894–1986), British publisher who became a leading Conservative; in Parliament 1924–29 and 1931–64. He opposed APPEASEMENT in the late 1930s and was a member of Winston CHURCHILL'S wartime cabinet, responsible for Mediterranean and southeastern European political affairs from 1942 until 1945. In later years he was criticized by opponents for allegedly having too easily acquiesced to the repatriation of displaced persons to Soviet-bloc nations. He held several cabinet-level positions before succeeding Anthony EDEN as prime minister in 1957, holding that office until his resignation in 1963. The PROFUMO AFFAIR further damaged his weakening Conservative government, which was then supplanted by the second postwar Labour government.

McNamara, Robert Strange (1916–   ), president of Ford Motor Company who became U.S. secretary of defense (1961–68), and as such was deeply involved in the succession of steps that drew the United States into the VIETNAM WAR. During 1965 he developed grave doubts about U.S. war strategy, in particular the bombing of North Vietnam, and by 1967 had come to oppose continued expansion of American involvement. In 1968 he resigned to become president of the WORLD BANK.

McNamara brothers, California labor leaders John J. and James B. McNamara, who pleaded guilty of having committed the LOS ANGELES TIMES BOMBING of 1910, as advised by their lawyer, Clarence DARROW.

Mach, ratio of the speed of an object to the speed of sound in the medium it is traveling through, so a craft traveling at the speed of sound is at Mach 1, and SUPERSONIC TRANSPORT traveling at twice the speed of sound is at Mach 2.

Machel, Samora (1933–86), Mozambique independence movement leader who joined Eduardo MONDLANE in FRELIMO in 1963 and in 1964 commanded guerrilla forces at the start of the long MOZAMBIQUE WAR OF INDEPENDENCE. He became leader of FRELIMO in 1970, after Mondlane's assassination by the Portuguese in 1969, and first president of independent Mozambique in 1975. A Marxist, he developed a one-party FRELIMO-dominated Socialist state, heavily supported by the Soviet Union. But economic problems and an increasingly successful continuing insurgency, supported by South Africa, caused him to moderate previous positions. Mozambique signed a nonaggression treaty with South Africa in 1984, and sought WORLD BANK loans and private investment. Machel died in a 1986 airplane crash.

Machu Picchu, long-lost Inca stronghold high in the Peruvian Andes, rediscovered by U.S. explorer Hiram BINGHAM in 1911, and later a major tourist attraction.

Mackle, Barbara Jane, American woman kidnapped on December 17, 1968, in Atlanta, Georgia, by Gary Steven Krist and Ruth Eisenmann-Schier. She was then buried alive in a shallow grave and found alive on December 20, after her $500,000 ransom was paid. Her kidnappers were captured, and most of the ransom was recovered; Krist was imprisoned for life, Eisenmann-Schier for 7 years.

Madagascar (Democratic Republic of Madagascar), until 1958 a French colony, then the autonomous Malagasy Republic. Full independence came on June 30, 1960, and the country's present name was adopted in 1975.

Madero, Francisco Indalécio (1873–1913), Mexican landowner and liberal, who ran for the Mexican presidency against Porforio DÍAZ in 1910; he was arrested before the election, and Díaz then declared himself the winner. Madero jumped bail and escaped to Texas, where he organized the armed revolt that became the MEXICAN REVOLUTION, bringing him to the presidency in October 1911. By early 1913, he had been accused of going too slowly on such matters as land reform and the condition of the poor; and many of his former supporters, including Emiliano ZAPATA, had risen against him, beginning the long civil war that was intertwined with the revolution. In February his own Mexico City garrison, led by Victoriano HUERTA, took power in a coup. Madero was assassinated by Huerta's forces on February 22, 1913.

Madrid, Siege of (November 1936–March 1939), the 28-month-long attack on Madrid by fascist Spanish, German, and Italian ground and air forces during the SPANISH CIVIL WAR.

Mafia, in Sicily, a centuries-old group of allied secret criminal societies, organized essentially along feudal lines; in the 20th century, they have developed the power to resist sucessfully many Italian government attempts to break them up or reduce their power. In the United States, the Mafia was a similar but independent set of organizations, developed by a few early Italian immigrants from the 1880s on, which proved equally resistant to public control. Until the late 1920s, these were Italian-American Mafia organizations; after the Castellammarese intra-Mafia factional war of that period and the advent of the far better organized and controlled national crime syndicate, which was in part also multiethnic, the term *Mafia* became in practice synonymous with such terms as "the Syndicate," "the Organization," and Cosa Nostra (Our Thing).

Magellan, U.S. space probe launched on a 15-month, 795-million-mile voyage toward VENUS in May 1989, the first such craft to be released from a SPACE SHUTTLE, the *ATLANTIS*, and due to reach its target in August 1990. In a sign of easing superpower relations, U.S.S.R. space scientists shared with their U.S. counterparts data from their earlier Venus probes, in preparation for the *Magellan* probe.

MAGIC, World War II code name for the long U.S. effort to break a series of secret Japanese codes, which succeeded to great effect before the Battle of MIDWAY, deeply affecting the outcome of that decisive battle of the Pacific war.

magic bullet, popular name for Paul EHRLICH'S arsenic treatment for SYPHILIS, developed in 1910.

Maginot Line, a huge system of French fortifications on the French-German border, built in the 1930s, in place at the beginning of World War II, and relied on by France to stop a German invasion with minimum casualties. Named after André Maginot, a key initiator, the Line provided only an illusion of safety, for it was never extended to the sea; in May 1940 the German army went right around it into the lightly defended ARDENNES, there making the breakthrough near Sedan that led to the fall of France.

magnetic recording tape, magnetized tape to record sounds or signals for later reproduction, first used during World War II by the Germans to make TAPE RECORDINGS.

magnetic resonance imager (MRI), alternate name for the NMR IMAGER.

Magsaysay, Ramón (1907–57), Filipino World War II anti-Japanese guerrilla leader who went into politics after the war, serving as Philippines defense minister 1950–53 and in that position playing a key role in the defeat of the Communist-led HUKBALAHAP insurgency. He became president of the Philippines in 1953, and was killed in an airplane crash in 1957.

Ma Haide, the Chinese name of George HATEM, American public health doctor who joined the Chinese Communist movement in the late 1930s and stayed on for half a century, becoming a leading public health doctor in China and throughout the world.

Mahathir bin Mohamad, Datuk Seri (1925–), Malaysian physician, in parliament 1964–69 and again from 1974, who was minister of education in 1974, deputy prime minister 1976–81, then prime minister from 1981.

Mahdi, Sadiq al- (1936–), Sudanese political leader and prime minister of the Sudan from 1986; he was a great-grandson of Muhammad Ahmad ibn as-Sayyid 'Abd Allah, the Mahdi who in the 1880s led the successful Sudanese revolt against Egyptian-British rule. A moderate, al-Mahdi opposed Islamic fundamentalist rule of the Sudan but was unable to reconcile the ruling Moslem north with the Christian and animist south to end the long SUDANESE CIVIL WAR. The war continued and with it growing insurgent domination of the south, massive international debt payment problems, and worsening famine, leading to the starvation of an estimated 1 million Chad and Ethiopian refugees in the Sudan and hundreds of thousands of Sudanese displaced by the civil war.

Makarios III (Michael Khristodoulou Mouskos; 1913–77), Greek Orthodox priest, who became archbishop of Cyprus in 1950 and leader of the Cypriot self-determination movement. Until 1959 he fostered the goal of *ENOSIS* (union with Greece) rather than continuing British colonial control. Exiled to the Seychelles by the British in 1956, he returned to live in Athens until 1959, when he negotiated Cypriot independence with the British, foregoing immediate *enosis*. He became first president of Cyprus in December 1959, while bitter Greek-Turkish guerrilla warfare on Cyprus, which had begun in the early 1950s, escalated in 1963 into the CYPRUS CIVIL WAR. The civil war drew Greek and Turkish military intervention and the continuing presence of UNITED NATIONS peacekeeping forces until 1967. In 1974 Makarios was forced to flee Cyprus after a successful Greek officers' revolt, organized by the military dictatorship in Greece. He returned in December, after

Turkish seizure of much of northern Cyprus, and after both the Greek and the Cyprus military governments had fallen. He was then reelected to the presidency, dying in office.

Malagasy Republic, the name of the Democratic Republic of MADAGASCAR from 1958 to 1975, when the name People's Republic of Madagascar was adopted.

Malan, Daniel François (1874–1959), South African minister and Afrikaner nationalist, who devoted his life to the restoration of Boer rule and 19th-century Boer racism in South Africa. He entered parliament in 1918, was opposition leader during the late 1930s and again in the early 1940s, and came to power as National party prime minister in 1948, then instituting the APARTHEID policies that were to tear South African society apart during the following four decades.

Malawi (Republic of Malawi), until 1953 Nyasaland, a British protectorate. In 1953 Nyasaland was joined to RHODESIA, but nationalist protests forced dissolution of the federation in 1963. Malawi became an independent state and COMMONWEALTH member on July 6, 1964, led by Prime Minister Hastings BANDA, who then continued as president from 1966.

Malaya (Independent Federation of Malaya), federation of various Malay states, until 1957 controlled by Great Britain and becoming an independent nation and COMMONWEALTH member on August 31, 1957. On September 16, 1963, Malaya joined with Sarawak, Sabah, and Singapore (which later withdrew) to form MALAYSIA.

Malaya, Battle of (December 1941–January 1942), early World War II campaign, starting on December 8, 1941, when Japanese invasion forces landed in northern Malaya; in the next 2 months they fought their way south to SINGAPORE against ineffective British and Malay opposition. By January 31 the Japanese had taken mainland Malaya and faced Singapore across the Strait of Johore.

Malayan Civil War (1948–60), a protracted Communist-led guerrilla war, in which mainly ethnic Chinese-Malayan forces led by Chen Ping were ultimately defeated by British, colonial, and ethnic Malayan forces. The latter succeeded in blocking rebel sources of supply, winning the allegiance of large numbers of rural Malays with promises and then delivery of full independence from Britain, and developed effective airborne and base-area guerrilla war techniques.

Malaysia, until 1957 various Malay states controlled by Great Britain, using a variety of governmental forms. Following the suppression of the post–World War II Malayan insurrection came the August 31, 1957, formation of the Independent Federation of Malaya, with COMMONWEALTH membership. On September 16, 1963, this was supplanted by Malaysia, which then included SINGAPORE, Sarawak, and Sabah; Singapore later withdrew.

Malaysian National Front, the ruling and by far the strongest party in Malaysia. It is a coalition of several component parties, including the United Malaya National Organization (UMNO), which carried the main thrust of the Malayan independence movement and of the succeeding Alliance party under the leadership of Tunku ABDUL RAHMAN in the post–World War II period; the Malaysian Chinese Association (MCA); the Malaysian Indian Congress (MIC); and several smaller parties.

Malcolm X (Malcolm Little; 1925–65), Black Muslim leader of the 1960s and founder of the newspaper *Muhammad Speaks*. He was a leader of the Nation of Islam, then headed by Elijah Muhammad, until leaving to form the Muslim Mosque in 1964. Malcolm X was assassinated in New York City on February 21, 1965.

Maldives (Republic of Maldives), until 1960 a British protectorate. The island nation achieved internal autonomy in 1960, gained independence as a sultanate on July 25, 1965, and became a republic in 1968.

malefactors of great wealth, phrase coined by U.S. president Theodore ROOSEVELT, in a speech at Provincetown, Massachusetts, on August 7, 1907.

Malenkov, Georgi Maksimilianovich (1902–   ), Soviet Communist party official, closely associated with Joseph STALIN from the 1920s and from 1932 Stalin's chief personal aide. He became a Politburo member and deputy prime minister in 1946, succeeded Stalin after his death in 1953, then took steps to change course away from Stalinist terror, even though he had been closely associated with that terror during his entire career. Domestically, he moved toward consumer goods production; internationally, away from confrontation with the United States. But his period of power was brief; within a few months he was engaged in a power struggle with Nikita KHRUSHCHEV, which Malenkov lost in 1955. In 1957 he and his supporters were removed from all major party posts, and he was later expelled from his party.

Mali (Republic of Mali), until 1958 Sudan, part of French West Africa. Internal autonomy was granted in 1958; independence came on June 20, 1960. During 1959 and 1960 Mali and SENEGAL were briefly joined in the Federation of Mali.

Malinowski, Bronislaw (1884–1942), Polish anthropologist, whose fieldwork in the Trobriand Islands and other Pacific cultures provided models that greatly influenced later generations of anthropologists. During his tenures at the University of London (1924–39) and at Yale (1939–42) he exerted a major influence on anthropological theory and practice. Among those he influenced were some of the colonial independence movement leaders then resident in Great Britain, including Jomo KENYATTA.

Malmédy Massacre (December 17, 1944), the murder of 86 U.S. prisoners of war by German SS troops during the BATTLE OF THE BULGE.

Malraux, André (1901–76), French writer, philosopher, and public official, who wrote

of his experiences early in the CHINESE CIV-
IL WAR and of his friend ZHOU ENLAI in his
seminal novel, *Man's Fate* (1933). In his novel *Man's Hope* (1938) he wrote of his experience in the SPANISH CIVIL WAR. Turning
away from his early radical views after
World War II, he became Charles DE
GAULLE'S culture minister 1959–69.

Malta (Republic of Malta), until 1964 a British colony, becoming independent and a
COMMONWEALTH member on September
21, 1964. In 1974 Malta became a republic.

Malta Summit (December 2–3, 1989), the
first BUSH-GORBACHEV summit, held
aboard Soviet and U.S. ships at anchor in
Marsaxlokk Bay, Malta. The meetings were
more general and exploratory than substan-
tive, with both presidents indicating progress in a post-COLD WAR atmosphere, but
no specific agreements eventuating.

Managua earthquake (December 23, 1972),
an earthquake that destroyed much of the
center of the Nicaraguan capital, killing an
estimated 5,000 people. The failure of the
corrupt SOMOZA government to distribute
international relief supplies was greatly re-
sented, contributing to the downfall of the
regime.

Mandela, Nelson Rohihlahia (1918–   ),
South African lawyer, an activist in the AF-
RICAN NATIONAL CONGRESS (ANC) from
1944, and a deputy vice-president of the
ANC from 1952. Until the SHARPEVILLE
MASSACRE of 1960 Mandela was a leading
South African advocate of nonviolence; after Sharpeville he engaged in sabotage. He
was imprisoned in 1962, that imprisonment
becoming a life sentence for himself and
seven others in 1964. While in prison he became the undisputed leader of the South
African freedom movement and a worldwide symbol of resistance to racism. During
the latter years of his imprisonment he was
repeatedly offered his freedom by the
South African government, subject to conditions, but he refused to accept less than an
unconditional release. He was released on
February 11, 1990, beginning a new era in
South African history.

Mandela, Winnie (1936–   ), South African social worker who became an AFRICAN
NATIONAL CONGRESS activist in 1956 and
married Nelson MANDELA in 1958. After
his imprisonment she became a leader of
the South African freedom movement, was
penalized by the South African government
on several occasions, and was placed in internal exile in 1977. In 1985 she defied government restrictions and began to make
public appearances, ignoring government
threats to imprison her. In 1988 her prestige and ability to lead were seriously impaired by her alleged involvement in
beatings and at least one murder allegedly
committed by her bodyguards.

Manhattan, U.S. ice-breaking oil tanker,
the first commercial ship to traverse the
NORTHWEST PASSAGE, north of North
America, in 1969.

Manhattan Project (1942–45), shortened
code name for the U.S. research and development effort that produced the first
ATOMIC BOMB, using NUCLEAR FISSION;
formally named the Manhattan District of
the Army Corps of Engineers. The multi-
pronged project, employing scientists at
many universities, was placed under the
direction of General Leslie R. GROVES in
1942. Enrico FERMI's research group,
working in a squash court at the University of Chicago, built the world's first NU-
CLEAR REACTOR and developed the first
successful CHAIN REACTION on December
2, 1942, in the process producing fissionable PLUTONIUM. In 1941, using the CY-
CLOTRON at the University of California
at Berkeley, Ernest O. LAWRENCE learned
how to separate out fissionable URANIUM,
techniques employed from 1943 on a larger scale at OAK RIDGE, Tennessee. In
1943 Harold UREY and John R. Dunning,
working at Columbia University, worked
out a gaseous diffusion method of extracting uranium 235 that was employed
at Oak Ridge from 1945. J. Robert OPPEN-
HEIMER supervised the actual design and
construction of the bomb from 1943 at
LOS ALAMOS, New Mexico; the first atomic bomb was set off at ALAMOGORDO, New

Mexico, July 16, 1945, in a test called TRINITY. The first atomic bombs used in warfare destroyed HIROSHIMA and NAGASAKI, Japan, on August 6 and August 9, 1945. The Manhattan Project was disbanded in 1946 and its functions taken over by the ATOMIC ENERGY COMMISSION (AEC).

Manifest Destiny, U.S. imperialist call for expansion into the Carribbean and the Pacific put forward by William Seward in the 1870s. It was revived by Alfred Mahan in the 1890s, and adopted by such early imperialists as Theodore ROOSEVELT and Henry Cabot LODGE. The theory was part of the rationale for American expansionism in the early 20th century.

Manley, Michael (1923–), Jamaican trade union official, political leader, and socialist, son of Norman Manley, who had founded the People's National party in 1939. Michael Manley became president of the People's National party in 1969 and was prime minister from 1972 to 1980, in that position embarking Jamaica on a set of ambitious socialist programs and emerging as a NONALIGNED MOVEMENT spokesperson in world affairs.

Mannerheim, Karl Gustaf Emil (1867– 1951), Finnish baron who commanded White forces during the FINNISH CIVIL WAR of 1918. He defeated Red forces with German aid, resisted German domination of Finland, and temporarily left public life after losing Finland's first presidential race in 1919. He became a field marshal in 1933, commanded Finnish forces during and after the SOVIET–FINNISH WAR OF 1939–40, and was president of Finland 1944–46.

Mannheim, Karl (1893–1947), Hungarian sociologist, a college teacher in Germany, 1919–33, and in Great Britain, 1933–47. His best-known work was *Ideology and Utopia* (1936), a study relating ideas to social and class origins and current status.

Mansi railroad disaster (June 7, 1981), disaster that occurred at Mansi, India, when an overloaded train stalled on a railroad bridge during a storm. Seven cars were swept off

the bridge; probably more than 500 people died, although official estimates came to 268.

Manson, Charles (1934–), mass murderer who, with four others, committed the cult murders of five people—including actress Sharon Tate and her unborn child—in Beverly Hills, California, on August 9, 1969. On August 11 the group committed two more cult murders. All five murderers were subsequently sentenced to life imprisonment.

Manstein, Erich von (1887–1973), German officer, who saw service in World War I, and early in World War II participated in the invasions of Poland and France; his plan to penetrate French defenses at Sedan was the key to the fall of France in May 1940. On the Eastern Front, forces under his command took SEVASTOPOL but failed to take Leningrad or STALINGRAD, and then began the long retreat that would end in BERLIN. He did not stay in command that long; in March 1944 he was relieved of his command by Adolf HITLER. He was later convicted of war crimes and imprisoned for 4 years.

Mao Tse-tung, the old-style name of Chinese leader MAO ZEDONG.

Mao Zedong (Mao Tse-tung; 1893–1976), the primary leader and chief theoretician of communism in China, who led the COMMUNIST PARTY OF CHINA through the CHINESE CIVIL WAR to power in 1949, was chairman of the PEOPLE'S REPUBLIC OF CHINA until 1959, and chairman of the party for the rest of his life. He formed his first Communist group shortly after becoming a Marxist in 1920, was present at the first congress of the Communist party in 1921, and was active in the KUOMINTANG until the SHANGHAI MASSACRE ushered in the Communist–Kuomintang split of 1927 and the Chinese Civil War. From then on he turned from the former Communist urban insurrection strategy to the rural base-building strategy that was to take the Communists to power 22 years later. He led the unsuccessful

AUTUMN HARVEST UPRISINGS of 1927 and subsequently fled, with a few hundred survivors, into the Ching-Kang Mountains of western Kiangsi, where he and ZHU DE turned to building People's Liberation Army guerrilla forces in central China. From then until 1934 he fought in central China, during the guerrilla period and the KIANGSI SOVIET period. In 1934, surrounded and about to be destroyed by stronger Nationalist forces, he recommended the flight that became the LONG MARCH to northern China. During the course of that march he became political leader of the Communist party, beginning the process that by the early 1940s made him undisputed leader of Chinese communism. In those years he effectively broke with Joseph STALIN and the COMMUNIST INTERNATIONAL, which until the mid–1930s had essentially directed Chinese Communist policy. After achievement of power in 1949 he became leader of the new Chinese government, at first attempting to build a new industrial system essentially on the Soviet model, and then in 1958 making a sharp break with previous policies and attempting to build a new set of urban and rural communes that would take China on a GREAT LEAP FORWARD. In the mid–1960s he went even further, initiating the CULTURAL REVOLUTION, with its RED GUARDS, enormous cultural and physical destruction, and virtual deification of Mao. In the 1970s he went into decline, and moderates led by ZHOU ENLAI and DENG XIAOPING vied with a faction led by Mao's third wife, JIANG QING, which was later to be named and tried as the GANG OF FOUR.

Mapai (Workers' Party), Israeli Social Democratic party formed under the leadership of David BEN GURION in 1930. The Mapai, with its successor, the Israel Labor party, formed in 1968, was the Israeli ruling party from 1948 to 1977; in the late 1980s it was led by Shimon PERES.

Maquis, a term describing both individual World War II French RESISTANCE fighters and guerrilla units, although often during that war used to describe only units of the London-affiliated French Forces of the Interior, or FREE FRENCH.

Marcantonio, Vito (1902–54), U.S. congressman from East Harlem, in New York City, who was elected to the House of Representatives in 1934 as a Republican, on Fiorello LAGUARDIA'S Fusion ticket, and thereafter on the American Labor party ticket. Marcantonio generally followed U.S. Communist party policies, although he was not an avowed Communist, and became a highly controversial figure during the early years of the COLD WAR and the onset of the MCCARTHY period.

March on Rome, the tactic used by Benito MUSSOLINI to seize power in Italy in late October 1922. On October 24 his Fascist party organized a BLACKSHIRT march on Rome, as the key element in a nationwide seizure of power. King VICTOR EMMANUEL III and the Italian army refused to oppose the Blackshirts; instead, the king asked Mussolini to become premier, and he took power on October 31.

March on Washington (August 28, 1963), a meeting of an estimated 250,000 civil rights advocates at the Lincoln Memorial in Washington, DC, at which Martin Luther KING, Jr., delivered his celebrated I HAVE A DREAM speech. The meeting was a major event in the development of the American CIVIL RIGHTS MOVEMENT.

Marconi, Guglielmo (1874–1937), Italian physicist who sent the first transoceanic RADIO message in 1901, using the WIRELESS telegraphy he had been developing over several years—first in Italy, then in Britain—work for which he was awarded the 1909 Nobel Prize for Physics. After World War I, he focused on MICROWAVES.

Marco Polo Bridge Incident (July 7, 1937), an armed clash between Chinese and Japanese troops at the Marco Polo Bridge, near Peking, that began the SINO-JAPANESE WAR.

Marcos, Ferdinand Edralin (1917–89), much-decorated World War II Filipino anti-Japanese guerrilla fighter, who went into politics after the war. He was a Liberal party member of the House of Representatives, 1949–59, and of the Senate, 1959–65; as Nationalist party candidate, he won the presidency in 1965. After his reelection in 1969, as continuing Moro and Communist-led insurgencies strengthened and Liberal party support grew, he turned toward repression of his political opponents, jailing thousands in 1971; from September 1972 he openly ruled under martial law, and thereafter by decree. He imprisoned Benigno Aquino, along with other Liberal party leaders, in 1972, held him until 1980, and then let him go abroad. He was widely accused of ordering the assassination of Aquino as he stepped off his airplane on his return to the Philippines in 1983. Marcos ordered a presidential election in February 1986; when he lost that election to Corazon AQUINO, he attempted to hold power by means of electoral fraud. He was forced to flee into exile on February 25, 1986. During the late 1980s attempts were mounted to prosecute him for financial malfeasance.

Marcuse, Herbert (1898–1979), German philosopher, who left Nazi Germany and settled in the United States in 1934. A Marxist with Freudian leanings, he posited the need for revolutionary change, and his thinking became important to many in the NEW LEFT movements of the 1960s.

Mariel boat people, the estimated 114,000 Cubans allowed in 1981 to leave Cuba for Florida, through the Cuban port of Mariel. Most were refugees, much like the hundreds of thousands who had emigrated to the United States in earlier years, many them leaving Cuba to join their families in the United States. Several thousand freed criminals also were allowed to emigrate; some continued their criminal careers in the United States.

Mariner, U.S. series of unmanned spacecraft to explore nearby planets, in 1962 and 1967 flying by and gathering data on VENUS and in 1964 and 1969 photographing the surface of MARS and making thermal maps of it, using INFRARED RADIATION. *Mariner 9,* placed into orbit around Mars in November 1971, revealed much new infor-

mation about the planet, its moons, and the possibility of its supporting life. In 1974 *Mariner 10* flew by Venus to reach the region of Mercury, where it went into orbit.

Mark I (automatic sequence control calculator), early electromechanical calculator developed at Harvard University, 1939–44, by Howard Aiken, working with IBM. Used for calculations during the war, it was a precursor to such all-electronic computers as the COLOSSUS and ENIAC.

Market Garden, Operation (September 1944), code name for the failed Allied limited offensive aimed at penetrating the SIEGFRIED LINE; it included the Battle of ARNHEM.

Marne, First Battle of the (September 5–10, 1914), battle that developed when German armies advancing south turned to take Paris, rather than attempting to sweep west and south to envelop the French and British armies, as envisaged in the SCHLIEFFEN PLAN. This enabled the French to strike and envelop the German right flank, and then to engage and stop the entire German offensive with the aid of their Paris reserves; the troops were brought from Paris to the front in any vehicles available, including a fleet of taxicabs. Paris was saved, the entire German advance was stopped, and the Schlieffen Plan had ultimately failed. Instead, both armies fought a series of battles along the Aisne and Yser Rivers and then to the North Sea, as they developed the lines of fortifications they would hold for the next 4 years. Attacking all along the front, the French failed to break through the German lines; at YPRES, German and British forces suffered huge casualties, but the Germans failed to break through to take the Channel ports. Had the Germans won the Marne battle, the course of World War I and of world history might have been very different. Instead, 4 years of TRENCH WARFARE in the west were to bring millions of war dead and the eventual defeat of Germany and its allies.

Marne, Second Battle of (July 15–August 5, 1918), this set of battles began as the fifth and last German offensive of 1918, as German armies attacked French and American forces in Champagne, reaching and crossing the Marne in the first few days of the offensive but then being forced to withdraw. Allied forces then went over to the offensive, regaining much of the ground that had been lost in the five German offensives of 1918. The Allies kept the initiative for the balance of the war.

Mars, planetary target of U.S.S.R and U.S. space probes. In 1965 *MARINER 4* flew by Mars, as did *Mariner 6* and *7* in 1969 and 1971, sending back photographs of craters on its surface. In May 1971 the Soviet Union sent aloft *Mars 1* and *2*, placing them in orbit and landing capsules that briefly sent back TELEVISION signals. The same month, the U.S. sent *Mariner 9* to Mars, placing it in orbit and transmitting television pictures and other data. In 1974 a Soviet craft crashed while attempting a landing on Mars; two U.S. craft, *VIKING 1* and *2*, successfully landed there in 1976, and *Viking 1* broadcast data for more than 5 years. Maps, photographs, and other resulting information gave a much more accurate picture of Mars and its moons, giving a negative (though not definitive) answer to the continuing question of whether Mars supports life. In 1988, the U.S.S.R. sent two craft, *Phobos 1* and *Phobos 2*, toward Mars, but both failed in early 1989 before they could complete their mission.

Marshall, George Catlett (1880–1959), U.S. officer, who saw service in World War I, was General John J. PERSHING'S aide for 5 years after that war, and in 1939 became chief of staff of the U.S. Army. In that position he organized the American run-up to participation in the war that had already started in Europe, including cooperation with the British. He was chief organizer of the two-front, Europe-first strategy that was the keystone of overall Allied strategy throughout the war, and chose the American military leaders of the war, including Dwight D. EISENHOWER to lead the NORMANDY invasion. He became a five-star general in December 1944. After the war he headed the

U.S. mission to China, November 1945–January 1947, which slowed but did not stop the CHINESE CIVIL WAR. In February 1947 he became secretary of state, in that position developing the huge American aid program that helped rebuild postwar Western Europe—the MARSHALL PLAN.

Marshall, Thomas Riley (1854–1925), U.S. lawyer and Democratic governor of Indiana (1909–13), who was twice Woodrow WILSON'S vice-president (1913–21); he was credited with originating the phrase "What this country needs is a really good five-cent cigar!" during a long, slow Senate debate on national priorities.

Marshall, Thurgood (1908–   ) U.S. lawyer, on the staff of the NATIONAL ASSOCIATION FOR THE ADVANCEMENT OF COLORED PEOPLE (NAACP) from 1936 and head of its legal staff, 1940–62. In that position he became the leading civil rights lawyer in the United States, fighting and winning a series of major legal battles, the most notable being the landmark school desegregation case, the 1954 BROWN V. BOARD OF EDUCATION OF TOPEKA, KANSAS. In 1962 President John F. KENNEDY named him a second Circuit Court of Appeals judge. In 1965 President Lyndon B. JOHNSON named him solicitor-general of the United States, and in 1967 Johnson appointed him the first Black member of the U.S. Supreme Court. On the Court, Marshall continued on his established course, becoming a leading member of the liberal wing of the Court, in the liberal majority during his early years and in the liberal minority as times and the Court changed.

Marshall mission, the failed 1945–47 attempt by General George C. MARSHALL, acting for U.S. president Harry S. TRUMAN, to mediate the CHINESE CIVIL WAR, which had resumed after the defeat of Japan in World War II. He did negotiate a truce in January 1947, but it had completely broken down by July 1947, and he left China in January 1948.

Marshall Plan, a U.S. program in aid of European post–World War II reconstruction and economic redevelopment, put forward by Secretary of State George C. MARSHALL in June 1947. It generated massive gifts and some loans to many non-Communist European nations in the late 1940s and early 1950s, and at the same time was a powerful tool in support of American COLD WAR and CONTAINMENT aims.

Martov, Julius (1873–1923), Russian Marxist who worked with LENIN from 1895 but broke with him in 1903, becoming a leader of the MENSHEVIK faction in the Russian socialist movement. He fled into exile after his party was outlawed in 1920.

Mary Rose, Henry VIII's flagship, which sank in Britain's Portsmouth Harbor in 1545 and was raised in 1982 in a massive exercise in underwater archeology. The remains found on board were preserved and later displayed.

Masaryk, Jan (1886–1948), Czech diplomat, the son of Tomás MASARYK and minister to Great Britain, 1925–38. He resigned in 1938, after the MUNICH AGREEMENT, and was foreign minister of the London-based Czech government-in-exile 1941–45, in that period also becoming a widely known broadcaster. He was Czech foreign minister, 1945–48, staying on for a little while after the Communist coup. On March 10, 1948, he fell to his death from a window in the foreign ministry building in Prague; whether it was murder, suicide, or an accident is unknown.

Masaryk, Tomás Garrigue (1850–1937), Czech philosopher, leader of the Czech independence movement, and first president of Czechoslovakia. From 1891 he worked within Austria-Hungary, in parliament 1891–1893 and 1907–14, and was a leading spokesman for Czech and other national groups throughout the period. He headed the London-based Czech National Council 1914–17, and went to Russia in 1917 to organize the CZECH LEGION, coming out through the United States in 1918. He returned home to become president of Czechoslovakia, 1918–35, retiring because of ill health. Jan MASARYK was his son.

maser (**M**icrowave **A**mplification by **S**timulated **E**mission of **R**adiation), device that produces an intense, concentrated beam of RADIO waves (originally high-frequency MICROWAVES), much as a LASER produces an intense, concentrated beam of light; first built in 1954 by a U.S. team led by physicist Charles Hard Townes. Its best-known use is probably in ATOMIC CLOCKS. Masers also have been found in the universe, brief intense signals produced from the gaseous clouds around newly found stars, and from 1981 they have been used to measure astronomical distances.

massive retaliation, a nuclear age theory postulating that the way to respond to any direct or indirect attack on one of the two superpowers, its friends, or its client states, is to promise convincingly to mount full-scale nuclear retaliation on the author of the attack. The theory was soon invalidated by events, as neither superpower proved in fact willing to mount such an attack and run the risk of possibly humanity-destroying nuclear war.

Masters, William Howell (1915–   ), gynecologist, and **Virginia Eshelman Johnson** (1925–   ), psychologist, U.S. sex researchers who in 1966 published the ground-breaking book, *Human Sexual Response*. Their best-selling, highly regarded work drew on controversial firsthand laboratory study of sexual activity at their Reproductive Biology Research Foundation in St. Louis, Missouri.

Masurian Lakes, First Battle of the (September 9–14, 1914), World War I battle in which the German armies of General Paul von HINDENBURG, after destroying the Russian Second Army at TANNENBERG in late August, moved north against General Paul Rennenkampf's Russian First Army. The battle at the Masurian Lakes was a second East Prussian disaster for the Russian army, which lost an estimated 125,000–150,000 men, though Rennenkampf was able to save most of his command in a precipitate retreat.

Masurian Lakes, Second Battle of (February 7–21, 1915), World War I battle that was the climax of the German Eastern Front winter offensive of 1915, in which attacking German armies encircled a Russian army corps, taking 90,000 prisoners, and forcing the balance of the defending Russians to retreat.

Mata Hari (Margaretha Geertruida Zelle; 1876–1917), Dutch dancer who was executed as a German spy by the French, October 15, 1917. The World War I case, with its considerable sexual connotations, is still a cause celèbre, generating much media and literary attention.

Matsushita, Konosuke (1894–1989), Japanese industrialist, founder of the Matsushita Electric Industrial Company in 1918, and a leader in the development of Japanese paternalistic industrial relations practices. As a member of the ZAIBATSU who played a substantial role in developing Japanese militarism, he was barred from major commercial activity during the early postwar period. He was allowed to resume his previous positions in 1948, and thereafter once again became a leading Japanese industrialist.

Matteotti, Giacomo (1885–1924), Italian socialist and anti-fascist member of parliament who, on June 10, 1924, was murdered by the fascists for opposing them and exposing fascist election frauds. Mussolini survived the ensuing political crisis, emerging from it the unchallengeable leader of fascist Italy, having effectively intimidated and thereby silenced his opponents.

Mau Mau Uprising (1952–56), Kenyan guerrilla war, pitting nationalist guerrilla members of the Mau Mau Society, drawn mainly from the Kikuyu people, against the British army. Armed actions accompanied the mounting campaign for Kenyan independence, which began in 1945 with the end of World War II. By 1952, large-scale guerrilla attacks on British plantations and settlements were occurring throughout the country. The British responded with substantial military actions against the Mau Mau, the Kikuyu, and the national movement, including the imprisonment of Jomo KENYATTA. The guerrilla war continued until early 1956, ending with Mau Mau defeat as guerrilla attacks subsided. Kenyatta was widely described as the arch-terrorist of the time, although he denied such charges. He remained imprisoned until 1961, ultimately emerging to become president of the Kenyan republic.

Mauritania (Islamic Republic of Mauritania), until 1958 a French protectorate, then gaining internal autonomy and on November 28, 1960, becoming an independent state.

Mauritius, until 1968 a British colony; it became a democratic independent state and COMMONWEALTH member on March 12, 1968.

Maurras, Charles Marie Photius (1868–1952), French writer and editor who founded the rightist ACTION FRANÇAISE group in 1899. He collaborated with the Nazis during World War II and was sentenced to life imprisonment after the war.

May, Alan Nunn (1911–   ), British atomic physicist, who became a Soviet spy during World War II, passing atomic energy information to the Soviet Union until his exposure and imprisonment in 1946.

May 4th Movement, Chinese student protest demonstrations against the pro-Japanese provisions of the VERSAILLES treaty, that began in Peking on May 4, 1919, and subsequently sparked demonstrations, strikes, and boycotts throughout the country. A new youth-oriented Chinese nationalist movement had been developing for several years, and the demonstrations served to focus that movement. Its young leaders were to become the leaders of both the KUOMINTANG and the COMMUNIST PARTY OF CHINA in the years ahead.

May 30th Movement, series of antiforeign demonstrations that swept China following the killing of 13 Chinese demonstrators on May 30, 1925, by British troops in Shanghai. More than 50 WHAMPOA MILITARY ACADEMY cadets also were killed during an armed clash on June 23, with British and French marines. The demonstrations lasted until early 1926.

***Mayaguez* Incident** (May 12–14, 1975), a Cambodian gunboat's capture of the U.S. merchant ship *Mayaguez* and its crew of 39 in international waters approximately 60 miles off the Cambodian coast. After negotiations failed, President Gerald FORD authorized a U.S. Marine rescue operation: air attacks on Cambodian naval vessels and airfields, and helicopter attacks on Tang Island, where the ship was being held. The Cambodians released the American crew in a fishing boat while the attack was in progress.

Mboya, Thomas Joseph (1930–69), Kenyan labor and independence movement leader, who was general secretary of the Kenya Federation of Labor 1953–63, a founder of the Kenya African National Union (KANU) in 1960, and minister for economic planning and development in Jomo KENYATTA'S first republican government. He was widely regarded as Kenyatta's political heir apparent until his 1969 assassination in Nairobi.

Mc: See **Mac.**

Mead, Margaret (1901–78), U.S. anthropologist, whose work in preindustrial, or "primitive," cultures focused on psychoanalytically based inquiry into comparative sexual practices, as influenced by cultural sexual and child-rearing practices. Her published works, such as *The Coming of Age in Samoa* (1928), were popular and widely circulated, contributing to the development of new U.S. attitudes toward sexual diversity.

Meany, George (1894–1980), U.S. plumber, who became a trade union official and in 1952 president of the AMERICAN FEDERATION OF LABOR (AFL). He brought the CONGRESS OF INDUSTRIAL ORGANIZATIONS (CIO) and the AFL together into the merged AFL-CIO in 1955, and was first president of the new organization. He also was a vice-president of the International Confederation of Free Trade Unions, and a

U.S. delegate to the UNITED NATIONS General Assembly.

Mecham, Evan (1924–   ), Arizona automobile dealer and sharply conservative Republican governor of Arizona, from his election in 1986 until his impeachment in February 1988. He was convicted and removed from office on April 4 by the Republican-dominated state senate, and later acquitted in a criminal trial of perjury and money-laundering charges. In office he had been an extremely controversial figure, his comments on minority groups isolating him even from his own party, and had been facing a massive recall campaign before his impeachment.

Medawar, Peter Brian (1915–87), Brazilian-born British-Lebanese zoologist, who worked out the mechanism that causes grafts or TRANSPLANTS to be rejected by the recipient's body. He was following through on Australian immunologist Macfarlane Burnet's idea that the graft or transplant was regarded as "foreign" by the body's immune system and hence to be destroyed, an idea for which they shared the 1960 Nobel Prize for Physiology or Medicine. Medawar's work was basic to the modern development of organ and tissue transplants, opening the way for selective immunosuppressive drugs; it also explained the mechanism behind auto-immune diseases, in which the body mistakenly attacks its own tissues.

Medellín cartel, a major drug-growing and drug dealing syndicate, powerfully placed throughout Colombia and neighboring countries, named after the Colombian city of Medellín. During the late 1980s the cartel grossed an estimated $6–7 billion per year, mainly from U.S. cocaine and marijuana sales, while successfully resisting Colombian and U.S. attempts to combat the drug trade.

Medicare and Medicaid, U.S. social welfare programs, introduced as part of President Lyndon B. JOHNSON's GREAT SOCIETY program, in the Mills Act of 1965, and further developed thereafter. Medicare provides for a federally subsidized system of voluntary health insurance for those over 65. Medicaid provides poor people with state-administered, federally subsidized medical care.

Medvedev, Roy Aleksandrovich (1925–), Soviet historian and dissenter, whose first major work, *Let History Judge* (1971 in English), was an attack on the crimes and repression of the Stalinist period; he was later expelled from the COMMUNIST PARTY for his criticism. He also wrote—with his twin brother, Zhores MEDVEDEV—*A Question of Madness* (1971 in English), which told the story of Zhores' imprisonment in a psychiatric institution and exposed such methods of imprisoning and punishing dissenters. He was reinstated to Communist Party membership in the GORBACHEV era.

Medvedev, Vadim Andreevich (1929–), Soviet economist, political theoretician, and Communist Party official (deputy propaganda chief of the Central Committee 1970–78) who was national science and technology department head until his surprise 1988 elevation to the Politburo. He then became ideology secretary, second only to GORBACHEV in the Soviet Union.

Medvedev, Zhores Aleksandrovich (1925–), Soviet biologist, whose attacks on Trofim LYSENKO's government-supported views on genetics led to his imprisonment in a psychiatric hospital, from which he was released only after international and Soviet protest. In *A Question of Madness* (1971), written with his twin brother, Roy MEDVEDEV, he exposed to the world the use of psychiatric detention to silence dissenters. While conducting research in London in 1973, his citizenship was revoked, so he remained in the West, continuing his critical works and reporting in 1979 on the previously unacknowledged nuclear disaster at BLAGOVESCHENSK in the Urals in 1958.

Meese, Edwin, III (1931–), U.S. lawyer, who became a key aide to Ronald REAGAN when he was governor of California (1967–75), and went with him to Washington in 1981. Meese served as counsellor to the president, 1981–85, and U.S. attorney-general, 1985–88. After charges of possible involvement in the WEDTECH case, Special Prosecutor James C. McKay investigated Meese for 14 months while top Justice Department aides resigned to protest Meese's continuing tenure. Meese resigned on July 5, 1988, after McKay's report had been filed but before its contents were revealed. McKay's report was made public on July 18, 1988; it alleged that Meese had "probably violated the criminal law" four times while in office, but that no basis for prosecution existed.

Megiddo, Battle of (September 19–21, 1918), the final battle of the Middle East campaigns during World War I. ALLENBY's British forces broke Turkish defensive positions near Jaffa, routed the Turkish forces, and pursued them through the Jordan valley, ultimately taking Damascus, Beirut, Homs, and Aleppo. Their advance ended with the Allied-Turkish armistice of October 30, 1918.

Mehendra Bir Bikram Shah Deva (1920–72), Nepalese king (1956–72), who instituted democracy with the constitution of 1959, canceled the new constitution in 1960, and imprisoned the elected leaders of Nepal; he banned all political parties and ruled as an absolute monarch. In 1962 he set up non-party representative assemblies, but in effect continued to hold all power until his death. He was succeeded by his son, BIRENDA BIR BIKRAM SHAH DEVA.

Mein Kampf, a two-volume work by Adolf HITLER, the first volume written in prison following the Munich BEER HALL PUTSCH of 1923, the second in 1925. The book was central to Nazi theory and practice, sounding the racist, anti-Jewish, and nationalist themes that would take Hitler to power and generate World War II.

Meir, Golda (Golda Meyerson; 1898–1978), American-Israeli Zionist, who emigrated from the United States to Israel at the age of 23, and in 1928 became a leader of the Palestine Jewish labor federation, the Histadrut; she was also active in the socialist

MAPAI party. In 1946 she became head of the political department of the Jewish Agency for Palestine and in 1948 was Israel's first ambassador to the Soviet Union. She was labor minister 1949–56, foreign minister 1956–66, and prime minister 1969–74, resigning after widespread criticism of the government's lack of preparation for the YOM KIPPUR WAR (FOURTH ARAB–ISRAELI WAR; OCTOBER WAR) of 1973.

Mellon, Andrew William (1855–1937), U.S. banker who, as head of Pittsburgh's Mellon National Bank, played a substantial role in the development of many major U.S. companies; he was secretary of the treasury from 1921 to 1932, through the boom of the 1920s, the CRASH of 1929, and the first years of the GREAT DEPRESSION. A conservative, he believed the U.S. economic system to be essentially self-regulating, and made no attempt to limit the boom and its accompanying speculative practices; after the Crash, he tried to revive the economy with modest, unsuccessful attempts to restimulate business.

melting pot, phrase coined by Israel Zangwill in act 1 of his play *The Melting Pot* (1908); from "America is God's crucible, the great melting pot where all the races of Europe are melting and reforming!"

Memel, Lithuanian seacoast city that had been part of Germany before the German defeat in World War I; it was then disputed by Poland, the Soviet Union, and Lithuania, until finally taken by Lithuania in 1923. Nazi Germany forced Lithuania to cede the area back to Germany in 1939; it became part of the Soviet Union after World War II.

Memorial Day Massacre, an alternate name for the Memorial Day 1937 LITTLE STEEL MASSACRE.

Mendes-France, Pierre (1907–82), French lawyer and socialist, in the national assembly 1932–58, with a World War II break in which he was imprisoned by the VICHY government and escaped to fly for the FREE FRENCH. He opposed the INDOCHINA WAR;

when he became premier in June 1954, he quickly ended the war. He was premier only until February 1955, and was not in office during the De Gaulle years. Briefly serving in the assembly again during 1967–68, he continued to be an active socialist leader.

Mengele, Joseph (1911–   ), Nazi doctor and mass murderer who participated in the killing of an estimated 60,000 "defectives," beginning in 1940; as chief medical officer at AUSCHWITZ, he was directly responsible for choosing many of those who were to be immediately murdered on arrival at the death camp. He also engaged in willfully cruel experimentation, using human subjects. He is thought to have escaped to South America after the war and was sought as a major war criminal for decades. His death has been reported on many occasions; there is a small possibility that he is still at large.

Mengistu, Haile Mariam (1937–   ), Ethiopian officer, who was a leader of the army coup that deposed Haile SELASSIE in 1974. Mengistu took full power after factional infighting in February 1977, ruling as dictator and developing a socialist state on the most conservative Soviet model, with substantial Soviet and Cuban military and other material assistance. He established the Workers' party in 1984, with himself as secretary-general.

Menon, Vengalil Krishnan Krishna (1897–1974), Indian lawyer, editor, nationalist, socialist, and diplomat, who practiced law in Great Britain from 1925 and was there secretary of the India League 1927–47, and a key Indian independence movement representative. With independence, he became Indian high commissioner in London, 1947–53; he was India's UNITED NATIONS ambassador 1952–60, and Indian defense minister 1957–62. He resigned his cabinet post after Indian defeat in the CHINESE–INDIAN BORDER WAR of 1962, continuing in the Indian parliament until his death.

Mensheviks, Russian word for the "minority," a name given by the BOLSHEVIK wing of the Russian Social-Democratic party to the somewhat more moderate major portion of the party at the party congress of 1903, when the Bolsheviks won votes on certain intraparty issues. The Mensheviks, led by Georgi PLEKHANOV and Julius MARTOV, were the main body of the Social-Democratic party; after the Bolsheviks split away to form their own party in 1912, the Mensheviks were the party. They were suppressed by the Bolsheviks after the OCTOBER REVOLUTION.

Menzies, Robert Gordon (1894–1978), Australian lawyer and conservative, a member of the Victoria legislature 1929–34 and of parliament 1934–66. He was United Australia party prime minister 1939–41 and Liberal prime minister 1949–66, a period of massive immigration, strong commercial development at home, and coordination of Australian and U.S. policies in southeast Asia. He took Australia into the KOREAN and VIETNAM WARS, and also participated in regional anti-Communist military alliances.

Mercury, series of U.S. spacecraft that first put Americans into orbit around the Earth. In suborbital flights, Alan SHEPARD flew in the Mercury craft *Freedom 7* on May 5, 1961 and Virgil (Gus) GRISSOM flew in *Liberty Bell 7* on July 21, 1961. Then on February 20, 1962, John GLENN had a 5-hour, three-orbit flight in *Friendship 7*. These Mercury flights, and the GEMINI ones that followed, helped prepare for the APOLLO landings on the Moon.

Mercury, planetary target of Soviet and American space probes, notably by *Mariner 10* in 1974, which flew by the planet several times.

mercy killing, alternate term for EUTHANASIA.

Meredith, James Howard (1933–   ), U.S. student, who in 1961 applied for admission to the University of Mississippi, was rejected because he was Black, and then, with the help of the NATIONAL ASSOCIATION FOR THE ADVANCEMENT OF COLORED PEOPLE (NAACP), used legal process to force admission, in a case finally decided by the

Supreme Court. Because the state of Mississippi refused to allow him to register, he was enrolled under federal protection, after President John F. KENNEDY had federalized state National Guard troops and sent them in to end rioting, which killed two and injured many more. In 1966 Meredith was shot while marching to encourage Mississippi voter registration, but he survived to complete the march later, with thousands of supporters.

Mers el-Kebir sinkings (July 3–4, 1940), early World War II attack by British warships on French naval units at Mers el-Kebir, Algeria, which had refused either to join the ALLIES or to take themselves out of the war by sinking or demilitarizing their ships. The British sank three French battleships at Oran. At Alexandria, Egypt, a French squadron responded by demilitarizing the ships.

Messerschmitt, Willy (1898–1978), German engineer and aircraft designer, who from 1923 designed and built a wide range of AIRPLANES, notably the Me-109, which set a world speed record in 1939. The Me-109 was the LUFTWAFFE's basic plane during World War II, supplemented by Messerschmitt bombers and other fighters. In his later career, Messerschmitt produced satellites and missiles.

Messina earthquake (December 28, 1908), a series of Sicilian and Italian earthquakes that caused an estimated 100,000–150,000 deaths, destroying Messina and many smaller towns and cities.

Metaxas, Ioannis (1871–1941), Greek officer and World War I army chief of staff whose fortunes were closely tied to those of the monarchy. He became premier in April 1936, took power as dictator in August, and ruled Greece until his death in January 1941.

Meuse–Argonne Offensive (September 26–November 11, 1918), World War I push in which U.S. and French forces attacked weakening German forces on the Meuse and in the Argonne Forest, and ultimately reached Sedan, stopping their drive only with the armistice, November 11, 1918.

Mexican earthquakes of 1985 (September 19–20, 1985), two massive earthquakes, one of them measuring 8.1 on the RICHTER SCALE, that struck Mexico City and portions of southern Mexico, killing an estimated 5,000–10,000 people, injuring tens of thousands more, and leaving hundreds of thousands homeless. Hundreds of large buildings at the center of Mexico City were leveled, as the area proved particularly vulnerable to earthquake shocks.

Mexican Revolution (1910–20), a revolution and civil war that began as an armed insurrection against the regime of Porfirio DÍAZ in 1910 and ultimately became a long civil war, with many leaders and factions, that cost an estimated 1 million lives. Díaz arrested the opposing presidential candidate, Francisco MADERO, in 1910 and had himself declared winner of the presidential race; Madero jumped bail, organized an armed insurrection, and took power in May 1911. Some Madero supporters, including Emiliano ZAPATA, soon split with Madero on several issues—but especially on the question of the speed of land reform—and civil war followed. In 1913 Madero's Mexico City commandant, Victoriano HUERTA, organized a coup, executed Madero, and became dictator, but almost immediately he lost the civil war to the forces led by Venustiano CARRANZA. Carranza then sucessfully pursued the civil war, defeating the forces of Francisco VILLA and Zapata. Zapata's forces retreated to their home bases in the south and resisted all government attempts to subdue them until Zapata's assassination in 1919. Villa's forces retreated to their home bases in the north, in 1916 attacking Columbus, New Mexico, precipitating a U.S. invasion of northern Mexico, which ended in early 1917. Carranza was assassinated in 1920 by the forces of his own general, Alvaro OBREGÓN, who had led a successful insurrection against the Carranza government. Obregón then became president, consolidated his power, and ended the civil war.

Mexican–U.S. border war (1916–17), conflict that began on March 15, 1916, when Mexican guerrilla forces led by Francisco VILLA attacked Columbus, New Mexico. A U.S. force of an estimated 10,000 men, led by John J. PERSHING, then invaded northern Mexico, seeking but not finding Villa and instead fighting several small-scale engagements with Mexican regulars attempting to limit their operations. U.S. forces withdrew in February 1917.

Mexico City explosion (November 19, 1984), explosion of a gasoline truck that set off a much larger explosion at a natural gas plant in Mexico City. An estimated 450 people were killed and 31,000 made homeless.

MGM Grand Hotel fire (November 21, 1980), a fire in a large new high-rise hotel in Las Vegas, Nevada, that had opened without smoke detectors and sprinklers in operating condition; 84 died and 500–600 more were injured.

MIAs, popular shorthand for missing in action; generally used in connection with U.S. troops missing in action during the VIETNAM WAR, some of whom may have been held as North Vietnamese prisoners; these were often called POWs/MIAs.

Michelson, Albert Abraham (1852–1931), U.S. physicist, who in 1920 first measured the diameter of a star, Betelgeuse, using a self-designed interferometer in which the canceling out or "interference" of some lines in rays of light allowed for measurement. For his earlier work—notably his 1878 measurement of the speed of light, refined in 1926—Michelson was the first American to win the Nobel Prize for Physics, in 1907.

microchip, popular name for the MICRO-PROCESSOR computer chip.

microprocessor, COMPUTER central processing unit, the formerly room-size set of heat-producing vacuum tubes much reduced and placed on a single silicon chip. Developed in 1971 by Marcian "Ted" Hoff of Intel, microprocessors—popularly called chips or microchips—made possible the miniaturization that led to inexpensive PERSONAL COMPUTERS.

microwave, type of high-frequency RADIATION, widely used in RADAR and in long-distance telephone and TELEVISION transmission. In 1921, in Britain, Albert W. Hull developed a microwave-producing ELECTRON TUBE called a magnetron, a significant aid in radar operations during World War II. Concern about the biological effects of microwaves have caused many countries to set occupational standards for exposure to them. Despite such concerns, microwave ovens, first patented in 1945, became extremely popular, with several million in use in the United States alone by the 1980s. Radio astronomers found microwaves among COSMIC RAYS, giving support to the BIG BANG THEORY of the universe's origin. Microwaves are also used in MASERS (**m**icrowave or **m**olecular **a**mplification by **s**timulated **e**mission of **r**adiation). From the 1980s scientists were experimenting with fuelless AIRPLANES, powered by microwave beams sent up from the ground.

MIDAS (**Mi**ssile **D**efense **A**lert **S**ystem), U.S. military surveillance SATELLITE system, the first launched on May 22, 1961.

Middle Congo, the former name of CONGO (People's Republic of the Congo), which was a French colony until 1958, and became an independent state on August 15, 1960.

Middletown, classic study of middle-class America, published in 1937 by Robert Staughton LYND and Helen Merrell LYND.

Midway, Battle of (June 4–6, 1942), the decisive battle of World War II in the Pacific. The Japanese sent a massive invasion fleet, including nine battleships and all of Japan's four major aircraft carriers, to take Midway Island, planning to later engage and defeat the remaining U.S. Pacific fleet, which they thought nowhere near Midway. The Americans, who had long known the Japanese secret communications codes, mobilized their three remaining aircraft carriers and a much smaller supporting fleet northeast of Midway, hoping to gain some advantage from Midway's contingent of fighter planes.

The Japanese were entirely surprised by the U.S. fleet, and lost all four of their aircraft carriers; the Americans lost only one carrier, the *Yorktown.* On June 6 the huge Japanese fleet headed for home; without air cover, it was helpless against carrier attack. The Allies were then able to take the offensive in the Pacific.

Mies van der Rohe, Ludwig (1886–1969), German-American architect, a leader in the theoretical development of the International Style in the 1920s and early 1930s, who directed the Bauhaus from 1930 to 1933, and put his "less is more" theories into practice after emigrating to the United States in the late 1930s. Two of his most influential works were his Chicago high-rise glass box apartment houses (1951), and his Seagram Building (1958), the latter built in collaboration with Philip JOHNSON.

Mihajlović, Draža (1893–1946), Yugoslav officer, who had fought with guerrilla units during the BALKAN WARS and in World War I, and who organized CHETNIK guerrilla forces after Germany's conquest of Yugoslavia in the spring of 1941. During World War II his pro-royalist forces fought German and Italian occupying forces, and TITO's partisans as well, in a three-way war. On the insistence of the Soviets at the TEHRAN CONFERENCE, Allied support of the Chetniks was withdrawn in late 1943 and early 1944, amid charges that the Chetniks had collaborated with German and Italian occupation forces. Mihajlović was captured by the partisans and executed in 1946.

Miki, Takeo (1907–88), Japanese political leader, in parliament from 1937, who opposed the growth of Japanese militarism in the late 1930s and emerged as a leader of the small liberal minority within the ruling conservative Liberal-Democratic party. He held several cabinet-level posts before becoming deputy prime minister in 1972 in the TANAKA government. He resigned in 1974, as financial scandal developed, then became prime minister after Tanaka's forced resignation. In 1976, he made the decision to pursue the LOCKHEED SCANDAL investigation and ultimately to prosecute

Tanaka. Miki lost power in 1976, remaining in parliament until 1986.

military-industrial complex, a phrase coined by U. S. president Dwight David EISENHOWER in his farewell address, in which he warned that government must guard against the "acquisition of unwarranted influence, whether sought or unsought, by the military-industrial complex."

Milk–Moscone murders (November 27, 1978), the shootings of gay San Francisco supervisor Harvey Milk and Mayor George Moscone by ex-supervisor Dan White. Having resigned from the board of supervisors because of financial pressures, White had wanted to be reappointed and Moscone had agreed to do so. Milk opposed White's return, Moscone changed his mind, and White murdered both. A jury convicted White of manslaughter, rather than murder, because of impaired capacity, a verdict sharply protested in San Francisco's gay community, which felt that the verdict reflected anti-gay sentiment on the part of the jury.

Milken, Michael R., U.S. securities industry figure who, during the 1980s headed the DREXEL, BURNHAM, LAMBERT "junk bond" department. He became the most important figure in the junk bond market, through which he arranged financing for many of the corporate takeovers of the time, while generating over $1 billion in personal compensation. In December 1988, as part of its settlement of massive securities fraud charges, Drexel agreed to fire Milken. On March 29, 1989, Milken and two former Drexel employees were indicted for allegedly committing a series of federal securities-related crimes; federal prosecutors said that they intended to ask for $1.8 billion in restitution.

Miller, Richard, a former FBI employee who was sentenced to life imprisonment as a Soviet spy in 1984. Soviet husband-and-wife émigrés Svetlana and Nikolai Ogorodnikov both pleaded guilty in the same case and received long prison sentences. Miller's conviction was later overturned on appeal.

Millikan, Robert Adrews (1868–1953), U.S. physicist who first measured the charge of an ELECTRON, helping to confirm both the fundamental PLANCK's constant and EINSTEIN's theories on the PHOTOELECTRIC EFFECT; he won the 1923 Nobel Prize in Physics. In 1925 he gave the name COSMIC RAYS to RADIATION emanating from outer space.

Mills, C. Wright (1916–62), U.S. sociologist, whose major interest was in the sociology of power, and whose main work, THE POWER ELITE (1956), described the United States as dominated by a set of somewhat overlapping elites. His work considerably influenced the thinking of the American reformers and radicals of the 1960s.

Mindszenty, Jozsef (1892–1975), Hungarian Roman Catholic priest who, as a bishop, was arrested for anti-Fascist activities during World War II; he became primate of Hungary in 1945 and a cardinal in 1946. Convicted of treason by the Communist government in 1949, he was sentenced to life imprisonment but was freed from what had by then become house arrest during the HUNGARIAN REVOLUTION of 1956. After the defeat of the revolution he took refuge in the American embassy for 15 years, refusing to leave until 1971, although he could have done so some years earlier.

Minh, Doung Van ("Big Minh;" 1916–), Vietnamese officer who led the army revolt that deposed NGO DINH DIEM in 1963, and was himself deposed in 1964, then fleeing abroad. Returning in 1968, he was an unsuccessful presidential candidate in 1971 and the last president of South Vietnam, for 2 days in 1975, before being captured by the North Vietnamese.

Minsk campaign of 1944 (June–July 1944), the Soviet summer offensive of 1944, late in World War II, that trapped and smashed German forces west of the Dnieper River. Minsk was retaken, with an estimated half million German casualties and prisoners and the loss of huge quantities of war materials.

Minton, Sherman (1890–1965), U.S. lawyer, Indiana Democratic senator 1935–39, and Seventh Circuit U.S. Court of Appeals judge 1941–49. He was appointed to the U.S. Supreme Court by President Harry S. TRUMAN in 1949 and thereafter took a generally conservative position on the Court, especially in regard to civil liberties matters.

Mir (Peace), modernized version of the U.S.S.R. SOYUZ space station, becoming the first permanently manned space station in 1986; built under the direction of Valentin GLUSHKO. Soviet cosmonaut Yuri V. Romanenko spent 326 days in the *Mir* station before returning to Earth in 1987, a record later broken by other Soviet cosmonauts. Cosmonauts were withdrawn from the *Mir* station in April 1989, presumably because of budget constraints.

Miranda v. *Arizona* (1966), a landmark and sharply controversial U.S. Supreme Court decision of June 13, 1966, that set rules covering the rights of criminal suspects. It required police to advise prisoners that they have the right to remain silent; that anything they say may be used against them; that they have the right to have a lawyer present while being questioned; that the court will appoint a lawyer if they cannot afford one; and that they may consult with a lawyer at any point, before continuing to speak. The Miranda ruling also stated that unless the prosecution could demonstrate at the trial that such warnings had been administered, and that prisoners had then waived such rights and continued to speak, no evidence obtained as a result of interrogation could be used against them. Later decisions of the BURGER and REHNQUIST courts considerably diluted the above guarantees.

MIRV (**m**ultiple **i**ndependently targetable **r**eentry **v**ehicle), a single MISSILE with many nuclear warheads, capable of being aimed to destroy many targets in a single flight, and therefore the subject of intense attention by nuclear arms reduction negotiators.

Miss America resignation, the forced resignation of the 1983 Miss America, Vanessa WILLIAMS, after *Penthouse* magazine revealed that she had earlier posed for nude photographs.

Mississippi civil rights murders (June 1964), the killings of civil rights workers James CHANEY, Andrew GOODMAN, and Michael SCHWERNER by white racists in Neshoba County, Mississippi. In 1967, seven men, including Deputy Sheriff Cecil Price and KU KLUX KLAN Imperial Wizard Sam Bowers, were convicted of federal civil rights violations in the case; no state charges in connection with the murders were filed. The murders were memorialized in the film *Mississippi Burning* (1988).

Mississippi Freedom Democratic Party, dissident Mississippi Democratic Party organization led by Fannie Lou HAMER, Charles EVERS, Hodding Carter III, and others. In 1964 it challenged as racist regular Democratic party delegates to the Democratic National Convention, blocked the seating of those delegates at the 1968 convention, and was itself seated as the regular delegation in 1972, thereby sharply altering the balance of forces within the Democratic party. The party was never an electoral force, although it sponsored some candidacies, including the gubernatorial campaign of Charles Evers in 1972.

Mississippi River floods (January–February 1937), the worst of many 20th-century floods in the Mississippi basin, causing an estimated 200–300 deaths and the evacuation of 600,000–700,000, as the river flooded most towns and cities along the Ohio and lower Mississippi. Major floods also occurred in 1912 and 1927.

Missouri, U.S. battleship on which the Japanese surrender in World War II was signed, in Tokyo harbor, on September 2, 1945.

Mitchell, John Newton (1913–88), U.S. lawyer, a municipal bond specialist, who met Richard M. NIXON when their Wall Street law firms merged in 1967, managed Nixon's 1968 presidential campaign, and became U.S. attorney-general in 1969. As attorney-general he mounted a major attack on antiwar and civil rights activists, that included indiscriminate wiretapping from 1969, prior restraint on publication of the PENTAGON PAPERS in 1971, and widespread harassment of dissenters and political opponents. His restraint order was stopped by the Supreme Court in 1971; his wiretapping activities were curbed by the Supreme Court in 1972. While attorney-general, Mitchell was deeply involved in the DIRTY TRICKS CAMPAIGN and the WATERGATE COVERUP. He resigned in February 1972 to head Nixon's reelection campaign, then resigned that position in June 1972, allegedly for family reasons. On January 1, 1975, he was convicted on several Watergate-connected charges, subsequently serving 19 months in prison. His wife, Martha Beall Jennings Mitchell, whose notable penchant for flamboyant public comment was much encouraged by the media and enormously destructive to John Mitchell, left him in 1974; she died two years later.

Mitchell, William "Billy" (1879–1936), U.S. officer, who saw service in the Spanish-American War and as an aviator and bomber group commander in World War I. During the early 1920s he strongly advocated the development of air power, especially naval air power, and was demoted. In 1925 he publicly and very sharply criticized his superiors after the loss of the dirigible *Shenandoah*, and was court-martialed, convicted, and resigned. As a civilian, he continued to advocate air power, raising the possibility of precisely the kind of attack that took place at PEARL HARBOR in 1941. He became a prophet with honor posthumously, a medal being voted him by Congress in 1946, 10 years after his death.

Mitscher, Marc Andrew (1887–1947), U.S. naval officer and pilot who commanded the aircraft carrier *Hornet* at the beginning of World War II and at the Battle of MIDWAY, in 1944 becoming a vice-admiral commanding the Fast Carrier Task Force and playing an important role in the liberation of the PHILIPPINES and the battle for OKINAWA.

Mitterand, François (1916–   ), French socialist political leader, who saw service in the RESISTANCE during World War II and

entered the national assembly in 1946, then served in many cabinet-level posts until 1958 and the triumph of Gaullism in France. He became president of France in 1981 and was reelected in 1988; he pursued increasing French participation in the EUROPEAN COMMUNITY and a moderate socialist program aimed at the nationalization of much of finance and industry, coupled with an increase in social welfare programs.

Mobutu Sese Seko (Joseph Désiré Mobuto; 1930–   ), Congolese officer, who became president of Zaire. With independence, in June 1960, he became army chief of staff. In September 1960, he briefly took control of the country, although the civilian government continued to be headed by President Joseph KASAVUBU. On November 25, 1965, he openly took power again, banned all opposition parties, set up a one-party authoritarian state, and successfully resisted several attempted coups. In 1971, in an effort to build national identity and unity, he Africanized the Congo, changing its name to Zaire, and changing many place and personal names, including his own, to their African equivalents.

Modane troop train crash (December 12, 1917), accident that killed 543 people when a troop train derailed close to Mt. Cénis tunnel in the Alps, near Modane, France; it was the world's worst railroad accident until the 1989 CHELYABINSK RAILROAD DISASTER. The accident was kept secret until after World War I ended.

Mogadishu rescue (October 18, 1977), sucessful West German commando attack, with the cooperation of the Somali government, on BAADER-MEINHOF GROUP hijackers holding 86 hostages aboard a Lufthansa airliner at Mogadishu airport.

Mohenjo-daro, center (with Harappa) of a major Bronze Age civilization in the Indus Valley, now in Pakistan, dating from about 2500–1500 B.C.; it was rediscovered and excavated from the 1920s by British archaeologist Mortimer WHEELER.

Mohorovicic discontinuity (Moho), thin boundary layer between the Earth's crust and the mantle below it, lying 5–40 kilometers below the surface and marked by sharp changes in the velocity of earthquake waves as they pass through Earth; it was discovered by Croatian seismologist Andrija Mohorovicic in 1909. In the 1961–66 Mohole Project, attempts by the U.S. research ship *GLOMAR CHALLENGER* to bring up samples of the Moho were abandoned because of expense; however, the techniques developed were helpful in later deep-sea drilling projects intended to enhance geological knowledge or to find new oil and gas deposits.

Moi, Daniel arap (1924–   ), Kenyan teacher, a founder of the Kenya African Democratic Union (KADU), the main opposition party in Kenya until its 1964 merger into the dominant Kenya African National Union (KANU), the party of Jomo KENYATTA. He served in the Kenyatta cabinet from 1961, became vice-president in 1967, and succeeded to the presidency in 1978, after Kenyatta's death. During his presidency substantial and increasing economic problems emerged, as did major internal political problems. The latter included an unsuccessful air force coup in 1982, the subsequent stifling of opposition, and the nominal reelection of Moi in 1988 without a popular vote, amounting to the straightforward establishment of an authoritarian government.

Molotov, Vyacheslav Mikhaylovich (1890–1986), Soviet diplomat and longtime associate of Joseph STALIN, who supported Stalin during the internecine Communist party struggles of the 1920s and the GREAT PURGE of the 1930s. He became chief Soviet diplomat in 1939, in that year negotiating the NAZI–SOVIET PACT. He accompanied Stalin at TEHERAN, YALTA, and POTSDAM and headed the Soviet UN delegation until 1949, representing the Soviet Union throughout the early years of the COLD WAR. He fell from favor in 1956, after having joined in an attempt to remove KHRUSHCHEV from office, and was dismissed and stripped of all power by Khrushchev in 1957.

Moltke, Helmuth von (1848–1916), German World War I chief of staff, 1906–14, whose modification of the SCHLIEFFEN PLAN made it possible for French and British forces to resist the first main German attack on France in 1914, and to stop the German armies at the Battle of the MARNE. After the German offensive stalled, he was replaced by General Erich von FALKENHAYN.

Mondale, Walter Frederick (1928–   ) U.S. lawyer, and Democratic senator from Minnesota (1964–77), who served one term as Jimmy CARTER's vice president (1977–81) and was his party's presidential nominee in 1984. He lost the election to Ronald REAGAN by a large margin, carrying only Minnesota and the District of Columbia. Throughout his career he was a liberal, focusing domestically on such matters as CIVIL RIGHTS and social welfare, and internationally on such matters as nuclear arms control, although for a time in the 1960s he supported JOHNSON administration policies in VIETNAM.

Mondlane, Eduardo (1920–69), Mozambican independence movement leader; educated abroad, he was employed by the UNITED NATIONS and was a university teacher before returning to Africa in 1962 to found FRELIMO (Mozambique Liberation Front) and take it into the long MOZAMBIQUE WAR OF INDEPENDENCE in 1964. He pursued that war as leader of FRELIMO until his assassination by the Portuguese in 1969.

monkey trial, media-generated name for the 1925 SCOPES TRIAL which tested the Tennessee law prohibiting the teaching of evolution.

Monod, Jacques Lucien (1910–76), French biologist and director of Pasteur Institute in Paris who shared a 1965 Nobel Prize for Physiology or Medicine for his work on how living cells use a FEEDBACK mechanism to control the manufacturing of vital substances. A hero of the French RESISTANCE, Monod is probably best known for his 1970 book, *Chance and Necessity*, in which he postulated that the whole of evolution has resulted from pure chance and that there is no plan or intention in the universe. This view, for Monod the result of attempted pure scientific objectivity, had links with EXISTENTIALISM, as expressed by his friend Albert CAMUS.

Mons, Battle of (August 23, 1914), one of the World War I Battles of the FRONTIERS, in which German forces sweeping south and west through Belgium forced back British and Belgian forces as part of a general Allied retreat.

Montagu, Montague Francis Ashley (1905–   ), British-American anthropologist, who wrote widely on a number of controversial topics, notably race, sexual equality, CREATIONISM, and human aggression. Perhaps his best-known work was *Man's Most Dangerous Myth: The Fallacy of Race* (1942), from which he drew his draft of UNESCO's 1950 "Statement on Race."

Montenegro, an independent nation at the beginning of the 20th century and a kingdom from 1910. Montenegro fought on the Allied side during World War I, being occupied by Austrian and German forces from 1916. It became part of Yugoslavia after World War I, was occupied by Italian troops, 1941–45, and became part of Yugoslavia again after World War II.

Montesorri, Maria (1870–1952), Italian physician—the first woman medical doctor in her country since medieval times—who helped transform early childhood education. At her Children's House in Rome, founded in 1907, she developed methods and materials designed to free a child's creative energy and develop coordination and perception, with the teacher as guide and inspiration rather than as instructor. These formed the model for the private Montessori schools later founded around the world, and they strongly influenced public-sponsored elementary education as well.

Montgomery, Bernard Law (1887–1976), British officer, who saw service in India and during World War I and was a divisional commander in the BRITISH EXPEDITIONARY FORCE early in World War II, leaving France with his division at DUNKIRK. He commanded the British Eighth Army during the North African campaign, winning the Battle of EL ALAMEIN and ultimately linking up with Allied forces in Tunisia. He commanded British armies invading Sicily and then Italy, leaving the Italian campaign to prepare for the coming invasion of NORMANDY. He served under General Dwight D. EISENHOWER during and after that invasion, though often in extremely abrasive disagreement as to many major aspects of the European campaign. In 1944, he became a field marshal, and after the war he held important British and NATO posts.

Montgomery bus boycott, the 381-day Black boycott of public transportation in Montgomery, Alabama, organized by Martin Luther KING, Jr. and Ralph D. ABERNATHY after the December 1, 1955, arrest of Rosa PARKS for refusing to give up her seat on a public bus. The campaign, which resulted in the desegregation of the city's buses, was the first major action of the modern American CIVIL RIGHTS MOVEMENT, catapulting King into national leadership, and beginning the long series of actions that in the next decade would mount a major attack on racism in the United States.

Moon, Earth's natural satellite and the target of various space activities, including the U.S.S.R.'s series of LUNIK SATELLITES, which first landed on the Moon in 1959; the U.S. RANGER, SURVEYOR, and LUNAR ORBITER series, which also landed on the Moon, gathering data for a manned visit; and the U.S. APOLLO series which put the first humans on the Moon in 1969.

Moon, Sun Myung (1920–   ), South Korean minister, who founded the Unification Church in 1954; he also developed considerable commercial interests in South Korea and the United States, some of them as an individual and some as church-run enterprises. His mostly young converts, popularly known as "Moonies," were pressed to develop total financial and personal commitment to the church. Moon moved his headquarters to the United States in 1973; in 1982 he was convicted of U.S. income tax evasion, receiving an 18-month sentence.

Mooney, Thomas J., and WARREN K. BILLINGS, labor leaders who were convicted of bombing a San Francisco Preparedness Day parade on July 22, 1916, killing 10 and injuring scores of others. Mooney received a death sentence; Billings was sentenced to life imprisonment. A worldwide movement, the weakness of the trial evidence, and the intervention of President Woodrow WILSON secured commutation of Mooney's sentence to life imprisonment, and in 1939 he received a pardon. In the same year, Billings's sentence was reduced, and he was released.

Moonlight Sonata, German code name for the terrorist bombing raids conducted during the moonlight hours of November 14–15, 1940, on the British city of COVENTRY. The British had foreknowledge of the attack but could not use it, because of the need to protect crucial ULTRA information.

Moore, Sara Jane, would-be assassin who shot at but missed President Gerald R. FORD in San Francisco, on September 22, 1975; she was immediately captured and subsequently sentenced to life imprisonment.

Moral Majority, U.S. conservative political organization founded by the Reverend Jerry FALWELL in June 1979, that developed continuing campaigns on several major issues, including abortion, communism, homosexuality, women's rights, and pornography, all of which it opposed; and the American family, school prayer, and a strong military, all of which it favored. It was dissolved by Falwell in June 1989.

Morgan, John Pierpont (1837–1913), U.S. investment banker who became the most powerful financier of the late 19th and early 20th centuries. By the early 1900s he controlled a widespread financial and industrial empire that included what was then the largest corporation in the world, the United States Steel Corporation, which he organized in 1901. He also controlled banks, securities firms, major railroads, shipping lines, and other industrial companies. Morgan was powerful enough to organize the private financial effort that controlled the brief PANIC OF 1907 but not strong enough to withstand the political power of the trust-busting progressive Republicans of his day, led by President Theodore ROOSEVELT. In 1904 his Northern Securities Company, a massive railroad trust, was broken up by the landmark Supreme Court decision in the NORTHERN SECURITIES CASE, and in 1912 the PUJO COMMITTEE hearings subjected his holdings to extensive public scrutiny. He was also a very substantial philanthropist and art collector; much of his art collection went to the Metropolitan Museum of Art on his death, and his book collection became the Morgan Library.

Morgan, Thomas Hunt (1866–1945), U.S. biologist, who laid the foundation of modern genetics, for which he was awarded the 1933 Nobel Prize for Physiology or Medicine, the first U.S.-born American and the first nonphysician so honored. In breeding experiments (1907–10) using the common fruit fly, *Drosophila*, Morgan showed for the first time that GENES were units of heredity, and that some inherited characteristics are sex-linked, ideas outlined in several works, notably *Theory of the Gene* (1926).

Morocco (Kingdom of Morocco), until 1956, split into French and Spanish protectorates although formally an independent nation. Morocco was not easily held: the RIF WAR of the 1920s was the most powerful of many risings against European rule, and the country was not fully conquered until the mid-1930s. Independence came on March 2, 1956.

Morocco Crisis of 1905, a crisis that occurred when Germany challenged French colonial interests in Morocco. It led to the Algeciras Conference of 1906, resulting in British support of France against Germany.

Morocco Crisis of 1911, a second Morocco crisis, which occurred when Germany again challenged the French, sending the gunboat *Panther* to the Moroccan port of Agadir. With Britain supporting France, a general war seemed very close, but Germany withdrew after a face-saving agreement with France. Both Morocco crises were part of the run-up to World War I.

***Morro Castle* sinking** (September 7–8, 1934), the sinking of the excursion liner *Morro Castle* off New Jersey after a fire that went out of control. The crew fought the fire ineffectually, then took the first lifeboats, leaving most of the passengers on board; 134 passengers died in the fire and sinking.

Mosca, Gaetano (1858–1941), Italian political theorist, who from the early 1880s and most influentially in his *Elements of Political Science* (1896), posited that all societies are dominated by ruling elites. A liberal legislator and diplomat, he left public life after the victory of fascism in Italy. His theories, which in no way favored fascism, were used by Italian fascists to justify totalitarian rule.

Moscow, Battle of (November–December 1941), the decisive early battle on the Russian front in World War II. German forces, advancing uninterruptedly since the June 22 invasion, neared Moscow in October; slowed in mud and developing cold weather, they paused to regroup. With reinforcements and the commitment of much of Germany's remaining air force in the east, they renewed their offensive, ultimately reaching Moscow's suburbs. But Russian reinforcements from the Far East arrived in early November, the defenses of Moscow held, and Soviet forces began a major and successful counteroffensive on December 6. The long German offensive ended, short of Moscow. HITLER then compounded German problems by relieving several of his generals and taking personal command of the situation.

Moscow, Treaty of (July 1920), recognized the independence of Lithuania after the LITHUANIAN WAR OF INDEPENDENCE (1918–20).

Moscow summit (May 1988), the fourth meeting between U.S. President Ronald REAGAN and U.S.S.R. premier Mikhail GORBACHEV, at which they exchanged for-

mal INF TREATY ratification documents, continued their attempts to resolve regional conflicts and long-standing superpower differences throughout the world, and signed a series of less important agreements, all in continuance of the new set of Soviet-American relationships that had begun with the transfer of Soviet power to Gorbachev in early 1985.

Moscow trials, three major show trials held in Moscow, in 1936, 1937, and 1938, during the GREAT PURGE, in which many of the Soviet Union's best-known Communists, all of them at some time opposed to Joseph STALIN, confessed themselves guilty of a wide assortment of wholly fabricated crimes and were subsequently executed, many of them to later be "posthumously rehabilitated."

Moslem Brotherhood, Sunni Islamic fundamentalist movement largely based in Egypt from its founding in 1928, which developed considerable strength and much terrorist activity during the 1940s. The organization was banned in Egypt, and greatly damaged by the government of Gamal Abdal NASSER in the 1950s, suffering thousands of arrests and the execution or imprisonment of much of its leadership. It has experienced some resurgence in the 1980s through covert alliances with legal parties. In Syria, the movement developed strength as a legal party after its founding in the late 1930s and through the BA'ATH coup of 1963 but was then outlawed, moving into guerrilla and terrorist warfare against the government. A Moslem Brotherhood–led insurrection at Hama in 1982 was defeated by the Iraqi army, with thousands killed.

Moslem League (All-India Moslem League), a Moslem political and civil rights organization formed in 1906 in British India that became a mass political organization under the leadership of Mohammad Ali JINNAH in the late 1930s. In 1940 the League called for the formation of the separate Islamic state of Pakistan and won British and Indian agreement to the creation of an independent Pakistan after the massive Hindu-Moslem civil disorders of 1945. The League became the ruling party of Pakistan after independence in 1947 but was banned from 1958 to 1962, as were all political parties. It reorganized in 1962, renamed itself the Pakistan Moslem League, and nominally returned to power, remaining in power until the rise of the Pakistan People's party in 1977. During the rule of Mohammad ZIA UL-HAQ, the party was allowed to form a cabinet with Mohammed Khan Junejo as prime minister, but all real power resided in Zia and the Pakistani army.

Mosley, Oswald (1896–1980), British fascist, racist, and founder of the British Union of Fascists in 1932; he began his political career as a Conservative in 1918, switched to Labour in 1924, and was a Labour MP 1926–30. Mosley became a MUSSOLINI-style fascist in 1932, later leaning more toward the more overtly anti-Jewish Nazi style of fascism. During the 1930s his party attempted to develop a Nazi paramilitary force in Britain, with largely unsuccessful street actions in London's then predominantly Jewish East End. It provoked counterviolence, and the government then banned the development of such private armed forces. Mosley was arrested and interned, 1940–43, thereafter serving mainly as an inspirational symbol to later British fascist movements.

Mossadeq, Mohammed (1880–1967), Iranian political leader and lifelong opponent of the PAHLEVI shahs of Iran, who became head of Iran's National Front party in the late 1940s and premier of Iran when his party took power in 1951. The Mossadeq government nationalized Iran's oil industry, precipitating a major dispute with Great Britain, and simultaneously attempted to develop a new social system in Iran. In August 1953 U.S. and British intelligence organizations tried and failed to organize a coup against the Iranian government; Shah Mohammed Reza Pahlevi then fled the country. Three days later an army revolt toppled the government, the shah returned, and Mossadeq was imprisoned. He left prison 3 years later, but was kept under house arrest until his death.

Mother Cabrini, the popular name of Frances Xavier CABRINI, a Catholic nun who worked with poor immigrants and was sainted in 1946.

Mother Jones, the popular name of Mary Harris JONES, U.S. labor organizer of the late 19th and early 20th centuries.

Mother Teresa (Agnes Gonxha Bojaxhiu; 1910–   ), Roman Catholic nun, from 1928, who taught in India; in 1948 she founded a school in Calcutta dedicated to working with the poor, and in 1950 founded what became the worldwide Missionaries of Charity order, which worked with the poor and ill. She received the 1979 Nobel Peace Prize for her work.

Mount St. Helens eruption (May 18, 1980), a huge volcanic eruption in the state of Washington that killed 40–60 people and caused great physical damage. Although there was adequate warning, the eruption was much more powerful than had been anticipated.

Mountbatten, Louis (Lord Mountbatten; 1900–79), British naval officer and cousin to the British royal family, who became chief of British combined operations 1942–43 and supreme Allied commander in southeast Asia 1943–46; he commanded the Allied forces that took back Burma from the Japanese. He was the last viceroy of India, and as British governor-general worked with both sides during the PARTITION OF INDIA. He was assassinated by the IRISH REPUBLICAN ARMY on August 28, 1979, while on holiday off the coast of Ireland.

Mount Ogura crash (August 12, 1985), crash of a Japan Air 747 into Mt. Ogura, Japan, killing 520 of 524 aboard; it was the world's worst single-plane disaster to date.

Mount Pelée eruption (May 8, 1902), a volcanic eruption that killed an estimated 30,000, destroying the city of Saint-Pierre on the island of Martinique. The deaths occurred largely because the local government chose to ignore abundant signs and specific scientific warnings of an impending eruption.

MOVE bombing (May 13, 1985), police bombing of the Philadelphia building housing the radical MOVE organization after earlier efforts to evict MOVE members had led to a police siege. The bombing—set off in an attempt to force evacuation—killed 11 people, several of them children, and started a fire that destroyed 61 neighborhood homes.

Mozambique (People's Republic of Mozambique), until 1975 a Portuguese colony. It became independent on June 25, 1975, after the MOZAMBIQUE WAR OF INDEPENDENCE.

Mozambique National Resistance, formal name of RENAMO, the Portuguese and South African–backed insurgent organization in Mozambique.

Mozambique War of Independence (1964–74), a 10-year guerrilla war fought by FRELIMO (Mozambique National Liberation Front) forces against the Portuguese army with considerable success. It ended with the April 1974 coup in Portugal which overthrew the SALAZAR government. The new Portuguese government, headed by Antonio SPINOLA, made peace with FRELIMO, headed by Machel SAMORA; independence came to Mozambique in June 1975.

MPLA, initials of the POPULAR MOVEMENT FOR THE LIBERATION OF ANGOLA, by which the organization is best known.

MRI (magnetic resonance imager), alternate name for the NMR IMAGER.

Mubarek, Mohammed Hosni (1928–   ), Egyptian air force officer, who became air force chief of staff in 1969, armed forces commander-in-chief in 1972, and Anwar al-SADAT'S vice-president in 1975. His prestige soared after his forces scored substantial early successes during the YOM KIPPUR WAR (FOURTH ARAB–ISRAELI WAR) of 1973. After Sadat's assassination in 1981, Mubarek succeeded to the Egyptian presidency, thereafter essentially continuing Sadat's moderate foreign policies, combatting Islamic fundamentalism at home, and attempting to deal with Egypt's very serious economic problems.

muckrakers, a body of U.S. writer-reformers who described a wide range of corrupt practices and attitudes throughout American society in the early years of the 20th century, with special attention to corporate practices in the period 1902–12. Their work came to public attention with the publication of Ida TARBELL's 1902 series on the Standard Oil Corporation, but the name "muckraker" was first applied to them by Theodore ROOSEVELT in 1906. Their work furthered some of his most strongly supported legislative reforms, including the PURE FOOD AND DRUG ACT (1906), and the Beef Inspection Act (1906), which followed soon after publication of Upton SINCLAIR's THE JUNGLE, a novel that powerfully and effectively attacked meatpacking practices.

Mueller v. *Allen* (1983), a landmark U.S. Supreme Court decision validating a Minnesota law that allowed state tax deductions for tuition, textbooks, and transportation to private elementary and secondary schools.

Mugabe, Robert Gabriel (1924–   ), Zimbabwean teacher, nationalist, and socialist who was a founder of the Zimbabwe African National Union (ZANU) in 1963. He was imprisoned, 1964–75, emerging to join the intensifying guerrilla war against Ian SMITH'S white Rhodesian government. He became leader of ZANU in 1976, quickly forming a troubled but effective alliance with Joshua NKOMO'S Zimbabwe African People's Union (ZAPU) in the Patriotic Front. The two parties campaigned independently in the free, British-supervised elections of 1980; ZANU won a clear majority, and Mugabe became first prime minister of the new Republic of Zimbabwe. His party won again in 1985, Mugabe becoming executive president. His ZANU forced ZAPU to merge with it with in 1987; in that year, the Mugabe government also abolished the reservation of 20 parliamentary seats for whites. Zimbabwe then became a one-party state led by Mugabe, with a very large cabinet that included Nkomo.

Muhammad, Elijah (Elijah Poole; 1897–1975), U.S. BLACK MUSLIM, who succeeded Wali Farad as leader of the NATION OF ISLAM in 1934. He was imprisoned, 1942–46, for counseling draft evasion.

Mujaheddin, in Afghanistan, a general term encompassing all of the diverse antigovernment, anti-Soviet groups and guerrilla fighters engaged in the AFGHAN–SOVIET WAR of the 1980s. It is also the name popularly applied to an umbrella guerrilla organization, the Islamic Alliance of Afghan Holy Warriors, which emerged as a government-in-exile, based in Pakistan, in 1985.

Mujaheddin-e-Khalq (People's Warriors), an Iranian socialist and Islamic political and military organization that opposed the shah and became the major source of armed resistance to Iran's Islamic fundamentalist government. It engaged in guerrilla warfare, terrorism, and assassination throughout the country.

Mukden, Battle of (February 21–March 10, 1904), the decisive land battle of the RUSSO–JAPANESE WAR, in which the Japanese defeated the Russians.

Mukden-Chinchow, Battle of (October 27–30, 1948), the defeat and then destruction of the retreating Nationalist Manchurian army by Communist forces during the final stages of the CHINESE CIVIL WAR.

Mukden Incident (September 18–19, 1931), the seizure of Mukden, China, by Japan's KWANGTUNG ARMY; the alleged bombing of a Japanese railway line was the pretext used. The army then quickly seized all of Manchuria, renaming it Manchukuo, and set up Henry P'U YI as its puppet ruler.

Muldoon, Robert David (1921–   ), New Zealand accountant, a Conservative member of parliament from 1960 and prime minister 1975–84, who leaned toward the United States in foreign affairs and pursued a conservative course at home.

Mulroney, Martin Brian (1939–   ), Canadian lawyer and corporate executive, who entered parliament and became Progressive Conservative party leader in 1983. As prime minister (1984–   ) he negotiated a major trade treaty with the United States in January 1988, and won an electoral victory largely on the issue of approval of that treaty, in November 1988, while continuing to face substantial economic problems.

Munich Agreement (September 29–30, 1938), the agreement made in Munich, Germany, by which France and Great Britain acceded to German demands for "self-determination," meaning, in practice, immediate annexation by Germany of several largely German-speaking areas in western Czechoslovakia. The Nazis called the area the SUDETENLAND; it had been part of Czechoslovakia since the end of World War I. The agreement was made by prime ministers Neville CHAMBERLAIN and Édouard DALADIER without consulting the Czechs. It clearly meant immediate dismemberment of Czechoslovakia, predictably followed by German annexation of the rest of the country, which came in March 1939, without demur from Great Britain and France. It also very clearly encouraged HITLER to continue his adventurist policies and led directly to World War II, although Chamberlain told his people afterward that he had brought them "PEACE FOR OUR TIME."

Munich Olympics murders (September 1972), a BLACK SEPTEMBER terrorist group attacked Israeli athletes at the 20th Olympics, in Munich, killing two and taking nine hostages; all nine were killed when a rescue operation miscarried. Five terrorists were killed in the action; the others were later traded for hostages taken in an airline hijacking.

Muñoz Marín, Luis (1898–1980), Puerto Rican journalist and son of Luis Muñoz Rivera, a leader in the fight for freedom from Spanish rule before U.S. annexation of Puerto Rico. In 1938 he founded the Puerto Rican Popular Democratic party, thereafter leading his party to electoral majority. In 1948 he was elected the first Puerto Rican governor of the island and was reelected three times (1952–64).

Murder, Incorporated, the name given by the media of the 1930s to the assassination group of the MAFIA, or national crime syndicate. The leaders of the group were Albert Anastasia and Louis "Lepke" Buchalter.

Murdoch, Keith Rupert (1931–), Australian-American publisher who, starting in 1952 with a single small Australian newspaper, built a large, diverse worldwide communications enterprise. His publications include *The Times* of London, one of the world's oldest and most highly respected newspapers, as well as a wide variety of other publishing, broadcasting, and related companies.

Murmansk Run, during World War II, the North Atlantic convoy route from assembly areas near Iceland to Murmansk; in warmer weather, some convoys went to Archangel. From early 1942 enormous quantities of American war material flowed to the Soviet Union along this route.

Murphy, Frank (1890–1949), U.S. lawyer, who pursued a varied career as practicing attorney, prosecutor, judge, mayor of Detroit, U.S. high commissioner of the Philippines, Democratic governor of Michigan (1936–38), and U.S. attorney-general (1939–40), before being appointed by Franklin D. ROOSEVELT to the Supreme Court in 1940. As governor and attorney-general, he had been a strong voice in defense of civil rights and sympathetic to union organization; he continued to pursue those interests on the Court.

Murray, Philip (1886–1952), U.S. coal miner, and vice-president of the United Mine Workers of America (UMW) 1920–42. In 1936 John L. LEWIS appointed him head of the Steel Workers Organizing Committee, which went on to become the United Steelworkers of America; he became its first president in 1942. Murray was president of the CONGRESS OF INDUSTRIAL ORGANIZATIONS (CIO) 1940–52.

Murrow, Edward Roscoe (1908–65), U.S. journalist and broadcaster, whose World War II broadcasts from London ("THIS IS LONDON") during the BLITZ in 1940 developed great sympathy for the Allied cause in the United States. He became a television broadcaster in the 1950s, his "See It Now" becoming the most celebrated public service program of the time, as was his later "Person to Person." In the early 1950s he powerfully and effectively opposed the witchhunts generated by Senator Joseph MCCARTHY and his associates.

Muskie, Edmund Sixtus (1914–), U.S. lawyer, Democratic governor of Maine, 1955–59; senator, 1959–80; and secretary of state, May 1980–January 1981. In 1968 he unsuccessfully ran for the vice-presidency, and in 1972 unsuccessfully sought his party's presidential nomination. He was the Democratic frontrunner during much of the nomination campaign, but his campaign was seriously damaged by the DIRTY TRICKS CAMPAIGN organized and financed by the staff of President Richard M. NIXON, then seeking reelection.

Mussolini, Benito "Il Duce" (1883–1945), Italian teacher, journalist, and one-time socialist who became fascist leader of Italy, 1922–43. In 1912 he became editor of the socialist newspaper *Avanti*, strongly opposing the oncoming world war. In 1914 he changed his position, became editor of a pro-war newspaper, and was expelled from the Socialist Party. In 1919 he founded the first Italian fascist organization and in 1921 became a fascist member of parliament, in the same period organizing the BLACKSHIRTS into terrorist street-fighting groups that became a national paramilitary force. In 1922 the fascist MARCH ON ROME in late October was unopposed by King VICTOR EMMANUEL III and the Italian army; Mussolini became prime minister and soon dictator of Italy, known as Il Duce (The Leader). In that position he destroyed Italian democracy and murdered, jailed, and exiled his opponents. He also became extremely popular with the great mass of the Italian people for his oratory, grandiose building schemes, the seeming stability and relative prosperity he brought to the country, and his empire building. In 1935 his armies invaded ETHIOPIA, ignoring inadequate LEAGUE OF NATIONS sanctions. In 1936 the Italian government began sending massive support to the fascist side in the SPANISH CIVIL WAR, including an estimated 50,000 troops and more than 1,500 airplanes, at that time much of the Italian air force. In 1939 Italy occupied ALBANIA. On June 10, 1940, Mussolini took his country into World War II on the side of his German ally, Adolf HITLER. His forces proved totally inadequate for modern warfare. The Italian army was defeated in Greece, needing German help to ultimately defeat the much smaller, poorly equipped Greek army. In the early days of the war in North Africa major elements of the Italian army were destroyed by much smaller British forces, with hundreds of thousands of Italian prisoners taken. On July 24, 1943, after the Allied invasion of Sicily on July 23, Mussolini was stripped of power and imprisoned by his own Fascist Grand Council. The Germans rescued him, took him to Munich, and then set him up in a puppet government in northern Italy; the fighting on the Italian front was taken over by German troops. At the end, April 28, 1945, he and his mistress, Claretta Petacci, were killed by Italian partisans, who found him trying to escape over the border to Germany disguised as a German soldier.

mustard gas, popular name for 2,2'-dichlorodiethyl sulfide, the "king of poison gases," introduced in 1917 in World War I as part of CHEMICAL AND BIOLOGICAL WARFARE.

Muste, Abraham Johannes (1887–1967), U.S. pacifist minister, who was executive secretary of the FELLOWSHIP OF RECONCILIATION, 1940–53, and a leading antinuclear activist and peace movement leader after the use of the atomic bomb AT HIROSHIMA and NAGASAKI and the development of the COLD WAR in the late 1940s. Earlier, during the 1920s and 1930s, he had been a labor

organizer and Marxian socialist revolutionary.

Muzorewa, Abel Tendekayi (1925–), Zimbabwean United Methodist bishop and black nationalist, a moderate who did not join the large-scale move into intensified civil war in 1975–76 and who was, in 1979, briefly prime minister of the white-organized multracial government of Rhodesia that preceded the establishment of the Republic of Zimbabwe.

My Lai Massacre (March 16, 1968), the mass murders of Vietnamese civilians, mostly women, children, and old men, in the hamlet of My Lai in Quang Tri province, Vietnam, by soldiers of the Americal Division, U.S. Army. The platoon, commanded by Lieutenant William L. CALLEY, Jr., murdered an estimated 347 unarmed civilians after pushing them into a ditch, and were then joined in a daylong orgy of atrocities by other U.S. soldiers in the area. A later court martial convicted only Lieutenant Calley of mass murder, all 12 other indicted soldiers escaping any penalty. Calley was sentenced to life imprisonment; his sentence was later commuted to 10 years, and he was paroled in September 1974.

Myrdal, Alva Reimer (1902–86), Swedish teacher, social planner, public official, diplomat, and peace activist, who directed social welfare departments of the UNITED NATIONS and UNESCO 1949–56, was Swedish ambassador to India 1956–61, a member of parliament 1962–70, Geneva Disarmament Conference delegate 1962–73, and minister for disarmament and church affairs 1966–73. Throughout her life, Alva Myrdal was deeply concerned with world population control, social welfare, and disarmament. She shared a Nobel Peace Prize with Alfonso García Robles in 1982. Her husband was Gunnar MYRDAL.

Myrdal, Gunnar (1898–1987), Swedish economist and sociologist, whose interest in the related matters of worldwide poverty, population control, race relations, and integrated economic development produced a series of major and very influential works, including the classic study of U.S. race relations, *An American Dilemma* (1944), and *Asian Drama* (1968). He was Swedish minister of trade and commerce, 1945–47, and executive secretary of the UNITED NATIONS Economic Commission for Europe, 1947–57. His term "stagflation," used to describe the combination of stagnation and inflation he believed characterized most Western economies in the 1970s and 1980s, became part of the language. He shared a Nobel Memorial Prize in Economic Science with Friedrich HAYEK in 1974. His wife was Alva MYRDAL.

N

NAACP, the initials of the NATIONAL ASSO-CIATION FOR THE ADVANCEMENT OF COLORED PEOPLE.

Nader, Ralph (1934–   ), U.S. lawyer, who became a leading consumer advocate. He began his work soon after graduation from law school in 1958, and published his book *Unsafe at Any Speed*, an attack on the safety of U.S. motor vehicles, in 1965, later organizing a group of like-minded reformers who took up a wide range of consumer safety issues.

Nagasaki, site on Japan's Kyushu Island where the second ATOMIC BOMB was used in warfare. At 9:30 A.M., on August 9, 1945, a B-29 bomber of the U.S. Air Force dropped the bomb on the city of Nagasaki, a secondary target, after the pilot failed to sight the prime target at Kokura. It was the only atomic bomb then in existence, the first having been used in the TRINITY test and the second to bomb HIROSHIMA on August 6. Nagasaki, like Hiroshima, was a relatively undamaged minor military target; the bombing was intended as a demonstration of the killing power of the atomic weapon and an attempt to force Japan to surrender unconditionally. The Nagasaki bomb immediately killed an estimated 40,000–70,000 people, injuring an equal number and destroying approximately half of the city's structures. An estimated 50,000–100,000 more people later died of RADIATION sickness, CANCER, and other bomb-related injuries, most of them within a few years of the bombing; victims and their children are still dying today of the bomb's effects. The city was rebuilt after the war, away from the ra-

diation-damaged area; part of it is now a peace park.

Nagorno-Karabagh, largely Armenian enclave in Azerbaijan, the genesis of the AZERBAIJANI-ARMENIAN CIVIL WAR that began in early 1988.

Nagumo, Chuichi (1887–1944), Japanese naval officer who, as commander of the First Air Fleet, directed major Japanese air attacks during the early years of World War II, including the attack on PEARL HARBOR on December 7, 1941. He commanded the Japanese carrier fleet at the Battle of MIDWAY, losing four carriers and with them Japanese hopes of winning the Pacific war. He was later relieved of carrier force command, and committed suicide in July 1944.

Nagy, Imre (1896–1958), Hungarian Communist leader, who joined the BOLSHEVIKS while a Russian war prisoner during World War I, returned to do clandestine Communist organizing work in Hungary, 1921–30, and lived in the Soviet Union, 1930–44, working as an agronomist. He returned to Hungary after World War II as agriculture minister in the RÁKOSI government. After STALIN's death in 1953 he replaced Rákosi as prime minister, immediately instituting the more liberal policies favored by new Soviet prime minister, Georgi MALENKOV; he lost power to Rákosi in 1955 and was expelled from his party later that year. He became prime minister again on October 24, 1956, during the HUNGARIAN REVOLUTION, immediately instituted major democratic reforms, released Cardinal MINDZENTY, and announced Hungary's neutrality and coming withdrawal from the WARSAW PACT. After the Soviet invasion that ended the revolt he was executed. He was posthumously rehabitated in 1989, and reburied, with honors.

Najibullah, Mohammad (1947–   ), Afghani political leader, who succeeded Babrak KARMAL as ruling party head in May 1986 and formally took power in Afghanistan in December 1986. Before that he had been head (1979–85) of the secret police.

Nakasone, Yasuhiro (1918–   ), Japanese political leader, a World War II naval officer, in parliament from 1947, who held a series of cabinet-level posts in the 1960s and 1970s and was leader of the ruling conservative Liberal Democratic party and prime minister 1982–87. In 1988 a massive stock scandal was exposed, revealing that several of Nakasone's key associates and aides had engaged in illegal activities while in office, as far back as 1984.

Namibia, until 1918, as South West Africa, a German colony. It was occupied by South African forces during the World War I and afterward; it became a South African–administered LEAGUE OF NATIONS mandate territory in 1920 and a UNITED NATIONS trust territory after World War II. After 1946 South Africa continued to occupy Namibia in defiance of the UN and from the mid-1960s attempted to apply its own APARTHEID policies to Namibia. The long NAMIBIAN WAR OF INDEPENDENCE began in 1966 and ended in 1988. Namibia became an independent nation in March 1990.

Namibian War of Independence (1966–88), a guerrilla war conducted by the SOUTH-WEST AFRICA PEOPLE'S ORGANIZATION OF NAMIBIA (SWAPO), operating out of bases in Angola, against the South African occupiers of Namibia, who were holding Namibia under authority of a mandate that was withdrawn by the UNITED NATIONS General Assembly in October 1966. SWAPO forces were supplied by the Soviet Union and backed by Cuban and Angolan forces. The South African army was able to contain the low-level insurgency, making many incursions into Angola against

SWAPO forces, often fighting Cuban and Angolan forces as well, sometimes in support of the South African–backed guerrillas of the Jonas SAVIMBI'S NATIONAL UNION FOR THE TOTAL INDEPENDENCE OF ANGOLA (UNITA). The long insurgency continued, however, side by side with the long ANGOLAN CIVIL WAR, accompanied by unremitting United Nations condemnation of the South African occupation of Namibia. In November 1988, as part of an attempted general peace settlement in the region and with Cuban and South African forces withdrawing, South Africa agreed to Namibian independence. The independence process was almost upset at the outset, as SWAPO guerrillas moved across the Angolan border soon after the cease-fire in violation of the peace agreement. They were forced back over the border with considerable losses, and the peace agreement held, supervised by a UN peacekeeping force.

Nanchang Uprising (August 1927), the first major armed clash of the long CHINESE CIVIL WAR. The Communist forces were defeated, their remnants fleeing to the Ching-kang Mountains of western Kiangsi.

Nansen, Fridtjof (1861–1930), Norwegian oceanographer and statesman. From the 1880s Nansen was an Arctic explorer, his most famous expedition being 1895–1896 when, with his specially built ship *Fram* (*Forward*), he explored the drift of polar ice, nearly reaching the NORTH POLE. He continued oceanographic explorations and teaching and from 1906 was a public official as well. In newly independent NORWAY he served as minister to Britain (1906–08) and head of his country's LEAGUE OF NATIONS delegation (1920). From then until his death he headed commissions, for the League and for the International Red Cross, designed to repatriate prisoners of war and help resettle displaced persons; he developed for them a special identity card, popularly dubbed the "Nansen passport." Awarded the 1922 Nobel Peace Prize for this work, he donated the prize money to the cause.

Narayan, Jaya Prakash (1902–79), Indian nationalist and socialist, a follower of Mahatma GANDHI in his youth, who led an armed insurgency against British rule during World War II. Narayan left political life in the early 1950s but came out of retirement to challenge Indira GANDHI'S government in 1974, charging corruption and a worsening of the condition of the masses of the Indian poor. He was chief organizer of the Janata party coalition that defeated Gandhi in the 1977 elections; that done, he retired again in 1978.

Narvik, key site in the 1940 Battle of NORWAY, early in World War II.

NASA, initials of the NATIONAL AERONAUTICS AND SPACE ADMINISTRATION.

Nasser, Gamal Abdel (1918–70), Egyptian officer, who in 1948 saw service in the FIRST ARAB–ISRAELI WAR (ISRAELI WAR OF INDEPENDENCE). In June 1952, then a colonel, he was the chief organizer of the EGYPTIAN REVOLUTION, an army coup that ended the rule of FAROUK I and established the Egyptian republic. He became premier in 1954, president in 1956, and thereafter led Egypt until his death of a heart attack in 1970. He was the first major leader of modern Egypt, fostering modernization, land reform, secular institutions, military strength, and massive public works projects, the largest of which was the construction of the ASWAN HIGH DAM on the Nile. Withdrawal of promised British and U.S. funds for that project led to his nationalization of the Suez Canal in 1956. The subsequent SUEZ CRISIS and the SINAI–SUEZ WAR (SECOND ARAB–ISRAELI WAR) led to military defeat and the loss of the Sinai Peninsula, while greatly increasing Nasser's Arab world prestige. This, in turn, led to the short-lived formal union with Syria (1958–61) as the United Arab Republic. Nasser died shortly after successfully mediating the Jordanian–Palestinian conflict of 1970–71.

Nation, Carry Amelia Moore (1846–1911), PROHIBITION activist of the late 19th and early 20th centuries, best known for her campaign against alcohol-serving establishments. From 1901 she carried on the hatchet-wielding violence against liquor stocks and furniture that became her trademark.

Nation of Islam, the formal name of the BLACK MUSLIMS.

National Aeronautics and Space Administration (NASA), body in charge of the U.S. space program from October 1, 1958, created following the Soviet Union's 1957 SPUTNIK flight and replacing the earlier, research-oriented National Advisory Committee on Aeronautics (NACA). Much of NASA's developmental work was carried out in Huntsville, Alabama, home of the U.S. Army Ballistic Missile Arsenal; the space flights themselves were launched from CAPE CANAVERAL (CAPE KENNEDY, 1963–73), Florida, and coordinated from the JOHNSON SPACE CENTER in Houston. The SPACE SHUTTLE's frequent landing site is EDWARDS AIR FORCE BASE in California.

National Association for the Advancement of Colored People (NAACP), the leading U.S. civil rights organization of the 20th century; from its founding in 1909, it engaged in a series of major battles for racial and sexual equality. Focusing heavily on equality before the law, it won a series of major court cases, from *Guinn* v. *United States* (1915), which outlawed the "grandfather clause," to *BROWN* v. *BOARD OF EDUCATION* (1954), outlawing school segregation. It was biracial from the start, though moving over to mainly Black leadership in 1919, and has been led by such major figures as William E. DU BOIS, James Weldon JOHNSON, Walter WHITE, and Roy WILKINS. In the 1960s, the NAACP began to share leadership with more directly activist groups, such as Martin Luther KING's SOUTHERN CHRISTIAN LEADERSHIP CONFERENCE (SCLC), but remained a key U.S. civil rights organization.

National Front for the Liberation of Angola (FNLA), organization founded in 1962 and led by Holden ROBERTO. FNLA set up a government in exile and fought the ANGOLAN WAR OF INDEPENDENCE in northern Angola to victory in 1974. During 1975 it entered into a coalition with the POPULAR

MOVEMENT FOR THE LIBERATION OF AN-GOLA (MPLA) and the NATIONAL UNION FOR THE TOTAL INDEPENDENCE OF ANGO-LA (UNITA), but late in 1975 joined UNITA against the MPLA in the ANGOLAN CIVIL WAR. By 1979 it had been broken by Cuban and MPLA forces; Roberto fled abroad, but some FNLA remnants fought on into the early 1980s.

National Health Service, British government–operated medical and dental service initiated by Clement ATTLEE'S post–World War II Labour government in 1946 and put into full operation in 1948. It was a major element of the British "safety net" and a goal long sought by Labour. At the start it was hoped that all services could be fully government-paid, but by 1951 some charges had been instituted, although the service continued to be operated by the government at far less cost to patients than private health care services.

National Industrial Recovery Act (1933), U.S. federal law that set up the NATIONAL RECOVERY ADMINISTRATION (NRA), a NEW DEAL agency.

National Labor Relations Act (1935), the formal name of WAGNER ACT, the major U.S. labor relations law of the GREAT DE-PRESSION.

National Labor Relations Board, a U.S. federal agency created by the WAGNER ACT of 1935 and, until amended by the TAFT-HARTLEY ACT of 1947, a NEW DEAL agency that made it much easier to organize unions than was possible before its passage or after its amendment. The Taft-Hartley Act and the Landrum-Griffin Act of 1959 considerably altered the regulatory balance between labor and management.

National Labor Relations Board **v.** *Jones & Laughlin Steel Corporation* (1937), a landmark U.S. Supreme Court decision validating the NATIONAL LABOR RELATIONS ACT, which had made it far easier for trade unions to organize and had been providing legal support for the organization of the CONGRESS OF INDUSTRIAL ORGANIZATIONS

(CIO). A wave of industrial union organization followed this decision.

National Organization for Women (NOW), a U.S. organization formed in 1966 to advocate and drive toward complete equality for women under the law, in practice, and in every portion of society. To those ends it mounted a wide series of attacks on discriminatory practices, lobbied for women's rights legislation, and initiated and entered court cases involving women's rights. It played a major role in pushing an EQUAL RIGHTS AMENDMENT through Congress in the early 1970s, but was unable to secure ratification by a sufficient number of states.

National Party (NP), the ruling party of the Republic of South Africa from 1948, the party of Daniel MALAN, Johannes STRIJDON, Hendrik VERWOERD, Pieter BO-THA, and F.W. DECLERK. The party instituted APARTHEID following the 1948 election and steadfastly pursued a policy of racial segregation and suppression of dissent, coupled with a sustained, violent attack on South African civil and political liberties.

National Recovery Administration (NRA), a U.S. NEW DEAL agency created in June 1933 by the National Industrial Recovery Act, which made an attempt to develop industrial self-government, largely by the establishment of industrial codes regulating business and labor practices. Its BLUE EA-GLE symbol was promoted nationally, and more than 500 industrial codes were ultimately adopted. The major provisions of the enabling act were declared unconstitutional by the Supreme Court in *SCHECTER POULTRY CORPORATION* v. *UNITED STATES* (1935), and the agency then became powerless; it was discontinued in January 1936.

National Socialist German Workers' Party, the Nazi Party of HITLER and Germany.

National Union for the Total Independence of Angola (UNITA), group organized in 1966 by Jonas SAVIMBI that fought the Portuguese in southern Angola until victory in 1974. During 1975 it was briefly in coalition with the POPULAR MOVEMENT FOR THE LIBERATION OF ANGOLA (MPLA) and THE NA-

TIONAL FRONT FOR THE LIBERATION OF ANGOLA (FNLA), but late in 1975 joined the FLNA against the MPLA in the ANGOLAN CIVIL WAR. It secured substantial South African support, including South African troop incursions into Angola in pursuit of Namibian guerrillas, leading to several battles between Cuban and South African forces in Angola. UNITA was not a party to the joint Angolan–Cuban–South African agreement of August 1988, which declared a cease-fire in Namibia and Angola and provided for Cuban and South African troop and support pullout. UNITA declared that it intended to fight on against the Angolan government. A UNITA–MPLA truce was signed on June 22, 1989, but held for only 2 months.

National Youth Administration (NYA), a U.S. NEW DEAL program, part of the WORKS PROGRESS ADMINISTRATION (WPA) that supplied part-time jobs to large numbers of young people during the mid-1930s.

Nationalist China, alternate name for the Republic of CHINA from 1926 and especially after 1949 on Taiwan.

NATO, the initials of the NORTH ATLANTIC TREATY ORGANIZATION, a multinational Western military organization established in 1952.

Nauro (Republic of Nauro), until 1918 a German colony. The island became a British mandate territory in 1919, was occupied by Japanese forces during World War II, and became a UNITED NATIONS trust territory in 1947. It gained independence and COMMONWEALTH status on January 31, 1968.

Nautilus, world's first nuclear-powered submarine, launched in 1954, its production largely sparked by U.S. admiral Hyman RICKOVER. In 1958 it was the first ship to reach the NORTH POLE underwater.

Nazi Party (National Socialist German Workers' Party), political organization that began as the German Workers' Party in 1919, changed its name in 1920, and was the party of Adolf HITLER from 1921. The party drew national attention after its failed

Bavarian BEER HALL PUTSCH of November 1923; while in jail following that attempt, Hitler wrote *MEIN KAMPF*. It continued to be a minor party until the late 1920s, when it built substantial street-fighting strength, and in 1930 became a major factor in the Reichstag. With increasingly substantial army and business support in the conditions created by the GREAT DEPRESSION, Hitler and his party won power in 1933, from then on turning Germany into an increasingly totalitarian, racist state, bent on winning the full support of the German people, committing genocide against German Jews, and taking Germany into a new world war; it did all three.

Nazi–Soviet Pact (German–Soviet Nonaggression Pact, August 23–24, 1939), an agreement between Adolf HITLER and Joseph STALIN, negotiated and signed by Joachim von RIBBENTROP and Vyacheslav MOLOTOV, providing for the PARTITION OF POLAND between Germany and the Soviet Union should the Germans attack that country. It contained a secret agreement providing a German sphere of influence in Lithuania and Soviet spheres of influence in Finland, Latvia, Estonia, and Bessarabia. The agreement freed Germany to attack Poland, which it did on September 1, 1939, beginning World War II. On September 17, Soviet troops invaded and took the eastern portions of Poland, as provided by the treaty. On September 28 the treaty was amended to provide further German penetration into Poland and a Soviet, rather than German, sphere of influence in Lithuania. On October 10 Soviet troops entered Latvia, Lithuania, and Estonia. Finland refused to accede to Soviet demands, and on November 30, 1939, the Soviet Union invaded Finland, beginning the FINNISH–RUSSIAN WAR.

Negrín, Juan (1894–1956), doctor and professor of physiology who became the last prime minister of the the Spanish Republic; he was later prime minister of the Republican government-in-exile.

Nehru, Jawaharlal (1889–1964), Indian lawyer and socialist, who became active in the CONGRESS PARTY in 1919, after the AM-RITSAR MASSACRE. He and his father, Moti-lal Nehru, gave up their law practices and devoted their lives to the independence movement. From the early 1930s he was one of Mohatma GANDHI'S leading associates. He spent a total of 9 years in jail, his final release coming in June 1945; he then emerged as Congress Party leader in the run-up to Indian independence. In 1947 he became the first prime minister of India, serving until his death in 1964. As prime minister, he pursued a nonaligned course while fostering the development of a modern industrial economy and a secular, democratic state. His daughter was Indira GANDHI, and his sister was Vijaya PANDIT.

Nehru, Motilal (1861–1931), Indian lawyer who, with his son, Jawaharlal NEHRU, became a committed nationalist leader after the AMRITSAR MASSACRE of 1919. He gave up his law practice, was imprisoned twice for civil disobedience, and worked closely with his son and Mohatma GANDHI in the Indian independence movement.

Neill, Alexander Sutherland (1883–1973), Scottish educator and psychologist who in 1921 founded the SUMMERHILL SCHOOL, a revolutionary self-governing school centered on the students rather than on an institutional regime.

Nelson, George "Baby Face" (1908–34), psychopathic killer, bank robber, and associate of John DILLINGER; killed by Federal Bureau of Investigation agents near Barrington, Illinois, on November 27, 1934.

Nenni, Pietro (1891–1980), Italian journalist and socialist leader, an antifascist who went into exile in 1926, fought on the Republican side during the SPANISH CIVIL WAR, and led the Socialist party from 1949 to 1969. In coalition with the Communists until the HUNGARIAN REVOLUTION of 1956, he then moved into the Christian Democratic–Socialist coalition, which dominated Italian politics until the mid-1970s.

NEP, the NEW ECONOMIC POLICY, introduced by LENIN and followed by the Soviet Union from 1921 to 1928.

Neptune, planetary target of U.S. space probes, flown past by *PIONEER 10* on its way out of the solar system in 1983 and by *VOYAGER 2* in 1989. While studying Neptune early in the century, Percival LOWELL predicted the existence of the planet later found and called PLUTO.

Nesbit, Evelyn, the wife of Harry K. THAW, and a principal player in the triangle that resulted in Thaw's 1906 murder of architect Stanford White.

Netherlands East Indies, the former name of INDONESIA (Republic of Indonesia), which became an independent nation on August 17, 1945, thereafter fought a 4-year-long war of independence.

Neto, Augustinho (1922–79), Angolan physician and nationalist, active in Angolan freedom movements from the early 1950s and in the POPULAR MOVEMENT FOR THE LIBERATION OF ANGOLA (MPLA) from 1957. He escaped from a Portuguese prison in 1962, returned to Angola to become president of the MPLA, and then led the MPLA during the long ANGOLAN WAR OF INDEPENDENCE. On November 11, 1975, after the Portuguese had left Angola, Neto announced formation of the Soviet-backed People's Republic of Angola, with himself as president, ending the short-lived three-way coalition of the MPLA, the NATIONAL FRONT FOR THE LIBERATION OF ANGOLA (FNLA), and the NATIONAL UNION FOR THE TOTAL INDEPENDENCE OF ANGOLA (UNITA). The 14-year war of independence was over; then began the long civil war. Neto's presidency ended with his death while being treated for cancer in Moscow.

Neuilly, Treaty of (November 27, 1919), the Bulgarian peace treaty, following World War I, which provided for reparations, territorial concessions, and military restrictions on the Bulgarian armed forces.

Neumann, John (Janos) von (1903–57), Hungarian-American mathematician, who made major contributions in mathematics, physics, GAME THEORY, and COMPUTER science. In Europe he did key early work on set theory, and in 1926 he wrote his groundbreaking *Mathematical Foundations of Quantum Mechanics.* Emigrating to the United States in 1930, von Neumann worked at the Institute for Advanced Study, Princeton, New Jersey, from its founding in 1933 to his death. There he developed mathematical theory basic to analysis of continuously varying space (rather than dimensional space expressed in whole numbers), introducing a "ring of operators" now called Von Neumann algebras. His 1920s development of game theory bore fruit later in the 1944 *Theory of Games and Economic Behavior,* written with Oskar Morgenstern. It was von Neumann who, in 1946, first suggested the use of stored programs in computers, as opposed to rewiring for each new task, as was necessary in ENIAC. In his 1946 paper "Preliminary Discussion of Logical Design of an Electronic Computing Instrument," written with two others, he set the pattern for the development of DIGITAL COMPUTERS. A U.S. military adviser during World War II, he built a special computer called MANIAC (**m**athematical **a**nalyzer, **n**umerical **i**ntegrator, **a**nd **c**omputer), which provided the mathematical calculating power necessary for the development of the HYDROGEN BOMB; he also served on the ATOMIC ENERGY COMMISSION from 1954. Even after his death, a late work titled *Theory of Self-Reproducing Automata,* published in 1966, broke new ground in the discussion of CYBERNETICS and ROBOTS.

neutrino, chargeless and nearly or wholly massless subatomic PARTICLE, proposed first by Wolfgang PAULI in 1930 to account for a seeming mass–energy imbalance in the ATOMIC STRUCTURE and first found in 1956. Given off as part of the RADIOACTIVE decay of a NEUTRON, it is the focus of much research as a clue to the origin of the universe.

neutron, PARTICLE in an atom's NUCLEUS, similar to a PROTON, but with no electric charge. First posited by William Draper Hawkins in 1921, it was discovered by James Chadwick in 1932, and placed in the ATOMIC STRUCTURE by 1948. Experiments in bombarding elements with neutrons, by Enrico FERMI and others in the 1930s, disclosed the possibility of NUCLEAR FISSION with URANIUM, the result being a self-sustaining CHAIN REACTION of neutron bombardment, as in an ATOMIC BOMB or a NUCLEAR REACTOR. Stars composed mostly of neutrons, probably PULSARS, occupy a late stage in STELLAR EVOLUTION. By the early 1960s scientists had found that the neutron was not an indivisible particle but included other smaller particles, including NEUTRINOS.

Never in the course of human history was so much owed by so many to so few, statement by British prime minister Winston CHURCHILL, speaking to the House of Commons on August 20, 1940, in praise of the Royal Air Force during the BATTLE OF BRITAIN.

New Deal, phrase coined by Franklin Delano ROOSEVELT in his speech accepting the presidential nomination at the Chicago Democratic National Convention on July 2, 1932: "I pledge you, I pledge myself, a new deal for the American people." In the years that followed, "New Deal" became a slogan to describe the whole program of economic and social reforms introduced during the Roosevelt era, which included a quick BANK HOLIDAY, the end of PROHIBITION, and establishment of the NATIONAL RECOVERY ADMINISTRATION (NRA) and the AGRICULTURAL ADJUSTMENT ADMINISTRATION (AAA), both of the latter declared unconstitutional in their early forms, but greatly stimulative during their lifetimes. The New Deal also initiated the CIVILIAN CONSERVATION CORPS (CCC), PUBLIC WORKS ADMINISTRATION (PWA), FEDERAL EMERGENCY RELIEF ADMINISTRATION, WORKS PROGRESS ADMINISTRATION (WPA), FEDERAL DEPOSIT INSURANCE CORPORATION (FDIC), HOME OWNERS LOAN CORPORATION (HOLC), the TENNESSEE VALLEY AUTHORITY (TVA), and SOCIAL SECURITY. Effective securities regulation began with establishment of the SECURITIES AND EXCHANGE COMMISSION. Labor organization was encouraged by passage of the WAGNER ACT and establishment of the NATIONAL

LABOR RELATIONS BOARD, which were followed by a wave of industrial organization.

New Economic Policy (NEP; 1921–28), a set of policies successfully instituted by LENIN in 1921, after the famine and political strains caused by WAR COMMUNISM. They were aimed at providing private sector incentives that would better supply food and other consumer goods to a starving and restless Soviet people.

New Fourth Army Incident (January 6, 1941), an attack by Nationalist troops on the headquarters of the Communist New Fourth Army during the period of the united front against Japan. The Communist force was destroyed, with thousands of casualties, and resumption of the civil war was narrowly averted.

New Freedom, a slogan developed by Woodrow WILSON during the U.S. presidential campaign of 1912, calling for increased antitrust regulation, better organization of the American banking system, and reduced and reorganized tariffs.

New Frontier, a slogan coined by John F. KENNEDY in his speech accepting the presidential nomination at the Democratic National Convention of 1960, calling in general terms for a move to meet new challenges facing the American people in the years ahead. The slogan was not translated into a specific legislative program, as were the NEW DEAL of Franklin Delano ROOSEVELT and the FAIR DEAL of Harry S. TRUMAN, his Democratic predecessors.

New Georgia, Battle of (July–August 1943), World War II amphibious landings by U.S. troops on this major Japanese base in the Solomon Islands, which led to a month of heavy jungle fighting, followed by almost a month of mop-up operations. By late August, Allied forces held the entire island of New Georgia.

New Guinea campaign of 1944 (April–July 1944), World War II Allied attack on Japanese-held western New Guinea; in late April, U.S. troops landed near the large Japanese base at Hollandia, captured the Aitape airfield, and took Hollandia. From May through July, further Japanese bases were captured; the remaining Japanese retreated into the jungle for the rest of the war.

New Hebrides, a former joint British-French colony that became the new nation of VANUATU on July 30, 1980.

New Left, a term generally applied to the U.S. radical student movement of the 1960s and early 1970s, led most visibly by the STUDENTS FOR A DEMOCRATIC SOCIETY but including a wide range of other activist student organizations and individuals. The New Left was heavily involved in student protests against the VIETNAM WAR, and in such student demonstrations and movements as the BERKELEY FREE SPEECH MOVEMENT, the COLUMBIA SIT-INS, and the several marches on Washington. Its members were deeply influenced by the thinking of such academics, writers, and revolutionaries as Herbert MARCUSE, Franz FANON, C. Wright MILLS, and Che GUEVARA.

New London school explosion (March 18, 1937), explosion that destroyed the consolidated school in New London, Texas, where raw gas was being improperly used in place of more expensive natural gas. The school filled with odorless, highly explosive gas that was somehow touched off, killing 413 children and 14 teachers.

New Nationalism, The, title of a 1910 speech by Theodore ROOSEVELT at Osawatomie, Kansas, in which he called for much increased federal welfare programs and greater corporate regulation. It provided much of the basis for his platform as unsuccessful BULL MOOSE PARTY presidential candidate in the election of 1912.

New People's Army, a Filipino Maoist guerrilla army founded in 1969 as the armed force of the Communist Party of the Philippines—Marxist-Leninist. It mounted a nationwide guerrilla insurgency against the Philippine government, despite attempts by Corazon AQUINO's administration to negotiate with the insurgents, freeing major insurgent leaders as a gesture of good will.

New Right, a conservative, mainly evangelical-Christian–based U.S. political movement that developed in the mid-1970s, coalesced around the MORAL MAJORITY organization founded by the Reverend Jerry FALWELL in 1979, and grew into a major political force during the administrations of President Ronald REAGAN, whom it generally supported. It focused on such issues as the RIGHT TO LIFE, school prayer, anticommunism, opposition to the EQUAL RIGHTS AMENDMENT and other feminist-supported issues, and pornography.

New York City Parking Violations Bureau scandal, a 1986 municipal corruption case involving Bronx borough president Stanley M. Friedman, Queens borough president Donald Manes, city officials Michael Lazar, Lester Shafran, and Geoffrey G. Lindenauer, and businessman Marvin Kaplan. Manes committed suicide in March 1986; Lindenauer turned state's evidence; Friedman, Lazar, Shafran, and Kaplan were found guilty. The scandal, along with several lesser New York municipal scandals of the period, severely damaged the administration of New York City mayor Edward Koch.

New York Times Company v. *Sullivan* (1964), a landmark U.S. Supreme Court decision, providing that a public official must prove "actual malice" to be able to win damages for libel.

Newton, Huey Percy (1942–89), U.S. Black activist of the 1960s, a founder of the BLACK PANTHER PARTY in 1966. Newton was involved in a series of violent incidents during the late 1960s; he was imprisoned (1968–70), freed on appeal, fled abroad to avoid a murder charge in 1974, and was exonerated after his return to face trial in 1979.

Nguyen That Thanh, the given name of Vietnamese leader HO CHI MINH.

Nhu, Ngo Dinh (1910–63), brother of NGO DINH DIEM, and head of the South Vietnamese secret police until the army coup of 1963. He and his brother were executed the day after the coup.

Nicaraguan Civil War (1978–88), a continuing low-level guerrilla war was conducted by Cuban-supported SANDINISTA forces against the SOMOZA government from 1961. In 1978, as opposition to the dictatorship grew, Sandinista forces were able to mount major attacks against government forces, briefly seize the national palace, and effectuate a hostages-for-prisoners exchange with the government. In the spring of 1979, Sandinista forces mounted a successful offensive; Somoza fled into exile on July 17, and a Sandanista government took power on July 19. Former government forces, operating largely in the north out of bases in Honduras, with substantial U.S. support, became guerrilla insurgents known as CONTRAS (Againsts). Contra groups also formed in the south; these were composed mainly of former Sandinistas, in opposition after finding the new government turning sharply toward authoritarianism. A long insurgency developed; but the insurgents made little headway, and in the late 1980s they found U.S. public opinion turning against providing further aid, a trend that became decisive after the emergence of the IRAN–CONTRA AFFAIR. The cease-fire of March 1988 effectively ended the civil war, though some sporadic fighting continued. The democratic elections of February 1990, toppled the Sandinista government, opening a new chapter in Nicaraguan history.

Nicholas II (1868–1918), the last Romanov emperor (czar) of Russia. He became czar in 1894, succeeding his father, Alexander III, and ruled Russia through the lost RUSSO-JAPANESE WAR and the RUSSIAN REVOLUTION OF 1905. After that revolution, his OCTOBER MANIFESTO instituted a modified constitutional government, but by 1907 he had veered once again toward autocracy. He led Russia to defeat in World War I, was deposed by the FEBRUARY REVOLUTION of 1917, and abdicated on March 15, 1917; he and his family then became prisoners of the PROVISIONAL GOVERNMENT. After the OCTOBER REVOLUTION, on July 16, 1918, he, his wife (Alexandra Fyodorovna), and their family were killed at Sverdlovsk (then

Yekaterinburg) by their BOLSHEVIK captors. Afterward there was some dispute as to whether or not one of their children, ANASTASIA, had survived.

Niebuhr, Reinhold (1892–1971), U.S. Protestant minister, educator, and philosopher, an exponent of political realism within the context of religiously based ethics, whose thinking deeply influenced three generations of American and British political leaders. He was a socialist and pacifist in the early 1930s, but from the mid-1930s he advocated violent resistance to fascism, if necessary, and supported World War II. In 1952 he was a founder of AMERICANS FOR DEMOCRATIC ACTION (ADA).

Niemöller, Martin (1892–1984), German Protestant leader who in 1934, with Karl BARTH, formed a coalition of anti-Nazi church leaders called the Synod of Barmen. A German submarine commander in World War I, later a Protestant minister, Niemöller was arrested in 1937 for his strong and public opposition to the Nazis and Adolf HITLER. Freed from DACHAU in 1945, he then became a major church leader and pacifist, speaking against German involvement in the COLD WAR.

Niger (Republic of Niger), until 1958 a French colony, although strong Taureg resistance and weak French colonial commitments to this very poor country made French control of the interior desert regions tenuous. Niger was granted internal autonomy in 1958 and became an independent state on August 3, 1960.

Nigeria (Federal Republic of Nigeria), until 1954 a British colony; it first gained internal autonomy, then became an independent state and COMMONWEALTH member on October 1, 1960. It became a republic in 1963. In 1967 ethnic tensions generated the NIGERIA–BIAFRA WAR.

Nigeria–Biafra Civil War (1967–70), conflict that began with the secession of the eastern region of Nigeria, led by Ibo military governor Chukwuemeka Odumegwu OJUKWU, on May 20, 1967, after a series of coups and countercoups had fanned long-standing tensions between the mostly northern Moslem peoples and mostly southern Christian Ibos. Thousands of Ibos in the northern portions of the country had been massacred, and hundreds of thousands more fled into the Ibo eastern region. Ojukwu became president of the new state of Biafra; the Nigerian government, led by Yakubu GOWON, refused to accept the Biafran secession. A bitter civil war followed, with the deaths of an estimated 1.5–2 million before the war ended with Biafran surrender on January 15, 1970. Most of those who died were noncombatants, many of them children, who succumbed to starvation and disease despite a worldwide Biafran relief effort.

Night of the Long Knives (June 29–30, 1934), the date of the BLOOD PURGE in Germany, when the leading Nazi STORM TROOPERS (SA) were killed, by HITLER's order, to please the rival SS.

Nimbus, U. S. weather SATELLITE system from the late 1960s.

Nimeiry, Gaafar Mohammed al- (1930–   ), Sudanese officer who led a successful young officers' coup in 1969, achieved full power in 1971, and thereafter ruled a one-party Sudanese state along increasingly Moslem fundamentalist lines. In 1972 he granted autonomy to the predominantly Christian and animist Black provinces of the south, temporarily halting the then 17-year-old SUDANESE CIVIL WAR. Faced with difficult economic problems that were exacerbated by the presence of an estimated 1 million refugees from Ethiopia and Chad and with increasing internal opposition to his severe Islamic law policies, he was deposed in a 1985 military coup.

Nimitz, Chester William (1885–1966), U.S. naval officer who took command of the Pacific Fleet after PEARL HARBOR and directed it through the crucial Battle of the CORAL SEA and the decisive Battle of MIDWAY. His forces captured GUADALCANAL and in 1943 began a sustained series of offensives in the Pacific, ultimately taking the air war to the Japanese homeland. He ended the war as fleet admiral in command of by far the largest navy in the world.

1984, a George ORWELL novel (1949), in which a viciously manipulative totalitarian state, masquerading as a Utopia, is exemplified by the slogan BIG BROTHER IS WATCHING YOU, seen everywhere.

Nineteenth Amendment, the WOMAN SUFFRAGE amendment to the Constitution of the United States, stating that "the right of citizens of the United States to vote shall not be denied or abridged by the United States or by any state on account of sex." It was introduced in 1887 and ultimately ratified in 1920.

Nivelle, Robert Georges (1856–1924), French World War I general who became the victorious hero of the second Battle of VERDUN in June 1916. However, his much-heralded offensive of April 1917 failed, costing France an estimated 120,000 casualties; he was replaced as commander of the French northern armies.

Nivelle Offensive (April 16–20, 1917), a powerful World War I French offensive in the Champagne region, with 1,200,000 men in the attacking French armies. It failed completely, with heavy losses, and was followed by massive FRENCH ARMY MUTINIES.

Nixon, Richard Milhous (1913–   ), U.S. lawyer, a California Republican congressman (1947–51) and senator (1951–53), vice-president under Dwight EISENHOWER (1953–61), and 37th president of the United States (1969–74). Nixon was defeated by John F. KENNEDY in the presidential election of 1960; he defeated Democrats Hubert H. HUMPHREY in 1968, and George MCGOVERN in 1972, resigning in 1974 to avoid impeachment, after his role in the WATERGATE scandal had been revealed. As a congressman and senator, he was one of the leading anti-Communists of the MCCARTHY period, from his position as a member of the HOUSE UN-AMERICAN ACTIVITIES COMMITTEE. As president, he and his secretary of state, Henry KISSINGER, continued to try to end the VIETNAM WAR while still prosecuting the war: they mounted substan-

tial operations in Cambodia and Laos, mined North Vietnamese harbors, and increased the bombing of North Vietnam. Peace was not attained, but a negotiated American withdrawal from the countries in the area occurred during 1973. In February 1972, he accomplished a new American OPENING TO CHINA, following it with much improved Chinese-American relations. In May 1972 he concluded a STRATEGIC ARMS LIMITATIONS TREATY with the Soviet Union, and in a series of summit meetings concluded nuclear arms and other agreements aimed at reducing tensions between the two superpowers. Domestically, his administration sponsored few legislative initiatives, being preoccupied with foreign affairs and facing a great deal of antagonism in Congress and out in the country because of continuing American involvement in the Vietnam War. During the early 1970s, he and those around him became deeply involved in efforts to identify and suppress opposition, involving themselves and the national security agencies in a series of wiretap and surveillance activities, some of which surfaced during prosecution of the PENTAGON PAPERS case, and many more of which surfaced when the White House "plumbers" were captured during the WATERGATE break-in. After the easy presidential reelection of 1972, a number of illegal acts and subsequent illegal attempts to cover up those acts were revealed by media investigators and the WATERGATE COMMITTEE, ultimately resulting in the convictions of many of those who had functioned in and around the White House in the Nixon years. About to be impeached, Nixon resigned instead. His elected vice-president, Spiro AGNEW, having had to resign, Nixon was succeeded by his appointed vice-president, Gerald R. FORD, on August 9, 1974, receiving a pardon from President Ford in September 1974.

Nixon–Brezhnev summits, a series of three early 1970s summit meetings between U.S. president Richard M. NIXON and Soviet premier Leonid BREZHNEV. The May 1972 Moscow meeting resulted in a signed SALT I agreement and several other arms limitation and mutual cooperation agreements. The June 1973 Washington meeting resulted in several minor agreements and statements of principle furthering the DETENTE process. The June 1974 Moscow meeting failed to make any substantial arms-reduction progress, but some minor agreements were signed.

Nkomo, Joshua (1917–   ), Zimbabwean nationalist leader, head of several successive parties in Rhodesia, including the Zimbabwe African People's Union (ZAPU), before his imprisonment (1964–74). He emerged from imprisonment to lead his party into intensified guerrilla war against the Rhodesian government, and in 1976 into an effective but always troubled Patriotic Front coalition with the Zimbabwe African National Union (ZANU), led by Robert MUGABE. The two organizations ran separate slates in the 1980 elections, ZANU winning and Mugabe becoming prime minister and then president of Zimbabwe. Nkomo joined the government, but guerrilla warfare then began between ZAPU and ZANU forces; he was forced out of government in 1984. His party was merged into ZANU in 1987, as Zimbabwe became a one-party state, and Nkomo rejoined the Mugabe government.

Nkrumah, Kwame (Francis Nwia Kofi; 1909–72), Ghanian political scientist, who became a pan-African student leader in the United States in the early 1940s. He returned home in 1947, and organized the Convention People's party in 1949, leading it to power in 1951 after having been imprisoned for nationalist agitation. He became prime minister of the Gold Coast in 1951, of Ghana when independence was achieved in 1957, and first president of the Republic of Ghana in 1960. In those years he also became one of the leading pan-African Black leaders of his time. As president of Ghana, he attempted to build socialism, developed a repressive one-party state, and was deposed in 1966, thereafter continuing to be a powerful pan-African leader and writer from sanctuary in Guinea.

NKVD (People's Commissariat of Internal Affairs), the massive national Soviet secret police organization, the chief instrument used by Joseph STALIN to carry out the GREAT PURGE of 1934–39, as well as other acts of repression. The NKVD was the successor organization to the OGPU, itself a successor of the original Soviet secret police, the CHEKA. These functions were later taken over by successor organizations, from 1952 by the KGB.

NLRB, the initials of the NATIONAL LABOR RELATIONS BOARD, originally a NEW DEAL U.S. federal agency created by the WAGNER ACT.

NMR imager (*n*uclear *m*agnetic *r*esonance imager, also called MRI, or *m*agnetic *r*esonance *i*mager), medical diagnostic device that, like a CAT SCAN, takes pictures of the body at different planes. But where a CAT scan reflects the ELECTRON density of tissues, involves RADIATION, and must physically move the camera to photograph different sections of the body, the NMR reflects PROTON density, uses no radiation but instead variations in absorption of high-frequency radio waves in electromagnetic fields by the nuclei of different atoms, and can angle its camera electronically. The NMR, introduced in Britain in 1973, has less sharp pictures than the CAT scan, but NMR images are more useful medically, providing better information to physicians about the biological and chemical state of the tissues.

Nobile, Umberto (1885–1978), Italian aviator and explorer who, in 1926, with Roald AMUNDSEN and Lincoln ELLSWORTH, first flew over the NORTH POLE in a dirigible. Two years later, Amundsen lost his life on a flight to rescue Nobile, who survived to lead many Arctic expeditions for both Italy and the U.S.S.R.

Noel-Baker, Philip John (1889–1982), British pacifist and socialist, an Olympic silver medalist in 1920, a Quaker noncombatant ambulance driver in World War I, Labour member of parliament (1929–31, 1936–70), and a lifelong campaigner for world peace.

He was awarded the Nobel Peace Prize in 1959. After his unsuccessful quest for peace during the interwar period, he supported the British World War II war effort, later held several posts in the postwar Labour government, and became a leading postwar advocate of multilateral nuclear disarmament.

No Man's Land, the strip of land, as little as 30 yards wide in some places, that ran the length of the German and Allied systems of fortifications from Switzerland to the North Sea on the Western Front during World War I.

Nomura, Kichisaburo (1887–1964), Japanese naval officer and diplomat, who became ambassador to the United States in 1939 and was engaged in negotiations with the American government in Washington when the surprise Japanese attack on PEARL HARBOR took place. He was then interned and returned to Japan in 1942.

Nonaligned Movement, an international organization established in 1961, now consisting of more than 100 mostly THIRD WORLD African, Asian, and Latin American member countries; at its inception it focused on anticolonialism, and during the 1970s and 1980s added economic goals as an additional main focus, with special attention to the problem of third-world debt.

Norgay, Tenzing (1914–86), Sherpa mountaineer who, with Edmund HILLARY, first reached the top of Mt. Everest, the world's highest mountain, arriving on May 29, 1953, after almost reaching it with another climber the year before.

Noriega, Manuel Antonio (1938–), Panamanian officer, head of intelligence from 1970, head of the armed forces from 1982, and in effect head of government and dictator of Panama from 1982. Noriega cooperated closely with U.S. Latin American military and intelligence operations during the 1970s and 1980s while at the same time engaging in highly profitable drug trade operations on behalf of one or more Latin American drug cartels. He was indicted on drug trade–connected charges in Florida in

February 1988, triggering a major confrontation with the United States and massive but unsuccessful anti-Noriega demonstrations in Panama. These were followed by several unsuccessful coup attempts as negotiations to speed his departure broke down. He ran a fraudulent presidential election in 1989, nullifying that election after it became clear that his candidate had lost, as attested by independent observers who included former U.S. president Jimmy CARTER. Noriega was deposed by the U.S. invasion of December 20, 1989. He took refuge in the Vatican Panama City embassy on December 24, and surrendered to U.S. forces on January 3, and was then taken to the United States to stand trial on longstanding drug charges.

Normandy invasion (D-Day, June 6, 1944), late World War II invasion of Europe by the ALLIES. Following the plans detailed in OPERATION OVERLORD, an invasion fleet of more than 5,000 ships crossed the English Channel to Normandy on June 6. After the fleet and thousands of aircraft had bombarded coastal fortifications, Allied assault forces landed on five beaches, designated Utah, Omaha, Juno, Sword, and Gold; three airborne divisions were dropped inland. All of the landings succeeded, although there was substantial resistance on Omaha Beach, and by nightfall all five beachheads had been secured. Allied troops then slowly moved inland against well-fortified, strong opposition, although the Germans withheld crucial armored divisions for a time, thinking that the main Allied thrust would come at their heavily fortified positions at the Pas de Calais, the shortest way across the Channel. By early July, Allied forces 1 million strong were in France. In late July, Allied forces broke through German defenses at St. Lo, and by late August the Allies had liberated Paris and advanced to the Seine, having taken Brussels and Antwerp. By mid-September 1944, Allied troops faced the Germans on the SIEGFRIED LINE.

***Noronic* disaster** (September 17, 1949), killing of 128 people when the Canadian Great

Lakes cruise ship *Noronic* caught fire while docked at Toronto; its passengers were caught aboard when the single exit from the ship was blocked by the fire.

Norris, George William (1861–1944), U.S. lawyer, a Nebraska Republican congressman 1903–13 and senator 1913–43. In 1910 Norris was a leader of the fight against the rule of speaker Joseph Cannon in the House of Representatives. He opposed American entry into World War I and the postwar LEAGUE OF NATIONS. Domestically, he was a progressive Republican, a sponsor of the NORRIS–LA GUARDIA ANTI-INJUNCTION ACT of 1932 and of the TENNESSEE VALLEY AUTHORITY (TVA), which gave his name to its first dam.

Norris–La Guardia Anti-Injunction Act (1932), U.S. federal legislation affirming the right to organize unions, specifically making "yellow dog contracts"—by which workers agreed that union membership would be grounds for dismissal—unenforceable, and thereby severely limiting the use of anti-union injunctions in labor disputes.

North, Oliver Laurence (1943–   ), U.S. Marine officer who saw service in Vietnam, 1968–69, and from 1981 was attached to the National Security Council (NSC) as deputy director of the military affairs bureau; he was dismissed on November 25, 1986, for his role in the IRAN–CONTRA AFFAIR. During those years, working out of the White House, he was involved in many covert operations, considerably beyond those of the Iran–Contra affair. In July 1987, his testimony before the Iran–Contra congressional investigating committees was nationally televised, and for a short time he became a major celebrity. After a 14-month grand jury investigation directed by federal special prosecutor Lawrence E. Walsh, North was indicted on Iran–Contra-connected charges, on March 14, 1988. He left the marine corps on March 16, and began a series of lecture tours to muster financial and popular support. In May 1989, after a long trial, he was convicted on three felony

counts in connection with the Iran–Contra Affair.

North Africa, final campaign in (April 1–May 13, 1943), last World War II engagements in North Africa. During most of April 1943 strengthening Allied forces pursued retreating Axis forces, in late April engaging and in early May defeating the remaining German and Italian armies in North Africa. On May 7 Tunis fell, and in the next week an estimated 250,000 German and Italian troops surrendered, ending the war in North Africa.

North Atlantic Treaty Organization (NATO), an international military organization established in 1949, pursuant to the terms of the North Atlantic Treaty, and providing a framework for joint Allied military activities in Europe in the event of Soviet military action. Its 16 member countries are Belgium, Canada, Denmark, France, Federal Republic of Germany, Great Britain, Greece, Iceland, Italy, Luxembourg, the Netherlands, Norway, Portugal, Spain, Turkey, and the United States.

Northcliffe (Alfred Harmsworth, Lord Northcliffe; 1865–1922), British publisher, who pioneered in developing a popular, sensationalist press and in the process built the largest publishing organization of his time, ultimately controlling the *The Times* of London, the *Daily Mail*, the *Evening Standard*, the *Sunday Dispatch*, *The Observer*, and scores of other publications.

Northeast Passage, seaway north of Eurasia between the Atlantic and the Pacific; an iceclogged route, it was traversed only once before the 20th century but was turned into a major seaway in the 1930s. Boris Vilkitski, starting in 1914, and Roald AMUNDSEN, starting in 1918, were only the second and third explorers to sail the route, both having to winter over because of ice. In 1932 the Soviet ship *Sibiriakov* first traveled the Northeast Passage without wintering over. The Russians then fielded a fleet of icebreakers to keep open the sealane they call the Northern Sea Route. The passage was a vital route for supplies in World War II, and is now generally kept open from June to October.

Northern Expedition (1926–28), the KUO-MINTANG offensive north from Canton, which, with Soviet aid and advice, quickly captured Hankow, Nanking, and Shanghai; its first phase ended with the Kuomintang–Communist split and the SHANGHAI MASSA-CRE. The drive north resumed in the spring of 1928, ending with the defeat of the armies of the northern warlords; Peking was taken in June 1928.

Northern Ireland (Ulster), six northern Irish counties; until the settlement of the IRISH WAR OF INDEPENDENCE, in 1921, they were part of the United Kingdom, then became an autonomous province. In 1972, as the NORTHERN IRELAND CIVIL WAR worsened, direct British rule over Northern Ireland was reinstituted.

Northern Ireland Civil War (1969–   ), unrest in Northern Ireland that grew into substantial demonstrations in 1968; in 1969, major demonstrations and a long, terrorist-oriented guerrilla insurgency was mounted by the PROVISIONAL IRISH REPUBLICAN ARMY (Provisionals), which had broken away from the IRISH REPUBLICAN ARMY. In August 1969, British forces were sent to Northern Ireland and have been there ever since, in divisional strength. On January 30, 1972, BLOODY SUNDAY, British troops killed 13 unarmed Catholic demonstrators in Londonderry, sharply escalating the level of violence; in March 1972 the British government imposed direct rule on Northern Ireland. The guerrilla war continued, with terrorist actions in Northern Ireland, Ireland, Great Britain, and on the mainland of Europe, drawing counteraction by Protestant Irish paramilitary and guerrilla forces and continuing armed British rule in a cycle unbroken in two decades of war.

Northern Peru earthquake (May 31, 1970), an earthquake that destroyed many populated places throughout northern Peru and set off the Mount Huascarán avalanche; in all, an estimated 50,000–70,000 died, with enormous attendant physical damage.

Northern Rhodesia, a former British protectorate, in 1953 it became part of the Federation of Rhodesia and Nyasaland, and gained independence as the new nation of ZAMBIA on October 24, 1964.

Northern Sea Route, Soviet name for the NORTHEAST PASSAGE.

Northern Securities* v. *United States (1904), a landmark U.S. Supreme Court decision, breaking up the railroad holding company controlled by J. Pierpont MORGAN and James J. HILL that held most American railroad lines between Chicago and the Pacific Northwest. It was a major victory for the trust-busting activities of President Theodore ROOSEVELT.

North Pole, northern end of the Earth's axis, target of numerous landmark 20th-century expeditions. From 1898 Robert E. PEARY made several attempts to reach it; he was finally successful in 1909 though some disputed his claim even into the 1980's. The first flights over the North Pole occurred in 1926, when Richard E. BYRD and his co-pilot, Floyd BENNETT, made the trip by airplane; Roald AMUNDSEN, Lincoln ELLSWORTH, and Umberto NOBILE also arrived in a DIRIGIBLE in 1926. Both claims were later disputed by some. The U.S. nuclear submarine *NAUTILUS* was the first ship to cross the North Pole underwater, in 1958; 2 years later, the U.S. *Skate* was the first to surface at the North Pole. In 1977 the Soviet icebreaker *Arktika* was the first surface vessel to reach the North Pole.

Northwest Passage, sea route north of North America between the Atlantic and Pacific, long sought by American explorers and first traversed in 1903–06 by Roald AMUNDSEN in his sloop *Gjöa*. Knut RASMUS-SEN was the first to trace the route by dogsled (1921–24), from Greenland across to Point Barrow, Alaska. In 1940–42 the Canadian ship *St. Roch* was the first to travel west to east on the route. The ice-clogged seaway was too difficult for regular use, however, and not until the 1960s, with the discovery of oil in northern Alaska, did the first commercial ship journey through the passage; it was the American specially built ice-breaking tanker, *Manhattan*, in 1969.

Norway (Kingdom of Norway), until 1905 a Swedish territory; Norway became an independent state on September 23, 1905.

Norway, Battle of (April–June 1940), invasion of Norway by Germany early in World War II, beginning with an attack on April 9, 1940. By April 10, German troops had landed on both coasts, had taken Oslo by air and sea, and were pushing inland with air support against small Norwegian defense forces with negligible air support. On October 14, Allied troops without significant air support landed near Trondheim and Narvik, but soon all but the Narvik positions were evacuated because of heavy air attacks. From late April through late May, reinforced Allied forces numbering an estimated 25,000 men attacked and then took Narvik, but the Allies evacuated Narvik and ended the Norway campaign June 8–9, because of the massive German successes in Western Europe, which made their position untenable.

Novorossisk collision (August 31–September 1, 1986), a nighttime collision between the freighter *Pyotr Vasev* and the cruise ship *Admiral Nakhimov*, on the Black Sea near the Soviet city of Novorossisk; 398 people were killed.

Novotný, Antonín (1904–75), Czech Communist Party leader, who fought in the Czech underground early in World War II and was imprisoned by the Nazis 1941–45; he then became a party leader in the postwar period. Succeeding Klement GOTTWALD as head of the party in 1953, he continued Gottwald's repressive policies, attempted some very modest reforms under heavy popular pressure in 1967, and was replaced by reformer Alexander DUBCEK in 1968.

NOW, initials of the NATIONAL ORGANIZATION FOR WOMEN, by which that feminist organization, founded in 1966, is best known.

Noyon-Montdidier Offensive (June 9–13, 1918), the fourth of five major German offensives in 1918. German troops attacking toward Paris advanced only 9 miles against strong French resistance, which stopped the offensive with heavy German casualties.

NRA, the initials of the NATIONAL RECOVERY ADMINISTRATION, by which this NEW DEAL U.S. federal agency of the 1930s was best known, its symbol being the BLUE EAGLE.

Nu, U (1907–   ), Burmese teacher, socialist, and nationalist leader who was active in anti-British activities during the 1930s and joined the Japanese during World War II; he became foreign minister of the Japanese-sponsored Burmese puppet government, 1943–45. After the assassination of AUNG SAN in July 1947, he became chief Burmese independence negotiator and in January 1948 the first prime minister of Burma. He held power until the army takeover of June 1958, dealing with multiple continuing insurgencies, maintaining Burma's nonaligned position, and beginning to build a national social welfare network. The army relinquished power in 1960, and U Nu again became prime minister, this time only until the Ne WIN army coup of March 1962, after which he was imprisoned until 1966, and then went into exile. He was allowed to return to Burma in 1980. In 1988 he emerged as one of the leaders of the new popular opposition to the military government, though his attempt to form a provisional government failed.

Nuclear Accidents Agreement (1971), a U.S.–U.S.S.R. agreement providing for notification in the case of a nuclear accident that might cause a nuclear weapon to explode, missile launchings seemingly aimed at the other superpower, or detection of any other nuclear activity of concern to either nation; it was aimed at reducing the risk of accidental nuclear war.

nuclear energy, energy binding together the PARTICLES in an atom's nucleus, released when the atom changes form—either in a slow, natural process; in a controlled process, as in a NUCLEAR REACTOR; or in an artificially induced, speeded-up process, as in NUCLEAR FISSION or NUCLEAR FUSION.

nuclear fission, process by which NUCLEAR ENERGY is released when an atom absorbs an extra NEUTRON into its NUCLEUS, becomes unstable, and then splits into two nuclei. Ernest RUTHERFORD first split a nucleus in 1919; in the 1930s Enrico FERMI systematically bombarded elements with neutrons, observing their effects; and German researchers Otto Hahn, Fritz Strassman, Lise Meitner, and Otto Richard Frisch focused specifically on URANIUM, the latter two using a CLOUD CHAMBER to photograph the tracks following the splitting of uranium. In 1939 Meitner, by then exiled from Germany by the Nazis, published the first report describing the process, naming it "nuclear fission." Also in 1939, Frédéric JOLIOT-CURIE and others suggested the possibility of a CHAIN REACTION; that is, if extra neutrons are released, then more and more atoms are split, in a self-sustaining process. That same year Niels BOHR, John Wheeler, and others found that fission mainly occurred with URANIUM 235 (U-235), a rare ISOTOPE of uranium 238 (U-238). In 1940 Glenn T. SEABORG and Edwin M. McMillan discovered PLUTONIUM and determined that the plutonium 239 (Pu-239) isotope also was fissionable. European research was hampered during World War II; bombing and early miscalculations slowed German fission work under Werner HEISENBERG. In the United States, work was coordinated from 1942 under the MANHATTAN PROJECT, directed toward the building of the ATOMIC BOMB; but after the war, under the ATOMIC ENERGY COMMISSION (AEC), other applications of nuclear fission were explored. By the early 1950s electric power was being generated from nuclear energy in the United States, becoming commercially available a few years later. Meanwhile, nuclear technology spread to other countries, including Canada, the Soviet Union, Great Britain, France, and China. Despite the 1968 NUCLEAR NONPROLIFERATION TREATY, nuclear technology later

spread to some other countries as well, probably including Israel and South Africa.

nuclear freeze movement, the movement to freeze nuclear armaments at current levels; it began at the Pugwash multinational scientific meeting of 1981 and generated nuclear freeze movements in many countries during the 1980s. Support for the movement waned after the Soviet Union and the United States moved to reduce, rather than freeze, nuclear weapons.

nuclear fusion, process by which hydrogen nuclei merge, or fuse, producing helium and energy, the type of reaction that produces energy in the Sun and stars, as first outlined in 1939 by Hans BETHE. On Earth the uncontrolled reaction leads to an explosion, as in the HYDROGEN BOMB; but if controlled, it can be a powerful energy source. By 1942 Enrico FERMI and Edward TELLER had conceived of a bomb employing nuclear fusion; it was built by Teller 1949–52. Controlled nuclear fusion proved more elusive, even after attempts from the 1950s by various countries, including the superpowers, to share nuclear fusion information. DEUTERIUM, the main fuel used in nuclear fusion, is readily available, as in sea water, and efficient nuclear fusion would hold the promise of cheap, almost unlimited energy. Into the late 1980s, however, nuclear fusion, produced under extremely high temperatures, was very far from fulfilling that promise, the energy put in outweighing the gain overall. But the promise is so great that when, in early 1989, B. Stanley Pons of the University of Utah and Martin Fleischmann from Britain's University of Southampton announced that they had achieved nuclear fusion at room temperatures—so-called cold fusion—it was front-page news for weeks, with controversy raging over whether they had, in fact, achieved nuclear fusion or some other type of reaction.

nuclear magnetic resonance imager, formal name of the NMR IMAGER.

Nuclear Nonproliferation Treaty, 1968 treaty signed by more than 100 nations, agreeing not to acquire or help in the acquisition of nuclear weapons. France and China, possessors of nuclear weapons, were not signatories, nor were several non-nuclear-power nations.

nuclear power, energy released from atoms through NUCLEAR FISSION or NUCLEAR FUSION, especially controlled energy used for peaceful purposes.

nuclear reactor (atomic pile), structure in which NUCLEAR FISSION reactions are induced and controlled to produce a flow of usable energy or to produce materials needed for nuclear weapons; the first was created in 1942 by Enrico FERMI'S MANHATTAN PROJECT research team in a University of Chicago squash court.

Nuclear Regulatory Commission (NRC), U.S. agency that, with the Energy Research and Development Administration (ERDA), replaced the ATOMIC ENERGY COMMISSION (AEC) from 1975.

Nuclear Test Ban Treaty (1963), a Soviet-American-British agreement banning atmospheric, underwater, and outer space testing of nuclear weapons but permitting underground testing to continue. The agreement was later signed by many other nations.

nuclear winter, theoretical result of atomic warfare, as particles aloft in the atmosphere exclude the Sun's warming rays, leading to worldwide cooling and widespread crop failures and extinctions. Sparked by Luis and Walter ALVAREZ's 1980 theory of mass extinction following a meteorite crash some 65 million years ago, and the subsequent concern of scientists such as Carl SAGAN, an interdisciplinary group in 1984 published their grim forecast of a nuclear winter in a key paper titled "Long-Term Biological Consequences of Nuclear War."

nucleus, positively charged mass in an atom, placed at the center of ATOMIC STRUCTURE by Ernest RUTHERFORD in 1911. In 1919 Rutherford first artificially bombarded the nucleus of an atom, splitting it; later experiments along these lines led to modern NUCLEAR FISSION. By the 1930s, scientists had found that the nucleus includ-

ed the uncharged NEUTRON and the positively charge PROTON, which by the 1950s were found to have been made up of other still smaller PARTICLES, notably QUARKS, held together by GLUONS.

Nujoma, Sam (1929–   ), Namibian political leader, a co-founder and first president of the SOUTHWEST AFRICA PEOPLE'S ORGANIZATION OF NAMIBIA (SWAPO) in 1959; from 1966 he led SWAPO guerrilla external forces in the long NAMIBIAN WAR OF INDEPENDENCE, returning to Namibia in 1989.

Nuremberg Laws, Nazi anti-Jewish decrees, promulgated on September 15, 1935, and linked with the ideas of EUGENICS. They deprived German Jews of full citizenship, forbade marriage or intercourse between Jews and others, introduced a period of even more severe anti-Jewish persecution throughout Nazi Germany, and helped prepare Germans for the eventual murder of millions of Jews in Nazi DEATH CAMPS.

Nuremberg Trials (November 1945–October 1946), the war crimes trials of prominent Nazis by the International Military Tribunal in Nuremberg, Germany, the first of many such trials after World War II, at Nuremberg, other German locations, the Soviet Union, Yugoslavia, and other countries. Later trials at Nuremberg included the war crimes prosecutions of some of the Nazi DEATH CAMP doctors, a considerable number of other CONCENTRATION CAMP personnel, and members of the SS special squads in the Soviet Union. Similar war crimes trials were held in Tokyo. The trials produced massive evidence of Nazi crimes, dating back to the seizure of power in Germany in 1933 and including the huge mass murders of the Nazi period. At the conclusion of the trials two of the defendants were sentenced to death, including Martin BORMANN (in absentia), Hans FRANK, Wilhelm FRICK, Hermann GOERING, Alfred JODL, Ernst KALTENBRUNNER, Wilhelm KEITEL, Joachim von RIBBENTROP, Alfred ROSENBERG, Fritz Sauckel, Arthur Seyss-Inquart, and Julius STREICHER. All but Goering, who committed suicide in his cell, and

Bormann, who was never captured, were executed. Seven other defendants were sentenced to imprisonment, and three were acquitted.

Nuts! comment by U.S. general Anthony C. MCAULIFFE during the World War II Battle of BASTOGNE, on receiving a German ultimatum to surrender.

Nyasaland, the former name of MALAWI (Republic of Malawi), a British protectorate and then part of RHODESIA, which became an independent nation on July 6, 1964.

Nyerere, Julius Kambarage (1922–   ), Tanzanian teacher, a moderate socialist and pan-African leader who was founding president of the Tanganyika African National Union (TANU) in 1954. He became prime mover in the drive for Tanganyikan national independence that culminated in full autonomy within the COMMONWEALTH in 1961, and in the establishment of the Tanganyikan republic in 1962. He was president of Tanganyika 1962–64, and then of the union of Tanganyika and Zanzibar, which became the new nation of Tanzania, 1964–85. He established a socialist-oriented one-party state, achieved major social welfare and educational advances, and became one of Africa's leading statesmen. In 1984 his government successfully went to war against Uganda, helping depose the Idi AMIN dictatorship. He left the presidency in 1985, an elder statesman and the most influential of his country's leaders.

O

Oak Ridge, Tennessee site of the plant that from 1943 produced fissionable URANIUM for early ATOMIC BOMBS, notably the one exploded at HIROSHIMA.

OAS, the French Algerian terrorist SECRET ARMY ORGANIZATION of the early 1960s.

OAS, the initials of the multinational ORGANIZATION OF AMERICAN STATES.

OAU, the initials of the multinational ORGANIZATION OF AFRICAN UNITY.

Obote, Apollo Milton (1924–   ), Ugandan nationalist and socialist, who founded the Ugandan People's Congress in 1960, and became first prime minister of the Republic of Uganda in 1962, within the framework of a constitution that granted autonomy to Buganda and three other earlier kingdoms within Uganda. In 1966 he deposed the president and vice-president and abolished the constitution and the autonomy it provided, becoming president. In 1969 he established a one-party socialist state, repressing all opposition parties. In 1971 he was himself overthrown in a military coup led by Idi AMIN; he then went into Tanzanian exile. After Amin was toppled by the Tanzanian army in the UGANDA–TANZANIA WAR of 1979, Obote's party won majority support, and he became president again. He then instituted a reign of terror of his own, first against political opponents and then during the civil war that followed, in which an estimated 200,000 people died. In 1985 he was again deposed, and went into exile.

Obregón, Alvaro (1880–1928), Mexican farmer who raised a company of soldiers to fight with Francisco MADERO in the MEXICAN REVOLUTION and became general of Venustiano CARRANZA's forces. His forces ultimately defeated the forces of Francisco VILLA in a series of battles in 1915, including the decisive Battle of CELAYA. He led a revolt against the Carranza government in 1920, became president of Mexico 1920–24, and was assassinated in 1928.

Ochs, Adolph Simon (1858–1935), U.S. publisher who purchased the *New York Times* in 1896, introduced the slogan "All the News That's Fit to Print," added such features as the *Times* book review, and developed it into one of the most respected newspapers in the United States.

O'Connor, Sandra Day (1930–   ), U.S. lawyer, prosecutor, Arizona Republican state legislator (1969–74), judge (1975–79), and court of appeals judge (1979–81). In 1981 she became an associate justice of the Supreme Court, the first woman to hold that position.

October Manifesto, the October 17, 1905, document in which Czar NICHOLAS II, seeking to ease the pressure on his regime caused by the RUSSIAN REVOLUTION of 1905, inaugurated a short-lived period of limited constitutional government in Russia.

October Revolution, the second Russian revolution of 1917, which overthrew Alexander KERENSKY's PROVISIONAL GOVERNMENT, brought the BOLSHEVIKS to power, and began the RUSSIAN CIVIL WAR of 1917–22. On November 6, 1917, RED GUARD and military units organized by the PETROGRAD SOVIET, by then under Bolshevik control and directed by Bolshevik leader Leon TROTSKY, headquartered in the SMOLNY INSTITUTE, began to forcibly occupy government centers in Petrograd. On the night of November 7, they completed their occupation, storming and taking the WINTER PALACE, headquarters of the Provisional Government. Throughout the country, Soviet armed forces undertook similar action, meeting heavy armed resistance only in the Ukraine and in Moscow. In the Ukraine that resistance continued; the more general civil war began in May 1918. Between October and May, the Bolsheviks took Russia out of World War I by the Treaty of BREST-LITOVSK (March 3, 1918); established a new secret police, the CHEKA, and began to suppress all dissent; and organized the Red Army. They also began to carry out such programmatic promises as the nationalization of private property, including land, industry, and the financial system; legal equality for women; separation of church and state and, in practice, the attempted destruction of religious organizations; and development of a new judicial system.

October War (October 6–24, 1973), an alternate name for the YOM KIPPUR WAR, also known as the FOURTH ARAB–ISRAELI WAR.

Odessa, liberation of (April 10, 1944), freeing of the Russian city by Soviet forces driving southwest toward Rumania, late in World War II.

Odinga, Ajuma Oginga (1911–), Kenyan Luo tribal leader and teacher, who became an associate of Jomo KENYATTA in the Kenyan national movement in 1948, a vice-president of the Kenya African National Union (KANU) in 1960, and vice-president of Kenya 1964–66. A socialist, he split with Kenyatta and the KANU in 1966, forming the Kenya People's Union. He was then forced to resign his vice-presidency and was succeeded by Daniel Arap MOI, who later became president of Kenya. In 1969, after the assassination of Thomas MBOYA, Odinga's party was banned; he was arrested, jailed until 1971, and then not allowed to run for public office. He was again arrested after the unsuccessful air force coup of 1982, as was his son, Raila Odinga.

Office of Price Administration (OPA), a U.S. federal agency, created in April 1941, that controlled prices and rents and administered rationing programs during World War II.

Office of Strategic Services (OSS), U.S. World War II special operations intelligence organization, headed by Colonel William J. DONOVAN; it was involved in a considerable variety of espionage, sabotage, and other covert operations. The organization was regarded by many military and intelligence professionals of the period as a group of free-wheeling, rather unstable amateurs, although it was able to claim credit for many successful operations. The OSS was the forerunner of the CENTRAL INTELLIGENCE AGENCY (CIA).

officers' plot, failed bombing attempt to assassinate HITLER, carried out on July 20, 1944, by Col. Klaus von STAUFFENBERG on behalf of a group of German army officers. An armed forces purge and many executions followed; one of the casualties was General Erwin ROMMEL, who had been implicated and committed suicide.

OGPU, a later name and form of the Soviet secret police organization that began in 1917 as the CHEKA.

Ohio State Penitentiary fire (April 21, 1930), fire that broke out at the terribly overcrowded state prison at Columbus, Ohio. Fearing escapes, prison guards refused to open the cell doors, trapping prisoners in the burning prison; 320 died in their cells.

oil embargo (October 1973–March 1974), the cutoff of all oil supplies to the industrialized nations of the world, imposed by the ORGANIZATION OF PETROLEUM EXPORTING COUNTRIES (OPEC), in response to the Israeli victory in the ARAB–ISRAELI WAR of 1973. The embargo was lifted after the disengagement of the combatants.

Ojukwu, Chukwuemeka Odumegwu (1933–), Nigerian officer, an Ibo who became military governor of the eastern region of the country in 1966, and resisted central government control during and after the Ibo massacres of 1966–67. On May 30, 1967, the eastern region seceded, becoming the Republic of Biafra; Ojukwu was its president, leading his new state throughout the NIGERIA–BIAFRA CIVIL WAR. After the lost war he went into exile, returning to Nigerian political life in the early 1980s.

Okies, the destitute migrant refugees from the DUST BOWL of Oklahoma and several neighboring states during the 1930s, and the subject of John Steinbeck's *The Grapes of Wrath*. Many settled in California and in such northern cities as Detroit, finding war work during the 1940s and becoming integrated into their new communities.

Okinawa, Battle of (April–June 1945), capture of this Pacific island by U.S. forces late in World War II. Unopposed amphibious landings began on April 1; heavy fighting between American forces and Japanese defenders, numbering 130,000–140,000 men, began a few days later as the main attacking force moved against strongly defended mountain positions. On April 7, strong Japanese aerial attacks, including hundreds of KAMIKAZE suicide attacks, did some damage to the invasion fleet but failed to put any of its major fighting vessels out of action. On the same day the remaining Japanese superbattleship, the *Yamoto*, attacked the invasion fleet, but without air cover it was easily sunk. Kamikaze attacks continued through mid-April, resulting in some damage to the invasion fleet and the loss of over 3,000 more Japanese planes and pilots. A long land battle on the island ended on June 22, when Japanese resistance ended. An estimated 125,000–130,000 Japanese died defending the island, most of the defenders electing to fight to the death, although there were more than 7,000 Japanese prisoners. Of 50,000 American casualties, there were over 12,000 dead.

Olympic boycott, boycott of the 1980 Moscow summer Olympics, initiated by President Jimmy CARTER, in response to the 1979 Soviet invasion of AFGHANISTAN. The boycott was ultimately joined by over 50 other countries.

Olympic games, a modern revival of the ancient Greek games, as a quadrennial set of international summer and winter games and a celebration of essential human unity. The Athens Olympiad of 1896 began the modern games; aside from major breaks during World Wars I and II, they have been held regularly ever since, although sometimes marred and intruded upon by current conflicts. Nazi racism directed against Black American athlete Jesse Owens marred the 1936 Berlin games, as did the Arab terrorist mass murder of Israeli athletes at the MUNICH GAMES of 1972. Two Americans caused a furor by responding with BLACK POWER salutes (a clenched fist raised in the air) during their victory celebrations at Mexico City, in 1968, while continuing disputes in southern Africa caused withdrawal threats in 1972 and many withdrawals in 1976. The Soviet invasion of AFGHANISTAN generated U.S. and other Western withdrawals from the 1980 Moscow games; the Soviets retaliated by boycotting the 1984 Los Angeles games. The 1988 Seoul games seemed for a time threatened by possible mass demonstrations against an unpopular Korean government and possible terrorist attacks, but went off without incident. While sometimes seriously threatened, the Olympic games and their ideal have endured.

Oman (Sultanate of Oman), until 1951 a British protectorate. Though an independent state since December 20, 1951, and with British bases no longer in operation after 1977, Oman remains strongly influenced in external affairs by Great Britain.

one third of a nation, statement by U. S. president Franklin Delano ROOSEVELT, in his second Inaugural Address, January 20, 1937; from "I see one third of a nation illhoused, ill-clad, ill-nourished."

Onishi, Takijiro (1891–1945), Japanese naval officer who, as air force commander in the Philippines during the American invasion of 1944, originated the KAMIKAZE tactics used there and even more fully during the Battle of OKINAWA. He committed suicide after the Japanese surrender in 1945.

only thing we have to fear is fear itself, The, statement by U. S. president Franklin Delano ROOSEVELT in his first Inaugural Address, March 4, 1933.

OPA, the initials of the OFFICE OF PRICE ADMINISTRATION, by which this most ubiquitous of all the U.S. wartime federal agencies was best known.

OPEC, the initials of the multinational ORGANIZATION OF THE PETROLEUM EXPORTING COUNTRIES

Open Door Policy, the stated policy of the United States toward China from 1899, calling for the protection of China from foreign dismemberment and for equal trading rights for all countries in China; it became United States policy in the early years of the century.

open-heart surgery, direct surgery on the heart—unbeating, drained of blood, and open to the surgeon's view—while the patient's circulatory system is kept functioning by a heart-lung machine. Until the mid-20th century heart surgery was rare, minor, and tentative, for the heart kept beating and the surgeon had to work "blind" on tissue obscured by blood. Only if the body was chilled to reduce its need for oxygen could the heart be open to the surgeon's view and then for only about 10 minutes. Even so, during World War II surgeons were forced to operate on the wounded; one physician, Dwight Emary Harken, reportedly removed 134 "missiles" from the heart area, 13 from the heart itself, without losing a patient. In 1944 Albert BLALOCK introduced surgery to repair heart defects in BLUE BABIES. But only with the development of practical heart-lung machines—essentially external ARTIFICIAL HEARTS—were doctors able to do complex, intricate, time-consuming work on the heart. In 1953, John Gibbon, Jr., first used a heart-lung machine to keep his patient, Cecelia Bavolek, alive during heart surgery. The techniques of open-heart surgery led to HEART TRANSPLANTS, the first of which was done by Christiaan BARNARD in 1967, and to other innovations, such as the CORONARY BYPASS, first done by U.S.

surgeon Rene Favalaro, also in 1967. Much open-heart surgery focused on less drastic operations, such as repair or replacement of valves.

opening to China, the February 1972 visit of U.S. president Richard M. NIXON to the PEOPLE'S REPUBLIC OF CHINA, which ended the decades of estrangement that had started with American support of CHIANG KAI-SHEK during the latter stages of the CHINESE CIVIL WAR and then became bitter enmity during the KOREAN WAR.

Oppau explosion (September 21, 1921), explosion of an industrial gas generator at Oppau, Germany, destroying a chemical plant and much of the city; more than 1,000 people died.

Oppenheimer, Julius Robert (1904–67), U.S. physicist and teacher, who played a major role in the development of the ATOMIC BOMB as part of the MANHATTAN PROJECT, from 1943 organizing and directing the LOS ALAMOS, New Mexico, laboratory in which the bomb itself was developed. In the late 1930s, he had done key early work relating to PULSARS and BLACK HOLES. During the postwar period, he was greatly concerned with the survival of humanity because of the bomb he had helped create; serving as adviser to the ATOMIC ENERGY COMMISSION and the U.S. Mission to the United Nations, Oppenheimer supported international control of atomic energy and opposed the building of the HYDROGEN BOMB. He became director of the Institute for Advanced Study at Princeton in 1947. In 1953, during the witchhunts of the MCCARTHY period, he was accused of having Communist friends and of possible disloyalty and was denied further security clearance. He was later officially rehabilitated, receiving the Fermi Award in 1967.

oral contraceptive, alternate name for BIRTH CONTROL PILL.

Oran sinkings (July 4, 1940), a World War II British attack on French warships anchored in the harbor at Oran, Algeria, after the French refused to join the British, intern themselves, or sink their ships in the harbor. Three French battleships were sunk, the VICHY government broke relations with Great Britain, and a good deal of animosity developed between the British and the French, which lasted throughout the war and into the postwar period.

organ transplant, replacement of a diseased human organ with a healthy one from a donor; TRANSPLANTS of kidneys and other organs were attempted from the 1900s but with little success until the 1950s. The first successful KIDNEY TRANSPLANT was done in 1954 and the first HEART TRANSPLANT in 1967.

Organization of African Unity (OAU), a multinational African forum established in 1963; its 50 members include almost all African nations, with some temporary withdrawals and returns as disputes develop. An exception is South Africa, which is the object of much of the anticolonial focus of the organization, along with opposition to some superpower activities in Africa. During the 1980s, considerable attention also has been paid to the continent-wide problems of mounting debt and large, often starving refugee populations.

Organization of American States (OAS), a multinational inter-American organization established in 1948; its 32 members include almost all of the nations of Latin America and the United States. Cuba, although a member nation, has been barred from participation since 1962, although many sanctions against Cuba were removed in 1975, and the late 1980s saw much pressure to reestablish full Cuban participation. The OAS is active in the assertion of human rights throughout Latin America, in attempts to settle disputes between and within its member nations, and in opposition to moves against its members, as in its support of Argentina during the FALKLANDS WAR. It is increasingly involved in attempts to solve the great problems caused by the foreign debt crisis faced throughout Latin America.

Organization of the Petroleum Exporting Countries (OPEC), a multinational oil-pro-

ducing cartel, composed of Algeria, Ecuador, Gabon, Indonesia, Iran, Iraq, Kuwait, Libya, Nigeria, Qatar, Saudi Arabia, United Arab Emirates, and Venezuela. It was established in 1960, and has since attempted to control world oil prices, with varying success. During the mid-1970s, OPEC was able to force major oil price increases, in one 2-month period, October–December 1973, increasing prices 373%. That winter, OPEC sucessfully imposed an OIL EMBARGO on the industrialized nations of the world. But with oversupply and a world economic slowdown from the late 1970s, OPEC became much less able to control world oil prices, although they remained far higher than pre-1973 prices.

Organization, The, an alternative name for the U.S. MAFIA.

Orlando, Vittorio Emanuele (1860–1952), Italian political leader, a member of parliament from 1897, at cabinet level during the early years of the century, and premier of Italy 1917–19. He led the Italian delegation at the PARIS PEACE CONFERENCE, but was disappointed by the terms of the Treaty of VERSAILLES. He subsequently resigned as premier, but became leader of Italy's Chamber of Deputies. He supported Benito MUSSOLINI'S rise to power, but broke with him after the Fascist murder of Giacomo MATTEOTI in 1924; in 1925 he retired from public life in protest against the fascist government. He returned to public life after the fall of fascism, and was a senator from 1948–52.

Ortega Saavedra, Daniel (1945–), Nicaraguan Marxian socialist and SANDINISTA leader, a guerrilla fighter from 1963 and imprisoned 1967–74; he was one of the five-member junta that ruled the country following the flight of dictator Anastasio SOMOZA in July 1979. Ortega became leader of the farther-left three-member junta that ruled from March 1981, and president of Nicaragua in January 1985. He was defeated in the free elections of February 1990.

Orwell, George (Eric Arthur Blair; 1903–50), British writer who focused on political matters in his essays and fiction. Some of his best-known works are the novel *1984* (1949), which powerfully attacked authoritarianism masquerading as a kind of socialism, *ANIMAL FARM* (1946), *Homage to Catalonia* (1938), and *The Road to Wigan Pier* (1937).

OSO (**O**rbiting **S**olar **O**bservatory), series of U.S. research and observation SATELLITES recording solar data and transmitting it on command, the first launched on March 7, 1962.

OSS, the initials of the OFFICE OF STRATEGIC SERVICES, the U.S. World War II predecessor of the CENTRAL INTELLIGENCE AGENCY (CIA).

Oswald, Lee Harvey (1939–63), assassin of President John F. KENNEDY in Dallas, Texas, on November 22, 1963. Oswald was murdered by Jack RUBY in the Dallas city jail, in full view of a huge worldwide televison audience, 2 days later, November 24, 1963.

Oświęcim, alternate name for the AUSCHWITZ-BIRKENAU German concentration camp.

Ottoman Empire, an alternate name for the Turkish Empire, the empire of the Ottoman Turks who ruled much of Europe and the Near East at the beginning of the 20th century. Turkish control over the empire deteriorated throughout the 19th century and the early years of the 20th century; the empire became widely known as the SICK MAN OF EUROPE. World War I, in which the Turks became German allies in a losing war, brought the coup de grace. The empire was dismantled, its surviving central portion becoming the Turkish Republic.

Ouchy, Treaty of (1912), agreement ending the ITALO-TURKISH WAR.

overkill, excess of nuclear weapons over what would be needed to destroy or defeat an enemy at war, a term that came into use after World War II in relation to the superpower arms race.

Overlord, Operation, code name for the ALLIES' June 1944 NORMANDY invasion plan in World War II.

Oxford Pledge, the pacifist resolution of Britain's Oxford Union in February 1933, that "this House will not fight for King and Country," reflecting continuing widespread revulsion against what were then seen as the needless deaths of millions in World War I, and strong support, especially among the young, for the LEAGUE OF NATIONS and the cause of disarmament. The pledge was very soon ignored in practice by the same young people who had made it; as fascism came, some of them went to Spain to fight on the Loyalist side, and the vast majority of them fought without reservation in World War II.

ozone layer (ozonosphere), layer of air about 50,000–120,000 feet high in the Earth's atmosphere; it is heavy with ozone, a form of oxygen created by electricity or, in this case, ULTRAVIOLET RADIATION from the Sun. The ozone layer protects humans from the most harmful effects of ultraviolet radiation, but from at least 1974 it was clear that certain chemicals can deplete the layer by converting ozone back into normal oxygen; a British team in 1985 even detected a hole in the ozone layer over Antarctica. In addition to gases from volcanic eruptions, oustanding culprits were identified as chlorofluorocarbons (CFCs), also called chlorofluoromethanes (CFMs) or Freons, commonly used as spray propellants or refrigerants. The United States banned CFCs in aerosol sprays in 1978, and in 1988 was the first to ratify an international treaty banning them, but few other actions were taken there or elsewhere in the intervening years.

P

pacemaker, small electrical device implanted in a patient's chest to stimulate regular pumping action in the heart. Bulky external electrical devices had been used for that purpose from the 1930s, but the development of miniature batteries and TRANSISTORS allowed the development of small implants in the United States by 1952, the first implant being made in 1958.

Pact of Paris, an alternate name for the KELLOGG-BRIAND PACT of 1928, a multinational attempt to outlaw war.

Paderewski, Ignacy Jan (1860–1941), eminent pianist and Polish nationalist, who played a large role in winning world support for the cause of Polish independence; he became first premier and foreign minister of the new Polish Republic in 1919. He left the government in 1920, returning to his musical career. During the early years of World War II, he was a leading member of the Polish government in exile.

Pahlevi, Muhammed Reza Shah (1919–80), the last shah of Iran (1941–79), who became shah after the forced abdication of his father, Reza Shah PAHLEVI, in 1941. He became little more than a figurehead ruler in 1951, with the accession to the premiership of National Front leader Mohammed MOSSADEQ, and the nationalization of the Iranian oil industry. He fled the country on August 16, 1953, after supporting an unsuccessful coup against the Mossadeq government, sponsored by U.S. and British intelligence organizations, but returned as ruler of Iran 3 days later, when an Iranian army revolt toppled that government. He then ruled Iran, continuing and greatly expanding the westernization program begun by his father, but as an American ally, deeply involved in the COLD WAR. He survived the anti-government rioting of June 1963, subsequently exiling its leader, Ayatollah Ruhollah KHOMEINI; ultimately, in January 1979, his government fell to a coalition of Khomeini's Islamic fundamentalist followers, democratic groups opposed to his increasingly savage and corrupt regime, and left-wing socialist groups. Pahlevi then fled into Egptian exile.

Pahlevi, Reza Shah (Reza Khan; 1878–1944), Iranian general in command of the Cossack Brigade, who seized power from the government of Ahmad Shah in February 1921, then built a powerful military force and took full control of the country. He became premier in 1923, and shah, head of the new house of Pahlevi, in 1925. For the next 16 years he ruled Iran, increasingly as an absolute monarch, attempting to steer an independent course while using greatly increasing oil revenues to develop Iran into a modern nation. In the process, he sharply attacked the power of the Islamic clergy; a major symbolic move was the abolishing of the veil in 1936. He refused to enter World War II on the side of the Allies, and Iran was invaded by British and Soviet troops after the German invasion of the Soviet Union in 1941; he was then forced to abdicate, going into exile after passing the crown to his son, Mohammed Reza Shah PAHLEVI.

Pakistan (Islamic Republic of Pakistan), until 1947 part of British India, which also dominated many minor, nominally independent states on the subcontinent. With independence came the disastrous partition of India (INDIA, PARTITION OF), emergence of the new nations of Pakistan and INDIA, and continuing disputes over some of the other states on the subcontinent, including Kashmir. Pakistan, led by Mohammed Ali JINNAH, became a Moslem state, with two main divisions, East and West Pakistan. East Pakistan won its own independence in 1971, as BANGLADESH, in the 1971 BANGLADESH WAR OF INDEPENDENCE, which was accompanied by the INDIA–PAKISTAN WAR OF 1971. After the 1988 death of dictator Mohammed ZIA UL-HAQ, Pakistan embarked on a new, democratic course under the leadership of Benazir BHUTTO.

Pakistan People's Party, the socialist and Islamic party founded in Pakistan in 1967 by Zulfikar Ali BHUTTO. It took power on December 20, 1971, when Bhutto became chief martial law administrator and then prime minister after the lost INDIA–PAKISTAN WAR OF 1971. The party won the March 1977 elections, but was banned following the July army coup that brought general Mohammad ZIA UL-HAQ to power. Bhutto was executed in 1979, but his daughter, Benazir BHUTTO, who had been held under house arrest for some years and had then gone abroad, returned to lead the party in opposition to the Zia Ul-Haq dictatorship in 1986. In 1988 she led it to power in a democratic Pakistan, after the death of Zia in an airplane crash.

Palestine, partition of (1948), partition was recommended by the British Peel Commission in 1937, in response to the the PALESTINIAN GENERAL STRIKE AND REVOLT of 1936. In 1947 the UNITED NATIONS recommended partition of Palestine into Arab and Jewish states, setting October l, 1948, as the date of British withdrawal. As civil war threatened in Palestine, Britain decided to withdraw earlier, setting May 14, 1948, as the date. Israel declared itself an independent nation, effective on that date; civil war and the ISRAELI WAR OF INDEPENDENCE (FIRST ARAB–ISRAELI WAR) immediately followed, ending with de facto partition of the country, although without peace treaties.

Palestine Liberation Organization (PLO), Palestinian Arab political organization founded in 1964 as a semigovernmental body aiming ultimately to achieve a Palestinian Arab state, primarily by political means and through development of a regular Palestinian army. In 1967, after Arab defeat in the THIRD ARAB–ISRAELI WAR (SINAI–SUEZ WAR), the PLO began to focus more on guerrilla warfare. In 1969 Yasir ARAFAT was named PLO chairman, and his organization, FATAH, became the most important group in the PLO. The PLO suffered a major setback with its 1970–71 defeat by and expulsion from Jordan. It then headquartered in Lebanon and became engaged in the long LEBANESE CIVIL WAR, meanwhile continuing its guerrilla war against Israel. The 1982 Israeli invasion of Lebanon severely damaged PLO fighting forces, as did internal dissension. From the mid-1970s, the PLO took what was perceived by its hard-line elements and by some Arab states as too moderate a position vis-à-vis Israel; the resulting dissidence, including some secessions, weakened the PLO considerably, contributing to its eventual expulsion from Lebanon in 1983. Although a much weakened fighting force, the PLO continued to be recognized as the main Palestinian Arab political organization, and Yasir Arafat as the main spokesperson of the Palestinian national movement. In the late 1980s, especially as the INTIFADA developed on the WEST BANK, the PLO achieved worldwide recognition as the leading force in what was seen as a Palestinian government-in-exile, and Arafat was recognized as the leader of the Palestinian independence movement.

Palestinian general strike and revolt (1936–39), a 6-month general strike that grew into a 3-year guerrilla war throughout Palestine, in opposition to growing Jewish settlement and land purchase and to continuing British occupation of the country. In response, the British Peel Commission in 1937 recommended the partition of Palestine. The White Paper of 1939 limited Jewish immigration and land purchase, while restating the goal of ultimate partition of Palestine into Jewish and Arab states.

Palmach, an Israeli front-line fighting force formed in 1941; some Palmach commando units fought with the British in the Middle East during World War II. From 1945 through the end of the ISRAELI WAR OF INDEPENDENCE (FIRST ARAB–ISRAELI WAR) the Palmach was an elite fighting force within the HAGANAH; after independence it was disbanded, its members either absorbed into the Israeli armed forces or going into civilian life.

Palme, Olaf (1927–86), Swedish Social Democratic party leader, in parliament from 1958 and premier 1969–76 and 1982–86, who was active on international disarmament and development matters. He was assassinated in Stockholm, on February 28, 1986.

Palmer, Alexander Mitchell (1872–1936), U.S. lawyer, Pennsylvania Democratic congressman (1909–15), and United States attorney general (1919–21) who was the key mover in the development of the RED SCARE of 1919–20, which featured the PALMER RAIDS, and resulted in the jailing without adequate legal process of thousands and the deportation of hundreds of radical and aliens, the most prominent of whom were Emma GOLDMAN and Alexander BERKMAN.

Palmer Raids, the mass arrests of more than 4,000 alleged subversives throughout the United States, initiated by U.S. attorney general A. Mitchell PALMER on January 2, 1920. They were arrested as part of the RED SCARE of 1919–20, a period of antialien, antiradical hysteria following World War I and the RUSSIAN REVOLUTION. All but a few of those arrested in the Palmer Raids were ultimately acquitted or not even brought to trial, although hundreds of those arrested earlier, including Emma GOLDMAN and Alexander BERKMAN, were deported.

Pan-African movement, an attempt to build an African anticolonial movement, begun in 1900 with the first Pan-African Congress,

organized by W. E. B. DU BOIS and other U.S. and West Indian Black leaders in London. Five such Pan-African Congresses were held, in 1900, 1919, 1921, 1923, and 1927. As World War II was ending, a far stronger African anticolonial movement emerged and with it formation of the Pan African Federation in 1944 and the watershed Sixth Pan-African Congress of 1945, held in Manchester and attended by many future African national leaders, including Jomo KENYATTA and Kwame NKRUMAH. Independence came to many African nations during the early postwar period; the next Pan-African meeting was the 1958 Accra, Ghana, meeting of independent African states, which developed in 1963 into the continent-wide ORGANIZATION OF AFRICAN UNITY.

Panama (Republic of Panama), until 1903 part of Colombia, becoming an independent nation on November 3, 1903, after a brief revolution sponsored by the United States to clear the way for the building of the PANAMA CANAL. The new nation granted the United States long-term rights to the PANAMA CANAL ZONE and became a de facto U.S. protectorate. Panama and the United States renegotiated the Canal Zone treaties in 1977, easing considerable strain between the two countries. In the late 1980s, a continuing U.S.–Panama dispute over the alleged drug-related activities of Panamanian strongman Manuel NORIEGA developed. It escalated into a substantial confrontation on the issue of Panama's nullified presidential election of May 1989.

Panama Canal, the U.S.-built canal across the Isthmus of Panama, linking the Atlantic and Pacific oceans; it became a central facility for the world's ocean shipping from the day the first ship passed through, August 3, 1914. It succeeded the failed French-led attempt to build such a canal, begun under Suez Canal builder Ferdinand de Lesseps in 1881. The canal traverses the 10-mile-wide CANAL ZONE, granted to the United States by Panama by treaty in 1904, after president Theodore ROOSEVELT had encouraged a Panamanian revolution against

Colombia to secure a compliant treaty partner. Building began in 1904, took 10 years, and was completed by engineer George W. GOETHALS. The virtual U.S. sovereignty over the Canal Zone was disputed by many Panamanians from the beginning, leading ultimately to armed clashes in 1964 and renegotiation of the basic agreement by the treaty of 1979.

Panama, invasion of, U.S. forces in divisional strength invaded Panama on December 20, 1989, joining forces already stationed in that country; total U.S. forces involved ultimately numbered 24,000–25,000 troops. The small Panamanian army, the Self Defense Force, was quickly overwhelmed, in less than 4 four days of fighting. Panamanian military casualties included an estimated 400–500 dead, including members of the paramilitary Dignity Battalions. Several hundred Panamanian civilian noncombatants were also killed, an estimated 2,000 more were injured, and an estimated 13,000–14,000 were left homeless. U.S. military casualties included 24 dead and 323 wounded; there were also 3 U.S. civilian deaths. Panamanian leader Manuel NORIEGA, the target of the attack, took refuge in the Vatican Panama City embassy on December 24. He surrendered to U.S. forces on January 3, and was taken to the United States, to stand trial on longstanding drug charges. On December 20, the U.S. installed a new Panamanian government, headed by president Guillermo Endara. U.S. forces continued to occupy Panama during the early months of 1990.

Pan-Arab movement, a movement that, in its 20th-century form, developed as the rebellion of the Arab national movement against Turkish rule led by HUSEIN IBN ALI and his sons, in alliance with the British, during World War I. As a group of often-competing Arab states developed, Arab unity continued as an ideal, coming sharply into focus in the 1930s and 1940s on the Palestine issue; in 1945, with the formation of the ARAB LEAGUE; and in 1948, with the FIRST ARAB–ISRAELI WAR, on formation of the state of Israel. During the postwar period the pan-Arab and socialist BA'ATH PARTY, organized in 1947, also gained strengh throughout the Arab world, coming to power in Syria in 1963 and in Iraq in 1968; Egypt's Gamal Abdel NASSER also expressed Pan-Arab goals. The long Arab–Israeli conflict and common oil interests have preserved considerable pan-Arab unity during the 1970s and 1980s, but conflicting national interests and the advent of Islamic fundamentalism have created major new divisive problems in the Arab world.

Panay Incident (December 12, 1937), the Japanese bombing of several U.S. and British gunboats and the sinking of the U.S.S. *Panay* in the Yangtse River, near Nanking; the action was part of the run-up to World War II. The sinking was a cause célèbre in the United States, which was not satisfied by Japanese apologies.

Pandit, Vijaya Lakshmi (1900–), Indian nationalist leader, daughter of Motilal NEHRU and sister of Jawaharlal NEHRU. An independence movement activist, she was imprisoned on several occasions by the British in the 1920s, served in the Uttar Pradesh legislature in the 1930s, and after independence became a key Indian diplomat. She was India's ambassador to the Soviet Union 1947–49, to the United States 1949–51, and to Great Britain 1954–61. In 1953–54, she was the first woman president of the UNITED NATIONS General Assembly. She was active in Indian political life from 1962 to 1968, as a provincial governor and then as a member of parliament.

Pangaea, single supercontinent believed to have existed some 200 million years ago, according to Alfred WEGENER's CONTINENTAL DRIFT theory (1912).

Panic of 1907, a U.S. financial crash that for a time threatened to send the United States into a major depression; it was averted by the concerted private action of a group of financiers led by J. Pierpont MORGAN. The next such U.S. panic resulted in the CRASH of 1929, in which such private efforts were mounted but failed.

Pankhurst, Emmeline (1858–1928), British women's rights leader and chief organizer of the successful battle for WOMAN SUFFRAGE in Britain. From 1903, when she organized the Women's Social and Political Union, to 1912, she and her daughters, Christabel Pankhurst (1880–1958) and Sylvia Pankhurst (1882–1960), led a highly visible movement. In that period, they and their followers were very often arrested and imprisoned by an intransigent British government, while conducting peaceful demonstrations, and they resorted to the attention-getting tactic of the hunger strike while in prison. From July 1912, her movement turned toward violence, including some incidents of arson. At the beginning of World War I, she and her organization ended their campaign, and thereafter fully supported the British war effort in return for a promise of woman suffrage after the war.

Panmunjom negotiations, the 2-year-long truce negotiations that ultimately led to the KOREAN WAR armistice of July 27, 1953. The talks were held at the village of Panmunjom, in the no-man's-land between the opposing armies.

Panzers, TANK divisions of the German army, used to great effect in World War II.

Papadopoulos, George (1919–　　), Greek officer who took power in a 1967 military coup, and then ruled Greece by decree until he was toppled by another military coup in 1973. He was sentenced to death by the democratic government that came to power in 1974, but the sentence was not carried out.

Papandreou, Georgios (1886–1968), Greek socialist and political leader, in parliament 1923–35, and founder of the Democratic Socialist party in 1935; he was exiled by the METAXAS dictatorship 1936–40 and imprisoned by AXIS occupation forces until his escape in 1944. He headed the Greek government-in-exile, was three-time Greek premier between 1945 and 1965, held other cabinet-level posts, and when not in power was the head of the opposition. He was arrested by the PAPADOPOULOS government after the 1967 military coup, dying a year later. Andreas George PAPANDREOU was his son.

Papandreou, Andreas George (1919–　　), Greek socialist, economist, and political leader, the son of Georgios PAPANDREOU. He lived in the United States 1939–63, in that period becoming a U.S. citizen, serving in the navy during World War II, and teaching in a university. In 1963, he returned to Greece to serve in his father's cabinet, went into parliament, and was arrested and imprisoned by the PAPADOPOULOS government after the 1967 military coup. In exile from 1967 to 1974, he returned to Greek politics and became premier 1981–89, pursuing a socialist course domestically and a nonaligned course in international affairs.

Papen, Franz von (1879–1969), German military officer and diplomat, who was chancellor June 1–December 2, 1932. In January 1933, he was instrumental in bringing HITLER to power in Germany; until June 1934 he was Hitler's vice-chancellor and thereafter a Nazi diplomat. He was acquitted of war crimes at the NUREMBERG TRIALS but later spent some time in jail for having been a major Nazi figure.

Pap smear, a simple test for cervical CANCER involving microscopic analysis of cells taken from a woman's vagina; developed by Greek-American cell biologist George Papanicolaou in 1933 from his earlier work, and later used as a routine screening procedure.

Papua New Guinea, until 1975 controlled by Australia; part of it had been the long-time British New Guinea colony, and its northeastern portion, formerly a German colony, had been acquired after World War I as a LEAGUE OF NATIONS mandate territory. It became an independent nation on September 16, 1975.

Paris, liberation of (August 25, 1944), World War II taking of Paris by Allied troops pursuing the retreating German army; the first Allied troops into the city were French.

Paris Peace Accords (January 27, 1973), the agreement negotiated by LE DUC THO and Henry KISSINGER, after years of U.S.–North Vietnamese negotiation, which ended American participation in the VIETNAM WAR. Remaining U.S. forces were withdrawn in return for a promise to return American prisoners of war. North and South Vietnam entered into a period of truce, although substantial North Vietnamese forces remained in South Vietnam. Small-scale hostilities soon resumed, and in 1975 a final North Vietnamese offensive destroyed South Vietnamese resistance. After the Paris Peace Accords there were allegations that many Americans were still being held in North Vietnam and Laos, and a campaign was launched to free any still being held.

Paris Peace Conference (January 18–June 28, 1919), conference of the victorious World War I ALLIES, which organized the LEAGUE OF NATIONS; agreed on the disposition of several former CENTRAL POWERS' colonial possessions, setting up a mandate system for some of them; set the level and form of reparations; and agreed on the Central Powers' territorial losses and restrictions. It also set up several new European nations and adjusted the boundaries of others. The conference concluded with the Treaty of VERSAILLES, signed on June 28, 1919, after considerable German resistance and preparation for military action on the part of the Allies. Also signed were the Treaty of SAINT-GERMAIN with Austria, the Treaty of NEUILLY with Bulgaria, the Treaty of TRIANON with Hungary, and the Treaties of SÈVRES and LAUSANNE with Turkey.

Park Chung Hee (1917–79), South Korean officer who fought in the Japanese army during World War II, becoming a South Korean army officer after the war. In May 1961, then a general, he took power in a coup, and kept power as an elected president until 1971. Facing growing opposition, he openly assumed dictatorial power in 1971, ruling by decree and intensifying his repression of all opposition, while successfully focusing on the industrialization of South Korea. He was assassinated on October 26, 1979, by the head of his own Central Intelligence Agency.

Parker, Alton Brooks (1852–1926), U.S. lawyer and judge, who was the Democratic presidential nominee in 1904, and was defeated by Theodore ROOSEVELT, thereafter resuming his legal career.

Parker, Bonnie, and **Clyde Barrow,** U.S. criminals of the early 1930s, who as "Bonnie and Clyde" committed at least 13 murders and scores of armed robberies throughout the Southwest, before being killed in police ambush near Giblans, Louisiana, in May 1934. Parker had a strong appetite for publicity, sending photos and writing letters and poems to newspapers, among them "The Ballad of Bonnie and Clyde," which was later set to music. The pair became folk heroes in their time and place; in 1967 Faye Dunaway and Warren Beatty played them in the motion picture *Bonnie and Clyde*.

Parkinson's disease (parkinsonism), neurological disease often involving muscular rigidity, slow movement, and tremors, identified in the 19th century, but only in the 20th century found to result from lack of dopamine needed to ensure proper neural connections in the brain. From the late 1960s, many Parkinson's disease patients were helped by a medication called levodopa, or L-dopa, which causes the body to produce the missing dopamine. In 1986, Mexican physician Ignacio Navarro Madrazo claimed great benefits from implanting adrenal tissue in the brain, but other physicians were unable to reproduce successful results.

Parks, Rosa (1913–   ), U.S. Black civil rights trailblazer, whose action in refusing to give up her seat to a White bus passenger in Montgomery, Alabama, on December 1, 1955, led to the organization of the MONTGOMERY BUS BOYCOTT, the emergence of Martin Luther KING, Jr., as a civil rights leader, and the development of the modern American CIVIL RIGHTS MOVEMENT.

particle accelerator, alternate name for an ACCELERATOR or "atom smasher."

particles, in physics, the minute subdivisions of matter that make up the atom. In the early 20th century, the basic pieces in the ATOMIC STRUCTURE were thought to be the NEUTRON, PROTON, and ELECTRON. But by mid-century it became clear that these were themselves made up of—and "decayed" into—smaller particles. In 1946 Murray GELL-MANN and other researchers found previously unknown particles with qualities later called STRANGENESS; in 1964 Gell-Mann and Richard FEYNMAN (and independently, George Zweig) outlined a theory based on various particles called QUARKS. In the century's last decade research continued, with no one sure that the absolutely fundamental, indivisible particles had yet all been identified.

particle-wave duality, alternate name for WAVE-PARTICLE DUALITY.

Parti Québécois, Quebec separatist party formed in 1968 by René LÉVESQUE; it became the ruling party in Quebec from 1976 to 1985, with Lévesque as premier. The party lost the 1980 referendum on opening sovereignty negotiations with the Canadian government, and became a small minority party after its 1985 electoral defeat.

Passchendaele, an alternate name for the third Battle of YPRES (July 31–November 10, 1917), in which British forces suffered an estimated 320,000 casualties, while gaining only 5 miles, finally taking the small Belgian village of Passchendaele.

Pasternak, Boris Leonidovich (1890–1960), Soviet novelist and poet who was recognized as a major poet in the early 1920s but then fell into disfavor with the Soviet government. In 1955 he wrote DR. ZHIVAGO, the classic testament of an artist who remained free despite an authoritarian government; it was published in Italy in 1957. He was awarded the Nobel Prize for Literature in 1958, but was pressured by his government to reject it, his work emerging only later in the Soviet Union.

Pathet Lao, the army of the Communist movement in Laos, organized in 1950 to fight the French during the INDOCHINA WAR; it went on to win the LAOTIAN CIVIL WAR. A key organizer of the Pathet Lao was Prince SOUPHANOUVONG, later Laotian head of state; another was KAYSONE PHOMVIHANE, later prime minister.

Patton, George Smith (1885–1945), U.S. officer, who saw service in Mexico and as a tank officer in World War I. During World War II he commanded substantial American forces during the invasions of North Africa and Sicily, but became involved in a much-publicized incident of physical and verbal abuse of a wounded soldier and lost his command. He headed the U.S. Third Army during the European campaign, relieved besieged BASTOGNE during the Battle of the BULGE, and led his forces across Germany to meet the advancing Soviets at the end of the war. He was military governor of Bavaria after the war, but his propensity to talk himself into difficulty once again surfaced, and he was relieved of his command in October 1945; he died in an automobile accident that December.

Paul VI, Pope (Giovani Battista Montini; 1898–1978), Italian priest, ordained in 1920, who became a cardinal in 1958 and pope 1963–78. He succeeded JOHN XXIII in 1963. In 1965 he finished VATICAN II, which John XIII had initiated, and then spent much of his tenure working with the issues raised by Vatican II. On societal matters, he tended to pursue the objectives of Vatican II, fostering ecumenicism, moves toward peace, and aid to developing nations. On personal, religous, and church matters he took a more conservative view, braking moves toward organizational reforms and sharply restating opposition to birth control.

Pauli, Wolfgang (1900–58), Austrian-American physicist, who in 1925 developed the exclusion principle, stating that only one ELECTRON could occupy a specific, single state within an atom, for which he was awarded the 1945 Nobel Prize for Physics. In 1931, concerned with a mass-energy imbalance within the then-current ATOMIC STRUCTURE, he proposed the existence of a massless, chargeless PARTICLE (later named a NEUTRINO), which was finally discovered in 1956. Working mostly in America from the 1930s, Pauli also made major contributions to QUANTUM THEORY.

Pauling, Linus Carl (1901–   ), U.S. chemist, who did key work in the 1930s on bonds between atoms, as outlined in his highly influential *Nature of the Chemical Bond* (1939). In the early 1950s, he suggested that protein molecules had a helical, or spiraling, form; this idea was later used by Francis CRICK and James WATSON in their model of DNA, which has a DOUBLE HELIX structure. For that and other work on molecular structure, notably on enzymes, Pauling was given the 1954 Nobel Prize for Chemistry. After the development of the ATOMIC BOMB, Pauling became an active campaigner for nuclear disarmament, winning the 1962 Nobel Peace Prize, only the second person (after Marie CURIE) to win two Nobel Prizes. In 1970 he made the controversial contention that VITAMIN C was a preventative for the common cold.

Paulus, Friedrich (1890–1957), commander of the German Sixth Army who failed to take STALINGRAD and then failed to extricate his forces, ultimately surrendering what remained of his army, to the great discomfort of Adolf HITLER. Taken prisoner, he later defected to the Soviets.

Pavlov, Ivan Petrovich (1849–1936), Russian physiologist, whose work on animal behavior laid the basis for modern BEHAVIORISM. In his most famous experiment, he found that a dog used to a bell sounding when food is given, soon learns to salivate at the sound of the bell alone. He called this pattern of learned response to a given stimulus a conditioned reflex, and spent more than 30 years exploring this form of learning, which he called conditioning.

payola disc jockey scandal, scandal generated by a 1959–60 congressional investigation of record company bribery of disc jockeys to play their records on the air. The investigation resulted in the firings of many disc jockeys, some prosecutions, and the anti-payola law of 1960.

Paz Estenssoro, Victor (1907–   ), Bolivian economist and democratic political leader, founder in 1941 of the Nationalist Revolutionary Movement, and three-time president of Bolivia (1952–56, 1960–64, 1985–   ). He was in exile from 1946 to 1951 after an army coup, and again from 1964 to 1971, after a coup toppled his government.

PC, popular shorthand for PERSONAL COMPUTER, a compact but capacious device introduced in 1975.

PCBs (polychlorinated biphenyls), toxic chemical used from the 1920s in a wide range of products, including an oil found in electrical transformers; by 1977 it was found to be linked to CANCER, birth defects, and liver disorders. Though banned that year from production in the United States, PCBs were still to be found in many parts of the environment, including TOXIC WASTE DUMPS, being extremely slow to break down and requiring concerted effort for effective cleaning up, as in New York's Hudson River in the 1980s.

Peace Corps, U.S. volunteer international service organization, proposed by then-Senator John F. KENNEDY during the 1960 presidential campaign, and established by law in 1961. Volunteers live in the communities in which they work; most teach or work in agriculture, health services, or other developmental projects.

peace for our time, hopeful phrase by British prime minister Neville CHAMBERLAIN, broadcasting to the nation on his return from MUNICH, September 30, 1938; from "I believe it is peace for our time."

peace, land, and bread, a BOLSHEVIK slogan before and during the OCTOBER REVOLUTION of 1917.

Pearl Harbor attack (December 7, 1941), the Japanese surprise air attack on the U.S. Pacific fleet, at anchor in Pearl Harbor, Oahu, Hawaii, and on the military airfields of the island, bringing the United States into World War II. The Japanese fleet, from which the 360 planes of the attack force came had been at sea since November 25. Three U.S. battleships were sunk, one capsized, and four were heavily damaged; many other smaller vessels were sunk or damaged; and over 250 American planes were destroyed, most of them on the ground. There were almost 5,000 American casualties; Japanese losses were light. But the key vessels in the Pacific fleet, the carriers *Lexington*, *Saratoga* and *Enterprise*, were at sea and survived the disaster; the Japanese attack did not destroy the main elements of the American Pacific fleet, as was soon made clear at MIDWAY.

Pearse, Patrick Henry (1879–1916), Irish poet and teacher, who was an early member of the IRISH VOLUNTEERS, a chief organizer of the EASTER RISING of 1916, and commander-in-chief of Irish forces during the rising. Pearse was executed in Dublin on May 3, 1916.

Pearson, Lester Bowles (1897–1972), Canadian diplomat from 1928, who was a founder of the UNITED NATIONS, ambassador to the United States, 1945–46, and head of Canada's UN delegation before becoming Canada's minister of external affairs, 1948–57. He entered parliament as a Liberal in 1948. Pearson played a major role in resolving the Palestine crisis of 1947–48, in other peacekeeping efforts, and especially in the resolution of the SUEZ CRISIS, for which he received the 1957 Nobel Peace Prize. He became Liberal party leader in 1958, and was prime minister 1963–68, during his tenure authorizing the arming of U.S. nuclear weapons on Canadian soil and resisting a growing QUEBEC SEPARATIST MOVEMENT.

Peary, Robert Edwin (1856–1920), U.S. explorer who led the first party to reach the NORTH POLE, for which he was named an honorary rear admiral by the U.S. Navy. Earlier a surveyor in Central America and explorer in Greenland, Peary made several failed attempts on the North Pole. He finally succeeded on April 6, 1909, accompanied by Matthew A. HENSON and four Eskimos, though some disputed his claim even into the 1980s. A former associate, Dr. Frederick A. Cook, claimed to have reached the North Pole in 1908, though his claim was generally discounted.

Peenemünde, site of ROCKET research laboratories on the northern German coast, where the V-1 and V-2 BOMBS were developed and tested during World War II, and therefore the target of massive Allied bombing raids, notably in 1943.

Peking Man, fossil remains of early humans, formerly called *Sinanthropus Pekinensis* but now simply regarded as belonging to the species *Homo erectus*. They were found in Choukoutien (Zhoukoudian) Cave near Peking (Beijing), China, in 1927 by paleoanthropologists, including P'ei Wen-chung, Davidson Black, and Pierre TEILHARD DE CHARDIN. The remains, perhaps 250,000–500,000 years old, were mysteriously lost during World War II, though casts had been taken and like fossils were later found.

Pelton, Ronald, a U.S. National Security Agency employee who sold classified communications information to the Soviet Union during the early 1980s; he was arrested in 1985 and sentenced to life imprisonment.

P'eng Te-huai (1898–1974), Chinese soldier who became a Communist general, second only to ZHU DE, during the course of the 22-year CHINESE CIVIL WAR. He led Communist advance forces during the LONG MARCH, was field commander of the Eighth Route Army during the SINO–JAPANESE WAR, and was commander of Chinese forces in the KOREAN WAR. In 1959 he opposed MAO ZEDONG's GREAT LEAP FORWARD and was expelled from the Communist party, also losing all official positions. He was later posthumously rehabilitated.

penicillin, wonder drug of the 20th century, an ANTIBIOTIC effective as a cure for a wide range of diseases, including SYPHILIS, tuberculosis, and bacterial infections such as scarlet fever. Produced by a mold, penicillin was discovered by Alexander FLEMING in 1928 and isolated and refined for medical use in England in 1940 by Australian-British pathologist Howard Walter Florey and German-British biochemist Ernst Boris Chain, the three sharing the 1945 Nobel Prize for Physiology or Medicine. Rapid large-scale production made penicillin available for use in the armed forces during World War II and then widely in the general public. Penicillin's structure was established in 1949 by Dorothy HODGKIN, using an early COMPUTER. Even after the development of other antibiotics, penicillin remained the drug of choice in many situations, though some people developed a severe ALLERGY, leading to possible deadly anaphylactic shock.

Pentagon Papers, a Defense Department top secret study of Southeast Asian policy that detailed a long series of government secret decisions and falsehoods. Daniel ELLSBERG, a U.S. military adviser who had come to oppose the VIETNAM WAR, took parts of the study to the *New York Times,* which published them beginning in June 1969. The federal government attempted to prohibit publication, but on June 30 the Supreme Court upheld the newspaper's right to publish; the publication contributed greatly to adverse public perceptions regarding the war. Ellsberg and Anthony Russo were later prosecuted, but government wiretapping and the burgling of Ellsberg's psychiatrist's office by a White House special unit—the same "plumbers'" unit that figured so largely in the WATERGATE scandal—caused withdrawal of all charges in May 1973, after mistrials had been declared. In 1974 several former White House figures were convicted in connection with the break-in.

Pentagon procurement scandal, an alleged multibillion dollar set of frauds, involving many defense contractors, consultants, and defense department procurement personnel; it was generally charged by the U.S. federal government in June 1988, after a 2-year investigation. Specific indictments, suspensions, guilty pleas, and convictions began to flow in late 1988 and early 1989.

People's Republic of China, name of CHINA from 1949.

People's Temple, the cult led by James "Jim" JONES into the JONESTOWN mass suicides and murders of 1978.

Peres, Shimon (Shimon Persky; (1923–), Israeli political leader who was defense minister 1974–77, after a long career in subcabinet-level positions. He was prime minister in the 1984–86 coalition government.

perestroika, a Soviet political slogan introduced by Mikhail GORBACHEV, literally meaning "restructuring" and describing large-scale Gorbachev-era reforms of the Soviet economy and of Soviet society, including the development of a far more market-oriented economy, considerable private ownership of land and other productive resources, and decentralization of economic planning, production, and distribution. Perestroika and GLASNOST were the main early themes of the GORBACHEV era.

Pérez de Cuéllar, Javier (1920–), Peruvian lawyer and diplomat who had been Peru's ambassador to the Soviet Union (1969–71), head of Peru's UNITED NATIONS delegation (1971–75), and a UN mediator and undersecretary before becoming fifth UN secretary-general in 1982. In that position, he faced a series of major and continuing regional conflicts and continuing disputes, most of them requiring superpower mediation, but he played a significant peacemaking role in mediating the negotiations leading to the end of the IRAN-IRAQ WAR.

Perkins, Frances (1882–1965), U.S. teacher, social worker, and economist, who from 1910 became active in developing research and reform legislation aimed at safeguarding and improving the safety, health, working conditions, and compensation of working women and children. From 1919 to

1933 she was successively a member of New York State's Industrial Commission, member and chairman of the state Industrial Board, and state industrial commissioner, in 1933 going with Franklin Delano ROOSEVELT to Washington when he became president. As secretary of labor, 1933–45, she played a major role in developing and administering a wide range of NEW DEAL labor and social programs, with special emphasis on the the FAIR LABOR STANDARDS ACT. She was the first woman to hold a cabinet position.

Peron, Juan Domingo (1895–1974), Argentinian officer, who became minister of labor after participating in the 1943 military coup and in that position began building the labor support that would become a mainstay of his future power. He was imprisoned briefly in 1945, after another military coup, emerging to successfully run for the presidency in 1946. From then until September 1955, in close association with his wife, Eva (Evita) PERON, until her death in 1952, he developed a dictatorship in Argentina. He repressed opposition, destroyed freedom of expression, and attempted to develop nationalized industries into a corporate state along Italian fascist lines. Peron was deposed by a military coup in 1955, fleeing into exile, but returned to Argentina in 1972, and was reelected to the presidency 1973–74. He died in office and was succeeded by his wife, Isabel, who ruled until the military coup of 1976.

Peron, Maria Eva "Evita" (Maria Eva Duarte; 1919–52), Argentinian actress who was the wife and political partner of Juan PERON. She played a major role in developing labor support for Peron and in purging the labor movement and Argentine society of opponents after coming to power. Her death, of natural causes in 1952, was a huge and perhaps fatal blow to her husband's regime. *Evita*, a popular play of the U.S. musical theater, was very loosely based on her life story.

Pershing, John Joseph "Blackjack" (1860–1948), U.S. general, who commanded the U.S. Expeditionary Force that invaded Mexico in pursuit of Pancho VILLA's forces in 1916–17, and who in 1917 became commander of what was ultimately the 2-million-strong American Expeditionary Force in Europe. In 1919, he became the first American General of the Armies.

Persian Gulf War, an alternate name for the IRAN–IRAQ WAR of 1980–88.

personal computer (PC), small, powerful COMPUTER, using many prepackaged "plug-in" programs, widely used in homes, schools, and small businesses. The Altair PC, sold in kit form in 1975, was the first personal computer. The first fully assembled PC, the Apple II, went on the market 2 years later.

Pétain, Henri Phillippe (1856–1951), French World War I general whose Second Army held VERDUN for 6 months against heavy German attacks in 1916. He became French commander-in-chief in 1917 and held that position until the end of the war; he was made a marshal of France in 1918. In 1925–26 he commanded French forces during the RIF WAR, and held other official positions during the interwar period. He became premier of France on June 16, 1940, immediately sought an armistice, and formed the VICHY government of unoccupied France on July 10. He collaborated with the Nazis for the balance of the war, and was sentenced to death afterward, a sentence commuted to life imprisonment by Charles DE GAULLE.

Petlyura, Simon Vasilievich (1879–1926), Ukrainian nationalist leader, who attempted to set up an independent Ukrainian state after World War I. He was a Polish ally in the SOVIET–POLISH WAR of 1920. His forces also engaged in severe anti-Jewish pogroms in the Ukraine during this period, and in an attempt to take revenge for those pogroms he was assassinated in Paris on May 26, 1926.

Petrograd Soviet (Council) of Workers and Soldiers Deputies, a council set up in March 1917, composed of elected representatives from workers' groups and military detachments in the Petrograd area. It developed substantial nationwide influence in the months that followed, and also served as a model for other such councils throughout Russia. In September the Petrograd and other key soviets throughout the country were won over by the BOLSHEVIKS, and the Petrograd Soviet became the key instrument used by the Bolsheviks in activating the OCTOBER REVOLUTION.

Phalange party, Lebanese Maronite Christian conservative political party and militia organized in 1936 and to some extent influenced by the thinking of Spanish fascism and its FALANGE. It was led by Pierre GEMAYEL until his son, Bashir, acceded to leadership in the mid-1970s. The organization fought on the side of Camille CHAMOUN during the LEBANESE CIVIL WAR of 1958, and became the main Christian militia force during the LEBANESE WARS of the 1970s and 1980s; in the mid-1970s it also made war on and destroyed other Christian militias. The Phalange was covertly allied with the Israelis during the 1970s, that alliance becoming open during the 1982 invasion of Lebanon. On September 15, 1982, one day after the assassination of Bashir Gemayel, Phalange forces massacred 400 or more men, women, and children at the SABRA AND SHATILLA Palestinian camps in Beirut. Israeli forces did nothing to stop them, inaction that brought worldwide charges of Israeli complicity in the murders, charges the Israelis denied.

Philby, Kim (Harold Adrian Russell Philby; 1912–88), leading British spy who, in fact, was a Soviet spy from his college days at Cambridge in the 1930s, along with his college friends and Soviet espionage network colleagues Anthony BLUNT, Guy BURGESS, and Donald MACLEAN. From 1940, when he joined British military intelligence, to 1963, when he fled to the Soviet Union, he was an important Soviet espionage agent, working in both Britain and the United States. He continued to work in Soviet intelligence after his arrival in the Soviet Union.

Philip, duke of Edinburgh (1921–   ), son of Prince Andrew of Greece and Princess Alice of Battenberg and great-great-grandson of Queen Victoria of Britain; he was named duke of Edinburgh before his marriage to Princess Elizabeth in 1947; she became ELIZABETH II in 1952. Prince Philip saw service in the Royal Navy during World War II.

Philippine Revolution (February 1986), a series of events generated by the national election of February 7, 1986, which pitted Corazon AQUINO against incumbent Ferdinand MARCOS, whose 21-year dictatorship had been greatly weakened since the 1983 assassination of Benigno Aquino, husband of Corazon Aquino. Although Aquino won the election, fraudulent government figures gave the election to Marcos. She claimed victory, setting off 2 weeks of massive demonstrations; civil war threatened. U.S. representatives strongly pressed Marcos to resign, and support for Aquino grew in both the Philippines and the United States. On February 22 Army Chief of Staff Fidel Ramos and Defense Minister Juan Ponce Enrile went over to Aquino, as did substantial sections of the armed forces, and public demonstrations grew. Marcos flew to Hawaiian exile on February 25, later to be threatened with prosecution the United States for alleged financial malfeasance; Aquino set about restoring constitutional government though forced to continue the long war against Communist insurgents, and to withstand several rightwing coup attempts in the years after the revolution, most notably the failed coup of early December 1989, involving elements of the army, with the covert support of several highly placed Philippine politicians.

Philippine Sea, Battle of the (June 19–20, 1944), a major World War II sea battle occurring side by side with the invasion of SAIPAN. Japanese naval forces attacked far stronger U.S. naval forces, in the process losing three of Japan's remaining aircraft carriers, more than 450 airplanes and their pilots, and many smaller ships. American losses were limited to fewer than 100 airplanes, most of whose pilots and crew were saved, and no major ships.

Philippine War of Independence and **Philippine–American War,** conflict that began in 1896 with a successful rebellion against Spanish rule, led by Emilio AGUINALDO. But the United States took and held the Philippines in 1898, during the Spanish-American War. Aguinaldo became first president of the Philippine republic on January 23, 1899, and war with the United States began on February 4. By 1900, the war had spread throughout the Philippines, involving 50,000–60,000 American troops led by General Arthur MacArthur and smaller numbers of Filipinos, in Aguinaldo's army and associated guerrilla forces. Aguinaldo was captured on March 23, 1901, and declared his allegiance to the United States in April; some elements of his forces and some Moslem forces in the south held out until 1906. There were an estimated 100,000–200,000 Filipino war dead—most succumbed due to famine and disease—and 4,000–5,000 American fatalities.

Philippines (Republic of the Philippines), former Spanish colony; at the turn of the century the site of the PHILIPPINE WAR OF INDEPENDENCE and PHILIPPINE–AMERICAN WAR. After U.S. victory in the SPANISH–AMERICAN WAR and then over the Philippine forces of Emilio AGUINALDO, the country was a U.S. protectorate until its occupation by Japanese forces during World War II. On July 4, 1946, the republic became an independent nation. The 21–year dictatorship of Ferdinand MARCOS was ended by the PHILIPPINE REVOLUTION of February 1986; the government of Corazon AQUINO then restored democracy.

Philippines, Battle of the (December 1941–May 1942), World War II battle, on December 8, 1941, that followed the Japanese bombers' destruction at CLARK FIELD of most of the U.S. air force in the Philippines. Japanese amphibious landings began on December 10, and on December 22 the main Japanese invasion force landed on Luzon. Manila, an open city, was taken 4 days later, the much stronger Japanese forces then pursuing U.S. and Philippine forces south, engaging them on BATAAN peninsula in March, and forcing surrender on April 9. The Japanese then besieged and bombarded the island of CORREGIDOR, and mounted an amphibious assault on May 5. The island surrendered on May 6, and defense forces on several other islands also surrendered in May, although Philippine and American guerrillas continued to fight the Japanese throughout the war.

Philippines, Liberation of the (January–August 1945), retaking of the Philippines by the Allies during World War II. On January 9, 1945, American troops landed at Lingayen Gulf on Luzon and began to fight their way south toward Manila. By late January they were approaching Manila, joining troops landed near Manila beginning January 30. Manila fell in the first week of February, an estimated 17,000 of its 18,000–20,000 Japanese defenders fighting to the death until late February. Bataan and Corregidor fell in February, although mopping-up operations continued through April. The remaining Japanese then fled into the mountains, there holding out until the end of the war, as did Japanese forces on Mindanao.

Phony War (September 1939–May 1940), on the Western Front the period between the outbreak of World War II and the German attack on France, Belgium, and Holland, a period characterized by so little military activity as to seem to its participants hardly a war at all.

phosgene, one of the toxic gases widely used in WORLD WAR I as part of CHEMICAL AND BIOLOGICAL WARFARE.

photoelectric effect, ejection of ELECTRONS from a metal plate in the presence of light, forming the basis of TELEVISION and RADAR, an effect discovered in the 19th century but explained in 1905 by Albert EINSTEIN, using Max PLANCK's idea of energy existing in QUANTUM form. The effect itself could be used in ELECTRON TUBES as light detectors, where light was converted to electrical signals. The first practical photoelectric cell was developed in 1904 by Johann Phillip Ludwig Elster.

photon, discrete unit—or quantum—of electromagnetic energy, originally specifically referring to light. The existence of such discrete units was first suggested in 1900 by Max PLANCK, and was supported by Albert EINSTEIN's explanation of the PHOTOELECTRIC EFFECT (1905). In 1923, Arthur Holly COMPTON introduced the idea of the photon, a particle of light with a dual nature, acting in some ways like a wave and in others like a particle, a key contribution to QUANTUM THEORY.

photosynthesis, process by which plants use the green pigment CHLOROPHYLL and sunlight to transform carbon dioxide and water into vital nutrients, such as proteins, carbohydrates, and fats. This key sequence of chemical reactions was first worked out 1945–57 by Melvin CALVIN.

Piaget, Jean (1896–1980), Swiss psychologist, who pioneered in studying how children develop basic concepts such as space, causation, and time. Using a series of now-classic experiments, some involving what appear to young children as optical illusions, Piaget developed a theory that children pass through a regular sequence of stages, in each of which key new understandings force them to modify their view of the world.

Piccard, Auguste Antoine (1884–1962), **and Jean Félix Piccard** (1884–1963), Swiss twins, a physicist and a chemist, respectively, who made significant contributions to the study of both atmosphere and ocean. For experiments on COSMIC RAYS in the upper atmosphere, with its dangerously low pressure, Auguste developed a balloon with a pressurized cabin, an innovation later adopted in AIRPLANES. In 1931 he and Paul Kipfer ascended to a world record of nearly 52,000 feet; they were feared lost, becoming celebrities when they landed safely in Austria. In 1934, Jean and his American wife Jeannette Ridlon ascended to nearly 58,000 feet, later making several innovations in balloon technology; after his death she worked for the NATIONAL AERONAUTICS AND SPACE ADMINISTRATION (NASA) as an expert on the upper atmosphere. Auguste also

applied pressurized cabin technology to ocean study, developing the BATHYSCAPE in 1948. His son Jacques (1922–   ), built the bathyscape *Trieste*, which in 1953 descended over 10,000 feet, setting a world record; by 1960 Jacques and U.S. Navy lieutenant Don Walsh had descended over 35,000 feet to explore the Pacific floor. Jacques also focused on building self-contained submersibles for long-term use; in 1969 his *Ben Franklin* took a six-man crew on a 1,650-mile journey, floating with the Gulf Stream.

Pickering, Thomas Reeve (1931–   ), U.S. diplomat, a career foreign service officer from 1959, who held a long series of diplomatic posts, including ambassadorships to Jordan, Nigeria, El Salvador, and Israel, before being named United Nations ambassador by President George BUSH, December 6, 1988.

Pierre Hotel robbery (January 2, 1972), the looting of safe deposit boxes at New York City's Pierre Hotel by a band of armed robbers, which realized at least $4 million in jewels, securities, and cash, and was the largest hotel robbery in U.S. history. Although some of the stolen property was later recovered, the robbery was never solved.

pile (atomic pile), early alternate name for a NUCLEAR REACTOR, more specifically the conglomerate of material massed for the NUCLEAR FISSION reaction.

Pilsudski, Jósef Klemens (1867–1935), commander of Polish forces and leader of Poland during the SOVIET–POLISH WAR of 1920. From youth Pilsudski was involved in the anti-Russian underground, and he spent 15 years (1887–1902) in Siberian exile. He was a leader of the Polish Socialist party, organized underground terrorist groups before World War I, and fought on the German side as leader of the Polish Brigade during the early years of World War I; later he refused to support the Germans and was imprisoned. After the 1918 armistice, he became Polish commander-in-chief. In partial eclipse during the early years of the Polish Republic, he led a military coup in May 1926, and from then until his death was de facto dictator of Poland.

Piltdown Man, supposed human-like fossil remains found on Piltdown Common, in England's Sussex, 1911–12 by Charles Dawson, and named *Eoanthropus dawsoni* (Dawn Man). Always questioned by some, the remains were proved fraudulent in the 1950s after comparative analyses with other fossil finds, RADIOCARBON DATING, and chemical analyses showed them to be only a few centuries old, and doctored. The hoax's perpetrator remains unknown.

Pincus, Gregory Goodwin (1903–67), American biologist, who in 1951–55 developed the BIRTH CONTROL PILL, using synthetic HORMONES to interrupt a woman's monthly ovulation-menstruation cycle, so preventing conception.

P'Inghsingkuan, Battle of (September 25, 1937), the ambush of a Japanese division by a division of the Chinese Communist Eighth Route Army. The action was of little military significance, but was a considerable morale builder for the Chinese.

Ping-Pong diplomacy, the popular term for the April 1968 Chinese Communist invitation of the U.S. Ping-Pong team to China, signaling a new willingness to begin the process of normalization of relations between the two countries, after almost two decades of estrangement.

Pinochet Ugarte, Augusto (1915–   ), Chilean dictator, who as army commander-in-chief mounted the September 11, 1973, military coup that toppled the elected government of Chile and whose military government then embarked on a long reign of terror. From the mid-1980s, Pinochet was faced with growing internal opposition to the dictatorship. He attempted to appease his opponents with small concessions and in late 1988 made major concessions, including an October plebescite, which he lost. In November 1988, he announced that he would not be a presidential candidate in the scheduled December 1989 presidential election, though he and his associates continued to control the country.

Pioneer, series of U.S. observational and research SATELLITES. *Pioneer 10,* launched in 1971, was the first spacecraft to fly by the planet JUPITER, passing within 81,000 miles in December 1973, before hurtling beyond NEPTUNE in 1983. The first human-made object to leave the solar system, it was still broadcasting data about the solar wind in the late 1980s. *Pioneer 11* reached the vicinity of Saturn in 1979, revealing previously unknown moons.

Piper Alpha explosion (July 6, 1988), a series of explosions followed by a massive fire, destroying the North Sea oil rig *Piper Alpha* off Aberdeen, Scotland, and killing 167 people. It was the worst such disaster since the beginning of North Sea oil operations in 1968.

Pius X, Saint (Giuseppe Melchiorre Sarto; 1835–1914), Italian priest, ordained in 1858, cardinal and patriarch of Venice 1893, and pope from 1903 to 1914; he was beatified in 1951 and canonized in 1954. Deeply conservative, Pius X opposed the doctrine of modernism, which sought to reconcile Catholic doctrine with the main intellectual movements of the modern world, stressing instead close day-to-day personal involvement in religious observance and social action directed by the church hierarchy.

Pius XI (Ambrogio Damiano Achille Ratti; 1857–1939), Italian priest, ordained in 1879, who became a cardinal 1921, and was pope from 1922 to 1939. In 1929 he signed the LATERAN TREATY, recognizing the legitimacy of the Italian fascist government, in return for government recognition of Catholicism as the state religion, and of the independence and sovereignty of the Vatican. In 1933, he signed a treaty with Nazi Germany, acquiescing to Nazi curbs on Catholic political action, although in 1937 he condemned both German fascism and all communism; in 1938, he generally condemned anti-Semitism.

Pius XII, (Eugenio Pacelli; 1876–1958), Italian priest, ordained in 1899, who became a cardinal in 1929, Vatican secretary of state

1930–39, and pope 1939–58. He negotiated the 1933 treaty with Germany, acquiescing to Nazi curbs on Catholic political action, although concurring in the late-1930s denunciations of Nazism and communism issued by PIUS XI. He maintained Vatican neutrality during World War II; afterward he was sharply attacked for having done little or nothing to try to avert or stop the Nazi mass murders of millions of Jews or the mass murders of millions of Gypsies, Poles, Russians, and others. During the postwar period he played a major political role in Italy, attacking communism and fostering Christian Democratic party growth.

Planck, Max Karl Ernst Ludwig (1858–1947), German physicist, who laid the basis for QUANTUM THEORY. In 1900, while working out a puzzling RADIATION problem, Planck made a key assumption: that energy exists in discrete units, which he called quanta (Latin for "units"). He also worked out the constant ratio between the size of a quantum and the frequency of radiation, the result now called Planck's constant. Though he himself had difficulty at first with the revolutionary nature of his quantum theory, by 1905 Albert EINSTEIN had used it to explain the PHOTOELECTRIC EFFECT, as Niels BOHR did by 1913 in developing his model of ATOMIC STRUCTURE. Planck's work, which won him the 1918 Nobel Prize for Physics, marked the end of classical physics and the beginning of modern physics.

plastics, synthetic substances that can be shaped into a wide variety of usable products. Made of long molecule chains called POLYMERS, plastics can be heated without melting and, while softened, can be molded into shapes that are retained on cooling. Building on 19th-century experiments with softening natural substances (which produced celluloid), Belgian-American chemist Leo Baekeland in 1909 developed the first wholly synthetic plastic, Bakelite. It was not used in commercial products until 1928, by which time the polymer polyvinyl chloride (PVC) had been discovered (1912). In 1937 Wallace A. Carothers of the U.S. firm of E.

I. du Pont de Nemours developed the "superpolyamide" called nylon, which became popular for stockings and clothing during World War II, when silk supplies from Asia were cut off. Polyethylene, invented by the British and brought to the market in 1939, was a vital substance for use in RADAR and film; later it was commonly used to form trash cans, milk containers, shopping bags, and the like. Polyurethane, common in foam rubbers and adhesives, came along in 1937; epoxy resins, used as coatings and adhesives, in 1943. These and other types of plastics transformed manufacturing and packaging; from 1921 new machines were developed to produce plastics in sheets, a thin coating, molded containers, blown containers, or whatever shape might be desired. Plastics were so durable that they retained their cohesiveness long after their usefulness had ended, creating by the 1970s a major garbage problem, and on both land and sea sometimes strangling animals. Some governments tried to meet the problem by collecting the plastic for reuse, offering a few cents per container for return. By the 1980s, scientists had even developed plastics that were deliberately designed to break down after some weeks in light or water.

plate tectonics, geological theory that the Earth is composed of some 20 plates of crust, several continent size, "floating" on a molten mantle. Earthquakes and volcanoes occur where the plates scrape against each other or slide one under another to be destroyed. New crust is formed at rifts, especially in sea floors, where the plates are moving apart—the basic theoretical mechanism supporting Alfred WEGENER's CONTINENTAL DRIFT theory. The key idea of seafloor spreading was proposed by U.S. geologist Henry H. Hess in 1960, later modified by British geophysicists F. J. Vine and D. H. Matthews in 1963, and confirmed by surveys of the ocean floor showing the periodic reversals of Earth's magnetism in a series of strips on either side of ocean rifts.

Platt Amendment, an amendment to a U.S. appropriations bill in 1901, introduced by

Senator Orville Platt, providing the terms on which the United States was to make its promised withdrawal of armed forces from Cuba, while holding Cuba as essentially a protectorate. The terms were embodied in the Cuban-American treaty of 1903.

Plekhanov, Georgi Valentinovich (1856–1919), Russian Marxist theoretician, the founder of the first Russian Marxist organization in 1883 and a founder of the Russian Social Democratic Labor party in 1898. In 1903, when that party split, he at first favored LENIN and the BOLSHEVIK side but soon returned to the more moderate views of the MENSHEVIKS. He later went into exile, returning to Russia after the first RUSSIAN REVOLUTION of 1917. He fled the country again after the OCTOBER REVOLUTION, and died soon thereafter in Finland.

PLO, the initials of the PALESTINE LIBERATION ORGANIZATION.

Ploesti Raids (August 1, 1943), Allied bombing raids on the Ploesti oil fields in Rumania. They cost many planes, did some damage, and were notable for what were then long distances traveled by the bombers from their North African bases.

Pluto, ninth planet in the solar system, unknown before the 20th century; predicted from observations of astronomical irregularities by Percival LOWELL in 1905 and discovered in 1930 by Clyde Tombaugh.

plutonium, radioactive element first discovered in 1940 by Glenn SEABORG and others. The plutonium 239 (Pu-239) ISOTOPE is widely used for NUCLEAR FISSION in NUCLEAR REACTORS and military weapons. Pu-239 can be made by bombarding the more common form of URANIUM, U-238, and less Pu-239 is needed for fission than when uranium (U-235) alone is used. The world's first nuclear reactor, built by Enrico FERMI's team in 1942, demonstrated how to produce plutonium, which was used in the TRINITY test of the ATOMIC BOMB at ALAMOGORDO and the atomic bomb at NAGASAKI in 1945.

Poincaré, Raymond (1860–1934), French political leader who, as premier in 1912 was deeply involved in the building of the Allied coalition that went into World War I; he was wartime president of France. As premier again, 1922–24, he sent French troops into the RUHR when Germany failed to make reparations payments. He was the last premier (1926–29) of a then-stable France, before the onset of the GREAT DEPRESSION.

Poindexter, John Marlan (1936–   ), U.S. naval officer who, in 1981, became military assistant to White House national security advisor Richard Allen. In 1983 he was deputy national security adviser and then national security adviser, in that position fostering increased U.S. intervention in Central America and Libya, and becoming deeply involved in the IRAN–CONTRA AFFAIR. On November 25 he resigned as national security adviser, and in December refused to testify before congressional committees on Fifth Amendment grounds. In July 1987, with limited immunity, he did testify, admitting the withholding of information from Congress while defending his intent and asserting that President Ronald REAGAN knew nothing of the movement of Iranian arms payment money to the Contras. On March 16, 1988, he was indicted on several Iran–Contra-related charges; pretrial maneuvering continued during 1989.

Point Four Program, U.S. post–World War II foreign aid program generated in 1950 by the fourth point of President Harry TRUMAN'S 1949 inaugural address; it called for the supply of U.S. investment capital and personnel in agricultural and industrial development, science, health, education, and administration. Implementation of the programs was sporadic; they were also used as instruments of U.S. COLD WAR policy, to persuade and reward friendly countries.

poison gas, popular name for toxic chemicals used in CHEMICAL AND BIOLOGICAL WARFARE.

Poison Squad, popular name for Harvey Washington WILEY's U.S. Department of Agriculture chemists, who in the early 20th century tested food additives and adulteratives on themselves.

Poland (Polish People's Republic), until the end of World War I a country partitioned among Russia, Germany, and Austria. It was an independent nation during the interwar period. The German invasion of Poland on September 1, 1939, began World War II. The country was then partitioned again, pursuant to the NAZI-SOVIET PACT; occupied by German forces after the Nazi invasion of the Soviet Union in 1941; and occupied by Soviet forces after World War II. Some multiparty opposition was briefly tolerated after 1945, but the 1947 elections firmly established Poland as a one-party Soviet bloc state. During the GORBACHEV era Poland embarked on a new political course, in 1989 establishing the first non-Communist government in eastern Europe for 40 years.

Poland, invasion of (September 1, 1939), attack on Poland by massive German armies, beginning World War II. The attack was accompanied by powerful air attacks, which caught and destroyed most of the small Polish air force on the ground, destroyed roads and communications, and terrorized the population. The attack was led by armored formations, using BLITZKRIEG tactics, that easily penetrated and then routed thinly spread Polish armies. German armor reached Warsaw on September 8, and the Germans then besieged the city. Warsaw held out until September 27, 1939, and some smaller pockets of resistance lasted until early November.

Poland, partition of, division of Poland by Soviet and German forces, as agreed on by the terms of the NAZI–SOVIET PACT of August 1939. On September 17, 1939, Soviet troops invaded Poland from the east, taking part of Poland; German forces met them at the agreed-on partition line.

Polaroid Land Camera, camera that includes both negative film and positive paper, putting out a print within seconds; it was invented in 1947 by Edwin Herbert LAND.

Polhill, Robert one of the American LEBANON HOSTAGES, an American University professor, who was kidnapped on January 24, 1988.

polio (poliomyelitis or infantile paralysis), highly communicable viral disease causing paralysis and sometimes death, affecting not only children but also adults, such as Franklin Delano ROOSEVELT. In the United States alone, a major polio epidemic in 1916 caused more than 27,000 cases, with whole regions of the country quarantined; panic resulted as many tried to leave crowded cities. The worst series of epidemics occurred in the United States between 1942 and 1953, though outbreaks also occurred elsewhere, notably in Europe and Asia. In 1953, Jonas SALK introduced his POLIO VACCINE, at first experimentally, quickly making the disease a rarity in the United States. Albert SABIN'S vaccine, developed in 1956, had many advantages, and was adopted by the WORLD HEALTH ORGANIZATION (WHO) in 1957, for use in controlling polio in the rest of the world.

polio vaccine, protective serum against POLIO, first developed in 1952 by Jonas SALK. To act against all three polio strains, Salk developed a vaccine made from killed polio viruses, which produced immunity. He tested it in 1953, in the midst of an epidemic, and then moved to large-scale vaccination in 1954. Albert SABIN then developed a vaccine from deactivated live polio viruses, in 1956. Because the Sabin vaccine was cheaper to make, easier to store, offered lifetime immunity, and could be given orally, it became the vaccine of choice, though it involved some risk; it was adopted in 1957 by the WORLD HEALTH ORGANIZATION (WHO) for use throughout the world.

Polisario (Popular Front for the Liberation of Saguia el Hamra and Rio de Oro), western Saharan revolutionary organization formed in 1973 to win independence from Spain. When Spain withdrew from the area in 1976, Polisario formed the Saharan Arab Democratic Republic; but the area was then claimed by Morocco and Mauritania, beginning a long guerrilla war in which Polisario operated first from Mauritania and then from Algeria. Mauritania withdrew in 1979, but Morocco then occupied all of the disputed area, and the war continued.

Polish campaign of 1944 (July–August 1944), the continuing late World War II summer offensive by Soviet armies moving into Poland, almost to Warsaw. There they paused for 2 months while the Germans across the Vistula River massacred tens of thousands of Polish Jews and other Poles engaged in the WARSAW GHETTO RISING.

Polish Corridor, the disputed Polish avenue to the sea along the Vistula River, between East Prussia and the rest of Germany; it was made part of Poland in the Treaty of VERSAILLES, but did not include the city of Danzig (Gdánsk), which was made a free city. The Corridor and Danzig were major sources of Polish-German tension during the interwar period. Nazi intentions to annex the Corridor and Danzig in March 1939 were blocked by British guarantees of Polish independence; those guarantees were the proximate cause of Britain's entry into World War II, after the German of invasion of Poland in September.

Polish October (October 1956), part of the wave of unrest sweeping all Communist parties after KRUSHCHEV'S SECRET SPEECH, which in Poland was coupled with long-standing nationalist and economic unrest, and was strong enough to topple the hardline Stalinist government and bring Wladislaw GOMULKA to power.

Politburo, the committee, or political bureau, at the top of the hierarchic organization of the COMMUNIST PARTY OF THE SOVIET UNION, its membership being drawn from the Central Committee of that party. The name is also applied to the top committees of other Communist parties.

political power grows out of the barrel of a gun, statement by Chinese Communist leader MAO ZEDONG.

Pollard, Jonathan J., an employee of the U.S. Naval Intelligence Support Center, who was a spy for Israel. He and his wife, Anne Henderson Pollard, were convicted of espionage in 1987; he was sentenced to life imprisonment, she to a 5-year term.

Pol Pot (Tol Saut; Saloth Sar; 1928–), Kampuchean (Cambodian) political leader, who became general secretary of the Communist Party of Kampuchea and organizer of the KHMER ROUGE army in 1963. He led the Khmer Rouge until their victory in the CAMBODIAN CIVIL WAR, then became first prime minister of Kampuchea in 1976. He was the chief organizer of the CAMBODIAN HOLOCAUST, which killed millions of his own people. He resigned as prime minister after the successful Vietnamese invasion of Kampuchea during the KAMPUCHEA-VIETNAM WAR, to lead guerrilla forces fighting the Vietnamese.

polychlorinated biphenyls, full scientific name of PCBs, substances known since 1977 to be carcinogenic.

polymers, giant molecules consisting of long chains of linked shorter molecules, called monomers, repeating over and over; the name is Greek for "many units." Polymers occur in nature, but as German chemist Hermann Staudinger first discovered in 1922, PLASTICS are also made up of polymers. These long chains untangle themselves when heated but retain their molecular bonds, giving plastics their valued moldability and cohesiveness. Silicon, widely used in MICROPROCESSORS in modern COMPUTERS, is a naturally occurring polymer.

Pompidou, Georges (1911–74), French teacher and banker, a leading Gaullist who worked closely with DE GAULLE from 1944, helping to negotiate an end to the Algerian war in 1961, and serving as premier 1962-1968. He succeeded De Gaulle as president of France in 1969, and died in office.

Ponzi, Charles (1877–1949), 1920s investment broker, who guaranteed very large returns to small investors, and paid them with the funds supplied by new investors. After media exposure of his criminal record his flow of new investment money stopped, and so did his ability to pay previous investors. The entire structure collapsed, with large losses by small investors and Ponzi's ultimate conviction and imprisonment. Such pyramiding arrangements, known as "Ponzi schemes," have since become illegal.

Popieulskco, Jerzy, Polish priest and SOLIDARITY sympathizer who was murdered by Polish government security agents in 1984. Four security policemen were later convicted of his murder; their sentences of imprisonment were reduced in 1986 and 1987.

Popper, Karl Raimund (1902–), Austrian–British philosopher of science, linked with the idea that much of scientists' work is to find hypotheses *false* rather than true, the strongest theories being those that have stood up to the most severe tests.

Popular Front, a French left coalition of the mid-1930s, in power under the leadership of Premier León BLUM 1936–37. The Popular Front was in the same period an alternate name for the UNITED FRONT strategy of the COMINTERN, which from 1935 sought to build as broad as possible a movement against the developing threat of fascism. It did so until the 1939 NAZI–SOVIET PACT created a classic "flip-flop," as Communist parties all over the world responded to the new Soviet foreign policy.

Popular Movement for the Liberation of Angola (MPLA), the ruling party of the People's Republic of Angola, formed in 1956 as a nationalist movement against Portuguese rule. The MPLA fought the 1961–74 ANGOLAN WAR OF INDEPENDENCE in central Angola, with increasingly strong Soviet backing, which included the arrival of Cuban troops during the long civil war that followed Angolan independence. Its leader from 1962 through his death in 1979 was Augustinho NETO. He was succeeded in party leadership and the presidency by José Eduardo dos Santos.

Port Chicago explosion (July 17, 1944), collision and explosion of two ammunition ships at Port Chicago, near San Francisco; 322 were killed and hundreds injured.

Port Huron statement, a declaration of principles, adopted by the STUDENTS FOR A DEMOCRATIC SOCIETY at Port Huron, Michigan, in 1962, calling for massive changes in the American political system and for action to produce those changes. It was written by Thomas HAYDEN, then a student at the University of Michigan.

Portsmouth, Treaty of (1905), agreement ending the Russo-JAPANESE WAR.

Portuguese Armed Forces Movement, the group of young officers, including António EANES, who on April 24, 1974, toppled the Portuguese dictatorship in a bloodless coup and then went on to reestablish democracy in Portugal and pull Portuguese forces out of Angola, Mozambique, and Guinea.

Portuguese Guinea, the former name of GUINEA-BISSAU, which became an independent nation on September 10, 1974.

positron, particle of ANTIMATTER, first predicted in 1928 by Paul DIRAC as an antielectron, the positively charged counterpart of the negatively charged ELECTRON, and discovered by Carl Anderson in 1932.

Post, Wiley (1899–1935), American aviator who made the first round-the-world flight in 1931 with Harold Gatty in the *Winnie Mae*, taking 8 days and nearly 16 hours; he then in 1933 made the first solo flight circling the globe. A barnstormer and stunt parachutist from the 1920s, Post later developed a pressure suit for high-altitude flights. He was killed with his passenger, comedian Will Rogers, when their plane crashed at Point Barrow, Alaska, on a flight to Asia.

Potemkin, a battleship of the Russian navy; a sailors' mutiny on the ship was a major incident in the RUSSIAN REVOLUTION of 1905. The mutiny was the subject of the classic Sergei Eisenstein film, *Potemkin* (1925).

Potsdam Conference (July–August 1945), a post–World War II Allied conference that organized the occupations of Germany and Berlin, set up the International Military Tribunal that conducted the NUREMBERG TRIALS, and agreed on the removal and resettlement of many millions of German-speakers from Eastern Europe to Germany. It also handled a miscellany of questions dealing with the government and people of Germany and the coming peace treaties.

Powell, Adam Clayton, Jr. (1908–72), U.S. minister, civil rights activist, and reformer, the first Black member of the New York City Council (1941–45), and New York Democratic congressman (1945–71). In 1967, the House of Representatives refused to seat him, charging financial irregularities; it did seat him, with penalties, after his reelection in a 1968 special election. In 1969, the Supreme Court found the House's failure to seat Powell in 1967 unconstitutional.

Powell, Lewis Franklin, Jr. (1907–), U.S. lawyer, president of the American Bar Association 1964–65, the American Association of Trial Lawyers 1969–70, and the American Bar Foundation 1969–71. He was named to the U.S. Supreme Court by president Richard M. NIXON in 1971, retiring in 1987. On the Court he was generally a moderate-to-conservative influence, often operating as a swing vote between the more sharply liberal and conservative groups in the Court.

power elite, the, a phrase coined by U.S. sociologist C. Wright MILLS, in his 1956 book of that name.

Powers, Francis Gary, U.S. pilot of the reconnaissance plane involved in the May 1, 1960 U-2 INCIDENT. He was imprisoned in the Soviet Union, and exchanged for Soviet spy Rudolph ABEL in 1962.

POWs/MIAs, Vietnam, U.S. prisoners of war (POWs) and those listed as missing in action (MIAs) still unaccounted for after the Vietnam War, the subjects of a long campaign by their families and others, who believed many to still be alive and in Vietnamese or Laotian hands many years after the war.

Poznán Revolt (June 1956), two days of rioting in Poznań, Poland, by workers and intellectuals, ultimately suppressed by Soviet troops with more than 50 killed, hundreds injured, and an estimated 1,000 arrests. The riots were part of a wave of strikes and demonstrations throughout the country, and part of the unrest that swept Eastern Europe in the wake of KHRUSHCHEV'S SECRET SPEECH.

Prague Spring (January–August 1968), brief period in which the Czechoslovak Communist Party, led by reformer Alexander DUBCEK, initiated a series of democratic reforms, including guarantees of religious and press freedom. Soviet and Soviet-allied troops invaded Czechoslovakia on August 20, 1968, took the country, and forced its leaders to reverse course.

Preppie murder case (August 26, 1986), the media-developed name for the murder of Jennifer Levin in New York City's Central Park, for which Robert Chambers, Jr., was later tried. He pleaded guilty to manslaughter while a deadlocked jury was arguing the highly publicized case. Both Levin and Chambers were prep school graduates from well-to-do families; hence the name of the case.

Primo de Rivera, Miguel (1870–1930), Spanish soldier who led the 1923 coup that made him dictator of Spain until his resignation in 1930, and who led Spanish forces in the 1925 RIF WAR.

Prince of Wales and Repulse sinkings (December 10, 1941), early World War II sinkings of the British battleship *Prince of Wales* and battlecruiser *Repulse*. Without air reconnaissance, the ships unsuccessfully sought the Japanese southeast Asian battle fleet, and were themselves found by Japanese land-based aircraft off the coast of Malaya. Being without air support they were easily sunk.

Prinz, Joachim (1902–88), German rabbi, ordained in 1925, who publicly opposed the Nazis before and after their rise to power, finally leaving Germany in 1937 after many arrests. He was president of the American Jewish Congress 1958–66 and, with Martin Luther KING, Jr., an organizer of the 1963 MARCH ON WASHINGTON. An advocate of civil rights and other liberal causes, he was often accused of communism during the MCCARTHY period. He sucessfully sued the periodical *Common Sense* for having made the charge.

Profumo Affair (1963), British political scandal involving John Profumo, then war minister, and call girl Christine Keeler, who was also in touch with a Soviet official. Although no national security breach was alleged, enormous media attention forced Profumo's resignation and further weakened the Conservative government led by Harold MACMILLAN.

Progressive Party, the name of three short-lived 20th century U.S. political parties. The first was Theodore ROOSEVELT'S BULL MOOSE party organization of 1912–16. The second was the Wisconsin state Progressive party (1934–46), led by Senator Robert LA FOLLETTE, Jr. The third was the Progressive party of Henry A. WALLACE, its presidential candidate in 1948, who left the party when it opposed the KOREAN WAR, the party then surviving as a minor organization until its disappearance in 1952.

Prohibition, period that began with the passage of the Eighteenth Amendment to the Constitution, ratified on January 15, 1919, ending the long campaign to prohibit alcoholic beverages in the United States, led by the Women's Christian Temperance Union (founded in 1869) and the Anti-Saloon League of America (founded in 1893). The Volstead Act, enforcing the new amendment, went into effect on January 16, 1920. From then until December 5, 1933, when ratification of the Twenty-first Amendment once again legalized alcohol, the sale or making of beverages containing more than 0.5% alcohol was outlawed. The unpopular prohibition law was also unenforceable; it created a large new illegal alcoholic beverage industry, with manufacture, distribution, and sale of such beverages wholly and very profitably in the hands of criminals, and it spurred the development of large criminal gangs and ultimately of a national crime syndicate. The careers of such criminals as Al CAPONE, Charles "Lucky" LUCIANO, and Arthur "Dutch Schultz" Flegenheimer were fully developed during the Prohibition period.

Project Blue Book, U.S. Air Force project (1948–69) to gather and evaluate information on sightings of UNIDENTIFIED FLYING OBJECTS.

proton, PARTICLE in an atom's NUCLEUS, similar to a NEUTRON but with a positive charge; it was first discovered by Ernest RUTHERFORD in 1914. By the early 1960s, scientists had discovered that the proton was not an indivisible particle, but included other smaller particles, in general called QUARKS, held together by GLUONS.

Provisional Government, the revolutionary government that took over control of Russia after the FEBRUARY REVOLUTION of 1917; it was led by Prince Georgy Lvov and later by Alexander KERENSKY. This government continued Russian participation in World War II until the CENTRAL POWERS' success on the Eastern Front and failure of supply caused disintegration of the main fighting forces of the Russian army. At the same time, food shortages, strikes, and demonstrations made governing Russia all but impossible. In October the extremely weak Provisional Government quickly fell to BOLSHEVIK assaults. The civil war that immediately began was dominated by ex-czarist army generals, rather than by deposed Provisional Government people.

Provisional Irish Republican Army (Provisionals), guerrilla fighting force in Northern Ireland, which split off from the IRISH REPUBLICAN ARMY in 1969, and thereafter engaged in a terrorist-oriented insurgency against the governments of Northern Ireland and Great Britain. It claimed responsibility for scores of bombings and assassinations in Northern Ireland, Ireland, Great Britain, and on the European mainland. The striking force of the organization is numbered only in the hundreds, but it is supported by substantial elements in the Irish Catholic communities of Ireland, Great Britain, and North America.

Przemyśl, Siege of (1914–15), Russian siege of an Austrian fortress in Galicia, which held out for almost 7 months before ultimately surrendering its garrison of 110,000.

psychedelic drugs, alternate name for HAL-LUCINOGENIC DRUGS, meaning "mind-man-ifesting."

psychoanalysis, type of "talking therapy" that has the patient associate ideas freely and without reservation, in an effort to by-pass normal personal defenses and reach the root cause of neuroses, often thought linked to sexual life and fantasies. Devel-oped by Sigmund FREUD at the turn of the 20th century, the psychoanalytic approach involves several therapeutic sessions a week for some years. It was exported around the world by Freud's followers, especially to the United States after World War II, though questions as to its worth, compared to other therapies, continued to be raised.

public opinion polls, surveys of public views on issues of the day begun in a scien-tific way, using statistical sampling tech-niques, in the 1930s. That decade saw the founding of Elmo Burns ROPER's Roper Re-search Associates (1933) and George GAL-LUP's American Institute of Public Opinion (1935); such organizations were founded al-so in Britain and other parts of the world, especially after World War II. Polls were used widely in market research and adver-tising, but their most influential use was probably in connection with political cam-paigns. In 1936 scientific polling gained a boost in public confidence when several key polls, notably those by Roper, Gallup, and Archibald Crossley, predicted a ROOSEVELT win, whereas earlier-style nonscientific polls predicted a Landon landslide. Although in the 1948 U.S. presidential election most ma-jor polls erroneously predicted that Thomas E. DEWEY would win, campaign polling be-came ever more sophisticated over the de-cades, especially with the use of COMPUTERS. In the 1960 presidential cam-paign, John F. KENNEDY employed pollster Louis HARRIS as a personal consultant, and soon many candidates had their own sur-veying organizations. TELEVISION networks used exit polls—surveys of people leaving voter booths—to predict election results even before the votes were counted. By the 1980s, surveying organizations were doing daily "tracking polls" to chart shifts of pub-lic opinion.

Public Works Administration (PWA), a U.S. NEW DEAL agency created during the first HUNDRED DAYS of the ROOSEVELT ad-ministration and administered by Harold ICKES; it supplied grants and loans to a wide variety of building projects, such as dams, bridges, housing projects, schools, and highways. The agency made little impact during the early days of the Roosevelt era, largely because of the caution of Harold Ickes; in aggregate, however, PWA funding was important in the creation of many ma-jor public works projects.

***Pueblo* Incident** (1968), the seizure of the *U.S.S. Pueblo* and its 83-man crew by North Korean forces in the Sea of Japan. After 11 months of negotiations, 82 surviving crew members were released.

Pujo Committee (1912), special U.S. con-gressional committee, chaired by Arsene Pujo, that studied and revealed the opera-tions of the "money trust," a group of banks exerting substantial control of many major financial and business institutions, through a system of financial controls and interlock-ing directorates. The committee gained a great deal of public attention through the reluctant testimony of financier J. Pierpont MORGAN; its work made a considerable con-tribution to the development of bank regu-lation and the FEDERAL RESERVE SYSTEM.

pulsar, rapidly rotating NEUTRON star that emits regular bursts or pulses of RADIA-TION, the remnant of a SUPERNOVA in a late stage of STELLAR EVOLUTION. J. Robert OP-PENHEIMER and George Volkoff predicted the existence of pulsars in 1938; the first one was discovered and named by Jocelyn Bell in 1967 (for which her supervisor, Anthony Hewish, but not Bell, received the 1974 Nobel Prize for Physics).

Pumpkin Papers, a high-security file of State Department documents that figured prominently in the 1949 and 1950 trials of Alger HISS, in the form of rolls of microfilm that Whittaker CHAMBERS claimed had been given him by Hiss in 1937 and 1938 and that he had subsequently hidden in a hollow pumpkin on his farm in Maryland. Hiss denied the charge, was indicted for perjury, and was released after a hung jury could not agree on a verdict; he was convicted of perjury in his second trial.

Pure Food and Drug Laws, a group of U.S. laws greatly expanding the power of federal regulatory agencies over food and many other commodities; the Pure Food and Drug Act (1906), the Meat Inspection Act (1906), and the Pure Food, Drug, and Cosmetic Act (1908). The reforms embodied in these laws were strongly supported by President Theodore ROOSEVELT, and passage was greatly assisted by such exposés as Upton SINCLAIR's novel *THE JUNGLE* which attacked the meatpacking industry, and also by pressure from inside the Department of Agriculture, especially Harvey Washington WILEY's analysis of widespread food additives and adulteratives. Other laws followed, most notably the 1938 Food, Drug, and Cosmetic Act, setting up the FOOD AND DRUG ADMINISTRATION (FDA).

purge trials, an alternate name for the MOSCOW TRIALS of the 1930s.

P'u Yi, Henry, the name later taken by HSÜAN T'ung, who as a child was the last Manchu emperor of China; he was the subject of the 1987 film, *The Last Emperor.*

PWA, the initials of the PUBLIC WORKS ADMINISTRATION, a NEW DEAL U.S. federal agency of the 1930s.

Pyeshkov, Aleksei Maximovich the given name of author Maxim GORKY.

Q

Qaddafi, Muammar al- (1942–   ), Libyan officer who took power in a 1969 military coup and has since ruled Libya, systematically destroying all opposition while establishing an Islamic fundamentalist, socialist state with pan-Arab inclinations, as delineated in his *Green Book.* Qaddafi nationalized much of the oil industry, effectively expelled the Libyan Italian and Jewish communities, and attempted short-lived unions with several other Arab states. He has involved Libya in the long CHAD WAR, a series of acts of international terrorism, and serious confrontations with Egypt and United States, which included American air and sea attacks on Libyan targets in April 1986.

Qatar (State of Quatar), until World War I, a Turkish protectorate; in 1916, it became a British protectorate. An absolute monarchy, the country became an independent state on September 1, 1971.

Qin Shih Huang Di Tomb, burial site near Xian (Sian) of the first emperor and unifier of China, Qin Shih Huang Di (Ch'in Shih Huang Ti), who died in 210 B.C. and was buried with thousands of life-size terra-cotta soldiers to guard him; discovered in 1974.

Quang Tri, Battle of (March–April 1972), a successsful divisional-strength attack by North Vietnamese forces across the North–South border zone (DMZ) into Quang Tri province, taking the city of Quang Tri and large numbers of South Vietnamese prisoners. South Vietnamese forces retook the city in September.

quantum theory, idea that energy exists in discrete units called quanta (Latin for "units"), first proposed by Max PLANCK in 1900. That energy was not infinitely subdivisible but existed in PARTICLES was a revolutionary notion fundamental to many 20th-century discoveries in physics and so marked the beginning of modern physics. Albert EINSTEIN used it in his 1905 special theory of RELATIVITY, as did Niels BOHR in formulating his view of ATOMIC STRUCTURE in 1913. Quantum theory required an equally new mathematical substructure, called wave mechanics or quantum mechanics, to which many scientists contributed, including Paul DIRAC, Erwin SCHRÖDINGER, Werner HEISENBERG, Wolfgang PAULI, and Richard FEYNMAN.

quarks, supposed basic building blocks of matter, subatomic PARTICLES with fractional charges that make up PROTONS, NEUTRONS, and other atomic particles, held together by GLUONS, a concept first introduced in 1964 by U.S. physicist Murray GELL-MANN and independently by George Zweig and Richard FEYNMAN. Several types of quarks exist; in the language of particle physics, they are said to come in various "flavors," including up, down, charm, STRANGE, probably top and bottom, and perhaps more. Unlike many other particles, quarks were posited, in 1973, as having the strongest attraction to each other at the greatest distance. The existence of quarks with the flavor of charm was supported by the 1974 discovery of the J/psi particle. Other scientists in the same decade suggested that quarks were the end of "strings" in the universe. A 1984 claim to have observed a top quark was not immediately confirmed.

quasar, extremely bright object of star-like appearance, originally called variously radio star, quasi-stellar radio source, quasi-stellar object, or QSO; discovered in 1960 by California Institute of Technology astronomers Allan Rex Sandage and Thomas Matthews, using both optical telescopes and RADIO ASTRONOMY. At first judged to be relatively near Earth's galaxy, quasars were found, by the 1963 analysis of Maarten Schmidt and Jesse Greenstein, also of Caltech, to have an extreme RED SHIFT, indicating that quasars are probably the most distant objects yet observed; since their light has taken so long to reach us, they may reflect conditions near the beginning of the universe. Because their great brightness implies enormous energy resources, some astronomers have linked quasars with BLACK HOLES, some with the energy-producing mutual annihilation of matter and ANTIMATTER.

Quayle, James Danforth "Dan" (1947–), U.S. lawyer, Indiana Republican congressman (1977–81), senator (1981–89), surprise vice-presidential candidate in 1988, and vice-president of the United States from 1989. As was true of President George BUSH before him and of most vice-presidents, in the early period of his vice-presidency Quayle exerted little influence over policies or events.

Quebec Conference of 1943 (August 14–24, 1943), a World War II ROOSEVELT–CHURCHILL meeting in which a May 1, 1944, target date was set for the Allied invasion of western Europe, a position favored by the Americans over the Italian-Balkan invasion strategy favored by the British. The Italian campaign was to be pursued as well, as were the Pacific and Southeast Asia campaigns, but the continued main emphasis was to be the cross-Channel invasion.

Quebec Conference of 1944 (September 12–16, 1944), a World War II ROOSEVELT-CHURCHILL meeting held, with the defeat of Germany in World War II in clear sight, to plan for the postwar period, with particular attention given to the future occupation of Germany and developments in Eastern Europe and also to plan Allied cooperation in the coming invasion of Japan.

Quebec separatist movement (1960–80), movement developed under the leadership of Liberal Quebec premier Jean Lesage (1960–66), reaching its greatest strength under PARTI QUEBECOIS leader René LEVESQUE (1968–75). The movement resulted in the development of bilingualism and biculturalism, as well as significant economic concessions, but it fell far short of its main goals; in 1980 Quebec voters defeated the proposal to open negotiations seeking sovereignty. It was accompanied by the development of a terrrorist movement; from 1963 activists of the Federation for the Liberation of Quebec engaged in bombing and other terrorist acts in and around Montreal. In 1967 Charles DE GAULLE visited Quebec, calling for the establishment of a French-Canadian nation ("Vive le Québec libre!"). In 1969–70, terrorist groups, called the Quebec Liberation Front (Front de Libération du Québec) engaged in a major series of bombings and kidnappings, murdering Quebec labor minister Pierre La Porte and precipitating the "October Crisis" of 1970. The Canadian government responded with mass arrests and by sending army units into Montreal. The separatist movement then focused on electoral solutions but lost much of its support after the 1980 sovereignty referendum.

Quemoy and Matsu, China Sea islands held by the Taiwan government after the Chinese Communist mainland victory of 1949, and maintained with U.S. protection. In 1958 U.S. ships supplied Quemoy through a period of blockade and air-sea attacks, and in 1962 U. S. warnings stopped a possible invasion from the mainland.

Quinlan, Karen Ann (1954–81), key figure in the U.S. case that established the legal RIGHT TO DIE. Comatose from April 1975 after ingesting alcohol and tranquilizers, Quinlan was placed on a respirator. In September 1975, her parents, acting on her behalf, petitioned to remove the respirator; the court refused, but in March 1976 the New Jersey Supreme Court granted their request. Quinlan was taken off the respirator on May 22, 1976, but surprisingly survived—still comatose—for more than 5 years, before dying of pneumonia in a nursing home on June 11, 1981. The Supreme Court had refused to hear the case in November 1976, letting stand the New Jersey ruling.

Quisling, Vidkun (1887–1945), Norwegian fascist who headed a puppet government during the German World War II occupation of his country. He was executed for treason in October 1945. During the war and after, the term "Quisling" became synonymous with "traitor."

Qumran Cave, desert site in modern Israel where, in 1947, the first of the DEAD SEA SCROLLS were found.

R

Ra II, reed boat, made in early Egyptian style, sailed across the Atlantic in 1969–70 by Norwegian explorer Thor HEYERDAHL.

Rabi, Isidor Isaac, (1898–) Austrian-born, U.S.-educated physicist, who in the 1930s developed ways to accurately measure magnetism in atoms and molecules, work that won him the 1944 Nobel Prize for Physics. During World War II he worked on RADAR and on the ATOMIC BOMB, later succeeding J. Robert OPPENHEIMER as chairman of the ATOMIC ENERGY COMMISSION's General Advisory Committee (1952–56).

Rabin, Yitzhak (1922–), Israeli officer who saw service during the ISRAELI WAR OF INDEPENDENCE (FIRST ARAB–ISRAELI WAR) in 1948 and rose to become army chief of staff (1964–68). He was ambassador to the United States (1968–73), briefly labor minister in 1974, and prime minister (1974–77). He became defense minister in the 1984 coalition government, taking direct responsibility for Israeli army operations against the Palestinian populations of the WEST BANK and Gaza Strip during the INTIFADA of the late 1980s.

radar (**ra**dio **d**etecting **a**nd **r**anging), method of spotting and locating objects using reflection of RADIO waves, first patented by German engineer Christian Hülsmeyer in 1904, based on earlier work, but not really developed until the 1930s. Researchers followed independent lines in America and several European countries, though Scottish physicist Robert Alexander Watson-Watt is often credited with the first practical radar for detecting aircraft in 1935. In World War II, Britain made some key technical breakthroughs, including the development of a MICROWAVE-producing tube called a magnetron and a klystron tube that made the radar beam more precise, aiding the RAF significantly in the BATTLE OF BRITAIN, especially because radar development was given low priority in Germany. In 1963, during the COLD WAR, the United States set up an extensive "early warning" radar system in Greenland, Britain, and Alaska for detecting INTERCONTINENTAL BALLISTIC MISSILES (ICBMs). Radar also appeared in civilian life, especially used by air traffic controllers, weather forecasters, and police.

Radek, Karl Bernhardovich (Karl Sobelsohn; 1885–1939), Russian Social Democrat who fought in Poland during the RUSSIAN REVOLUTION OF 1905, became a BOLSHEVIK leader in exile, and returned to Russia with LENIN in 1917. He became a leader of the COMINTERN in the early 1920s but was expelled from his party as a Trotskyist in 1927, returning in 1930 to become an editor of *Izvestia*. He was imprisoned during the MOSCOW TRIALS of 1937 and died in prison 2 years later. He was posthumously rehabilitated during the GORBACHEV era.

radiation, energy being transmitted in apparently different forms, first understood as belonging to one continuous electromagnetic spectrum only in 1905, following EINSTEIN's theory of RELATIVITY. Along the spectrum, running from the highest to the lowest frequency, are found RADIO waves, MICROWAVES, INFRARED rays, light (the very narrow visible spectrum from red to violet), ULTRAVIOLET rays, X-RAYS, and GAMMA rays. Until 1911 scientists assumed that all radiation came from the Earth; then Victor Hess, making measurements during balloon flights, recognized the existence of COSMIC RAYS. Radiation was also assumed to be wavelike until the 1923–24 work of Arthur Holly COMPTON and Louis DE BROGLIE showed that in some respects it behaved like particles, giving rise to the idea of WAVE-PARTICLE DUALITY. Scientists in the 20th century have developed a wide range of applications for the various types of radiation, as in RADIO ASTRONOMY and medicine. Much popular discussion of radiation has focused on the danger of the invisible emissions, as from X-rays and microwaves.

radio, transmission and detection of radio waves—that is, RADIATION from the radio portion of the electromagnetic spectrum—carrying informational signals through space; a form of telecommunication overlapping many areas, including TELEVISION, RADAR, RADIO ASTRONOMY, and telephones. Radio grew out of 19th-century work in WIRELESS telegraphy, especially by Guglielmo MARCONI, who founded the first commercial wireless telegraphy service in 1898, providing Lloyd's of London with information about incoming ships. In December 1900, American electrical engineer Reginald Aubrey Fessenden transmitted the human voice for the first time, to a receiver a mile away. Then, in 1901, Marconi tapped out the letter S in Morse code, sending the first trans-Atlantic signal from St. John's, Newfoundland, to a waiting receiver in Poldhu, Cornwall, confounding those who thought radio signals could be sent no farther than 100–200 miles. By 1902 he had sent a signal 700 miles during the day and 2,000 miles at night; the difference was later found to be in the nature of the IONO-SPHERE, an atmospheric layer that reflects radio waves. The first known radio program in the United States was broadcast on Christmas Eve 1906, transmitted by Fessenden from Brant Rock, Massachusetts; his audience was mostly wireless operators on nearby ships and a few amateurs on land. The following year he conducted the

first two-way radio-telephone transmission between Brant Rock and Scotland. By 1910 wireless telegraph messages were commonly passed between land and ships, and that year they were transmitted for the first time between land and an AIRPLANE. Within 8 years the first message was transmitted from England to Australia. Into the 1920s some early receivers used crystal detectors, introduced in 1901 by Karl Braun, so radios were sometimes called crystal sets; though precursors of modern TRANSIS-TORS, they were soon replaced by ELEC-TRON TUBES. These could generate, detect, and amplify signals, allowing radio development to boom. ELECTRONICS inventor Lee DE FOREST gained great publicity for fledgling radio by broadcasting Enrico Caruso singing live at the Metropolitan Opera in 1910, and offering the first radio news report in 1916. Bell Telephone engineers, working with De Forest's electron tubes, made the first transoceanic voice transmissions in 1915. The following year David SARNOFF of the American Marconi company suggested building stations for transmitting speech and music, to be received by "radio music boxes" in the home. Pioneer radio operators began regular broadcasts as early as 1919 in The Hague and in 1920 in Montreal. The first regular radio station in the United States was KDKA in Pittsburgh, Pennsylvania, which started broadcasting on November 2, 1920, with the Harding-Cox presidential election returns. By July 2, 1921, a radio blow-by-blow account of the Dempsey–Carpentier fight had an audience of approximately 300,000 people; the first paid commercial was broadcast a year later. In 1926 the National Broadcasting Company (NBC) formed the first permanent network of radio stations. In 1912 and again in 1927, the U.S. Congress passed radio acts to regulate the industry, in 1934 setting up the FEDERAL COMMUNICATIONS COMMISSION (FCC), which assigned radio wavelengths to stations. The British began to license both transmitters and receivers in 1922, and 5 years later formed a public broadcast authority, the BRITISH BROADCASTING COR-PORATION (BBC), funded by licensing fees. By the end of the 1920s radio service had spread throughout Europe and the British Commonwealth. A series of international agreements, effected from 1926, extended gradually around the world and allotted the wavelengths on which each country's stations could broadcast. Early radio stations all varied their power output to convey sound or signal; that is, they used amplitude modulation (AM). But in 1935 Edwin Armstrong developed a signal varied with frequency modulation (FM), the resulting sound being steadier and less subject to interference. Today both types of stations exist side by side. Being a powerful propaganda tool, radio is kept under strict state control in some countries, but it recognizes no borders. The BBC, widely known for its international broadcasting of high-quality programming, started its foreign-language broadcasts in 1938. But from the 1920s many other countries also have transmitted programs designed for people outside their borders—sometimes openly propagandistic. As the Soviet Union has long beamed programs in English to the people of North America, so the U.S. VOICE OF AMERICA and RADIO FREE EUROPE have transmitted programs in various languages to people behind the IRON CURTAIN. Sometimes governments have attempted to "jam," or scramble, signals from outside their borders; listening to foreign radio broadcasts could sometimes even lead to imprisonment. In World War II radio provided vital means of communications, often coded, with resistance fighters behind enemy lines; ever since, intelligence services have listened avidly to other countries' radio communications for information about their intentions. Though challenged in the popular affection by both motion pictures and TELEVISION, radio remains a powerful medium; immediacy and interaction are two of its main attractions. All-news stations, which arrived on the U.S. scene in 1975, and call-in shows take advantage of both of these attractions. From the 1950s,

when transistors began to replace VACUUM TUBES, radios also became smaller, more portable, and ubiquitous. Listeners tuning in on shortwave bands can hear programming from thousands of miles away, especially at night, and "ham radio" operators are able to talk with fellow amateurs from all over the world.

radioactivity, property of an atom spontaneously decaying, or disintegrating, while giving off RADIATION and PARTICLES; the natural products of radioactivity are gamma rays, a type of low-frequency radiation; alpha particles, the nuclei of helium atoms without the ELECTRONS; and beta particles, speeded-up electrons. Radioactivity was first discovered in 1896 by Antoine-Henri Becquerel, and explored in the following decades by Marie Sklodowska CURIE and Pierre Curie. In 1900 French physicist Paul Villard discovered gamma rays, which Ernest RUTHERFORD quickly realized were similar to X-RAYS but of shorter wavelengths; Rutherford also discovered and named both alpha and beta particles in the early 1900s. Rutherford and Frederick SODDY first understood in 1902–1903 that radioactive emissions were actually the result of an unstable atom decaying into another more stable one. The length of time it takes for half of a given amount of a radioactive element to decay into another is called its HALF-LIFE. Radioactivity can occur naturally, as in URANIUM, or it can be artificially induced, as first done by Rutherford in 1919. Additional types of particles are produced with artificially induced radioactivity, as during NUCLEAR FISSION or bombardment in an ACCELERATOR, a process much studied by modern particle physicists. Radioactive ISOTOPES, or radioisotopes, are widely used in medicine, as in the treatment of cancer or as tracers in the body to aid diagnosis.

radio astronomy, observation of objects in the universe, not by optical means but by analysis of the RADIO waves they emit, the waves themselves being first discovered in 1931 by Bell Labs radio engineer Karl Guthe JANSKY. By 1937 U.S. astronomer

Grote Reber had built the first radio telescope, a dish-like affair 31 feet across; others followed, and by the 1980s a single VERY LARGE ARRAY (VLA) radio telescope, with many dishes arranged to work together, had the observational capacity of a 17-mile-wide radio "dish," focusing radio waves and collecting them for analysis by computer. Radio astronomers showed that the universe contained far more objects than those previously seen and, working with optical telescope astronomers, they began to identify new types of objects in the sky, such as QUASARS; they also discovered background cosmic RADIATION, supporting the BIG BANG THEORY of the universe's origin. Since World War II, astronomers also have used various devices to "observe" the universe by collecting and analyzing other types of radiation, such as INFRARED RAYS. The American Orbiting Astronomical Observatory is a series of SATELLITES used to map the entire electromagnetic spectrum of the universe from beyond the distortion of the Earth's atmosphere.

radiocarbon dating, method of dating the remains of ancient life by measuring how much of the radioactive ISOTOPE carbon 14 it contains; knowing carbon 14's very long HALF-LIFE of 5,730 years, and its proportion in living tissue, scientists can tell how long ago remains were alive. Use of the carbon 14 dating technique, developed in 1946 by American chemist Willard Frank LIBBY and refined by others over the decades, transformed archeology, anthropology, and paleontology in general, showing that many settlements were far older than previously thought.

Radio Free Europe, broadcast service funded by the U.S. government and aimed at the people of Eastern Europe and the Soviet Union from 1952; during the COLD WAR, it was often staffed by political refugees and emigrants from behind the IRON CURTAIN.

radioisotopes, radioactive form of ISOTOPE widely used for medical analysis and treatment; often artificially created for the purpose, following Irène JOLIOT-CURIE and Frédéric JOLIOT-CURIE's 1934 discovery of artificially induced RADIOACTIVITY. Radioactive iodine, for example, allows doctors to analyze the functioning of the thyroid gland and also can be used to destroy some tissue in cancerous or overactive thyroid glands. In the field of nuclear medicine, certain imaging procedures also require that the patient be given radioisotopes before a scan.

radon, odorless, colorless, radioactive gas, existing in several forms and having a short HALF-LIFE; it was discovered in 1900 by German physicist Friedrich Ernst Dorn. Released from rocks and springwater in the earth, radon is an unseen source of cancer-causing RADIATION. With more efficient insulation, especially after the OIL EMBARGO of the 1970s, it came to be trapped in buildings, causing the Environmental Protection Agency to suggest in 1988 that all homes and lower-floor apartments should be checked for radon levels.

Raeder, Erich (1876–1960), German naval officer who saw service during World War I, becoming commander-in-chief and then grand admiral of the German navy during the interwar period; he was relieved of command by Adolf HITLER in 1943. Sentenced to life imprisonment at the NUREMBERG war crimes trials, his sentence was later commuted.

Rahman, Mujibur (Sheikh Mujibur; 1920–75), the first president of Bangladesh; he was a MOSLEM LEAGUE activist until 1947 and in 1948 one of the founders of the Awami League, which became the main force in the campaign for an independent Bangladesh, then East Pakistan. In 1970 he and his party won an overwhelming electoral victory in East Pakistan, and enough votes in West Pakistan to have made him president. But the military government of Pakistan refused to convene the new national assembly, arresting him and triggering the BANGLADESH WAR OF INDEPENDENCE and the INDIA–PAKISTAN WAR OF 1971, which led to the establishment of an independent Bangladesh. Released from imprisonment, he became first president of

Bangladesh in December 1971. As president, Rahman attempted to develop a moderately socialist economy in a very poor country against a backdrop of recurrent natural disasters, epidemic disease, and continuing civil unrest. He was assassinated, along with his wife and five children, on August 15, 1975, during an attempted army coup.

Rainbow Warrior incident (July 1985), the sinking by French agents of the ship *Rainbow Warrior*, operated by the Greenpeace anti-nuclear-testing group who were in Auckland Harbor preparing an attempted disruption of French South Pacific nuclear weapons tests. The New Zealand government arrested two French agents and convicted them of manslaughter. Both were later freed but only after a bitter dispute between France and New Zealand was mediated by UNITED NATIONS secretary general Javier PEREZ DE CUELLAR. The French government paid $7 million in compensation.

Rajk, Laszlo (1909–49), Hungarian Communist who fought in the SPANISH CIVIL WAR, was a resistance leader during World War II, served as interior minister 1946–48, and became foreign minister in 1948. In 1949 he was charged with treason; he confessed while undergoing a show trial and was executed. The charges were wholly false; in 1956 he was posthumously rehabilitated by MÁTYAS RÁKOSI, whose government had executed him.

Rákosi, Mátyas (1892–1971), Hungarian Communist leader, who fled to the Soviet Union after the defeat of the BELA KUN government in 1919, returned in 1925, and was imprisoned from 1925 to 1940, when his release was negotiated. In 1945 he became head of the Hungarian Communist Party, which seized full power in 1947, installing him as head of the Hungarian government. He was replaced by more liberal Imre NAGY in 1953, returned to power in 1955, and in 1956 unsuccessfully resisted the powerful reformist pressures generated by the February KHRUSHCHEV SECRET

SPEECH. He resigned in July 1956, and returned once more to the Soviet Union.

Ramsay, Bertram Home (1883–1945), British naval officer, who came out of retirement to serve in World War II. He planned the successful British evacuation of DUNKIRK in 1940, was deputy fleet commander during the 1942 North African invasion, and commanded all naval forces in the NORMANDY invasion of 1944. He died in an aircraft accident in France, in January 1945.

Ramstein air show disaster (August 28, 1988), 49 people were killed and 350 injured, when three Italian precision-flying-team jets crashed into a crowd of 300,000 spectators at the annual U.S. Ramstein Air Base air show near Frankfurt, West Germany. Acceding to angry West German public opinion, which had previously built pressure to ban such shows as dangerous, the government then prohibited them until further notice, over U.S. protests.

Randolph, Asa Philip (1889–1979), U.S. labor organizer and civil rights activist, who in 1925 founded the Brotherhood of Sleeping Car Porters and was its president from 1925 to 1968. During World War I he worked to organize Blacks into unions and founded *The Messenger*, a magazine devoted to that work. During World War II he successfully lobbied for establishment of the FAIR EMPLOYMENT PRACTICES COMMISSION (FEPC) after threatening to organize a march on Washington. In 1955, he became a vice-president of the AFL-CIO, and in 1963 was chief organizer of the MARCH ON WASHINGTON at which Martin Luther KING, Jr. delivered his I HAVE A DREAM speech.

Ranger, series of U.S. unmanned spacecraft exploring the MOON in the 1960s, preparatory to the APOLLO flights, transmitting television pictures of the Moon before making a "hard," or crash, landing onto it.

Rank, Otto (Otto Rosenfeld; 1884–1937), Austrian psychoanalyst and early Freud protégé, who split with his mentor in 1924, on publication of his book *The Trauma of Birth*. Later in Paris and then New York,

Rank developed a therapy aimed at reliving the birth trauma.

Rankin, Jeannette (1880–1973), U.S. social worker, woman suffrage activist, and a Montana Republican congresswoman (1917–19, 1941–43), in 1917 becoming the first woman to serve in either house of Congress. A lifelong antiwar activist, she opposed U.S. entry into World War I. In 1941 she was the only member of Congress to vote against the declaration of war on Japan after the attack on PEARL HARBOR; she left Congress at the end of her term. She was also active in opposition to the VIETNAM WAR.

Rapallo, Soviet–German Treaty of (April 16, 1922), a treaty by which Germany became the first major country to recognize the Soviet Union. All war debts or reparations between the two countries were disclaimed, laying the basis for favorable trade relations.

Rapallo, Yugoslav–Italian Treaty of (November 12, 1920), a treaty that temporarily settled the status of disputed Fiume, making it a free city. Fiume was taken by Italy in 1924, and became part of Yugoslavia after World War II.

Rape of Nanking (December 13, 1937), the fall of Nanking to Japanese troops during the SINO–JAPANESE WAR, so described throughout the world because of the extremely brutal behavior of the Japanese troops that took the city.

Rasmussen, Knud Johan Victor (1879–1933), Danish explorer and ethnologist, Greenland-born and part Eskimo, who from 1902 led many expeditions to map remote areas of Greenland and study Eskimo culture; from 1910 he worked from THULE, a base he founded in northern Greenland. He also made wider Arctic explorations; he was the first to travel the route of the NORTHWEST PASSAGE by dogsled (1921–24) from Greenland across to Point Barrow, Alaska, visiting the many Eskimo tribes along the way.

Rasputin (Gregory Yefimovich Novykh), Russian monk and faith healer who, from 1905, strongly influenced Czarina Alexandra, wife of NICHOLAS II, and whose rough and highly sexual conduct scandalized Russian court and related circles of the time. The czarina's influence over Russian nonmilitary affairs peaked during World War I, and with it Rasputin's influence. He was assassinated by three prominent Russian conservatives on December 16, 1916.

Rathenau, Walter (1867–1922), German industrialist who helped organize Germany's war effort during World War I, became foreign minister of the Weimar Republic, and established normal relations with the Soviet Union with the 1922 Treaty of RAPALLO. He was attacked by the German far right as a Communist sympathizer and also as a Jew, and was assassinated by rightists on June 24, 1922.

Rather, Dan (1931–   ), U.S. journalist and broadcaster, who as a CBS correspondent, reported the assassination of John F. KENNEDY from Dallas, and went on to cover many of the main stories of the 1960s and 1970s. He became a major figure during his tenure as CBS White House correspondent (1966–74), as he sharply questioned and helped expose Richard M. NIXON'S role in the WATERGATE scandal. He was named CBS television news anchor in 1981, succeeding Walter CRONKITE.

Rava Ruska, Battle of (September 3–11, 1914), World War I battle, in which Austrian forces invading Russian Poland were decisively defeated by the Russians after initial successes, and retreated 100 miles to the Carpathian Mountains. At the end of this campaign the Russians held most of Galicia.

Ray, James Earl (1928–   ), assassin of Martin Luther KING, Jr., in Memphis, Tennessee, on April 4, 1968. Ray was captured in London on June 8, 1968, pleaded guilty to the murder, and received a 99-year jail term.

Rayburn, Samuel Taliaferro (1882–1961), U.S. lawyer, a long-time Texas Democratic member of the House of Representatives (1913–61), and Speaker of the House for a total of 17 years, during the administrations

of presidents ROOSEVELT, TRUMAN, EISEN-
HOWER, and KENNEDY. He played a major
role in the development and passage of
much of the NEW DEAL legislation of the
1930s.

Reagan, Ronald Wilson (1911–   ), U.S.
sportscaster, actor, president of the Screen
Actors Guild, governor of California, and
40th president of the United States (1981–
89). He was a popular Hollywood actor
from the late 1930s through the 1950s, becoming active in film industry matters and
serving as president of the Screen Actors
Guild 1947–52. During that period he began the swing from the liberal Democrat he
had been to the conservative Republican he
became. He became active in Republican
party affairs in 1964 and was governor of
California from 1967 to 1975. He unsuccessfully sought the Repubican presidential
nomination in 1968 and 1976, before winning it and then the presidency in 1980, defeating incumbent Jimmy CARTER. He was
wounded in John HINCKLEY'S assassination
attempt of March 30, 1981, but completely
recovered. He won a landslide second-term
victory in 1984, defeating Democrat Walter
MONDALE in all but Minnesota and the District of Columbia. As president he pursued
a conservative agenda domestically, sharply
cutting social welfare expenditures and reducing federal regulation in several areas.
At the same time he greatly increased military expenditures and cut taxes, with resulting net budget deficits that by 1988 had
created a national debt approaching $2 tril-
lion. In foreign affairs his main preoccupa-
tion was with the Soviet-American cold war;
a staunch anti-Communist from Screen Actors Guild days, he began his administration by publicly calling the Soviet Union an
"evil empire." He ended it with the INF
TREATY and a series of increasingly cordial
and productive meetings with Soviet premier Mikhail GORBACHEV. These resulted in
Soviet withdrawal of troops from the AF-
GHANISTAN CIVIL WAR, negotiation toward
settlement of many regional conflicts, and
moderation—perhaps even the ending—of
the cold war. His other foreign policy initia-

tives met with mixed success: continuing involvement in the NICARAGUAN and
SALVADOREAN civil wars; the successful
1983 invasion of Grenada; the peacekeeping effort in Lebanon, which ended with
the 1983 terrorist attack on U.S. marines in
Beirut; the STAR WARS initiative; the repeated attacks on Libya; and the disastrous
IRAN–CONTRA AFFAIR.

Reagan–Gorbachev summits, four superpower meetings, at GENEVA (1985), REYKJA-
VIK (1986), WASHINGTON (1987), and
MOSCOW (1988), eventuating in the INF
TREATY, a substantial reduction in regional
conflicts all over the world, and a major
change in American–Soviet relations.

recombinant DNA, short segments of DNA
that have been "cut and pasted"—that is,
separated and spliced together in new
ways—as part of GENETIC ENGINEERING.
Recombinant DNA was almost a scare word
to the public in the mid-1970s, because of
concern that artificially created life forms
might escape from the laboratory and run
amok. The result was stringent government
controls on working with recombinant
DNA, somewhat relaxed after 1980.

Reconstruction Finance Corporation (RFC),
a U.S. federal lending agency created in
January 1932, in a HOOVER administration
attempt to meet the problems of the GREAT
DEPRESSION by making sizable federal loans
available to large business organizations. In
July 1932 its purposes were broadened to
include a wider range of Depression-related
objectives. During the first HUNDRED DAYS
of the ROOSEVELT administration, it became
a major NEW DEAL instrument for direct
loans to family farms and small businesses,
as well as a provider of a much wider variety
of loans to and investments in larger businesses.

Recruit stock scandal, a Japanese financial
corruption scandal that broke in July 1988,
involving many high government officials
and business leaders. The Recruit Cosmos
real estate company sold insider stock to
many high government officials, business
leaders, and journalists before taking the

company public. The company also made direct payments to government officials, some of them in the form of campaign contributions. The stock transactions were apparently legal under Japanese law but were seen as unethical. They generated a major scandal and caused the resignations of the finance, economics, and justice ministers, some business leaders, and several key aides to both Prime Minister Noboru TAKESHITA and his predecessor, Yasuhiro NAKASONE. As the scandal widened and deepened, it also directly involved Takeshita, forcing his April 24, 1989, announcemnt that he would resign.

Red Army Faction, the formal name of the BAADER-MEINHOF GROUP and also the name of the terrorist organization that succeeded the group after the 1972 captures of Andreas Baader, Ulrike Meinhof, and other original members of the group.

Red Baron, popular name for Manfred von RICHTHOFEN, the leading German fighter pilot of World War I.

Red Brigades, an Italian left terrorist organization that committed many assassinations in the 1970s and 1980s, including the March 1978 assassination of former Italian prime minister Aldo Moro. It is loosely affiliated with several similar organizations, including the Union of Fighting Communists, which committed several assasssinations in the late 1980s.

Red Front, the German Communist party street-fighting organization during the Weimar Republic period; smashed by the Nazis, it then went underground.

Red Guards (Chinese), roving groups of "levelers" formed by millions of young people all over China during 1966–67, aiming to purge Chinese life of all unorthodox "bourgeois" tendencies in response to MAO ZEDONG's call during the CULTURAL REVOLUTION. In practice this caused an enormous upheaval throughout the country, with tremendous human, economic, cultural, and educational damage, including the destruction of many of China's most treasured cultural artifacts and art treasures.

Red Guards (Soviet), the workers' militia developed by the SOVIETS during the PROVISIONAL GOVERNMENT period of 1917. The Red Guards of the PETROGRAD SOVIET, along with regular military units, took the WINTER PALACE and the city, during the OCTOBER REVOLUTION of 1917. Other Red Guard units did much the same in their areas of operation throughout Russia; together they formed much of the basis for the new Red Army that fought the RUSSIAN CIVIL WAR.

Red Orchestra (Rote Kapelle), large-scale Soviet intelligence network successfully functioning throughout Germany and occupied Europe during the early years of World War II.

Red Scare (1919–20), a time of antiradical hysteria in the United States; also known as the period of the PALMER RAIDS.

red shift, the apparent movement of starlight toward the red—or longer-wavelength—end of the electromagnetic spectrum. It was first observed by U.S. astronomer Vesto Melvin Slipher in 1920, an early confirmation of Albert EINSTEIN's general theory of RELATIVITY. A kind of Doppler effect, shown by objects swiftly receding from one another, the red shift tends to support the BIG BANG THEORY and is of special interest in the study of galaxies and QUASARS.

Red Terror, the name given by the BOLSHEVIKS to the tactics used to destroy opposition after the OCTOBER REVOLUTION of 1917; it involved the use of such extralegal means as mass arrests and summary executions.

Reeb, James, Boston Unitarian minister and civil rights activist beaten by racists in Selma, Alabama, on March 9, 1965, while in the city to participate in the SELMA MARCHES. He died on March 11. In December 1965, three whites were acquitted of his murder.

Reed, Frank, one of the American LEBANON HOSTAGES, director of the Lebanese International School, who was kidnapped on September 9, 1986.

Reed, John Silas (1887–1920), U.S. journalist and socialist who reported on American labor matters, the MEXICAN REVOLUTION, World War I, and the RUSSIAN REVOLUTION. A BOLSHEVIK partisan, his best-known work was a sympathetic report on the OCTOBER REVOLUTION, *Ten Days That Shook the World*. He became a leader of the Communist Labor Party of the United States in 1919, was indicted for sedition, and fled to the Soviet Union, where he died in 1920. Reed was the protagonist of Warren Beatty's 1981 film, *Reds*.

Reed, Walter (1851–1902), U.S. physician and bacteriologist, who identified the mosquito as the carrier of YELLOW FEVER. In the wake of the Spanish-American War, Reed headed a commission to Havana, Cuba, to explore the causes of yellow fever, a dangerous task that had taken the lives of several co-workers. Once Reed had identified the mosquito carrier in 1900, William GORGAS oversaw a mosquito-eradication campaign there and in PANAMA, allowing the canal to be built. The U.S. Army hospital at Washington, D.C., was named in Reed's honor.

Regan, Donald Thomas (1918–   ), U.S. stockbroker, head of Merrill Lynch, Pierce, Fenner, and Beane until becoming secretary of the treasury in 1981. In 1985 he swapped positions with James BAKER, becoming chief of staff to President Ronald REAGAN. In February 1987 he was dismissed from that post, after a highly publicized set of disagreements with Nancy Reagan.

Regents of the University of California **v.** *Bakke* (1978), a landmark U.S. Supreme Court decision on educational quota systems, better known as the BAKKE CASE.

Rehnquist, William Hubbs (1924–   ), U.S. lawyer and assistant federal attorney general heading the Office of Legal Counsel, 1969–71, who strongly defended NIXON administration policies, including military surveillance of anti-VIETNAM WAR activists. Nixon appointed him an associate justice of the Supreme Court in 1971; he was confirmed by the Senate in a 68–26 vote, after a nomination fight in which liberals accused him of being a doctrinaire radical right conservative. He was appointed chief justice by President Ronald REAGAN in 1986 and confirmed 65–33, again after a nomination fight. A generally extremely conservative associate justice, he seemed to move to a somewhat more conciliatory position within the court in his early years as chief justice.

Reich, Wilhelm (1897–1957), Austrian-American psychiatrist who believed that the orgasm—for him, the discharge of sexual energy, or "orgone"—was vital to personal health. Associated with Sigmund FREUD in the 1920s, and with sexual freedom movements in Germany in the early 1930s, Reich tried to harmonize COMMUNISM and PSYCHOANALYSIS, an effort that barred him from both movements. Arriving in the United States in 1939, he founded the Orgone Institute and later developed the orgone box, which he claimed restored sexual energy and cured diseases such as CANCER. The orgone box, branded a fraudulent therapy by the FDA, brought Reich a 2-year jail term, during which he died.

Reichenau, Walther von (1884–1942), German officer and early Nazi, who rose to the rank of field marshal in 1940. He commanded substantial German forces during the Austrian, Polish, French, and Soviet invasions, dying of natural causes in 1942.

Reichstag Fire (February 27, 1933), a key Nazi strategem on the road to power. The Nazis, still a minority party, arranged to burn the Reichstag, the WEIMAR REPUBLIC seat of government, and blame it on Communists. Using the resultant anti-Communist hysteria, HITLER took power the next day, suspending all constitutional protections; a month later, March 23, 1933, the Reichstag voted itself out of existence, recognizing the fact of the Nazi dictatorship.

Reilly, William Kane (1940–   ), U.S. lawyer and leading conservationist, president of the Conservation Fund from 1973 and of the World Wildlife Fund from 1985;

on December 22, 1988, was named head of the Environmental Protection Agency (EPA) by president George BUSH.

Reith, John Charles Walsham (1889–1971), British executive who directed the BRITISH BROADCASTING COMPANY (BBC) in its formative years, 1922–38. He was responsible for maintaining the quasi-public authority's independence and for setting standards of excellence in programming that made the BBC's RADIO and, from 1936, TELEVISION broadcasts famed throughout the world.

relativity, in physics, a revolutionary view of the universe, put forth by Albert EINSTEIN in 1905 and more widely in 1915, positing that all measurement of motion, space, and time is relative to a particular frame of reference, which led to his famous equation of $E = MC^2$ and to the recognition of a SPACE-TIME CONTINUUM. Corollary to this was the revolutionary idea that, as a system approaches the speed of light, mass increases, clocks slow, and lengths contract, nothing being quite what it seems in our everyday life. The importance of the observer's frame of reference was registered in many other fields during the century.

Remagen bridgehead, the first Allied bridgehead over the Rhine in World War II. On March 7, 1945, U.S. forces seized the Ludendorff Bridge at Remagen before it could be fully destroyed by the retreating Germans. A bridgehead over the Rhine was established relatively easily, a crossing that had been expected to be extremely costly and difficult. At Remagen the successful Allied invasion of Germany from the west was assured.

RENAMO (Mozambique National Resistance), Mozambican Lisbon-based insurgent movement financed and supplied by Portuguese expatriates and the South African government; it developed in the 1970s with the initial assistance of the Rhodesian government. During the 1980s RENAMO mounted a strongly terrorist insurgency, focusing on guerrilla attacks on civilians. Beginning in 1987, the South African

government began to distance itself publicly from RENAMO, although continuing to covertly support that organization.

Republican Party, one of the two major U.S. political parties, formally adopting its name in 1854. During the 20th century, the party has been in power 49 of 89 years, during the presidencies of William MCKINLEY, Theodore ROOSEVELT, William Howard TAFT, Warren G. HARDING, Calvin COOLIDGE, Herbert HOOVER, Dwight D. EISENHOWER, Richard NIXON, Gerald R. FORD, Ronald REAGAN, and George BUSH. A strongly business-and-finance-oriented party at the turn of the century, it became a progressive, as well as conservative, party during the administrations of reformer Theodore Roosevelt, splitting and losing power in 1912, returning to power in the boom years of the 1920s, and then staying in power even when widespread Harding administration corruption culminated in the TEAPOT DOME scandal. It lost power to Franklin D. ROOSEVELT's NEW DEAL coalitions of the 1930s and through the TRUMAN years, reasserting itself and coming to power again in the prosperous 1950s. From 1968 to 1989, with a national shift toward conservatism, the Republican Party held the presidency for 17 of 21 years, although Democrats in most periods continued to control one or both houses of Congress.

Republic of China, name of CHINA from 1926 to 1949 and thereafter the government on Taiwan.

Republic of Cyprus, name of CYPRUS from its 1961 independence.

Republic of Korea, an independent state from August 15, 1948, consisting of that portion of KOREA below the 38th parallel. From its inception the country has been involved in a continuing "cold war" with its northern neighbor, the DEMOCRATIC PEOPLE'S REPUBLIC OF KOREA, which in 1950 became the hot KOREAN WAR, involving the United States, the UNITED NATIONS, and China and eventuating in a decades-long stalemate between the two Koreas.

Resistance, French, a loose confederation of anti-German forces fighting underground in France during the Nazi occupation of World War II; it included FREE FRENCH forces tied to the government-in-exile led by Charles DE GAULLE, often called MAQUIS, along with Communist-led units, former army units continuing to fight on after the surrender, and a miscellany of smaller anti-Nazi groups.

Resurrection City, the squatters' settlement established in Washington, D.C., by the Poor People's Campaign of 1968, led by the SOUTHERN CHRISTIAN LEADERSHIP CONFERENCE and its president, Ralph ABERNATHY, who had taken over leadership after the assassination of Martin Luther KING, Jr.

return to normalcy, the 1920 presidential election campaign slogan of Warren G. HARDING.

Reuben James (October 31, 1941), the first U.S. warship sunk in World War II, a destroyer torpedoed by a German submarine in the North Atlantic while on convoy duty.

Reuther, Walter Philip (1907–70), U.S. automobile worker, who in 1935 founded and became a local president of the United Automobile Workers (UAW), and in 1936 led the first SITDOWN STRIKE, leading to organization of General Motors and Chrysler in 1937. He became head of the UAW General Motors Department, president of the UAW in 1946, and president of the CONGRESS OF INDUSTRIAL ORGANIZATIONS (CIO) in 1952, leading the CIO back into the AFL-CIO in 1955. He took the UAW out of the AFL-CIO in 1968; it rejoined in 1981. He was also a political activist and social reformer in such areas as social welfare and civil rights. During the COLD WAR he was a vice-president of the anti-Communist International Confederation of Free Trade Unions.

Revive China Society, organization founded in Hawaii in 1894 by Chinese Republican leader SUN YAT-SEN, beginning the long campaign to overthrow the Manchus that ultimately led to the CHINESE REVOLUTION of 1911.

Reykjavik summit (October 1986), the second meeting between U.S. president Ronald REAGAN and U.S.S.R. premier Mikhail GORBACHEV, at which they failed to move ahead, foundering on Soviet insistence on and American refusal to restrict the Reagan STRATEGIC DEFENSE INITIATIVE (STAR WARS) to limited laboratory testing.

Reynaud, Paul (1878–1966), French political leader, who as a cabinet minister opposed Munich and became premier in March 1940. He wanted to fight on as long as possible after the French military disaster in the spring of 1940, and resigned rather than sign an armistice with the Germans. After liberation he reentered politics as a member of the Chamber of Deputies, and was a cabinet member in several postwar governments.

Reynold v. Sims (1964), a landmark U.S. Supreme Court decision, applying the principle of "one man, one vote," which had been enunciated in earlier decisions, to state offices. By requiring that members of the House of Representatives and state legislators be elected from districts with approximately equal populations, the Court forced a massive redrawing of electoral district lines throughout the United States.

Reza Khan, an alternate name for Reza Shah PAHLEVI, who in 1925 became the first Pahlevi shah of Iran.

RFC, the initials of the RECONSTRUCTION FINANCE CORPORATION, a U.S. federal lending agency of the GREAT DEPRESSION.

Rhee, Syngman (1875–1965), South Korean political leader who fled from Japanese-occupied Korea in 1912 and lived in exile in the United States until 1945, then returning to Korea. He became the first president of South Korea (1948–60). He led his country during the KOREAN WAR but later became a virtual dictator, presiding over a corrupt police state. He was turned out by an uprising in 1960, retiring to Hawaii.

Rhesus (Rh) factor, protein substance found in the blood of at least 85 out of 100 people, discovered in 1940 by Karl LANDSTEINER and Alexander S. Wiener; Rhesus referred to the kind of monkey used in their initial experiments. The mixing of Rh-positive blood (with the factor) with Rh-negative (without) can cause blood cells to be destroyed; in the case of an Rh-negative mother and an Rh-positive fetus, the blood mixing can (if not identified and remedied) damage the fetus, causing retardation or death. The discovery of the factor allowed blood intended for transfusions to be properly typed for use, opening the way for widespread development of BLOOD BANKS.

Rhine, Joseph Banks (1895–1980), U.S. psychologist, who coined the phrase EXTRA-SENSORY PERCEPTION (ESP) to cover phenomena such as telepathy, clairvoyance, precognition, and often psychokinesis. Trained as a botanist, Rhine (with others) founded the Parapsychology Laboratory at Duke University in 1930: it was designed to scientifically test various claims to the existence of ESP.

Rhineland, German territory on both sides of the Rhine, which was demilitarized and occupied by the ALLIES after World War I and then evacuated in 1930, still demilitarized. The Rhineland was successfully reoccupied by German troops on March 7, 1936, in violation of the VERSAILLES and LOCARNO treaties, and subsequently remilitarized. The action, which drew no military response, was a key victory for Adolf HITLER in the run-up to World War II.

Rhodesia, as SOUTHERN RHODESIA a former British colony that declared its independence in 1965 and eventually (1980) became the nation of Zimbabwe.

Ribbentrop, Joachim von (1893–1946), German diplomat, who was HITLER's personal representative abroad during the 1930s, German ambassador to Great Britain 1936–38, and from 1938 German foreign minister. He negotiated several major agreements for Hitler, including the 1936 ANTI-COMINTERN PACT with Japan, the 1936 Rome-Berlin Axis, the 1939 German-Italian alliance, the MUNICH agreement, and the NAZI–SOVIET PACT of 1939, which paved the way for the start of World War

II. He was adjudged a war criminal at the NUREMBERG TRIALS and was hanged on October 16, 1946.

Richter scale, geological scale developed in 1935 by U.S. seismologist Charles F. Richter to rate the magnitude of earthquakes. Each point indicates at least 10 times the strength of the previous one, a 6.0 earthquake being 10 times as powerful as a 5.0 one.

Richthofen, Manfred von ("The Red Baron;" 1892–1918), the leading German fighter pilot of World War I, who was credited with shooting down 80 enemy planes. He was killed in aerial combat on April 24, 1918, by Canadian aviator Roy Brown.

Rickenbacker, Edward "Eddie" Vernon (1890–1973), leading U.S. fighter pilot of World War I, credited with shooting down 22 enemy planes. A Congressional Medal of Honor winner, he survived the war and later became president of Eastern Airlines.

Rickover, Hyman George (1900–   ), Polish-American career officer in the U.S. Navy who sparked the 1950s development of nuclear submarines. His work, from 1947, as head of the atomic submarine division of the Navy's Bureau of Ships produced the first nuclear submarine, the *Nautilus*, in 1954 and led to his becoming vice-admiral in 1958 and then admiral in 1973, 9 years after his retirement. Rickover was also a strong proponent of civilian use of NUCLEAR ENERGY.

Ride, Sally K. (1951–   ), U.S. astrophysicist and the first American woman astronaut in space, launched aboard the SPACE SHUTTLE *CHALLENGER* on its second flight, June 18, 1983.

Ridgway, Matthew Bunker (1895–   ), U.S. officer, who in World War II commanded the 82nd Airborne Division during the invasions of SICILY, ITALY and NORMANDY, becoming a corps commander late in the war. In 1950 he took command of American Eighth Army and UNITED NATIONS ground forces in KOREA, and in 1951 became commander of all American and UN forces in that war and Allied commander in Japan. From 1953 until his retirement in 1955 he was U.S. Army chief of staff.

Rif War (1921–26), a guerrilla war between Moroccan republican forces led by ABD EL-KRIM and much larger Spanish and French colonial armies. In July 1921, at the Battle of Annual, Rif forces ambushed Spanish forces moving into the Rif Mountains; of approximately 20,000 in the Spanish force 12,000 were killed, most of the rest surrendering. In April 1925, Rif forces moved against the French, destroying a string of French blockhouses and almost capturing Fez. But from September 1925 to May 1926, combined French and Spanish forces totaling approximately 200,000 men successfully pursued the guerrillas; the war ended with Abd el-Krim's surrender.

Riga, Treaty of, agreement that ended the SOVIET–POLISH WAR of 1920, settling the Polish–Soviet border until the Soviet invasion of 1939, following the NAZI–SOVIET PACT and the German invasion of Poland, beginning World War II.

right to die, legal right of a person to refuse medical aid that might sustain life. In the second half of the 20th century, with the proliferation of machines such as respirators, questions arose about the responsibility of physicians to keep their patients alive by all available means, versus the patient's right to refuse medical aid or the family's right to make that decision on the patient's behalf. In the United States the 1976 ruling allowing the parents of Karen Ann QUINLAN to remove her from the respirator was a key case in establishing the right to die. Many people also felt that the right to die should include the right of a person, especially someone who is terminally ill, to commit suicide—sometimes called voluntary EUTHANASIA—though such an idea had little legal status in most countries.

Right to Life movement, a U.S. antiabortion movement that developed after the landmark 1973 Supreme Court decision in *ROE* v. *WADE*, which established the fundamental right of pregnant women to make their own choices as to abortion. In the late

1980s Right to Life advocates moved into civil disobedience in an attempt to publicize their position, by blocking the operation of abortion clinics. Some extremists in the Right to Life movement went even further, embarking on a terrorist bombing campaign.

River Plate, Battle of the (December 13, 1939), a sea battle between the German pocket battleship *GRAF SPEE* and the three lighter British cruisers that caught up with it at the mouth of the River Plate. The Graf Spee disabled the British heavy cruiser *Exeter* and severely damaged both light cruisers but was itself damaged and forced to make port in Montevideo, Uruguay. The two light cruisers were joined by another heavy cruiser, and other British ships were on the way. The captain of the *Graf Spee*, refused more than 72 hours of sanctuary by the neutral Uruguayan government, sank his own ship outside the harbor.

RNA (ribonucleic acid), molecule that works with DNA to reproduce hereditary material in the GENE.

Roberto, Holden Alvaro (1925–   ), Angolan nationalist, leader of the the NATIONAL FRONT FOR THE LIBERATION OF ANGOLA (FNLA) during the 1961–74 ANGOLAN WAR OF INDEPENDENCE; he was head of the Angolan government in exile and then leader of FNLA forces during the long civil war that followed. By 1979 his forces had been defeated by the Cuban–Angolan forces of the People's Republic of Angola. Roberto ultimately found political asylum in France.

Roberts, Oral (1918–   ), U.S. evangelist, founder of the Oral Roberts Evangelistic Association and Oral Roberts University, and a major figure in the worldwide fundamentalist Christian evangelical movement. At least twice in the late 1980s, he threatened to commit suicide if his fundraising goals were not met.

Roberts, Owen Josephus (1875–1955), U.S. lawyer, law professor, and TEAPOT DOME prosecutor; he was appointed to the Supreme Court by Herbert HOOVER in

1930. He was a moderate on the Court, in some instances finding NEW DEAL legislation constitutional and in others refusing to do so. He headed the commission that studied the Japanese attack on PEARL HARBOR, his 1942 report castigating the leadership of the U.S. armed forces.

Robertson, Marion Gordon "Pat" (1930–), U.S. evangelical minister, ordained in 1959 and from 1960 the first television evangelist and host of the "700 Club." During the 1970s and 1980s, he built his Christian Broadcasting Network (CBN) into a considerable business enterprise, and then used his religious following as a base for his unsuccessful 1987–88 run for the Republican presidential nomination.

Robeson, Paul Bustill (1898–1976), U.S. lawyer, actor, singer, and Black activist. He was simultaneously one of the leading performing artists of his time and a major figure on the political left in the anti-fascist and American civil rights movements of the 1930s and 1940s. He was accused of Communist sympathies during the MCCARTHY period and suffered intense harassment by the witchhunters of the day, ultimately finding it impossible to pursue his career in the United States. In 1950, in an attempt to silence him, he was denied a passport by the U.S. government, an action nullified by the Supreme Court in 1958. He thereafter lived for some years in Great Britain, while working in many parts of the world as a theater and concert artist. Seriously ill, he returned to the United States in 1963.

Robinson, Jack Roosevelt "Jackie" (1919– 72), U.S. athlete who in 1947 became the first Black major league baseball player and the first to break the color line in U.S. professional sports; his dignity and professional accomplishment helped to pave the way for all who were to follow. He was a star player for Branch Rickey's Brooklyn Dodgers 1947–57.

robot, sophisticated machine, mostly run by COMPUTER, designed to do tasks once performed by humans; from the Czech word *robota* (slave or forced labor). After Karel Capek introduced the term in his 1921 play *R.U.R.* (Rossum's Universal Robots), robots were a science fiction staple, usually depicted in humanoid form. Researchers in the 1930s and 1940s, notably Norbert WIENER, developed ideas about FEEDBACK—essentially, the ability of a machine to "learn" from experience and modify its workings to meet changing conditions, that being the difference between basic preprogrammed robots and the still-ideal robots able to "learn" through trial and error. In 1946 American inventor George Devol invented a device to control machines and 8 years later a "programmable arm." The first firm to make and sell industrial robots was Unimation, founded in 1960 by Devol and Joe Engelberger; the first robot was installed the following year at a New Jersey General Motors plant. Early rudimentary robots, called universal transfer devices (UTDs), were used for simple repetitive tasks such as spot welding, spray painting, and stacking. But the 1971 development of the MICROPROCESSOR, which resulted in the miniaturization of computers and their consequent drop in cost, made more sophisticated robots a practical possibility. By the 1980s robots were generally being used in automobile, robot-making, and general manufacturing operations. Japan led the way in robot use and in the attempt to develop "smarter" robots, drawing on work done on ARTIFICIAL INTELLIGENCE. By the late 1980s, well over 100,000 robots were being used worldwide, almost two thirds of them in Japan.

Rockefeller, John Davison (1839–1937), U.S. 19th-century petroleum industry magnate, whose Standard Oil trust dominated more than 90% of the U.S. petroleum industry and had massive holdings in other extractive industries and transportation, until the court-ordered dissolution of Standard Oil of Ohio in 1892. In 1911 a landmark decision of the Supreme Court dissolved its successor, Standard Oil of New Jersey. Rockefeller then became a major 20th-century philanthropist who, among other gifts, initiated several major foundations. His son, John D. Rockefeller, Jr., who was also a major industrialist and philanthropist, had five similarly minded sons, one of whom was Nelson A. ROCKEFELLER.

Rockefeller, Nelson Aldrich (1908–79), U.S. four-term Republican governor of New York (1958–73), who served one term as Gerald R. FORD'S appointee to the vice-presidency (1974–77). (The WATERGATE scandal had caused Richard M. NIXON to resign the presidency shortly after Spiro T. AGNEW's resignation of the vice presidency in 1973, while facing charges of tax evasion.) A liberal, Rockefeller failed to gain the Republican presidential nomination in 1960, 1964, and 1968. He was the grandson of John Davison ROCKEFELLER.

rocket, aircraft moved by JET PROPULSION but (unlike JETS) carrying both fuel and oxygen on board. Modern rocketry began when American physicist Robert Hutchings GODDARD sent up the first liquid-propellant rocket in 1926. Goddard and others developed devices such as gyroscopes to stabilize rockets; in particular, Theodore von KÁRMÁN developed solid propellants. Others worked in Europe, among them French test pilot Robert Esnault-Petrie, who coined the term "astronautics," and Sergei KOROLEV, key Soviet rocket and later spacecraft engineer. Leading the German rocket technicians was Wernher von BRAUN, whose team developed the V-1 AND V-2 BOMBS of World War II. After the war von Braun and about 100 other rocket experts went to the United States, helping to develop research rockets, GUIDED MISSILES, and spacecraft. In the Soviet Union, Korolev and his successor, Valentin GLUSHKO, developed the rockets that sent into space the world's first artificial SATELLITE, *SPUTNIK*, and the U.S.S.R.'s first INTERCONTINENTAL BALLISTIC MISSILE (ICBM), both in 1957.

Roe* v. *Wade (1973), a landmark U.S. Supreme Court decision, clearly establishing the fundamental right of pregnant women to make their own choices as to abortion. The decision was followed by long, powerful antiabortion and proabortion campaigns.

Roehm, Ernst (1887–1934), organizer and leader of the Nazi STORM TROOPERS (SA); he was murdered by order of Adolf HITLER on June 30, 1934, as part of the Nazi BLOOD PURGE.

Rogers, Carl Ransom (1902–87), U.S. psychologist, whose ideas spurred the human potential movement from the 1960s. After early work with troubled children, Rogers began to develop what he called client-centered therapy, in which a nondirective psychologist helped "clients" focus on personal growth and communication, as opposed to the Freudian or medical doctor–patient relationship. His work helped form the underpinning for variously named encounter groups or sensitivity training, permissive interpersonal gatherings aimed at spontaneity in expressing feelings and sensitivity to feelings of others.

Rojas Pinilla, Gustavo (1907–75), Colombian officer who became armed forces commander-in-chief in 1950 and dictator after the coup of 1953. He ruled until 1957, during the worst years of LA VIOLENCIA, and was then peacefully removed in negotiations led by the next president of Colombia, Alberto LLERAS Camargo.

Rokossovski, Konstantin Konstantinovich (1896–1968), Soviet officer, who saw service during World War I and the RUSSIAN CIVIL WAR. He was a corps and then army commander in 1941, his forces playing a substantial role in the defense of MOSCOW, and in 1942 was overall commander of Soviet forces engaged in the Battle of STALINGRAD. Ultimately, forces under his command struck deep into Germany. He held a series of key Soviet military positions during the postwar period.

Rome, Fall of (June 4, 1944), peaceful taking of Rome by Allied troops pursuing the retreating Germans north; it had previously been declared an open city.

Rommel, Erwin (1891–1944), German officer, who saw service in World War I and rose under Adolf HITLER to command an armored division during the Battle of FRANCE in 1940. In early 1941 he became commander of German forces in North Africa, soon generating a string of victories that took his forces almost to Alexandria and earned him the popular name "The Desert Fox." But his forces lost the key Battle of EL ALAMEIN, retreating across North Africa before stronger Allied forces, and he was recalled to Germany. In 1944 he commanded German armies in France facing the NORMANDY invasion, subsequently retreating before the advancing Allies. He had become disillusioned with Hitler's leadership, starting in North Africa, and had agreed to cooperate with those who attempted to end Hitler's regime in July 1944; injured in an air attack, he was hospitalized on July 20, the day of the attack. However, Hitler learned of his complicity and ordered his death. Rommel committed suicide on October 14, 1944; his death of war wounds was announced, and he was buried with honors, for he was Germany's most popular World War II general.

Roosevelt, Anna Eleanor (1884–1962), U.S. political leader and reformer who became a world figure and one of the leading women of her time. She was a niece of president Theodore ROOSEVELT and married future President Franklin D. ROOSEVELT in 1905. She was active in Red Cross work during World War I, in such liberal organizations as the LEAGUE OF WOMEN VOTERS in the 1920s, and from the early 1920s in the Democratic Party. She became a national figure after her husband's presidential election, developing an active, independent political life and stance of her own, and powerfully influencing the development of NEW DEAL social programs through direct influence on the president and as a lecturer, radio personality, and the writer of the nationally syndicated newspaper column, "My Day." After Franklin Roosevelt's death in 1945, she continued her work. She was a member of the U.S. delegation to the UNITED NATIONS 1945–52 and was largely responsible for the passage of the UN Declaration of Human Rights. She was also active in reform Democratic politics and became one of the best-known speakers and

authors of the period. Her books include the three autobiographical works *This Is My Story* (1937), *This I Remember* (1949), and *On My Own* (1958).

Roosevelt, Franklin Delano (1882–1945), U.S. lawyer, New York state legislator (1911–13), assistant secretary of the navy (1913–20), twice governor of New York (1929–33), and 32nd President of the United States (1933–45); he led his country during an unprecedented four terms in office, through the GREAT DEPRESSION and World War II, although he had from 1921 been crippled by polio. A Democrat, he defeated incumbent Republican Herbert HOOVER in 1932 and Republicans Alfred M. LANDON in 1936, Wendell WILLKIE in 1940, and Thomas E. DEWEY in 1944. In his 1932 acceptance speech at the Democratic National Convention, he promised a "NEW DEAL for the American people"; in office, his domestic program came to be known by that name. As president, with the American system greatly threatened by the massive crisis of the Depression, and with the assistance of his BRAIN TRUST, he introduced and vigorously promoted a series of stimulative economic moves and major legislative and regulatory changes, many of them in the first HUNDRED DAYS of his first administration. Among the most important of these were a quick BANK HOLIDAY, the end of PROHIBITION, and establishment of the NATIONAL RECOVERY ADMINISTRATION (NRA) and the AGRICULTURAL ADJUSTMENT ADMINISTRATION (AAA); both of the latter were later declared unconstitutional in their early forms but were greatly stimulative during their lifetimes. He also pushed through the CIVILIAN CONSERVATION CORPS (CCC), PUBLIC WORKS ADMINISTRATION (PWA), FEDERAL EMERGENCY RELIEF ADMINSTRATION, CIVIL WORKS ADMINISTRATION, WORKS PROGRESS ADMINISTRATION (WPA), FEDERAL DEPOSIT INSURANCE CORPORATION (FDIC), HOME OWNERS LOAN CORPORATION (HOLC), the TENNESSEE VALLEY AUTHORITY (TVA), and SOCIAL SECURITY. Effective securities regulation began, with establishment of the

SECURITIES AND EXCHANGE COMMISSION. Labor organization was encouraged, with passage of the WAGNER ACT and establishment of the NATIONAL LABOR RELATIONS BOARD, which were followed by a wave of industrial organization. Abroad, he faced the growth of FASCISM, and although early attempting to maintain neutrality, he cooperated with Great Britain very closely after the major Nazi successes of 1940. In the Pacific the growth of militarism in Japan forced war in December 1941; thereafter he was the wartime president who, with his British, Soviet, Chinese, and French counterparts, formed the coalition of Allies that brought victory over the Axis. He did not live to see that entirely through, dying in office while at Warm Springs, Georgia, on April 12, 1945.

Roosevelt, Theodore (1858–1919), U.S. reformer, conservationist, trustbuster, sometime imperialist, writer, rancher, New York Republican state assemblyman (1882–1884), U.S. Civil Service Commission member and head (1889–1895), New York City police commissioner (1895–1897), assistant secretary of the navy (1897–1898), colonel of the Rough Riders and leader of the charge up San Juan's Kettle Hill during the Spanish-American War, New York governor (1899–1901), vice-president, and 26th president of the United States (1901–09). He succeeded to the presidency on the assassination of William McKINLEY, who died in Buffalo on September 14, 1901, and defeated Democrat Alton B. PARKER in 1904. As president he became deeply involved in a series of attempts to regulate monopolies and curb monopolistic business practices. To those ends he initiated the NORTHERN SECURITIES CASE, which ultimately broke up that immense railroad trust; intervened to force settlement of the long anthracite coal strike of 1902; and in 1906 pushed through both the PURE FOOD AND DRUG ACT and the HEPBURN ACT, which gave the Interstate Commerce Commission some railroad rate regulatory powers, following up on the Elkins Act of 1903, which began the regulatory process in this area. As a

conservationist he supported a wide variety of initiatives aimed at creating new national parks and monuments and large new forest and national resource reserves; in 1905 he initiated the U.S. Forest Service. As an imperialist, he fomented a Panamanian revolution against Colombia and then took a large strip of land for the PANAMA CANAL, which he actively encouraged. He also sent U.S. forces into the Dominican Republic in 1904, although withdrawing American forces from Cuba in 1902 and acting as mediator in the Far East. And as a progressive Republican reformer, he put forward the SQUARE DEAL slogan after the election of 1904, anticipating the NEW DEAL of another Roosevelt (a cousin) 28 years later. He ran for the presidency again in 1912 but failed to gain the Republican presidential nomination; instead he ran as a PROGRESSIVE (BULL MOOSE) candidate that year, losing to Democrat Woodrow WILSON.

Roosevelt Corollary, a U.S. Western Hemisphere foreign policy position stated by President Theodore ROOSEVELT in his December 1904 message to Congress, as an amendment to the Monroe Doctrine; it maintained that the United States had the right to intervene in the internal affairs of any Western Hemisphere nation guilty of financial and other "misdeeds" against foreign nations. It served as justification for the Cuban and several other such interventions until replaced by Franklin Delano ROOSEVELT'S GOOD NEIGHBOR POLICY of the 1930s.

Root, Elihu (1845–1937), U.S. lawyer, who became secretary of war in the cabinets of presidents William McKINLEY and Theodore ROOSEVELT, 1899–1904, in that position administering Cuba, the Philippines, and other formerly Spanish territories, and sending troops against the forces of Emile AGUINALDO during the PHILIPPINE–AMERICAN WAR. He was Roosevelt's secretary of state 1905–09, and a New York Republican senator, 1909–15; after World War I he actively supported the INTERNATIONAL COURT OF JUSTICE and the LEAGUE OF NATIONS.

Roper, Elmo Burns, Jr. (1900–71), U.S. public-opinion analyst, who was an early figure in the development of modern public opinion polls. In 1933 he founded Roper Research Associates, doing surveys for *Fortune* magazine from 1936. A pioneer in scientific political polling, Roper became famous for accurately predicting the vote in the 1936, 1940, and 1944 U.S. presidential elections, when earlier nonscientific polls had wildly inaccurate predictions.

Rosenberg, Alfred (1893–1946), a Nazi racist theoretician who provided much of the ideological justification for the mass murders of millions of Jews, Russians, Poles, Gypsies, and other "inferior" peoples before and during World War II. He was found guilty of war crimes at the NUREMBERG TRIALS and was hanged on October 14, 1946.

Rosenberg, Ethel Greenglass (1915–53) and **Julius Rosenberg** (1918–53), U.S. Communists convicted in 1951 of espionage during World War II, resulting in the passage of ATOMIC BOMB secrets to the Soviet Union; on April 5, 1951, they were sentenced to death by Judge Irving R. Kaufman. All appeals having failed, including clemency appeals to presidents TRUMAN and EISENHOWER and a massive worldwide campaign to free them, they were killed at Sing Sing, on June 19, 1953. They were the first Americans to be executed in peacetime for espionage. Their trial, convictions, and executions occurred at the height of the MCCARTHY period. Although they were found guilty, the severity of the sentence and its ultimate execution were widely attributed to the anti-Communist hysteria of the time.

Rote Kapelle, the RED ORCHESTRA, a large Soviet intelligence network operating before and during World War II in Nazi-held Europe.

Roth* v. *United States (1957), a landmark U.S. Supreme Court decision defining obscenity, holding it unprotected by the First Amendment, and thereby making it possible to legislate against it, and to make it a criminal offense.

Rothschild, Edmond de (1845–1934), French banker, head of the House of Rothschild in France, who from 1882 became financial patron of the Lovers of Zion and other Zionist organizations. His support helped establish the agricultural settlements, towns, cities, industries, educational and scientific institutions, and physical infrastructure that laid the basis for the establishment of the Palestine Jewish community that ultimately became the modern state of Israel.

Rotterdam bombing (May 13, 1940), the German bombing and destruction of much of the Dutch city early in World War II. The terror bombing of Rotterdam, a nonmilitary target, was part of a pattern of such bombings, aimed at breaking Dutch and Belgian will to resist the German invasion.

Rubin, Jerry (1938–), an anti-VIETNAM WAR activist who became a leader of the YIPPIE movement and who was convicted and later acquitted as one of the CHICAGO SEVEN after the CHICAGO DEMOCRATIC CONVENTION disorders of 1968.

Ruby, Jack (1911–67), murderer of Lee Harvey OSWALD in the Dallas, Texas, city jail on November 24, 1963, while a massive worldwide television audience watched; two days earlier, on November 22, Oswald had murdered President John F. KENNEDY. Ruby died in prison on January 3, 1967.

Ruhr, the key center of German heavy industry, which was occupied by France and Belgium in 1923, because of German failure to pay reparations provided by Treaty of VERSAILLES. It was evacuated in 1925 after substantial German reparations payments.

Rumania, until 1878, part of the Ottoman Empire; in the 20th century, a winner in the SECOND BALKAN WAR and WORLD WAR I, and an autocratic state during the interwar period, increasingly dominated by the Iron Guard. The fascist dictatorship of Ion ANTONESCU took Rumania into World War II on the Nazi side. The country was occupied by Soviet troops in 1944, and officially became an orthodox People's Republic on December 30, 1947, led by GHEORGE GHEORGIU-DEJ. In the early 1960s, he moved the country away from complete Soviet domination, and toward his own version of Communism. He was succeeded in 1965 by Nicolae CEAUSESCU, who for the next 25 years developed an increasingly rigid, repressive dictatorship, until overthrown by the RUMANIAN REVOLUTION.

Rumanian campaign of 1944 (August–September 1944), late World War II attack on Rumania by advancing Soviet armies. Rumania surrendered on August 23, its armies then going over to the Soviets, while the German–Soviet conflict in Rumania continued. Bucharest was taken on September 1, while the remaining German troops retreated, having taken substantial losses.

Rumanian Revolution (December 16–28, 1989), uprising that began with large pro-democracy demonstrations on December 16 in Timosoara, Transylvania; security forces clashed with demonstrators, and on December 17 killed hundreds, in the TIMOSOARA MASSACRE. Unrest swept the country as reports of the massacre began to circulate. On December 21 demonstrators in Bucharest interrupted a nationally televised CEAUSESCU speech; security forces then opened fire. Mass demonstrations in Bucharest on December 22 went over into armed revolt, with the army quickly joining the revolutionaries against the security forces, as fighting spread throughout the country. The revolutionaries were led by a hastily organized National Salvation Front. President Nicolae Ceausescu and his wife, Elena Ceausescu, were captured on December 22, and executed by the new government on December 25. Security forces continued to resist, but the revolution had been completed by December 28.

Runstedt, Karl Rudolph Gerd von (1875–1953), German officer, who saw service in World War I, became an army commander during the early years of the Nazi government, and commanded an army group during the invasion of Poland in 1939. During the Battle of FRANCE he commanded the army group that broke through from the Ardennes to the North Sea, forcing the surrender of the Belgians, the evacuation of the British, and the fall of France; after that campaign he became a field marshal. During the invasion of the Soviet Union his army group penetrated the Ukraine; they took Kiev and with it an estimated 1 million Soviet troops but were stopped at Rostov. Transferred to Western Europe to prepare for the coming Allied invasion, he commanded all German forces in western Europe at the time of the NORMANDY invasion. Unable to stop the Allied armies, and sure that Germany was losing the war, in July 1944 he urged Hitler to sue for peace. Instead Hitler relieved him of command, only to return him to command in September. He was captured by British troops in May 1945.

Rural Electrification Administration (REA), a U.S. NEW DEAL agency established in 1935, that encouraged the development of farmers' cooperatives to build transmission lines and supply electricity to rural areas; the REA played a substantial role in the electrification of rural America.

Rushdie, Salman (1947–), British author, best known as a novelist, whose novel *Midnight's Children* won a 1981 Booker award. His 1988 novel, *THE SATANIC VERSES*, generated worldwide Islamic fundamentalist protests and drew a February 14, 1989, death threat from Iranian Ayatollah Ruhollah KHOMEINI, who offered a $1 million reward to his murderer. The death threat generated enormous controversy, which resulted in the renewed isolation of Iran from the Western world. *The Satanic Verses* became a best-seller in many countries, though banned in much of the Islamic world; its author went into hiding.

Rusk, David Dean (1909–), U.S. diplomat, who served in the war and state departments during the post–World War II period, was head of the Rockefeller Foundation 1952–61, and was secretary of state 1961–69, through the KENNEDY and JOHNSON administrations. An advocate of increased U.S. commitment to the VIETNAM WAR, Rusk became Lyndon B. Johnson's chief Vietnam adviser, also serving as chief administration spokesman in defense of Johnson's Vietnam policies until deescalation of the war and peace negotiations began in 1968.

Russell, Bertrand (1872–1970), British philosopher, mathematician, writer, and radical reformer, who taught at Cambridge until fired in 1916 because of his opposition to World War I. His *Principia Mathematica* (1910–13), co-authored with Alfred North WHITEHEAD, was a landmark in attempting to develop a stronger, more certain logical base for mathematics, work soon undercut by that of Kurt GÖDEL. He was a sexual and educational reformer, a socialist, and after the use of the ATOMIC BOMB at HIROSHIMA and NAGASAKI in 1945, a leader of worldwide antinuclear activities. In his mid-90s, he was a leading opponent of the VIETNAM WAR.

Russian Civil War (1917–22), a 5-year-long series of widely separated military actions throughout the country, fought by the new BOLSHEVIK government after the OCTOBER REVOLUTION of 1917. Heavy and protracted fighting developed between the new Red Army and "White" military forces in southern Russia and the Ukraine, Finland, the Baltic provinces, Poland, along the Trans-Siberian railway, and in Siberia, with insurgent forces augmented and supported by foreign expeditionary forces from many nations. In 1917 Cossack and Red forces fought each other in the Don basin; by 1919 the fighting had become a large conflict between the Red forces and White armies led by General Anton DENIKIN. In May 1918 some 40,000–70,000 former Czech and Slovak World War I prisoners, trying to fight their way out of Russia via the Trans-Siberian Railroad, formed the CZECH LEGION and supported the White forces in eastern Russia and Siberia, led from late 1918 by Admiral Alexander KOLCHAK. In early 1918 Finnish forces led by Baron Karl Gustaf MANNERHEIM, supported by German forces, took and held Finland. In Au-

gust 1918 White forces nearly took Moscow, and Ukrainian nationalist forces led by General Simon PETLYURA attempted to set up an independent Ukrainian state in November 1918. In 1919 White forces led by Kolchak, Denikin, and General Nicolai YUDENICH attacked the Red Army from the east, south, and northwest, but all ultimately failed. In 1920 the brief RUSSO–POLISH WAR, the capture and execution of Kolchak, the Red success in the Crimea against General Piotr WRANGEL'S army, and the securing of Latvian, Lithuanian, Estonian, and Finnish independence completed the major actions of the civil war. Only White forces in Siberia remained, supported by the Japanese army. When the Japanese withdrew, late in 1922, the civil war was over. There had been considerable intervention by other governments. In December 1917 a substantial Japanese force took Vladivostock and was followed into Siberia in 1918 by a smaller American force. In March 1918 a small combined British, French, and American expeditionary force took Murmansk and supported White armies in northern Russia while smaller French forces landed in Odessa, and French and British supplies reached White armies in southern Russia.

Russian Revolution, a rather general term that has come to embrace the entire sequence of events beginning with the FEBRUARY REVOLUTION of 1917, continuing with the OCTOBER REVOLUTION of 1917, and concluding with the end of the RUSSIAN CIVIL WAR and the withdrawal of the last foreign troops in 1922.

Russian Revolution of 1905, uprising that began on BLOODY SUNDAY, January 9, 1905, when troops at the Winter Palace in St. Petersburg killed and wounded hundreds of unarmed petitioners. A wave of demonstrations and armed forces mutinies followed, the most notable of these being the mutiny on the battleship *POTEMKIN*. In August, in an attempt to ease the situation, Czar NICHOLAS II promised to create an elected national body, the Duma, but it would have no real power. The revolution continued and grew, with strikes, demonstrations, and armed clashes, and the creation of the first workers' councils (SOVIETS). The Czar then issued his OCTOBER MANIFESTO, promising much more substantial reforms and the inauguration of a constitutional monarchy, thereby considerably blunting the thrust of the revolution, and making it possible for his armed forces to suppress remaining pockets of armed resistance.

Russo–Japanese War (1904–05), conflict that began with a successful surprise Japanese attack on the Russian Far Eastern fleet, at anchor in Port Arthur harbor on February 4, 1904; the Japanese did not declare war until February 10. The Japanese besieged the city for 7 months and took it. On land, the Japanese army took Korea and much of Manchuria, ultimately decisively defeating the Russian army at the Battle of MUKDEN, February 21–March 10, 1904, in an engagement involving 600,000 men. Meanwhile, the main Russian naval force, the Black Sea fleet, steamed east around Africa and Asia to engage the Japanese navy, most of it going around the Cape of Good Hope. At the Battle of TSUSHIMA, on May 27, 1905, the much larger, obsolete, poorly maintained and trained Russian fleet was destroyed by the Japanese fleet, the Russians losing eight battleships and all but one cruiser and five destroyers and the Japanese losing three torpedo boats. The war ended with the Treaty of PORTSMOUTH, New Hampshire, mediated by U.S. president Theodore ROOSEVELT, in which Japan won Port Arthur, half of Sakhalin Island, and a major role in Korea, as well as driving the Russians out of Manchuria.

Rustin, Bayard (1912–87), U.S. pacifist, Quaker, socialist, and civil rights rights activist, a field secretary of the CONGRESS OF RACIAL EQUALITY (CORE) in 1941, race relations director of the Fellowship of Reconciliation 1941–53, head of the War Resisters League 1953–55, and an aide of Martin Luther KING, Jr., 1955–60. He was a longtime associate of A. Philip RANDOLPH in civil rights and socialist activities. In 1963

he organized the massive MARCH ON WASHINGTON, at which King delivered his I HAVE A DREAM speech. In his later years he continued to advocate pacifism and interracial cooperation, sometimes against criticism generated by separatist Black leaders.

Rutan, Richard, American pilot who, with Jeana YEAGER, made the first nonstop airplane flight around the world, in the *VOYAGER* in 1986.

Rutherford, Ernest (1871–1937), New Zealand-born British physicist who, with Frederick SODDY, developed the theory (1902–03) that RADIOACTIVITY resulted in the transformation of one element to another. In the same period he studied the three natural products of radioactivity, discovering and naming alpha and beta particles, and recognizing gamma rays as a type of RADIATION similar to X-RAYS; he also developed the concept of HALF-LIFE. In 1911, with Hans GEIGER and Ernest Marsden, he developed the basic model of ATOMIC STRUCTURE with a NUCLEUS at the center, later modified by Niels BOHR and others. In 1914 he discovered the PROTON, and 5 years later he was the first to induce radioactivity artificially. Winner of the 1908 Nobel Prize for Chemistry, Rutherford was widely respected as a teacher and long-time head of Britain's Cavendish Laboratory.

Rutledge, Wiley Blount (1894–1949), U.S. lawyer, law professor, and judge, who was appointed to the Supreme Court by Franklin D. ROOSEVELT in 1943; on the Court he was generally a liberal.

Rwanda (Republic of Rwanda), until World War I a German protectorate; taken by the Allies during the war, it became part of the Belgian-administered Rwanda-Urundi LEAGUE OF NATIONS trust territory during the interwar period and an independent republic on January 28, 1961.

Rwanda Civil War (1962–63), a failed attempt by the former Tutsi leadership to regain control of the country after the Hutu electoral victories of 1960 and 1961 and the establishment of the Hutu-dominated

Rwandan republic. After the failure of the revolt, 1963–64, Hutu massacres of Tutsis resulted in an estimated 10,000–15,000 deaths and generated an estimated 200,000 Tutsi refugees.

S

Saar, an industrial area on the French-German border. Its coal mines were awarded to France for 15 years by the Treaty of VERSAILLES under LEAGUE OF NATIONS administration, with a plebescite providing choice of affiliation thereafter. The plebescite of January 13, 1935, resulted in an overwhelming vote for return to Germany.

Saarinen, Eliel (1873–1950) and Eero Saarinen (1910–61), Finnish-American architects, a father and son who made major contributions to the development of modern architecture. Eliel Saarinen was the leading Finnish architect of his time; before his emigration to the United States in 1923 his most notable building was the Helsinki railroad terminal (1910–14). Eero Saarinen designed such major structures as the MIT auditorium and chapel (1955) and the TWA terminal at John F. Kennedy Airport in New York (1962).

Sabin, Albert Bruce (1906–   ), Polish-American physician and medical researcher who in 1956 developed a POLIO VACCINE made from deactivated live viruses. Taken orally, it was cheaper, easier to store, and effective for longer than Jonas SALK's earlier vaccine, and became the vaccine of choice throughout the world.

Sabin vaccine, live-virus POLIO VACCINE developed in 1956 by Albert SABIN.

Sabra and Shatilla massacres (September 16–18, 1982), the mass murders of 400 or more men, women, and children at the Sabra and Shatilla Palestinian refugee camps at Beirut, Lebanon, by PHALANGE militia, one day after the assassination of Phalange leader Bashir GEMAYEL. Israeli troops in the area did nothing to bar Phalange entry into the camps or to stop the massacres in progress, and were accused throughout the world of complicity. Israel's Kahane Commission denied Israeli complicity but accused Menachim BEGIN, Ariel SHARON, and several high Israeli officers of failure to prevent the massacres.

Sacco-Vanzetti case, controversial trial involving shoemaker Nicola Sacco and fish peddler Bartolomeo Vanzetti, both anarchists and foreign-born Italian-Americans. Convicted on July 14, 1921, of being members of a group that killed two men during the course of an April 15, 1920, payroll robbery in Braintree, Massachusetts, Sacco and Vanzetti were executed on August 23, 1927, after 6 years of worldwide protests. Fifty years later they were posthumously exonerated by the state of Massachusetts, for, as claimed at the time by their defense attorneys, their trial was conducted with extreme prejudice by Judge Webster Thayer, and in an antianarchist, anti-Italian, anti-immigrant climate that made a fair trial impossible.

Sadat, Anwar al- (1918–1981), Egyptian officer and revolutionary, who was imprisoned for anti-British activities during and after World War II, and was closely associated with Gamal Abdel NASSER in the EGYPTIAN REVOLUTION of 1952. He held several leading positions under Nasser, including the vice-presidency, and succeeded to the presidency after Nasser's death in 1970. Sadat expelled his Soviet advisers in 1972. In 1973 he initiated the FOURTH ARAB–ISRAELI WAR (YOM KIPPUR WAR) with successful surprise attacks on Israel, although the war ended with Israeli victory. After the war Sadat helped organize the Arab OIL EM-BARGO, which forced emergency American mediation of the remaining issues; he then moved into a closer relationship with the United States and an attempt to peacefully resolve some of the major Arab–Israeli disputes. In 1977 he offered to go to Israel if that would help bring peace, and subsequently did so, beginning the sequence of negotiations that led to the Egyptian–Israeli peace treaty of 1979 and Israeli evacuation of the Sinai Peninsula; he and Menachim BEGIN jointly received the Nobel Peace Prize in 1978. Although the rest of the Arab world condemned the treaty, he continued to press for peace in the area, including Palestinian autonomy after Israeli withdrawal from the WEST BANK and the Gaza Strip. He was assassinated by Islamic fundamentalists in Cairo October 6, 1981, while reviewing a parade.

Sagan, Carl (1934–), U.S. astronomer, who played a key role in planning planetary space probes with NASA, his own specialty being planetary atmospheres and the possibility of life on other planets or beyond, as described in popular books, such as *Intelligent Life in the Universe* (1966), and television series, notably "Cosmos" (1980). He was among the group whose concern over the effects of atomic warfare led to 1984 predictions of a NUCLEAR WINTER.

Sahel drought and famine (1965–), the continuing long-term drought in the African lands abutting the southern Sahara desert. The presence of millions of refugees because of continuing wars in the region, and the long-term overgrazing of diminishing pasturelands, have combined to create a massive and continuing famine, which has been exacerbated by the periodic refusal of some of the combatants to allow relief shipments into famine-stricken areas. Famine has been particularly severe in southern Sudan and Ethiopia.

Said, Nuri al- (1888–1958), Iraqi officer, who saw service in the Turkish army during the early years of World War I and joined the ARAB REVOLT in 1916, becoming FAISAL'S chief of staff and Iraqi chief of staff in

1921. During the 1920s he held several cabinet-level posts, and became prime minister in 1930; he then became Iraq's strong man. He was assassinated in the 1958 coup that toppled the monarchy of King Faisal II, and brought to power the republican government led by Abdul Karim KASSEM. Faisal also was assassinated during the coup.

Saigon evacuation (Operation Frequent Wind; April 1975), the evacuation of an estimated 7,000 Americans and Vietnamese by air from Saigon as North Vietnamese troops approached the city. More than 2,000 were evacuated from the U.S. embassy near the center of Saigon.

Saint Christopher and Nevis, until 1967 British colonies, gaining internal autonomy in 1967 and becoming an independent state and COMMONWEALTH member on September 19, 1983.

St. Francis Dam collapse (March 13, 1928), the collapse of a California dam that cost an estimated 450–700 lives and much property damage, because of the failure to evacuate those living in the Santa Clara valley.

Saint-Germain, Treaty of (September 10,1919), the Austrian peace treaty following World War I that dismembered Austria-Hungary, passing large territories to the new countries of Czechoslovakia, Poland, and Yugoslavia, and to Italy and Rumania. The treaty also provided for reparations and ended Hapsburg rule, with establishment of the Austrian republic.

St. Laurent, Louis Stephen (1882–1973), Canadian lawyer and president of the Canadian Bar Association, 1930–32, who joined MACKENZIE KING'S wartime cabinet as justice minister in 1941. He entered parliament as a Liberal in 1942, was minister of internal affairs, 1946–48, and was Canada's second French-Canadian prime minister, 1948–58.

St. Lawrence Seaway, major Canadian–U.S. waterway that from 1959 connected the Atlantic Ocean with the Great Lakes, making it possible for large oceangoing ships to travel into the North American heartland. The seaway includes large hydroelectric power plants.

Saint Lucia, until 1967 a British colony. The island gained internal autonomy in 1967 and became an independent state and COMMONWEALTH member on February 22, 1979.

St.-Mihiel Offensive (September 12–16, 1918), World War I push in which U.S. and French forces attacked retreating German forces in the St.-Mihiel salient, cleared the salient, and prepared the way for the final Allied offensives of the war.

St. Roch, Canadian ship that was the first to sail west to east along the NORTHWEST PASSAGE, north of North America, in 1940–42.

St. Valentine's Day Massacre (1929), the murder of seven people in Chicago on the orders of AL CAPONE.

Saint Vincent and the Grenadines, until 1967 British colonies, gaining internal autonomy in 1969 and becoming an independent state and COMMONWEALTH member on October 27, 1979.

Saipan, Battle of (June–July 1944), World War II U.S. marine and army landings at the Pacific island of Saipan on June 15, following bombardment by a powerful fleet on its way to the Philippines. Very costly hand-to-hand fighting followed; although the Americans had captured the island's airfield within 3 days and the outcome of the invasion was clear, the great majority of the Japanese defenders chose to fight to the death. Fighting ended July 9; by then an estimated 25,000–30,000 Japanese soldiers, sailors, and civilians had died. Some of them, including Japanese commanders Chuichi Nagumo and Jisaburo Ozawa, committed suicide when the end was near. There were over 16,000 American casualties, including more than 3,000 dead.

Sakharov, Andrei Dmitriyevich (1921–1989), leading Soviet nuclear physicist, a key figure in developing the U.S.S.R.'s HYDROGEN BOMB, who became a world figure as a democratic dissenter within the Soviet Union during the 1960s, winning the 1975 Nobel Peace Prize for his continuing work on behalf of human rights. He was not allowed to leave the country, and in 1980 he and his wife, Elena Bonner, were internally exiled by the Soviet government at Gorky. He was released from internal exile and allowed to travel abroad during the GORBACHEV era, then choosing to remain in the Soviet Union and continue his fight to bring democracy to Soviet society, even winning political office.

Salad Oil fraud, an early 1960s U.S. fraud developed by commodity-futures buyer Anthony (Tino) De Angelis, who supplied false warehouse receipts for stored salad oil that did not exist; the receipts were then used by their recipients as collateral for massive loans. After his Allied Corporation went bankrupt in 1963, the fraud was discovered, with resultant losses to others of $150–200 million and further losses of $15–20 million to commodities brokers with whom De Angelis had purchased futures on margin. De Angelis was later convicted and imprisoned.

Salan, Raoul Albin Louis (1899–   ), French officer, who saw service in World War II and Indochina and was Algerian commander-in-chief when Charles DE GAULLE took power in France in 1958. He opposed Algerian independence, but during 1958–59 he was stationed in Paris by De Gaulle, which removed him from direct command in Algeria. However, that did not stop him from organizing the unsuccessful 1961 French officers' revolt in Algeria and the SECRET ARMY ORGANIZATION (OAS), which for a time attempted to organize an insurrection in France. He was later sentenced to life imprisonment but was released in the June 1968 amnesty.

Salang Tunnel disaster (November 2, 1982), death of at least 700 people during the AFGHAN CIVIL WAR, when a motorized army convoy moving through the Salang Tunnel in Afghanistan suffered a fuel truck explosion, subsequent fire, and dense, killing smoke.

Salazar, Antonio de Oliviera (1889–1970), Portuguese economist who became finance minister in the 1928 military government and prime minister, 1932–68, ruling for 36 years as the fascist dictator of a corporate state on the Italian model. He supported Francisco FRANCO during the SPANISH CIVIL WAR and German and Italian fascism as well, although keeping his country out of World War II. He brought Portugal into the NORTH ATLANTIC TREATY ORGANIZATION (NATO) in 1949, and strongly resisted colonial independence movements throughout his tenure.

Salerno railroad disaster (March 2, 1944), suffocation of an estimated 500 passengers by carbon monoxide fumes when an overloaded train carrying sleeping passengers stalled in a railroad tunnel near Salerno, Italy.

Salk, Jonas Edward (1914–   ), U.S. physician and medical researcher, who in 1952 developed the first POLIO VACCINE against poliomyelitis, or infantile paralysis. It was introduced experimentally the following year and on a large scale in 1954 and proved immediately effective, though later it was largely replaced by Albert SABIN's polio vaccine. Salk's early work with influenza VIRUSES resulted also in a flu vaccine in 1953. Later he devoted himself to searching for a vaccine against CANCER.

Salk vaccine, killed-virus POLIO VACCINE developed in 1952 by Jonas SALK.

SALT I, the media-developed name for the STRATEGIC ARMS LIMITATION AGREEMENTS OF 1972.

SALT II, the media-developed name for the STRATEGIC ARMS LIMITATION AGREEMENT OF 1979.

Salyut, series of U.S.S.R. space stations, with the SOYUZ spacecraft being used to ferry astronauts back and forth from Earth; later replaced by the *MIR* permanently manned station. *Salyut 1* received three astronauts from *Soyuz 10* on April 24, 1971, becoming the world's first space station. The first crew change in space occurred in 1985 with *Salyut 7*.

Sambre River, Battle of (August 22–23, 1914), one of the World War I Battles of the FRONTIERS, in which German forces sweeping south and west through Belgium pushed back French forces on the Sambre River.

Samuelson, Paul Anthony (1915–   ), U.S. economist and econometrician, whose textbook *Economics* was by far the most widely used college economics text in the world. He was a Keynesian who refined and applied KEYNES's work to the post–World War II world, making a substantial and diverse body of contributions to economic theory. He received the Nobel Prize in Economics in 1970.

Samuelson, Victor E., U.S. Exxon company executive kidnapped on December 6, 1973, by guerrillas in Campana, Argentina, and later freed after Exxon paid a record $14.2 million ransom.

Sandinistas (Sandinist National Liberation Front), the governing party in Nicaragua, named after Nicaraguan guerilla martyr César Augusto SANDINO; it began as a Cuban-supported guerrilla group in the early 1960s, mounted a low-level guerrilla insurgency against the SOMOZA government that grew into the NICARAGUAN CIVIL WAR, and took power in July 1979, then fighting a long continuing war against the insurgent CONTRAS. The Sandinistas were defeated in the peaceful, democratic elections of February 1990.

Sandino, César Augusto (1893–1934), Nicaraguan guerrilla general, a Liberal leader during the Liberal-Conservative fighting of 1926–27, in which the U.S. intervened on the side of the Conservatives. His forces withdrew to the mountains after the truce of 1927, continuing to fight both U.S. Marine occupation forces and the government, until U.S. forces withdrew in 1933. He was murdered in 1934 by the forces of Anastasio SOMOZA, then head of the National Guard, while discussing peace terms. He became a martyr and guerrilla hero throughout Latin America; the Nicaraguan SANDINISTA movement was inspired by his example and took its name from his.

San Francisco Conference (April–June 1945), the large international meeting that established the UNITED NATIONS. The United Nations Charter was signed by the 51 original members of the organization on June 26, 1945, and became effective on October 24.

San Francisco earthquakes On April 18, 1906, a California San Andreas Fault earthquake leveled most of the city and its surrounding areas, causing an estimated 700–800 deaths and $300–400 million in property damage. On October 17, 1989, San Francisco's second major earthquake of the century, measuring 6.7 on the RICHTER scale, caused an estimated 62 deaths, 2,000 injuries, and several billion dollars of property damage, in an extended area centered at Hollister, 80 miles southeast of San Francisco. An estimated 42 died in the collapse of a section of the Nimitz Freeway; part of the Bay Bridge also collapsed.

Sanger, Margaret Higgins (1883–1966), U.S. nurse who became an advocate of birth control while handling maternity cases, many of them involving self-induced abortions, on Manhattan's Lower East Side. She founded the National Birth Control League in 1914, coining the term "birth control" in that year, and organized the first American BIRTH CONTROL CLINIC in 1916, in the Brownsville section of Brooklyn. She was arrested in 1917, her case generating a landmark New York State court decision that first made it possible for doctors to legally supply birth control advice to patients. In 1921 she founded the American Birth Control League, which later became the Planned Parenthood Federation; she was president of the International Planned Parenthood Federation.

São Tomé and Principe, until 1975, Portuguese colonies; the islands achieved independence on July 12, 1975, after several years of low-level insurgency, as part of general Portuguese colonial divestiture at that time.

Sarajevo, Bosnian city, now in Yugoslavia, in which Archduke FRANCIS FERDINAND, heir to the Austro-Hungarian throne, and his wife were assassinated on June 28, 1914, by Bosnian nationalists trained and equipped by the BLACK HAND, a Serbian secret society. Austria-Hungary soon went to war against Serbia; Russia declared war on Austria-Hungary; and within days both sets of great powers in Europe had begun World War I.

Sarikamish, Battle of (January 1–3, 1915), World War I battle in which invading Turks were defeated by Russian forces in the Caucasus, with approximately 30,000 dead and 30,000 other casualties, including desertions, out of an attacking force of 80,000.

Sarney Costa, José (1930–), Brazilian lawyer and political leader, who held a series of Maranhao state and national positions 1956–85 and was a Liberal Party leader when elected to the vice-presidency in January 1985. He became president on April 22, 1985, after the death of President-elect Tancredo de Almeida Neves, and was elected to the presidency in June 1988. His term expired in March 1990 after 5 years in office; succeeding Brazilian presidents were to serve 5-year terms.

Sarnoff, David (1891–1971), Russian-American engineer and executive, who rose at the Radio Corporation of America (RCA) to become its chairman, helping shape the development of RADIO and TELEVISION. Sarnoff came to public attention in 1912 when he was the first to pick up the *TITANIC*'s distress signals, reporting for 72 hours on the sinking and rescue efforts. By 1921 he was general manager of RCA, where he made the key early decisions to manufacture radio sets and to establish the National Broadcasting Company (NBC) as a programming arm. Later in the decade he hired Vladimir ZWORYKIN and gave him the funds to make the first practical, all-electronic television in 1932, backing the manufacture of black-and-white sets in the 1930s and color sets and color transmission in the late 1940s, at every step ahead of his competitors.

Sartre, Jean Paul (1905–80), French philosopher and writer who, during the early post–World War II period, popularized the concept of EXISTENTIALISM, a theory of personal freedom positing that life has no meaning beyond direct personal engagement and commitment based on personal experience, free of the limiting influences of society. He refused the 1964 Nobel Prize for Literature as an expression of his existential beliefs. In political matters Sartre was a person of the French Left, later moving toward Marxism, and attempting, without great success, to merge Marxism and existentialism. He was a lifetime companion of Simone de BEAUVOIR.

Satanic Verses, The (1988), a novel by Salman RUSHDIE that generated protests from many Moslems throughout the world, especially from Islamic fundamentalists, for its treatment of Mohammed, Abraham, Mohammed's wives, the Koran, and other aspects of the Islamic faith. In January 1989 the book was publicly burned in Bradford, England, and there were violent fundamentalist-inspired demonstrations in India and Pakistan on February 12 and 13, resulting in at least nine deaths. On February 14 Iranian Ayatollah Ruhollah KHOMEINI called for Rushdie's murder, offering a $1 million reward to his murderer. Subsequently, Khomeini, other Iranians, and several Islamic terrorist groups in other countries called for the murder of many connected with the publication of the book, including the employees of its publisher, Viking Penguin. Many Moslem countries subsequently banned the book, as did South Africa. Bookstore bombings occurred in several Western cities, including Los Angeles and London, and there were many threats of bombings elsewhere. But even in the Moslem world, where the book and its author were widely attacked, the Khomeini call to murder was little supported outside the fundamentalist groupings. And in the Western world, the reaction was immense. Viking Penguin stood firm and continued to publish and reprint the book. Great Britain condemned Khomeini's action and broke newly normalized relations with Iran. France, Canada, the Vatican, and a score of other countries, including the entire EUROPEAN COMMUNITY (EC), also condemned Khomeini and his associates, the EC also breaking relations with Iran. The U.S. government was not as forthcoming on the issue, but it opposed the call to murder. Some American bookstore chains attempted to back away from distribution of the book but were forced to reconsider after a powerful anticensorship public and publishing community reaction. The book became an international best-seller; its author remained in hiding.

satellite, artificial, human-made craft launched into orbit from Earth, the first being the U.S.S.R.'s SPUTNIK in 1957. Many artificial satellites have been used as research stations; workhorse satellite series like EXPLORER and PIONEER have been used, for example, to gather information on cosmic RADIATION. The American OSO (*O*rbiting *S*olar *O*bservatory) satellites recorded solar data and transmitted them on command from 1962. The first communications satellite (comsat), *ECHO*, launched in August 1960, used "passive" reflection to transmit sounds and pictures; it was replaced by "active" satellites that received, amplified, and transmitted RADIO, TELEVISION, and telephone signals worldwide in a system called INTELSAT (*I*nternational *Tele*communications *Sat*ellite Organization). The weather satellite TIROS (*T*elevision and *I*nfra-*R*ed *O*bservation *S*atellite), which first charted hurricanes in 1960, was superseded by more sophisticated meteorological satellite systems such as Nimbus. Navigational satellites helped ships and airplanes pinpoint their positions; others were dedicated to military surveillance, such as the Amerian MIDAS (*M*issile *D*efense *A*lert *S*ystem) and VELA HOTEL, aimed at detecting nuclear explosions.

Sato, Eisaku (1901–75), Japanese government official, brother of Nobusuki KISHI, who held transportation ministry positions before and during World War II and went on to hold several cabinet-level posts in the postwar period. He was prime minister 1964–72, a period in which Japan gained massive economic strength. During his tenure Japan also regained Okinawa, the rest of the southern Ryuku Islands, and the Bonin Islands. He was, with Sean MAC-BRIDE, co-recipient of the 1974 Nobel Peace Prize for his work on and signing of the NUCLEAR NON-PROLIFERATION TREATY of 1968.

Saturday night massacre (October 20, 1973), a key event in the WATERGATE scandal, in which U.S. president Richard M. NIXON attempted to resist exposure by the content of the Watergate tapes by firing Special Prosecutor Archibald COX and Deputy Attorney-General William Ruckelshaus; instead he entirely destroyed his own credibility and remaining public support.

Saturn, planetary target of space probes, most notably the U.S. *PIONEER 11* spacecraft, which flew by in 1979 and discovered previously unknown moons, and the U.S. *VOYAGER 1* and 2, which sent back striking pictures of Saturn's rings and found more moons.

satyagraha, the philosophy and form of nonviolent resistance developed by Mahatma GANDHI, which stressed civil disobedience without anger and with full acceptance of all penalties. It was first used by Gandhi during the South African Indian campaign for civil and political rights, 1906–13, and then used by him as a powerful weapon during the long campaign for Indian independence that ended in 1947.

Saudi Arabia (Kingdom of Saudi Arabia), nation established by the forces of Ibn SAUD during the 30-year period 1902–32. Before and during World War I he took control of several portions of Arabia formerly dominated by the Ottoman Empire; in the 1920s his forces defeated those of HUSSEIN Ibn Ali; and in the 1930s he consolidated power, formally establishing the Saudi Arabian kingdom on September 23, 1932.

Savannah River nuclear plant, the U.S. nuclear weapons fuel production plant at Savannah River, South Carolina, that—it was disclosed in October 1988—had for 31 years experienced a series of very substantial problems endangering the health and safety of its employees and of hundreds of thousands in the surrounding area. These included fuel rod and potential core meltdowns, RADIATION exposures, and widespread plant contamination. A congressional committee hearing indicated that the U.S. government had secretly and knowingly concealed these problems, although the plant's operator, E. I. Dupont de Nemours & Co, had repeatedly reported problems and incidents as they occurred. It appeared to be part of a pattern of secrecy and breakdown throughout the U.S. nuclear weapons production system.

Savimbi, Jonas (1934–   ), Angolan nationalist, founder of the NATIONAL UNION FOR THE TOTAL INDEPENDENCE OF ANGOLA (UNITA) in 1966 and leader of UNITA through the 1961–74 ANGOLAN WAR OF INDEPENDENCE and the long civil war that followed.

savings and loan bailouts, major U.S. government expenditures aimed at meeting government deposit guarantees and preserving financial stability, as hundreds of savings and loan associations were found to be insolvent. Tens of billions of dollars had been spent by early 1990; total government costs in the $100–200 billion range were anticipated.

Say it ain't so, Joe, the lament of baseball fans in 1919 after the BLACK SOX SCANDAL broke, directed at the great Chicago White Sox outfielder "Shoeless Joe" Jackson, since then a taunt directed at those accused of betraying the trust of others.

Scalia, Antonin (1936–   ), U.S. lawyer, law professor 1967–74 and 1977–82; assistant attorney general in the Justice Department Office of Legal Counsel, 1973–77; and U.S. Court of Appeals judge, 1982–86. He was appointed an associate justice of the Supreme Court by President Ronald REAGAN in 1986, the youngest and thought to be one of the most conservative members of the Court.

Scarsdale Diet murder (March 10, 1980), the murder of Dr. Herman Tarnower, the cardiologist who had developed the Scarsdale Diet, by Virginia private school headmistress Jean Harris in a lovers' quarrel. It was followed by one of the most highly publicized trials of the time, and the imprisonment of Harris for second-degree murder.

Schacht, Hjalmar Horace Greeley (1877–1970), American-born German banker who became a key financial planner and head of the Reichsbank (1923–29) during the WEIMAR REPUBLIC period. He was Nazi Reichsbank president, 1933–39, and a Nazi cabinet minister, 1934–37. However, he opposed HITLER's war plans and was sent to DACHAU concentration camp in 1944. He was accused of war crimes but acquitted at the NUREMBERG TRIALS in 1946; released by the German courts in 1946, he became a banker again in West Germany.

Schecter Poultry Corporation v. United States (1935), a landmark U.S. Supreme Court decision invalidating the NATIONAL INDUSTRIAL RECOVERY ACT (NIRA), a major piece of NEW DEAL legislation.

Schenck v. United States (1919), a landmark U.S. Supreme Court decision, affirming the conviction of a socialist antiwar protester under the Sedition Act for sending out antiwar leaflets. Justice Oliver Wendell HOLMES enunciated the "clear and present danger" doctrine. The unanimous Court decision was part of the post–World War I RED SCARE that also generated the PALMER RAIDS.

Schick test, skin test developed in 1913 by Hungarian-American physician Béla Schick to indicate susceptibility to diphtheria, a widespread and much-feared childhood disease in the days before ANTIBIOTICS. If no redness or swelling appeared on the skin at the site of a small injection of diphtheria toxin, a child was known to be immune and did not have take the full injection, which could have serious side effects.

Schirach, Baldur von (1907–74), an early Nazi who became a youth activist and was head of the Hitler Youth organization from 1933. He was convicted of war crimes at the NUREMBERG TRIALS and imprisoned for 20 years.

Schleicher, Kurt von (1882–1934), German army officer who represented army interests throughout the WEIMAR REPUBLIC period and was briefly German chancellor before HITLER took power. He was killed by the Nazis on June 30, 1934, during the BLOOD PURGE.

Schlieffen Plan, the main German strategic plan for World War I, developed by General Alfred von Schlieffen; it envisaged a two-front war in which the main body of German army would first defeat France, while small forces engaged in a holding action against Russia, and then turn toward the Russians. The Germans followed the plan but with ultimately disastrous modifications, in their attempt to pull the French army forward and then drive around it to the sea through Belgium and the Netherlands in 1914.

Schmidt, Helmut Heinrich Waldemar (1918-   ), West German political leader who served in the German army during World War II, became active in the Social Democratic party in 1946, and entered the federal parliament in 1953. He then held a succession of party and administrative positions, becoming defense minister, 1969–72, and finance minister, 1972–74; he succeeded Willy BRANDT as chancellor, 1974–82. As chancellor he continued Brandt's policies of DETENTE with the Soviet bloc to some extent, supported nuclear armament negotiations and full development of the EUROPEAN COMMUNITY, and moved somewhat closer to the United States in military matters.

Schneiderman, Rose (1882–1972), U.S. labor leader, an early organizer of the International Ladies Garment Workers Union (ILGWU) and the Women's Trade Union League. She was a labor adviser to President Franklin D. ROOSEVELT during the GREAT DEPRESSION.

Schrank, John N. (1876–1943), would-be assassin who shot and wounded Theodore

ROOSEVELT in Milwaukee, Wisconsin, on October 14, 1912. Roosevelt was seriously wounded; Schrank was immediately captured, declared insane, and institutionalized for the rest of his life.

Schrödinger, Erwin (1887–1961), Austrian physicist who, inspired by Louis DE BROGLIE's work on WAVE-PARTICLE DUALITY, developed the Schrödinger wave equation in 1926 to describe the wavelike behavior of fundamental particles; his work formed part of the mathematical underpinning for QUANTUM THEORY. He shared the 1933 Nobel Prize for Physics with Paul DIRAC, that same year leaving Berlin and later Austria in opposition to the Nazis. He worked at the Dublin Institute for Advanced Studies with Dirac, 1940–56. His 1944 work, *What Is Life?*, outlined how a set of chemical codes might determine genetic inheritance, inspiring the work of James WATSON and Francis CRICK in discovering the structure of DNA.

Schuman Plan, a 1950 proposal by French foreign minister Robert Schuman to establish a European common market for coal and steel, which was the inspiration for the formation of the EUROPEAN COAL AND STEEL COMMUNITY (ECSC) and later the EUROPEAN ECONOMIC COMMUNITY (EEC), or COMMON MARKET, and the EUROPEAN ATOMIC ENERGY COMMUNITY (EURATOM), the three component parts of the EUROPEAN COMMUNITY (EC).

Schuschnigg, Kurt von (1897–1977), Austrian lawyer and politican who was a member of the cabinet of Engelbert DOLLFUSS in 1932 and became chancellor after the assassination of Dollfuss in 1934. Earlier in 1934 Schuschnigg had joined Dollfuss in creating the Austrian dictatorship, and in the forcible repression of the protests that followed. As chancellor he continued the dictatorship, attempted and failed to resist German annexation, and stepped down. He was later jailed by the Germans; after the war he taught in the United States.

Schwab, Charles Michael (1862–1939), U.S. steel industry executive who joined the Carnegie Steel Company as a laborer, be-

came its president in 1897, was chief negotiator of the Carnegie sale to J. P. MORGAN's new United States Steel Company in 1901 and was first president of the new company, then the largest industrial company in the world. Starting in 1903, he developed his own Bethlehem Steel Company into the second largest U.S. steel company and ultimately became a major industrialist, though financial reverses later in his life caused him to lose his fortune.

Schweitzer, Albert (1875–1965), German physician, philosopher, writer, and musician, who left his career as a renowned organist in 1913, became a medical missionary, and spent most of his long life operating his hospital and leper colony at Lambaréné, in Gabon. He was awarded the 1952 Nobel Peace Prize for his work and became one of the most highly regarded humanitarians of his time.

Schwerner, Michael, young civil rights worker who, with James CHENEY and Andrew GOODMAN, was murdered in Neshoba County, Mississippi, in June 1964, in the MISSISSIPPI CIVIL RIGHTS MURDERS.

SCLC, the initials of the SOUTHERN CHRISTIAN LEADERSHIP CONFERENCE, a leading organization of the CIVIL RIGHTS MOVEMENT of the 1960s.

Scopes trial, popularly called the "monkey trial," in which biology teacher John T. Scopes of Dayton, Tennessee, was tried for teaching evolution rather than the literal interpretation of the Bible prescribed by Tennessee law. The 1925 trial attracted worldwide media attention; one of the reporters present was H. L. Mencken. Clarence DARROW led the Scopes defense, and William Jennings BRYAN led the prosecution. Although Bryan won a minor conviction and fine, later reversed by a higher court, he was much overmatched by Darrow in the courtroom and was treated unmercifully by the media. Bryan soon became ill, and died 5 days after the trial. The Tennessee law in question was repealed in 1967, though supporters of CREATIONISM continued to fight the teaching of evolution in the schools. The 1960 film *Inherit the Wind* was a fictional re-creation of the Scopes trial.

Scorpion sinking (May 21, 1968), the disappearance of the U.S. nuclear submarine *Scorpion* in the Atlantic, with the loss of its entire crew of 99. The last message from the ship was information about its position, about 250 miles off the Azores, without any trouble report.

Scott, Robert Falcon (1868–1912), British explorer who led the second party to reach the SOUTH POLE. After 1901–04 explorations in the Antarctic with the British Royal Navy, he set out for the South Pole in 1910, reaching it on January 17, 1912, only to find that Roald AMUNDSEN had been there before him, on December 14, 1911. On their return to camp Scott and his party died in a blizzard; their remains and records were found months later.

Scottsboro case, conviction of nine young Black men for allegedly raping two young White women aboard a freight train in Alabama in March 1931. Eight were sentenced to death, and one, a 13-year-old, to life imprisonment—all on tainted evidence, by a demonstrably prejudiced judge and jury in an atmosphere that precluded the possibility of a fair trial, and without adequate counsel. A major civil rights protest ensued, and attorney Samuel S. Liebowitz became lawyer for the defendants. The Supreme Court reversed two successive convictions but ultimately let five convictions stand, with long jail sentences. All but Haywood Patterson were ultimately paroled; he escaped from jail in 1948, was later imprisoned for another crime, and died in jail in 1952. Defendant Clarence Willie Norris, who had violated the terms of his parole by leaving Alabama in 1946, was pardoned in 1977.

Scowcroft, Brent (1925–   ), U.S. Air Force Officer, who held a series of staff and teaching positions, 1947–68; moved into staff national security positions in the defense department, 1968–71; and became a military aide to president Richard M. NIXON, 1971–72. In 1972 he became White House assistant to the president for national security affairs, under Henry KISSINGER, and was National Security Council head during the FORD administration, continuing to work on arms control matters during the CARTER administration. In 1986 he was appointed to the TOWER COMMISSION and joined in its sharp criticism of REAGAN administration involvement in the IRAN–CONTRA AFFAIR. On November 23, 1988, Scowcroft was named national security advisor by President-elect George BUSH.

scuba (**s**elf-**c**ontained **u**nderwater **b**reathing **a**pparatus), underwater breathing apparatus, formally called the Aqualung, developed in 1943 by Jacques COUSTEAU and Émil Gagnan.

SDI, the initials of the U.S. STRATEGIC DEFENSE INITIATIVE (Star Wars).

SDS, popular shorthand for STUDENTS FOR A DEMOCRATIC SOCIETY, by which that organization, founded in 1960, is best known.

Seabed Non-nuclearization Treaty (1971), a U.S.–U.S.S.R. agreement not to place nuclear weapons on or under the ocean floor.

Seaborg, Glenn Theodore (1912–   ), U.S. nuclear chemist who in 1940, with Edwin M. McMillan, first discovered the element PLUTONIUM. During World War II he worked with the MANHATTAN PROJECT, producing the plutonium used in the first ATOMIC BOMB, tested at ALAMOGORDO, New Mexico, in July 1945, and in the second atomic bomb used in warfare, dropped on NAGASAKI, Japan, in August 1945. After the war he resumed his research on elements, discovering eight more by bombarding URANIUM in a CYCLOTRON, work for which he shared with McMillan the 1951 Nobel Prize for Chemistry. A strong proponent of NUCLEAR ENERGY, Seaborg was later chairman of the U.S. ATOMIC ENERGY COMMISSION (AEC).

Seale, Bobby (1937–1989), U.S. Black activist of the 1960s, a founder of the BLACK PANTHER PARTY in 1966.

Sea Lion, Operation, the German code name for the plan to invade Britain in 1940, which required air supremacy and the neutralization of the British navy by the German air force, followed by a large-scale amphibious invasion of Britain. It was frustrated by the victory of the British air force in the Battle of BRITAIN, which made the rest impossible.

SEATO, the initials of the SOUTHEAST ASIA TREATY ORGANIZATION.

Second Arab-Israeli War (October 29–November 6, 1956), an alternate name for the SINAI–SUEZ WAR.

Second Balkan War (1913), the second of the two BALKAN WARS, in which Bulgaria was defeated by Serbia, Greece, Rumania, and Turkey; part of the run-up to World War I.

Second International, the international organization of the world's socialist parties, from its foundation in 1889 until its split over participation in World War I. Before the war it had pledged itself to call on its members not to participate, should a war come; but when war came in 1914, the great majority of the member parties and unions chose to support the war efforts of their countries. It was split irrevocably in 1919 when LENIN organized the COMMUNIST INTERNATIONAL and was succeeded first by the Labor and Socialist International of the interwar period and then by the Socialist International of the postwar period, which is still in being.

Second Vatican Council, the formal title of VATICAN II, the most important Catholic Church meeting of the 20th century and probably of the preceding several centuries as well.

Second World War (1939–45), alternate name for WORLD WAR II.

Secord, Richard V., retired U.S. general who, with his partner, Albert HAKIM, became a figure in the IRAN–CONTRA AFFAIR, allegedly being deeply involved in the arms-for-hostages and Nicaraguan CONTRA arms supply arrangements. In March 1988 he was indicted in connection with the scandal, in May 1989 was indicted on several other related charges, and early in 1990 settled outstanding charges with minor penalties.

Secret Army Organization (OAS), Algerian French terrorist organization, led by general Raoul SALAN, which from April 1961 mounted a substantial series of terrorist attacks against Algerian Moslems, usually with the tacit approval of French army forces in the region. Simultaneously, the OAS developed a terrorist campaign against the French government, aiming to reverse DE GAULLE's Algerian independence policy. Both terrorist campaigns failed; Salan was sentenced to life imprisonment but was released during the 1968 amnesty.

Securities and Exchange Commission (SEC), a U.S. NEW DEAL agency established by the securities laws of 1933 and 1934, which together provided for registration of the stock exchanges and regulation of new securities issues. The legislation gave the SEC broad regulatory powers, in an attempt to curb the manipulative practices that had helped lead to the CRASH of 1929. Its first chairman was Joseph P. KENNEDY; its second, William O. DOUGLAS. Its jurisdiction was later extended, but by the 1980s it was severely limited, in the greatly altered worldwide financial industry that had by then emerged.

Sedition Act (1918), U. S. World War I law that, together with the Espionage Act of 1917, prohibited a wide range of antiwar activities, including free speech. It was used as a witchhunting tool, primarily against socialists and other radicals, and also to bar from the mails and thereby damage or destroy antiwar foreign language and radical periodicals. More than 1,500 people were prosecuted under these laws; one of them was Socialist leader Eugene V. DEBS, imprisoned for an antiwar speech and jailed for 32 months of a 10-year sentence until pardoned by President Warren G. HARDING. In a mass trial of 100 leaders of the INDUSTRIAL WORKERS OF THE WORLD (IWW) all were found guilty; 15 were sentenced to 20-year prison terms, 35 to 10-year terms, and 50 to shorter terms, all with heavy fines.

Selma marches (March 1965), two civil rights marches from Selma to Mongomery, the state capital of Alabama, both led by Martin Luther KING, JR.. On March 7 some 500 marchers were attacked, beaten, and gassed by Alabama state troopers in an action condemned by civil rights activists and sympathizers throughout the United States, who then traveled to Selma in considerable numbers to join in subsequent marches. On March 9 a much larger march was stopped by court order. On that day civil rights activist and Boston Unitarian minister James REEB was beaten by racists in Selma; he died on March 11. On March 17 a court-permitted Selma-to-Montgomery march began, led by King and Ralph BUNCHE; on March 21 it was completed as a march and demonstration of 25,000 in Montgomery, in which most of the leading Black figures and many of the leading white leaders of the time participated.

Semple, Ellen Churchill (1863–1932), U.S. geographer and influential academic, who focused on the ways in which the land and environment help shape human settlements and culture, as in her *Geography of the Mediterranean Region: Its Relation to Ancient History* (1931).

Sendero Luminoso, alternate name for the Peruvian SHINING PATH guerrilla army.

Senegal (Republic of Senegal), until 1960 a region under French control, as a colony from 1895. It was granted internal autonomy in 1958, joined Mali in the Federation of Mali in 1959, became independent as part of the federation on June 20, 1960, and established itself as a separate nation on September 5, 1960. The major leader of the Senegalese independence movement was poet Léopold SENGHOR, who became first president of the new country, remaining in the presidency until 1980. On February 1, 1982, Senegal joined Gambia in the confederation of SENEGAMBIA.

Senegambia (Confederation of Senegambia), the February 1, 1982, merger of the neighboring states of SENEGAL and much smaller GAMBIA, which by the late 1980s had not actually been realized.

Senghor, Léopold Sédar (1906–   ), Senegalese poet, Africanist, Socialist, and political leader, who was a pioneer African poet in the 1930s and became leader of the Senegalese national movement after World War II. Senghor served in the French national assembly 1946–58, founded the Senegalese Progressive Union in 1949, and became president of the Repubic of Senegal in August 1960. He was president for 20 years, stepping down voluntarily in 1980 after his election to a fourth 5-year term in 1978. During his presidency Senegal was nonaligned but also continued to be closely associated with France, leaning west rather than east. After an attempted opposition coup in 1962 Senghor presided over a one-party state. He moved toward limited democracy during the 1970s, a movement continued by his successors during the early 1980s, but with increasing hesitation as economic and political problems developed.

Separate educational facilities are inherently unequal, judgment by U.S. Supreme Court Chief Justice Earl WARREN in his landmark opinion (1954) on school desegregation, in the case of *BROWN V. BOARD OF EDUCATION OF TOPEKA.*

Serbia, an independent kingdom at the beginning of the 20th century; Serbian nationalism and opposition to Austria helped generate the recurrent Balkan crises leading to both the first and second BALKAN WARS, and to the June 1914 assassinations of Austrian Archduke Francis Ferdinand and his wife at SARAJEVO that precipitated World War I. Serbia became part of Yugoslavia after World War I, was occupied by German troops during World War II, and became part of Yugoslavia again after World War II.

Serbia, Fall of (autumn 1915), successful World War I invasion of Serbia by German, Austrian, and Bulgarian forces, who attacked on October 6, 1915, smashed the much smaller Serbian army, and drove to the Adriatic, occupying Serbia and then Montenegro.

Sessions, William Steele (1930–), U.S. lawyer, in the Justice Department 1969–71, West Texas U.S. attorney 1971–74, and federal district judge in Texas 1974–87. In November 1987 he became director of the FEDERAL BUREAU OF INVESTIGATION (FBI).

SETI (search for extraterrestrial intelligence), project that involved scanning the sky with RADIO telescopes for messages from outer space and sending messages to other possible beings in the universe. The project centered in the 1970s at Arecibo, Puerto Rico, and after that was conducted at several international sites, especially from 1983.

Sevastopol, Battles of (June–July 1942), World War II engagements in the Crimea as German forces resumed their southern offensive in the spring of 1942. By early June they besieged Sevastopol, which fell on July 2, 1942, with heavy Soviet losses. The city was retaken by Soviet forces in May 1944, most of its German garrison being evacuated by sea.

Seveso pesticide disaster, 1976 accident at a Seveso, Italy, pesticide plant when a cloud of toxic gas, heavily laden with DIOXIN, was spilled over the region, killing many animals but—at least immediately—no humans, though all were moved from the area.

sex change, use of HORMONES and operations to change one's sex, one of the first to have done so being Christine (né George) JORGENSON in 1952.

Seychelles (Republic of Seychelles), until 1976 a British colony, with some internal autonomy since 1967. It became an independent state and COMMONWEALTH member on June 29, 1976, and a one-party state in 1977, after the coup that brought President France Albert Rene to power.

Shackleton, Ernest Henry (1874–1922), British explorer who made four expeditions to the Antarctic. Forced by sickness to leave the first, 1901–04, with Robert SCOTT, he returned (1907–1909) to discover Mt. Erebus and approach to within 100 miles of the SOUTH POLE. In 1915, after his ship was

crushed by ice, he led a dramatic 800-mile journey to a remote whaling station on South Georgia Island, where on a later trip he died and was buried.

Shamir, Yitzhak (Yitzhak Yzernitzsky; 1915–), Polish-Israeli Zionist, who emigrated to Israel at the age of 20, there joining the terrorist IRGUN ZVAI LEUMI in 1937. He left the Irgun for the even more terrorist-oriented STERN GANG in 1940, became Stern Gang chief of operations in 1942, and in that capacity directed a substantial number of terrorist operations. He was an Israeli intelligence agent (1955–65), became a leader of the HERUT party (1970), was foreign minister in the BEGIN government (1980–83), and succeeded Begin as prime minister (1983–84). In 1984 he became coalition government foreign minister and from 1986 was Israeli prime minister.

Shanghai, Battle of (1932), the first Battle of Shanghai (January 28–March 8, 1932), which followed the MUKDEN INCIDENT, the Japanese annexation of Manchuria, and the China-wide boycotts of Japanese goods that followed. A substantial Japanese punitive expedition landed in Shanghai and was held on its beachheads by the Chinese 19th Route Army until breaking through Chinese positions late in February. Defeated, the Chinese called off their anti-Japanese boycotts, and the Japanese army withdrew.

Shanghai, Battle of (1937), the second Battle of Shanghai (August 8–November 8, 1937), one of the major early battles of the SINO–JAPANESE WAR. Invading Japanese troops were once again held by the Chinese in heavy fighting until heavy reinforcements and new landings forced the Chinese to retreat.

Shanghai Massacre (April 12, 1927), an attack by China's Nationalist forces led by CHIANG KAI-SHEK on Communist militia and labor organizations in Shanghai; 5,000–6,000 of these former allies were executed by Chiang's forces, as were Communists in several other cities, signaling the real beginning of the 22-year-long CHINESE CIVIL WAR. The event is graphically described, from the Communist point of view, in André Malraux's novel, *Man's Fate*, in which the central character is modeled after ZHOU ENLAI, who directed Communist forces in Shanghai at the time.

Shantung Question, the dispute over those provisions of the Treaty of VERSAILLES granting Germany's former concessions in the northeastern province of Shantung to Japan. The concessions aroused great opposition in China, generating the demonstrations of the MAY 4TH MOVEMENT, which played a major role in the further development of Chinese republican and revolutionary movements.

Shapiro v. *Thompson* (1969), a landmark U.S. Supreme Court decision striking down state residency requirements regarding welfare recipients, which made it possible for those qualifying for welfare under the laws of any jurisdiction to move there and receive welfare payments.

Shapley, Harlow (1885–1972), U.S. astronomer working at the Harvard Observatory who in 1918 described the shape of the Milky Way, placing the Earth for the first time on the fringes of the galaxy. He was also noted for his work on Cepheid variables, showing that they are pulsating stars, and for his popular writings, such as *The View from a Distant Star* (1964).

Sharon, Ariel (1928–   ), Israeli officer, who saw service during the ISRAELI WAR OF INDEPENDENCE (FIRST ARAB–ISRAELI WAR) in 1948, conducted antiguerrilla operations during the mid-1950s, and was a paratroop commander during the SINAI–SUEZ WAR (SECOND ARAB–ISRAELI WAR). He commanded an armored divison during the SIX-DAY WAR (THIRD ARAB–ISRAELI WAR) of 1967 and again commanded an armored divison during the YOM KIPPUR WAR (FOURTH ARAB–ISRAELI WAR; OCTOBER WAR) of 1973. He became defense minister in 1981, was deeply involved in every major aspect of the 1982 Israeli invasion of Lebanon, and was forced to resign as defense minister after the SABRA AND SHATILLA

MASSACRES, though remaining in the Israeli cabinet.

Sharpeville massacre (March 21, 1960), killing of 67 people and wounding of approximately 200 more when South African police opened fire on unarmed demonstrators at Sharpeville, near Johannesburg. Subsequent protest demonstrations were violently repressed, and the government declared a countrywide state of emergency. The massacre generated worldwide condemnation and within a year had led to South Africa's withdrawal from the COMMONWEALTH. The event also helped push the AFRICAN NATIONAL CONGRESS away from its traditional nonviolent commitment and toward armed action, helping initiate the long guerrilla war that followed, part of the ongoing destruction of South African society.

Shastri, Lal Bahadur (1904–66), Indian CONGRESS PARTY activist, who became general secretary of the party in 1951, served in Jawaharlal NEHRU'S cabinet during the 1950s and early 1960s, and succeeded Nehru as prime minister 1964–66. He died while negotiating the Tashkent peace talks that ended the INDIA–PAKISTAN WAR OF 1965.

Shaw, George Bernard (1856–1950), major literary and intellectual figure, who, with Beatrice WEBB and Sidney WEBB, provided much of the ideological focus for British socialism through their work in the FABIAN SOCIETY. Many of his plays, such as *Pygmalion* (1913), *Heartbreak House* (1920), *Major Barbara* (1905), and *Misalliance* (1910), became 20th century classics.

Shcharansky, Anatoly (1948–   ), Soviet mathematician, who became a leading Jewish dissident during the 1970s. He was refused permission to leave the country, imprisoned in 1977 on false espionage charges, and in 1986 released in a Soviet–American swap of alleged spies; he then emigrated to Israel.

Sheean, James Vincent (1899–1975), U.S. journalist, whose reportage from Africa and Eurasia during the interwar period illuminated some of the major continuing stories and events of the century. In the 1920s he reported on the RIF WAR, the early stages of the long Arab–Israeli conflict in what was then Palestine, on the beginning of the long CHINESE CIVIL WAR, and on Mussolini's MARCH ON ROME. In the 1930s he reported on the SPANISH CIVIL WAR and the rise of fascism and in the 1940s on the assassination of Mohandas K. GANDHI.

Sheffield soccer stadium disaster (April 15, 1989), a panic causing 94 deaths and at least 169 injuries, as thousands of football fans pushed into enclosed stands at Hillsboro, England, near Sheffield; many were crushed against steel crowd-control fences. It was the worst sports disaster in British history.

Shepard, Alan Bartlett, Jr. (1923–   ), the first U.S. astronaut, who made a 15-minute suborbital flight in the MERCURY spacecraft *Freedom 7* on May 5, 1961, reaching a height of 116 miles.

Sheppard murder (July 4, 1954), the Cleveland, Ohio, murder of Marilyn Sheppard, whose husband, osteopath Samuel Sheppard, was 3 weeks later charged with the murder while a public campaign for his conviction was being conducted in the press. His trial attracted national attention; he was convicted and sentenced to life imprisonment, protesting his innocence. In 1964 he succeeded in reopening the case and was granted a new trial after an appeal that went to the U.S. Supreme Court, which agreed that his original trial had been conducted in an atmosphere that prevented a fair trial. He was acquitted on appeal; the murder was never solved.

Sherman, James Schoolcraft (1855–1912), U.S. lawyer and Republican congressman from New York (1887–1891, 1893–1909) who was Willam Howard TAFT'S vice-president for one term (1909–12); he died while running for reelection in what became the losing Taft candidacy of 1912.

Shevardnadze, Eduard Amvroslyevich (1928–   ), Soviet Communist party official, who first drew national attention in 1972 when he replaced the Georgian party leader, Vasilii Mzhavanadze, after leading a successful anticorruption campaign. He became a member of his party's Central Committee in 1976, and was Mikhail GORBACHEV'S surprise choice to replace Andrei GROMYKO as foreign minister in 1985, initiating a new, seemingly far more relaxed era in Soviet foreign policy.

Shigumetsu, Mamoru (1887–1957), Japanese lawyer and diplomat who was foreign minister from 1943 to 1945 with a brief break in mid-1945. He was a signatory to the Japanese surrender on the battleship *Missouri*, in Tokyo harbor, on September 2, 1945. He was later convicted of war crimes and imprisoned for 7 years. Paroled in 1950, he reentered the Japanese foreign office in 1954.

Shining Path (Luminous Path; Sendero Luminoso), Peruvian Maoist guerrilla army, from 1980 fighting mainly in southern Peru, though engaged in some bombings at Lima; although numbering less than 5,000, an increasingly serious threat to the government in the late 1980s.

Shirer, William Lawrence (1904–   ), U.S. journalist and broadcaster, who reported from Europe during the interwar period; his reportage and late-1930s CBS RADIO broadcasts helped to expose the nature and threat of the Nazi movement. His definitive *Rise and Fall of the Third Reich* (1960) built on his early experience.

Shockley, William Bradford (1910–1989), English-American physicist who, with John Bardeen and Walter Houser Brattain, developed the TRANSISTOR and laid the basis for modern solid-state ELECTRONICS, winning them the 1956 Nobel Prize for Physics. Shockley caused considerable controversy in later decades with his outspoken belief in the genetic inferiority of Blacks.

shock treatment, use of electrical stimulation or drugs to cause temporary loss of consciousness in mental patients. Vienna psychiatrist Manfred Sakel first used deliberately induced INSULIN shock to treat patients in 1933. Four years later Italian physicians Ugo Cerlutti and Lucio Bini developed the technique of administering controlled electrical shocks to mental patients, in what was called electroconvulsive therapy (ECT). Both kinds of techniques were widely used over the next two decades, although serious questions were raised about their long-term aftereffects. Their use declined only after the development of TRANQUILIZERS in the mid-1950s.

Shriver, Robert Sargent (1915–   ), U.S. editor and writer, a brother-in-law of John F. KENNEDY, who worked in Kennedy's 1960 presidential campaign and became first director of the PEACE CORPS (1961–66), first director of the Office of Economic Opportunity (1964), and ambassador to France (1968–70). In 1972 he replaced Senator Thomas EAGLETON as the Democratic vice-presidential candidate after Eagleton withdrew from the race. He unsuccessfully sought the Democratic presidential nomination in 1980 and later became a television newscaster.

Shroud of Turin, cloth in a Turin, Italy, church long believed by some to have covered the body of Jesus Christ after his crucifixion, but shown in 1988, by RADIOCARBON DATING, to have been made during the 13th century.

Shultz, George Pratt (1920–   ), U.S. economist active in industrial relations, who was labor secretary (1969–70), Office of Management and Budget director (1970–72), treasury secretary (1972–74), economic adviser to presidents EISENHOWER and REAGAN, and secretary of state (1982–89), in that post pursuing Reagan adminstration foreign policy objectives. He entirely disavowed any knowledge of the IRAN–CONTRA AFFAIR, staying on to play a key role in developing the series of REAGAN–GORBACHEV SUMMIT meetings that led to the INF TREATY, the Soviet withdrawal from Afghanistan, the settlement of several major regional conflicts, and the end of the COLD WAR.

shuttle bombing, from late June 1943, the World War II bombing of Axis targets in Europe by Allied planes from Britain, which flew on to North Africa, there refueling and often bombing European targets again on the way home. In June 1944 the Allies organized shuttle bombing runs from Britain to the Soviet Union and back.

shuttle diplomacy, a media description of the personal diplomacy of U.S. secretary of state Henry KISSINGER, as he flew back and forth between the several parties in the Middle East, trying to defuse recurrent crises and build a basis for a lasting peace in the area. It was later used quite aptly to describe that general kind of diplomatic approach.

Siad Barre, Mohammed (1920–   ), Somali officer, who became armed forces commander in chief in 1966, and led a coup that installed him as Somali ruler in 1969. As president he led a one-party, totalitarian socialist state, which largely failed to develop his arid, very poor country. Until the late 1970s Siad Barre was closely allied with the Soviet Union. But after the Somali invasion of the Ogaden desert region in 1977 had generated the lost SOMALI–ETHOPIAN WAR of 1977–78, in which Soviet and Cuban forces helped Ethiopia to defeat his forces, Siad Barre turned to the United States for arms and other support.

Sian Incident (December 12–25, 1936), the detention of CHIANG KAI-SHEK by his own forces, when he went to Sian (now Xian) to personally lead an anti-Communist offensive. General CHANG HSUEH-LIANG insisted that Chiang negotiate with the Communists to establish a united front against the Japanese; Chiang did negotiate with ZHOU ENLAI, a truce resulted, and Chiang was released. Chang left Sian with Chiang, was arrested, and spent the next quarter century under house arrest, on the mainland and later on Taiwan.

Sicily, Invasion of (July 9–August 17, 1943), World War II landings on the Sicilian southern coast, on July 9, by seaborne Allied forces led by generals PATTON and MONTGOMERY, who held their beachheads and within a few days were moving inland. By the end of July, they were moving north toward Messina, after taking western Sicily. Italian and German troop evacuations to the mainland soon began; the Allies took Messina on August 17, ending the Sicilian campaign.

sick man of Europe, a phrase describing the OTTOMAN EMPIRE, which had been weakening throughout the 19th century, and was in terminal condition during the run-up to World War I.

Siegfried Line (Westwall), World War II line of German fortifications on the French-German border, built in the 1930s. It was not tested during the 1939–40 PHONY WAR period on the WESTERN FRONT, but proved a significant obstacle to ALLIED troops moving westward toward Germany in 1944–45.

Sierra Leone (Republic of Sierra Leone), until 1961 a British colony, becoming an independent state and COMMONWEALTH member on April 27, 1961.

Sihanouk, Norodom (1922–   ), Cambodian leader, king of Cambodia 1941–55, who helped turn his country into a constitutional monarchy after World War II. He led his country to independence in 1953, abdicated in 1955 to become prime minister, and was elected head of state in 1960. From 1959, when civil war came to Vietnam, he attempted to be neutral, although he did not oppose the building of the HO CHI MINH TRAIL through his country by the North Vietnamese. He was overthrown in 1970 in a coup led by LON NOL, then setting up a Cambodian government-in-exile in Peking. After the victory of the Chinese-backed KHMER ROUGE he was Cambodian head of state again for a year; he then resigned and left political life, returning to Cambodian politics in the late 1980s.

Sikorsky, Igor Ivan (1889–1972), Russian-American aeronautical engineer, who developed the modern HELICOPTER. Inspired by Leonardo Da Vinci's ideas, Sikorsky had by age 20 built his first helicopter. Lacking the resources to develop it properly, in 1911 he turned to designing and flying AIRPLANES, before emigrating during the Russian Revolution. In the United States from 1919, he

founded his own aircraft firm in 1923, designing both commercial and military planes, most notably the famous CLIPPERS. In 1939 Sikorsky returned to his first love and developed a truly practical helicopter; that and his later models set the standard for such craft in the late 20th century.

Silent Spring, Rachel CARSON's cautionary work (1962), describing a future in which chemicals, especially pesticides, and pollution in general choke out the Earth's diversity of life; it helped lay the basis for development of worldwide environmental concern and GREEN MOVEMENTS.

Silkwood, Karen Gay (1946–74), U.S. atomic worker, who collected evidence of health and safety hazards while working at a Kerr-McGee's PLUTONIUM production plant in Oklahoma; she died in an automobile accident on her way to meet a *New York Times* reporter and a union official. Authorities ruled her death accidental; her notes were never found, and there were widespread, though unproven, allegations that she had been murdered. A long series of court cases followed; the Kerr-McGee Corporation eventually settled the safety violations claims of her estate out-of-court. Meryl Streep played Karen Silkwood in the movie *Silkwood* (1983).

Simpson, Wallis Warfield (1896–1986), the American woman for whom EDWARD VIII gave up the British throne during the ABDICATION CRISIS of 1936, when his proposed marriage to her proved unacceptable to the main British decision makers of the time, led by prime minister Stanley BALDWIN. Edward and Wallis then became the duke and duchess of Windsor.

Sinai–Suez War (Second Arab–Israeli War, October 29–November 6, 1956), a war that erupted after Egyptian president Gamal Abdel NASSER nationalized the Suez Canal, partly because of the U.S. and British withdrawal of funds for construction of the ASWAN HIGH DAM, precipitating the SUEZ CRISIS. Britain and France decided to seize the canal, and Israel agreed to attack Egypt, providing a rationale for British-French military action. As planned, Israeli paratroops and armor attacked on October 29. A British-French ultimatum was issued, and British-French seaborne invasion forces left Malta on October 30. Anglo-French bombing of the canal area began on October 31, and paratroops attacked Port Said on November 5; seaborne forces began landings at Port Said on November 6. Meanwhile, Israeli troops attacked withdrawing Egyptian troops in the Sinai, taking Sharm el-Sheikh on November 5. However, the United States opposed the invasion and forced withdrawal of the forces of all three invading countries. The disputed Suez Canal area was occupied by a UNITED NATIONS peacekeeping force until 1967, shortly before the outbreak of the SIX-DAY WAR (THIRD ARAB–ISRAELI WAR).

Sinanthropus Pekinensis, old alternate name for PEKING MAN.

Sinclair, Upton Beall (1878–1968), novelist and reformer, whose muckraking novel *The Jungle* (1906), an exposé of the Chicago meat-packing industry, helped spark the early PURE FOOD AND DRUG LAWS. A lifelong crusader, Sinclair wrote dozens of novels and pamphlets in support of social causes, including birth control, child labor laws, and socialism, in addition to his Lanny Budd series of novels, one of which won a Pulitzer Prize. He also ran many times for public office as a socialist, almost winning in the California gubernatorial race of 1934, and helped found the AMERICAN CIVIL LIBERTIES UNION.

Singapore (Republic of Singapore), until 1959 a British colony. The island was occupied by Japanese forces during World War II, gained internal autonomy in 1959, and was part of Malaysia 1963–65, becoming an independent state and COMMONWEALTH member on August 9, 1965. From 1963 Singapore was led by Prime Minister Lee Kuan Yew.

Singapore, Battle of (February 8–15, 1941), the taking of Singapore, whose massive fortifications faced the sea. The Japanese invaders of MALAYA came by land after having taken all of mainland Malaya from the British in December and January. On February 8, 1941, preceded by an aerial bombardment, Japanese armored barges with air cover crossed the Strait of Johore to attack Singapore. On February 15, after the city's water supply had been taken by the Japanese, the city's 70,000 defenders surrendered.

Singh, Mithileshwar, one of the LEBANON HOSTAGES, an American University professor who was kidnapped on January 24, 1988, and released on October 3, 1988.

Singh, Vishwanath Pratap (1931–), Indian political leader, in the Uttar Pradesh assembly from 1969, in parliament as a CONGRESS PARTY representative from 1971, and in several cabinet-level posts during the 1970s. He was head of the Uttar Pradesh state government 1980–1982, and minister of finance and then of defense in the Rajiv GANDHI government, going into opposition in 1987. He succeeded Gandhi, as the National Front prime minister of India, on December 1, 1989.

Sinn Fein, the political arm of the Irish Republican movement, which became a political party in 1905 and the majority party in the elections of 1918, after the executions of the leaders of the EASTER RISING of 1916. They proclaimed the Irish Republic in April 1919, naming Eamon DE VALERA as first president of the Irish republic. Sinn Fein organized and operated the provisional Irish government during the IRISH CIVIL WAR. The party split over the agreement ending that war, which partitioned Ireland, and it was never again a powerful force, essentially replaced by De Valera's Fianna Fail party in 1926.

Sino-Japanese War (1937–45), conflict between China and Japan that began on July 7, 1937, with the MARCO POLO BRIDGE INCIDENT near Peking, China. By the end of 1937, the Japanese had taken Peking, Tientsin, much of the north China plain, Shanghai, and Nanking, and the Chinese had moved their capital to Hankow. During 1938, the Japanese continued their advance, taking more of north and central China, including Süchow, Kaifeng, and finally, in October, Hankow and Canton. They had suffered a major reverse in June when the Chinese broke the YELLOW RIVER DIKES, flooding the river plain and drowning a Japanese offensive. The Chinese then moved their capital to Chungking, where it stayed for the rest of the war. Meanwhile, the Communists were fighting a guerrilla war against the Japanese in north China and extending their network of bases and influence. As Chinese resistance hardened rather than collapsing, as the Japanese had hoped, the Japanese advance stalled in 1939 and remained stalled while they began their run-up to World War II, including their 1940 invasion of Indochina. During the early years of World War II the war in China settled into a Japanese occupation, with periodic small Japanese offensives aimed at cutting Chinese food supplies. But in 1943 and 1944 Allied air forces achieved clear superiority throughout the eastern theater, the Japanese responding with a successful offensive aimed at Allied airfields late in 1944, an offensive that was resumed in early 1945. By the spring of 1945, facing the threat of massive Soviet Far Eastern armies and Allied offensives in the Pacific and southeast Asia, the Japanese began to pull back in China and were continuing to pull back as the war ended in August.

Sirhan Sirhan (1944–   ), assassin of Robert F. KENNEDY in Los Angeles on June 5, 1968. He was immediately captured and, on conviction, was sentenced to death, a sentence that because of a change of California law was later commuted to life imprisonment.

Sirica, John Joseph (1904–   ), U.S. lawyer and judge, a Republican who in 1957 was appointed by President Dwight D. EISENHOWER to the U.S. district court for the District of Columbia. He was chief judge of that court in 1973, when he presided over the original WATERGATE burglars trial and then a series of subsequent Watergate-related actions, including the tapes actions that led directly to the threatened impeachment and ultimate resignation of President Richard M. NIXON.

sit-down strikes, a strike technique used by U.S. labor during the mass-production-industry organizing strikes of the mid-1930s, in which striking workers continued to occupy their workplaces, refusing to be evicted other than by force. It was most notably employed during the massive United Automobile Workers–General Motors organizing strike of January–February, 1937, when Flint, Michigan, police attempted to bar food supplies to the sit-down strikers inside the struck plants, and a battle ensued. The violence was stopped by Governor Frank MURPHY of Michigan, who ordered in the National Guard, allowed food to flow to the strikers, and mediated the dispute, with the help of an appeal for cooperation from President Franklin D. ROOSEVELT. The union was recognized, the strike was won—and the sit-down strike technique was declared illegal by the Supreme Court in 1939.

Six-Day War (Third Arab–Israeli War; June 5–10, 1967), a successful set of surprise attacks by Israel against Egypt, Jordan, and Syria, after weeks of preparation by the Arab states and Israel for a major new war. In mid-May Egyptian president Gamal Abdel NASSER declared a state of emergency and demanded withdrawal of UNITED NATIONS peacekeeping forces from the Suez Canal; UN Secretary-General U THANT did so immediately. Israel and the Arab states then mobilized for war. On June 5 Israel launched preemptive air strikes against Egypt, Jordan, and Syria, destroying most of the air forces of all three countries on the ground and damaging Iraqi air strength as well. Then, in 6 days, Israel defeated the Egyptian army, taking the entire Sinai Peninsula; defeated the Jordanian army, taking the balance of Jerusalem and the entire WEST BANK; and defeated the Syrian army, taking the Golan Heights. No peace treaty followed the war; Israel continued to occupy the territories taken.

Sixteenth Amendment, amendment to the U.S. Constitution (1913) empowering Congress to levy federal income taxes.

Skate, U.S. submarine that was the first to surface at the NORTH POLE, in 1960.

Skinner, Burrhus Frederic (1904–   ), U.S. psychologist, who was a key exponent of BEHAVIORISM from the late 1930s. To Skinner, ideas of freedom and human will are, at best, illusions because human behavior is the result of learning and experience. He believed that education should be controlled and behavior engineered so that individuals act for the good of the group, rather than in disruptive ways, ideas developed in his widely circulated 1948 book, *Walden Two.* Aiming to make learning more rigorously controlled and efficient, Skinner developed the idea of programmed instruction, incorporated in a "teaching machine." The machine did not last, but Skinner's approaches had considerable influence on education, especially on the structuring of material for learning.

Skokie Nazi march (1978), a public march, at which the SWASTIKA would be displayed, planned for Skokie, Illinois, by the American NAZI party, generating a long train of litigation. Ultimately, the U.S. Supreme Court overruled lower courts that had banned the march and then struck down local ordinances that also would have resulted in banning the march. The AMERICAN CIVIL LIBERTIES UNION supported the constitutional right of the Nazis to march and lost one third of its Illinois membership and 20% of its national membership as a direct result. After winning the legal battle, the Nazis decided to call off their march; instead, they held a public meeting at Marquette Park in Chicago on July 9, 1978. Approximately 20–25 uniformed Nazis came, along with an estimated 2,000–3,000 spectators.

Skylab, U.S. orbital space station dedicated to scientific experiments, especially exploring possible commercial and scientific opportunities in space, launched on May 14, 1973. Damaged on launch, it was repaired by the first three-man crew after their arrival on May 25, at the start of their 28-day stay. Two other Skylab missions were launched in 1973, the last and longest lasting for 84 days. Later abandoned, the Skylab station fell back to Earth in 1979, breaking up with no harm over Australia.

Slánský show trials, the November 1952 trial and conviction for treason, on wholly false charges, of Rudolph Slánský, Czech Communist party secretary-general, 1945–51, and 13 other leading Czech Communists. Slánsky and 11 of the others were Jews; less than 2 months later Joseph STALIN'S anti-Semitism was to cause the arrest of the Soviet doctors who were falsely accused in the DOCTOR'S PLOT. Slánsky and 10 others were hanged in December; the remaining 3 were imprisoned and later released; all 14 were rehabilitated, 11 of them posthumously.

Slim, William Joseph (1891–1970), British officer, who saw service in World War I, and during World War II was a divisional commander in the Middle East before being sent to Burma in 1942, there retreating with his forces to India before advancing Japanese forces. In early 1944, his Fourteenth Army began the series of victories that ultimately drove the Japanese from Burma.

smallpox, first disease to be totally eradicated by medical intervention. Though effective vaccines had been available since the 19th century, millions of cases and thousands of deaths were still caused annually by smallpox as late as 1967, the year of the last major epidemic, in India and Pakistan. But in the late 1960s the WORLD HEALTH ORGANIZATION (WHO) mounted an inoculation campaign to eliminate smallpox altogether. The last known case of smallpox was reported in October 1977, the last to die being a Somali citizen, except for a British photographer who in 1978 was inadvertently infected by smallpox viruses being used in research at Birmingham University.

Smith, Alfred Emanuel (1873–1944), U.S. political leader, a four-term Democratic governor of New York State (1919–20; 1923–28), who in 1928 became his party's presidential nominee, losing to Herbert HOOVER in an election marred by anti-Catholic bias against Smith.

Smith, Ian (1919–   ), Zimbabwean white political leader, in the Southern Rhodesian parliament from 1948 and prime minister of SOUTHERN RHODESIA 1964–79, who led the unsuccessful effort to maintain minority white rule in his country. In 1965, facing world and COMMONWEALTH condemnation, he led Southern Rhodesia to declare its independence from Great Britain, and from the early 1970s he was engaged in the long ZIMBABWE CIVIL WAR. In 1979 he stepped down, participated in the brief MUZOREWA government, and was thereafter a white representative in the Zimbabwe parliament.

Smith Act trials, a series of trials of U.S. Communist leaders, beginning in 1948 and extending into the 1950s, under the Smith Alien Registration Act of 1940, which proscribed the teaching or advocacy of violent overthrow of the U.S. government, as well as organization of or membership in any organization so advocating. The convictions of 11 Communist leaders were upheld by the Supreme Court in *DENNIS V. UNITED STATES* (1951); other trials and convictions followed thereafter, until the Court reinterpreted the law to mean specific incitement to violent overthrow in *YATES V. UNITED STATES* (1957), the anti-Communist hysteria of the MCCARTHY period by then having subsided.

Smolny Institute, BOLSHEVIK Petrograd headquarters during the OCTOBER REVOLUTION; from there Leon TROTSKY directed the military forces that took control of the city and stormed the WINTER PALACE.

Smoot-Hawley Tariff (1930), the law establishing very high U.S. protective tariffs, initiated by U.S. senator Reed Smoot following the CRASH of 1929. It sharply cut worldwide trade as other countries followed suit, and thereby made a major contribution to the acceleration of the worldwide GREAT DE-PRESSION of the 1930s and the onrush of fascism and war.

Smuts, Jan Christian (1870–1950), South African lawyer, who became a guerrilla general during the BOER WAR, afterward working with Louis BOTHA to secure self-government for the Transvaal and the Orange Free State and to create the Union of South Africa. He was defense minister 1910–20 and commander of South African forces and then of Allied East African forces during World War I; in 1917 he joined the LLOYD GEORGE war cabinet. At the PARIS PEACE CONFERENCE he was active in developing the LEAGUE OF NATIONS, then returned home to become prime minister (1919–24), leaving politics for 9 years after being defeated by James HERTZOG in 1924. In 1933 he joined Hertzog's coalition cabinet as justice minister, taking office as prime minister when Hertzog refused to support South African participation in World War II. He was a leading COMMONWEALTH statesman throughout the war and into the postwar period, and among those who drafted the UNITED NATIONS charter. But his internationalist and developing multiracialist approach did not long survive in South Africa's postwar period. He was defeated by Daniel MALAN in 1948; what followed was APARTHEID and four decades of racism that destroyed much of what he had labored to build.

Snow, Edgar Parks (1905–72), U.S. journalist, in China from 1928, who in 1936 went to YENAN, there interviewing and becoming friendly with many of the leaders of Chinese communism, including MAO ZEDONG and ZHOU ENLAI. He brought the Chinese Communists and their movement to the Western world for the first time in his book *Red Star over China* (1937), thereafter continuing to report and write on China and Chinese communism until his death.

Soares, Mario Alberto Nobre Lopez (1924–   ), Portuguese lawyer and socialist, often imprisoned by the SALAZAR dictatorship and in exile 1970–74; he returned to Portugal after the PORTUGUESE ARMED FORCES MOVEMENT coup of 1974 to become a leader of the new government. He was foreign minister 1974–75, in that position bringing Portuguese African colonial rule to an end, and prime minister 1976–78 and 1983–85, becoming president in 1986.

socialism, a considerable range of related theories, all calling to some extent for public economic ownership, from the ownership of only some major public utilities to the total public ownership of every aspect of economic life, with such ownership exercised in a wide range of state forms. In the 20th century those calling themselves socialists have been democrats and totalitarians, moderates and radicals, from Clement ATTLEE, Eugene DEBS, and Jawaharlal NEHRU to V.I. LENIN, Joseph STALIN, and MAO ZEDONG— and also DENG XIAOPING and Mikhail GORBACHEV, who late in the century sharply redefined the Communist branch of socialism. During World War I many of the world's socialist parties split over whether or not to support their warring national governments, most of them choosing to do so, despite previous vows to oppose a war. After the RUSSIAN REVOLUTION socialism split into two well-defined branches, one a group of moderate socialist parties organized into the SECOND INTERNATIONAL, the other a group of Communist parties organized into the THIRD (COMMUNIST) INTERNATIONAL, or COMINTERN. In Europe, socialist parties were in power during part of the interwar period in Germany and France and after World War II in many countries, including Great Britain and the Scandinavian states. Parties describing themselves as socialist or socialist-oriented also came to power in many new nations, including India, Indonesia, Israel, such Arab socialist states as Iraq and Syria, and a wide range of other developing nations, some of them democracies and some one-party states.

Socialist Party of the United States, a political body formed in 1901 in a merger of the Socialist Labor party and the Social Democratic party of America. It was led by Eugene V. DEBS and achieved considerable electoral strength before the United States entered World War I. Debs was Socialist presidential candidate in 1904, 1908, 1912, and 1920, receiving more than 900,000 votes in the elections of 1912 and 1920; the 1912 total was over 6% of the total vote. The party came under heavy attack for its antiwar position during World War I, Debs and other leaders being imprisoned under the Espionage and Sedition Acts. In 1919 the Communist-oriented wing of the party split off, in two splinters that in 1920 joined to form the COMMUNIST PARTY. The Socialist party never regained its prewar strength, although it continued, with Norman THOMAS as its main standard-bearer.

Socialist Revolutionary party, the largest revolutionary party in Russia, until its suppression by the BOLSHEVIKS after the OCTOBER REVOLUTION of 1917, and the party of Alexander KERENSKY, premier of the PROVISIONAL GOVERNMENT. In a largely rural Russia it was a party of agrarian reform; it was also committed to terrorist tactics, its members routinely engaging in political assassination.

Social Security, in the United States, the system of federally guaranteed retirement benefits originally established by the NEW DEAL's Social Security Act of 1935. It has since grown into a massive set of federal–state social insurance collections, guarantees, and payments, covering later-years, survivors, disability, health care, unemployment compensation, and a miscellany of welfare provisions.

Soddy, Frederick (1877–1956), British chemist who with Ernest RUTHERFORD developed the theory (1902–03) that RADIOACTIVITY resulted in the transformation of one element to another. Exploring this radioactive disintegration, he discovered that many elements exist in variant forms, which in 1913 he named ISOTOPES, a discovery that won him the 1921 Nobel Prize for Chemistry.

SOE, the initials of the British covert operations SPECIAL OPERATIONS EXECUTIVE.

solar energy, energy collected from the Sun's RADIATION, which humans have been able to concentrate for human use only in the 20th century. In 1913 a solar collector of over 13,000 square feet was built in Egypt to turn water into steam to run an irrigation pump. In 1939 scientists at the Massachusetts Institute of Technology built an experimental house heated by flat-plate solar collectors on its roof, improved by various innovations in the following decades. Little use was made of such solar-heating possibilities, however, until the OIL EMBARGO of the 1970s, after which some people added solar panels to their homes; incentive declined with the oil glut of the 1980s. Meanwhile, French scientists explored large-scale uses with the first large solar furnace, built 1948–52 at Montlouis, a prototype for others in the United States, Japan, and France—notably at Odeillo, a massive alignment of 9,600 mirrors covering 20,000 square feet. Solar furnaces are often used in studying high-temperature properties of materials. Of greater long-term interest is the possibility of converting solar to electrical energy. In 1954 Bell Laboratories scientists D. M. Chapin, C. S. Fuller, and G. L. Pearson developed the first solar cell to do just that, using silicon crystals to form TRANSISTORS. Though used in space, the cost of solar cells is relatively high and the efficiency low, so they have not so far had a major impact on human society. At the world's largest solar energy plant, Solar One, built in California's Mojave Desert 1980–81, for example, electricity initially cost five to ten times as much as normal, though that improved somewhat and innovations such as SUPERCONDUCTORS could totally change the picture. In the late 1960s some scientists proposed launching a huge satellite energy collector into space, returning energy to Earth in a MICROWAVE beam, but cost and concerns about radiation hampered development of such a project.

Solidarity (Independent Self-Governing Trade Union Solidarity), Polish national trade union confederation, formed on September 18, 1980, after the nationwide series of strikes generated by the successful GDANSK LENIN SHIPYARD STRIKE and led from its inception by Lech WALESA. In less than a year Solidarity grew to include an estimated 10 million workers, second only to the government as a force in Poland. It was officially outlawed by the martial law decree of December 1981, going underground while remaining a major force in the country. In late 1988 and early 1989, during the GORBACHEV era, a series of Solidarity—government talks were conducted, ultimately leading to the 1989 legalization of Solidarity. The organization won a major electoral victory in the 1989 Polish elections, the first free elections to be held in Poland in 40 years.

Solomon Islands, until 1975 a British colony, gaining internal autonomy in 1976 and independence on July 7, 1978.

Solzhenitsyn, Alexander Isayevich (1918–), Soviet novelist and dissenter, imprisoned and internally exiled, 1945–56; his work indicted STALIN'S government and the Soviet system from which it developed. Such works as *The Gulag Archipelago* (1973–75), *The First Circle* (1968), and his early *One Day in the Life of Ivan Denisovich* (1962) exposed the Soviet prison system, won him the 1970 Nobel Prize for Literature and caused his deportation in 1974; he then settled in the United States, there continuing his work.

Somalia (Somali Democratic Republic), an independent nation formed on July 1, 1960, by a merger of BRITISH SOMALILAND with what had earlier in the century been ITALIAN SOMALILAND, taken by the British after World War II and administered by Italy as a UNITED NATIONS trust territory 1950–60. French Somaliland later became DJIBOUTI. Somali claims to the Ogaden region, held by ETHIOPIA, generated the SOMALI–ETHIOPIAN WAR of 1977–78. Somali is a one-party state, led by Mohammed SIAD BARRE from the 1969 military coup.

Somali–Ethiopian War (1977–78), conflict that began with a Somali invasion of the disputed Ogaden desert region. From July through early September 1977 Somali forces enjoyed some early successes. The Somalis besieged Harar in late September but failed to take the city, partly because of Soviet and Cuban support of their Ethiopian allies against their Somali allies. In November 1977 Somali expelled Soviet forces and closed Soviet bases. In February 1978 Ethiopian and Cuban forces, supported by Soviet advisers, relieved Harar, and broke Somali strength at Diredawa-Jijiga (March 2–5). The Somalis requested a cease-fire on March 8, 1978, and subsequently withdrew from the Ogaden region.

Somme, Battle of the (July 1–November 13, 1916), a 4½-month-long World War I assault by major British and French forces against heavily fortified and strongly defended German positions in the Somme valley, which gained only 8 miles; cost an estimated 650,000 British, 420,000 German, and 195,000 French casualties; and failed to break through the German defense. The British introduced TANKS on the Somme.

Somme Offensive (March 21–April 5,1918), the first of five major German offensives in 1918, all of them aimed at winning World War I with the help of the Eastern Front troops freed by Soviet withdrawal from the war. German forces attacked British armies on the Somme and advanced 40 miles before they were stopped—close enough to bombard Paris with their BIG BERTHA long-range seige guns.

Somoza Debayle, Anastasio (1925–80), Nicaraguan officer, son of Anastasio SOMOZA Garcia. A West Point–educated soldier, he took control of the National Guard after his father's 1956 assassination, and in 1963 became dictator, succeeding his brother Luis. He continued his family's dictatorship but lost a great deal of public support after diverting large amounts of aid to personal use following the MANAGUA EARTHQUAKE of 1972. He continued to lose support as his government turned even more corrupt, ultimately also losing the support of the U.S. government. His army proved unable to withstand increasing SANDINISTA military pressure in the late 1970s; he fled the country in July 1979. He

was assassinated in Asunción, Paraguay, on September 17, 1980.

Somoza Garcia, Anastasio (1896–1956), Nicaraguan political leader, who became head of the National Guard and took control of Nicaragua in 1933, after the departure of the U.S. Marine occupation force. He was dictator of Nicaragua until his assassination in 1956, in command of the National Guard at all times—although in some periods ruling through puppet presidents—and always in close cooperation with U.S. commercial interests in his country. He built a very large family fortune during his tenure, as did his sons, who succeeded him, Luis becoming dictator 1956–63 and Anastasio succeeding Luis 1963–79.

sonar (**so**und **n**avigation **a**nd **r**anging), technique of transmitting high-frequency sound waves, then plotting and analyzing the echoes received, the underwater equivalent of RADAR. Conceived shortly after the *Titanic* sinking in 1912, sonar was developed in 1915 by French inventor Paul Langevin. At first it was used largely to spot underwater icebergs but was also used during both World War I and II to help ships scan the seas for mines and submarines. By 1922 sonar was being employed to check ocean depths, leading to the 1925 discovery of the Mid-Atlantic Ridge, which later figured in theories of CONTINENTAL DRIFT. Sonar continued to be developed throughout the century and, with the addition of increasingly efficient ELECTRONICS, developed into a highly sophisticated technique; the sound echoes were transformed into electrical signals, which formed a picture on a CATHODE RAY TUBE. Sonar was also used on fishing boats to help locate schools of fish, and the technique inspired the use of ULTRASOUND techniques in many other areas, such as medicine.

sonic boom, shock wave created when an aircraft reaches the speed of sound and breaks through the SOUND BARRIER, either on acceleration or deceleration, first experienced on Charles YEAGER's 1947 flight.

Son of Sam, name assumed by 1970s New York mass murderer David BERKOWITZ, in his letters to newspapers, after which it was adopted by the media.

Soong, Ch'ing-ling (Madame Sun Yat-sen; 1892–1981); sister of Mei-ling SOONG and Chinese financier T. V. SOONG, and like them educated in the United States; she married SUN YAT-SEN in 1914 and was widely known thereafter as Madame Sun Yat-sen. With her husband, she broke with CHIANG KAI-SHEK and the KUOMINTANG, after the split between them and the Communists, which in 1927 began the CHINESE CIVIL WAR. She then lived in the Soviet Union, returning to China in 1937 and becoming active in war relief work. She supported the Communist side in the civil war, taking official positions in the PEOPLE'S REPUBLIC OF CHINA after 1949 and becoming, as Sun's widow, an important national figure.

Soong, Mei-ling (Madame Chiang Kai-shek; 1897–   ), wife of Chinese leader CHIANG KAI-SHEK, known throughout the world as Madame Chiang Kai-shek; sister of Ching-ling SOONG (Madame SUN YAT-SEN) and of Chinese financier T. V. SOONG and like them educated in the United States. Her marriage to Chiang in 1927 perfected his lifelong alliance with the Soongs; at that time he also converted to Christianity. She worked very effectively for the Chinese Republic from then on, especially in the United States.

Soong, T. V. (1894–1971), brother of Ch'ing-ling SOONG (Madame SUN YAT-SEN) and Mei-ling Soong (Madame CHIANG KAI-SHEK). Educated in the United States, like his sisters, Soong was finance minister of NATIONALIST CHINA's government in 1925, and after Chiang's marriage to his sister in 1927 was his key financial ally, during Chiang's rise to power and until Communist victory in 1949.

Sorel, Georges (1847–1922), French philosopher of SYNDICALISM, whose advocacy of violence to achieve political aims proved attractive to the syndicalists for whom it was intended, and also for French, German, and Italian fascist and other rightist movements.

Sorge, Richard (1895–1944), an extremely successful Soviet spy who, during the 1930s, penetrated the German embassy in Tokyo; until late 1941 he passed a great deal of vital information as to German and Japanese intentions to the Soviet Union, including the coming German invasion of the Soviet Union and Japanese Southeast Asia invasion plans. He was arrested in October 1941 and later executed.

Soudan, the former name of MALI (Republic of Mali), then part of French West Africa. Mali became an independent nation on June 20, 1960.

sound barrier (sonic barrier), increase in frictional drag on an object approaching the speed of sound, an apparent wall broken through by Charles YEAGER in the first supersonic flight in 1947, followed by a SONIC BOOM.

Souphanouvong (1909–   ), Laotian engineer and political leader, a PATHET LAO founder who fought beside VIETMINH forces during the war for Indochinese independence in the early 1950s, and throughout the long LAOTIAN CIVIL WAR headed the Lao Patriotic Front, which was associated with the Pathet Lao. He participated in the 1960–62 coalition government organized by his half-brother, Prince SOUVANNA PHOUMA, and in 1975 became head of state of the new Communist government of Laos. He resigned because of illness in 1986, though remaining chairman of the Lao Front for National Reconstruction, which succeeded the Patriotic Front.

South Africa (Republic of South Africa), nation formed after British victory in the BOER WAR. The former Boer republics of the Transvaal and Orange Free State became British colonies, but were soon (1906 and 1907) granted internal autonomy, and in 1910 joined the British Cape Colony and Natal to form the Union of South Africa, which became a COMMONWEALTH member in 1934. In 1961, after South African racial policies—as expressed by the increasing application of APARTHEID and the SHARPEVILLE MASSACRE of 1960—had isolated the country from much of the world community, South Africa withdrew from the Commonwealth, establishing a republic. It became increasingly isolated from the rest of the world in the decades that followed, as worldwide condemnation of its racialism grew, but entered a new era with the advent of the DE KLERK government in September 1989, and the release of Nelson MANDELA in February 1990.

South Carolina v. *Katzenbach, Attorney General* (1966), a landmark U.S. Supreme Court decision upholding certain challenged sections of the VOTING RIGHTS ACT OF 1965 and supporting the aims of that antidiscrimination law.

Southeast Asia Treaty Organization (SEATO), 1954–77 military alliance of Australia, France, Great Britain, New Zealand, Pakistan, the Philippines, Thailand, and the United States, in pursuit of common interests in southeast Asia. It included a commitment to supply military assistance to Cambodia (Kampuchea), Laos, and South Vietnam. Some SEATO allies sent contingents to join U.S. forces during the VIETNAM WAR.

Southern Christian Leadership Conference (SCLC), U.S. civil rights organization founded in 1957 by Martin Luther KING, JR., Ralph ABERNATHY, and other leaders of the modern CIVIL RIGHTS MOVEMENT, most of them Black southern clergymen. It was the leading organization of the CIVIL RIGHTS MOVEMENT from its formation through the 1960s. King led the organization until his assassination in 1968, and was then succeeded by Ralph Abernathy.

Southern France campaign of 1944 (August–September 1944), execution of Operation ANVIL-DRAGON late in World War II, beginning on August 15, 1944, with Allied air-sea landings on the lightly defended French Mediterranean coast east of Marseilles. French forces quickly captured Marseilles and Toulon, taking 45,000–50,000 prisoners. American forces pursued and trapped the retreating Germans in the Rhône Valley, ultimately taking over 30,000 prisoners.

Southern Rhodesia, a former White-dominated, racist British African colony, which became independent in 1965, a republic in 1969, and then entered the period of the ZIMBABWE-RHODESIA CIVIL WARS, from which in 1980 emerged the new nation of ZIMBABWE.

Southgate Supper Club fire (May 28, 1977), a smoky kitchen fire that spread through this large, rambling Kentucky supper club, ultimately killing 162 people, some in the resulting panic and most through smoke inhalation.

South Pole, southern end of the Earth's axis, target of numerous landmark 20th-century expeditions. After several earlier attempts, by Ernest SHACKLETON among others, Roald AMUNDSEN in 1911 led the first party to reach the South Pole, with Robert SCOTT's ill-fated party arriving a month later. The first flight over the South Pole was made by Richard E. BYRD with co-pilot Bernt Balchen on November 29, 1929. Lincoln ELLSWORTH flew over wide areas of the Antarctic, including the South Pole, 1933–39. During the 1957–58 INTERNATIONAL GEOPHYSICAL YEAR, Edmund HILLARY led the third party to reach the South Pole, arriving by tractor on January 4, 1958.

Southwest Africa People's Organization of Namibia (SWAPO), Namibian nationalist organization formed in 1959, to press for the withdrawal of South African forces and the establishment of an independent Namibia. In 1966 SWAPO went over to armed insurrection, with Angola-based groups beginning a low-level guerrilla war of independence, mounted by what SWAPO called its "external" forces. Simultaneously, SWAPO "internal" forces within Namibia continued to use legal means to press for independence, which was promised as part of the 1988 general peace agreements in the Angola-Namibia area. Namibia became an independent nation in March 1990.

South Yemen, alternate name for YEMEN PEOPLE'S REPUBLIC, an independent nation since 1967.

South Yemen Civil War (January 1986), a short, bloody week of fighting in Aden between rival groups within the ruling Yemen Socialist party, which cost an estimated 4,000 lives. Fighting began with an attempt by party chairman Ali Nasir Mohammed to massacre his opponents and ended with his defeat and flight.

Souvanna Phouma (1901–84), Laotian engineer, administrator, and political leader, a moderate who led the Laotian government from 1951 to 1975, except for a period as ambassador to France in 1958–59. During 1960–62 he led a coalition government that included his half-brother, Prince SOUPHANOUVONG. He was Western-oriented for the balance of the period, which included the 1950–75 LAOTIAN CIVIL WAR. After the PATHET LAO victory he stayed on in Vientiane in an advisory capacity.

soviet, the Russian word for council. The first soviets formed during the RUSSIAN REVOLUTION OF 1905 and then disbanded. In 1917, before and during the FEBRUARY REVOLUTION and the PROVISIONAL GOVERNMENT period, the Petrograd and other soviets throughout the country formed a network of representative bodies, becoming the main vehicle for BOLSHEVIK development of the OCTOBER REVOLUTION of 1917 and then the main descriptor for Russian society itself.

Soviet collectivization famine (1932–34), the famine resulting from the disastrous drop in agricultural production following forced collectivization, coupled with the export of well over l.5 millions of tons of grain per year. The famine and accompanying health problems caused the death of at least 1.5 million and probably 5–6 million Soviet citizens.

Soviet–Japanese War of 1945 (August 9–14, 1945), short-lived conflict at the end of World War II. On August 9, 1945, 3 days after the HIROSHIMA bombing, the Soviet Union declared war against Japan, then immediately launched a major attack from Outer Mongolia and Siberia on Japan's KWANGTUNG ARMY in Manchuria. Overcoming early Japanese resistance, the much stronger Soviet armies had within 4 days smashed the Kwangtung Army, overrun much of Manchuria, and were on August 14, the day of Japan's surrender, across the Yalu River into Korea.

Soviet–Polish War (1920), post–World War I conflict in which, on April 25, 1920, Polish armies led by General Jósef PILSUDSKI and allied with Ukrainian forces led by Simon PETLYURA, attacked Soviet forces in eastern Poland and the Ukraine. Poland had been newly reconstituted after the end of World War I; the Russians were engaged in the RUSSIAN CIVIL WAR. Pilsudski's forces scored early successes, taking Kiev, while Petlyura's forces engaged in severe anti-Jewish pogroms in the occupied areas. In mid–May, Soviet forces led by Generals Mikhail TUKHACHEVSKY and Semën BUDËNNY counterattacked; by late July they were nearing Warsaw. At the decisive Battle of WARSAW (August 16–25, 1920), the Polish army smashed the Soviet force then moved east, their advance stopping only with the armistice of October 12, 1920. On March 18, 1921, the Treaty of RIGA defined Poland's eastern borders.

Soviet Union, an alternate and the most widely used name of the UNION OF SOVIET SOCIALIST REPUBLICS.

Soweto riots (June 1976), massive riots that erupted in Soweto, a large Black township southwest of Johannesburg, when the South African government attempted to force the use of the Afrikaans language in all South African schools. In a week of rioting that began in Soweto and spread to other parts of the country, an estimated 600 Black and other non-white South Africans were killed by the police and thousands more were injured. The forced use of Afrikaans was dropped.

Soyuz, series of U.S.S.R. workhorse spacecraft used from April 23, 1967. The first flight was a disaster, with cosmonaut Vladimir M. Komarov killed on emergency reentry, as would happen to the three-man crew of the *Soyuz 11* on June 30, 1971. But the Soyuz went on to success, with many "firsts" to its credit. On January 15–16, 1969, *Soyuz 4* and *5* linked together in the first space docking by two piloted craft; *Soyuz 10* on March 23, 1971, docked with *SALYUT 1*, the first space station. In the first joint U.S.-Soviet mission, *Soyuz 19*, launched on July 15, 1975, docked with an APOLLO ASTP craft. *Soyuz 34*, launched unmanned on June 6, 1979, carried cosmonauts back from the Salyut space station.

Spaak, Paul-Henri (1889–1972), Belgian lawyer, socialist, and political leader, who entered parliament in 1932, and from 1935 to 1966 held a long series of cabinet posts. He was premier three times (1938–39, 1946, 1947–50), was the first president of the UNITED NATIONS General Assembly in 1946, secretary-general of NATO 1957–61, and a founder of the EUROPEAN COMMON MARKET.

Spaatz, Carl (1891–1974), U.S. Air Force officer, who in 1942 took command of American air forces in Britain, then in North Africa, and from January 1944 until reassignment to the Pacific theater in early 1945 commanded all U.S. air forces in Europe. He then commanded all American Pacific air forces until the Japanese surrender.

space race, U.S.–U.S.S.R competition in the exploration and exploitation of space, for prestige, power, and knowledge, sparked by the Soviet SPUTNIK flight in 1957.

space shuttle, U.S. series of reusable spacecraft used from 1981, formally called the Space Transportation System (STS) craft, including *COLUMBIA, CHALLENGER, ATLANTIS*, and *DISCOVERY*.

space-time continuum, the idea that space and time are not separate and distinct entities but merge into one another. Inspired by EINSTEIN's 1905 theory of RELATIVITY, in 1907 Russian-German mathematician Hermann Minkowski posited that time was a kind of fourth dimension of the universe,

an idea that Einstein employed in his 1915 general theory of relativity.

Space Transportation System (STS), formal name of the series of U.S. spacecraft popularly called the SPACE SHUTTLE, used from 1981.

space walk, movement by an astronaut outside a spacecraft, wearing a spacesuit, first done by Soviet cosmonaut Aleksei Leonov in March 1965 in the *VOSKHOD* 2; such astronauts were always tethered to their craft until 1984 when the first U.S. astronauts moved into space wearing jet-propelled backpacks.

Spanish Civil War (1936–39), a successful insurrection, led by fascist Francisco FRANCO, against the Loyalist forces of the Spanish Republic, which cost an estimated 1 million war dead. The war was also, in part, a rehearsal for World War II. Nationalist forces were joined by German and Italian troops, tanks, airplanes, other armaments, and advisers, and were heavily supplied by those countries with war materials. Loyalist forces were joined by smaller numbers of Soviet advisers, pilots, and armaments, as well as the troops of the INTERNATIONAL BRIGADES, and were able to buy some war materials abroad, including French airplanes. The democratic nations declared their neutrality, to the great advantage of the Nationalist forces, which, from early in the war, were far better equipped and supplied than the Loyalists. The war began on July 18, 1936, with army and navy revolts in Morocco and Spain; by November, Nationalist troops had begun the long siege of MADRID. The war was won essentially in the north; Bilbao fell in June 1937, and Barcelona in January 1939, a few months after the decisive Battle of the EBRO. Madrid and Valencia surrendered in March 1939.

Spanish flu epidemic, an alternate name for the INFLUENZA PANDEMIC of 1918–19.

Spartacist Revolt (1919), the failed armed Communist insurrection in Berlin against the new German socialist government, in January 1919. It was led by Rosa LUXEMBURG and Karl LIEBKNECHT of the Spartacist League, who were murdered by their FREIKORPS captors on January 15, 1919.

Speak softly and carry a big stick; you will go far, statement by U.S. president Theodore ROOSEVELT, September 2, 1901.

Special Operations Executive (SOE), British World War II covert operations organization, which developed intelligence and field operations in several theaters of war, functioning especially to supply and coordinate European anti-Nazi resistance movements.

Speck, Richard Benjamin, U.S. mass murderer who killed eight student nurses in Chicago, July 13–14, 1966; he was captured and sentenced to life imprisonment.

Speer, Albert (1905–81), Nazi who after 1942 became head of Germany's war production organization; he was tried and convicted as a war criminal at NUREMBERG after the war, and sentenced to 20 years in prison.

Spengler, Oswald (1880–1936), German philosopher and historian whose major work, *THE DECLINE OF THE WEST* (1922), summed up his thinking, which posited immutable laws of societal change and development, attacked democracy as a symptom of decay, and urged Germans to jettison democracy in favor of authoritarianism. Although entirely useless as historical analysis, his work found favor with those attacking Wiemar democracy in the 1920s and helped to provide the ideological conditions for the rise of German fascism.

sperm bank, storehouse of sperm frozen for later use in artificial insemination; an idea suggested in the 1950s by U.S. geneticist Hermann Joseph Muller. The sperm is often drawn from men regarded as superior, as in intellectual ability, physical development, and freedom from known genetic defects. It is, in effect, a form of modern EUGENICS, likewise often being associated with non-scientific racism or elitism.

Spinola, Antonio Sebastiao Ribiero de (1910–   ), Portuguese officer, who led antiguerrilla forces in Guinea 1968–72, was army chief of staff 1972–74, and became president of the new democratic government after the PORTUGUESE ARMED FORCES MOVEMENT coup of April 1974, although he did not join in the coup. He resigned in September, in disagreement with the policy of rapid withdrawal from the African colonies. In March 1975 he fled to Brazil, after the failure of a military coup.

Spirit of St. Louis, The, the airplane in which Charles A. LINDBERGH made the first solo flight across the Atlantic, on May 20–21, 1927.

split brain, recognition that the two halves of the brain, while working together in a complementary way, have special areas of dominance, the left side of the brain focusing on language skills and the right hand, eye, and ear; the right side, on shapes, emotions, and other nonverbal skills and the left hand, eye, and ear. From the mid-1940s some operations had been performed dividing the brains of patients, to halt the otherwise crippling effects of severe epilepsy. Building on experience with such patients, and on studies of animals with experimentally split brains, scientists in the 1960s began to more systematically explore the role of the two sides of the brain, in the process learning more about its normal workings and about how to help people with impaired brains, such as stroke victims.

Spock, Benjamin McLane (1903–   ), U.S. pediatrician and author, who became a leading anti-VIETNAM WAR activist and 1972 presidential candiate of the People's Party. In 1968 he was convicted of illegally counseling draft resistance, but the conviction was reversed on appeal.

Spruance, Raymond Ames (1886–1969), U.S. naval officer, who took command during the Battle of MIDWAY and played a major role in the winning of that decisive victory. In 1943 he commanded Amercan naval forces in a series of island-hopping invasions of the Gilbert and Marshall island groups, becoming a full admiral in early 1944; in 1944–45 he commanded U.S. naval forces at IWO JIMA and OKINAWA.

Sputnik, series of U.S.S.R. SATELLITES; *Sputnik 1* was the first artificial satellite to orbit the Earth, on October 4, 1957. The 184-pound capsule was boosted into orbit by a converted ICBM powered by a ROCKET built by Valentin GLUSHKO; it circled the Earth every 96 minutes, reaching a high point of 584 miles before returning in early 1958, burning up on reentry. *Sputnik 2*, launched later that year, carried LAIKA, the first dog in space. Other Sputnik flights followed, some carrying other animals, during which the Russians tested various life-support and reentry systems. They prepared the way for manned flights, spurred the U.S. space program directed by the NATIONAL AERONAUTICS AND SPACE ADMINISTRATION (NASA), and inaugurated the SPACE RACE.

Spycatcher **case,** the unsuccessful 2½-year British government effort to suppress the book *Spycatcher*, an exposé by former MI5 intelligence agent Peter Wright. In 1985 British publication was suppressed by the government, and the suppression was made permanent in 1986. Wright arranged for Australian publication, but in September 1985 the British government secured a restraining order in Australia as well. However, in 1987 the Australian courts upheld the right to publish, and the book became a best-seller in several countries, including the United States, while still banned in Britain. Late in 1988 several British newspapers defied the ban, publishing stories about the book and its accusations, and the Sunday *Times* of London serialized it. On October 13, 1988, Britain's Law Lords upheld publication of the stories about the book, effectively ending the controversy.

Square Deal, a term used by U.S. president Theodore ROOSEVELT to describe his domestic reform policies, and as a slogan during his presidential campaigns of 1904 and 1912.

Sri Lanka (Democratic Socialist Republic of Sri Lanka), until 1948, Ceylon, a British colony, the island became an independent state and COMMONWEALTH member on February 4, 1948.

Sri Lankan Civil War (1981–), a bitter communal war between minority Tamils and majority Sinhalese, with Tamil United Liberation Front demands for an autonomous Tamil area in northern and eastern Sri Lanka strongly resisted by the majority Sinhalese government. In the early 1980s the Indian government of Indira GANDHI supported Tamil demands, providing support for Tamil exile groups in the largely Tamil south Indian province of Tamil Nadu. The Rajiv GANDHI government, however, took a different view, attempting to mediate a peace settlement between the parties that did not envisage the establishment of an autonomus Tamil state, and then sending in Indian peacekeeping forces. Tamil guerrillas, originally responsive to Indian efforts, ultimately fought Indian forces, which were progressively reinforced; by mid-1989 they numbered an estimated 30,000 troops and even at that level were unable to end or even very well contain the insurrection.

SS (Schutzstaffel; Blackshirts), the Nazi secret police, which also supplied CONCENTRATION CAMP personnel and later developed a military organization; led by Heinrich HIMMLER from 1929. Before HITLER came to power in 1933 the SS was a small paramilitary organization. After he came to power the SS quickly became the Nazi political police, destroying the competitive SA (Brownshirts) in the BLOOD PURGE of 1934 and providing the concentration camp personnel (the Death's Head battalion), who would ultimately murder many millions of people, including most of the 6 million Jews who died in the JEWISH HOLOCAUST. During World War II the SS military organization (WAFFEN SS) grew very quickly and by the end of the war had challenged the German general staff for control of the army.

SST, widely used initials for SUPERSONIC TRANSPORT, AIRPLANES capable of traveling faster than the speed of sound.

stagflation, term coined by Swedish economist Gunnar MYRDAL to describe the combination of economic stagnation and inflation he believed characterized most Western economies in the 1970s and 1980s.

Stalin, Joseph (Joseph Vissarionovich Dzhugashvili; 1879–1953), Soviet leader, who played a small role in the OCTOBER REVOLUTION of 1917, but by 1928 had risen to sole control of the Communist party apparatus and with it the Soviet Union, in the process defeating and expelling his rival, Leon TROTSKY. In 1929, using the secret police, the CHEKA, as his main instrument, he began the processes of repression, forced collectivization, and quick industrialization that were to bring about the deaths of millions of Soviet citizens through mass famine and accompanying disease, the deaths of millions more in labor camps, and the internal exile of still more millions, while at the same time helping to develop the Soviet Union into a powerful industrial nation. In 1934, after the murder of Leningrad Communist party leader Sergei KIROV, he embarked on the GREAT PURGE, the series of systematic accusations, show trials, and executions of tens of thousands of old BOLSHEVIKS, military leaders, and cultural leaders. They included such old allies and colleagues as Lev KAMENEV, Grigori ZINOVIEV, and Nicolai BUKHARIN, as well as Marshal Mikhail TUKHACHEVSKY and most of the Soviet officers' corps. The MOSCOW TRIALS of this period, resulting in the execution of the highest-ranking Communist party and military leaders, were the showpieces of a much greater set of killings. In 1939 Stalin signed a nonagression pact with Germany and moved Soviet forces into eastern Poland. During World War II he added the role of commander in chief to that of dictator, taking personal control of the Soviet war effort. In the postwar period, under his direction, Soviet forces took control of most of Eastern Europe, and he participated fully in developing the COLD WAR. It is probable that he was in the process of beginning another major Soviet purge at the time of his death, reportedly of a brain hemorrhage, on March 5, 1953. The massive crimes typical of the Stalin era were partially exposed by the KHRUSHCHEV SECRET SPEECH of 1956 and the THAW that followed and were much more fully exposed during the GORBACHEV era.

Stalingrad, Battle of (August 23, 1942–February 2, 1943), the decisive World War II Soviet victory that stopped the German southern advance and turned the tide of the war; at Stalingrad, Soviet armies began the series of offensives that were to take them to Berlin. From August 23, when German Sixth Army forces, commanded by General Friedrich PAULUS, reached the Volga at Stalingrad, Soviet and German infantry fought a long, house-to-house battle for the city. At the same time, Soviet armies, ultimately numbering an estimated 1 million men, built up on the German flanks. On November 19, preceded by an enormous barrage, Soviet armies attacked on both flanks; within 5 days they had executing a pincers movement that encircled 250,000–300,000 German and satellite troops. Hitler forbade Paulus from attempting to break out to the rear, which he might have done early in the encirclement; then the German troops slowly froze, starved, and ran out of ammunition. The entire remaining German force surrendered on February 2.

Standard Oil Company of New Jersey v. United States (1911), a landmark U.S. Supreme Court decision, breaking up the massive Standard Oil trust, which controlled much of the American petroleum industry, and many other large transportation and industrial companies; a major victory for the antitrust forces of the time.

***Stark* incident** (May 17, 1987), the killing of 37 American sailors in a surprise Iraqi missile attack on the *U.S.S. Stark*, operating in the Persian Gulf during the Iran–Iraq War. Iraq apologized for the error; the United States soon afterward began to escort reflagged Kuwaiti tankers through the Persian Gulf, and was thereafter involved in several other engagements in the Gulf against Iran.

Starkweather, Charles, U.S. mass murderer who killed 11 people in Nebraska and Wyoming in December 1957 while accompanied by 14-year-old Carol Ann Fugate; three of the first four killings were those of Fugate's mother, stepfather, and 2-year-old sister. Starkweather was executed; Fugate was sentenced to life imprisonment and later paroled.

stars, evolution of, the theory that the stars are not eternal but undergo a series of changes called STELLAR EVOLUTION.

Star Wars, popular term for the STRATEGIC DEFENSE INITIATIVE (SDI), an experimental space-based nuclear defense system under development from 1983.

Stauffenberg, Klaus Schenck von (1907–44), German anti-Nazi World War II colonel, wounded in action and thereafter reassigned to Berlin; he unsuccessfully attempted to assassinate Adolf HITLER, as the key element of the army OFFICERS' PLOT. He was able to carry a bomb into a staff conference in Hitler's headquarters at Rastenburg, in East Prussia, on July 20, 1944. The bomb went off but failed to kill Hitler, and Stauffenberg's associates did not succeed in taking power. He was seized and executed later in the same day. A purge and many executions followed; Hitler lived until his suicide in Berlin, on May 30, 1945.

Stavisky affair, an early 1930s French scandal involving financier Serge Stavisky, who in December 1933 was accused of bond fraud and committed suicide on January 3, 1934. Stavisky was a Russian Jew, suspected of having close ties with highly placed members of the leftist government then in power. Rightist French organizations, such as the ACTION FRANÇAISE and the CROIX DE FEU, used the case to build large, violent antirepublican, anti-Jewish riots and were able to bring down the government, which was succeeded by a center coalition that ended the massive riots, and saved France from what was becoming an attempt to overthrow the republic.

steady state theory, cosmological theory that the universe is expanding and new matter continually being created to form new stars and galaxies. Put forward in 1920

by British physicist James JEANS, the steady state theory was most popular after 1948, when Austrian-British mathematician Hermann Bondi, British astronomer Fred HOYLE, and Austrian-American astronomer Thomas Gold revised it. But the theory declined in popularity as 1960s discoveries tended to confirm the rival BIG BANG THEORY.

Steel Strike of 1919, a massive AMERICAN FEDERATION OF LABOR (AFL) strike for union recognition and the 8-hour day in the steel industry, led by William Z. FOSTER and involving an estimated 300,000–350,000 steelworkers. The strike began on September 22, 1919, and was broken by early January 1920, with a great deal of violence.

Steen, Alann, one of the American LEBANON HOSTAGES, an American University professor, who was kidnapped on January 24, 1988.

Stefansson, Vilhjalmur (1879–1962), Canadian-American explorer of Icelandic descent, famed for his Arctic explorations, most notably the 5 years (1913–18) spent continuously above the Arctic Circle, living off the land and discovering several previously uncharted islands. He advised Pan American Airways on polar routes (1932–45) and the U.S. government on Arctic resources and, during and after World War II, on survival techniques for troops.

Steffens, Joseph Lincoln (1886–1936), U.S. journalist and leading MUCKRAKER, whose *The Shame of the Cities* (1904) and other early works were powerful indictments of the American monied elites of the time. He later became a socialist and after the RUSSIAN REVOLUTION supported the Soviet model of socialism.

Stein, Marc Aurel (1862–1943), British archeologist and explorer, who became the preeminent European historian, explorer, and rediscoverer of the ancient Asian Silk Road and of the cultures that met and interpenetrated along that travel and trade route for some thousands of years. Stein's work contributed greatly to the development of archeology, and to modern understandings of the real relationships between China and the other cultures of the ancient world. He was also a major antiques-taker, an activity much deplored in China; during several early 20th-century expeditions he took massive amounts of antiquities out of China's Tarim Basin, including the DIAMOND SUTRA, the oldest full printed book known, dated from about 868 A.D.

Steinbeck, John (1902–68), U.S. writer whose novel *The Grapes of Wrath* (1939) told the story of the "Okies," the DUST BOWL farmers forced to become migrants during the GREAT DEPRESSION. His book, and the film of the same name, were together one of the most powerful and effective populist statements of the period and by far his best work.

Steinberg, Joel, New York City lawyer who, on January 30, 1989, was convicted of the November 1, 1987, beating-murder of 6-year-old Lisa Steinberg, whom he claimed to have adopted but had not. Steinberg's conviction rested largely on evidence given by his common-law wife, Hedda Nussbaum, herself severely beaten by Steinberg. The murder attracted enormous public attention in a nation newly sensitive to the issue of child abuse.

stellar evolution, theory that stars, rather than being fixed and immutable, evolve through a regular life sequence, first suggested in the 1880s but developed in the 20th century. As proposed by German physicist Hans BETHE in 1906 and independently by Carl von Weizsäcker in 1912, interstellar gases condense to bodies in which thermonuclear reactions convert hydrogen to helium over a long "middle age." A star's final fate varies partly with its size. Stars about the size of our Sun dwindle to become white dwarfs and finally black dwarfs, essentially dead stars. A larger star—above a limit identified in 1931 by Subrahmanyan CHANDRASEKHAR—may explode massively in a nova or SUPERNOVA and then either become a NEUTRON star (probably a PULSAR), with a heavy metal core surrounded by a halo of neutrons, or collapse upon itself into a BLACK HOLE. The key to stellar evolution

theory is the relationship between brightness and stellar types, developed by Danish astronomer Ejnar Hertzsprung in 1911 and independently by U.S. astronomer Henry Norris Russell, who in 1913 depicted that relationship in the HERTZSPRUNG-RUSSELL DIAGRAM. The discoveries of Arthur EDDINGTON in 1924, that the luminosity of a star is directly related to its mass, and that stars are gaseous, their energy traveling to the surface not by convection but by RADIATION, also form part of the basis for the stellar evolution theory.

Stephenson, William ("Intrepid;" 1896–1989), Canadian inventor and industrialist who saw service as a flyer in World War I and began taking on assignments for British intelligence during visits to Germany in the 1930s. From 1940 he was chief foreign intelligence organizer for Great Britain in the Americas, working out of New York City, playing a major role in the development of the American OFFICE OF STRATEGIC SERVICES and training espionage agents in Canada for placement in occupied Europe. His code name was "Intrepid," as in the title of his book, *A Man Called Intrepid* (1976).

Steptoe, Patrick (1913–88), British gynecologist-obstetrician who developed IN VITRO FERTILIZATION, producing and later delivering the world's first TEST-TUBE BABY, Louise BROWN, in 1978.

Stern Gang (Lehi; Fighters for the Freedom of Israel), a terrorist organization named after its founder, Abraham Stern, who was killed by British Palestinian occupation forces in 1942. Stern was an IRGUN ZVAI LEUMI activist, who broke with the Irgun and formed his own organization in 1940, when the Irgun made a wartime decision to stop armed attacks on the British in Palestine. His organization continued on a terrorist course, its most notable actions being the assassination of Lord Moyne in 1944, its participation in the DEIR YASIN MASSACRE of 1948, and the assassination of UNITED NATIONS mediator Folke BERNADOTTE in 1948, an act that finally caused the group to be outlawed by the new Israeli government.

Yitzhak SHAMIR was a leading member of the Stern Gang.

steroids, class of compounds sharing some of the same chemical makeup, including CORTISONE and sex hormones such as TESTOSTERONE, ESTROGEN, and PROGESTERONE; they often control metabolic and growth processes. Used since the 1950s to treat a wide range of ailments, steroids have increasingly been taken in large doses for nonmedical purposes by athletes wanting to maximize their speed, endurance, and power, even though the likely cost is ultimately a shortened or physically distorted life. The widespread abuse of steroids became an open scandal in the 1980s, with many athletes disqualified from competition for failing tests designed to detect steroids.

Stethem, Robert, U.S. Navy diver murdered in 1985 by ISLAMIC HOLY WAR terrorists aboard a hijacked TWA airliner at Beirut airport.

Stevens, John Paul (1920–), U.S. lawyer, who was appointed to the Seventh Circuit U.S. Court of Appeals in 1970. He was named to the Supreme Court by President Gerald FORD in 1975. On the Court he functioned generally as a moderate, often becoming a swing vote between liberals and conservatives on close decisions.

Stevenson, Adlai Ewing (1900–65), U.S. lawyer, who held a series of diplomatic posts during World War II and was an adviser to the U.S. UNITED NATIONS delegation 1946–47. He was Democratic governor of Illinois 1949–53. Stevenson was his party's presidential nominee in 1952 and 1956, losing twice to Dwight D. EISENHOWER, and served as U.S. ambassador to the United Nations 1961–65.

Stewart, Potter (1915–), U.S. lawyer, who was appointed to the Sixth Circuit U.S. Court of Appeals in 1954 and to the Supreme Court by President Dwight D. EISENHOWER in 1958. On the Court he usually strictly construed the applicable law, while at the same time usually finding with the liberal majority, often in a separately written concurring opinion.

Stimson, Henry Lewis (1867–1950), U.S. lawyer and antitrust prosecutor during the administration of Theodore ROOSEVELT. He was secretary of war 1910–13, secretary of state 1929–33, and in his seventies World War II secretary of war 1940–45. A Republican member of the Democratic cabinets of presidents ROOSEVELT and TRUMAN, he played a major role in developing the American war effort.

Stockton schoolyard murders (January 17, 1989), the mass murders of five schoolchildren in the playground of Cleveland Elementary School in Stockton, California, by Patrick Edward Purdy (alias West), who fired 110 rounds from his semiautomatic assault rifle in the course of the murders, and then committed suicide. All of the children killed were Southeast Asian refugees. In the wake of the murders, state and national pressure to ban such weapons grew, greatly assisted by the American law enforcement community.

Stolypin, Pyotr Arkadievich (1862–1911), Russian official, who was made premier by Czar NICHOLAS II in 1906 and thereafter forcibly suppressed dissent with such tactics as the mass hangings of revolutionaries. He reversed the reforms inaugurated after the czar's OCTOBER MANIFESTO of 1905. Stolypin was assassinated in Kiev in September 1911.

Stone, Harlan Fiske (1872–1946), U.S. lawyer, law professor, and U.S. attorney general (1924), who was appointed to the Supreme Court by Calvin COOLIDGE in 1925. A liberal, he found much of the NEW DEAL legislation of the 1930s constitutional, also defending the individual protections afforded by the Bill of Rights. In 1941 Franklin D. ROOSEVELT appointed him Chief Justice.

Stone, Isadore Feinstein (I. F. Stone; 1907–89), U.S. journalist and dissenter, who, after two decades as a staff writer and columnist on such then-liberal publications as *The New York Post, The Nation,* and *PM,* published his own newsletter, *I. F. Stone's Weekly* (1953–72). During that period he was the leading muckraking dissenter of his time, opposing the COLD WAR and the VIETNAM WAR, and so effectively exposing federal waste and corruption as to become required reading for tens of thousands of journalists, government people, academics, lobbyists, and other interested parties, whether they supported or opposed his political views.

Stonehenge, huge circle of standing stones (c. 1800–1400 B.C.) on England's Salisbury Plain, long known to be a religious site, but from 1965, after publication of Gerald HAWKINS's book *Stonehenge Decoded*, believed also to be an ancient observatory, aligned with solar and lunar eclipses.

Stopes, Marie Charlotte Carmichael (1880–1958), British BIRTH CONTROL advocate who in 1921 founded Britain's first clinic for the dissemination of contraceptive information. Trained as a paleobotanist, from 1916 Stopes focused on birth control issues, writing two widely influential best-selling books, *Married Love* (1918) and *Contraception: Its Theory, History and Practice* (1923).

Storm Troopers (SA), the NAZI PARTY streetfighting and terrorist organization from 1920, led by Ernst ROEHM, which played a substantial role in bringing Adolf HITLER to power in 1933. After power had been achieved, the army and SS soon felt the organization and its leaders to be a competitive force, and persuaded Hitler to authorize the murder of its leaders and many of its members. That was done on June 29–30, 1934, the NIGHT OF THE LONG KNIVES, in what has since become described as the Nazi BLOOD PURGE.

strangeness, quality of certain subatomic PARTICLES, first discovered in 1946 and described and given the label "strange" in 1953 by Murray GELL-MANN, working independently of T. Nakano and Kasuhiko Nishijima. Part of the strangeness of these particles is their asymmetry which, in 1956, led to the downfall of the longheld idea that righthandedness and lefthandedness were indistinguishable in the universe.

Strategic Arms Limitation Agreement of 1979 (SALT II), a U.S.–U.S.S.R. agreement that placed limitations on the numbers of INTERCONTINENTAL BALLISTIC MISSILES (ICBMS), missile launchers, and MULTIPLE INDEPENDENTLY TARGETABLE REENTRY VEHICLES (MIRVs).

Strategic Arms Limitation Agreements of 1972 (SALT I), U.S.–U.S.S.R. agreements limiting the use of ANTIBALLISTIC MISSILE SYSTEMS (ABMs), and suspending additional INTERCONTINENTAL BALLISTIC MISSILE (ICBM) deployment for 5 years.

Strategic Defense Initiative (SDI, or Star Wars), U.S. space-based nuclear defense system greatly favored by President Ronald REAGAN, which engaged great attention and much research outlay from 1983 but did not, at least in the early years, yield promising results. It became a major stumbling block in U.S.–U.S.S.R. arms negotiations from the mid-1980s.

Stratten, Dorothy (1960–80), young Canadian actress, who while still a teenager, was found and exploited by Paul Snider, later her husband. She became a *Playboy* centerfold nude in 1979 and "Playmate of the Year" in 1980. She was beaten, raped, and murdered by her then-estranged husband on August 18, 1980; he then committed suicide.

Strauss, Franz Josef (1915–88), West German political leader, who served in the German army during World War II, cofounded the conservative Bavarian Christian Social Union in 1945, and entered the federal parliament 1949. He then rose through a series of posts to become defense minister 1956–62, in that position fostering West German rearmament and attempting to develop nuclear weapons. He was forced to resign in 1962, because of his major, unsuccessful attack on press freedom, in which he accused the magazine *Der Spiegel* and some of its personnel of treason. He was finance minister 1966–69, and chancellor of Bavaria from 1978 until his death.

Streicher, Julius (1885–1946), Nazi propagandist and publisher of the racist, anti-Jewish newspaper, *Der Stürmer*, who played a major role in the development of German genocidal theories and actions. He was convicted of war crimes at the NUREMBERG TRIALS and executed in 1946.

Strijdom, Johannes Gerhardus (1893–1958), South African lawyer, a committed segregationist as a NATIONAL PARTY member of parliament 1929–58, and a rigid upholder of APARTHEID as prime minister 1954–58.

Stroessner, Alfredo (1912–   ), Paraguayan officer, who fought in the CHACO WAR and was armed forces commander in chief when he seized power in the military coup of 1954, then a ruling dictator for 35 years, the longest period of rule in Paraguayan history. He was toppled by a military coup led by his second-in-command, General Andres Rodriguez, on February 2–3, 1989, and went into exile in Brazil.

Stroud, Robert ("Bird-man of Alcatraz;" 1890–1963), double murderer imprisoned for life (1909–63), often in solitary confinement, who became an ornithologist. From about 1920 Stroud began to raise canaries, then widened his scope to study diseases of birds in general, especially while at Leavenworth federal prison, the result being his classic *Stroud's Digest of the Diseases of Birds* (1942). After 1942, at Alcatraz, he was forbidden to work with birds or to publish. His life was the subject of a 1955 biography and a 1962 movie starring Burt Lancaster.

structuralism, wide-ranging philosophical movement of the 20th century, centered in France, that focused on the system or structure being studied, rather than its elements or content. Among the thinkers especially linked with structuralism are Claude LÉVI-STRAUSS, Michel FOUCAULT, Roland BARTHES, and Noam CHOMSKY.

STS (Space Transportation System), formal name of the series of U.S. spacecraft popularly called the SPACE SHUTTLE, used from 1981.

Students for a Democratic Society (SDS), U.S. reformist and then revolutionary student group, part of the NEW LEFT. Organized in Chicago in 1960, in its early years SDS focused on civil rights and antipoverty issues, moved in the mid-1960s into anti-VIETNAM WAR action, and in 1969 fragmented into several small factions, one of them the WEATHERMEN.

submarine warfare, series of major naval confrontations during World War I and II. German submarines sank approximately 6,000 Allied ships totaling 12 million tons during World War I, losing 200 submarines. The 4-year Battle of the Atlantic was by far the most important naval aspect of the war; the survival of Allied forces on the Western Front depended on it. Improved antisubmarine technology and the successful development of the convoy system in 1917 made it possible for supplies to continue to flow to Britain throughout the war. German submarine warfare also developed strong anti-German feeling in the United States and greatly contributed to American entry into the war. During World War II the Allies and Germans fought a second crucial Battle of the Atlantic; the combined forces of the British and American navies, coupled with adoption of the convoy system, ultimately defeated the German submarine fleet. This made it possible for the United States, functioning as the ARSENAL OF DEMOCRACY, to supply its allies on both major fighting fronts. Enormous amounts of American supplies went to the Soviet Union via the MURMANSK RUN; even larger quantities of supplies went directly to Great Britain, fueling continued resistance early in the war, then as part of the buildup to the multiple assaults on Europe that culminated in the NORMANDY invasion and Nazi defeat.

subway vigilante, the media-supplied name for BERNHARD GOETZ.

Süchow, Battle of (December 1948–January 1949), the decisive battle of the CHINESE CIVIL WAR, in which attacking Communist armies, approximately 500,000 strong as they moved toward Canton, met and destroyed defending Nationalist armies of equal strength. Nationalist casualties were an estimated 250,000 men, and the morale of the remaining Nationalist armies was greatly weakened.

Sudan (The Republic of Sudan), until 1954 a British protectorate, though nominally jointly governed by Egypt and Great Britain. Internal autonomy was gained in 1954, and was followed by the beginning of what would become decades of civil war. Independence came on January 1, 1956.

Sudanese Civil War (1955–   ), the long continuing insurgency that began shortly after Sudan achieved full autonomy from British-Egyptian rule in 1954. The civil war pitted the Christian and animist Black provinces of the south against the dominant Moslems of the north, who controlled the Sudanese government. In 1972 President Gaafar Mohammed al-NIMEIRY seemed to conclude the war, with a treaty that promised full autonomy for the southern provinces, but in 1980 his government reneged on certain key elements of the agreement. This stirred renewed rebel activity, which by 1985 had burst into full-scale civil war. The war was accompanied by continued widespread starvation suffered by local and refugee populations, including an estimated 1 million refugees from Chad and Ethiopia, and by periodic blockage of international relief shipments by the warring parties.

Sudetenland, a single name given by the Nazis to several predominantly German-speaking areas that had become part of Czechoslovakia after World War I. Some of them were near the Sudetes Mountains, and most of them were near the Czech–Polish border. Although the Sudeten Nazi party won large concessions from the Czech government in 1937 and 1938, Germany insisted on "self-determination," meaning annexation; at MUNICH, on September 29–30, 1938, France and Great Britain forced Czechoslovakia to accede to the Nazi demands; after Munich, the onset of World War II was clearly in sight.

Suez Crisis (July–November 1967), a Middle East confrontation that began in late July 1967, when the United States and Great Britain withdrew promised financing for Egypt's ASWAN HIGH DAM. In retaliation, Egyptian president Gamal Abdel NASSER nationalized the Suez Canal on July 26, creating an impasse that negotiations failed to resolve. France and Britain resolved to take the canal by force; Israel agreed to invade the Sinai, threatening the canal and providing a rationale for Anglo-French military intervention. Israel fulfilled its agreement, invading Egypt on October 29, and beginning the SIX-DAY WAR (SECOND ARAB–ISRAELI WAR). France and Britain then proceeded to attack Egyptian airfields and to move on the canal with air- and seaborne forces, as planned; by November 6, the Egyptians had evacuated the Sinai, and Anglo-French forces had landed at Port Said. The United States, however, sharply opposed the action and forced all three nations to withdraw, a UNITED NATIONS peacekeeping force then moving into the area. The withdrawal had enormous emotional and political repercussions in Great Britain, where there was widespread feeling that this bending to the will of the United States was a humiliation that marked the end of British great-power status. The resignation of British prime minister Anthony EDEN, which soon followed, was widely thought to be at least partly due to his handling of the Suez crisis, although ill health was the stated reason for his resignation.

Suharto (1921–   ), Indonesian soldier, in the Dutch army, the Japanese occupation army during World War II, and the insurgent army during the INDONESIAN WAR OF INDEPENDENCE. A general by 1965, he commanded army forces in putting down the attempted Communist Party of Indonesia coup of 1965 and during the massive political massacres that followed. He took power from SUKARNO in March 1966, thereafter controlling the country (1966–   ). As president he turned his country away from China and the Soviet Union and toward the West, continued to suppress domestic opposition, and banned all but government-financed political parties.

Sukarno (1901–70), Indonesian engineer, socialist, and active nationalist from the mid-1920s, who supported the Japanese during World War II, and in August 1945 proclaimed Indonesian independence. He

then led his country through the INDONE-
SIAN WAR OF INDEPENDENCE, and became
the first president of Indonesia in 1949. As
president he faced continuing Moslem insurgency and severe economic problems, as
he attempted to build a socialist state. In the
late 1950s he moved away from democracy,
in 1959 entering a period of government by
decree, which he called "guided democracy," while developing strong ties with the
Communist Party of Indonesia and with
China and the Soviet Union. After the attempted Communist coup of 1965 and the
anti-Communist INDONESIAN POLITICAL
MASSACRES that followed, he lost much of
his popularity and power. He was deposed
in March 1966, turning power over to General SUHARTO without resistance and leaving public life.

sulfa drug, an early "wonder drug," a kind
of antibacterial medicine, the first of which
was discovered by German chemist Gerhard
Domagk in 1932. Four sulfa drugs were developed by the end of World War II, and
though their effect was overshadowed by
the development of PENICILLIN and other
ANTIBIOTICS, sulfa drugs are still widely
used, especially where antibiotics are ineffective, even though some sulfa-resistant
bacteria have developed.

Sullivan, Harry Stack (1892–1949), U.S.
psychiatrist, who helped develop the interpersonal school of psychiatry. Seeing mental disturbances as resulting not from inner
causes but from a person's relations with
others, Sullivan pioneered in the use of
group therapy.

Sullivan, Louis Wade (1933–　), U.S.
physician, medical professor, and administrator, who had been dean of medicine at
Morehouse College since 1974, when
named secretary of health and human services by president George BUSH on December 22, 1988.

Summerhill School, self-governing child-
centered school founded in England's Sussex by A. S. NEILL in 1921, the premise being "to make the school fit the child" instead
of the reverse. Though too revolutionary to

be widely copied, Neill's experiences at
Summerhill still considerably contributed to
the gradual relaxation and increasing openness of 20th-century education, especially in
the United States.

Sunday, William Ashley "Billy" (1862–
1935), U.S. Christian fundamentalist revivalist, a former professional baseball player,
who from 1896 conducted often-huge revival meetings throughout the United States,
becoming the best-known revivalist of his
time.

Sununu, John H. (1939–　), U.S. engineer, university professor, New Hampshire
state legislator (1973–74), and governor
(1983–89), who became a member of the
BUSH 1988 presidential campaign staff and
was named White House chief of staff on
December 17, 1988.

Sun Yat-sen (1866–1925), the Chinese republican revolutionary who led the movement to overthrow the Ch'ing (Manchu)
dynasty, to bring democracy to China, and
to bring China into the mainstream of the
modern world. He spent some time in Hawaii as a youth, trained to become a doctor
in China and Hong Kong, and began his
revolutionary career back in Hawaii, in
1894, founding the REVIVE CHINA SOCIE-
TY. His first attempt to organize a revolution was in Canton in 1895; it quickly failed,
and he fled abroad. From then until 1911
he lived abroad, gathering money and support for the republican revolution and from
1900 to 1911 organizing eleven more attempted revolts in China. From 1905 he
headed a group of revolutionary organizations loosely formed into the Alliance Society. In 1911, learning of the Wuhan revolt
against the Manchu government, he returned home to a revolutionary China and
became provisional president of the new republic. To unite the revolutionary forces, he
agreed to step down in favor of former government minister YÜAN SHIH-K'AI, and Yüan became president after the resignation of
the emperor in 1912. He parted from Yüan
in 1913, leading a second revolution, which
was defeated, and then fled to Japan; he returned to China after Yüan's death in 1916.

He spent the next 7 years attempting to form and re-form a republican government. In 1923 he accepted Soviet aid and with it the support of the Chinese Communist party. He reorganized the KUOMINTANG along Soviet lines and set about organizing the NORTHERN EXPEDITION, which, under the leadership of CHIANG KAI-SHEK, would bring China under Kuomintang control and at the same time begin the 22-year-long CHINESE CIVIL WAR. But Sun did not live to see the beginning of the expedition, dying of cancer in Peking, on March 12, 1925, from then on to be regarded as father of the Chinese revolution by Nationalists and Communists alike.

Sun Yat-sen, Madame, the name by which Ch'ing-ling SOONG, the wife of SUN YAT-SEN, is best known.

superconductivity, loss of resistance to electricity in certain materials when cooled; first discovered in 1911 by Dutch physicist Heike Kamerlingh Onnes, though a working theory of the phenomenon was not developed until 1957. To achieve superconductivity—that is, to lose little or no electrical energy to resistance or friction—materials had to be cooled to near absolute zero; that being very difficult and expensive, superconductive materials had limited applications for some decades, notably in particle ACCELERATORS and NUCLEAR MAGNETIC RESONANCE imaging machines. In 1986 two IBM researchers, K. Alex Müller and J. Georg Bednorz, found new ceramic materials that became superconductive at much higher temperatures, for which they were awarded the 1987 Nobel Prize for Physics. Other scientists quickly found similar materials and at even higher temperatures as they began exploring for some whose physical properties would make them suitable for everyday use, with the promise of revolutionary changes in many areas.

supernova, explosion of a massive star in a late stage of STELLAR EVOLUTION, such as that thought to have produced the Crab Nebula. The term was introduced in 1934 by German-American astronomer Walter Baade and Bulgarian-Swiss astrophysicist Fritz Zwicky, whose predictions that NEUTRON stars result after supernovas was confirmed in 1968.

supersonic transport (SST), AIRPLANE capable of traveling faster than the speed of sound—that is, at MACH 1 or above—creating a shock wave called a SONIC BOOM. U.S. Air Force captain Charles YEAGER first broke the SOUND BARRIER in a research jet, the Bell X-1, in 1947, but the first supersonic airliner was the Soviet Tupolev TU-144, unveiled in 1968. The first regularly scheduled supersonic airliner was the Anglo-French Concorde, which went into service in 1976. The United States had decided in 1971 not to pursue supersonic transport development. Craft traveling at Mach 5 or more are termed hypersonic.

Suriname (Republic of Suriname), until 1975, Dutch Guiana, a Netherlands colony, with internal autonomy from 1954. It became an independent state on November 25, 1975.

Surveyor, series of U.S. unmanned spacecraft exploring the MOON in the 1960s, developing the techniques for making a "soft" landing on the Moon, preparatory to the APOLLO flights.

Sutherland, Thomas, one of the American LEBANON HOSTAGES, American University agriculture dean, who was kidnapped on September 9, 1986.

Suzman, Helen (Helen Gavronsky; 1917–), South African economist and liberal, who won her first parliamentary seat in 1953 and founded the Progressive party in 1959; it became part of the opposition Progressive Federal party in 1977. She was a leading opponent of APARTHEID and of suppression of political and civil liberties, a proponent of a democratic, multiracial South African solution.

Svoboda, Ludvik (1895–1979), Czech officer who, during World War II, led the Czech corps fighting beside Soviet forces on the Eastern Front. He was defense minister in the postwar government and stayed on after the Communist coup of 1948. He survived the purges of the SLÁNSKY SHOW TRI-

ALS period and was Czech president 1968–75.

Swaggart scandal, the February 1988 scandal following charges of sexual misconduct on the part of television evangelist Jimmy Swaggart, accused of consorting with at least one prostitute, a credit quickly claimed by New Orleans prostitute Debra Murphree. Swaggart tearfully delivered a nationally televised "I HAVE SINNED!" speech on February 21, 1988. In March his ministry was revoked by the Assemblies of God, removing him from his pulpit and from the air for a year. Swaggart ignored the order and went back to televangelism on May 22, 1988, soon proving able to hold his audience.

Swann* v. *Charlotte-Mecklenburg Board of Education (1971), a landmark U.S. Supreme Court decision validating a school busing plan for Charlotte, North Carolina, which had been ordered by a lower court.

SWAPO, initials of the SOUTHWEST AFRICA PEOPLE'S ORGANIZATION OF NAMIBIA, by which the organization is best known.

swastika, the NAZI PARTY insignia, adopted by Adolf HITLER in 1919, which thereafter became the symbol of his party and therefore in 1933 of the Nazi German state. The word is Sanskrit, and both word and symbol were thought by the Nazis to be "Aryan," although the symbol itself had been used by several of the world's peoples for some thousands of years before the Nazis adopted it. In German hands the symbol came to represent mass murder, fascism, and war, becoming the most hated and feared symbol of the 20th century.

Swaziland (Kingdom of Swaziland), until 1967 a British protectorate, then gaining internal autonomy and becoming an independent state and COMMONWEALTH member on September 6, 1968.

Symbionese Liberation Army (SLA), the organization that kidnapped Patricia "Patty" HEARST in 1974.

Symington, William Stuart (1901–88), U.S. industrialist, who entered government as head of the post–World War II Surplus Property Board and stayed on in a series of appointive posts during the TRUMAN administration. He was a Missouri Democratic U.S. senator 1953–77 and an unsuccessful candidate for his party's presidential nomination in 1960. He was an arms race proponent during the early years of the COLD WAR, but was also an opponent of American involvement in Vietnam.

syndicalism, a movement aiming to organize workers into unions capable of ultimately paralyzing and destroying existing governments by means of the general strike and then taking control of the means of production. In practice, syndicalists and anarchists generally operated together as ANARCHO-SYNDICALISTS, whether or not so describing themselves, as occurred in the French and Spanish labor movements before World War II and in the American INDUSTRIAL WORKERS OF THE WORLD (IWW).

Syndicate, The, an alternative name for the U.S. MAFIA.

Synod of Barmen, anti-Nazi church coalition formed in 1934 by European religious leaders such as Karl BARTH and Martin NIEMÖLLER.

syphilis, worldwide type of venereal disease, often fatal if untreated, for which cures were found in the 20th century. The microorganism causing syphilis was first observed by German bacteriologists Fritz R. Schaudinn and P. Erich Hoffmann in 1905, and in 1906 their countryman, August von Wasserman, developed the first blood test for the disease. In 1910 German bacteriologist Paul EHRLICH introduced the first drug to cure syphilis, an arsenic compound called salvarsan but quickly dubbed the "magic bullet." Treatment was long and difficult, however, involving a series of injections. Later PENICILLIN was found to cure syphilis, as do some other ANTIBIOTICS. However, social problems hindered treatment of those who most need it, so syphilis and other venereal diseases remained common around the world, and the number of cases increased in the last quarter of the century.

Syria (Syrian Arab Republic), until the end of World War I, part of the Ottoman Empire, then becoming a French-administered LEAGUE OF NATIONS mandate territory, and an independent state on April 17, 1946. During the period 1958–61 Syria and EGYPT briefly joined in the UNITED ARAB REPUBLIC. After the March 1963 military coup, Syria became an Arab Islamic socialist state, led by the BA'ATH PARTY.

Szilard, Leo (1867–1964), Hungarian-American nuclear physicist, who played a major role in the development of the ATOMIC BOMB. A student, then professor, in Germany, Szilard fled the Germans in 1933, working first in England and later in the United States, joining in early work on NUCLEAR FISSION with Enrico FERMI and others. Szilard drafted the letter sent by Albert EINSTEIN to president Franklin ROOSEVELT urging the United States to develop the atomic bomb before the Germans did, and when approval came he actively participated in the MANHATTAN PROJECT. Afterward he pressed for demilitarization and international control of nuclear technology, eventually becoming a leader in antinuclear peace activities and forsaking physics for biology.

T

Taeyokale hotel fire (December 25, 1971), a fire at the Taeyokale Hotel, at Seoul, South Korea, that killed 163 people, the world's worst hotel fire to date.

Tafari, Ras, the given name of Ethiopian leader HAILE SELASSIE.

Taft, Robert Alphonso (1889–1953), U.S. lawyer, the son of President William Howard TAFT; he was an Ohio Republican state legislator (1921–38), and senator (1939–53). He was a conservative, sharply opposed to Franklin Delano ROOSEVELT and the NEW DEAL, and an isolationist who opposed any moves he felt might lead to American involvement in World War II. After the war he continued in opposition, winning passage of the TAFT-HARTLEY ACT in 1947, which sharply limited the New Deal's labor legislation.

Taft, William Howard (1857–1930), U.S. lawyer and judge who was an Ohio superior court judge before becoming federal solicitor general (1890–1892), federal district court judge (1892–1900), colonial administrator of the Philippines (1900–04), secretary of war (1904–09), 27th president of the United States (1909–13), and chief justice of the United States (1921-1930). A Republican, Taft defeated Democrat William Jennings BRYAN in the 1908 presidential election. He won the contested Republican nomination of 1912 from Theodore ROOSEVELT but lost the election to Democrat Woodrow WILSON. As president he initiated few major changes, instead backing away from the reforms of the previous Roosevelt administration and occupying a very weak position; he suffered from a growing split with the Progressives in his own party and Democratic control of the House of Representatives for most of his term. As chief justice his main contribution was administrative; no landmark opinions bear his name or imprint.

Taft-Hartley Act (1947), a series of major amendments to the WAGNER ACT, that outlawed the closed shop, jurisdictional strikes, and secondary boycotts; made the union shop more difficult to institute; denied protection for wildcat strikes; reinstituted antistrike injunctions in some situations, partly nullifying the NORRIS-LA GUARDIA ACT of 1932; included anti-Communist provisions; and in aggregate made it far more difficult for unions to organize and to use the strike weapon.

Takahashi, Korekiyo (1854–1936), Japanese banker and public official, head of the Bank of Japan, who became finance minister 1913–14 and again in 1918. He was prime minister 1921–22, and finance minister in several cabinets. He was assassinated during the failed young officers' coup of 1936.

Takeshita, Noboru (1924–   ), Japanese political leader, in parliament from 1958, who held a series of cabinet-level posts, including the finance ministry, before becoming prime minister on November 6, 1987. As prime minister he continued to negotiate with the United States regarding trade imbalances, developed further economic ties with the People's Republic of China, and developed some internal tax reforms, but from July 1988 his otherwise relatively uneventful administration was dominated by the developing RECRUIT STOCK SCANDAL, which caused the resignations of his finance, economics, and justice ministers, some top business leaders, and several key aides to both Takeshita and his predecessor, Yasuhiro NAKASONE. On April 24, 1989, after the widening and deepening scandal had directly involved Takeshita, he announced that he would resign.

Tambo, Oliver (1917–   ), South African lawyer, who became active in the national movement in the 1950s in close collaboration with Nelson MANDELA, being banned or imprisoned for much of the period. He became a deputy president of the AFRICAN NATIONAL CONGRESS (ANC) in 1958 and went into exile abroad in 1960, functioning for the ANC out of Zambia and becoming president of the ANC in 1967. During the next two decades he led the ANC in what became a guerrilla war against the South African government, including military assaults, terrorist attacks against noncombatants, and the organization of internal resistance movements.

Tampico Incident, the arrest of several U.S. sailors at Tampico, Mexico, in 1914, which provided the pretext for the American occupation of VERA CRUZ.

Tampomas 2 **sinking** (January 27, 1981), sinking of the Indonesian passenger *Tampomas 2*, which caught fire in the Java Sea during a storm; after almost 2 days of rescue attempts, the ship finally sank, and an estimated 580 of its 1,200 passengers and crew died.

Tanaka, Kakuei (1918–   ), Japanese entrepreneur, who went into politics in 1947 and held ministerial posts from 1962 to 1972, then becoming prime minister 1972 to 1974. He resigned under attack for financial malfeasance while in office. He was indicted in 1976 for accepting bribes from the Lockheed Corporation while prime minister, and was convicted in 1983 after a long trial that exposed a major scandal but did not dislodge his Liberal Democratic party from power.

Tanganyika, a former German East African colony, that after World War I became a British-administered LEAGUE OF NATIONS mandate terrritory; after World War II it became a UNITED NATIONS trust territory. It gained independence in 1961, and merged with ZANZIBAR and Pemba to form the new nation of TANZANIA on April 26, 1964.

Tangshan earthquake (July 28, 1976), a series of earthquakes that destroyed much of the center of this North Chinese city, killing a reported 242,000 people and injuring 164,000 more; the actual figures may be even higher.

tanks, armored vehicles running on tracks and therefore able to carry soldiers and weapons over rough terrain and through many types of barriers. The tank was first developed in Britain by Ernest Dunlop Swinton, with Winston CHURCHILL's support, in 1915, though such ideas had been proposed and rejected by the governments of several countries from the turn of the century. The British and French, who built their own models, first used tanks in the Battle of the SOMME in 1916, but their first great success was in 1917 at CAMBRAI, where a concentrated force of Allied tanks broke through the HINDENBURG LINE. The Germans sometimes fought back in captured Allied tanks. In the interwar period arguments raged about light versus heavy tanks and about how to use tanks. The Germans and Russians learned the effectiveness of massed tank thrusts in the SPANISH CIVIL WAR. Such lessons laid the basis for Hitler's BLITZKRIEG attacks with armored PANZER units against Poland and later Russia and the striking desert tactics of Erwin ROMMEL in North Africa. By contrast, although the Allies had far more tanks, they often dispersed them to support infantry, diluting their effectiveness; this included the Russians, most of whose experienced generals had been removed during STALIN's purges. The largest single tank battle occurred near Kursk, in the U.S.S.R., in 1943, involving almost 3,000 tanks. Tanks also were widely used by the Allies in Western Europe following the 1944 NORMANDY INVASION, by the Russians in Manchuria against the Japanese in 1945, and to a lesser extent by U.S. forces in the Pacific, often with amphibious vehicles. Afterward huge numbers of tanks remained in place in Europe, the trend being toward lighter vehicles, sometimes basically armored personnel carriers armed with GUIDED MISSILES. Tanks were heavily used in battle by the Arabs and Israelis and by the Indians and Pakistanis in the 1950s and 1960s, but changing patterns of war and defenses made tanks less important militarily in places such as Vietnam.

Tannenberg, Battle of (August 26–31, 1914), a decisive early battle on the Eastern Front in World War I, at Tannenberg, in East Prussia, in which the Russian Second Army suffered a major defeat, losing an estimated 125,000 men and a great deal of much-needed war material. The Russian commander, General Alexander Samsonov, committed suicide after his troops were surrounded and his command cut to pieces by better-led, better-trained, better-equipped German forces under generals Paul von HINDENBURG and Erich LUDENDORFF.

Tanzania (United Republic of Tanzania), a union of TANGANYIKA and ZANZIBAR. Until World War I Tanganyika was a German colony; after the war it became a British mandate territory, and after World War II a British-administered UNITED NATIONS trust territory, achieving independence and COMMONWEALTH status in 1961. The Tanganyikan independence movement was led by President Julius Kambarage NYERERE, who led Tanganyika and then Tanzania until 1985. The islands of Zanzibar and Pemba were a British colony until gaining independence and Commonwealth membership in 1963. On April 26, 1964, the two new countries merged into the United Republic of Tanganyika and Zanzibar, later renamed Tanzania.

tape recording, use of magnetized tape to record sounds or signals for later reproduction. As early as 1900 Danish inventor Valdemar Poulsen had a U.S. patent to record using a magnetized wire, but the first known use of magnetic tape recording was during World War II by the Germans, to broadcast at chosen times speeches by Hitler and other Nazi leaders. Spurred by this use, the Ampex Corporation developed a tape recorder in the United States in 1948, first used by ABC for the Bing Crosby Show. By 1950 magnetic tape was being used for scientific data and tried out with the UNIVAC computer, being put into more general use with computers from 1956. Video tape recorders were first developed in 1956, though they did not become widespread among consumers until the 1980s. In the early 1960s music-quality tape cartridges were developed for personal use; cassettes were introduced by the Dutch firm of Philips in 1963, taking a large share of the market once held by long-playing records and becoming seemingly ubiquitous with the arrival of hand-size tape recorder-players.

Taranto bombing (November 11, 1940), World War II attack of Italian naval units at Taranto, Italy, by British carrier-based bombers. Three battleships were sunk and several smaller ships damaged in a major disaster for the Italian navy.

Tarawa, Battle of (November 20–24, 1943), World War II attack that began with an extremely costly U.S. Marine amphibious assault on heavily fortified Betio Island. Because of the shallowness of the water near the landing area, the American landing craft could not even reach the beach, and the Americans suffered many casualties as they waded ashore. There were over 3,000 Marine casualties, almost 1,000 of them dead, over 4,500 Japanese dead, and few Japanese survivors, as almost all of the island's defenders chose to fight to the death.

Tarbell, Ida Minerva (1857–1944), U.S. journalist and MUCKRAKER, whose *History of the Standard Oil Company* (1904) was one of the first major exposés of U.S. monopolistic practices, helping to create the climate within which trustbusting activities flourished.

Tasaday, small hunting-and-gathering tribe found in the Philippines in 1972 and regarded by many as relics from the primitive life-style of the Stone Age. From at least 1986, some charged that the Tasaday had been a hoax, though others pointed out that by then they had had 14 years of contact with the modern world.

Tate, Sharon, U.S. actress killed by mass murderer Charles MANSON on August 9, 1969.

Taussig, Helen Brooke (1898–1986), U.S. pediatric cardiologist who first diagnosed the heart defects that led to blue pallor (cyanosis) in BLUE BABIES and who with her surgeon-colleague Albert BLALOCK devised an operation to correct them.

Tawney, Richard Henry (1880–1962), British historian, whose work in economic history as it influenced and intertwined with the history of ideas is expressed in his best known work, *Religion and the Rise of Capitalism* (1926). He was active in socialist and reform causes and was president of the Worker' Educational Association 1928–44.

Taylor, Maxwell Davenport (1901–86), U.S. officer, who commanded the 101st Airborne Division during the invasion of NORMANDY in 1944, and throughout the subsequent European campaign. He later commanded the American Eighth Army in Korea, was chairman of the Joint Chiefs of Staff, 1962–64, and was American ambassador to South Vietnam, 1964–66.

Teapot Dome, a cabinet-level U.S. bribery scandal, in which Secretary of the Interior Albert B. Fall in 1922 took bribes amounting to $400,000 in return for leases on federal oil reserves, without competitive bidding. He granted Harry F. Sinclair a lease on the Teapot Dome, Wyoming, federal oil reserve, and Edward O. Doheny, a lease on the Elk Hills, California, reserve. A Senate investigation led by senator Thomas J. Walsh disclosed the leases and bribes; prosecutions followed after a Justice Department coverup failed. The Supreme Court nullified the leases in 1927. Fall was convicted of bribery in 1929; Sinclair eventually served a short term for contempt of court.

Tedder, Arthur William (1890–1967), British air officer, who saw service in World War I. During World War II he commanded British air forces in North Africa, all Allied air forces in the Mediterranean, then all Allied air forces in the European theater, as deputy supreme commander to Dwight D. EISENHOWER.

Tehran Conference (November 28–December 1, 1943), the first ROOSEVELT–CHURCHILL–STALIN wartime summit meeting, at which several major decisions were reached, affecting the course of World War II and the shape of the postwar world. The conferees agreed to set May 1944 as the time of the coming Allied invasion of Western Europe, Stalin agreed to make war on Japan after the defeat of Germany, the basic structure of the UNITED NATIONS was agreed on, and Iranian, Polish, Yugoslav, and several other postwar independence and territorial matters were partially settled.

Teilhard de Chardin, Pierre (1881–1955), French paleontologist and theologian, best known for his view that humans and indeed the whole universe are evolving toward spiritual unity. Because his Jesuit superiors mistrusted his attempt to reconcile evolution and Catholicism, he was allowed to publish only strictly scientific papers during his lifetime. His philosophical works were mostly published posthumously. Stationed in China from the 1920s, he helped locate and place in context the early human fossil remains known as PEKING MAN, found in 1927.

television, electrical transmission of pictures and sound; explored since the 1880s but achieved only in the 20th century, when it became a major force in linking the peoples of the Earth into what Marshall MCLUHAN called a GLOBAL VILLAGE. Building on the previous two decades' developments, Scottish inventor John Logie BAIRD and American inventor Charles Francis Jenkins both developed experimental versions of television in 1923. Baird made the first public demonstration of television in London in 1926 and the first trans-Atlantic transmission 2 years later. Early types of television used a crude mechanical method of transmitting signals; a rotating disk converted light into electrical impulses, causing a flickering image. A more successful approach, employed by Russian-American inventor Vladimir ZWORYKIN, involved electron-beam scanning, using a CATHODE RAY TUBE. In 1923–24, Zworykin patented the two basic elements of modern television: the iconoscope camera tube and the kinescope picture tube. By 1932 he had actually built the first all-electronic television. Technical improvements and experimental broadcasts were made through the 1930s. Color television was developing, too. A German patent was filed as early as 1904; both Zworykin and Baird had color television patents in the 1920s, with Baird making a color television demonstration in 1928; several Bell Laboratories scientists made key innovations in 1929; and CBS Laboratories' Peter GOLDMARK made a successful color broadcast in 1940. In Britain television service was begun in 1936 under the quasi-governmental BRITISH BROADCASTING CORPORATION (BBC), which the following year broadcast the coronation procession of GEORGE VI. In the United States, Zworykin's RCA television was demonstrated at New York City's World's Fair in 1939, the year of the first television pictures of a U.S. president (Franklin ROOSEVELT), a major league baseball game, and a college football game—and the first television sets for sale to the public. Network television made its official debut with an NBC broadcast from the General Electric station, WRGB, at Schenectady, New York, on February 1, 1940; by mid-year there were 22 other American television stations. That year also saw the first broadcast of presidential conventions (not live, but television pictures of film). Commercial television authorized by the FEDERAL COMMUNICATIONS COMMISSION (FCC) formally began on July 1, 1941, with 15 hours of programming from New York City's WNBT. CBS television reported the attack of Pearl Harbor on December 7, 1941, but World War II temporarily halted the spread of television, with all but six sta-

tions being shut down. Not until 1945 did NBC put together its first "network," linking New York, Philadelphia, and Schenectady. But by 1949, more than 1,000,000 television receivers were in use in the United States; by 1951, that number had jumped to 10,000,000, reaching 50,000,000 by 1959. In Britain the BBC resumed television broadcasting in 1946, joined in 1954 by commercial television stations. Color television, with its more complex technology, developed more slowly, but by 1971 the sales of color television in America surpassed those of black and white. By that time television had changed the face of the modern world. In addition to the popular entertainment programs, viewers saw presidential conventions, space launchings, wars, uprisings, sports contests, and myriad other events live or on MAGNETIC TAPE (introduced in 1956). The EISENHOWER–NIXON presidential campaign of 1952 was the first to be televised live; by the 1980s, presidential campaigns had become largely media (for which read "television") events. Images from Joseph MCCARTHY to Oliver NORTH could be made—and broken—on the "tube." Distant parts of the world were linked ever more closely together after 1962, when the SATELLITE *TELSTAR* made its first trans-Atlantic broadcasts, both black-and-white and color, between the United States and England and France. By the 1980s multiple satellites allowed immediate two-way communication, not simple transmission, between distant parts of the world. Bell Labs' 1969 development of an imager COMPUTER chip led to the development of eversmaller hand-held television cameras, including, by 1985, a paperback-size video camera for home use. The use of satellites and hand-held television cameras led to a proliferation of local news coverage, by the 1980s decreasing somewhat the power of the networks. American and British programming has been widely exported and, for better or worse, has played a major role in Westernizing many other cultures and in helping to make English the unofficial world language. The power of television as a propaganda tool has caused many governments around the world to keep it under state control; other countries mix commercial with nonprofit systems. From 1975, with Sony's introduction of the first video cassette recorder (VCR), many people were able to exercise more choice in their viewing, being able to rent or buy videotaped material or to record programs for later watching. Cable and satellite dishes also made available a much wider range of programming, cutting into the networks' traditional share of the viewing audience. Though widely criticized for its excesses in sensationalizing news and for creating mindless, often violent entertainments, television has probably been underrated for its role in increasing viewers' understanding of themselves and the world around them.

television quiz show scandal, scandal generated by 1959 New York grand jury and congressional investigations of charges that some of the most popular televison quiz shows of the period were "fixed," by show staff coaching of contestants. Charles Van Doren, winning contestant on the "$64,000 Question," confessed to such fixing on November 2, 1959, ending the quiz show fad until their resurgence in the 1970s and 1980s.

Teller, Edward (1908–   ), Hungarian-American nuclear physicist, called the father of the HYDROGEN BOMB. After training in Germany and study with Niels BOHR in Denmark, Teller emigrated from Nazi Germany in 1935, settling in the United States. Working with Enrico FERMI on NUCLEAR FISSION from 1941, he joined the MANHATTAN PROJECT, working to develop the ATOMIC BOMB. As early as 1942 Teller and Fermi conceived of a bomb they called the "Super," using NUCLEAR FUSION with an atomic bomb as a trigger. From 1949 he led development of this hydrogen bomb, in the process breaking bitterly with J. Robert OPPENHEIMER, and for decades pushed for development of nuclear weapons and nuclear energy. Late in his life he was a key theoretician behind the STAR WARS proposal.

Telstar, first communications SATELLITE to relay TELEVISION signals, including color, launched from Cape Canaveral on July 10, 1962; a precursor of the worldwide INTELSAT system.

Tenerife airport disaster (March 27, 1977), the collision of two full Boeing 747s on the ground at Tenerife airport, causing both to burst into flames, killing 576 people and creating the worst airplane disaster in history.

T'eng Hsiao-ping, the old-style name of Chinese leader DENG XIAOPING.

Tennessee Valley Authority (TVA), a massive U.S. NEW DEAL utilities project that built a series of large dams in the Tennessee River basin, as well as ultimately buying existing private power installations, which generated and sold electric power to municipalities, associations, and large businesses in the basin at low rates. They developed a considerable range of flood control, farm help, and conservation projects in the valley.

Terauchi, Count Hisaichi (1879–1946), Japanese officer who held many key army and government positions before World War II, including that of war minister in the mid-1930s. From 1937, he commanded Japanese forces in north China and was then Southeast Asia commander-in-chief 1941–45, becoming a field marshal in 1943.

Tereshkova, Valentina Vladimirovna (1937–   ), Soviet cosmonaut who on June 16, 1963, in VOSTOK 6, became the first woman in space, orbiting the Earth 48 times in a 71-hour flight.

terrible beauty is born, a a line by William Butler Yeats; from *Easter, 1916,* about the EASTER RISING.

terrorism, in the late 20th century, a term generally used to describe such actions as assassination, hijacking, bombing, and the mass murder of defenseless civilians, carried out by such organizations as the BAADER-MEINHOF GROUP, the RED BRIGADES, and BLACK SEPTEMBER; for example, the MUNICH OLYMPICS MURDERS and the ACHILLE LAURO hijacking. Many governments have used similar tactics, as in the sponsorship of DEATH SQUADS, the destruction of the homes, imprisonment, and exile of dissenters, the use of poison gas against civilian populations, and the operation of genocidal CONCENTRATION CAMPS.

Teruel, Battle of (December 1937–February 1938), a Republican offensive during the SPANISH CIVIL WAR, that captured but could not hold the city.

testosterone, male sex HORMONE, first identified and synthesized in 1935 by Croatian-Swiss chemist Leopold Ruzicka and others; it is a STEROID sometimes used to enhance muscular development in athletes.

test-tube baby, child born of a human egg fertilized outside of and later implanted into the womb, by the process of *IN VITRO* FERTILIZATION, the first such baby being Louise BROWN in 1978.

Tet Offensive (January–February 1968), a major attack by the North Vietnamese regular army and accompanying guerrillas on cities and military installations throughout South Vietnam, attack teams even penetrating the U.S. Embassy compound in Saigon. Although the offensive was ultimately repelled, it was the turning point in the VIETNAM WAR, demonstrating that after years of heavy bombing and reassuring American predictions of imminent victory, no victory was in sight; there was no "light at the end of the tunnel." The already-powerful American peace movement was greatly strengthened, and the JOHNSON administration was so disheartened that deescalation of the war, the opening of peace negotiations, and Lyndon B. Johnson's decision not to seek reelection all quickly followed.

Texas City explosions (April 16, 1947), explosion of a nitrate-carrying freighter in the city harbor in Texas, reaching a Monsanto chemical plant on shore and setting off a huge explosion that destroyed much of the city's business district. Later that night, a second nitrate-carrying freighter exploded in the harbor. An estimated 500–1,000 people were killed, with thousands injured and massive property damage.

Texas Tower sniper, former U.S. marine Charles Whitman, later found to have had a brain tumor, after killing his wife and mother, mounted the University of Texas observation tower and on August 1, 1966, killed 16 people, wounding 30 others, before police killed him.

Thaelmann, Ernst (1886–1944), the leading German Communist of the 1920s and early 1930s, and his party's unsuccessful presidential candidate in 1925 and 1933. He followed COMINTERN policy in attacking the German Social Democrats as "social fascists," splitting the opponents of fascism and making the Nazi rise to power far easier than it might otherwise have been. He was murdered by his Nazi captors in BUCHENWALD in September 1944.

thalidomide, a drug widely prescribed for pregnant women in Great Britain and Germany, and experimentally in many other countries, from 1957 until it became clear in 1961–62 that it caused serious birth defects, including major malformations in newborn babies. Some of the parents of "thalidomide babies" later won money settlements from governments and drug companies after years of protest and litigation. In the United States the FDA did not approve the drug for use, but it was used experimentally on tens of thousands of pregnant women and their children; afterward, U.S. drug laws were examined and greatly tightened to prevent recurrence of that kind of error.

Thant, U (1909–74), Burmese diplomat and UNITED NATIONS representative 1957-1961, who was third secretary-general of the UN 1961–71. During his tenure he was able to develop little impact on the major events of the time; he maintained an essentially neutralist position in the COLD WAR while stressing matters important to the THIRD WORLD at the UN. His decision to withdraw UN peacekeeping forces from the Sinai and Gaza in 1967 was both criticized as helping pave the way for the subsequent Arab–Israeli war and praised as lifesaving realism in contemplation of a war that the UN could not stop.

That's one small step for a man, one giant leap for mankind, comment by U.S. astronaut Neil ARMSTRONG, alighting on the MOON, July 16, 1969.

Thatcher, Margaret (Margaret Roberts; 1925–   ), British chemist and barrister, who became a Conservative member of Parliament in 1959 and was education and science minister 1970–74. She became Britain's first woman major political party leader in 1975 and first woman prime minister in 1979. Leading the most conservative wing of her party, she moved to privatize previously nationalized industries, sharply cut social welfare and cultural funding, and fostered legislation aimed at reducing union power. She also attempted to limit both criticism and possible national security breaches, in part by suppressing publication by former government employees, as in the *SPYCATCHER* case. The British victory in the 1982 FALKLANDS WAR greatly helped the national self-esteem of many in Great Britain and also helped her to continue in office in a period of some domestic difficulty. The civil war in Northern Ireland, accompanied by IRISH REPUBLICAN ARMY terrorist actions directed at her personally and at British citizens in many locations, was a continuing major unsolved problem.

Thaw, Harry Kendall (1872–1947), the man who shot and killed architect Stanford White at the dinner-theater on the roof of Madison Square Garden in New York City, on June 25, 1906, after Thaw's wife, Evelyn Nesbit Thaw, had accused White, her former lover, of seducing her before her marriage to Thaw. The case attracted great public interest and media attention, for Nesbit had been a well-known model and stage performer before her marriage to Thaw; and the sex practices of all three protagonists were deemed lurid for the time and place. After two trials Thaw was acquitted for reasons of insanity, and institutionalized. He later escaped, in 1915 was legally declared sane, was later recommitted, and was freed again in 1922.

Thaw, the, in the Soviet Union, the period of relaxation of internal tensions that fol-

lowed the death of Joseph STALIN in 1953, a period in which the use of the KGB's internal security apparatus was considerably limited, thousands of prisoners were released from labor camps, and voices of dissent were heard for the first time since the early 1930s. In 1956, with KHRUSHCHEV'S SECRET SPEECH, exposing many of the crimes of the Stalin period, the process accelerated, then also being called DE-STALINIZATION. After the removal of Khrushchev, in October 1964, the Soviet government again began to harass and in 1966 to prosecute dissidents, although never returning to the mass terrorism of the Stalin years.

There is no right to strike against the public safety by anybody, anywhere, any time, comment by Calvin COOLIDGE, then governor of Massachusetts, breaking the BOSTON POLICE STRIKE of 1919.

thermonuclear weapon, explosive device, such as the HYDROGEN BOMB, that produces its energy through NUCLEAR FUSION, creating much heat in the process.

They shall not pass, French slogan at the Battle of VERDUN (1916) during World War I, and SPANISH REPUBLICAN slogan at the SIEGE OF MADRID during the SPANISH CIVIL WAR.

Thieu, Nguyen Van (1923–   ), South Vietnamese officer and VIETNAM WAR general who joined in the army coup that deposed Ngo Dinh DIEM in 1963 and in the coup that deposed Nguyen Cao KY in 1965. Thieu became president of South Vietnam in 1967; he fled abroad in 1975 after his forces were defeated.

Third Arab–Israeli War (June 5–10, 1967), an alternate name for the SIX-DAY WAR.

Third International, an alternate name for the COMMUNIST INTERNATIONAL, denoting that it was a successor to the socialist SECOND INTERNATIONAL, which had split over the issue of participation in World War I.

Third Reich (1933–45), the third German empire, the first being the Holy Roman Empire, the second imperial Germany 1871–

1918, and the third the Nazi name for HITLER'S Germany.

Third World, the nonaligned poorer countries of the world. The term came into general use as the COLD WAR developed in the 1950s and with it what were at that time two definable Western and Soviet blocs. The third world was never well defined; politically, it was soon superseded by the NONALIGNED MOVEMENT and economically by the equally spongy "developing nations" term.

This House will not fight for King and Country, the OXFORD PLEDGE of February 1933.

This is London, the salutation of Edward R. MURROW, broadcasting from London to the United States during the 1940 BLITZ. His broadcasts did much to develop American sympathy for the Allies.

Tho, Le Duc (1911–   ), chief North Vietnamese negotiator during the Paris peace talks that led to the agreement of January 1973 ending American involvement in the VIETNAM WAR. In 1973 he and U.S. negotiator Henry KISSINGER were jointly awarded a Nobel Peace Prize, which Le Duc Tho declined.

Thomas, Norman Mattoon (1884–1968), U.S. minister, pacifist, socialist, and civil libertarian, who was a founder of the AMERICAN CIVIL LIBERTIES UNION in 1920 and of the League for Industrial Democracy in 1922. He was six-time presidential candidate of the SOCIALIST PARTY 1928–48.

Thomson, Joseph John (1856–1940), British physicist who discovered the ELECTRON in 1897 during work on cathode rays, sparking a wide range of 20th-century developments, most notably in the field of ELECTRONICS. He won the 1906 Nobel Prize for Physics. In 1904 he first posited the idea of electrons circling in orbits. As long-time head of the Cavendish Laboratory at Cambridge University, Thomson influenced a whole generation of scientists, such as Ernest RUTHERFORD.

Thornburgh, Richard Lewis (1929–   ), U.S. lawyer, a federal prosecutor as U.S. at-

torney for western Pennsylvania, 1969–75, and Justice Department criminal division assistant attorney general 1975–77. He was governor of Pennsylvania 1979–87, and was named U.S. attorney general by President Ronald REAGAN in July 1988. In September 1988, during a presidential campaign in which Republican presidential candidate George BUSH was attacking the AMERICAN CIVIL LIBERTIES UNION (ACLU), Thornburgh publicly delared that he had been an ACLU member but had resigned that membership. He was renamed U.S. attorney general by President-elect George Bush on November 21, 1988.

Thorndike, Edward Lee (1874–1949), U.S. psychologist, whose work focused on studies of human intelligence and learning methods. In his early work with animals Thorndike developed some now-standard experiments and tests, including the maze and the puzzle box; the results of his work on trial-and-error learning helped form the basis for BEHAVIORISM. He also developed tests for a wide range of human skills and aptitudes, the best known being the INTELLIGENCE TESTS he created for U.S. Army use in World War I. His textbooks on educational psychology were widely used and highly influential.

Three Mile Island (March 28, 1979), nuclear plant near Middletown, Pennsylvania, where a series of events brought the Unit 2 NUCLEAR REACTOR within what later reports said to be 1 hour from meltdown. A considerable amount of RADIOACTIVE material was released into the surrounding environment, although disagreement continues as to the amount of human and environmental damage caused. The event, accompanied by enormous media coverage, greatly heightened public concern as to the safety of NUCLEAR ENERGY.

***Thresher* sinking** (April 10, 1963), the sinking of the U.S. nuclear submarine *Thresher* off the New Hampshire coast after its hull failed at a depth of 1,000 feet, with the loss of its entire crew of 129.

Thule, town in northern Greenland founded in 1910 by Danish explorer Knut RASMUSSEN as a base for expeditions and given the Greco-Roman name for a northernmost land. During and after World War II, Thule became, by U.S.–Danish agreement, an important defense station.

thyroxine, vital HORMONE produced by the thyroid gland, first isolated as a crystal by Edwin C. Kendall in 1914, later synthesized and used to treat patients with insufficient thyroid hormone production.

Tiananmen Square, huge central Beijing square that was the site of the CHINESE STUDENT DEMONSTRATIONS OF 1989 and of the bloody attacks by the Chinese army on June 4, 1989, in which hundreds and perhaps thousands of Chinese citizens were killed.

Tiger, the, Georges CLEMENCEAU, French statesman who came out of semiretirement at the age of 76 to lead France to victory in World War I.

Till, Emmett (1941–55), a 14-year-old Black Chicago schoolboy visiting in the south, whose body was found in the Tallehatchie River, in Le Flore County, Mississippi, on August 31, 1955. He had been lynched, apparently for whistling at a White woman in a local store. Two White men were acquitted of the murder, having been tried before an all-White Mississippi jury. Coming when it did, at the beginning of the modern CIVIL RIGHTS MOVEMENT, the lynching of Emmett Till became a cause *célèbre*.

Times Beach, Missouri site of a major toxic chemical disaster. In 1971 thousands of gallons of DIOXIN, waste from a herbicide plant, were poured on Times Beach's dirt roads to keep down dust. By 1974 the deaths of many local animals had been traced to the chemical, but authorities did nothing, thinking that dioxin broke down quickly in the environment. But by 1982 it was clear that the dioxin was still heavily concentrated—100 to 300 times safe levels. The next year, unable to come up with an effective plan to deal with the dioxin, the Environmental Protection Agency bought all the homes in the town and evacuated the whole population.

Timosoara Massacre (December 17, 1989), the killing of hundreds of unarmed pro-democracy demonstrators by Rumanian security police at Timosoara, Transylvania, by order of Rumanian dictator Nicolae CEAUSESCU. The massacre stirred nationwide protests, which quickly grew into the RUMANIAN REVOLUTION.

Timoshenko, Semyon Konstantinovich (1895–1970), Soviet officer, who saw service in the RUSSIAN CIVIL WAR. In 1940 he commanded Soviet forces in the FINNISH-SOVIET WAR, afterward becoming a field marshal. He commanded defending forces at Smolensk and in the south early in the war, but fell from favor after the Soviet reverse at Kharkov in 1942, then leading somewhat lesser forces for the balance of the war.

Tinbergen, Nikolaas (1907–88), Dutch-British zoologist who in the 1930s, with Konrad LORENZ, founded ethology, the scientific study of animal behavior, for which they (and Karl von Frisch) shared the 1973 Nobel Prize for Physiology or Medicine. Tinbergen especially focused on the relationship between physiological or environmental stimulus and behavioral response in animals, attempting to use such studies to cast light on human behavior and communication, notably with autistic people.

Tiros (*T*elevision and *I*nfra-*R*ed *O*bservation *S*atellite), world's first weather SATELLITE, launched in 1960.

Tirpitz, Alfred von (1849–1930), German admiral who, as naval chief of staff, built a powerful German navy during the run-up to World War I. Although his early advice to pursue unrestricted SUBMARINE WARFARE was rejected, his submarine fleet ultimately did great damage to Allied shipping; but his large surface force was never a significant factor, save for the inconclusive battle of JUTLAND, for it was bottled up by the much stronger British fleet throughout the war.

Titanic, "unsinkable" British luxury liner on its first voyage across the North Atlantic, which sank after striking an unseen iceberg off Newfoundland on April 15, 1912. The ship, later judged to have been traveling too fast and with inadequate lifeboats and safety drills, sank in a little less than 2 hours, with a loss of an estimated 1,500 passengers and crew, among them some of the notable people of the time. Young wireless operator David SARNOFF, working in New York City, was the first to pick up the *Titanic's* distress signals, reporting for 72 hours about the sinking and rescue efforts; but the radio operator of a ship only 10 miles away from the *Titanic* had gone off duty. As a result of the tragedy, liners were required to have sufficient lifeboat space and emergency drills; ships were required to keep a 24-hour radio watch; and an International Ice Patrol was established for the North Atlantic. In 1985 the *Titanic* was located on the seabed by oceanographer Robert Ballard.

Tito (Josip Broz; 1892–1980), Yugoslav Communist leader who became a Communist after having been captured by the Russians in 1915 while serving in the Austrian army; he then fought with the Red Army during the RUSSIAN CIVIL WAR. He was a leading Yugoslav Communist of the interwar period, becoming active in the COMINTERN, and was his party's general secretary from 1937. During World War II he led a powerful anti-Nazi partisan movement in Yugoslavia, which in some periods also fought against the CHETNIK forces of Draza MIHAJLOVIC. After the war he became undisputed leader of the Yugoslav Communist Party and state, formally becoming president in 1953 and life president in 1974. He broke with the Soviet Union in 1948 and thereafter led his country on an independent course, developing a market-oriented, socialist, multiethnic state, four decades before the GORBACHEV era. At the same time he suppressed internal dissent, such as that of Milovan DJILAS. He maintained an independent international course as well, after his break with the Soviet Union maintaining relations with the West

and becoming an initiator of the NONALIGNED MOVEMENT.

Tobruk, a fortress on the Libyan seacoast, that was held by the British during a long AXIS siege (April–December 1941) and relieved after a desert battle that ended with German withdrawal. On June 20–21, 1942, German-Italian forces, advancing from Libya into Egypt after their victory at BIR HACHEIM a week earlier, paused to assault and take the fortress of Tobruk, and with it 33,000 Allied prisoners and much war material.

Togliatti, Palmiro (1893–1964), Italian Communist leader, a socialist who became a founder of the Italian Communist Party in 1921, and from 1926 was secretary-general of his party, operating from exile. In 1935 he became secretary of the COMINTERN. He fought with the INTERNATIONAL BRIGADES during the SPANISH CIVIL WAR, spent World War II in the Soviet Union, and returned to Italy to head the Italian Communist Party in 1944. During the postwar period he built it into the largest Communist Party outside the Soviet and Chinese blocs and served in early postwar governments, but after 1947 he was not accepted into the Christian Democrat–dominated coalition governments that followed.

Togo (Republic of Togo), FRENCH TOGOLAND, which became Togo, gained internal autonomy in 1956 and independence on April 27, 1960.

Togoland, former West African German protectorate, which became a LEAGUE OF NATIONS mandate territory after World War I. In 1922 it was split into FRENCH (East) TOGOLAND and BRITISH (West) TOGOLAND, both LEAGUE OF NATIONS mandate territories during the interwar period. After World War II both Togolands became UNITED NATIONS trust territories. On March 6, 1957, British Togoland became part of the new nation of GHANA. On April 27, 1960, French Togoland became the new nation of TOGO.

Tojo Hidecki (1884–1948), Japanese soldier and militarist leader, who became Kwangtung army chief of staff in Manchuria, minister of war, and in October 1941 prime minister of Japan. He bore great responsibility for leading Japan into World War II, resigned after serious wartime defeats in 1944, and was arrested, tried, and hanged as a war criminal after the war.

Tokyo firebombing (March 9, 1945), dropping of large numbers of incendiary bombs on Tokyo by U.S. bombers late in World War II, creating firestorms that destroyed much of the city and caused an estimated 200,000 casualties, of whom at least 100,000 ultimately died. Subsequent American incendiary raids created firestorms in several other Japanese cities, with very large additional casualties.

Tokyo Rose (Iva Ikuko Toguri D'Aquino, 1916–), American who broadcast Japanese propaganda aimed at U.S. troops in the South Pacific during World War II, the propaganda being ignored and the music rather enjoyed by its audience. After the war she was convicted of treason and imprisoned for six years but was later pardoned by U. S. president Ford, in the belief that she had been forced to so broadcast by the Japanese.

Tokyo–Yokohama earthquake (September 1, 1923), an earthquake and following fire that caused an estimated 140,000 deaths and destroyed much of both cities.

Tombaugh, Clyde William (1906–), U.S. astronomer, who in 1930 first discovered the planet PLUTO; its existence had been predicted in 1905 by Percival LOWELL.

Tonga (Kingdom of Tonga), until 1958 a British protectorate, Tonga gained independence and COMMONWEALTH membership on June 4, 1970.

Tonkin Gulf Resolution (August 7, 1964), a U.S congressional resolution, enabling president Lyndon B. JOHNSON to take the United States into the undeclared VIETNAM WAR. It passed unanimously in the House of Representatives and with two dissenting votes in the Senate. The situation generating the resolution resulted from two reported attacks on U.S. naval vessels by North

Vietnamese torpedo boats in the Gulf of Tonkin. Later, critics charged that the resolution had been prepared before the attacks had been reported and that the situation had been manufactured by the administration for the purpose of legitimizing planned American intervention in Vietnam.

Tontons Macoutes, Haitian paramilitary force and secret police organization developed by dictator François DUVALIER, which terrorized the people of Haiti during the 29 years in which he and his son ruled.

Torch, Operation, code name of the Allied plan for the invasion of North Africa in 1942, involving landings by mainly American troops at French-held Casablanca, Oran, and Algiers. All three landings (November 8–11) were successful after some resistance; at Algiers, VICHY French Admiral DARLAN was captured, went over to the Allied side, and ordered all French troops in North Africa to do the same.

Torrey Canyon **oil spill** (March 18, 1967), a major oil spill and environmental disaster created when the U.S. oil tanker *Torrey Canyon* grounded off Cornwall, England; the spill damaged an estimated 120 miles of British and French coastline.

Torrijos, Omar (1929–81), Panamanian officer and nationalist leader, who took power from President Arnulfo Arias in the coup of 1968, and negotiated the 1979 PANAMA CANAL treaties aimed at returning the canal to Panamanian sovereignty. He died in a 1980 plane crash.

Touré, Ahmed Sékou (1922–84), Guinean union official, nationalist, and socialist who, as head of the Guinean Democratic party, became first president of Guinea in 1958, when independence from France was achieved. He developed a strongly socialist economy in the early years and became a major figure on the left in the pan-African movement. He also developed a repressive one-party state, moderated his policies somewhat in the later years of his rule, and held power until his death.

Tower, John Goodwin (1925–), U.S. political scientist and university professor, four-term Republican senator from Texas, 1961–85, and international business and banking consultant from 1985. After leaving the Senate he was U.S. nuclear arms negotiator at Geneva, 1985–86, and was head of the TOWER COMMISSION, which reviewed the IRAN-CONTRA AFFAIR in 1987. He was nominated secretary of defense by President-elect George BUSH on December 16, 1988, but ran into serious confirmation problems during the January 25–February 1, 1988, hearings of the Senate Armed Services Committee, because of allegations of previous drinking problems. On February 2 the committee postponed a vote on the nomination, pending further investigation, and on February 23 voted against his nomination. The issue went to the floor of the Senate on March 2, after Tower had publicly pledged future sobriety in three February 26 national television appearances. Although the administration continued to fully back the Tower nomination, on March 9 it was voted down 53–47 by the Senate, becoming the first major defeat of the new Bush administration.

Tower Commission (President's Special Review Board), U.S. 1986–87 commission, appointed by President Ronald REAGAN and headed by John TOWER—the other two members being Edmund MUSKIE and Brent SCOWCROFT—that made the first major investigation of the IRAN-CONTRA AFFAIR, and issued a report that severely criticized the administration for its policy and operational failures.

toxic shock syndrome, rare, sometimes fatal, bacterial infection found most often in menstruating women, first recognized in 1978. Its worst year was 1980, with 819 cases in the United States, including 69 deaths. In 1981 the disease was linked with use of superabsorbent tampons, causing certain types to be taken off the market, and in 1984 with misused contraceptive sponges.

toxic waste dump, site where dangerous, health-threatening chemicals have been piled or poured, often illegally and certainly irresponsibly, with results as predicted in Rachel CARSON's *SILENT SPRING* (1962). A worldwide problem, it has received the most publicity in the United States, from the 1970s, with the finding of sites such as LOVE CANAL. Though the Environmental Protection Agency declared in 1983 that toxic wastes in general, and DIOXIN in particular, were a top priority, even the inadequate money allocated was sometimes not spent, and the problem worsened.

***Toya Maru* sinking** (September 26, 1954), the sinking of the harbor ferry *Toya Maru* in Tsugaru Strait, off Japan, during a typhoon, when the railroad cars it was carrying were torn loose by the storm; 1,172 people died.

Toynbee, Arnold Joseph (1889–1975), British historian whose 12-volume work *The Study of History* (1934–61) was an attempt to develop a systematic analysis of the history of civilization, along with a religiously based theory of regenerative development. His work was widely popular in its time, although major inadequacies made it useless as a basis for further theoretical or practical work.

Tracy, Edward Austin, one of the American LEBANON HOSTAGES, a writer who was kidnapped on October 21, 1986.

tranquilizers, type of drug developed in the mid-1950s that revolutionized treatment of mental patients. In 1952 a tranquilizing drug called reserpine was isolated from a long-known Indian root and first used on patients the following year, but its use declined quickly. In 1954 a synthetic tranquilizer, chlorpromazine (Thorazine), was first used. The main advantages of these drugs and of the others that followed was that they helped to control anxiety, lessen hallucinations, and increase responsiveness to therapy. Tranquilizers quickly came to replace SHOCK TREATMENT for most patients, and within just a few years—in the United States by 1956—the population of mental hospitals, which had been rising for years, began to fall. Tranquilizers were so effective at calming patients that critics began to charge that hospitals were drugging their patients into a stupor to make them easier to care for. The drugs came to be widely used among the general population as well.

transistor, type of ELECTRONIC device that largely replaced the cumbersome, heat-producing VACUUM TUBE after the 1950s and allowed for modern miniaturization in many items such as COMPUTERS and RADIO. Transistors are made of crystals of certain metals with special properties, called semiconductors, for they are neither conductors or insulators; because ELECTRONS move through the solid semiconducting crystals, rather than through a vacuum, transistors form the basis of solid-state electronics. Though crystal radio detectors had been introduced by Karl Braun in 1901, transistors in their modern form were developed in 1948 by Bell Laboratories researchers William SHOCKLEY, John Bardeen, and Walter Houser Brattain. In the 1960s, when multiple transistors were built into integrated circuits put on MICROPROCESSOR CHIPS, the age of microelectronics began.

Transjordan, early alternate name for JORDAN.

transplant, in medicine, replacement of a diseased human organ or tissue with a healthy like part from a donor, or from elsewhere on the patient's own body. Tissue transplants go back at least 4,000 years, but grafts from one person to another often failed. In 1903 Danish veterinarian Carl Oluf Jensen was the first to recognize that such rejections were caused by the body's immune system. Transplants of whole organs awaited development of modern surgical techniques. In the first decade of the 20th century several human kidney transplants were attempted; in Germany doctors attempted to transplant a pig or dog kidney to a human. Scientists such as Alexis CARREL developed necessary surgical techniques by transplanting limbs and organs among animals, often dogs. In the process they learned that the closer the genetic relationship between donor and recipient, the more successful the transplant. In 1912 James B. Murphy experimented at the Rockefeller Institute with the first immu-

nosuppressive drug, designed to minimize transplant rejection. Years later, in 1944, Peter MEDAWAR outlined the modern theory of transplantation immunity: basically, that a donor's body fights "foreign" tissue as if it were a disease. In 1954 a Harvard medical team led by Joseph E. Murray performed the first successful kidney transplant. Shortly thereafter an Organ Transplant Registry was begun in the United States to permanently record data on transplants. More difficult and less widely used were liver transplants, first performed at the University of Colorado by Thomas E. Starzl in 1963; lung transplants, done in 1964 at the University of Mississippi (Jackson) by James D. Hardy; and pancreas transplants performed by Swiss surgeons in 1971, based on work by University of Minnesota researchers. The first successful HEART TRANSPLANT was performed in 1967 by Christiaan BARNARD. By the 1970s even bone marrow was being transplanted, saving the lives of many leukemia victims; and by the 1980s cornea transplants—less subject to rejection than most organs or tissues—were becoming almost routine. The immunosuppressive drug cyclosporine, approved by the FDA in 1983, was a breakthrough in controlling transplant rejection. Organ and tissue banks were set up around the world as methods were developed to preserve organs and tissue, where possible, for later use. By the late 1980s a major ethical question had emerged as to who should receive the limited number of organs available. Some desperate people mounted campaigns, picked up widely by the media, to publicize their need for organs and funds.

trash bag murders, a media-developed name for a series of 28 California murders committed between 1972 and 1977; in all cases the bodies of those murdered were dismembered and dispersed in trash bags. Patrick Kearney confessed to 21 of the murders in 1977 and was sentenced to life imprisonment.

Treblinka, Nazi DEATH CAMP in Poland in which hundreds of thousands of Jews and other Eastern Europeans were murdered by the Germans during World War II.

tree-ring dating, alternate name for DEN-DROCHRONOLOGY, a dating system developed by Andrew Ellicott DOUGLASS by about 1920.

trench warfare, term for the 4-year-long battle from entrenched fortifications between the Allied and German armies during World War I, from the failure of the German offensive in 1914 to the German surrender in 1918, in a war of attrition costing millions of lives. This was also the main form taken by the IRAN–IRAQ WAR (1980–88).

Trepper, Leopold (1905–77), Polish revolutionary, who emigrated to Palestine in 1924, was expelled for Communist activities in 1929 and was trained as a Communist activist in the Soviet Union during the early 1930s. He entered France as a Soviet intelligence agent in 1937 and built a major espionage network headquartered in Brussels, Belgium, that the NAZIS later called the RED ORCHESTRA. It consisted of approximately 300 agents and radio operators. Late in 1940 he warned the Soviet Union of the impending German invasion, a warning STALIN chose to ignore. Ultimately captured, he escaped and worked in the French RESISTANCE for the rest of the war. After the war, back in the Soviet Union, he was arrested, imprisoned for 10 years, and then "rehabilitated"; he then went home to Poland. Having decided to emigrate to Israel in 1967, during the anti-Jewish attacks encouraged by the GOMULKA government as a means of diverting public attention from aborted liberalization, he was instead held under house arrest. A worldwide campaign forced his release to Israel in 1974.

Tresca, Carlo (1870–1943), Italian-American anti-fascist who was assassinated in New York in 1943. The murder was unsolved, but was widely attributed to American Mafia assassins allegedly acting under orders from Benito MUSSOLINI.

Triangle Shirtwaist Company fire (March 25, 1911), New York City garment factory fire in which 146 workers, most of them young Jewish-American and Italian-American women, were burned or jumped to their deaths, because the exit doors of the firetrap factory were barred. Great public outrage developed after the fire; with it came a full investigation and the adoption of pioneering health and safety legislation in New York State.

Trianon, Treaty of (June 4, 1920), the Hungarian peace treaty following World War I, delayed because of the Hungarian revolution of 1919; it provided for Hungarian territorial and military concessions and for the payment of reparations.

Trinidad and Tobago (Republic of Trinidad and Tobago), until 1962 a British colony, gaining independence and COMMONWEALTH membership on August 31, 1962. From 1956 the leader of Trinidad and Tobago's independence movement was Dr. Eric WILLIAMS, his country's prime minister until his death in 1981.

Trinity, name of the test at LOS ALAMOS, New Mexico, where the first ATOMIC BOMB was set off on July 16, 1945, as part of the MANHATTAN PROJECT.

Tripartite Pact (September 27, 1940), the treaty formally creating the German-Japanese-Italian military alliance that fought World War II.

Triple Entente, the informal alliance of Great Britain, France, and Russia in the years before World War I that became the formal war alliance of 1914.

tritium, radioactive ISOTOPE of hydrogen with three times the normal mass, like DEUTERIUM a form of heavy hydrogen; it was discovered in 1934 by Australian physicist Marcus Laurence Oliphant. Tritium is used for various purposes, notably in the process of NUCLEAR FUSION, in ACCELERATORS as a bombarding particle, and as a tracer in biological or medical research.

Triton, U.S. nuclear-powered submarine, launched in 1958, that made the first undersea voyage around the world, in 1960.

Trotsky, Leon (Lev Davidovich Bronstein; 1879–1940), the military leader of the OC-

TOBER REVOLUTION and commander in chief of the Red Army, which he built, during the RUSSIAN CIVIL WAR. Trotsky was a revolutionary while still in his teens, and became a Marxist during a period of exile in Siberia. He was sent to Siberia again after the RUSSIAN REVOLUTION OF 1905 and later went to the United States, returning home in 1917 to join the new Russian Revolution. Although he had been a MENSHEVIK from 1903 to 1917, he joined the BOLSHEVIKS then, soon became LENIN'S second in command, and as chairman of the PETROGRAD SOVIET directed the armed forces that carried out the October Revolution. But after negotiating the BREST LITOVSK TREATY that took Russia out of World War I and leading the Red Army throughout the civil war, he unsuccessfully opposed Joseph STALIN'S rise to power. From 1924 through 1929 he suffered a series of reverses, ultimately being expelled from the Communist Party, sent into internal exile, and then deported from the Soviet Union. He continued to oppose Stalin from abroad during the 1930s, saw many of his old colleagues executed during the show trials of the 1930s GREAT PURGE, and was himself assassinated, probably by Stalin's agents, in Mexico City, on August 20, 1940.

Trucial States, former name for the UNITED ARAB EMIRATES.

Trudeau, Pierre Elliot (1919–), Canadian lawyer, who became justice minister in 1967 as a French-Canadian counterweight to the growing QUEBEC SEPARATIST MOVEMENT. He became Liberal party leader in April 1968, succeeding Lester PEARSON, and was prime minister from 1968 to 1979 and again from 1980 until his resignation in 1984. As prime minister he resisted Quebec separatism, granting the police great latitude in antiterrorist activities, while at the same time fostering bilingualism and national recognition of French-Canadian identity.

Trujillo Molina, Rafael Leonidas (1891–1961), Dominican Republic officer, dictator of his country, 1930–61, whose long tenure was marked by the suppression of all oppo-

sition, the murder of many of his opponents, and the financial aggrandizement of his friends and family. He was assassinated by a group of army officers, beginning a period of instability that resulted in the DOMINICAN REPUBLIC CIVIL WAR.

Truman, Harry S. (1884–1972), U.S. judge and political leader, a Missouri county judge before becoming a Democratic senator from Missouri (1935–45), who became vice-president in 1945 and succeeded Franklin Delano ROOSEVELT in the presidency on April 12, 1945, becoming 33rd president of the United States (1945–53). He defeated Republican Thomas E. DEWEY and Progressive Henry A. WALLACE in the 1948 elections. As president he made the decision to drop the first ATOMIC BOMBS used in warfare, on HIROSHIMA (August 6 1945), and NAGASAKI (August 9, 1945), an act that has colored every life on Earth ever since. He was a postwar president, and both of his administrations were greatly concerned with international matters, as the United States became one of only two superpowers and a participant in what became the COLD WAR. Some of his administration's major initiatives were the TRUMAN DOCTRINE, the MARSHALL PLAN's European recovery program, the development of the NORTH ATLANTIC TREATY ORGANIZATION (NATO), and the BERLIN AIRLIFT. In the Far East the United States was involved in the long occupation of Japan, attempted unsuccessfully to support CHIANG KAI-SHEK against the Communists in the final stages of the CHINESE CIVIL WAR, and ultimately found itself fighting the KOREAN WAR. Domestically, the Truman administration prosecuted the COMMUNIST PARTY while at the same time attempting to resist witchhunting as developed by Senator Joseph MCCARTHY and his supporters. Truman was largely frustrated by postwar conservative opposition to the continuation of NEW DEAL programs that he called the FAIR DEAL. He was succeeded in office by Dwight David EISENHOWER.

Truman Doctrine, a U.S. COLD WAR strategy first stated by President Harry S. TRUMAN, speaking to Congress on March 12, 1947, in which he asked for massive financial aid to Greece and Turkey, and declared U.S. policy to be that of aid to those opposing communism throughout the world.

Tshombe, Moïse Kapenda (1919–69), Congolese political leader who on July 11, 1960, led the Katanga province secession from the newly independent Congo. He was supported by Belgian industrial interests, who in this way sought to hold the mineral wealth of Katanga, and by Belgian and white mercenary troops, many of them South Africans. In February 1961, his troops murdered former Congo prime minister Patrice LUMUMBA, then imprisoned in Katanga. On September 17, 1960, UNITED NATIONS secretary-general Dag HAMMARSKÖJLD died in a plane crash over the Congo while en route to negotiate a cease-fire with Tshombe. By 1963 UN peacekeeping forces in the Congo had defeated Tshombe's army, and he fled abroad. In 1964 he was recalled by Congo president Joseph KASAVUBU to serve as prime minister. He was dismissed by Kasavubu in 1965 for alleged electoral fraud and again went into exile.

Ts'u Hsi (1835–1908), Chinese leader known in the west as the Dowager Empress of China; during the latter half of the 19th century she ultimately became the very conservative regent and real ruler of China. In 1900 she supported the BOXER REBELLION, fleeing Peking afterward and returning in 1902. From then on she supported many of the reforms she had earlier resisted, but it was too late; the revolution of 1911 occurred 3 years after her death. She was succeeded by the child emperor HSÜAN T'UNG (Henry P'u Yi).

Tsushima, Battle of (1905), a major Japanese defeat of the Russian navy during the Russo-JAPANESE WAR.

Tuchman, Barbara (1912–89), U.S. historian and writer, whose major works brought her two Pulitzer Prizes (1963, 1971) and were in several instances best-sellers. These included *The Guns of August* (1962), *The Proud Tower* (1966), *Stillwell and the American Experience in China, 1911–45*, (1971), and *A Distant Mirror* (1978).

Tudeh, the Soviet-oriented Iranian Communist party, which was allied with the MOSSADEQ National Front government in the early 1950s and was underground thereafter, until the IRANIAN REVOLUTION of 1979. Although it supported the new government, it was outlawed again in 1983, allegedly for pro-Soviet links.

Tukhachevsky, Mikhail Nikolayevich (1893–1937), Soviet general during the RUSSIAN CIVIL WAR and the SOVIET–POLISH WAR, who became army chief of staff, a marshal of the Soviet Union, and a leading Soviet expert on modern warfare. He was executed in Moscow on June 11, 1937, on false treason charges, his execution paving the way for the purge of the entire army by Joseph STALIN and his followers. The result was enormous early losses in World War II, when a virtually leaderless Soviet army met modern German armies led by an intact officers corps.

Tunisia (Republic of Tunisia), until 1956 a French protectorate, gaining internal autonomy in 1955 after 3 years of guerrilla insurgency, and achieving independence on March 20, 1956. From 1934 the leader of Tunisia's independence movement was Habib BOURGIBA, who became his country's first president; he left office in 1987.

Tuparamos (National Liberation Movement), a Uruguayan leftist guerrilla movement, originating in the early 1960s and named after Inca leader Túpac Amaru, which initially engaged in nonlethal urban guerrilla actions but in the late 1960s moved into bombing, murder, and kidnapping, with great impact on Uruguay. In February 1973 the Uruguayan army took over police functions, and during 1973 it smashed the Tuparamos, imprisoning hundreds and forcing most of the remaining members of the organization into exile. In late 1984, as constitutional government was restored after a long period of military rule, many Tuparamos members returned from exile, and in 1985 the main body of Tuparamos prisoners were released. In December 1985, reconvened as a legal party, the organization renounced violence and moved into electoral politics.

Tupolev, world's first SUPERSONIC airliner, unveiled in the U.S.S.R. in 1968.

Turing, Alan Mathison (1912–54), British mathematician who did key work in COMPUTER logic. In the 1930s he conceived of a theoretical "Turing machine" that could help analyze what problems were solvable by mathematics and by logical machines in general, his analysis helping to shape the computers that were to come. Under the secrecy of war in 1943 he built an all-ELECTRONIC, special-purpose DIGITAL COMPUTER, the COLOSSUS, to help break the German codes, notably those using the ENIGMA machine. Later he became involved in Britain's fledgling computer program and also theorized extensively on the possibilities of ARTIFICIAL INTELLIGENCE.

Turkey (Republic of Turkey), until the end of World War I the center of the OTTOMAN EMPIRE, the SICK MAN OF EUROPE, which by then had been fragmenting for a century. In 1923 what remained of the empire was replaced by the Turkish republic, led by ATATÚRK.

Turkish Republic of Northern Cyprus, independent though disputed nation established on CYPRUS in 1974.

Turner, Frederick Jackson (1861–1932), U.S. historian, whose main work dealt with the influence of the frontier on the development of American ideas and qualities. His classic work on the closing of the American frontier was done in the 1890s, and published as *The Frontier in American History* (1920).

Turner, Jesse, one of the American LEBANON HOSTAGES, an American University professor who was kidnapped on January 24, 1988.

Tutankhamen, full name of the Egyptian pharaoh (c. 1350 B.C.) better known to the public as King Tut; his tomb was excavated by English archeologist Howard CARTER in 1922 and much caught the public fancy.

Tutu, Desmond Mpilo (1931–   ), South African minister, head of the Anglican Church in South Africa, and leading advocate of nonviolence and peaceful reconciliation between the opposing forces in South Africa within the framework of a democratic, multiracial society. Ordained in 1961, he became the first Black Anglican dean of Johannesburg in 1975, general secretary of the South African Council of Churches in 1978, bishop of Johannesburg in 1984, and archbishop of Johannesburg in 1986. Leader of a worldwide campaign for social justice in South Africa, he won the Nobel Peace Prize in 1984.

Tuvalu, until 1975, the Ellice Islands, part of the British Gilbert and Ellice Islands, a protectorate until 1915, then a colony. In 1975 the Ellice Islands were split away from the Gilberts, gaining independence and COMMONWEALTH membership on October 1, 1978.

TVA, the initials of the TENNESSEE VALLEY AUTHORITY, a major U.S. NEW DEAL utilities project of the 1930s.

Twentieth Amendment, the "Lame Duck amendment" to the U.S. Constitution (1933), which moved the date of the presidential and vice-presidential inaugurations from March 4 to January 20, and also provided for the new Congress to take office on January 3.

Twenty-first Amendment, 1933 amendment to the U.S. Constitution, ending PROHIBITION.

Twenty-second Amendment, the "two-term amendment" to the U.S. Constitution, approved by Congress in 1947 and by the states in 1951, providing that no president could serve more than two terms or one full term and more than 2 years of an unexpired term. It was adopted in direct response to the four-term presidency of Franklin Delano ROOSEVELT.

Twenty-third Amendment, amendment to the U.S. Constitution (1961) that granted presidential election votes to the citizens of the District of Columbia.

Twenty-fourth Amendment, 1964 amendment to the U.S. Constitution outlawing the poll tax, which had been used since the post–Civil War period to disenfranchise Black Americans in the south.

Twenty-fifth Amendment, 1967 amendment to the U.S. Constitution that provided a procedure for the transfer of power from president to vice-president, should the president be disabled, and a procedure to fill a vacant vice-presidency.

26th July Movement, failed Cuban armed insurrection led by Fidel CASTRO, in which a small band of revolutionaries attacked the Moncada barracks on July 26, 1953; Castro was subsequently imprisoned for 2 years.

Two Cultures and the Scientific Revolution, influential 1960 essay by British physicist, public official, and novelist Charles Percy Snow, lamenting the mid-20th-century split between scientists and humanists, as reflected in ignorance of and inability to understand each other's work and intellectual motives.

two-term amendment, the TWENTY-SECOND AMENDMENT to the U.S. Constitution, prohibiting presidents from serving more than two terms or one full term and more than 2 years of an unexpired term.

Tylenol capsule murders, seven 1982 murders in Chicago, all caused by cyanide inserted into Tylenol capsules. The murders were not solved and were followed by a series of copycat poisonings and attempted poisonings in other parts of the United States. After a February 1986 poisoning death in Peekskill, New York, the makers of Tylenol, Johnson and Johnson, took nonprescription capsules off the market.

U

UFO, popular shorthand for UNIDENTIFIED FLYING OBJECT.

Uganda (Republic of Uganda), until March 1962 a British protectorate, gaining independence and COMMONWEALTH membership on October 9, 1962, under Prime Minister Milton OBOTE. The country became a republic in 1967 and a one-party state ruled by Obote in 1969. In 1971 power was taken in a military coup led by Idi AMIN, who then developed a murder-laden reign of terror until being deposed during the UGANDA–TANZANIA WAR.

Ugandan Civil War (1980–   ), a guerrilla war between the forces of President Milton OBOTE and National Resistance Army forces led by Yoweri Musaveni; it began with Obote's resumption of the presidency in late 1979, after Idi AMIN had been deposed during the UGANDA–TANZANIA WAR. Obote was deposed by officers of his own army, led by General Tito Okello, in July; peace talks followed, which yielded a peace agreement in mid-December. But Musaveni refused to accept the agreement; he renewed the war in January, took Kampala on January 27, 1986, and assumed the presidency. The defeated forces of the previous government fought on, as insurgents, in the north and east.

Uganda–Tanzania War (January–June 1979), an invasion of Uganda by Tanzanian troops in support of forces hostile to Ugandan president Idi AMIN. Tanzanian forces took Kampala on April 11, overcoming Ugandan and supporting Libyan troops. Amin fled to Libya; in late May, the party of former president Milton OBOTE, who had been deposed by Amin in 1971, won an electoral victory, and Obote resumed the presidency. Tanzanian forces remained in Uganda until June 1981.

Ulanhu (1906–88), Mongolian political leader who joined the Chinese Communist movement in 1923, fostered Mongolian independence during the interwar period, and fought with Communist forces during the CHINESE CIVIL WAR and the SINO-JAPANESE WAR. After Communist victory in 1949 Ulanhu became de facto ruler of Inner Mongolia, on behalf of the new government, and a deputy prime minister of the new People's Republic of China. He lost power in 1967 during the CULTURAL REVOLUTION. After his rehabilitation in 1973 he once again held high government offices, functioning in Beijing, but did not resume power in Inner Mongolia.

Ulbricht, Walter (1893–1973), German carpenter, who became a Communist leader, fought on the Republican side during the SPANISH CIVIL WAR, spent World War II in the Soviet Union, and came home with the Red Army. He was secretary general of the Socialist Unity party and East German leader 1950–71, taking his country on a course of rapid industrial growth and developing a one-party, Soviet-oriented state.

Ulster Defence Association, the main Protestant paramilitary force in Northern Ireland, from 1969 unifying many Protestant paramilitary organizations.

Ulster Volunteers, Protestant Northern Irish military organization formed in 1913 to fight, if necessary, for continuing ties to Britain and against Irish Home Rule. During the IRISH WAR OF INDEPENDENCE, and since then, it has been a powerful force opposing a united, independent Ireland and for continuing Northern Ireland ties with Great Britain.

ULTRA, British security classification for information gained from the German ENIGMA code, broken early during World War II. The Germans did not know that the Enigma transmitting machine had been reproduced by Polish intelligence just before the outbreak of the war and given to the British, who then broke the code. The Allies therefore had a critically important intelligence advantage throughout the war—so crucial that the British government felt unable to forewarn COVENTRY of the MOONLIGHT SONATA bombings slated for November 14–15, 1940. The existence of ULTRA was disclosed publicly only in the mid-1970s.

ultrasound (ultrasonic waves), high-frequency sounds above the range of hearing, used in SONAR-inspired techniques in which pulses of ultrasonic waves are sent out and the resulting reflected echoes translated, through ELECTRONICS, into an image on a CATHODE RAY TUBE. Various researchers in America and Europe experimented with ultrasound in medicine from the 1940s, but not until the early 1960s, in the work of Scottish physician Ian Donald, were ultrasound "pictures" good enough for diagnostic use. From then, ultrasonography was widely used, especially by obstetricians and gynecologists, who can scan the fetus for signs of trouble, and by physicians seeking to examine internal organs, and to check for tumors or stones. Ultrasonic waves also were used therapeutically as early as 1944, when physicians found that they could be used to destroy tumors; unfortunately, they destroyed healthy tissue as well. But at lower levels ultrasound has been used to aid healing, and in specially designed machines called lithotripters they are used to break up kidney and gall stones, eliminating the need for an operation. Ultrasound also has been used in industry to detect faults or flaws in structures or products and to speed up chemical reactions.

ultraviolet (UV), type of low-frequency RADIATION beyond the violet end of the visible-light part of the electromagnetic spectrum, called "black light" because it is invisible, though its effects can be seen; known since 1801, it was put to wide use only in the 20th century. Since 1900, when Danish physician Niels Ryberg Finsen discovered that ultraviolet rays killed germs, UV lamps have been used to sterilize rooms in institutions such as hospitals and also vaccines, blood plasma, and body tissues. Although small amounts of ultraviolet light are beneficial, helping the body make VITAMIN D and preventing rickets, the larger amounts in sunlight can cause skin cancer. In the late 20th century, depletion of the ultraviolet-shielding OZONE LAYER by chemicals such as CHLOROFLUOROCARBONS (CFCs), created concern about the danger to humans of increased ultraviolet rays.

uncertainty principle, theory in physics, propounded by Werner HEISENBERG in 1927, that the position and the momentum of a body cannot both be calculated at the same time with full accuracy; the more accurate the one measurement, the less accurate the other. The uncertainty principle undercut the idea that it was possible to know everything about the universe, given sufficient information. That idea troubled many scientists, among them Albert EINSTEIN, prompting his famous demurral: "God may be subtle, but He is not malicious."

UNESCO, initials of the UNITED NATIONS EDUCATIONAL, SCIENTIFIC AND CULTURAL ORGANIZATION, a UNITED NATIONS special agency.

UNICEF, initials of the UNITED NATIONS INTERNATIONAL CHILDREN'S FUND, a UNITED NATIONS special agency.

unidentified flying object (UFO), phenomenon in or from the sky that cannot be otherwise explained by the observer or by scientific evaluators. From the late 1940s people from many parts of the world, though especially in the United States, reported sighting seemingly extraterrestrial objects. A 1947 Washington observer dubbed one a "flying saucer," a name that stuck, even being translated into "flying sickle" in the Soviet Union. In 1948 the U.S. Air Force started Project Blue Book, designed to gather reports of UFO sightings, accumulating more than 12,600 in 21 years; other countries kept similar, though sometimes spottier, records. Many sightings were quickly identified with known events, such as meteors, satellites, unusual aircraft, and other meteorological, astronomical, or man-made phenomena; others were dubbed "unidentified," hence their current name. In the United States, periodic scientific evaluations of the records, notably in 1952, 1966, and 1968, rejected the notion of extraterrestrial visitations; after the 1969 report prepared by Edward U. Condon, Project Blue Book was ended. Some scientists dissented, however, noting the small number of unexplained sightings, and continued studying UFOs and exploring the psychology of UFO experiences. Meanwhile, sightings continued, though apparently declining somewhat after the 1960s.

unified field theory, so far, a vain attempt to reconcile in one comprehensive theory both gravitation and electromagnetic phenomena; an attempt at which Albert EINSTEIN and many other 20th-century scientists failed. American physicists Steven Weinberg and Sheldon Lee Glashow, and Pakistani physicist Abdus Salam, in 1967 independently developed the electroweak theory, an attempt to reconcile electromagnetism with the "weak" force leading to RADIOACTIVE decay; it won them the 1979 Nobel Prize for Physics. More recently, attempts to unify the various forces have been called grand unification theories (GUTs), starting with the one put forth in 1974 by Glashow and Howard M. Georgi.

Union of Soviet Socialist Republics (U.S.S.R., Soviet Union), successor state to the Russian Empire, which ended with the FEBRUARY REVOLUTION of 1917 and the establishment of the PROVISIONAL GOVERNMENT led by Alexander KERENSKY. That government was in turn destroyed by the OCTOBER REVOLUTION of 1917, which brought to power the BOLSHEVIKS, led by LENIN. On July 10, 1918, the Bolsheviks established the Russian Federated Socialist Republic (RSFSR). On conclusion of the RUSSIAN CIVIL WAR in 1922 the Soviet Union was formally established as the Union of Soviet Socialist Republics, in form a federation of autonomous republics, but in practice a highly centralized one-party Communist state. Both form and reality continued through the long dictatorial rule of Joseph STALIN and during the rules of his successors, until the reforms of the GORBACHEV era brought massive change to Soviet political and economic life.

UNITA, popular shorthand for the NATIONAL UNION FOR THE TOTAL INDEPENDENCE OF ANGOLA, by which the organization is best known.

United Arab Emirates, until 1968 a group of absolute monarchies along the Persian Gulf that were de facto British protectorates, called Trucial States after the early 19th-century treaties concluded with the British, which promised British protection in return for abstention from piracy. Great Britain announced its intention to withdraw its armed forces from the area in 1968; in the period December 1971–February 1972, Abu Dhabi, Ajman, Dubai, Fujaira, Ras al-Khaima, Sharja, and Umm al-Qaiwain federated into the United Arab Emirates.

United Arab Republic, the name of EGYPT, 1958–71, first taken during the 1958–61 union with Syria and kept until adoption of the country's present name, the Arab Republic of Egypt.

United Front, a Communist policy initiated by Comintern head Georgi DIMITROV in his 1935 "United Front" speech to the COMMUNIST INTERNATIONAL, in which he called for unity against the growing menace of fascism. Stressing cooperation with liberal, socialist, and democratic forces throughout the world, it was a major departure from previous policy, which had stressed independent Communist operation and sharp attacks on socialist organizations. In Germany that policy had enormously helped the rise of fascism. The United Front policy was followed until the NAZI–SOVIET PACT of 1939, which abruptly severed Communist links with anti-fascists throughout the world, until the Nazi attack upon the Soviet Union in 1941 made cooperation once again permissible. During the late 1930s Communists in many countries entered into such mainstream activities as the organization of the mass-production industries in the United States and the organization of the governing POPULAR FRONT in France.

United Nations (UN), the international organization developed after World War II to replace the LEAGUE OF NATIONS; with its 159 nation-members it is humanity's main forum in the late 20th century, though never the world parliament envisaged by some of the founders of the League and of the UN. Need for and intent to develop the UN were stated at several Allied World War II conferences; practical organization went forward at the DUMBARTON OAKS CONFERENCE of 1944, and the UN and its Charter were formally born at the SAN FRANCISCO CONFERENCE of June 1945. The UN's five secretary-generals, Trygve LIE, Dag HAMMARSKJÖLD, U THANT, Kurt WALDHEIM, and Javier PEREZ DE CUELLAR, have scored limited peacekeeping successes, mediating conflicts in Cyprus and the Congo in the early 1960s, helping to settle the 1980s IRAN–IRAQ WAR, and stationing peacekeeping observers in the Middle East and south Asia. Several specialized UN organizations, such as the postwar UN RELIEF AND REHABILITATION ADMINISTRATION (UNRRA), the WORLD HEALTH ORGANIZATION (WHO), the UN INTERNATIONAL CHILDREN'S EMERGENCY FUND (UNICEF), the FOOD AND AGRICULTURE ORGANIZATION (FAO), the UN EDUCATIONAL, SCIENTIFIC AND CULTURAL ORGANIZATION (UNESCO), and related bodies have made made substantial contributions to world health, productivity, and welfare. The United Nations Declaration on Human Rights, adopted in 1948 under the leadership of Eleanor ROOSEVELT, has attempted, though with limited success, to provide a human rights standard throughout the world. Perhaps the most visible contribution of the UN, however, has been the development of a stable international forum through which the smaller nations of the world can reach a worldwide audience.

United Nations Educational, Scientific and Cultural Organization (UNESCO), a UNITED NATIONS special agency established in 1946 to foster international cultural, educational, and scientific cooperation and to promote intellectual freedom. It has since developed a very wide range of projects and activities, but has also encountered considerable criticism for allegedly wasteful expenditures and, from the late 1970s, for activities allegedly aimed at limiting freedom of the press rather than promoting intellectual freedom.

United Nations High Commissioner for Refugees, Office of the (UNHCR), a special agency formed by the UNITED NATIONS in 1951, succeeding the UN Relief and Rehabilitation Administration (UNRRA) and the International Refugee Organization as the main UN organization dedicated to helping those millions in many countries displaced by wars, revolutions, and other massive disorders, as in China, Chile, Hungary, Algeria, and dozens of other countries during the past four decades. UNHCR won the 1954 Nobel Peace Prize.

United Nations International Children's Fund (UNICEF), a UNITED NATIONS special agency established in 1946 as the UN International Children's Emergency Fund and then dedicated to meeting the emergency needs of young people in hard hit countries during the immediate post–World War II period. Its role was later expanded to include both emergency and long-term programs for young people throughout the world. UNICEF won the 1965 Nobel Peace Prize.

United Nations Relief and Rehabilitation Administration (UNRRA), an international organization that actually predated formation of the UNITED NATIONS, being organized in 1943 by the ALLIES to provide emergency and refugee aid in areas freed from AXIS control; it continued until 1947 as a UN special agency. UNRRA, working primarily in China and Eastern and Southern Europe, played a major role in postwar reconstruction, in the return of millions of displaced persons to their homes, and in the resettlement of those who did not wish to go home after the war. Its first two directors in the critical early years were Herbert H. LEHMAN and Fiorello H. LA GUARDIA.

United Nations Relief and Works Agency for Palestine Refugees (UNRWA), from 1949 the main UNITED NATIONS agency attempting to help Palestine refugees and to that end operating camps and feeding, housing, and providing medical care, schools, and other necessities for an estimated 1.5 million refugees throughout the Middle East.

United States v. *Butler* (1936), a landmark U.S. Supreme Court decision invalidating the AGRICULTURAL ADJUSTMENT ACT (AAA), a major piece of NEW DEAL legislation.

United States v. *Darby* (1941), a landmark U.S. Supreme Court decision validating the Fair Labor Standards Act, which for the first time provided federally guaranteed minimum wages and overtime pay.

United States v. *Nixon* (1974), a landmark U.S. Supreme Court case that forced president Richard M. NIXON to produce the WATERGATE tapes and to supply them to the special prosecutor. His subsequent compliance led directly to his resignation, for after the contents of the tapes were disclosed, he faced impeachment.

United States v. *United States District Court for the Eastern District of Michigan* (1972), a landmark U.S. Supreme Court case, in which the Court curbed the widespread wiretapping, bugging, and other electronic domestic surveillance activities of the NIXON administration's Justice Department, by forcing disclosure of the information derived to the defendants in a Michigan bombing case.

UNIVAC, first electronic COMPUTER available for commercial use and the first to store data on MAGNETIC TAPE. It was built in 1951 by John William Mauchly and John Presper Eckert, makers of the ENIAC, one of the earliest all-electronic computers, introduced in 1946. UNIVAC was used by CBS to make the first TELEVISION network predictions about the presidential election in 1952.

UNRRA, the initials of the UNITED NATIONS RELIEF AND REHABILITATION ADMINISTRATION, the major post–World War II UNITED NATIONS relief organization.

Unsafe at Any Speed (1965), the pioneering consumer safety book by Ralph NADER; it attacked motor vehicle safety and helped to begin the era of consumerism in the United States.

Upper Volta (Independent Republic of Upper Volta), the former name of BURKINA FASO. Upper Volta was a French colony until August 5, 1960.

Ur, city in southern Iraq, home of the biblical Abraham and center of the Sumerian civilization, which invented writing; it was rediscovered and excavated (1922–34) by Leonard WOOLLEY.

uranium 235 (U-235), rare ISOTOPE of uranium, occurring with the more common U-238 in a ratio of less than 1 to 100; material used for NUCLEAR FISSION, as in ATOMIC BOMBS and NUCLEAR REACTORS, from 1942, notably in the bomb used on HIROSHIMA in 1945.

Uranus, planetary target of space probes, most notably the U.S. *VOYAGER 2*, which arrived in the region in 1986 and broadcast striking pictures of its rings.

Urey, Harold Clayton (1893–1981), U.S. chemist, who in 1931 discovered DEUTERIUM, a hydrogen ISOTOPE with twice the mass of ordinary hydrogen, winning him the 1934 Nobel Prize for Chemistry. Urey continued to explore other isotopes and played a key role in developing for the MANHATTAN PROJECT a method for extracting the URANIUM isotopes needed for NUCLEAR FISSION. After the war he urged nuclear disarmament and turned away from nuclear research, to geophysics. In 1953 he and Stanley Miller pioneered in producing amino acids, basic to life, by sending an electrical spark through a chemical "stew" much like that thought to have existed when life began on Earth.

Urschel, Charles, a wealthy U.S. businessman kidnapped by George "Machine Gun" Kelly and others in Oklahoma City on July 22, 1933; he was released after a $200,000 ransom had been paid but was able to lead the police to Kelly, who was sentenced to life imprisonment. The case received enormous publicity, to a considerable extent promoted by J. Edgar HOOVER, then bent on further developing the FBI's public image.

Uruguay Round, the 1980s set of negotiations organized by the GENERAL AGREEMENT ON TARIFFS AND TRADE (GATT) in an attempt to reduce international trade and tariff barriers.

U.S.S.R., the initials of the UNION OF SOVIET SOCIALIST REPUBLICS (Soviet Union).

U-2 incident, shooting down by the Soviet Union of an American CIA U-2 reconnaissance plane in Soviet air space, and capture of its pilot, Francis Gary POWERS, on May 1, 1960. Powers was tried as a spy and imprisoned; he was exchanged in February 1962 for Soviet spy Rudolph ABEL.

V

V-1 and V-2 bombs (*Vergeltungswaffen*, or Vengeance Weapons), early ROCKET-powered GUIDED MISSILES, developed by Wernher von BRAUN's team, built and tested at PEENEMÜNDE, and used in World War II by the Germans to mount terror attacks against Britain. The V-1, or "buzz bomb," controlled by a preset guidance system, was first used in June 1944. The V-2, a longer-range missile (190 miles) bearing a ton of explosives, traveled faster than the speed of sound and so gave no approach warning; it was first used in September 1944 against Paris and then over London. Although neither was a decisive military weapon, the V-bombs did kill many civilians; they were taken out of action by capture of their production sites as the Allies moved into Europe. After the war Wernher von Braun and more than 100 other German rocket experts (most of the Peenemünde technical staff) came to the United States, providing much of the technical basis for developments in missiles and space rockets. Over 70 V-bombs were also brought to the United States and then set off at the White Sands Proving Ground in New Mexico 1946–51, providing rocket-handling experience crucial to the development of INTERCONTINENTAL BALLISTIC MISSILES (ICBMs) and SATELLITES for space exploration.

vacuum tube, type of ELECTRON TUBE that uses a vacuum rather than a gaseous medium, a device basic to 20th-century ELECTRONICS, as in COMPUTERS, until the development of TRANSISTORS in 1948.

Van Allen, James Alfred (1914–   ), U.S. physicist specializing in research of the upper atmosphere, who predicted the existence of the two wide bands of RADIOACTIVE particles circling the Earth; named the Van Allen Belts, they were discovered by the U.S. SATELLITE *EXPLORER 1* in 1958. In the late 1950s Van Allen helped spark the INTERNATIONAL GEOPHYSICAL YEAR and greatly influenced the U.S. space program.

Van Allen Belts, two wide bands of RADIOACTIVE particles circling the Earth, discovered by the U.S. SATELLITE *EXPLORER* 1 in 1958; they were predicted by and named after U.S. physicist James VAN ALLEN.

Vance, Cyrus Roberts (1917–   ), U.S. lawyer who, as secretary of the army 1962–63 and deputy defense secretary 1964–67, was deeply involved in growing American involvement in the VIETNAM WAR, which he at first supported and then opposed. By 1968 he was urging President Lyndon B. JOHNSON to disengage. He was a Vietnam peace negotiator in 1968–69, and secretary of state from 1977 to 1980, resigning in disagreement with President Jimmy CARTER over the failed commando attempt to free the IRAN HOSTAGES, which he had from the first opposed.

Vandenberg, Arthur Hendrick (1884–1951), U.S. journalist and Michigan Republican senator (1928–51). An isolationist before World War II, Vandenberg became an internationalist and strong supporter of the UNITED NATIONS, the NORTH ATLANTIC TREATY ORGANIZATION (NATO), and the MARSHALL PLAN during the postwar period. He was chairman of the Senate Foreign Relations Committee, 1946–48.

Vanguard, series of U.S. SATELLITES, first launched successfully on March 17, 1958.

Vanguard 1 showed that the Earth is not perfectly round. *Vanguard 2*, launched on February 17, 1959, sent back the first TELEVISION photographs of cloud cover, becoming essentially the first weather station in space.

Van Lawick-Goodall, Jane, married name of ethologist Jane GOODALL.

Vanuatu (Republic of Vanuatu), until 1980, as the New Hebrides, a joint British-French colony; it became an independent nation and COMMONWEALTH member on July 30, 1980.

Vardar, Battle of the (September 15–29, 1918), the final battle of World War I on the Balkan front. Allied forces attacked Bulgarian forces, soon breaking through the Bulgarian center and routing the Bulgarian army. The offensive ended with the Allied-Bulgarian armistice of September 29, 1918.

Vargas, Getúlio Dornelles (1883–1954), Brazilian political leader who unsuccessfully ran for the presidency in 1930; he charged election fraud and came to power in the coup of October 1930, then ruling as a dictator although titled provisional president. He was elected to the presidency by the Congress in 1934, but in 1937 took dictatorial power openly, ruling absolutely until the October 1945 military coup. Attaining the presidency in the free election of 1950, he committed suicide in 1954 when faced with an armed forces demand that he resign.

Vatican II (Second Vatican Council; 1962–65), by far the most important council of the Roman Catholic Church in the modern period, initiated by Pope JOHN XXIII to reexamine the role of the church in the modern world. It resulted in major restatements of Catholic goals, fostered greatly increased ecumenicism, asserted the right to religious liberty, condemned anti-Semitism, and significantly modified liturgical practices and approaches, including the use of many languages and of indigenous musical forms. The impact of Vatican II on Catholics was enormous and continued to be so, although substantial conservative rebalancing occurred in later years.

Vatican City State, the independent Catholic state set up within the city of Rome by the LATERAN TREATY of 1929.

Veblen, Thorstein (1857–1929), U.S. economist, a powerful and effective critic of unrestrained monopolistic ownership and practice, whose thinking, beginning with publication of his book *The Theory of the Leisure Class* (1899), considerably influenced the U.S. "trustbusters" of the early 20th century. In that book he coined the phrase "conspicuous consumption" to describe and pillory the conduct of many of the American rich; the phrase then moved into the language.

V-E Day (May 8, 1945), the day on which the ALLIES announced that WORLD WAR II ended in the European theater.

Vela Hotel, series of U.S. military SATELLITES designed to detect nuclear explosions, in use from 1963.

Velikovsky, Immanuel (1895–1979), Russian-American astronomer, whose theories of cosmic collisions with Earth caused wide controversy from 1950. A physician and psychologist by training, Velikovsky asserted in *Worlds in Collision* (1950) that the Earth had been struck by a comet in 1500 B.C. Many of his writings, drawing on myth and ancient history, proved widely popular though of questionable scientific soundness. Some of his suggestions, however, have been confirmed, such as his prediction of RADIO waves from JUPITER.

Venizelos, Eleutherios (1864–1936), Cretan lawyer, active in Cretan politics after 1896, who became Greek prime minister in 1910 and from then until 1932 was a leading figure in Greek politics. He led Greece during the successful first BALKAN WAR, into World War I on the Allied side, and through the negotiations of the postwar period. He was premier for the last time 1928–32, into the early years of the GREAT DEPRESSION; after losing power he was involved in an unsuccessful coup attempt in 1935, which drove him into exile.

Ventris, Michael George Francis (1922–56), English linguist who in 1952, with John Chadwick, deciphered the previously untranslated Mycenean script called Linear B, (recognizing it as an archaic form of Greek) uncovered on Crete during excavations led by Arthur EVANS.

Venus, planetary target of U.S.S.R and U.S. space probes. In 1965 the Soviets' *Venera 3* crashed into Venus, becoming the first spacecraft to reach another planet. Capsules from other Venera spacecraft were landed on Venus in 1969 and 1970, and cameras briefly sent back the first pictures from the planet. *Venera 8* made the first soft landing on Venus in 1972; *Venera 9* and *10* sent back the first pictures from the surface of Venus in 1975; *Venera 13* and *14* made the first successful "soft" landings on Venus in 1982. In 1962 and 1967 U.S. MARINER spacecraft flew by Venus and transmitted data; two PIONEER craft were launched toward Venus in 1978. These probes showed, among other things, that Venus rotates "backward" and is not covered with water, as was once thought. After an 11-year hiatus, in May 1989 the United States launched the space probe *Magellan* on a 15-month, 795-million-mile voyage toward Venus; it was the first such craft to be released from a SPACE SHUTTLE, the *Atlantis*. In a sign of easing relations, Soviet space scientists shared their Venus data with their U.S. counterparts.

Vera (September 1959), a Japanese hurricane estimated to have killed 4,500 people and injured 40,000 on Honshu, with huge property damage.

Vera Cruz, occupation of (April 1914), shelling and occupation of the Mexican port of Vera Cruz by the U. S. Navy, in an attempt to stop German arms from reaching Mexican dictator Victoriano HUERTA; the arrest of several American sailors at Tampico was used as a pretext for the action. The Americans held the city until November, some months after Huerta had been deposed.

Verdun, Battle of (February 21–December 18, 1916), a 6-month-long unsuccessful assault by major German forces against the French fortress of Verdun, in World War I. In the autumn of 1916 Allied forces went on the offensive on the SOMME and on the Eastern Front; French forces at Verdun then retook almost all of the ground previously captured by the Germans. An estimated 1 million casualties were suffered at Verdun; 550,000 of them French, 450,000 German. PHOSGENE gas was introduced by the Germans at Verdun.

Versailles, Treaty of (June 28, 1919), document signed on conclusion of the PARIS PEACE CONFERENCE of 1919. Germany admitted war guilt and agreed to pay heavy reparations. The newly recreated nation of Poland received (Poseń) and the POLISH CORRIDOR, which gave it access to the Baltic Sea. Danzig (Gdańsk), at the sea end of the Polish Corridor, was made a free city. France received ALSACE-LORRAINE and the SAAR, while several areas of Germany were to be occupied for 5–15 years, and the RHINELAND was demilitarized. All of the these key treaty provisions later became issues exploited by Adolf HITLER in his run-up to World War II, the issue of the Polish Corridor becoming the German excuse for the invasion of Poland that set off that war.

Verwoerd, Hendrik Frensch (1901–66), South African sociologist and newspaper editor, who in 1937 resigned his university post in protest against South African admission of German Jewish refugees. He edited a Nationalist newspaper from then until 1948, when he was appointed to the Senate. He became native affairs minister in 1950 and prime minister in 1958, in both positions fostering and more fully developing APARTHEID. He was prime minister during the 1960 SHARPEVILLE MASSACRE, the subsequent outlawing of the AFRICAN NATIONAL CONGRESS, the imprisonment of Nelson MANDELA, and South Africa's 1961 withdrawal from the COMMONWEALTH. He was assassinated on September 6, 1966, by an insane white government employee.

Very Large Array (VLA), series of large dishes for collecting radio waves, arranged to work together to scan significant portion of the sky; used in RADIO ASTRONOMY.

Vichy government, collaborationist government formed in Vichy, France, in July 1940, after the World War II fall of France to the Germans. The Vichy government ruled "unoccupied" France; in fact, it was a German puppet government, at first headed by Phillippe PETAIN and after April 1942 by Pierre LAVAL. Although the government nominally existed until the end of the war, the Germans took over physical control of the previously unoccupied parts of France in November 1942, and the puppet government fled to Germany as Allied forces liberated France.

Victor Emmanuel III (1869–1947), king of Italy (1900–44) after his father, Humbert I, was assassinated. In 1922 he refused to authorize Italian army opposition to Benito MUSSOLINI'S MARCH ON ROME, instead making Mussolini prime minister and paving the way for the Italian fascist regime. He cooperated with Mussolini thereafter, turning against him and fleeing from the Germans to Allied sanctuary in 1943. He then effectively left public life, abdicating in 1946.

Vienna Summit (June 1979), a meeting between U.S. president Jimmy CARTER and Soviet premier Leonid BREZHNEV, at which they signed the SALT II arms limitation agreements.

Vietcong, North Vietnamese guerrilla units fighting inside South Vietnam during the VIETNAM WAR.

Vietminh, the Vietnamese forces that defeated the French during the INDOCHINA WAR; they were composed of combined Communist and nationalist elements, all led by HO CHI MINH.

Vietnam (Socialist Republic of Vietnam), until 1954 part of French Indochina, which included CAMBODIA (KAMPUCHEA) and LAOS. Vietnam was split into North and South Vietnam after the INDOCHINA WAR and became a single nation after North Vietnamese victory in the INDOCHINESE CIVIL WAR, which was accompanied by the VIETNAM WAR; the present republic came into being on July 2, 1976. The leader of the Vietnamese independence movement was HO CHI MINH.

Vietnam Civil War (1954–75), conflict that began following the end of the INDOCHINA WAR as a low-level VIET CONG guerrilla insurrection in South Vietnam. During the 1950s and early 1960s this grew into an insurgency threatening the continued existence of the South Vietnamese government, with North Vietnamese regular army forces joining Viet Cong units. The United States began its long Vietnam commitment in the mid-1950s, moved into direct military involvement in 1961, and began its major commitment late in 1965. From then until American withdrawal in 1973 the VIETNAM WAR superseded the existing civil war, with South Vietnamese and U.S. military forces together fighting North Vietnamese and Viet Cong forces. After American withdrawal the end of the civil war was in sight. The North Vietnamese began their final offensive in late 1974; they took Saigon on April 30, 1975, ending the civil war.

Vietnam War (1965–73), the period of massive U.S. intervention in the 30-year sequence of conflicts that began with the VIETNAMESE WAR OF INDEPENDENCE (INDOCHINA WAR; 1945–54), which developed into the VIETNAMESE CIVIL WAR (1954–75), part of which was the major Southeast Asian conflict that was the Vietnam War. Some hundreds of U.S. advisers were in Vietnam after completion of French withdrawal in 1956; by mid-1964, 20,000–25,000 U.S. troops and hundreds of American airplanes were in Vietnam. However, it was clear that North Vietnamese regular troops and VIETCONG guerrillas were about to defeat South Vietnamese forces, and bring what was then 20 years of conflicts to an end. In February 1965, using the authorization provided by the TONKIN GULF RESOLUTION of 1964, President Lyndon B. JOHNSON ordered heavy bombing of North Vietnam. In March 1965 U.S. troops in battalion strength began to arrive, and in July 1965 the decision to commit hundreds of thousands of troops was made. Allied non-Vietnamese forces at maximum commitment in 1969 totaled approximately 700,000; 625,000 of them Americans, the others from Australia, New Zealand, the Philippines, South Korea, and Thailand. Allied forces sustained more than 50,000 battle-connected deaths, more than 160,000 wounded, and more than 5,000 prisoners of war or missing in action. South Vietnamese forces sustained approximately 200,000 battle-related deaths and 500,000 wounded. North Vietnamese regular armed forces and Vietcong guerrilla casualty figures are unavailable, as are civilian casualties, after many years of countrywide guerrilla warfare in South Vietnam and heavy, sustained U.S. bombing of North Vietnam, guerilla-held areas in South Vietnam, and substantial portions of Laos and Cambodia. Between mid-1965 and January 1968, U.S.–South Vietnamese efforts failed to destroy the guerrilla forces in South Vietnam, while casualties mounted and U.S. antiwar opinion rose; in that period the Vietnam War was the most unpopular war in U.S. history. Antiwar opinion became decisive after the North Vietnamese TET OFFENSIVE of early 1968, which failed in military terms but was the turning point in the war, because it was widely interpreted in the United States as providing convincing evidence that there was no "light at the end of the tunnel." The Tet Offensive was closely followed by President Johnson's bombing pause, his announcement that he would not seek another term, and the opening of peace talks in Paris. Then followed years of off-and-on peace talks, the attempt by the United States to "Vietnamize" the war by strengthening South Vietnamese forces so that they might stand on their own, renewal of U.S. bombing, incursions into Laos and Cambodia, the mining of North Vietnamese harbors, and continuation of the long war; meanwhile, U.S. antiwar forces continued to press for disengagement. Such matters as the MY LAI MASSACRE, the PENTAGON PAPERS revela-tions, the ELLSBERG break-ins, and the KENT STATE KILLINGS made U.S. withdrawal inevitable, even though it was clear that "Vietnamization" had not worked and that ultimate North Vietnamese victory was certain. U.S. withdrawal came after the cease-fire agreement of January 1973; North Vietnamese victory in the long civil war came with the fall of Saigon, on April 30, 1975.

Vietnam War of Independence, alternate name for the INDOCHINA WAR.

Viking, series of U.S. spacecraft that reached MARS in 1976, *Viking 1* transmitting data for over 5 years.

Villa, Francisco "Pancho" (Doroteo Arango; 1878–1923), Mexican bandit, who became a revolutionary general during the MEXICAN REVOLUTION, joining the forces of Francisco MADERO in 1910. In 1912 he was imprisoned by Victoriano HUERTA in Mexico City but escaped north over the border and was back in Mexico in 1913, then becoming a major factor in the civil war until his defeat at the Battle of CELAYA in April 1915. In March 1916 Villa's forces raided north over the border, attacking Columbus, New Mexico. U.S. forces led by General John J. PERSHING then invaded northern Mexico, seeking Villa, whom they never found. Reconciled with the Mexican government, which made him a general after making common cause with him against the Americans, Villa retired in 1920. He was assassinated in 1923.

Vimy Ridge (April 9, 1917), site of a World War I Canadian attack that cost 11,000 casualties during the first day of the Battle of ARRAS.

Vincennes incident (July 3, 1988), the shooting down of Iran Air Flight 655—an Airbus A300 carrying 290 people from Bandar Abbas in Iran across the Strait of Hormus to Dubai, by a surface-to-air MISSILE from the cruiser *U. S. S. Vincennes*, operating in the Persian Gulf during the IRAN–IRAQ WAR. The Americans had mistaken the Airbus for an F-14 with aggressive intentions. All of those aboard were killed.

The Iranian government charged that the action was deliberate, and the U.S. government defended the action as an error occurring minutes after a skirmish in which the *Vincennes* had been engaged. The U.S. government offered compensation to the families of those killed.

Vinson, Frederick Moore (1890–1953), U.S. lawyer, Kentucky Democratic Congressman (1923–29; 1931–38), federal court of appeals judge (1938–43), head of the wartime Office of Economic Stabilization (1943–45), and secretary of the treasury in the first TRUMAN administration (1945–46); in 1946 Harry S. Truman appointed him chief justice of the United States. On the Court, he was generally a liberal but also tended to support such Truman administration actions as the steel mill seizures of 1952 and the SMITH ACT Communist prosecutions.

Violencia, La, the COLOMBIAN CIVIL WAR of 1947–58, a protracted rural guerrilla war in which an estimated 200,000–300,000 people died.

viruses, disease-causing organisms on the border between life and nonlife, reproducing like living things, though normally dependent on living cells for growth and reproduction, but forming crystals like salt or sugar. In 1898 Dutch botanist Martinus Willem Beijerinck found an infectious agent he believed to be liquid and named it *virus* (Latin for "poison"); and as early as 1910 Francis Peyton Rous had recognized that viruses can cause some CANCERS in animals. By 1915–16 British researcher Frederick William Twort and French-Canadian researcher Félix-Hubert D'Hérelle had found, independently, that some viruses eat bacteria; D'Hérelle called them bacteriophages (bacteria-eaters). But not until 1935 did American biochemist Wendell Meredith Stanley first isolate a living virus, in crystal form, for which he shared the 1946 Nobel Prize for Chemistry. Two years later British plant pathologist Frederick Charles Bawden found that the virus contained RNA, nucleic acids common to living things. Too small for ordinary microscopes, viruses were first photographed in 1942 by Italian-American microbiologist Salvador Edward Luria with the aid of an ELECTRON MICROSCOPE. In 1946 Max Delbrück and Alfred Day Hershey independently found that genetic matter from different viruses could be combined to form a new virus, for which they shared with Luria the 1969 Nobel Prize for Physiology or Medicine; their discoveries laid the groundwork for later GENETIC ENGINEERING. Just after World War II, U.S. microbiologist John Franklin Enders was the first to successfully grow viruses in test tube cultures, using PENICILLIN to inhibit bacterial growth and allow the virus to grow unaffected; for this work he shared the 1954 Nobel Prize for Physiology or Medicine. By 1949 he had learned how to grow the POLIO virus in human tissues, laying the groundwork for Jonas SALK's and Albert SABIN's 1950s breakthroughs on the POLIO VACCINE. In 1955 German-American biochemist Heinz Fraenkel-Conrat confirmed earlier theories that a virus consisted of RNA plus a protein coat; the complete genetic structure of a virus was worked out by other scientists in 1978. With the development of genetic engineering, some viruses were tailored to serve as vaccines, the first, in 1986, being a vaccine against herpes in swine.

Vishinsky, Andrei Yanuarievich (1883–1954), Russian lawyer and diplomat, a Social Democrat who became a BOLSHEVIK, saw service during the RUSSIAN CIVIL WAR, and became a leading Soviet jurist during the 1920s and 1930s. He was chief government prosecutor during the MOSCOW TRIALS of the 1930s, later becoming a deputy foreign minister; he was foreign minister, 1949–53, and Soviet UNITED NATIONS representative, 1953–54.

vitamins, substances essential to the body in small amounts, their absence causing various deficiency diseases; from *vita* (Latin for "life") and *amino* (a nitrogen group found in many vitamins). Some foods were known from the 19th century to be effective in preventing certain diseases, but British biochemist Frederick G. Hopkins first recognized in 1906 that necessary substances he called "accessory food factors" existed. In 1912 Polish-American biochemist Casimir Funk named such substances and studied some of the group later called B vitamins. American biochemist Elmer V. McCollum (and others) discovered in 1913 that more than one vitamin existed and began designating them by letters. As more vitamins were discovered, many deficiency diseases were prevented or cured.

vitamin A, key VITAMIN discovered in 1913 by American biochemist Elmer McCollum and others, found to be important to vision and growth though toxic in large quantities. Vitamin A was first isolated in 1937 by Swiss chemist Paul Karrer and independently by Austrian-German chemist Richard Kuhn and others.

vitamin B, group of related VITAMINS in foods such as liver, whole grains, and beans, foods known from the 19th century to be effective in preventing various vitamin-deficiency diseases even though vitamins were as yet unknown. Austrian-American physician Joseph Goldberger showed (1915–25) that the B vitamins niacin and nicotinamide were a preventative for the disease pellagra. In 1925 he also isolated vitamin B_2, or riboflavin, synthesized for medical use by 1935. By 1926 scientists had discovered that vitamin B_1, or thiamine, was a preventative for the disease beriberi; by 1931 its formula had been established, and by 1936 it had been synthesized. The complex structure of vitamin B_{12} was worked out on a COMPUTER in 1956 by Dorothy HODGKIN; others quickly isolated the substance itself. But its effects had long been seen in the liver-diet treatment successfully employed against ANEMIA from 1926.

vitamin C (ascorbic acid), key VITAMIN common in citrus fruits and paprika, lack of which was long known to result in scurvy. Vitamin C was discovered independently in 1928 by Hungarian-American biochemist Albert Szent-Györgyi and American Charles King, who first isolated it from lemon juice in 1932; others synthesized it 2 years later. American biochemist Linus PAULING caused considerable controversy when in 1970 he suggested that vitamin C was a preventative for the common cold, causing millions to take large quantities of vitamin C tablets despite the lack of hard evidence.

vitamin D, key group of VITAMINS found in fish liver oils; such oils were long used to treat rickets, but vitamin D was unknown until 1931–6, when three key D vitamins were identified. Vitamin D was later found to be made more potent by exposure to the ULTRAVIOLET RAYS in sunlight.

Vittorio Veneto, Battle of (October 24–November 4, 1918), the final battle of World War I on the Italian-Austrian front. Allied forces split the Austrian army, which soon collapsed; 300,000 Austrian prisoners were taken. The offensive ended with the Austrian–Allied armistice of November 4, 1918.

V-J Day (August 15, 1945), the day on which the ALLIES announced that World War II had ended in the Pacific theater.

Vladivostok summit (November 1974), a superpower summit meeting at which U.S. president Gerald R. FORD and U.S.S.R. premier Leonid BREZHNEV developed some limited agreement on the ground rules for the continuing SALT II talks, although the worsening of American–Soviet relations that followed the 1979 Soviet invasion of AFGHANISTAN vitiated moves toward agreement on nuclear disarmament during that period.

Voice of America, U.S. foreign-language RADIO service, operating since 1942, run by the United States Information Agency and often staffed by immigrants and political refugees.

Volstead Act, the enabling 1920 federal law that began the enforcement of PROHIBITION.

Vorster, Balthazar (1915–83), South African lawyer and Afrikaner activist, a Nazi sympathizer who was imprisoned for pro-Nazi activities during World War II (1942–44). He became a NATIONAL PARTY member of Parliament in 1953 and was justice minister 1961–66, in that position taking a leading role in the outlawing of the AFRICAN NATIONAL CONGRESS, the imprisonment of Nelson MANDELA, and the violent suppression of civil and political liberties in his country. He became prime minister in 1966, succeeding assassinated Hendrik VERWOERD, and continued to rigidly enforce APARTHEID and suppress opposition. He resigned because of ill health in 1978, then became president. He left public life in June 1979 after widespread criticism of his role in the illegal use of government propaganda funds.

Voskhod, feries of U.S.S.R. spacecraft. *Voskhod 1* put the first three-person crew in space on October 12, 1964; *Voskhod 2*, launched on March 18, 1965, carried the first astronaut to take a SPACE WALK outside the spacecraft, Aleksei LEONOV.

Vostok, series of U.S.S.R. spacecraft, built under the direction of Sergei KOROLEV, that first put humans in orbit. On April 12, 1961, Yuri GAGARIN circled the Earth in *Vostok 1* on a 1.8-hour flight. *Vostok 6* launched the first woman into space, Valentina TERESHKOVA, on June 16, 1963.

Vostok I, the first spacecraft; it orbited Earth once, on April 12, 1961, piloted by Soviet cosmonaut Yuri GAGARIN.

Voting Rights Act of 1965, law that outlawed the series of discriminatory tests that had for generations been used by white voter registrars to disenfranchise Black Americans in the South, it provided for direct federal supervision, as necessary, of southern voter registration. Mass Black registration and voting followed and with it the emergence of powerful Black electoral influence in the southern states. After 1965 large numbers of Black elected officials emerged, with a new willingness to engage in coalition politics on the part of white political leaders throughout the south.

Voyager, series of U.S. spacecraft making interplanetary probes. *Voyager 1* and *2*, launched in 1977, flew by JUPITER in 1979 and SATURN in 1980 and 1981, photographing their rings and discovering new moons, then taking divergent paths. *Voyager 1* headed for outer space; *Voyager 2* headed for URANUS, photographing its rings from nearby in 1986, and for NEPTUNE in 1989, discovering 6 new moons and several unusual rings before passing beyond into space.

Voyager, specially built, very light airplane that in 1986 made the first nonstop flight around the world, taking 9 days; it was piloted by U.S. aviators Dick Rutan and Jeana Yeager.

Voyager sinking (February 10, 1964), the sinking of the destroyer *Voyager* at Jervis Bay, New South Wales, Australia, after it collided with the aircraft carrier *Melbourne:* 82 people died.

W

Waffen SS, the sizable front-line fighting force of the Nazi SS, among the more tenacious combat units of the German army during the last years of World War II, as they fell back before the Allied European armies. Waffen SS units committed many of the most serious Nazi atrocities in occupied Europe.

Wagner, Robert Ferdinand (1877–1953), U.S. lawyer, and New York legislator, judge, and four-term Democratic senator (1927–49), who initiated much pioneering labor and labor-related legislation at both state and federal levels, including the New York State workmen's compensation law and such major NEW DEAL measures as the WAGNER ACT (National Labor Relations Act), SOCIAL SECURITY Act, National Industrial Recovery Act, and the FEDERAL EMERGENCY RELIEF ACT.

Wagner Act (Wagner-Connery Act; National Labor Relations Act), U.S. NEW DEAL legislation enacted in July 1935, that established the NATIONAL LABOR RELATIONS BOARD (NLRB), specified a number of employer unfair labor practices, provided for single majority union representation in each bargaining unit, and gave the NLRB power to decide union certification questions, including the right to conduct a secret ballot to determine workers' bargaining preferences. Because of employer resistance, the Wagner Act did not go fully into effect until declared constitutional by the Supreme Court in *NATIONAL LABOR RELATIONS BOARD* v. *JONES & LAUGHLIN STEEL CORPORATION* in 1937; it then played a major role in the unionization of the mass pro-

duction industries and of many other industries as well.

Wainwright, Jonathan Mayhew (1883–1953), U.S. officer, who saw service in the Philippines before and during World War I. Back in the Philippines at the outbreak of World War II, he became commander of remaining U.S.–Philippine forces in 1942, after the evacuation of Douglas MACARTHUR, ultimately surrendering CORREGIDOR to the Japanese. He survived the BATAAN DEATH MARCH and subsequent imprisonment, and was present at the formal Japanese surrender aboard the *Missouri* in Tokyo Bay, on September 2, 1945.

Waite, Terry, one of the LEBANON HOSTAGES, a British Anglican church hostage negotiator, who was kidnapped by Moslem extremists on January 20, 1987.

Wake Island, Battle of (December 8–23, 1941), early World War II attack on the small Wake Island garrison by Japanese bombers on December 8, 1941. An amphibious assault on December 11 was unsuccessful, but a second assault, on December 23, took the island.

Wald, Lillian D. (1867–1940), U.S. nurse, who in 1893 organized the settlement house that became the HENRY STREET SETTLEMENT on New York's lower East Side. In 1902 she initiated the first public school nursing program, and became the leading U.S. public health nurse of her time.

Waldheim, Kurt (1918–   ), Austrian diplomat, who saw service in the German army during World War II, and pursued a long career in Austrian diplomacy and politics before becoming fourth secretary-general of the UNITED NATIONS 1972–81. In that position he pursued UN relief activities in the THIRD WORLD and maintained peacekeeping forces in the Middle East, but otherwise had little impact on the main events of the time. When he became president of Austria in 1986, a major international controversy arose over his alleged links to Nazi atrocities in Yugoslavia and Greece during World War II. He at first denied and then admitted seeing service in the area, and then denied participation in or even knowledge of the Nazi atrocities in question.

Walesa, Lech (1943–   ), Polish electrician who was fired for being a leader of the 1970 Gdańsk Lenin Shipyard demonstrations, continued his organizing work during the 1970s, and emerged as Poland's chief labor leader. As head of SOLIDARITY he led the 1980 GDAŃSK LENIN SHIPYARD STRIKE that forced government recognition and concessions. Although he was imprisoned for almost a year after the declaration of martial law and the outlawing of Solidarity in December 1981, he remained underground leader of the Polish labor movement, emerging again in 1988 with the Solidarity–government talks that led to the 1989 legalization of Solidarity.

Walker–Whitworth espionage ring, a U.S. espionage group that operated for an unknown time (at least 17 years) under the leadership of U. S. Navy warrant officer John Walker, who sold to the Soviet Union classified information that had been gathered by himself; his brother, Arthur Walker; his son, Michael Walker; and his associate, Jerry Whitworth. All four were arrested in 1985 and sentenced to long terms of imprisonment.

Wallace, George Corley (1919–   ), U.S. lawyer and Alabama Democratic state legislator, judge, and governor (1963–67), who was a leading Southern segregationist during the 1960s. He promised to and did "stand in the schoolhouse door" in an attempt to block school integration, the schoolhouse door being the registration facility of the University of Alabama in June 1963. Federalized National Guard troops cleared the door, as did federal law officers and troops elsewhere in Alabama. He was the presidential nominee of the American Independent party in 1968, carrying five southern states. He was wounded in an assassination attempt on May 15, 1972, at Laurel, Mississippi.

Wallace, Henry Agard (1888–1960), U.S. agricultural scientist and journalist, who became Franklin D. ROOSEVELT'S secretary of agriculture and developed the AGRICULTURAL ADJUSTMENT ADMINISTRATION (AAA). He was vice-president, 1941–45, and secretary of commerce, 1945–46. A liberal, he spoke against the foreign policy of the subsequent TRUMAN administration as the COLD WAR began to develop, and lost his cabinet position. In 1948 he ran as PROGRESSIVE PARTY presidential nominee; his party was widely attacked as being pro-Soviet, and although he received more than 1 million votes, his defeat was so decisive as to essentially end his political career. His career did not revive even though he broke with his party a few years later over his support of the UNITED NATIONS Korean action.

Wall Street bombing, explosion on September 16, 1920, that killed 30 people and injured hundreds more. No one claimed "credit," and the bombing was unsolved; anarchists were widely blamed for the action in that RED SCARE period.

Wang Ching-wei (1883–1944), Japanese-supported ruler of occupied China from March 30, 1940, who had in the early years of the century been a chief aide to SUN YAT-SEN and then head of the left faction of the KUOMINTANG. In the early 1930s he was president of the Kuomintang.

War Communism, the internal economic policies followed by the Soviet government from 1918 to 1921, a period in which the new BOLSHEVIK government attempted to take over direct control of every aspect of the country's economic life. The new government nationalized almost all of Soviet industry as the country experienced runaway inflation, increasingly severe famines, rural unrest, and the widespread confiscation of food supplies by government forces—all while the RUSSIAN CIVIL WAR was being fought. The KRONSTADT sailors' rebellion of 1921 signaled the depth of the crisis generated by War Communism, and precipitated LENIN'S more moderate NEW ECONOMIC POLICY.

War on Poverty, a slogan put forward by U.S. president Lyndon Baines JOHNSON in 1964, as a basis for the wide range of economic legislation that resulted in formation of the Office of Economic Opportunity and such programs as the Job Corps, VISTA, and Head Start. During the early 1970s most of the programs so generated were discontinued.

Warren, Earl (1891–1974), U.S. lawyer, prosecutor, Republican California governor (1943–53), and 1948 candidate for the vice-presidency, on the DEWEY ticket; in 1953 Dwight D. EISENHOWER appointed him chief justice of the United States. During the next 16 years his court generated a series of landmark decisions, outlawing school segregation and defending the civil rights of Blacks and other minorities, ending the civil liberties abuses of the MCCARTHY period, enunciating the "one man, one vote" rule, and expanding and clarifying the rights of suspects and defendants. He was also chairman of the WARREN COMMISSION, which investigated the assassination of President John F. KENNEDY.

Warren Commission, the 1963 U.S. federal commission appointed by President Lyndon B. JOHNSON to investigate and report on the assassination of President John F. KENNEDY; it was headed by Chief Justice Earl WARREN. After a 10-month investigation the Warren Commission reported that it could find no conspiracy, that Lee Harvey OSWALD had acted alone, and that Oswald's assassin, Jack RUBY, had not known Oswald. The report caused great controversy, many still continuing to hew to the conspiracy theory even decades later.

War Resisters' International (WRI), an international pacifist and antiwar organiza-

tion, founded in 1921, that advises and supports conscientious objectors, deserters, and other war resisters throughout the world.

Warsaw, Battle of (August 16–25, 1920), the most decisive battle of the SOVIET–POLISH WAR of 1920, in which the Polish army, led by General Jósef PILSUDSKI defeated the Soviet army, led by General Mikhail TUKHACHEVSKY.

Warsaw Ghetto rising (April–May 1943), revolt of Jews in the Warsaw Ghetto. After the Nazi conquest of Poland, the city's Jews had been forced into the Warsaw Ghetto. By the spring of 1943 the Nazis had sent an estimated 400,000–450,000 of them to DEATH CAMPS; the remaining 60,000 revolted, choosing to die with weapons in their hands rather than to be quietly led away to the Nazi gas chambers. They fought the Nazis for a month, ultimately running out of ammunition and supplies; few survived the battle and the Nazi murders that followed.

Warsaw Pact (Warsaw Treaty Organization), an international Soviet-bloc military organization established in 1955 pursuant to the terms of the Treaty of Warsaw, in response to the formation of the NORTH ATLANTIC TREATY ORGANIZATION (NATO) and the rearmament of the Federal Republic of Germany. The organization provides a framework for joint military activities in Europe. Its seven member countries are Bulgaria, Czechoslovakia, German Democratic Republic, Hungary, Poland, Rumania, and the Soviet Union.

Warsaw rising (August–October 1944), revolt of the Polish underground in Warsaw, trying to take the city from its small German garrison, as attacking Soviet forces approached Warsaw during the summer of 1944. The Soviet army stopped just across the Vistula River from the city while the Germans reinforced their garrison and in the next 2 months destroyed the poorly armed and supplied Polish resistance fighters, tens of thousands of noncombatants, and much of the city. The remaining Poles surrendered on October 2.

Washington, Booker Taliaferro (1856–1915), U.S. teacher, who during the late 19th century developed Tuskegee Institute in Alabama into the leading Black educational institution of the time; he was a major Black leader from the mid-1890s until his death. He publicly urged Blacks to accommodate to segregation and to develop practical skills and wealth, rather than to oppose racism directly and insist on equality. These views pleased some of the most powerful White political, social, and economic leaders of his time, who accepted him as the dominant leader of the American Black community. Their acceptance and material contributions helped him to become that leader, in fact, developing the power to reward his friends and punish his enemies within that community. A few Black leaders, such as William E. DU BOIS, took a far different view; they developed the NATIONAL ASSOCIATION FOR THE ADVANCEMENT OF COLORED PEOPLE (NAACP), and began the process that would ultimately result in the CIVIL RIGHTS MOVEMENT and the formation of the modern U.S. Black community.

Washington summit (December 1987), the third meeting between U.S. president Ronald REAGAN and U.S.S.R. premier Mikhail GORBACHEV, at which both signed the INF TREATY and discussed outstanding differences between the two superpowers, with special attention to the resoluton of regional conflicts, signaling a great relaxation of tension between the two nations and at least a substantial truce in the decades-long COLD WAR.

Watergate (1972–74), the massive U.S. political scandal first exposed by the tenacious investigation of Washington *Post* reporters Robert WOODWARD and Carl BERNSTEIN, assisted by their anonymous source, DEEP THROAT, which led to the resignation of president Richard M. NIXON after exposure of his complicity in a series of illegal acts directed at his domestic political opponents. The triggering event was the arrest of five burglars, Bernard L. Barker, Virgilio R.

Gonzalez, Eugenio R. Martinez, James W. McCord, Jr., and Frank A. Sturgis, after they had broken into the national Democratic party headquarters in Washington's Watergate apartment complex, on June 17, 1972, intending to install wiretaps. In January 1973 they and two others, E. Howard Hunt and G. Gordon Liddy, were indicted and pleaded guilty; following that the entire Watergate story unfolded—in court, before a grand jury, and before a select committee of the Senate. Ultimately, Watergate was shown to be the illegal action at which Nixon and his co-conspirators were caught, one of many such connected illegal actions, which included the DIRTY TRICKS campaign for which Donald Segretti was later imprisoned, the PENTAGON PAPERS break-ins, large illegal campaign contributions, and the illegal use of those contributions by the Committee to Reelect the President (CREEP). Nixon and those around him attempted to cover their tracks but failed, and in late 1973 they foundered entirely over the matter of the Watergate tapes, recorded in the White House and revealing Nixon's complicity in the scandal. On October 20, 1973, Nixon fired special prosecutor Archibald Cox and Deputy Attorney-General William Ruckelshaus in the SATURDAY NIGHT MASSACRE that entirely destroyed Nixon's credibility and remaining public support. He was forced to appoint a new prosecutor, Leon Jaworski, and yield the tapes to the court although in altered condition. Nixon refused a later Jaworski demand for more tapes and documents, and on July 24, 1974, was compelled by the Supreme Court to comply. Facing three counts of impeachment, Nixon resigned, effective August 9, 1974; he was later pardoned, and thereby shielded from prosecution, by President Gerald R. FORD. Several of Nixon's subordinates and associates were convicted and imprisoned in connection with Watergate, including White House Chief of Staff H. R. HALDEMAN, presidential assistant John D. EHRLICHMAN, and former attorney general and chairman of the

Committee to Elect the President John N. MITCHELL.

Watkins, James David (1927–   ), U.S. naval officer who, in a 37-year naval career, held a number of senior positions, becoming an admiral in 1979, commander of the U.S. Pacific fleet 1981–82, and chief of naval operations 1982–86. After his retirement, he was appointed chairman of the national AIDS advisory commission by President Ronald REAGAN, in September 1987. In June 1988, he released a commission report that strongly urged major new national initiatives to combat the AIDS epidemic and its societal impacts, including a ban on AIDS-connected discrimination. On January 12, 1989, he was named energy secretary by President-elect George BUSH.

Watkins v. United States (1957), a landmark U.S. Supreme Court decision, reversing the conviction of a witness before the HOUSE UNAMERICAN ACTIVITIES COMMITTEE for violations of Fifth Amendment due process, and at the same time directly attacking the witchhunting tactics of that committee. The decision reflected and contributed to changed national attitutudes as MCCARTHYISM waned.

Watson, James Dewey (1928–   ), U.S. molecular biologist and co-discoverer (with Francis CRICK) of the DOUBLE HELIX form taken by the DNA molecule, the substance that carries and duplicates basic hereditary information; he shared the 1962 Nobel Prize for Physiology or Medicine with Crick and Maurice WILKINS. Watson's *Double Helix* (1968), describing the process of the discovery, was a surprise best-seller.

Watson, John Broadus (1878–1958), U.S. psychologist, who founded the school of psychology called BEHAVIORISM. Watson's view, first outlined formally in 1913, was that a person's observable and measurable responses to stimuli were the proper subject of psychology, and that behavior resulted from training (conditioning) rather than from instinct or heredity. His theories eschewed introspective approaches that fo-cused on unobservable phenomena such as inner feelings.

Watson, Thomas John (1874–1956), U.S. computer industry executive, who pioneered in the development and sale of COMPUTERS and built International Business Machines (IBM) into the largest computer company in the world. His son, Thomas J. Watson, Jr., succeeded him, leading the company until 1979.

Watts and other 1960s race riots, a series of massive race riots initiated by dissatisfied Blacks in U.S. inner city areas, beginning with the summer riots of 1965 in the Watts district of Los Angeles, which set a pattern for riots during the following 4 years. These riots resulted in hundreds of deaths, thousands of wounded, tens of thousands of arrests, hundreds of millions of dollars of property damage, and the use of tens of thousands of federal and state troops. After 1968 the rioting subsided, although isolated riots continued to occur on into the 1970s and 1980s.

Wavell, Archibald Percival (1883–1950), British officer, who saw service in the BOER WAR and World War I, and who became British Middle East commander in chief early in World War II. His forces scored major victories against larger Italian forces in North Africa early in World War II, but were defeated by German forces, and Wavell was recalled. At the outbreak of the Pacific war in December 1941, forces under his command lost much of Southeast Asia to the Japanese. He was next-to-last viceroy of India, being recalled in 1947 when he opposed immediate independence.

wave-particle duality, idea that particles have wavelike aspects and waves have particle-like aspects. Drawing on the 1923 work of Arthur Holly COMPTON and on Albert EINSTEIN's 1905 notion that matter and energy were interconvertible, Louis DE BROGLIE first suggested in 1924 that particles such as ELECTRONS have the properties of both waves and particles. In 1926 Erwin SCHRÖDINGER provided some mathematical underpinning for such a theory, which was confirmed by several scientists using X-RAY CRYSTALLOGRAPHY in 1927.

Weathermen, a U.S. revolutionary group formed in 1969 as a terrorist-oriented splinter of the fragmented STUDENTS FOR A DEMOCRATIC SOCIETY. Its members went underground, many of them believing that U.S. society was ready to collapse; they were determined to speed that collapse and build a mass revolutionary movement aided by acts of random terror. Their estimates having proven entirely incorrect, some members of the organization began to reappear during the later 1970s and early 1980s, with several prosecutions resulting. While underground, some Weathermen destroyed themselves, in the highly publicized 1970 Greenwich Village explosion of their own small homemade-bomb factory. Others received long prison terms for their involvement in the abortive Nanuet, New York, Brink's robbery of 1981.

Webb, Beatrice Potter (1858–1943), and **Sidney James WEBB** (1859–1947), British economists and Socialists who, together and with George Bernard SHAW, stood at the intellectual center of British socialism through their leadership of the FABIAN SOCIETY. They were prolific writers: among their major works were *The History of Trade Unionism* (1894), *Industrial Democracy* (1897), *Soviet Communism: A New Civilization?* (1935), and her *Minority Report* as a member of the Royal Commission on the Poor Laws (1909). They were founders of the *New Statesman* and the London School of Economics; he was also a Labour MP, 1922–31, and a member of both Labour cabinets in the 1920s.

Weber, Max (1864–1920), German sociologist whose influential work, *The Protestant Ethic and the Spirit of Capitalism* (1904), linked the growth of capitalism to the ethos of Protestantism; his body of work stressed the importance of ideas in the development of societies and economic systems. His work on the laws of development of bureaucracy had major impact on later sociologists.

Webster, William Hedgcock (1924–   ), U.S. lawyer, federal district court judge in Missouri, 1971–73; Court of Appeals judge, 1973–78; and director of the FEDERAL BUREAU OF INVESTIGATION (FBI) 1978–87. In May 1987 President Ronald REAGAN appointed him head of the CENTRAL INTELLIGENCE AGENCY (CIA); he was reappointed by incoming president George BUSH in December 1988.

Wedtech, a Bronx, New York, company that during the 1970s and early 1980s successfully bribed government officials to secure Defense Department contracts and Small Business Administration grants and loans. In 1987 and 1988, Congressional investigations and federal prosecutors exposed what became a major scandal that ultimately contributed a count to the conviction of former White House aide Lyn Nofziger in February 1988, and triggered a major investigation of the possible role of Edwin Meese, then attorney general. Meese was not prosecuted, but resigned under fire in July 1988. In August 1988 Congressman Mario Biaggi, former Bronx borough president Stanley Simon, Wedtech founder John Mariotta, former Small Business Administration official Peter P. Neglia, Biaggi law partner Bernard G. Ehrlich, and Biaggi's son, Richard P. Biaggi, were all convicted in connection with the scandal.

Wegener, Alfred Lothar (1880–1930), German meteorologist and geologist, who in 1912 outlined the CONTINENTAL DRIFT theory described in his *Origins of Continents and Oceans*; he was also known for his Arctic climatological research, during which he lost his life.

Weimar Republic, the German republic that superseded the monarchy overthrown by the GERMAN REVOLUTION OF 1918; named after the Weimar Constitution of August 11, 1919, establishing it. The republic, always weak, ended on January 30, 1933, when Adolf HITLER became chancellor of Germany.

Weinberger, Caspar Willard (1917–   ), U.S. lawyer, active in California Republican politics during the 1950s and 1960s, who was Federal Trade Commission chairman in 1970; deputy director and the director of the Office of Management and Budget, 1970–73; secretary of health, education and welfare, 1973–75; and secretary of defense, 1981–87. As secretary of defense he strongly supported and secured greatly increased military expenditures.

Weir, Reverend Benjamin, one of the LEBANON HOSTAGES, an American who was kidnapped on May 6, 1984, and released on September 14, 1985, as part of a complex set of negotiations between the U.S. government and those holding the hostages during that period, actions that ultimately led to the IRAN–CONTRA AFFAIR.

Weiss, Carl, Louisiana doctor who assassinated Huey LONG at Baton Rouge, Louisiana, on September 8, 1935, and was then killed by Long's bodyguards.

Weizmann, Chaim (1874–1952), Russian-British chemist who became a leader of world ZIONISM, helping to develop the 1917 BALFOUR RESOLUTION. He was president of the World Zionist Organization (1920–29), president of the Jewish Agency for Palestine (1929–31, 1935–46), and provisional and then first elected president of Israel (1948–52).

Welch, Joseph Nye (1890–1960), U.S. lawyer who represented the U.S. Army in the televised ARMY–MCCARTHY HEARINGS (1954) and succeeded in discrediting Senator Joseph McCarthy and his associates before a national and international audience, thereby contributing greatly to the end of McCarthy's witchhunting career.

Welsh v. *United States* (1970), a landmark U.S. Supreme Court decision, making it possible for those opposing war for ethical and moral reasons to be granted conscientious objector status, joining those already able to do so because of religious convictions.

We shall fight on the beaches, ringing statement by British prime minister Winston CHURCHILL, speaking to the House of Commons on June 4, 1940, after the British cross-channel evacuation from DUNKIRK; from "We shall not flag or fail. We shall go on to the end. We shall fight in France, we shall fight on the seas and oceans, we shall fight with growing confidence and growing strength in the air, we shall defend our island, whatever the cost may be, we shall fight on the beaches, we shall fight on the landing grounds, we shall fight in the fields and in the streets, we shall fight in the hills; we shall never surrender."

We Shall Overcome, song that became the anthem of the U.S. CIVIL RIGHTS MOVEMENT.

West Bank, the west bank of the Jordan River; formerly Jordanian territory, occupied by Israel from 1967, and thereafter partially colonized by the Israelis. With a population of approximately 1 million Palestinians, the area was the main site of the INTIFADA (uprising) beginning in 1988; Jordan withdrew from the West Bank and the PALESTINE LIBERATION ORGANIZATION (PLO) proclaimed a Palestinian state, including the West Bank and the GAZA STRIP.

West Coast Hotel Company v. *Parrish* (1937), a landmark U.S. Supreme Court decision, validating a Washington state law providing minimum wages for women and minors and reversing *Adkins* v. *Children's Hospital* (1923).

Western Desert Campaign (December 9, 1940–February 7, 1941), series of World War II engagements in North Africa. In September 1940 five Italian divisions invaded Egypt; the Italian force soon grew to 9 divisions. On December 9, 1940, British forces about one quarter their size, but with some armor, attacked Italian positions at Sidi Barrani, routed much more numerous Italian forces, and took 38,000 prisoners. From January 1–7, British forces took Bardia and TOBRUK and ultimately captured a total of 130,000 Italians. The British suffered total casualties of fewer than 2,000 men.

Western Samoa (Independent State of Western Samoa), until World War I a German protectorate, then becoming a New

Zealand LEAGUE OF NATIONS mandate territory, a UNITED NATIONS trust territory, and an independent nation and COMMONWEALTH member on January 1, 1962.

Westmoreland, William Childs (1914–), U.S. officer, who saw service in World War II and Korea, and who in June 1964 became commander of U.S. assistance forces in Vietnam. He became commander of U.S. combat forces in Vietnam in August 1964, after passage of the TONKIN GULF RESOLUTION. He left Vietnam to become U.S. army chief of staff in the summer of 1968. As commander of American forces, he was both vigorously attacked and vigorously supported in the United States during the Vietnam years. In January 1982 he was strongly criticized in a CBS documentary and sued CBS for libel; the case was settled out of court in 1985, after a long trial, without damage payments.

West Virginia Board of Education v. Barnette (1943), a landmark U.S. Supreme Court decision invalidating a compulsory flag salute law in West Virginia that had been challenged by members of Jehovah's Witnesses.

Weygand, Maxime (1867–1965), French officer, who held key staff positions during World War I, and was army commander in chief during the mid-1930s. In 1939 he came out of retirement to head French Near East forces, and in May 1940 replaced General Maurice GAMELIN as head of all Allied forces in Western Europe. He soon called for capitulation to the Germans, and afterward served as VICHY defense minister. He was arrested by the Germans after their seizure of unoccupied France in 1942, and imprisoned for the balance of the war. He was later tried for treason and acquitted.

Whampoa Military Academy, a KUOMINTANG training school initiated by SUN YAT-SEN in 1923 and organized in 1924 by CHIANG KAI-SHEK, with Soviet advisers, after Chiang's return from military training in the Soviet Union; its graduates became key supporters of Chiang's rise to power.

What this country needs is a really good five cent cigar!, comment by U.S. vice-president Thomas R. MARSHALL in 1917 during a long, slow Senate debate on national priorities.

Wheeler, Robert Eric Mortimer (1890–1976), British archaeologist who rediscovered one of the greatest Bronze Age civilizations, centered at Harappa and Mohenjo-Daro in the Indus Valley of northern India, and dating from about 2500–1500 B.C. His fieldwork there and in Britain made him one of the seminal figures in modern archeology.

White, Byron Raymond (1917–), U.S. lawyer, who was a college and professional football star in the late 1930s and 1940s as "Whizzer" White. A political associate of John F. KENNEDY during the 1960 presidential campaign, he was an assistant U.S. attorney-general 1961–62, and was appointed by Kennedy to the Supreme Court in 1962. On the Court he was generally a moderate-to-conservative influence, often functioning as a swing vote between liberals and conservatives on close decisions.

White, Edward Douglass (1845–1921), U.S. lawyer, who saw service in the Confederate army during the Civil War, and was a senator from Louisiana when appointed by Grover Cleveland to the Supreme Court in 1894. On the Court he was generally a conservative, and continued to be so after William Howard TAFT appointed him chief justice in 1910.

White, Paul Dudley (1886–1973), U.S. cardiologist working at the Harvard Medical School, who pioneered in the use of the ELECTROCARDIOGRAPH (ECG or EKG) to record the heart's electrical activity. A founder of the American Heart Association in 1922, he early emphasized the role of diet, stress, and exercise in the health of the heart, becoming famous as physician to President EISENHOWER after his 1955 coronary.

White, Walter Francis (1893–1955), U.S. Black civil rights leader, who became active in the NATIONAL ASSOCIATION FOR THE ADVANCEMENT OF COLORED PEOPLE (NAACP) shortly after his graduation from

Atlanta University in 1916; he was assistant secretary (1918–31) and then executive secretary (1931–55) of the NAACP, leading it through the antilynching and fair employment practices campaigns of the 1930s and 1940s and through the early years of the modern CIVIL RIGHTS MOVEMENT.

Whitehead, Alfred North (1861–1947), British mathematician and philosopher who, with his protégé Bertrand RUSSELL, made a landmark attempt to develop a solid substructure of logic for modern mathematics in *Principia Mathematica* (1910–13), work soon undercut by that of Kurt GÖDEL. In Britain and from the 1920s in America, Whitehead also worked in the philosophy of science, writing for both scholarly and popular audiences, as in his *Science and the Modern World* (1925).

Whitlam, Edward Gough (1916–), Australian lawyer, a Labour member of parliament from 1952, and prime minister 1972–75, in that position pursuing a far more independent course in world affairs than the preceding MENZIES administration, while also encountering economic problems and political scandals at home. His government was dissolved by the governor-general in November 1975, and then lost the December general election.

WHO, the initials of the WORLD HEALTH ORGANIZATION, a UNITED NATIONS special agency.

Wiener, Norbert (1894–1964), U.S. mathematician, who developed the theory of CYBERNETICS (Greek for "the science of steering ships"). At first, Wiener focused largely on logic and mathematical fundamentals, studying with Bertrand RUSSELL and David HILBERT, and he continued to make key contributions to basic mathematics. But his work on RADAR and missiles during World War II, and associated work with then-developing COMPUTERS, turned him toward studying information flow and control in machines as communication systems analogous to nervous systems in animals. He summarized his ideas in a 1948 book called *Cybernetics or Control and Communication in the Animal and the Machine*. This and many of his later works focused on the problems humans face in an automated society; their appeal ranged far beyond the scientific and technical community.

Wiesel, Elie (1928–), Jewish-Rumanian-American writer and teacher. As an adolescent he spent most of World War II in Nazi CONCENTRATION CAMPS. In the mid-1950s he began a lifelong focus on the JEWISH HOLOCAUST, also writing on other Jewish-related themes, including the situation of Soviet Jews. He was awarded the Nobel Peace Prize in 1986.

Wiesenthal, Simon (1908–), Jewish-Polish architect, imprisoned by the Nazis (1941–43, 1944–45) who became a leading Nazi hunter during the post–World War II period. Immediately after the war he was employed as a war crimes investigator by the U.S. Army; he subsequently operated out of the Jewish Documentation Center, which he founded in 1947. His best-known success came in 1960 with the location of Adolf EICHMANN, who was seized by Israeli agents in Argentina and later tried and executed in Israel.

Wiley, Harvey Washington (1844–1930), U.S. chemist and leader in the early 20th-century fight against adulteration of food. A chemistry professor, Wiley was the U.S. Department of Agriculture's chief chemist from 1883 to 1912, expanding his Bureau of Chemistry from a handful of employees to more than 500. He and his staff, popularly called the Poison Squad, analyzed many foods for additives and adulteratives—sometimes testing them directly on themselves—and pressed for government regulation of the food industry. His efforts, along with widely read works by such MUCKRAKERS as Ida TARBELL and Upton SINCLAIR, spurred the passage of the landmark 1906 PURE FOOD AND DRUG ACT.

Wilhelm II (1859–1941), emperor of Germany (1888–1918), the "Kaiser" who led the Central European powers and their allies during World War I. He abdicated in 1918, as the GERMAN REVOLUTION OF 1918 was beginning, and fled to Holland, where he spent the rest of his life.

Wilhelmina (1880–1962), queen of the Netherlands, 1890–1948; during World War II she fled to London after the 1940 German invasion, there serving as a focus for continuing Dutch resistance. She abdicated in 1948 in favor of her daughter Juliana.

Wilkins, Maurice Hugh Frederick (1916–), New Zealand-British biophysicist whose work in X-RAY CRYSTALLOGRAPHY, along with that of Rosalind FRANKLIN, produced key data that aided James WATSON and Francis CRICK in uncovering the DOUBLE HELIX structure of DNA; he shared with them the 1962 Nobel Prize for Physiology or Medicine.

Wilkins, Roy (1901–81), U.S. Black journalist and civil rights leader who became assistant secretary of the NATIONAL ASSOCIATION FOR THE ADVANCEMENT OF COLORED PEOPLE (NAACP) in 1931, editor of its publication, *The Crisis*, in 1934, and successor to Walter WHITE as leader of the NAACP, 1955–77.

Williams, Eric Eustace (1911–81), Trinidadian historian and socialist who studied, taught, and wrote in Great Britain and the United States before founding the People's National Movement in 1956. From 1956 until his death he led Trinidad and Tobago as chief minister and then as prime minister.

Williams, Vanessa, the 1983 Miss America, forced to resign after revelations that in 1982, as a college freshman, she had posed for some nude photographs. In 1984 *Penthouse* magazine announced that it would publish her nude photographs; this precipitated a national furor that forced her to resign her Miss America position, and sold a great many magazines.

Williams, Wayne B., young Black man accused of the ATLANTA MASS MURDERS of 1979–81 and sentenced to life imprisonment.

Willkie, Wendell Lewis (1892–1944), U.S. lawyer, who became Republican presidential nominee in 1940, and was defeated by Franklin Delano ROOSEVELT. A liberal in his party, he supported the war effort fully during World War II, and in 1942 wrote the book *One World*, which called for international cooperation and organization in the postwar world.

Wilson, Charles Thomson Rees (1869–1959), Scottish physicist, who in 1911 developed the CLOUD CHAMBER, a device for tracking the path of subatomic PARTICLES and RADIATION, for which he won the 1927 Nobel Prize for Physics.

Wilson, Edward Osborne (1929–), U.S. zoologist, who was a founder of sociobiology, an interdisciplinary science that focuses on the genetic roots of social behavior in humans and other animals, as outlined in his *Sociobiology: the New Synthesis* (1975); the theory is sometimes criticized as being excessively deterministic.

Wilson, James Harold (1916–), British economist and teacher, who became a Labour member of Parliament in 1945, held several posts in the postwar Labour government, became party leader in 1963, and was prime minister 1964–70, encountering major economic problems that contributed to Labour's surprise electoral loss in 1970. He returned to office in 1974 as prime minister of a Liberal-Labour coalition government, resigning unexpectedly in 1976. During the 1980s charges emerged that senior intelligence service officers had conspired to discredit him while in office, but they lacked full substantiation.

Wilson, Thomas Woodrow (1856–1924), 28th president of the United States, 1912–20; also lawyer, college professor, college president, and governor of New Jersey. As a candidate for the presidency, Wilson's program featured the NEW FREEDOM, an economic program calling for enhanced antitrust and financial system regulation coupled with tariff reform. A Democrat, in 1912 he defeated Republican William Howard TAFT and Progressive Theodore ROOSEVELT, and in 1916 he defeated Republican Charles Evans HUGHES for the presidency. As president, he accomplished tariff reduction, introduced the first income tax law, and established the FEDERAL RESERVE SYSTEM and the FEDERAL TRADE COMMISSION. As second-term candidate, his chief slogan was "He kept us out of war." But on April 2, 1917, he asked Congress to declare a state of war against Germany, which was done on April 6. As wartime president, he established the War Industries Board, led by Bernard BARUCH, which exercised great control over the American economy throughout the war. On January 8, 1918, he introduced his FOURTEEN POINTS, a program for postwar settlements that included the establishment of the LEAGUE OF NATIONS; he took that program to the PARIS PEACE CONFERENCE of January 18, 1919, which culminated in the Treaty of VERSAILLES. But the Senate refused to ratify the treaty, balking at participation in the League of Nations, and the United States made a separate peace in 1921, after Republican Warren G. HARDING had become president.

Win, Ne (Maung Shu Maung; 1911–   ), Burmese officer and nationalist, who fought with the Japanese during World War II, then joined the anti-Japanese revolt of the Burmese National Army in March 1945. During the postwar period he became a general in the Burmese army. In 1958 he took power in a bloodless army coup, relinquished control in 1960, and took power again in 1962, then ruling until forced by massive demonstrations to resign in July 1988. However, he was widely thought not to have fully relinquished control, and to have been a major factor in the September 1988 coup that once again returned the army to power in Burma.

Windscale (Sellafield) nuclear accident (October 7, 1957), a fire in the reactor core of Pile No. 1 at Great Britain's Windscale PLUTONIUM production plant, causing the release of very large quantities of RADIOACTIVE iodine into the air. The fire, which was finally extinguished on October 12, resulted in much environmental contamination in the area. In the wake of the event all live-

stock and milk in the immediate area were destroyed. The event was kept secret by the British government until 1978.

Windsor, duke and duchess of, title given by Britain's King GEORGE VI to EDWARD VIII and his wife, the former Wallis SIMPSON, for whom he had given up the throne in 1936.

Winnie Mae, airplane in which Wiley POST and Harold Gatty made the first round-the-world flight in 1931.

Winter Palace, the czar's palace in St. Petersburg, Russia, where the RUSSIAN REVOLUTION OF 1905 began with the BLOODY SUNDAY massacres; later the Petrograd headquarters of Premier Alexander KERENSKY'S PROVISIONAL GOVERNMENT, which was assaulted and taken by BOLSHEVIK forces to begin the OCTOBER REVOLUTION and the RUSSIAN CIVIL WAR.

wireless, popular name both for early RADIO and for telegraphy using radio signals, as pioneered in 1901 by Guglielmo MARCONI.

Wise, Stephen Samuel (1874–1949), U.S. Reform Jewish rabbi, liberal, and Zionist leader who in 1898 was a founder of the American Federation of Zionists, which later became the Zionist Organization of America. In 1916 he was a founder and later president of the American Jewish Congress, and in 1936 he was a founder of the World Jewish Congress, which he served as president until his death. During the Nazi period he was one of the world's leading anti-fascists; throughout his life he was a major Zionist leader.

Wittgenstein, Ludwig Josef Johann (1889–1951), Austrian-British philosopher, who made major contributions to modern theories of logic and language. Inspired by study with Bertrand RUSSELL in Britain, he wrote his key work on thought and language, *Tractatus Logico-Philosophicus* (1922).

Wobblies, the popular name for members of the INDUSTRIAL WORKERS OF THE WORLD (IWW).

woman suffrage, the worldwide movement to gain equal voting rights for women that began in the United States and Great Britain during the 19th century. In the United States the movement resulted in the NINE-TEENTH AMENDMENT (1920) and in Great Britain equal voting rights for women over 30 were obtained in 1918 and full equality in 1928. Equal voting rights were gained in Australia, New Zealand, and Scandinavia earlier in the 20th century, in Canada and many European countries after World War I, and spread to other parts of the world after World War II.

Women's International League for Peace and Freedom (WILPF), an international nonviolent peace and disarmament organization, founded in 1919, that campaigns and educates on peace-related matters and has consulting relationships with several UNITED NATIONS bodies. Jane ADDAMS and Emily Greene BALCH were among its founders and early leaders.

women's liberation, a slogan and body of ideology, developed in the mid-1960s, that advocates complete equality for women in societal fact and by law, long-sought goals of the women's movement. The NATIONAL ORGANIZATION FOR WOMEN (NOW) was formed in 1966 to drive toward realization of those goals, joining many women's and dual-sex organizations already advocating women's rights and equality. NOW moved a proposed EQUAL RIGHTS AMENDMENT through Congress in 1971 and 1972 but failed to secure enough state victories to pass the amendment. Women's liberation was far more than a political movement, however; it was also a movement for social equality and freedom of choice in such areas as employment, reproduction, club membership, and education. Many women's liberation advocates called for special attention to foster long-deferred equality, in such areas as child care and professional training. A major and continuing national controversy developed on the issue of abortion, involving massive public pressure on both sides, a civil disobedience movement mounted by the RIGHT TO LIFE MOVE-MENT, and series of U. S. Supreme Court decisions, most notably *ROE* v. *WADE*.

women's suffrage, later alternate name for the movement called WOMAN SUFFRAGE.

Woodstock Festival, a massive August 1969 music festival attended by an estimated 400,000 young people, and a high point of the U.S. COUNTERCULTURE. The festival was a quasi-religious experience for some of those attending, whose belief in peaceful simplicity, away from industrial society, seemed borne out by the experience.

Woodward, Robert Upshur (1943–   ) and **Bernstein, Carl** (1944–   ), U.S. journalists, who uncovered and ultimately broke the WATERGATE story while reporters for the *Washington Post* in 1972. With the help of anonymous informer DEEP THROAT, they followed the story from the arrest of the "plumbers" to the NIXON resignation, winning Pulitzer prizes and writing the best-selling *All the President's Men* (1974; film, 1976) and *The Final Days* (1976).

Woolley, Charles Leonard (1880–1960), British archaeologist, whose major field-work at many Middle Eastern and North African sites—especially at Ur (1922–34) in southern Iraq—rediscovered the full scale and significance of the ancient Sumerian civilization and of Mesopotamia as a whole in human history.

Works Progress Administration (WPA), a U.S. NEW DEAL agency, created in May 1935 and administered by Harry HOPKINS, that provided millions with jobs and created massive public works projects during the GREAT DEPRESSION, including building construction, roadbuilding, recreational projects, dams, bridges, clinics, and arts projects of many kinds.

World Bank, an informal name for three UNITED NATIONS agencies: the INTERNA-TIONAL BANK FOR RECONSTRUCTION AND DEVELOPMENT (IBRD), the INTERNATION-AL DEVELOPMENT ASSOCIATION (IDA), and the INTERNATIONAL FINANCE CORPORA-TION (IFC).

World Court (International Court of Justice), a body originally established as the Permanent Court of International Justice in the COVENANT OF THE LEAGUE OF NA-

TIONS in 1920; in 1946 it became a UN agency. Headquartered in Geneva, it arbitrates and judges disputes submitted to it by member states, some of them provided for by treaties between those states. It sets no precedents and has no ability to enforce its decisions, functioning rather as a convenient way of settling some international disputes and as a moral voice as to others.

World Health Organization (WHO), a UNITED NATIONS special agency established in 1948 to promote worldwide public health activities, that has made enormous contributions to the health and medical care of humanity. These include the eradication of SMALLPOX and the development of other massive immunization programs, the widespread establishment of sanitary practices, and the diminution of many epidemic diseases, including leprosy, POLIO, cholera, and malaria.

world must be made safe for democracy, The, statement by U.S. president Woodrow WILSON in a speech before Congress on April 2, 1917, in which he asked for a declaration of war on the Central Powers.

World War I (1914–18), major international conflict of the early 20th century, also called the Great War. The war, which began as an attack by Austria-Hungary on its smaller neighbor, Serbia, after the assassination of Archduke FRANCIS FERDINAND at SARAJEVO, soon involved every major and all but a few minor European countries; by 1917 it had drawn in the United States, as well. It had been a war waiting to begin, as the European powers developed conflicting imperial ambitions, armed themselves, and settled into the two sets of alliances that quickly went to war in August 1914. The Allies were France, the British Empire, Russia, the United States, Serbia, Italy, Belgium, Greece, Rumania, Montenegro, Japan, and Portugal. The Central Powers were Germany, Austria-Hungary, Turkey, and Bulgaria. Together, they suffered 8 million war dead of the 65 million mobilized, plus 21 million wounded and an estimated 6–7 million civilian dead, which included those killed in the ARMENIAN HOLOCAUST; civil-

ian dead are probably underestimated if the famine and INFLUENZA PANDEMIC following the war are taken into account. The war brought revolution and civil war to Russia and revolution to Germany, dismembered Austria-Hungary, and laid much of the basis for World War II. It was, in sum, the worst catastrophe to befall humanity until then, and paved the way for the even greater catastrophes that were the combined wars and massacres of the interwar period and World War II. In the west, the war began with a successful German attack through Belgium and the Netherlands in conformance with the SCHLIEFFEN PLAN. After the initial Battles of the FRONTIERS, German forces raced to the Marne, where they were stopped at the decisive first battle of the MARNE. Three and a half years of inconclusive TRENCH WARFARE followed, with such battles as those at VERDUN, on the SOMME, and at YPRES causing millions of casualties. In 1918 the Germans made a final attempt to finish the war, using Eastern Front reinforcements freed by Soviet withdrawal from the war; but they failed, with the Allies, now including substantial American forces, going over to the offensive and ultimately breaking through the German front. Inevitable defeat was then hastened by revolution in Germany, bringing the armistice of November 11, 1918. In the east early Russian successes were reversed at the battles of TANNENBERG and the MASURIAN LAKES in August and September 1914. This was a more fluid war than that in the west but one with comparable casualties. After the GORLICE-TARNOW BREAKTHROUGH of 1915 the Central Powers were on the offensive until the summer of 1916. Then the Russians mounted the BRUSILOV OFFENSIVE which, after initial successes, ultimately ground to a halt with tremendous casualties. Then began the processes of general disaffection and army mutiny that brought about the OCTOBER REVOLUTION and took the Russians out of the war. On the Italian front there was a long stalemate from May 1915, when Italy entered the war, to October 1917. In that period the Italians unsuccessfully attacked eleven times on the ISONZO River. In October 1917 German and Austrian troops attacked across the Isonzo at CAPORETTO, taking hundreds of thousands of prisoners and driving to the Piave River. In October 1918 Allied forces destroyed the Austrian army at the battle of VITTORIO VENETO and began the final drive that ended with the Italian-front armistice of November 4, 1918. In the Balkans, the Serbs and Montenegrins first repulsed the invading Austrians, but by October 1915 Serbia and Montenegro had been taken by the Central Powers. Rumania entered the war on the Allied side in August 1916 but was defeated and signed an armistice on December 9, 1917. To the south, the British failed to take the Dardanelles and Gallipoli in 1915 and fought a 4-year war with Turkey in Mesopotamia and Palestine, eventually taking both; from 1916 they were allied with the revolutionary forces of the ARAB REVOLT against Turkey. Turkish and Russian forces also met in the Caucasus. German colonies in the Far East and East Africa were ultimately taken by Allied forces. At sea German SUBMARINE WARFARE seriously threatened Allied lifelines across the Atlantic until late 1917, when improved antisubmarine devices and the development of the convoy system altered the balance in favor of the Allies. The British navy kept the main German fleet out of the war; The Germans ventured out only once, in 1916, fought the British at JUTLAND, and then retired. The PARIS PEACE CONFERENCE began on January 18, 1919.

World War II (1939–45), the major international conflict of the mid-20th century. The war began on September 1, 1939, with the Nazi invasion of POLAND, a BLITZKRIEG that soon succeeded in destroying Polish armed resistance; it was followed by the Nazi-Soviet PARTITION OF POLAND, pursuant to the terms of the recently concluded NAZI–SOVIET PACT. Ultimately, it involved every major and most of the smaller nations in the world. Its coming was long foreseen, for World War I had not resolved many major Great Power problems, and the interwar pe-

riod brought the GREAT DEPRESSION of the 1930s, the rise of FASCISM and militarism in Germany, Japan, and Italy, the failure of the LEAGUE OF NATIONS, and the inability of the Western powers to take effective action against the new aggressors. The European fascists moved against ETHIOPIA, the RHINELAND, Republican Spain, AUSTRIA, and CZECHOSLOVAKIA with impunity, and the Japanese moved against MANCHURIA and CHINA without democratic intervention. After MUNICH war was coming. It did; the Allies were ultimately the United States, the Soviet Union, the British Commonwealth, France, China, Poland, Yugoslavia, and many other countries; the Axis powers were Germany, Japan, Italy, and several smaller countries. Together, they suffered an estimated 15–17 million war dead of the 90–100 million mobilized, plus 23–26 million wounded and an estimated 25–35 million civilian dead, which included those killed in the JEWISH HOLOCAUST. These figures do not include the millions more who died in the wave of civil wars and wholesale population movements that followed the war. World War II was by far the greatest catastrophe ever to befall humanity, and it ended with the use of the ATOMIC BOMB, thereby creating the threat of a nuclear war that could be an infinitely greater catastrophe. In Europe the Polish invasion of 1939 was followed by a period of quiet in the west; then the German invasion of Denmark and Norway, in April 1940, was followed in May by the invasion of France, Holland, and Belgium, with the armored breakthrough in the Ardennes leading to the fall of France, the Allied evacuation from DUNKIRK, and the threat of invasion of Britain. But the RAF won the BATTLE OF BRITAIN in 1940, and the invasion did not come. In April 1941 Germany attacked and quickly took Yugoslavia and Greece and in June invaded the Soviet Union, swiftly taking much of western part of the country, besieging LENINGRAD, and threatening MOSCOW. But the Soviet winter counteroffensive of 1941–42 saved Moscow, and the German spring and summer offensives of

1942 failed to break Soviet resistance. Soviet armies went on the offensive after the decisive victory at STALINGRAD in the winter of 1942–43, and ultimately fought their way into Germany. The United States entered the war with the Japanese attack on PEARL HARBOR, on December 7, 1941, which destroyed much of the battleship component of the Pacific fleet, leaving the vital aircraft carrier force unharmed. The Japanese then proceeded to take the Philippines, much of the South Pacific, and all of Southeast Asia, including Hong Kong, Singapore, Malaya, Burma, and Indonesia; but they failed to take Australia and New Guinea or to conclude their long war in China. In April 1942, at the Battle of the CORAL SEA, and in June, at the decisive Battle of MIDWAY, the U.S. carrier fleet turned the course of the war in the Pacific. From then on, starting with the U.S. victory at GUADALCANAL late in 1942, the Americans followed the Japanese across the Pacific, fed by the enormous American productive capacity that was able to aid the Soviets, supply the Allied invasions in NORTH AFRICA, SICILY, ITALY, and NORMANDY, and build the U.S. fleet into by far the most powerful naval force in the world. By 1945 they were preparing to invade the Japanese mainland. From 1942 the Allies went on the offensive around the western and southern perimeter of Europe. Although German submarine attacks were extremely effective against Allied shipping in the North Atlantic for much of the war, the combined British and American fleets kept the Atlantic supply lines open, sank many German submarines, and ultimately won the antisubmarine war. In North Africa a see-saw desert war was resolved by the British victory at EL ALAMEIN on November 4, 1942, coupled with an Allied North African seaborne invasion on November 8; North Africa was secured in the spring of 1943. Sicily and Italy were invaded in the summer of 1943, the Germans soon taking over the Italian war and beginning the long retreat north that would last for the rest of the war. And on June 6, 1944, the successful Allied landings at NORMANDY began the drive across Europe that ultimately took Allied troops into Germany to meet Soviet troops coming from the east. The European war ended with the unconditional surrender of Germany, the document of surrender being signed at Reims, France, on May 7, 1945. The end of the Pacific war came after the American atomic bombings of HIROSHIMA, August 6, 1945, and NAGASAKI, August 9, 1945. On August 14 the Japanese surrendered unconditionally. The surrender documents were formally signed on the U.S. battleship *Missouri*, in Tokyo harbor, on September 2, 1945.

WPA, the initials of the WORKS PROGRESS ADMINISTRATION, by which this U.S. NEW DEAL federal agency of the 1930s is best known.

Wrangel, Peter Nikolayevich (1878–1928), Czarist officer who fought under General Anton DENIKIN during the RUSSIAN CIVIL WAR and in 1920 succeeded Denikin to command of the White armies in southern Russia. His forces were defeated in late 1920; he and the remainder of his army were evacuated by the French navy to Constantinople.

Wright, Frank Lloyd (1867–1959), U.S. architect whose thoughts as to molding structures to fit human needs and reflect their environments, coupled with the structures themselves, exerted great influence on the development of modern architecture throughout much of his 70-year career and thereafter. Some of his most notable works are his own home at Taliesin, Wisconsin (1911, 1915, 1925), the Imperial Hotel, Tokyo (1922), Falling Water, Bear Run, Pennsylvania (1937), the Usonian homes of the 1930s, and New York's Guggenheim Museum, designed in 1943 and built in the late 1950s. Taliesin West, at Scottsdale, Arizona, remained an architecture school after his death.

Wright, James Claude, Jr. (1922–), U.S. political leader, a Texas Democratic congressman from 1954, a liberal on domestic economic and civil rights matters who supported American involvement in the VIETNAM WAR, but later in his career opposed REAGAN administration interventionist policy in Central America. He was elected Democratic majority leader of the House of Representatives, 1977–87, and Speaker of the House from 1987. During the 1988 presidential campaign, he came under Republican attack for alleged improprieties in office, an attack that continued in 1989 with a congressional committee investigation. The negative publicity led to his resignation in June 1989, the first House Speaker to be forced from office.

Wright, Wilbur (1867–1912) and **Orville Wright** (1871–1948), U.S. inventors, brothers who developed the first engine-powered AIRPLANE. After early work with bicycles, they studied and improved on the glider; in 1900 they began flying their engineless craft off the sandy dunes called Kill Devil Hills, near Kitty Hawk, North Carolina. By 1903 they had added an engine to the light structure, and on December 17, 1903, flew the *Flyer I* (popularly dubbed the *Kitty Hawk*) on four flights; the first, by Orville, covered 120 feet in 12 seconds. They continued to make improvements and in 1906 received a U.S. patent for their flying machine; 3 years later they incorporated the American Wright Company to manufacture them. Wilbur died in 1912; Orville continued to work as a consultant on aviation, notably during World War I.

Wu P'ei-fu (1874–1939), Chinese soldier, who served under YÜAN SHIH-KAI and in the early 1920s became chief warlord in northern China. He failed to achieve the wider power he sought, being defeated in 1924 by a rival warlord, CHANG TSO-LIN, and then finally defeated in 1926 by the forces of the NORTHERN EXPEDITION, led by CHIANG KAI-SHEK.

Wysznski, Stefan (1901–81), Polish Catholic priest who became primate of Poland in 1949 and a cardinal in 1953. An opponent of Poland's Communist government, he was imprisoned, 1953–56, and released during POLISH OCTOBER in 1956; he supported SOLIDARITY in the 1980s. He attempted to act as a mediator between Solidarity and the government, and resisted those forces within the labor movement and the country as a whole that wished to turn the Solidarity–government confrontation into an armed insurgency.

X

X-ray, type of low-frequency RADIATION, beyond ULTRAVIOLET in the electromagnetic spectrum; discovered in 1895 but understood and widely applied only in the 20th century. In 1912 Max Theodor Felix von LAUE developed the technique of X-RAY CRYSTALLOGRAPHY, passing X-rays through crystals, in the process discovering X-rays to be a form of electromagnetic radiation. William Henry BRAGG and his son, William Lawrence, used the technique to measure the wavelength of X-rays and also to study ATOMIC STRUCTURE by the pattern of X-rays reflected from atoms. Because X-rays have a very short wavelength and can pass through solids, they have been extremely useful in 20th-century medicine (identifying broken bones) and industry (identifying flaws in products). In 1926, Hermann J. Muller discovered that X-rays could cause mutations on GENES, but their harmfulness to tissues has been turned to medical advantage in the treatment of CANCERS.

X-ray crystallography, technique of passing X-RAYS through crystals, whose evenly spaced atoms act as a grate, reflecting on a photographic plate, allowing measurements to be made of things otherwise too minute to measure. The technique was originally the idea of Max Theodor Felix von LAUE in 1912 and was refined by William Henry BRAGG and William Lawrence BRAGG, who first measured the wavelengths of X-rays. By 1927 scientists had used X-ray crystallography to confirm the theory of WAVE-PARTICLE DUALITY. With X-rays of known wavelength, the technique was also used to study the ATOMIC STRUCTURE of crystals of various substances, allowing for major discoveries in theoretical chemistry. After World War II Dorothy HODGKIN pioneered in using X-ray crystallography—along with a COMPUTER to analyze the results—to discover the structure of complex organic molecules such as PENICILLIN, INSULIN, and VITAMIN B$_{12}$. In the 1950s British biochemists Maurice WILKINS and Rosalind FRANKLIN made X-ray crystallography studies of DNA, which aided Francis CRICK and James WATSON in uncovering the DOUBLE HELIX structure of the molecule of life.

xerography, inexpensive dry (*xero* in Greek) copying process developed in 1937 by Chester CARLSON and patented 2 years later. The xerographic process was first publicly demonstrated in 1948, and in 1959 the Xerox Corporation introduced the first xerographic copier for commercial use, revolutionizing paper handling in offices and schools around the world.

Y

Yablonski murders, the December 31, 1959, killings of United Mine Workers leader Joseph Yablonski and his wife and daughter by the agents of UMW president W. A. "Tony" BOYLE. Boyle was ultimately convicted of the murder; three others pleaded guilty.

Yalta Conference (February 4–11, 1945), the second ROOSEVELT–CHURCHILL–STALIN World War II summit meeting, which reached decisions that were to considerably affect the shape of the postwar world, especially regarding Eastern Europe. The conferees agreed that the Soviet Union was to keep most of the Polish territory it had seized in 1939, with Poland taking a substantial portion of eastern Germany. Poland was to have free elections; in fact, no such elections ever occurred, and Poland became part of the large Soviet Eastern European sphere of influence tacitly agreed on by the conferees. The Soviet Union repeated its TEHRAN CONFERENCE promise to make war on Japan after the defeat of Germany in return for several territorial concessions, and several questions regarding the UNITED NATIONS were resolved, along with a miscellany of other postwar territorial questions.

Yamamoto, Isoroku (1884–1943), Japanese naval officer who saw action in the RUSSO–JAPANESE WAR and was commander in chief of the Japanese fleet 1939–43. He was chief Japanese naval planner before and during the early portion of World War II, as such developing the attack on PEARL HARBOR. He was killed in the Solomon Islands, on April 18, 1943, when American fighters shot down his aircraft.

Yamani, Ahmed (Sheikh Yamani; 1930–), Saudi Arabian lawyer and oil minister (1962–86), who was an organizer of and often spokesperson for the ORGANIZATION OF PETROLEUM EXPORTING COUNTRIES (OPEC) and an initiator of the OIL EMBARGO of 1973. During the 1970s and early 1980s Yamani advocated oil output restrictions to drive up prices but with limited success, as worldwide recession, non-OPEC oil-producing competition, and covert dumping of oil supplies on world markets by OPEC members caused a worldwide oil supply glut.

Yamashita, Tomoyuki (1885–1946), Japanese officer, who commanded southeast Asian invasion forces in 1941. His forces took Singapore in February 1942. He later commanded a Japanese Manchurian army, and was made commander in the Philippines in 1944, where his troops continued to retreat before liberating U.S.–Philippine forces until the end of the war. He was executed as a war criminal in 1946.

Yangtse floods, series of floods in the rivers of China in the 20th century; major floods along the Yangtse and other rivers in 1939 caused an estimated 500,000 deaths.

Yarmouth Castle sinking (November 13, 1965), the sinking of the American cruise ship *Yarmouth Castle* off Nassau, with a loss of 89, after a fire that went out of control because of faulty firefighting equipment aboard.

Yates v. United States (1957), a landmark U.S. Supreme Court decision, reversing the convictions of 14 Communist party leaders, sharply limiting federal government ability to prosecute dissenters under the SMITH

ACT and reflecting changed national attitudes as McCARTHYISM waned.

Yeager, Charles Elwood (1923–), U.S. pilot, who first broke the SOUND BARRIER, flying his Bell X-1 craft faster than the speed of sound, on October 14, 1947. A World War II fighter pilot and later a test pilot, in 1953 Yeager also set a speed record, flying at 1,650 miles per hour, and helped prepare the first astronauts for the early U.S. space efforts.

Yeager, Jeana, U.S. pilot who, with Dick Rutan, made the first nonstop airplane flight around the world in the *VOYAGER* in 1986.

yellow fever, severe, often fatal viral disease most common in tropical and subtropical areas, especially in the Americas, as in a 1905 epidemic in New Orleans. Working in Havana, Cuba, in 1900, Walter REED first confirmed an earlier theory that yellow fever was a mosquito-borne disease. Acting on that information, William Crawford GORGAS developed a mosquito-eradication program in Cuba, which he later applied in Panama so successfully that construction of the PANAMA CANAL (1904–14) could proceed without the terrible loss of life earlier experienced. South African–American microbiologist Max Theiler developed a vaccine against yellow fever in 1937, but mosquito eradication campaigns continued to be the main way of combatting this scourge.

Yellow River dikes, flood barriers intentionally broken by the Chinese in June 1938, during the second year of the SINO–JAPANESE WAR, in a successful attempt to slow the Japanese advance in north central China. Much of the Yellow River plain was flooded, causing enormous damage, but also stopping the Japanese CHENGCHOW OFFENSIVE.

Yellowstone fires (September 1988), massive U.S. Northwest forest fires, especially severe at Yellowstone National Park, that destroyed an estimated 3 million acres of forest, bringing sharp public criticism of the National Park Service policy of letting such fires burn themselves out naturally, and causing a policy review.

Yeltsin, Boris Nikolayevich (1931–), Soviet engineer and Communist party official, a member of the presidium from 1984 and first secretary of the Moscow city party committee 1984–87, in that position functioning as mayor of Moscow. A GORBACHEV supporter and leading advocate of democratization and decentralization, he publicly disagreed with Gorbachev as to the pace of change and was demoted to first deputy chairman of the State Construction Committee in 1987. In the 1989 elections he swept Moscow with an overwhelming majority, emerging as a leading advocate of change, with massive popular support.

Yemen Arab Republic (North Yemen), until the end of World I, part of the Ottoman Empire, then becoming a British-influenced Arab religious state, which became a republic after the military coup of 1962. The coup generated the YEMENI CIVIL WAR, which was followed by continued instability, and recurrent attempts to join the country with its smaller neighbor, the YEMEN PEOPLE'S REPUBLIC (SOUTH YEMEN).

Yemeni Civil War (1962–70), conflict that began with the republican revolt and establishment of the Free Yemen Republic in September 1962. The monarchy was supported by Saudi Arabia, and the republicans by Egypt, which had an estimated 60,000–80,000 troops in Yemen until the cease-fire of 1965, and kept substantial forces in Yemen until Egyptian defeat in the SINAI–SUEZ WAR (THIRD ARAB–ISRAELI WAR) of 1967. In February 1968 Southern Yemen entered the war on the side of the republicans, and Saudi Arabia once again sent support to the royalist forces. In April 1970 the Saudis agreed to the establishment of a republican government that included royalist representatives.

Yemen People's Republic (People's Democratic Republic of Yemen; South Yemen), until 1967 a British protectorate including the colony of ADEN. After a low-level guerrilla insurgency, which included factional fighting within the South Yemen independence movement, South Yemen became an independent nation on November 30, 1967, becoming the People's Republic in 1970.

Yenan, the north China city in Shensi province that was the headquarters of the Chinese Communist army after the LONG MARCH of 1934–35, and until power was achieved in 1949. This was the "Yenan period" of Chinese communism; the city is now a national shrine.

Yezhov, Nikolai Ivanovich (1894–1939), Soviet Communist Party leader, who headed the NKVD 1936–38, bearing major direct responsibility for the massive imprisonments and murders of the GREAT PURGE. He was himself purged in 1938 and disappeared in 1939, probably murdered by his former NKVD colleagues.

Yippies (Youth International Party), an anarchist-oriented NEW LEFT student radical group of the 1960s that came to world attention during the CHICAGO DEMOCRATIC NATIONAL CONVENTION of 1968. They organized demonstrations that were met by the Chicago police with extraordinary brutality, and were televised to a world audience.

Yom Kippur War (Fourth Arab–Israeli War, October War; October 6–24, 1973), conflict that began on October 6, in that year the date of the Jewish holy day of Yom Kippur, with successful surprise air and ground attacks by Egyptian forces along the Suez Canal and by Syrian forces, supported by Iraqi and Jordanian forces, on the Golan Heights. Israeli forces were driven back on both fronts, suffering heavy losses. But the far stronger and better led Israelis reasserted air superiority; within a week they were bombing Damascus and other Syrian targets at will and by October 12 were threatening to take Damascus. On October 16 Israeli forces in divisional strength counterattacked across the canal, and by October 24, the date of the cease-fire, they were positioned to destroy the Egyptian Third Army. Until October 24, U.S. and Soviet involvement had been limited to large supply airlifts to

the combatants, but direct Soviet intervention to save threatened Egyptian forces then seemed possible. This possibility generated a sharply cautionary American response. This major threat to world peace was ended by the UNITED NATIONS–sponsored agreement of October 27, 1973 which provided for Suez and Golan Heights peacekeeping forces manned by the smaller nations. Disengagement agreements were concluded between Egypt and Israel in January 1974 and between Syria and Israel in May 1974.

York, Alvin Cullum (1887–1964), Congressional Medal of Honor winner for his action against a German machine gun battalion on October 8, 1918, near Chateau-Thierry, France. He became a major American hero of the war, and was later portrayed by Gary Cooper in the film *Sergeant York* (1941).

Yoshida, Shigeru (1878–1967), Japanese diplomat, who held a series of responsible positions, 1906–39, including that of ambassador to Great Britain, 1936–39. He was briefly imprisoned by his own government (June–August 1945) for opposing the continuation of World War II. He was foreign minister 1945–46 and prime minister 1948–54, in that position taking Japan through the balance of the Allied occupation, the postwar land reform, the adoption of a new constitution, and establishment of the material and political bases for the economic upsurge and long period of conservative dominance that followed.

Young, Andrew (1932–   ), U.S. Congregational minister, who became a leader of the CIVIL RIGHTS MOVEMENT and was closely associated with Martin Luther KING, Jr. as executive director and later executive vice-president of the SOUTHERN CHRISTIAN LEADERSHIP CONFERENCE (SCLC). In 1972 he became the first Black Congressman from Georgia since Reconstruction. He was U.S. ambassador to the UNITED NATIONS (1977–79) and later became mayor of Atlanta, Georgia (1981–   ).

Young, Whitney Moore, Jr. (1921–71), U.S. civil rights leader, a former social worker, teacher, and administrator who headed the

Urban League 1961–71. In that period he focused on enhancing economic opportunities for Blacks and developing government and private antipoverty programs, as part of the larger CIVIL RIGHTS MOVEMENT.

Young Plan, a 1930 plan providing for renegotiation to lower levels of the German World War I reparations established by the Treaty of VERSAILLES and the DAWES PLAN of 1924. The Young Plan, named after American lawyer Owen D. Young, who developed it, also set up the Bank of International Settlements.

Young Turks, a Turkish revolutionary organization that won army support, forced the Turkish constitutional reforms of 1908, and then came to power in the coup of 1913.

Younghusband Tibetan expedition (1903–1904), a British expedition into Tibet led by Francis Younghusband, British explorer, army officer, and diplomat, that fought its way to Lhasa against Tibetan opposition, and forced Tibet to accept British control of disputed lands along the Tibet–India border.

Youngstown Sheet and Tube Company v. *Sawyer* (1952), a landmark U.S. Supreme Court decision, in which the Court invalidated president Harry TRUMAN's steel plant seizure during a national steel strike as an abuse of executive power.

Youth International Party, the more formal name of the group popularly known as the YIPPIES.

You won't have Nixon to kick around anymore, statement by Richard Milhouse NIXON, prematurely telling the Washington press corps that he was conducting his last press conference, on November 7, 1962.

Ypres, Battles of, three major World War I battles at Ypres, a Belgian town near the North Sea. At the first Battle of Ypres (October 20–November 24, 1914), the British Expeditionary Force, supported by French forces, held their lines against heavy German attacks, blocking German attempts to take the North Sea ports. At the second Ypres battle (April 22–May 25, 1915), the

Germans used POISON GAS (chlorine) to help them break through the British lines, but were thrown back by reinforcements. At the third Ypres battle, also called PASSCHENDAELE (July 31–November 10, 1917), attacking British troops suffered an estimated 320,000 casualties and gained a total of 5 miles, finally taking the small village of Passchendaele.

Yüan Shih-k'ai (1859–1916), Chinese military leader who served under the Manchus and was a minister in the Manchu government; he negotiated the abdication of the child emperor HSÜAN T'UNG (Henry P'u Yi) and the end of the dynasty with SUN YAT-SEN and the revolutionary movement in 1912. He then became the first president of the Republic of China, succeeding Sun, who had been provisional president. In 1913 a second revolution, led by Sun, failed to remove him, and Sun fled to Japan.

Yudenich, Nicolai Nikolayevich (1862–1933), Czarist general and commander of the White army in northwest Russia during the RUSSIAN CIVIL WAR; his forces were defeated in 1919, and he went into exile.

Yugoslavia (Socialist Federal Republic of Yugoslavia), until 1918, a region belonging partly to the Austro-Empire. On December 1, 1918, SERBIA and MONTENEGRO, both independent states, merged with CROATIA, SLOVENIA, and BOSNIA-HERZEGOVINA to form the kingdom of the Serbs, Croats, and Slovenes, which in 1929 became Yugoslavia. The country was occupied by AXIS forces during World War II; developed a three-way war among Axis, CHETNIK, and PARTISAN forces; and emerged on November 29, 1945, as a one-party Communist state led by TITO.

Yugoslavia, invasion of (April 6–17, 1941), World War II attack on Yugoslavia and Greece by German forces, starting on April 6, 1941. Greece, which had been winning its war against Italy since October 1940, fell in 17 days to the Germans. Yugoslavia had not been previously invaded, but in March 1941 had agreed to join Germany and Italy in the war. But a Yugoslav army revolt reversed the decision, triggering a quick German invasion, in which the Germans suffered minimal casualties and the Yugoslav army was routed and destroyed, with tens of thousands of casualties and an estimated 250,000–300,000 prisoners taken. Belgrade fell on April 12, and Yugoslavia surrendered on April 17.

Yugoslav–Soviet break (1948), a break between TITO, Joseph STALIN, and their respective countries on the issue of Yugoslav independence. It had been building since the end of World War II, as Tito and his associates converted their powerful Partisan army into an independent national army, and began to pursue the "Yugoslav road to socialism," which involved decentralization, worker control of enterprises, and a measure of free expression, all unacceptable to Stalin. In June 1948 the break was made public, with COMINFORM expulsion of Yugoslavia. Military action did not follow, though war seemed imminent in the autumn of 1949, as the Yugoslavs made it clear that they would fight if invaded, and Stalin was not willing to run the risk of a war that might ultimately engage the United States.

Z

Zaharoff, Basil (Basileios Zacharias; 1849–1936), Turkish-French armaments dealer who represented several other dealers in the Balkans, Eastern Europe, and Russia from the early 1880s, becoming very rich and well connected in the process; in the popular press of the day he was a "mystery man." He became a French citizen in 1913, and was knighted by the British government in 1918, avowedly for services as an Allied intelligence agent during World War I.

Zahir Shah, Mohammad (1914–   ), the last king of Afghanistan (1933–73), who succeeded to the throne after the assassination of his father, Nadir Shah, in 1933. He became a constitutional monarch in 1963, and in 1973 he was toppled by a revolution led by his former prime minister and cousin, Sardar Mohammed DAUD KHAN; he then went into exile.

Zaibatsu, the large Japanese industrial organizations, usually run by single families, that dominated the Japanese economy early in the century and until 1945, when they were outlawed by Allied occupation forces. After the occupation ended, large industrial organizations intertwined with private and public financial organizations came back, once again dominating the economic life of the country.

Zaire (Republic of Zaire), until 1960, the Belgian Congo, a Belgian colony; it became an independent state on June 30, 1960, an event followed by the CONGO CIVIL WAR. In 1965 MOBUTU Sese Seko emerged as sole leader of the country.

Zaire Civil War, the CONGO CIVIL WAR, as it was known at the time it occurred.

Zakharov, Gennadi F., a former UNITED NATIONS employee who had been charged by the U.S. government as a Soviet spy in 1986, and was released in a swap for Nicholas DANILOF, whom the Soviets had arrested and accused of spying.

Zambia (Republic of Zambia), until 1964, NORTHERN RHODESIA, a British protectorate, becoming in 1953 part of the Federation of Rhodesia and Nyasaland, controlled by the white government of Southern Rhodesia. After a decade of Black nationalist protest, Northern Rhodesia gained independence and COMMONWEALTH membership on October 24, 1964. Its first and only president was Kenneth KAUNDA, who in 1972 turned his country into a one- party state.

Zangara, Joseph (?–1933), assassin who shot at but missed president-elect Franklin D. ROOSEVELT in Miami, Florida, on February 15, 1933; he wounded Chicago mayor Anton J. Cermak, who later died. Zangara was subsequently executed.

ZANU, the initials of the ZIMBABWE AFRICAN NATIONAL UNION, by which it is best known.

Zanzibar (and Pemba), a former British East African colony that became an independent nation in 1963 and merged with TANGANYIKA to form the new nation of TANZANIA on April 26, 1964.

Zapata, Emiliano (1879–1919), Mexican Indian peasant and agrarian reformer, who led a peasant revolutionary army in southern Mexico during the MEXICAN REVOLUTION. He fought alongside Francisco MADERO against Porfirio DíAZ in 1910–1911 but soon broke with Madero on the question of land reform, developing his own Plan of Ayala. He and Francisco VILLA fought the armies of Venustiano CARRANZA, taking Mexico City in 1914; but they were later forced to withdraw, Villa to the north and Zapata to the south, where his army successfully resisted all government attacks. Zapata was assassinated in 1919.

ZAPU, the initials of the ZIMBABWE AFRICAN PEOPLE'S UNION, by which it is best known.

Zeebrugge ferry sinking (March 9, 1987), capsizing of the British ferry *Herald of Free Enterprise* in the English Channel off Zeebrugge, Belgium, killing 188 people.

Zeppelin, Ferdinand von (1838–1917), German general, who turned aircraft designer late in life. He developed a rigid airship—named, after him, the zeppelin, but better known as the DIRIGIBLE—which first flew in 1900.

Zhao Ziyang (Chao Tzu-yang; 1919–   ), Chinese Communist leader, a party secretary in Guangdong (Canton) 1965–67 and 1972–74, with a 5-year break during his "purge" in the CULTURAL REVOLUTION. A protégé of DENG XIAO-P'ING, Zhao was Chinese premier, 1980–87, and became general secretary of his party in 1987. With Deng, Zhao committed China to the development of new incentive-providing economic forms, including decentralized economic controls, and private ownership of land and small businesses. A leading liberal, he lost power to LI PENG and the conservative wing of Chinese communism during the crisis generated by the CHINESE STUDENT DEMONSTRATIONS OF 1989 in Beijing.

Zhivkiv, Todor (1911–   ), Bulgarian Communist official, a resistance fighter in World War II, who became secretary-general of the Bulgarian Communist party in 1954, then remaining in control of his party and government while continuing to execute Soviet-bloc policy. He apparently had considerable difficulty in coming to terms with some major aspects of Soviet GLASNOST and PERESTROIKA at the beginning of the GORBACHEV era but attempted to apply those policies to Bulgaria. He resigned under pressure in 1989.

Zhou Enlai (Chou En-lai; 1898–1976), Chinese Communist leader who became first premier of the PEOPLE'S REPUBLIC OF CHINA 1949–76. He was imprisoned for revolutionary work in 1920 and then spent 4 years in France, from 1921 as a Chinese Communist Party organizer. From 1924 he was on the faculty of WHAMPOA MILITARY ACADEMY, and was in 1927 military leader of the Communist forces during the taking of Shanghai by the NORTHERN EXPEDITION and the SHANGHAI MASSACRE that followed. The central character in André MALRAUX's novel, *Man's Fate*, set at the Shanghai massacre, was based on Zhou. In 1931 he joined MAO ZEDONG and ZHU DE in KIANGSI, and made the LONG MARCH to Yenan in 1934. From 1935 to 1945 he was chief Communist Party diplomatic representative, arranging the release of CHIANG KAI-SHEK during the SIAN INCIDENT of 1936 and negotiating with KUOMINTANG and American representatives before and during World War II. After Communist victory in 1949 he became premier, and was also foreign minister until 1958. From 1935 until his death 42 years later, he was the Chinese Communist movement's leading diplomat and spokesperson.

Zhu De (Chu Teh; 1886–1976), Chinese officer, founder and long-time commander of China's Red Army. ZHU was a Yunnan Military Academy graduate, who joined the COMMUNIST PARTY OF CHINA while a student in Germany in the 1920s. He returned to China and became a Nationalist army officer in 1926, fought on the Communist side in the unsuccessful NANCHANG UPRISING of 1927, and then fled to the Chingkang Mountains of western Kiangsi, where he was joined by MAO ZEDONG and the other survivors of the AUTUMN HARVEST UPRISINGS. From then on he headed the Communist armies, through the years of the KIANGSI SOVIET, during the LONG MARCH and the YENAN and SINO–JAPANESE WAR years that followed, and then through the last years of the CHINESE CIVIL WAR. He held command of the People's

Liberation Army until 1954, remaining a senior military figure in China for the balance of his life, and taking no other major active role in Chinese affairs.

Zhukov, Georgi Konstantinovich (1896–1974), Soviet officer, who saw service in World War I and in the RUSSIAN CIVIL WAR. In 1939 forces under his command were successful in the JAPANESE–SOVIET BORDER WAR. He was Soviet chief of staff in 1941, participated in the defense of LENINGRAD, and planned the successful Soviet counteroffensive in Battle of MOSCOW. As Deputy Supreme Commander under Joseph STALIN, he was largely responsible for overall planning of the defense of STALINGRAD and the series of offensives that took the Red Army to Berlin. He personally directed the final Soviet attack on Berlin. During the postwar period he lost Stalin's favor, but held several key government posts after Stalin's death, finally losing all positions after losing a political struggle with Nikita KHRUSHCHEV in 1957. After Khrushchev's fall from power, Zhukov was rehabilitated and honored.

Zia Ul-Haq, Mohammad (1924–79), Pakistani officer, who was appointed army commander in chief in 1976 and who took power in an army coup in July 1977. Zia imprisoned former prime minister Zulfikar Ali BHUTTO, and had him executed on a murder charge in April 1979 despite worldwide protests. Zia became the military dictator of Pakistan, ruling under martial law until 1985 and then beginning to move very slowly toward restoration of some aspects of democracy; however, he abruptly dissolved all major democratic institutions and returned the country to military rule in May 1988. As president, he fostered a return to rigid, medieval Islamic law, closely allied Pakistan with the United States, built Pakistani military strength, and attempted to develop atomic weapons. He supplied and offered refuge to Afghan rebel forces and an estimated 3–5 million Afghan refugees during the 1980s. He died in an airplane crash, on August 17, 1988, and was succeeded by Benazir BHUTTO, the daughter of Zulfikar

Ali Bhutto, who restored democracy in her country.

Zimbabwe (Republic of Zimbabwe), until 1923 SOUTHERN RHODESIA, a British colony; it gained internal autonomy in 1923, with continuing white domination of the government. In 1953 it joined in the Federation of Rhodesia and Nyasaland, which dissolved in 1963, NORTHERN RHODESIA gaining independence in 1964 as ZAMBIA. Southern Rhodesia, under attack as a racist state, declared itself independent of Great Britain in 1965 and a republic in 1969; then developed the guerrilla insurgency that became the ZIMBABWE–RHODESIA CIVIL WARS.

Zimbabwe African National Union (ZANU), Zimbabwean political party formed in 1963, when its founding members left the Zimbabwe African People's Union (ZAPU). In the early 1970s it moved into guerrilla war against the dominant white minority government of South Rhodesia. From 1976 ZANU was led by Robert MUGABE, who led it into a Patriotic Front coalition with ZAPU that year. When independence came in 1980, ZANU became the Zimbabwean majority party, and Mugabe was named Zimbabwe's first prime minister. From then on, ZANU was the country's ruling party, merging with ZAPU and abolishing white representation guarantees in 1987, and so becoming the sole party in Zimbabwe.

Zimbabwe African People's Union (ZAPU), Zimbabwean political party led by Joshua NKOMO from its formation in the early 1960s. It became a major force in the Southern Rhodesia Black national movement, going over to guerrilla warfare in the early 1970s and into the Patriotic Front coalition with the Zimbabwe African National Union (ZANU) in 1976. It won a minority position in the 1980 Zimbabwean elections, with Nkomo then joining the MUGABE government. Intermittently involved in guerrilla warfare against the new government during the early 1980s, in 1987 it was merged with ZANU, as Zimbabwe became a one-party state.

Zimbabwe–Rhodesia Civil Wars (1971–1984), conflicts that began as sporadic insurgent attacks by dissident Black nationalist forces operating out of neighboring Black African countries. In 1975–76 they grew into a substantial guerrilla war, with ZIMBABWE AFRICAN NATIONAL UNION (ZANU) and ZIMBABWE AFRICAN PEOPLE'S UNION (ZAPU) forces attacking from their bases in Zambia and Mozambique, and Rhodesian forces striking back at those bases in what became a set of border wars. In 1976 ZANU leader Robert MUGABE and ZAPU leader Joshua NKOMO joined forces in the Patriotic Front, though their alliance was beset by friction and some armed clashes. By 1979 the long civil war and world condemnation of an isolated Southern Rhodesia had combined to force the government of Ian SMITH to step down, to be replaced by the short-lived government of Bishop Abel MUZOREWA. ZANU and ZAPU did not not accept the legitimacy of the new government; nor did the American and other governments. This forced a different solution, the supervison of new elections by the British government, which in 1980 yielded a ZANU majority and the formation of the first government of the new nation of Zimbabwe by Robert Mugabe, with ZAPU and white minority representation. But the civil wars were not yet over; sporadic fighting between formerly allied ZANU and ZAPU forces developed and continued until 1984, when the long series of negotiations that led to the 1987 ZANU-ZAPU merger began. After 1987 Zimbabwe became a one-party state.

Zimmerman note (January 19, 1917), a coded message from German secretary of state Arthur Zimmerman to the German ambassador in Mexico, proposing a German–Mexican alliance should the United States come into World War I. British intelligence deciphered the note; its publication caused great anger in the United States and helped push the United States into the war.

Zinoviev, Grigori Yevseyevich (1882-1936), leading BOLSHEVIK and collaborator with LENIN, who returned with Lenin to Russia in 1917 and was the first president of the COMMUNIST INTERNATIONAL. In the early 1920s Zinoviev and Lev KAMENEV joined with Joseph STALIN to defeat Leon TROTSKY; then, in the mid-1920s, they opposed Stalin's takeover of the Soviet Union. For this, Zinoviev was expelled from the Communist party and lost his official positions, but later after recanting, he was rehabilitated. In 1935 he was sentenced to 10 years imprisonment for allegedly participating in a plot that resulted in the murder of Communist party leader Sergei KIROV. He was executed in 1936, a victim of the first major show trials of the GREAT PURGE. In June 1989, during the GORBACHEV era, he was posthumously rehabilitated.

Zionism, a movement to establish a Jewish national homeland in Palestine on the land once occupied by the Biblical land of Israel. Attempts to accomplish this goal began in 1882, when the Eastern European Lovers of Zion movement began to establish agricultural settlements in Palestine. The term itself was coined by Austrian writer Nathan Birnbaum. In 1897 Theodor HERZL organized the Congress of Zionist Organizations and became its first president; and in the years before World War I, Jewish settlement in Palestine increased. The BALFOUR DECLARATION of 1917 indicated British willingness to cooperate with Zionist aims, and provided a focus for the following 31-year campaign to establish Israel. That campaign captured Western world support after the full extent of the JEWISH HOLOCAUST became clear, although the Arabs of Palestine were supported in their opposition to Zionist national aspirations throughout the Arab and Moslem worlds. The establishment of the state of Israel in May 1948, which was also the beginning of the Arab–Israeli wars, achieved the main Zionist goal; but some IRGUN ZVAI LEUMI and STERN GANG activists insisted that Israel was incomplete until it included all that historically had been Israel, including Jerusalem and the WEST BANK of the Jordan River.

Zodiac murders, the media-developed name for a series of unsolved murders, mostly of young women and girls, occurring in California and other western states during the late 1960s and early 1970s. The name developed from the mode of mutilation involved and from several self-advertising letters sent to the press, possibly by the murderer. The letters claimed "credit" for 37 murders, although police estimates were generally much lower.

Zworykin, Vladimir Kosma (1889-1982), Russian-American electrical engineer and inventor; sometimes called the father of TELEVISION. Immigrating to the United States in 1919, he joined Westinghouse, where in 1923–24 he patented the two basic components of the modern television system, the iconoscope camera tube and the kinescope picture tube; in 1928 he also obtained a color television patent. Westinghouse executives were unimpressed with his "impractical" project, so he left for RCA (Radio Corporation of America), then headed by David SARNOFF, who put up the millions needed for Zworykin and his team to produce the first all-electronic television in 1932, and then to make television a practical reality. He developed many other devices in his working life, including an early "electric eye," electronic control for MISSILES, and devices used in RADIATION detectors; while at RCA, he also fostered the work of others, such as James Hillier's work on the ELECTRON MICROSCOPE in 1937.